Lecture Notes of the Institute for Computer Sciences, Social Informatics and Telecommunications Engineering 287

More information about this series at http://www.springer.com/series/8197

Shuai Han · Liang Ye · Weixiao Meng (Eds.)

Artificial Intelligence for Communications and Networks

First EAI International Conference, AICON 2019
Harbin, China, May 25–26, 2019
Proceedings, Part II

 Springer

Editors
Shuai Han
Harbin Institute of Technology
Harbin, China

Liang Ye
Harbin Institute of Technology
Harbin, China

Weixiao Meng
Harbin Institute of Technology
Harbin, China

ISSN 1867-8211   ISSN 1867-822X (electronic)
Lecture Notes of the Institute for Computer Sciences, Social Informatics
and Telecommunications Engineering
ISBN 978-3-030-22970-2   ISBN 978-3-030-22971-9 (eBook)
https://doi.org/10.1007/978-3-030-22971-9

This Springer imprint is published by the registered company Springer Nature Switzerland AG
The registered company address is: Gewerbestrasse 11, 6330 Cham, Switzerland

Preface

We are delighted to introduce the proceedings of the first edition of the 2019 European Alliance for Innovation (EAI) International Conference on Artificial Intelligence for Communications and Networks (AICON). This conference brought together researchers, developers, and practitioners from around the world who are leveraging and developing artificial intelligence technology for communications and networks. The theme of AICON 2019 was "Artificial Intelligence for Communications and Networks: Applying Artificial Intelligence to Communications and Networks."

The technical program of AICON 2019 consisted of 93 full papers, including six invited papers in oral presentation sessions during the main conference tracks. The conference tracks were: Track 1—AI-Based Medium Access Control; Track 2—AI-based Network Intelligence for IoT; Track 3—AI-enabled Network Layer Algorithms and Protocols; Track 4—Cloud and Big Data of AI-enabled Networks; Track 5—Deep Learning/Machine Learning in Physical Layer and Signal Processing; and Track 6—Security with Deep Learning for Communications and Networks. Aside from the high-quality technical paper presentations, the technical program also featured four keynote speeches and four invited talks. The four keynote speeches were by Prof. Moe Win from the Laboratory for Information and Decision Systems, Massachusetts Institute of Technology, USA, Prof. Mohsen Guizani from the Department of Computer Science and Engineering, Qatar University, Qatar, Prof. Guoqiang Mao from the Center for Real-Time Information Networks, University of Technology Sydney, Australia, and Prof. Byonghyo Shim from the Department of Electrical and Computer Engineering, Seoul National University, South Korea. The invited talks were presented by Prof. Jinhong Yuan from the University of New South Wales, Australia, Prof. Shui Yu from the University of Technology Sydney, Australia, Prof. Bo Rong from the Communications Research Centre, Canada, and Prof. Haixia Zhang from Shandong University, China.

Coordination with the steering chair, Imrich Chlamtac, the general chairs, Xuemai Gu and Cheng Li, and the executive chairs, Qing Guo and Hsiao-Hwa Chen, was essential for the success of the conference. We sincerely appreciate their constant support and guidance. It was also a great pleasure to work with such an excellent Organizing Committee team and we thank them for their hard work in organizing and supporting the conference. In particular, we thank the Technical Program Committee, led by our TPC co-chairs, Prof. Shuai Han and Prof. Weixiao Meng, who completed the peer-review process of technical papers and compiled a high-quality technical program. We are also grateful to the conference manager, Andrea Piekova, for her support and all the authors who submitted their papers to the AICON 2019 conference.

We strongly believe that the AICON conference provides a good forum for all researchers, developers, and practitioners to discuss all scientific and technological aspects that are relevant for artificial intelligence and communications. We also expect that future AICON conferences will be as successful and stimulating as indicated by the contributions presented in this volume.

May 2019

Shuai Han
Liang Ye
Weixiao Meng

Organization

Steering Committee

Imrich Chlamtac   University of Trento, Italy

Organizing Committee

General Chairs

Xuemai Gu   Harbin Institute of Technology, China
Cheng Li   Memorial University of Newfoundland, Canada

Executive Chairs

Qing Guo   Harbin Institute of Technology, China
Hsiao-Hwa Chen   National Cheng Kung University, Taiwan

Program Chairs

Shuai Han   Harbin Institute of Technology, China
Weixiao Meng   Harbin Institute of Technology, China

Sponsorship and Exhibits Chair

Rose Hu   Utah State University, USA

Local Chair

Shuo Shi   Harbin Institute of Technology, China

Workshop Chairs

Yahong Zheng   Missouri University of Science and Technology, USA
Shaochuan Wu   Harbin Institute of Technology, China

Publicity and Social Media Chairs

Zhensheng Zhang   Retired
Lin Ma   Harbin Institute of Technology, China

Publications Chair

Liang Ye   Harbin Institute of Technology, China

Web Chairs

Xuejun Sha   Harbin Institute of Technology, China
Chenguang He   Harbin Institute of Technology, China

Posters and PhD Track Chair

Chau Yuen   Singapore University of Technology and Design,
                                   Singapore

Panels Chair

Xianbin Wang   University of Western Ontario, Canada

Demos Chair

Yi Qian   University of Nebraska Lincoln, USA

Tutorials Chair

Mugen Peng   Beijing University of Posts and Telecommunications,
                                   China

Conference Manager

Andrea Piekova   EAI

Technical Program Committee

Deyue Zou	Dalian University of Technology, China
Fan Jiang	Memorial University of Newfoundland, Canada
Lingyang Song	Peking University, China
Bo Rong	Communications Research Center, Canada
Wei Li	Northern Illinois University, USA
Xi Chen	Flatiron Institute, Simons Foundation, USA
Baoxian Zhang	University of China Academy of Sciences, China
Jalel Ben-Othman	University of Paris 13, France
Jun Shi	Harbin Institute of Technology, China
Ruiqin Zhao	Northwestern Polytechnical University, China
Feng Ye	University of Dayton, USA
Tao Jiang	Huazhong University of Science and Technology, China
Hossam Hassanein	Queen's University, Canada
Ruofei Ma	Harbin Institute of Technology, China
Jun Zheng	Southeast University, China
Wei Shi	Carleton University, Canada
Kun Wang	Nanjing University of Posts and Telecommunications, China
Xianye Ben	Shandong University, China
Shiwen Mao	Auburn University, USA
Mianxiong Dong	Muroran Institute of Technology, Japan
Wei Xiang	James Cook University, Australia
Yulong Gao	Harbin Institute of Technology, China

Contents – Part II

Cloud and Big Data of AI-Enabled Networks

AI-Based Network Intelligence for IoT

Contents – Part I

Deep Learning/Machine Learning in Physical Layer and Signal Processing

AI-Based Medium Access Control

Security with Deep Learning for Communications and Networks

VITEC: A Violence Detection Framework

Hany Ferdinando[1,2]([✉]) [iD], Tuija Huuki[1] [iD], Liang Ye[1,3] [iD],
Tian Han[1,4], Zhu Zhang[1,4], Guobing Sun[1,5], Tapio Seppänen[1] [iD],
and Esko Alasaarela[1]

[1] University of Oulu, Oulu, Finland
hany.ferdinando@oulu.fi
[2] Petra Christian University, Surabaya, Indonesia
[3] Harbin Institute of Technology, Harbin, China
[4] Harbin University of Science and Technology, Harbin, China
[5] Heilongjiang University, Harbin, China

Abstract. Hundreds of millions of youths suffer from various violence each year. The negative impacts motivate much research and numerous studies on violence. However, those attempts went their own way, making the achieved results, especially from engineering, not so useful. Based on the Sensor and Social Web (SEWEB) concept, Violence Detection (VITEC) was proposed as a possible framework to facilitate multi-disciplinary researchers in their fight against violence. At its core, it consists of a primary agent, which is violence detection using physiological signals and activity recognition, and a secondary agent, which is violence detection using surveillance video. The second layer of the proposed framework contains a cloud computing service with a Personal Safety Network (PSN) database. The cloud computing service manages all data, notifications, and some more thorough processing. The upper layer is for both observed young persons and members of the PSN. The proposed framework offers business opportunities. The existing school violence/bullying intervention programs can take advantage of VITEC by providing almost instant notifications of violent events, enabling the victims to get immediate help and intensifying coordination among different sectors to fight against violence. In the long run, VITEC may provide an answer related to the vision of having a world free from violence in 2030, as addressed by the UN Special Representative of Secretary-General on violence against children.

Keywords: Violent detection · Bullying detection · VITEC ·
Surveillance video · Physiological signals · Activity recognition

1 Introduction

Our societies change dramatically and drastically due to advancement in technologies. Information and news spread easily and quickly to enable fast learning and engagement. There are many online tutorials we can find not only in text form but also in audio/video/multimedia format. We can know what happened on the other side of the world almost instantly. Intercontinental video calls are now very affordable, with better quality. However, the negative side is unavoidable. Abuses of power emerge in new and

S. Han et al. (Eds.): AICON 2019, LNICST 287, pp. 3–17, 2019.
https://doi.org/10.1007/978-3-030-22971-9_1

unexpected ways, such as harassment in social media and cyberbullying. Consequently, feelings of insecurity may arise not only among adults but also among young people.

Indeed, hundreds of millions of youths suffer from different kinds of violence in educational environments [1–3] and on the streets [4] every year all over the globe. Addressing problems of violence in the lives of children has never been more relevant than in 2018. Highly valued research reviews inform us that the consequences of violence are diverse, immediate, and long-lasting. Young persons who experience violence are likely to have stomach pains, headaches, and difficulties eating and sleeping; they may become afraid of attending school, which may in turn interfere with their ability to concentrate in class or participate in school activities. Furthermore, a violent experience can cause depression, loneliness, low self-esteem, suicidal thoughts, interpersonal difficulties, antisocial and criminal behavior, and attempted suicide [5, 6]. Research has also shown how violence slows social progress by generating huge economic costs, hindering sustainable development, and eroding human capital. A study found that the global costs of violence against children could be as high as US $7 trillion per year [7]. All forms of violence infringe on the fundamental right to a safe life, create unsafe learning environments, and reduce the quality of lives for all children and youths.

Concerning these impacts, United nation children's fund (UNICEF) launched #ENDviolence in 2013 to bring them to an end. The UN Special Representative of the Secretary-General on violence against children (SRSG-VAC), Marta Santos Pais, emphasized the vision of building a world free from fear and violence as the result of adopting the 2030 Agenda for Sustainable Development in September 2015 [8]. Quoted from Article 19 [9], *"the child must be protected from all forms of physical or mental violence, injury or abuse, neglect or negligent treatment, maltreatment, or exploitation, including sexual abuse, while in the care of parent(s), legal guardian(s) or any other person who has the care of the child"*.

However, the progress on protecting children from violence around the world has been slow, uneven, and fragmented [10]. Furthermore, most of the promising intervention models rely on education systems, schools, and teachers, which often have limited capacities and resources to work efficiently enough to address violence. Coordination between the education sector and other sectors such as health, social service, and child protection, might not work efficiently in practice, making the action too slow. The reporting system must be anonymous and confidential to protect both victims and witnesses.

Recently, it has been discussed whether or not technological solutions might assist in tackling violence in young persons' lives. Technology has evolved to a level that would have been impossible to achieve a couple of decades ago. Recently, semiconductor technology, including sensor development has enabled systems to become smaller and more powerful than before. A smartphone, its apps and the internet have become part of contemporary life, which promote mobility for the users.

A smartphone can be considered a small computer. It is equipped with a processor, memory, and operating system. Moreover, a smartphone is also armed with several sensors, the most common one being the 3D acceleration sensor. It delivers information about the position of the smartphone, for example detecting if a smartphone is in a landscape or portrait position, so that the display can be adjusted. It also enables the possibility for developers to write apps, providing users with various applications that can be downloaded.

In terms of protecting young persons against violence, apps such as *STOP!t*, *Speak UP!*, *BullyButton*, and *BullyTag* have been developed to help victims and witnesses report violent events anonymously. They provide a safe way to send audio, video, and text about an acute violent situation to a corresponding database server. Investigation of the database report may lead to new insights about violence. Violence, however, is an iceberg phenomenon, where only limited cases are reported, due to, for example, feeling of ashamed or fear of revenge from the perpetrators.

However, those apps, for example Stop!t got about three out of five stars based on the users' rating [11]. Collecting from various apps ratings, a few people reported that they were helpful to report the violent event with no fear and got assistance from the school several days later [11] and one person put his hope in anti-bullying apps [12]. There was also a comment that someone might misuse the apps to make a joke or false claim [13]. In general, all these apps require a manual activation to generate reports. In a threatening situation, most likely the victim has no time, courage, or possibility to tap a button. Also, the bystanders may face similar barriers to reporting, which makes these apps less useful. The apps for reporting violence must not only be anonymous, but also be able to autonomously detect the violent event and automatically perform the required action.

In addition to the apps-based reporting systems, there have been several attempts to detect violent situations using various modalities such as video, audio, and physiological signals. Although they have offered some promising results, no significant impact to reduce violence rate has been delivered, because each modality has worked on its own with no specific framework on which the information and achievements from various resources would be gathered and shared easily. In an attempt to connect different modalities and a workable reporting system, in this paper we propose VITEC, a violence detection framework based on the Sensor and Social Web (SEWEB) concept [14], as a contribution from various disciplines to address violence among young people. To the best of our knowledge, there is not yet available such an interdisciplinary designed, research-based framework to address physical violence targeted at young people.

SEWEB has been offered to protect children and youth from various kinds of dangerous situations, including health issues and violence [14]. It can be extended to not only school-related violence [3] but also street violence [4] and rape [15]. It is about connecting wearable and mobile sensors to social media in human well-being applications. It involves technologies such as smartphone apps, cloud computing services, social media, wearable safety devices to process the activity, location, voice, health-related and well-being information of the subjects. The system identifies and categorizes phenomena such as stress level, emotional and mood states, physical activity level in various modalities, and location. The results are reported to some pre-defined contacts, for example parents, school staffs, and authorities.

2   Research in Violence Detection

In general, two approaches or sets of system exist in violence detection research. Firstly, the systems work as a witness to violent events. Included in this approach are violence detection using surveillance video signals [16–18] and physiological signals measured from the subjects who were watching the violent scenes, e.g. EDA [19], EEG [20]. Secondly, the systems use signals measured from the victims directly, for example, their human body movement [21] and ECG signal [22].

Nam, Alghoniemy, and Tewfik pioneered a study on violent scene characterization based on flame and blood detection [16]. It opened a research pathway on violence detection using video. In general, studies using video to detect violence can be separated into two groups based on the source of video signals, either from movies or surveillance cameras. The main differences reside in the availability of sound and colour, because videos from surveillance cameras have no sound and are in a grey scale format. Video from surveillance camera usually has low resolution. The VITEC framework takes more advantages from the studies using surveillance videos. Table 1 provides the most promising attempts to detect violence using surveillance video. Various methods have been proposed with encouraging results and contributions.

Table 1. Attempts in violence detection using surveillance-like video

Authors	Results/Contributions	Note
Souza et al. [25]	Accuracies were up to 99%, depending on the methods	It used the collected grey scale videos from various sources without audio
Nievas et al. [26]	Accuracies were up to 92%, depending on the methods	It ignored color and audio to detect either fight or non-fight scene
Bilinski et al. [27]	Accuracies were up to 99%, depending on the methods and data sets. The proposed method offered a fast-computational algorithm	Videos were from various data sets: Violent Flow, Hockey Fight, and Movie
Zhang et al. [28]	Accuracies up to 87%, depending on the data sets. The proposed method offered a moderately fast computational algorithm	Surveillance videos were from various data sets: BEHAVE, the CAVIAR, and Crowded Violence
Ribeiro et al. [17]	Accuracies were around 90% using various databases. The system can be used in various contexts	Videos were from both simulation and real surveillance

The relationship between electrodermal activities (EDA), which is represented as either skin conductance or resistance, and motion picture violence has been studied as a pilot several decades ago [23]. A correlation was found between EDA and reaction to violent scenes. Lorber conducted a meta-analysis of 95 studies to investigate the relationship of EDA and heart rate (HR) – the number of heart beats in a minute – with aggression, psychopathy, and conduct problems [24]. It was suggested that both HR and EDA were reliably though modestly associated to each other in many cases.

Furthermore, violent scene annotation using EDA signal was proposed based on the hypothesis that high-level information in EDA may reveal the affective state of the audiences, especially their reactions to violence [19]. This study found that EDA offers objective, reliable, and robust measurements of user reaction to help in violent scenes annotation. However, since the signal is sensitive to any affective stimulation, e.g. pleasure, it was recommended to be used with other modalities.

Violent events could also be detected using brain signals (EEG) measured from subjects watching violent scenes [20]. It was a breakthrough to address the problem of violence, as compared to the usual questionnaires, interviews, and psychological tests. It achieved an accuracy up to 98.7% and strengthened the idea of using physiological signals to detect violent events.

Another study found that the highest average HR and EDA changes occurred in subjects who played a violent video game, as compared to watching others playing a violent video game or watching a violent movie [29]. Although EEG was not included in this study, perhaps this type of signal also provides the same response. This work empirically revealed that two approaches to attack violence were available, one from the witness' and the other from the victim's point of view. Research on violence detection using surveillance video belongs to the first approach, as well as those using physiological signals measured from the subjects watching violent scenes.

Attempting to detect violence from the victim's point of view, Ye et al. used 3D acceleration and 3D gyroscope signals measured from the subject involved in violence simulations to detect violence based on their body movements [21, 30]. The study relied on the main idea that during a violent situation the victim's body movement are different than during anon-violent situation. The proposed system successfully distinguished some normal daily life body movements from the ones related to violence, achieving an average accuracy of 92%.

Using single channel ECG (electrical activity of the heart) signals measured in pupils involved in violence simulation, violent events could also be identified [22]. This work also emphasized on the violence detection from the victim's point of view. It required a wearable sensor able to measure ECG signals. Accuracies to classify violent and non-violent events using 6-s ECG signal were up to 87%.

3   VITEC Framework

Based on the SEWEB concept, an online multi-modal **VI**olence de**TEC**tion (VITEC) framework is proposed using several components working together to provide reliable performance: (1) violence detection system based on the witnesses' and victims' point of view, (2) geographical location acquired from the GPS of a smartphone, (3) indoor location acquired from an RFID-based system, (4) reliable communication channel, and (5) processing unit: both local and cloud computing services.

Table 2 compares the original SEWEB concept to VITEC, providing general overview of the proposed framework in relation to the SEWEB concept. Embedded sensors used in the proposed framework are a 3D accelerometer and 3D gyroscope [21] to measure body movement or activity. This choice is a bit problematic, because not all smartphones have a gyroscope sensor. So, research on body movement recognition using an accelerometer only is recommended. Ambient information is not relevant, but the physiological signals of the subject measured using a wireless wearable sensor are needed. The SEWEB used no CCTV, but VITEC takes advantage of research on violence detection using surveillance video signals. Both SEWEB and VITEC need location data from either the GPS or RFID-based system.

Table 2. Comparing the SEWEB's and VITEC's component side-by-side

	SEWEB	VITEC
Technologies used to identify and measure relevant signals		
Embedded sensors of smartphones	✓	✓
Microphone of smartphones	✓	
Cameras of smartphones	✓	
Processing capacity of smartphones	✓	✓
Wearable sensors	✓	✓
Ambient sensors	✓	
CCTV		✓
Data measured and collected by sensors		
Activity data	✓	✓
Location data	✓	✓
Voice data	✓	
Health-related data	✓	✓*
Well-being data	✓	
Video data		✓
Technologies used to collect, process, and share/display data		
Smartphone apps	✓	✓
Cloud computing service	✓	✓
Social media solutions	✓	✓
Wearable safety devices	✓	✓
Phenomena to identify, measure, and categorize		
Change in stress level	✓	
Emotional state changes	✓	
Fast and slow changes in mood	✓	
Changes in physical activity level and modality	✓	✓
Detailed location information	✓	✓

* Physiological signals such as ECG, EDA, EEG, temperature, etc.

Although we cannot avoid verbal bullying, voice data is not relevant to VITEC because recording voice outside an isolated area is problematic. When someone is shouting the voices are recorded through all surrounding microphones, and the traceability of the voice data to a specific subject is questionable. VITEC does not use the smartphone camera, because users have to direct the camera manually. It is unrealistic to assume that the victim would have the possibility to direct the camera towards the perpetrator(s) or himself/herself.

VITEC does not identify stress level and emotional/mood changes. Psychologists argue about what kind of emotions/moods emerge during violent events, but to the best of our knowledge no empirical study has yet been found, which map those changes to violent events. Perhaps in the future these modalities can be added.

The four main components that make up the VITEC framework are a primary and secondary detection system, a Personal Safety Network, and a cloud computing service. The primary detection system is a collection of numerous primary agents, which work on the young people and detect violence based on the victim's point of view. The secondary detection system contains several of CCTV cameras connected to local video processing that detect a violent event based on the witness' point of view. They serve as secondary agents. Figure 1 shows the connectivity diagram of the VITEC framework.

As mentioned above, pupil welfare systems and other child protection services have limited capacities to work efficiently to address violence. The primary and secondary systems together with the cloud service are able to track and report violence automatically, delivering an additional resource for child safeguarding and combating violence. The VITEC framework also provides an automatic reporting feature. Both primary and secondary agents initiate the report by sending a message about suspicious events to the cloud service. When the cloud service confirms that a violent act, that event is recorded in the database together with the ID of all agents, the geographical location, date, and time. Thus, the number of unreported violent events can be reduced. Furthermore, the database in the cloud service can be used to study phenomena related to violence, which can benefit schools, other child welfare services, policy makers, and parents. It also enables better coordination between education and other child welfare sectors, such as health and social services and child protection. The primary and secondary systems depend upon various research activities, and so does the cloud service. As a result, the VITEC framework arranges such spaces for researchers from various fields to work together to fight against violence. It also encourages more collaborative work to deliver more valuable results.

3.1   Primary and Secondary Agents

Each primary agent consists of a wireless wearable multi-modal sensor that measures signals from the body of a young person and regularly sends appropriate signals to their smartphone for further processing. Each young person in VITEC is equipped with a primary agent. The smartphone employs a pre-detection algorithm, which must be simple but powerful enough to run within the limited smartphone environment and resources, to identify whether or not a suspicious event has occurred. Once a suspicious event is identified, the primary agent sends signals carrying that suspicious event along with the primary agent's ID and geographical location acquired from GPS to the cloud for further processing. The contribution of detecting violence using human body movements [21, 30] and physiological signal [22] fit for this role.

The secondary system contains several CCTV cameras connected to local video processing. CCTV cameras are security cameras that monitor the area of interest, for example a school yard, parking area, or street corner. Each CCTV sends recorded surveillance video with its ID to a local computer server for further processing.

This local server sends the detection result to the cloud. Results presented in Table 1 are promising for this role, because installing CCTV cameras at every geographical spot is impossible. According to the SEWEB concept, the secondary system is an additional system.

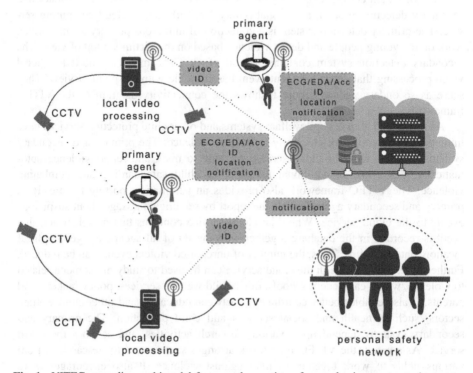

Fig. 1. VITEC, an online multimodal framework, consists of several primary agents (a smartphone and wearable sensors) and a number of secondary agents (CCTV connected to local video processing), and specific members of the Personal Safety Network connected to a cloud computing service.

Consequently, in the cloud service there are three possible cases based on the availability of the primary and secondary agents at a certain location. Upon receiving data from the primary agents, the cloud service must clarify if a violent event has occurred. It starts identifying the violent event using the signals from the primary agents. If a violent event is confirmed, the cloud service seeks for some notifications from the secondary agents in the area based on the location sent by the primary agents. The cloud services then decide which notifications should be fused to the result from the primary agents. This is the case when both agents are available. When there is no secondary agent available in the area of interest, the end result depends on the primary agents only. Another case is when there is no notification from the primary agents, but the secondary agents report a suspicious event at a certain location. The reason for this might be that the victim is one of the primary agents, but the battery power is low or that victim is not in the system yet. In this case the cloud service sends notification of the event to local authorities, for example the nearest police station, so the victim gets help immediately.

The primary agent solves problem about manual activation in the existing anti bullying apps. With automatic activation, the victims do not have to remember to press certain button when they experience violence. Furthermore, the system also sends notification to the authority on the victims' behalf. Some victims decide to report the violence events later, but most of them cancel or forget it.

3.2 Personal Safety Network

The Personal Safety Network is defined as the network connections a user wants to be in touch with in case of emergency or a socially challenging situation [14]. In other words, to whom should the notification be sent, depending on the context, e.g. location, type of challenging situation, time, type of help, etc. Those determine the members of the Personal Safety Network, so it is dynamically changing. For example, when a young person experiences violence on the street or on the way home from school, parents and the nearest authority can be notified. So, VITEC includes parents in all cases by default and dynamically changes other members of the Personal Safety Network based on the context.

3.3 Notifications

Notifications are sensor-initiated and user-initiated [14]. Within the VITEC framework, the sensor-initiated notification is a notification generated by the cloud services, because it is the end result after processing signals from sensors. The cloud sends a notification about a suspicious event to the members of the Personal Safety Network retrieved from the database as an alarm. The corresponding young person also receives a confirmation notification, indicating that the cloud has acknowledge the event. When a young person thinks that a confirmation notification should be received but he/she receives none, a user-initiated notification can be sent to the cloud manually, similar to the existing smartphone apps related to violence. Perhaps some situations cannot be measured by sensors, so that no notification is generated by the cloud services. This kind of situation is defined as a challenging situation. VITEC also sends notification about important messages, e.g. low battery power. Notification can be in a text message and/or as a status displayed in social media.

3.4 Context and Sensor Data

According to SEWEB, sensor data must be interpreted based on the context [14]. For example, in violence detection a primary agent interprets a violent event on the basis of pushing or tackling, also in cases of equally rough and tumble play. To decrease these kinds of false alarms, a multi-modal approach – including for example EDA and ECG – is needed to aid in violence detection. Both physiological signals are sensitive enough to affect stimulation, such that it may indicate that the subject is not in danger but having fun. Ferdinando et al. (2017) showed that it is possible, although not always, to separate some fun activities denoted as non-violence, e.g. playing, from simulated violence, e.g. pushing and hitting. It will require deeper investigation to get a more accurate algorithm to extract relevant information from the raw signals.

Figure 2 displays the position of each component in the VITEC framework in a layer diagram. This is a general layer diagram, as detailed layers on communication channels between layers are not provided. However, these follow a general data communication layer, consisting of certain standard internet protocols between clients and servers. The core of VITEC, as shown in Fig. 2, contains the primary and secondary agents, which detect violent events from the victims' and witnesses' points of view, respectively. Each agent only sends a message to the cloud when a suspicious event occurs.

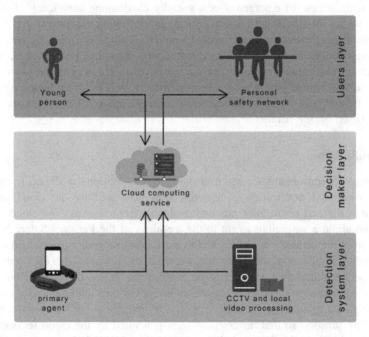

Fig. 2. Layer diagram of the VITEC framework presenting the position of each component and how each component interacts with the others.

The cloud computing service analyses the signals sent by primary agents more thoroughly and then combines with information from secondary agents to decide whether a violent event is occurred or not. If the violent event happens, the cloud service send notification to contact retrieved from database based on the context of the young person. A double arrow between the young person and the cloud represents a confirmation notification sent by the cloud to the young person and a user-initiated notification from the young person to the cloud, described above as a challenging situation.

4   The VITEC Service Platform and Business Concept

The VITEC service platform and business concept utilises a cloud computing service. The VITEC service platform can use either *Software as a Service* or *Platform as a Service*. If the system only provides services for end-users, then the *Software as a Service* should be used, where the vendor takes responsibility to maintain and develop the applications, and the users only provide data to the cloud. If there is the possibility to extend the services to other developers, then the right choice is the *Platform as a Service*. Instead of delivering service to end-users only, the *Platform as a Service* also provides services to developers who can create the applications for end-users. It allows for more collaboration among developers and expands the capability of the system to handle more complex problems.

Adopting the SEWEB business concept, VITEC offers a safety solution for young persons, location monitoring, and notifications for specified members of the Personal Safety Network to enable security knowledge with a potential market of around 10 million families [14]. The advantages offered by this business concept are the combined use of social media and sensor with shareable data for school or other related authorities. Some key operations within this business concept are apps and service developments, R&D, and marketing via various anti-bullying/anti-violence associations and school.

5   Social Contributions of VITEC

VITEC is a novel, innovative measure, designed through the multidisciplinary collaboration of academic scholars coming from the fields of engineering, psychology, and educational sciences for immediate recognition of acute physical violence among young persons. The affordances of VITEC are multiple across various age groups and across a range of spaces, places, geographical locations, and cultures. VITEC offers many ways forward for parents and other educators and public authorities, such as, school personnel, pupil welfare staff, social workers, and police by enabling efficient, immediate intervention when an acute violent situation is at hand. For the targets of violence, VITEC forms a unique personal alarm system that automatically contacts specified members of the social welfare network in case of a violent situation. It potentially increases the safety of not only young persons but also other potential targets of violent assault in locations and time of intensified risk for violence such as underpasses, empty or remote streets, on the way home from school, and at night-time. As for rape, there is an insistent myth (with hardly any supporting evidence) that girls and women lie about rape [31]. An automatic digital reporting system can potentially reduce the belief that rape is falsely reported, and so contribute to wider social change to address how rape is understood and responded to, and thus support in reducing sexual violence. Overall raised awareness of available digital applications for immediate intervention with increased risk of getting caught can make rape and other physical assaults less attractive to perpetrators.

6 Potential Future Research

The VITEC framework might open potential research in various fields. Machine learning has a wide range of research opportunities. For example, employing primary and secondary agents, the optimum way to fuse the results from both agents is still an open question. It ranges from the simplest method, e.g. a linear fusion with or without weight, to more complex methods, e.g. a Bayesian Network [32]. Another important example would be algorithms to choose the appropriate secondary agents based on the location. It is possible to get several secondary agents, which can contribute to detecting violent event, but perhaps not all agents are useful.

Researchers in machine vision have developed many useful methods to extract features from surveillance videos, and more advanced algorithms are coming to improve the present ones. Various scenarios may appear to verify the proposed methods. One possible scenario is when the recorded event is partially visible in a corner of the video frame only and no one knows whether a violent event has happened or not. The system must be able to decide whether such scenes are discarded or not. If motorized CCTVs are installed, the system may rotate the CCTVs' position when some suspicious events are detected at a street corners, for example, to make those scenes appear more clearly.

Perhaps what the primary agent requires most is a robust feature extraction method. ECG, for example, requires methods able to obtain powerful features from only several seconds signal, which is very challenging. Methods to harvest features from acceleration and gyroscope signals are on the horizon, and advancement in mathematics and programming languages supports them. Included in this part is a pre-detection algorithm running in the smartphone.

Presently, the primary agent relies on ECG signals and acceleration/gyroscope signals. To the best of our knowledge, there is no wearable sensor able to measure these three signals synchronously. Adding new modalities may require new sensors, which are not available yet. For example, using EEG signals require a new model of sensor, because wearing the available EEG sensor outside a laboratory or medical facility is not an option. This should motivate research on sensor development, e.g. a multi-modal wearable sensor with wireless connectivity, a wearable sensor with low energy consumption, etc.

VITEC depends on a reliable network, so data transmission should be made as efficient as possible. The primary agent sends data such as ID, location, raw signals, and notification of a possible violent event to the cloud service for further processing. The data transmission is only enabled when the primary agent receives a suspicious result, assuming that the pre-detection algorithm is mature enough. It allows saving the power and resources of the smartphone. The secondary agents also send data, e.g. detection result and ID to the cloud service. It means research on lossless data compression is in demand.

The proposed platform also drives research on apps development within the ubiquitous computing community. It includes but is not limited to (1) handling such a large number of nodes within the network communication to provide reliable operation; (2) dealing with resource constraint of the smartphone; (3) managing data transmission security and cryptographic protocol.

Research on violence detection using surveillance video also demands studies related to the optimum numbers and positions of cameras. It should minimize the number of cameras but offer large observation areas. This influences the number of dedicated local computers processing the data. Furthermore, recognition results from several angles or views that overlap must be fused carefully to provide reliable results. In the field of optimization, some strategies must be found to get the most appropriate number of CCTVs used in a certain area. This starts by defining some required parameters, e.g. possibility of occlusion, coverage area, percentage of overlapping areas, type of CCTV camera, etc. and continues to algorithm development and performance evaluation.

7   Discussions and Conclusions

Based on the SEWEB concept, the Violence Detection Framework – VITEC – was proposed as a response to problems related to violence among young people. It utilises sensors installed on the body of a young person and CCTV cameras to collect data to detect acute events of physical violence. It consists of a primary detection system (based on the victim's point of view) and secondary detection system(based on the witness' point of view). It also provides a framework to enable many researchers working on violence-related projects to work hand in hand to fight against violence.

VITEC places research on violence detection at its core to tackle the problem of school violence, providing researchers the means to transform their promising results into an applicable system. The primary agents detect violence using physiological and activity signals measured from the young persons. Although research on violence detection from the victim's point of view is not mature yet, advancements in mathematics, signal processing methods, computer technologies, and sensors development indicate that it is not beyond reach. Similarly, methods used in surveillance video-based violence detection in the secondary agent also take advantage of those advancements. The ultimate goal of these parts is to find a general model for both agents.

VITEC can be combined with existing school violence/bullying intervention programs to provide another way to report violent events. It also provides almost instant violent event notifications with location information. Furthermore, it may provide the answer of a world free from violence, as addressed by the UN Special Representative of Secretary-General on violence against children. VITEC is a kind of unique personal alarm system that automatically contacts specified persons.

Acknowledgment. This research and publication were supported by the Finnish Cultural Foundation, North-Ostrobothnia Regional Fund 2017.

References

1. United Nations: Protecting children from bullying - Report of Secretary-General. https://violenceagainstchildren.un.org/content/protecting-children-bullying-report-secretary-general. Accessed 2017
2. Sunnari, V., Kangasvuo, J., Heikkinen, M., Kuorikosi, N.: Gendered and Sexualized Violence in Educational Environments. Oulu University Press, Oulu (2002)

3. Barter, C., Berridge, D.: Children Behaving Badly? Peer Violence Between Children and Young People, pp. 1–262. Wiley-Blackwell, Chichester (2011)
4. Young, T., Hallsworth, S.: Young people, gangs, and street-based violence. In: Barter, C., Berridge, D. (eds.) Children Behaving Badly? Peer Violence Between Children and Young People. Wiley-Blackwell, Chichester, Chapter 5, pp. 59–69 (2011)
5. United Nations Educational, Scientific and Cultural Organization (UNESCO): School Violence and Bullying: Global Status Report, pp. 1–56. Unesco, Paris (2017)
6. United Nations Children's Fund: "UNICEF #ENDviolence,". https://www.unicef.org/end-violence. Accessed 2018
7. Pais, M.S.: The economic costs of violence against children, 13 July 2015. https://violenceagainstchildren.un.org/economic_costs_of_vac_viewpoint. Accessed 2018
8. Pais, M.S.: SRSG Santos Pais viewpoint: the 2030 agenda-implementation, follow up and review. http://srsg.violenceagainstchildren.org/viewpoint/2016-08-02_1478. Accessed 2018
9. Office of the United Nations High Commissioner for Human Rights: Convention on the Rights of the Child. http://www.ohchr.org/EN/ProfessionalInterest/Pages/CRC.aspx. Accessed 2018
10. SRSG on Violence against Children: Toward a World Free from Violence - Global Survey on Violence against Children, pp. 1–160. Unicef, New York (2013)
11. Google: STOPit - Apps on Google Play. https://play.google.com/store/apps/details?id=com.stopitcyberbully.mobile&hl=en. Accessed 2018
12. Google: Speak Up! (R) For Someone - Apps on Google Play. https://play.google.com/store/apps/details?id=com.rule14.socialvision. Accessed 2018
13. Apple Inc.: STOPit on the App Store. https://itunes.apple.com/us/app/stopit-app/id719179764?mt=8. Accessed 2018
14. Kinnunen, M., et al.: Wearable and mobile sensors connected to social media in human well-being applications. Telematics Inform. 33, 92–101 (2016)
15. Phipps, A., Ringrose, J., Renold, E., Jackson, C.: Rape culture, lad culture and every-day sexism: researching, conceptualizing and politicizing new mediations of gender and sexual violence. J. Gend. Stud. 27, 1–8 (2018)
16. Eyben, F., Weninger, F., Lehment, N., Schuller, B., Rigoll, G.: Affective video retrieval: violence detection in hollywood movies by large-scale segmental feature extraction. PLoS ONE 8, 1–9 (2013)
17. Ribeiro, P.C., Audigier, R., Pham, Q.C.: RIMOC, a feature to discriminate unstructured motions: application to violence detection for video-surveillance. Comput. Vis. Image Underst. 144, 121–143 (2016)
18. Zhang, T., Jia, W., Yang, B., Yang, J., He, X., Zheng, Z.: MoWLD: a robust motion image descriptor for violence detection. Multimed. Tools Appl. 76, 1419–1438 (2017)
19. Fleureau, J., Penet, C., Guillotel, P., Demarty, C.H.: Electrodermal activity applied to violent scenes impact measurement and user profiling. In: Conference Proceedings - IEEE International Conference on Systems, Man and Cybernetics, pp. 3310–3315 (2012)
20. Baltatzis, V., Bintsi, K., Apostolidis, G.K., Hadjileontiadis, L.J.: Bullying incidences identification within an immersive environment using HD EEG-based analysis: a Swarm Decomposition and Deep Learning approach. Sci Rep. 7, 1–8 (2017)
21. Ye, L., Ferdinando, H., Seppänen, T., Alasaarela, E.: Physical violence detection for preventing school bullying. Adv. Artif. Intell. 2014, 1–9 (2014)
22. Ferdinando, H., et al.: Violence detection from ECG signals: a preliminary study. J. Pattern Recogn. Res. 12, 7–18 (2017)
23. Kleinkopf, H.F.: A pilot study of galvanic skin response to motion picture violence. Thesis, Texas Tech University (1975)

24. Lorber, M.F.: Psychophysiology of aggression, psychopathy, and conduct problems: a meta-analysis. Psychol. Bull. **130**, 531–552 (2004)
25. de Souza, F.D.M., Chavez, G.C., Valle Jr., E.A., de Araujo, A.A.: Violence detection in video using spatio-temporal features. In: 23rd SIBGRAPI Conference on Graphics, Patterns and Images, pp. 224–230 (2010)
26. Bermejo Nievas, E., Deniz Suarez, O., Bueno García, G., Sukthankar, R.: Violence detection in video using computer vision techniques. In: Real, P., Diaz-Pernil, D., Molina-Abril, H., Berciano, A., Kropatsch, W. (eds.) CAIP 2011. LNCS, vol. 6855, pp. 332–339. Springer, Heidelberg (2011). https://doi.org/10.1007/978-3-642-23678-5_39
27. Bilinski, P., Bremond, F.: Human violence recognition and detection in surveillance videos. In: 13th IEEE International Conference on Advanced Video and Signal Based Surveillance (AVSS), pp. 30–36 (2016)
28. Zhang, T., Yang, Z., Jia, W., Yang, B., Yang, J., He, X.: A new method for violence detection in surveillance scenes. Multimedia Tools Appl. **75**, 7327–7349 (2016)
29. Jung, Y., Skoric, M., Kwon, J.H., Detenber, B.: Watching vs. playing: effects of violent media on presence, physiological arousal and aggressive cognitions. In: Proceeding of the International Society for Presence Research Annual Conference, pp. 1–7 (2011)
30. Ye, L., Ferdinando, H., Seppänen, T., Huuki, T., Alasaarela, E.: An instance-based physical violence detection algorithm for school bullying prevention. In: Proceeding of 2015 International Wireless Communications and Mobile Computing Conference (IWCMC), pp. 1384–1388 (2015)
31. McMillan, L.: Police officers' perceptions of false allegations of rape. J. Gend. Stud. **27**, 9–21 (2018)
32. Holmes, D.E., Jain, L.C.: Introduction to Bayesian networks. In: Jain, L.C. (ed.) Innovations in Bayesian Networks. Studies in Computational Intelligence, vol. 156, pp. 1–5. Springer, Heidelberg (2008). https://doi.org/10.1007/978-3-540-85066-3_1

Software Defect Prediction Model Based on Stacked Denoising Auto-Encoder

Yu Zhu[1(✉)], Dongjin Yin[2], Yingtao Gan[2], Lanlan Rui[1],
and Guoxin Xia[1]

[1] State Key Laboratory of Networking and Switching Technology, Beijing
University of Posts and Telecommunications, Beijing, China
915808818@qq.com, 1912696398@qq.com, 736070995@qq.com
[2] Beijing TangMIX Technology CO., Ltd., Beijing, China
576678349@qq.com, 541629067@qq.com

Abstract. Software defect prediction technology plays an important role in ensuring software quality. The traditional software defect prediction model can only perform "shallow learning" and cannot perform deep mining of data features. Aiming at this problem, we use the stacked denoising auto-encoder (SDAE) to superimpose into deep neural network. First, the deep network model was built through the stacked layers of denoising auto-encoder (DAE), then the unsupervised method was used to train each layer in turn with noised input for more robust expression, characteristics were learnt supervised by back propagation (BP) neural network and the whole net was optimized by using error back propagation. Simulation experiments prove that the prediction accuracy of our SDAE model is significantly improved compared with the traditional SVM and KNN prediction model.

Keywords: Software defect prediction · Stacked denoising auto-encoder · Deep learning

1 Introduction

With the wide application of computer software, the quality and reliability of software are increasingly valued. According to a report [1] by the National Institute of Standards and Technology, the success rate of complex specialized application software development in the United States is only 30%, and software defects cause the US economy to lose $55.9 billion annually. Therefore, how to establish a reasonable software defect prediction model is the focus of our research.

In recent years, many researchers have conducted various researches on software defect prediction technology, and proposed software defect prediction models based on machine learning and statistics. In 1993, Briand et al. [2] applied logistic regression, classification tree and OSR methods to the defect prediction study on 146 components of the ADA system. In 1998, Evett et al. [3] first applied genetic methods to the prediction of defects in military communication systems and telecommunication systems. The Multi-Layer Perception (MLP) proposed by Pizzi et al. [4] in 2002 is an effective software defect technique. Mahaweerawa et al. [5] first used fuzzy clustering

S. Han et al. (Eds.): AICON 2019, LNICST 287, pp. 18–27, 2019.
https://doi.org/10.1007/978-3-030-22971-9_2

to predict software defects in 2002. He applied Radial Basis Function (RBF) to predict software defects. In 2014, Jindal et al. [6] established a neural network prediction model to study software defects. Various optimization models for neural networks were proposed, such as PSO-BP and SA-BP. Yang et al. [7] introduced deep learning into the software defect prediction technology in 2015. In 2017, AV Phan et al. [8] proposes to automatically learn defect features for software defect prediction using precise graphs representing program execution flows, and deep neural networks.

Inspired by previous studies, this paper proposes a new software defect prediction model. Representative features are automatically extracted from unmarked condition monitoring data in an unsupervised manner by a stacked denoising auto-encoder (SDAE). By stacking the trained denoising auto-encoder, the deep neural network (DNN) is constructed to perform intelligent defect diagnosis after fine-tuning the model with several available marker data. In this approach, a large number of easily accessible unmarked status monitoring data is utilized to learn useful and robust features. Only a small amount of tag data is required, which is advantageous in practical applications. In addition, after further fine-tuning the trained DNN, the software defect prediction can be correctly classified by the proposed method. The rest of the paper is organized as follows. In Sect. 2, the prediction model based on SDAE are introduced in detail. In Sect. 3, the experiment on open source dataset MDP is discussed and the results are also displayed. Summary is made in Sect. 4.

2 Software Defect Prediction Model Based on SDAE

2.1 Data Preprocessing Method Based on SMOTE Algorithm

In the software system, the number of high-risk modules is relatively small, and the dataset is imbalanced dataset, and the class that is a small number is called a minority class. To solve this problem, Chawla et al. [9] proposed a synthetic minority over-sampling technique (SMOTE). The specific steps of the algorithm are as follows:

1. The training sample is T, and D is a minority sample set in T. For each minority class sample $x_i \in D$, calculate the Euclidean distance of x_i to other minority samples $x_j(j \neq i)$ and find the K neighbors of x_i according to the distance, denoted as $x_{i(near)}, near \in \{1, 2, \ldots k\}$.
2. Randomly select a sample $x_{i(j)} \in x_{i(near)}$ and generate a new minority sample according to the following formula: $x_{i1} = x_i + rand(0, 1) * (x_{i(j)} - x_i)$, where $rand(0, 1)$ represents a random number between 0 and 1.
3. Repeat step 2 according to the over-sampling rate M, then add all generated minority samples to D.

2.2 Stacked Denoising Auto-encoder

We propose a software defect prediction model that uses a deep neural network (DNN) based on stacked denoising auto-encoder. Representative features are learned by applying the denoising auto-encoder to the unlabeled data in an unsupervised manner. A DNN is then constructed and fine-tuned with just a few items of labelled data.

Auto-encoder. An auto-encoder is a three-layer neural network that tries to reconstruct the input at the output layer after being passed through an intermediate layer [10]. A sample auto-encoder is shown in Fig. 1 where it tries to learn a function $h_{W,b}(x) \approx x$, that is, the output layer is trying to be equal to the input layer. W, b correspond to the weight matrix and bias of the input respectively. There is no limit to the hidden layer's size, and the circle of "+1" means the biases.

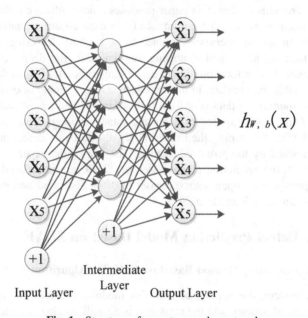

Fig. 1. Structure of an auto-encoder network.

The auto-encoder network's goal is to make the output is close to the input so that the output is the reconstruction of the input. In this way, the hidden layer can retained much of the information from the input data and may be a good expression of the input. Given a training set, with training examples, the cost function is formulated as:

$$
\begin{aligned}
J(W,b) &= \left[\frac{1}{m} \sum_{i=1}^{m} J(W, b; x^{(i)}, y^{(i)}) \right] + \frac{\lambda}{2} \sum_{l=1}^{n_l-1} \sum_{i=1}^{s_l} \sum_{j=1}^{s_l+1} (w_{ji}^{(l)})^2 \\
&= \left[\frac{1}{m} \sum_{i=1}^{m} \left(\frac{1}{2} ||h_{w,b}(x^{(i)}) - y(i)||^2 \right) \right] + \frac{\lambda}{2} \sum_{l=1}^{n_l-1} \sum_{i=1}^{s_l} \sum_{j=1}^{s_l+1} (w_{ji}^{(l)})^2
\end{aligned}
\tag{1}
$$

The first term in the formula is the mean square error, and the second term is the regularization, also called the weight decay, which is used to control the magnitude of the weight decay, thereby avoiding overfitting. $J(W, b; x^{(i)}, y^{(i)})$ is the square error relative to a single sample, and $J(W, b)$ is the loss function of the overall sample. λ is the coefficient of weight penalty.

In order to train the neural network, it is first necessary to initialize $W_{ji}^{(l)}$ and $b_i^{(l)}$ with an initial value close to 0, and then use the gradient descent algorithm to optimize the cost function $J(W, b)$.

The weights and bias of the network are updated using backpropagation algorithm as defined in [11]. Each iteration of the gradient descent algorithm updates the parameters W and b as follows:

$$W_{ji}^{(l)} = W_{ji}^{(l)} - \alpha \frac{\partial}{\partial W_{ji}^{(l)}} J(\text{W,b}) \tag{2}$$

$$b_i^{(l)} = b_i^{(l)} - \alpha \frac{\partial}{\partial b_i^{(l)}} J(W, b) \tag{3}$$

Where α is the learning rate.

$$\frac{\partial}{\partial w_{ji}^{(l)}} J(\text{w,b}) = \frac{1}{m} \sum_{i=1}^{m} \frac{\partial}{\partial w_{ji}^{(l)}} J\left(w, b; x^{(i)}, y^{(i)}\right) + \lambda W_{ji}^{(l)} \tag{4}$$

$$\frac{\partial}{\partial b_i^{(l)}} J(W, b) = \frac{1}{m} \sum_{i=1}^{m} \frac{\partial}{\partial b_i^{(l)}} J(W, b; x^{(i)}, y^{(i)}) \tag{5}$$

Denoising Auto-encoder. The denoising auto-encoder (DAE) is an improvement based on the ordinary auto-encoder, and its purpose is not to reduce noise, but to learn more features that are robust. The structure of DAE is showed in Fig. 2. First, the initial input x is corrupted into $\tilde{x}$ through the stochastic mapping $\tilde{x} \sim q_D(\tilde{x}|x)$. The mapping q_D can be described as: a fraction of the elements of data x chosen randomly is forced to 0. After corrupted input $\tilde{x}$ is got, the steps of encoder and decoder can be calculated as the ordinary auto-encoder to get the hidden output $y = f_\theta(\tilde{x})$ and reconstruction output $\hat{x} = g_{\theta'}(y)$. The cost function is the squared error loss $L_2(x - \hat{x}) = \|x - \hat{x}\|^2$, which is minimized by updating the parameters.

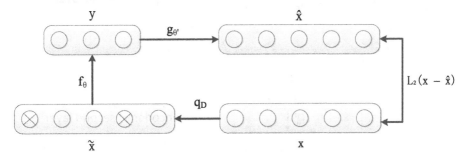

Fig. 2. Structure of a denoising auto-encoder network.

The difference between the DNA and the ordinary auto-encoder is that $\hat{x}$ here is a deterministic function of $\tilde{x}$ rather than x. It thus encourages the learning of a cleverer mapping than the identity: one that extracts features useful for denoising [12]. The layer-wise procedure is the same as the ordinary auto-encoder. The input corruption is used only for the training of each layer to learn useful representations. After the mapping f_θ is learnt, uncorrupted inputs are used to produce a representation that will serve as the clean input to the following layer. Different types of corruption processes may be considered such as additive isotropic Gaussian noise, salt-and-pepper noise and masking noise [13]. In this way, DAE utilizes the denoising as a training criterion to extract stable and robust features.

Stacked Denoising Auto-encoders. The stacked denoising auto-encoder network stacks multiple denoising auto-encoder networks to form a deep network model. The output of the previous hidden layer is used as the input of the latter denoising auto-encoder. The learning of denoising auto-encoder is performed layer by layer until the last hidden layer, and the output of this layer is the learned high-level output features. Note that the input corruption is only used for the initial denoising-training of each individual layer which acts as feature extractors. After the parameters are learned, the no corruption input is applied to produce the features that will be the clean input of the next layer [14]. The stacking procedure of denoising auto-encoders is shown in Fig. 3.

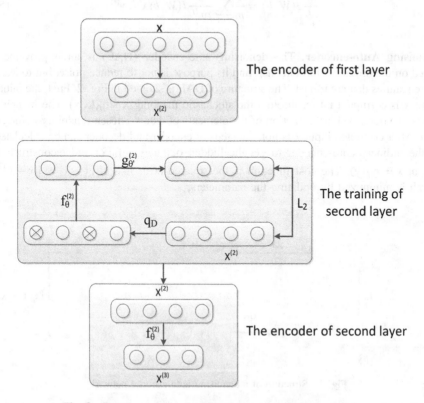

Fig. 3. Structure of a stacked denoising auto-encoder network.

Once the stack denoising auto-encoders (SDAE) is built, we can get the highest features from the last hidden layer. In order to get more discriminative features, a stand-alone supervised algorithm of Softmax regression is added on the top of the stack as illustrated in Fig. 4. The parameters of all layers then can be optimized using the stochastic gradient descent. And the classification accuracy result is able to be got from the Softmax model [15], too.

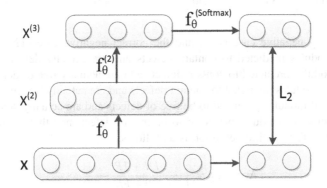

Fig. 4. Structure of softmax layer.

Step 1: Data pre-processing. Standardize the acquired data and then balance the data with the SMOTE algorithm.

Step 2: Initialization of the DNN. A DNN with N-hidden layers is initialized with random parameters.

Step 3: Unsupervised feature learning. Denoising autoencoder is applied here to learn representative features from the unlabeled data.

Step 4: Supervised fine-tuning of the model. After Step 3, a softmax layer is added on top of the DNN. Labelled condition data is used to fine-tune the parameters of the DNN by stochastic gradient descent.

Step 5: Fault diagnosis with the trained DNN. With the trained DNN, fault prediction can be carried out.

3 Experiments and Results

NASA dataset is widely used in the research of defect prediction technology. The data is derived from the source code of McCabe and Halstead attributes. We use NASA's MDP public data set, and select JM1, MC1 and PC5 three sub-data sets with a large amount of data. These three data sets are all imbalanced data sets, and the defect data is a minority class, as shown in the Table 1.

We rely on AMD Opteron (tm) Processor 6320, RAM 32 GB, 64-bit operating system, python 3.5.4 and so on. In the typical defect prediction technology research, the estimation results are usually evaluated using the confusion matrix related evaluation performance indicators, such as accuracy, precision, recall, F-measure and so on. The confusion matrix includes the correct positive case (TP), the wrong positive case

Table 1. Dataset summary.

Dataset	Number of samples	Number of attributes	Number of samples in the majority class	Number of samples in the minority class	Proportion of minority samples
JM1	7782	21	6110	1672	21.5%
MC1	1988	38	1942	46	2.3%
PC5	1711	38	1240	471	27.5%

(FP), the wrong negative case (FN), and the correct negative case (TN). TP is the number of modules predicted to contain defects and are actually defects. FP is the number of modules predicted to contain defects and are actually free of defects. FN is the number of modules predicted to contain defects and are actually free of defects. FN is the number of modules predicted to be free of defects and are actually defective, and TN is the number of modules predicted to be free of defects and that do not actually contain defects. The specific definition is as follows.

$$Accuracy = \frac{TN + TP}{TN + TP + FN + FP} \tag{6}$$

$$Precision = \frac{TP}{TP + FN} \tag{7}$$

$$Recall = \frac{TP}{TP + FP} \tag{8}$$

$$F - measure = \frac{(\alpha^2 + 1)Precision * Recall}{\alpha^2(Precision + Recall)} \tag{9}$$

Usually, $\alpha = 1$.

3.1 Data Preprocessing Based on SMOTE Algorithm

For imbalanced data sets, it is unreasonable to use only the confusion matrix-based metrics to evaluate the performance of the prediction model. For example, when the minority class proportion is less than 1%, even if all the minority samples are divided into the majority class, the total precision can still reach 99%, but such a model has no practical significance, and its classification accuracy rate for the minority is 0. Therefore, we will select the F-measure of the minority class and the overall AUC value as the evaluation indicators. The prediction of minority samples, that is, the defect samples, is what we need to pay attention to. F-measure can comprehensively consider the recall and precision of the samples. The ROC (Receiver Operating Characteristic curve) curve is a coordinate pattern analysis tool that can describe the classification performance of the classifier at different discriminant thresholds. The abscissa is the FP and the ordinate is TP. In practical applications, the performance of the classifier is generally evaluated by replacing the ROC curve with the AUC (Area Under the ROC Curve). We use SVM and KNN algorithms to classify data separately.

The Tables 2 and 3 lists the F-measure values of minority class and AUC values on the original and processed datasets using the SVM and KNN classifiers.

It can be seen from the table that after the imbalanced data is processed by the SMOTE algorithm, the classification effect of the minority samples is significantly improved, and the classification effect of the overall data is also improved.

Table 2. Metrics for the original dataset and the processed dataset using SVM.

Dataset		F-measure	AUC
JM1	Original dataset	0.23	0.56
	Processed dataset	0.60	0.65
MC1	Original dataset	0.00	0.50
	Processed dataset	0.76	0.75
PC5	Original dataset	0.11	0.52
	Processed dataset	0.61	0.62

Table 3. Metrics for the original dataset and the processed dataset using KNN.

Dataset		F-measure	AUC
JM1	Original dataset	0.23	0.55
	Processed dataset	0.75	0.72
MC1	Original dataset	0.00	0.50
	Processed dataset	0.87	0.86
PC5	Original dataset	0.33	0.56
	Processed dataset	0.69	0.68

3.2 Data Prediction Based on SDAE

We predict and classify the data processed by the SMOTE algorithm. Through experiments, we can determine that when the number of hidden layers in SDAE is 2, the number of cells per layer is [6, 11], and the learning rate is 0.1, the model performance is optimal. In order to verify the superiority of the proposed method with respect to the traditional classification method, the results were compared with SVM and KNN. The experimental results were evaluated by accuracy, recall, precision and F-measure. The detailed software defect prediction results were shown in the Table 4.

Obviously, when the SVM, KNN, and SDAE are measured using the Accuracy, Recall, Precision, and F-Measure metrics on the three software defect sets of JM1, MC1, and PC5, the metrics of SDAE are generally compared. It can be seen that the prediction performance has improved significantly. The reason why SDAE prediction and classification ability is stronger than SVM and KNN is that its deep nonlinear network abstracts the original data layer by layer, and obtains features that are more capable of describing the essence of the object and easy to classify. Denoising pre-training is performed for each layer of DAE. The robustness of the extracted features is further enhanced, and the spatial features of the data are more fully explored.

Table 4. Experimental results.

Dataset	Model	Accuracy	Precision	Recall	F-measure
JM1	SVM	0.65	0..65	0.65	0.64
	KNN	0.72	0.73	0.72	0.72
	SDAE	0.82	0.80	0.83	0.81
MC1	SVM	0.76	0.76	0.76	0.76
	KNN	0.86	0.87	0.86	0.86
	SDAE	0.87	0.89	0.86	0.87
PC5	SVM	0.66	0.66	0.66	0.66
	KNN	0.67	0.68	0.67	0.67
	SDAE	0.81	0.74	0.79	0.81

4   Summary

Aiming at the limitations of existing software defect prediction models that can't dig deeper into data features, this paper proposes to use the stack denoising auto-encoder in deep learning to learn the data of software defect datasets, mine data features, and build software defect prediction model. The actual data and comparative experimental results show that the SDAE model used in this paper has high predictability and practicability for software defects. In the following work, the differences between other non-neural network classification algorithms and SDAE in software defect prediction applications will be further studied, and the various parameter adjustment methods and structures of SDAE will be improved.

References

1. National Institute of Standards and Technology (NIST): Software Errors Cost U.S. Economy $59.5 Billion Annually. http://www.abeacha.com/NIST_press_release_bugs_cost.htm
2. Briand, L.C., Brasili, V.R., Hetmanski, C.J.: Developing interpretable models with optimized set reduction for identifying high-risk software components. IEEE Trans. Software Eng. 19(11), 1028–1044 (1993)
3. Evett, M., Khoshgoftar, T., Chien, P.D., et al.: GP-based software quality prediction. In: Proceedings of the Third Annual Conference Genetic Programming, pp. 60–65 (1998)
4. Pizzi, N.J., Summers, R., Pedrycz, W.: Software quality prediction using median-adjusted class labels. In: Proceedings: International Joint Conference on Neural Networks, vol. 3, pp. 2405–2409 (2002)
5. Mahaweerawat, A., Sophasathit, P., Lursinsap, C.: Software fault prediction using fuzzy clustering and radial basis function network. In: International Conference on Intelligent Technologies, pp. 304–313 (2002)
6. Jindal, R., Malhotra, R., Jain, A.: Software defect prediction using neural networks. In: IEEE 3rd International Conference on Reliability, Infocom Technologies and Optimization (ICRITO) (Trends and Future Directions), pp. 1–6 (2014)

7. Yang, X., Lo, D., Xia, X., et al.: Deep learning for just-in-time defect prediction. In: IEEE International Conference on Software Quality, Reliability and Security (QRS), pp. 17–26 (2015)
8. Phan, A.V., Nguyen, M.L., Bui, L.T.: Convolutional neural networks over control flow graphs for software defect prediction. In: IEEE 29th International Conference on Tools with Artificial Intelligence (ICTAI), vol. 1, pp. 45–52 (2017)
9. Chawla, N.V., Bowyer, K.W.: SMOTE: synthetic minority over-sampling technique. J. Artif. Intell. Res. **16**, 341–378 (2002)
10. Thirukovalluru, R., Dixit, S., Sevakula, R.K., et al.: Generating feature sets for fault diagnosis using denoising stacked auto-encoder. In: IEEE International Conference on Prognostics and Health Management, pp. 1–7 (2016)
11. Ng, A., Ngiam, J., Foo, C.Y., Mai, Y., Suen, C.: UFLDL tutorial. Accessed Mar 2016. http://ufldl.stanford.edu/wiki/index.php/UFLDL_Tutorial
12. Feng, X., Zhang, Y., Glass, J.: Speech feature denoising and dereverberation via deep autoencoders for noisy reverberant speech recognition. In: IEEE International Conference on Acoustics, pp. 1759–1763 (2014)
13. Vincent, P., Larochelle, H., Bengio, Y., et al.: Extracting and composing robust features with denoising autoencoders. In: ACM International Conference on Machine Learning, pp. 1096–1103 (2008)
14. Xiao, N., Liu, D., Luo, A., et al.: Adaptive feature extraction based on Stacked Denoising Auto-encoders for asynchronous motor fault diagnosis. In: IEEE International Congress on Image and Signal Processing, Biomedical Engineering and Informatics, pp. 854–859 (2017)
15. Ma, J., Lu, C., Zhang, W., et al.: Health assessment and fault diagnosis for centrifugal pumps using Softmax regression. J. Vibroengineering **16**(3), 1464–1474 (2014)

Deep&Cross Network for Software-Intensive System Fault Prediction

Guoxin Xia[1]($\boxtimes$), Dongjin Yin[2], Yingtao Gan[2], Lanlan Rui[1],
and Yu Zhu[1]

[1] State Key Laboratory of Networking and Switching Technology,
Beijing University of Posts and Telecommunications, Beijing 100876, China
736070995@qq.com
[2] Beijing TangMIX Technology Co., Ltd., Beijing, China

Abstract. With the development of information technology, the causes of software-intensive system failures become more complicated. This paper analyzes the correlation of various fault factors of software-intensive equipment and uses deep learning model to do fault prediction in complex electronic information system. Experimental results show that neural network model based on feature interaction can get better effect than some other methods.

Keywords: Software-intensive · Fault prediction ·
Field-aware Factorization Machine · Deep&Cross network

1 Introduction

With the rapid development of software and hardware and the continuous upgrading of various modern equipments, software has become more and more important, and it has more and more functions. Software-intensive systems have gradually become the mainstream form of software systems [1].

At the same time, the requirements of system availability and security become more stringent in such complex systems. What's more, maintenance is becoming more complicated after system error. Software is less reliable than hardware. Once a fault occurs, it not only causes the loss of the corresponding hardware function, but even causes the whole system to fall into paralysis. So it's important to predict which fault factors cause the error and to repair system targetedly based on the prediction.

The complexity of software grows exponentially with increasing demand, and the incidence of software-intensive system disasters due to software failures continues to increase. Some fault prediction methods for software-intensive systems are knowledge-based, mainly includes expert system [2] and fuzzy logic. Some fault prediction methods are based on models, like failure physical model and state space model. However, with the development of machine learning and deep learning theory, data-based fault prediction technology is starting to become a trend.

S. Han et al. (Eds.): AICON 2019, LNICST 287, pp. 28–39, 2019.
https://doi.org/10.1007/978-3-030-22971-9_3

There are 3 main reason for higher fault rate of software-intensive system:

Logical complexity: As code lines increase and modularize, interaction modules increase, it's difficult to control and predict the behavior of these interactions. Studies have shown that more and more failures occur because of abnormal interactions within the system.

Boundary erosion: software interactions and complex software-intensive peripheral hardware systems have become so frequent and complex software boundaries have been eroded by peripherals. The survey revealed that when the interaction between software and hardware fails, part or whole system will fall into trouble.

Longevity: Complex tasks require these systems to operate over long life cycles, during which the system must combat external and internal failure attacks and evolution to adapt to the environment but remain quasi-stable, which requires more attention and may cause system function failure in runtime, such as abnormal runtime data flow.

Longevity of system means more data can be collected. So data-based fault prediction can have a good effect. In this paper, we use Deep&Cross network to predict the fault factors of software-intensive systems. In particular, it makes following contributions: (1) Solving the problem of feature combination under sparse data while keeping different characteristics between different features, so training time and memory consumption will be less and generalization will be better; (2) The cross network layer introduced by DCN can express any high-order feature combination, while each layer retains low-order combination, and the vectorization of parameters also controls the complexity of the model. So logical complexity and boundary erosion of software-intensive systems are considered to predict more accurately.

2   Related Work

Fault prediction problems received a lot of attention from researchers. Some used autoregressive moving average (ARMA) model [3] or its variants to do fault prediction based on time series. And some did the same things by using LSTM (Long Short-Term Memory) [4] or its variants. When the software-intensive systems were not so complicated, some methods analyze and determine the location of defects by the basic tool that recorded running information of target software. These methods are based on the software failure mechanism, using the concept of control flow and data flow, analyzing the application of program slicing and dynamic slicing technology, and drawing on the idea of "software black box" [5, 6].

As complexity of software-intensive systems increases and large amount of data generate, methods based on deep learning play an increasingly important role. The fault prediction process is as shown below (Fig. 1):

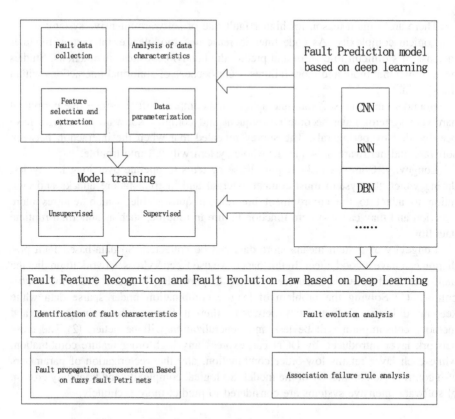

Fig. 1. Fault prediction process.

3   Fault Prediction in a Software-Intensive System

3.1   Fault Characteristics

In a software-intensive system, due to the embedding of lots of software programs which play an equally important role as its hardware system, the failure mode includes not only the software and the hardware but some new problems that hardware and software combination causes [7]. Generally there are three types as follows: (1) The software program is wrong and these errors are passed to the hard through the inter-action of software and hardware. And it causes hardware failure; (2) Hardware damage or failure affects the software associated with it, resulting in software errors; (3) There are no separate errors or malfunctions in software and hardware, but when a contact occurs in them, a system failure occurs, or the contact cannot be completed.

There are five typical characteristics in software-intensive systems: hierarchy, relevance, randomness, uncertainty and cross-propagation. These characteristics in software-intensive systems have become more and more obvious with increased software complexity. So expert knowledge system have more limitations and the difficulty of the definition of knowledge is also increasing. In the case of composite faults, each fault interacts with the system. The fault modeling and theoretical analysis of the composite fault cannot be performed using the certain mode. Deep learning does not rely on prior assumptions and automatically detects interactions.

3.2 Fault Factors

There are a variety of potential failure factors in a software-intensive system. For example, in software-intensive electronic information systems, some fault factors are as follows:

1. Software failure type: including input and output problems, program problems, performance problems, design/logic problems, timing problems, data problems
2. Environment type: temperature, humidity, electromagnetic, current exceed the threshold or change too much; typical misoperations such as mis-opening, mis-closing, etc.
3. Hardware failure type: hardware short circuit, open circuit, parameter problem, hardware damage or looseness.

3.3 Features and Feature Combination

We collected and processed a dataset about software-intensive electronic information system. After filtering, 76 features can be used to do prediction and 27 mainly fault factors exist. Some samples are in Table 1.

Table 1. Fault samples.

Number	Features closely connected to fault factors	Fault factors
1	Speed fluctuation of CPU fan	CPU fan is faulty
2	Server log alarm	Database content is lost
3	CPU temperature is too high for a long time && Computer crash	CPU burned down
4	CPU temperature is in normal && Unable to start server && CPU pin is abnormal	Poor CPU socket contact
5	Abnormal humidity	Hardware deformation
......	......	......

Considering communication and combination in features, we can turn this prediction into a feature combination problem. For example, CPU temperature exceeds eighty degrees may not cause fault. But if CPU have been working for a long time, the situation will be different.

After some features are correlated, their correlation with the prediction label will increase. A polynomial model is the most intuitive model that contains a combination of features. In a polynomial model, the combination of the features x_i and x_j is represented by $x_i x_j$. For a second-order polynomial model, the model's expression is as follows, where n represents the number of features of the sample, x_i is the value of the i-th feature, w_0, w_i and w_{ij} are model parameters.

$$y(x) = w_0 + \sum_{i=1}^{n} w_i x_i + \sum_{i=1}^{n} \sum_{j=i+1}^{n} w_{ij} x_i x_j \tag{1}$$

It's obvious in (1), the number of parameters of the combined feature is $\frac{n \times (n-1)}{2}$. However, after one-hot, features will be very sparse. Samples satisfying that xi and xj are not all zero are too enough to learn w_{ij} accurately. In FM (Factorization Machine) [8], w_{ij} form a symmetric matrix W which can be expressed as:

$$W = V^T V \tag{2}$$

In other words, $w_{ij} = <v_i, v_j>$. So FM's model equation is:

$$y(x) = w_0 + \sum_{i=1}^{n} w_i x_i \sum_{i=1}^{n} \sum_{j=i+1}^{n} <v_i, v_j> x_i x_j \tag{3}$$

In this equation, V_i is the hidden vector of the i-dimensional feature, $<,>$ represents the vector dot product. The length of the hidden vector is k (k << n), which contains k factors describing the feature. The parameter factorization makes the parameters of $x_h x_i$ and the parameters of $x_i x_j$ no longer independent of each other, so we can estimate the quadratic parameters of FM relatively reasonably in the case of sparse samples.

FM's embedding is shown as below (Fig. 2):

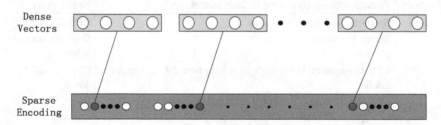

Fig. 2. FM embedding.

By introducing the concept of field, FFM (Field-aware Factorization Machine) [9] attributes features of the same nature to the same field. Taking the CPU temperature as an example, we set multiple levels at first. The three characteristics of 65–70 °C, 70–75 °C or 75–80 °C are all about CPU temperature and can be placed in the same field. In the same way, the data problem may be all the data loss, partial loss, data file virus infection, database operation error, database deadlock, etc. These dozens of features are all data problems, so they can also be put together in a field.

In FFM, feature x_i in each dimension learns a hidden vector v_{i,f_j} for each field f_j of other features. Therefore, the hidden vector is not only related to the feature, but also related to the field. That is to say, the "temperature of CPU is in 70–75 °C" feature uses different hidden vectors when it is associated with the "program input error" feature and the "current value size" feature.

Assuming that the n features of the sample belong to f fields, then the quadratic term of the FFM has n * f hidden vectors. In the FM model, there is only one hidden vector for feature of each dimension. FM can be seen as a special case of FFM, it is an FFM model that assigns all features to one field.

FFM's model equation is:

$$y(x) = w_0 + \sum_{i=1}^{n} w_i x_i + \sum_{i=1}^{n} \sum_{j=i+1}^{n} <v_{i,f_j}, v_{j,f_i}> x_i x_j \tag{4}$$

FFM's embedding is shown as below (Fig. 3):

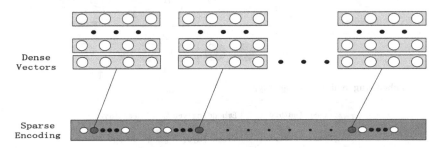

Fig. 3. FFM embedding.

4 Model Structure

DCN (deep & cross network) [10] model's structure is shown in Fig. 4. In this prediction problem, feature crossing is an important step, but many network structure only learns the secondary crossover at most. The Logistic Regression model uses the original artificial crossover feature, and Product-based Neural Network [11] uses the product method to do the second-order crossover. Neural Factorization Machines [12] and Attention Neural Factorization Machines [13] also use Bi-interaction to learn the second-order intersection of features. For higher-order feature intersections, others only let deep section learn. But DCN can express any high-order combination while each layer retains a low-order combination by cross layer network.

At first, we make data cleaning for our features collected. After that, we do FFM embedding for high dimensional sparse features and contact them with dense feature. So after embedding and stacking layer, the features can be shown as a vector like:

$$X_0 = [x_{embed,1}^T, \ldots, x_{embed,k}^T, x_{dense}^T] \tag{5}$$

After embedding and stacking layer, the network is divided into two ways. One way is the traditional DNN structure as follows

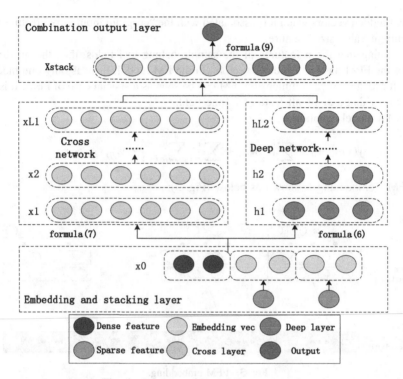

Fig. 4. Structure of Deep&Cross network.

$$h_{l+1} = Relu(w_l h_l + b_l) \tag{6}$$

When vector dimension of X0 is d and there are m units in each layer of DNN, the parameters that need to be learned in total are d * m + m * (m + 1) * (L2 − 1). Another way is DCN's core, cross network. Assuming that the network has L1 layers, the relationship between each layer and the previous layer can be expressed by the following relationship:

$$x_{l+1} = x_l x_l^T w_l + b_l + X_l = f(x_l, w_l, b_l) + x_l \tag{7}$$

In above, f is the function to be fitted, and x_l is the network input of the previous layer. The parameters that need to be learned are w_l and b_l. Since the dimension of x_l is d, and x_{l+1} is also d-dimension. The parameters w_l and b_l which need to be learned are also d-dimension vectors. Therefore, each layer has 2 * d parameters (w and b) that need to be learned.

After deep layer network and cross layer network, we use sigmoid function to output result:

$$x_{\text{stack}} = Concat(x_{l1}, h_{l2}) \tag{8}$$

$$\text{p} = \text{sigmoid}(W_{\text{logit}}x_{\text{stack}} + b_{\text{logit}}) \tag{9}$$

5   Experiments and Results

We do experiments based on a large number of test data from daily operations for complex electronic information systems.

After data preprocessing, 76 features are chosen for training and 27 fault factors exist. Fault data feature description are shown in the following Table 2. Discrete variables are converted to one-hot format.

Table 2. Fault data feature description.

Number	Raw feature	Discrete variable	Continuous variable	Example
1	Code length of each module		✓	1737
2	The extent to which the hardware reaches the specification	✓		[1, 0, 0, ...]
3	CPU temperature		✓	76 (°C)
4	CPU occupancy		✓	43 (%)
5	Memory occupancy		✓	66 (%)
6	Degree of constraint by size of main memory or storage availability	✓		[1, 0, 0, ...]
7	Satisfactoriness of system response time	✓		[1, 0, 0, ...]
8	Stability of hardware and system support	✓		[1, 0, 0, ...]
9	System runtime		✓	24276 (s)
10	Syslog level	✓		[1, 0, 0, ...]
11	Syslog refresh speed		✓	
......	......	......	......	......

We compared DCN method with other models, for example, DNN, SVM, NFM (Neural Factorization Machines) and FDES (fault diagnosis expert system). The goal is to predict fault factors and evaluation standard is precision, recall, F1-measure, accuracy and AUC (Area Under roc Curve). The calculation method of these indicators is the same as two classification problem by thinking of all incorrect categories as a negative sample. For example, when a test set is all predicted, there will be some samples predicted to be other classes while they are actually from class1, and some samples that are not actually from class1, predicted to be Class1, which leads to the following result:

Table 3. Classification situation.

	The predicted result is Class1 (Positive)	The predicted result is non-Class1 (Negative)
The prediction result is true (True)	Class1_TP: The number of samples that are predicted as Class1 and are actually Class	Class1_ TN: The number of samples that are not actually Class1 and are also predicted as other classes (non-Class1)
The prediction result is false (False)	Class1_ FP: The number of samples that are predicted as Class1 but are not actually Class	Class1_ FN: The number of samples that are actually Class1 but are predicted to be other classes (non-Class1)

According to the above Table 3, we can calculate:

$$Class1_{Precision} = \frac{Class1\_Tp}{Class1\_TP + Class1\_FP} \tag{10}$$

$$Class1_{Recall} = \frac{Class1\_TP}{Class1\_TP + Class1\_FN} \tag{11}$$

$$Class1_{F1Score} = \frac{2 * (Class1\_Precision * Class1\_Recall)}{Class1\_Precision + Class1\_Recall} \tag{12}$$

$$Class1_{Accuracy} = \frac{Class1\_TP + Class1\_TN}{count(Samples)} \tag{13}$$

Then final precision, recall, F1Score, accuracy can be calculated by taking the average of all classes' corresponding values.

We mainly used TensorFlow and python package scikit-learn to implement most of the models and have adjusted parameters to get the best performance for each single model. The results are as follow (ROC curve means receiver operating characteristic curve):

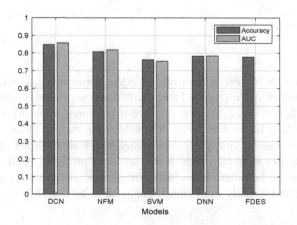

Fig. 5. Accuracy and AUC.

Table 4. Three evaluating indicators of 5 models.

Models	Indicators		
	Precision	Recall	F1Score
DCN	0.843	0.852	0.847
NFM	0.812	0.809	0.810
SVM	0.774	0.778	0.776
DNN	0.792	0.786	0.789
FDES	0.776	0.772	0.774

For FDES, we calculate only accuracy but not AUC, because FDES gives a result without probability. As we can see in Fig. 5 and Table 4. Deep&Cross network model gets the highest accuracy, AUC and F1Score. Obviously, multi-order intersection of features has significant effect. However, other models can't learn multi-order intersection of features effectively because of the lack of cross network structure. When we use FM embedding to replace FFM embedding in DCN model, the accuracy and AUC will drop a little bit. It means FFM embedding learned a more suitable hidden vector than FM embedding by distinguishing feature field.

As for training time, DCN with FFM takes about 12476 s and DCN with FM takes about 11382 s. There is not much difference in training time between the two methods. NFM takes 16232 s, DNN takes 17286 s and SVM takes 28109 s. FM and FFM make feature space small, so models can converge quickly. FFM is slower than FM due to diversity of feature combinations.

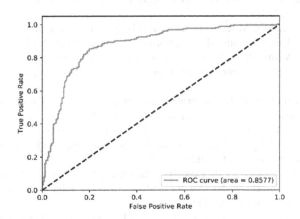

Fig. 6. ROC curve of DCN model.

Figure 6 shows the ROC curve of DCN model. An ideal ROC curve has a shape which covers the maximum area. From the experimental results above, we can see that DCN has a better effect than other models.

6 Summary

Software-intensive systems' failure mode are very complex. Fault characteristics from software and hardware are closely related. So mining associations between features is important to get a great result. DCN can express any high-order feature combination, while each layer retains low-order combination, and the vectorization of parameters also controls the complexity of the model. So it's suitable for prediction the failure point of software-intensive systems.

Acknowledgement. The work presented in this paper was supported by the National Natural Science Foundation of China (61302078, 61372108), 863 Program (2011AA01A102), National S&T Major Project (2011ZX 03005-004-02), and China Postdoctoral Science Foundation funded Project 2017M610827.

References

1. Shu, S., Wang, Y., Wang, Y.: A research of architecture-based reliability with fault propagation for software-intensive systems. In: Reliability and Maintainability Symposium, pp. 1–6. IEEE (2016)
2. Chen, W.B., Liu, X.L., He, C.J., et al.: Knowledge base design for fault diagnosis expert system based on production rule. In: Asia-Pacific Conference on Information Processing, APCIP 2009, pp. 117–119. IEEE (2009)
3. Baptista, M., Sankararaman, S., Medeiros, I.P.D., et al.: Forecasting fault events for predictive maintenance using data-driven techniques and ARMA modeling. Comput. Ind. Eng. **115**, 41–53 (2018)
4. Zhang, K., Xu, J., Min, M.R., et al.: Automated IT system failure prediction: a deep learning approach. In: IEEE International Conference on Big Data. IEEE (2017)
5. Mohan, K.K., Verma, A.K., Srividya, A.: Software reliability estimation through black box and white box testing at prototype level. In: International Conference on Reliability. IEEE (2011)
6. Li, N., Li, Z., et al.: Predicting software black-box defects using stacked generalization. In: Sixth International Conference on Digital Information Management. IEEE (2011)
7. Li, L., Lu, M.: Analyzing failure mechanism for complex software-intensive systems. In: IEEE International Symposium on Software Reliability Engineering Workshops. IEEE Computer Society, pp. 57–58 (2015)
8. Guo, H., Tang, R., Ye, Y., et al.: DeepFM: a factorization-machine based neural network for CTR prediction. In: Proceedings of the 26th International Joint Conference on Artificial Intelligence, pp. 1725–1731 (2017)
9. Juan, Y., Zhuang, Y., Chin, W.S., et al.: Field-aware factorization machines for CTR prediction. In: ACM Conference on Recommender Systems, pp. 43–50. ACM (2016)
10. Wang, R., Fu, B., Fu, G., et al.: Deep & Cross Network for Ad Click Predictions. In: Proceedings of the ADKDD 2017, pp. 1–7 (2017)
11. Qu, Y., Cai, H., Ren, K., et al.: Product-based neural networks for user response prediction. In: 16th International Conference on Data Mining, pp. 1149–1154 (2016)

12. He, X., Chua, T.: Neural factorization machines for sparse predictive analytics. In: Proceedings of the 40th International ACM SIGIR Conference on Research and Development in Information Retrieval, pp. 355–364 (2017)
13. Xiao, J., Ye, H., He, X., et al.: Attentional factorization machines: learning the weight of feature interactions via attention networks. In: 26th International Joint Conference on Artificial Intelligence, IJCAI 2017, pp. 3119–3125 (2017)

Research on Evaluation Method of Cooperative Jamming Effect in Cognitive Confrontation

Jing Ma[1], Bin Shi[1], Fei Che[2], and Sitong Zhang[2(✉)]

[1] Science and Technology on Special System Simulation Laboratory,
Beijing 100854, China
13301067916@189.cn, shibin1018@sohu.com
[2] Harbin Engineering University, Harbin 150001, China
chefei0627@126.com, zhangsitong0726@126.com

Abstract. In modern warfare, due to the increasingly complex electromagnetic environment, cognitive confrontation will become the main form of war. Effective interference with enemy radars is of great importance for taking the lead in the battlefield. The evaluation of the synergistic interference effect is an important indicator to measure the performance of the interference equipment. According to the evaluation result, the interference strategy can be changed in time to achieve the best interference revenue and provide a strong guarantee for the successful penetration of the target. In this paper, the discovery probability and positioning accuracy of radar network are used as evaluation indicators to establish an evaluation model. The interference power, interference frequency, interference timing and interference pattern are used as membership functions. The distance, false alarm probability and different interference strategies are studied. The simulation shows that proper false alarm probability, closer distance and proper interference strategy can improve the interference benefit and provide a theoretical basis for obtaining the best interference effect in the actual battlefield.

Keywords: Cognitive confrontation · Jamming effect evaluation ·
Evaluation index · Jamming strategy

1 Introduction

In the current war, as the battlefield environment becomes more and more complex, cognitive confrontation will become the main form of war in the future battlefield. Radar is an important part of cognitive confrontation, whose main task is to extract target information from the target echo by pulse compression and coherent accumulation, and realize the detection, localization and tracking of the target [1, 2]. As the opposite of the radar, the main task of the jammer is to intercept the radar's transmitted signal and then modulate and forward it, generating a deception or suppressing jamming signal similar to the target echo, so that the radar can not effectively detect the target [3, 4]. Coordination jamming assessment is an important indicator to measure the performance of jamming equipment [5]. According to the evaluation results, it can be

S. Han et al. (Eds.): AICON 2019, LNICST 287, pp. 40–51, 2019.
https://doi.org/10.1007/978-3-030-22971-9_4

judged whether the distribution of jamming resources is good or bad, which is conducive to the rational use of jamming resources, timely change the jamming strategy according to the evaluation results to achieve the best jamming revenue, and provide a strong guarantee for the successful penetration of the target [6, 7]. Therefore, it is of great significance to conduct a rapid, comprehensive and reasonable evaluation of the radar coordinated jamming effect [8, 9]. This problem has also been discussed in some previous studies. Literature [10] discussed the jamming effectiveness of the IR smoke projectile resist the IR imaging guided missile. Literature [11] proposed an online evaluation method based on support vector machine. The literature [12] evaluated the jamming effect based on the power criterion method. In literature [13], the method based on power criterion is used to study the reduction degree of enemy radar detection distance at different powers to evaluate the effect. Literature [14] uses the magnitude of the lure angle as the evaluation criterion. In the above study, the factors affecting the jamming effect are not comprehensive enough, and the evaluation effect will also change when the evaluation indicators are different. Therefore, when evaluating the jamming effect, it is necessary not only to accurately select the factors affecting the jamming effect, but also to select the appropriate evaluation indicators according to the different jamming objects. In this paper, the jamming effect of jammer on radar signal is studied. Four different membership functions are selected as the factors affecting the jamming effect. According to the characteristics of radar work, the discovery probability and location accuracy of radar are used as evaluation indicators to establish the jamming effect evaluation model.

2 Synergistic Jamming Membership Function

2.1 Jamming Power Membership Function

Firstly, we apply the ratio of jamming and signal (JSR) to describe the power suppression benefit which represents the suppressing effect to radar $R_j(j = 1, 2, \ldots, n)$ from jammer $u_i(i = 1, 2, \ldots, m)$. The power suppression benefit function can be expressed as q_{1ij}. Only when the ratio of the power of received jamming power and the power of the echo signal is greater than the minimum JSR, it is deemed that the jamming of the jammer is effective. The power of the jammer signal and the effective echo signal power received by the radar R_j are shown in Eq. (1).

$$P_{ji} = \frac{P_j G_j G_t \lambda^2}{(4\pi R_j)^2 L}, \quad P_{js} = \frac{P_t G_t G_r \lambda^2 \sigma}{(4\pi)^3 R_s^4} \tag{1}$$

where P_t and P_j separately represent the transmission power of radar and jammer, G_t is the radar main lobe gain, G_A is the gain of the jammer, σ is the scattering area of self-defense aircraft, A is the equivalent receiving area of radar antenna, R_j is the distance between radar and target and R_s is the distance between jammer and target.

K_j denotes the minimum ratio of jamming and signal, which indicates radar R_j required for normal work. Therefore, we can derive the decision-making criterions. After normalization, q_{1ij} can be expressed as Eq. (2)

$$q_{1ij} = \begin{cases} 1 & p_{ji}/p_{js} \geq 2K_j \\ \frac{2}{3}\left(\frac{p_{ji}/p_{js}}{K_j} - 0.5\right) & 0.5K_j \leq p_{ji}/p_{js} \leq 2K_j \\ 0 & p_{ji}/p_{js} \leq 0.5K_j \end{cases} \quad (2)$$

2.2 Jamming Frequency Membership Function

Then, the frequency alignment benefit function q_{2ij} is addressed to report the jamming suppression effect of jammer $u_i(i = 1, 2, \ldots, m)$ on radar $R_j(j = 1, 2, \ldots, n)$. The jammer u_i can only jam the radar R_j if the jammer's jamming frequency overlaps with the radar's operating frequency. (f_{i1}, f_{i2}) denotes the operating frequency of the jammer, and (f_{j1}, f_{j2}) denotes the operating frequency of the radar. Consequently, q_{2ij} can be expressed as Eq. (3).

$$q_{2ij} = \begin{cases} 1 & f_{i1} < f_{j1} \ and f_{i2} > f_{j2} \\ 0 & f_{i1} > f_{j2} \ or f_{i2} < f_{j1} \\ \frac{\min(f_{i2},f_{j2}) - \max(f_{i1},f_{j1})}{f_{j2} - f_{j1}} & other \end{cases} \quad (3)$$

2.3 Jamming Timing Membership Function

Next, the time-benefit function is used to express the jamming suppression effect of the jammer $u_i(i = 1, 2, \ldots, m)$ on the radar $R_j(j = 1, 2, \ldots, n)$. The effect of suppressing time benefit on jamming benefit can be expressed as q_{3ij}. Similar to the frequency alignment benefit function, q_{3ij} can be expressed as Eq. (4).

$$q_{3ij} = \begin{cases} 1 & t_{j1} < t_{r1} \ and \ t_{j2} > t_{r2} \\ 0 & t_{j1} > t_{r2} \ or \ t_{j2} < t_{r1} \\ \frac{\min(t_{r2},t_{j2}) - \max(t_{r1},t_{j1})}{t_{r2} - t_{r1}} & other \end{cases} \quad (4)$$

2.4 Jamming Style Membership Function

Finally, the jamming patterns benefit function q_{4ij} is adopted to describe the jamming patterns benefit which represents the jamming suppression effect of jammer $u_i(i = 1, 2, \ldots, m)$ on radar $R_j(j = 1, 2, \ldots, n)$. Suppose that each radar (possibly of different system type) have valid m types of jamming patterns, and been sorted according to the advantages and disadvantages of theoretical jamming effects. If jammer u_i contains the jamming patterns which are effective for radar R_j, then the higher the jamming pattern is in ranking, the greater the value of the jamming pattern benefit function is. Otherwise, $q_{4ij} = 0$. q_{4ij} can be expressed as Eq. (5).

$$q_{4ij} = \begin{cases} 0 & \text{jammer does not contain the jamming pattern} \\ 1 - \frac{n}{m} & \text{other} \end{cases} \tag{5}$$

In the battlefield environment, there are m jammers to jam the radar network composed of n radars. According to the above membership function calculation, the membership matrix of the m jammers $u_i(i = 1, 2, \ldots, m)$ to interfere with a certain radar in the radar R_j network is as Eq. (6).

$$q_j = \begin{bmatrix} q_{11j} & q_{12j} & \cdots & q_{1mj} \\ q_{21j} & q_{22j} & \cdots & q_{2mj} \\ q_{31j} & q_{32j} & \cdots & q_{3mj} \\ q_{41j} & q_{42j} & \cdots & q_{4mj} \end{bmatrix} \tag{6}$$

According to the expert's experience, the weight vector of the four indicators is recorded as $\omega = [\omega_1, \omega_2, \omega_3, \omega_4]$, which represents the weight of the four indicators of jamming power, jamming frequency, jamming timing and jamming pattern. The jamming benefits of the m jammer to a radar in the radar network are as Eq. (7).

$$Q_j = \omega \cdot q_j = [\omega_1, \omega_2, \omega_3, \omega_4] \cdot \begin{bmatrix} q_{11j} & q_{12j} & \cdots & q_{1mj} \\ q_{21j} & q_{22j} & \cdots & q_{2mj} \\ q_{31j} & q_{32j} & \cdots & q_{3mj} \\ q_{41j} & q_{42j} & \cdots & q_{4mj} \end{bmatrix} \tag{7}$$

$$= [q_{1j}, q_{2j}, \ldots, q_{mj}]$$

Since the jammer can produce effective jamming benefits from the above four aspects at the same time, when solving the jamming benefit of a single jammer to a single radar, the Zadeh "$\wedge$" operator should be used to perform small operations.

$$q_{ij} = \omega_1 \cdot q_{1ij} \wedge \omega_2 \cdot q_{2ij} \wedge \omega_3 \cdot q_{3ij} \wedge \omega_4 \cdot q_{4ij} \tag{8}$$

The jamming benefit matrix of the m-frame jammers to the n radars in the radar network can be obtained.

$$Q = [Q_1^T, Q_2^T, \ldots, Q_n^T] = \begin{bmatrix} q_{11} & q_{12} & \cdots & q_{1n} \\ q_{21} & q_{22} & \cdots & q_{2n} \\ \cdots & \cdots & \cdots & \cdots \\ q_{m1} & q_{m2} & \cdots & q_{mn} \end{bmatrix} \tag{9}$$

3   The Model of Collaborative Jamming Effect Evaluation

According to the role of radar network in cognitive confrontation, this paper selects the radar's discovery probability and location accuracy as indicators for the evaluation of coordinated jamming effects. The model of collaborative jamming effect evaluation is shown in the Fig. 1.

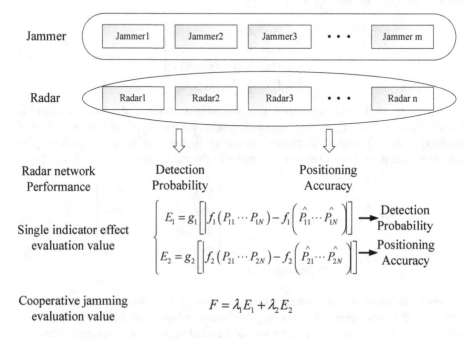

Fig. 1. The model of collaborative jamming effect evaluation

3.1   Effectiveness Evaluation Based on Radar Discovery Probability

The discovery of the probability is one of the important factors to measure the performance of a radar detection. This paper chooses the discovery probability as the evaluation index of radar network detection performance.

Under the condition of false alarm probability P_{fa}, let $x = \frac{r^2}{2\sigma^2}$ denote the ratio of signal plus noise to noise in the radar receiver. According to the Niemann-Pearson criterion used in radar detection, the probability of finding the false alarm probability and the envelope r can be obtained. The function is as Eq. (10)

$$P_d = \exp(-\frac{S}{N}) \int_{-\ln P_{fa}}^{\infty} \exp(-x) I_0(2\sqrt{x} \cdot \frac{S}{N}) dx \qquad (10)$$

We bring the jamming benefit matrix into the radar discovery probability. Then, the signal-to-jamming ratio received by the radar is:

$$\frac{S}{J} = \frac{P_t G_t \sigma L_1 \sqrt{n}}{4\pi R^2 P_j G_j L q_{ij}} \tag{11}$$

At this time, the expression of the radar discovery probability P_{dj} under the influence of the jamming signal is as Eq. (12).

$$P_{dj} = \exp(-\frac{K}{R^2 q_{ij}}) \int_{-\ln P_{fa}}^{\infty} \exp(-x) I_0(\frac{2}{R}\sqrt{x \cdot \frac{K}{q_{ij}}}) dx \tag{12}$$

At this point, the estimated jamming effect under the probability indicator is found to be:

$$E_1 = P_d - P_{dj} \tag{13}$$

3.2   Effectiveness Evaluation Based on Radar Positioning Accuracy

In addition to finding the probability, the positioning accuracy is also one of the important factors to measure the performance of a radar. It represents the accuracy level of the radar network to determine the target position. This paper chooses the positioning accuracy as another evaluation index of radar network detection performance. Geometric accuracy factor GDOP (Geometric Dilution of Precision) is one of the important criteria for measuring the accuracy of positioning systems.

The GDOP expression of the radar network is as Eq. (14).

$$P_g = \sqrt{\sigma_x^2 + \sigma_y^2 + \sigma_z^2} \tag{14}$$

Where σ_x, σ_y, σ_z is the positioning error mean square error in the x, y, and z axis directions, and x, y, and z are the position vector of the target.

When the radar network is cooperatively interfered, the signal received by the radar receiver is affected by the jamming signal, and the dry signal ratio of the received signal changes with different jamming strategies. The positioning error of the radar detection distance, azimuth and elevation angle The mean square error also changes, and the positioning accuracy of the radar network is affected.

The radar positioning accuracy expression under certain jamming strategy is as Eq. (15).

$$\hat{p}_g = \sqrt{\sigma_{xj}^2 + \sigma_{yj}^2 + \sigma_{zj}^2} \tag{15}$$

At this point, the estimated jamming effect under the positioning accuracy index is found to be:

$$E_2 = \hat{p}_g - p_g \tag{16}$$

4   Simulation Analysis

We set up two sets of experiments to verify the impact of different influencing factors on radar network discovery probability and positioning accuracy.

Experiment 1: The typical radar and jammer parameters are selected for simulation to verify the influence of different factors on the probability of radar discovery. The parameters of the three radars are:

$$P_t = 630\,\text{kw},\ \ G_t = 33\,\text{dB},\ \sigma = 5,\ L = 3\,\text{dB},\ n = 10$$

The parameters of the three radars are:

$$P_j = 150\,\text{w},\ \ G_j = 9\,\text{dB},\ L = 3\,\text{dB},\ n = 10$$

Under different false alarm probabilities, the relationship between radar discovery probability and signal-to-jamming ratio is simulated as Fig. 2.

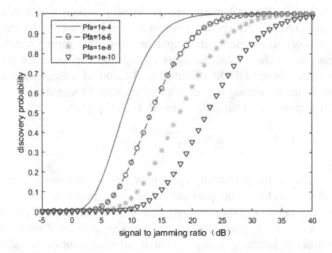

Fig. 2. The curve of radar discovery probability and signal to jamming ratio

At present, it is generally found that the probability of less than or equal to 0.1 is effective as an opaque jamming standard. It can be seen from the figure that this standard can be achieved. As can be seen from Fig. 2, in the case where the signal-to-jamming ratio is constant, as the probability of false alarm decreases, the probability of discovery decreases, and the radar detection performance becomes weak, and the more obvious the jamming effect is.

Fix the value of q_{ij} to 0.6, the simulation result of the relationship between radar probability and distance under different false alarm probabilities is as Fig. 3.

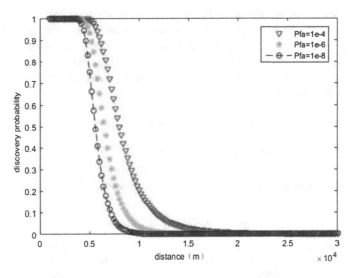

Fig. 3. The curve of radar probability and distance

It can be seen from the Fig. 3 that under a certain false alarm probability, as the distance increases, the probability of discovery gradually decreases. After the distance between the two reaches 12 km or more, the probability of radar discovery drops below 0.1, meeting the standard.

In order to study the influence of jamming benefit on the probability of discovery, the false alarm probability is fixed to $P_{fa} = 10^{-6}$. Under different jamming benefit values, the relationship between radar probability and distance is as Fig. 4.

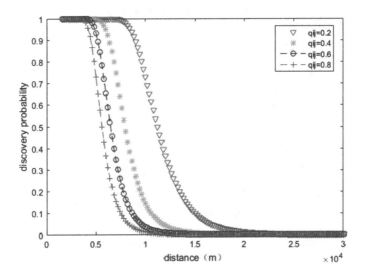

Fig. 4. The curve of radar discovery probability and jamming benefit value

It can be seen from the figure that in the case of false alarm probability and distance determination, with the increase of the jamming benefit value, the radar discovery probability is significantly reduced. The simulation shows that increasing the jamming benefit value plays an important role in reducing the radar discovery probability.

Experiment 2: We select typical radar and jammer parameters for simulation. The parameters of the three radars are:

$$P_t = 500\,\text{kw}, \ G_t = 40\,\text{dB}, f_c = 2.4\,\text{GHz} ,$$

$$B_r = 10^6\,\text{Hz} , \ L_t = 6\,\text{dB}, \ n = 10$$

The parameters of jammers are shown in the following Table 1

Table 1. Parameters of jammers

Number	Transmit power P_j (kw)	Transmit gain G_j (dB)	Center frequency f_c (GHz)	Bandwidth B_j (MHz)	Jammer loss L_j (dB)	Jammer pattern n
1	40	10	2.4	4	6	1
2	60	10	2.4	2	6	3
3	110	10	2.4	0.5	6	4

In the absence of jamming to the radar network, the two-dimensional plane simulation of the GDOP value of the radar network as a function of the distance between the radar and the target is shown in Fig. 5.

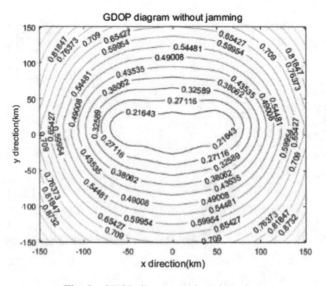

Fig. 5. GDOP diagram without jamming

We apply jamming to the radar network. Due to the different parameters of the jammer, the jamming effects of different jamming strategies are different. The three different jamming strategies and their corresponding jamming benefit values are shown in Table 2.

Table 2. The corresponding jamming benefit values of different jamming strategies

Radar Jammer	1	2	3	Jamming benefit
Strategy 1	1	2	3	0.8406
Strategy 2	3	1	2	0.8655
Strategy 3	2	1	3	0.8679

The GDOP diagram of the radar network under different jamming strategies is shown in Figs. 6, 7 and 8.

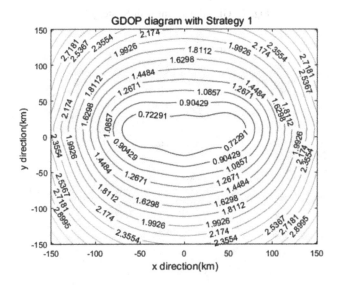

Fig. 6. GDOP diagram with Strategy 1

As can be seen from the figure, different jamming strategies have a great influence on the positioning accuracy of the radar network. Taking (0, 50, 0) as an example, the positioning accuracy of the point is 0.27 km without jamming, and the positioning accuracy of the point under the three jamming strategies is 0.90 km, 2.66 km and 7.17 km, respectively.

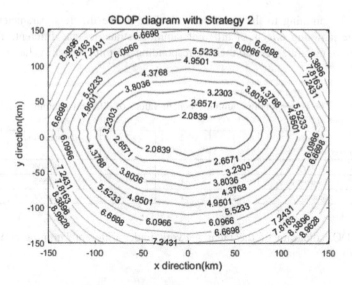

Fig. 7. GDOP diagram with Strategy 2

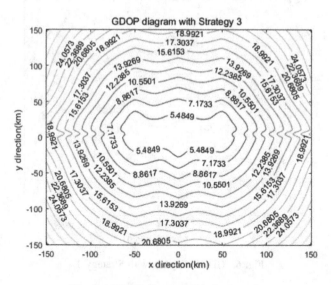

Fig. 8. GDOP diagram with Strategy 3

5 Conclusion

In cognitive confrontation, due to the wider application of radar networking, as an interfering party, the importance of jamming to radar networking is increasing. In order to measure the jamming effect, the evaluation of the jamming benefit has been paid more and more attention. In this paper, we take the discovery probability and location accuracy of radar network as evaluation indicators, and study the effects of distance, false alarm probability and different jamming strategies on the jamming benefit. Simulations show that proper false alarm probability, closer distance and proper jamming strategy can improve the jamming benefit. Since the false alarm probability and distance are not easy to change in the actual battlefield, it is an effective means to improve the jamming effect by making the appropriate decision to get the maximum jamming benefit.

Acknowledgment. The paper is funded by the National Natural Science Foundation of China (Grant No. 61701134), National key research and development program of China (Grant No. 2006YFF0102806), the Natural Science Foundation of Heilongjiang Province, China (Grant No. F2017004), and the Fundamental Research Funds for the Central Universities of China (No. HEUCFM180802 and No. HEUCFM180801), and the International Exchange Program of Harbin Engineering University for Innovation oriented Talents Cultivation.

References

1. Brooker, M., Inggs, M.: A signal level simulator for multistatic and netted radar systems. Trans. IEEE Aerosp. Electron. Syst. **47**(1), 178–186 (2011)
2. Deng, H.: Orthogonal netted radar systems. IEEE Aerosp. Electron. Syst. Mag. **27**(5), 28–35 (2012)
3. Ye, F., Chen, J., Li, Y.B.: Improvement of DS evidence theory for multi-Sensor conflicting information. Symmetry **9**, 69 (2017)
4. Ye, F., Zhang, X., Li, Y., Tang, C.: Faithworthy collaborative spectrum sensing based on credibility and evidence theory for cognitive radio networks. Symmetry **9**(3), 36 (2017)
5. Li, Y., Chen, J., Ye, F., Liu, D.: The improvement of DS evidence theory and its application in IR/MMW target recognition. J. Sens. **2016**, 1–15 (2016)
6. Lee, Y.J., Park, J.R., Shin, W.H., et al.: A study on jamming performance evaluation of noise and deception jammer against SAR satellite. In: International Asia-Pacific Conference on Synthetic Aperture Radar. IEEE, pp. 1–3 (2011)
7. Niu, C., Li, Y., Hu, R., et al.: Fast and efficient radio resource allocation in dynamic ultra-dense heterogeneous networks. IEEE Access, 1 (2017)
8. Gao, W., Tie, W.: Evaluation of electronic jamming effect based on seeker captive flight test and missile flight simulation. In: Proceedings of the SPIE, vol. 322, p. 1032209 (2017)
9. Bao, Z.C., Cui-Qiong, M.O., Wang, Z.: Jamming effect evaluation of PD radar seeker. Shipboard Electronic Countermeasure (2017)
10. Wang, L., Liu, Z., Wang, F.: Jamming effectiveness analysis of IR smoke projectile based on sight optical observation. In: International Symposium on Photoelectronic Detection and Imaging 2013: Infrared Imaging and Applications. International Society for Optics and Photonics, p. 890743 (2013)
11. Wang, W., Yang, J.A., Cui, L, et al.: Online communication jamming effect evaluation based on support vector machine. Electronic Information Warfare Technology (2017)
12. Bachmann, D.J., Evans, R.J.: Game theoretic analysis of adaptive radar jamming. IEEE Trans. Aerosp. Electron. Syst. **47**(2), 1081–2000 (2011)
13. Ruan, M., Wang, H., Li, Q.: Multi-point source support interference evaluation based on minimum interference distance. In: Systems Engineering and Electronics, vol. 31, no. 9, pp. 2110–2114 (2009). [61]
14. Du Plessis, W.P.: Platform skin return and retrodirective cross-eye jamming. IEEE Trans. Aerosp. Electron. Syst. **48**(1), 490–501 (2012)

Navigation Performance Comparison of ACE-BOC Signal and TD-AltBOC Signal

Chunxia Li, Jianjun Fan[✉], Min Li, and Yang Gao

Beijing Satellite Navigation Center, Beijing 100094, China
xiaomangps@163.com

Abstract. With the development of intellectual property rights and navigation performance optimization, recently two new four-components signal multiplex modulation methods, ACE-BOC & TD-AltBOC have been brought forward by scholars. The navigation performances of them are aimed to be compared in this paper. Based on analyzing of the power spectrum density function of these two modulation methods, their main navigation performances of code tracking precision, anti-multipath capability, anti-jamming capability and compatibility are compared. The results show that the navigation performance of ACE-BOC modulation signal is 1.0 dB–2.1 dB prior to that of the TD-AltBOC modulation signal. This is because of the difference of their power spectrum density function figures and that of the 1.2 dB distributed power level. The study production can be referred to choose the better one between these two new modulation methods.

Keywords: ACEBOC · TD-AltBOC · Multiplex · Modulation · Performance

1 Introduction

Both the GPS L5 signal and the Galileo E5 signal are used to design the signal of civil aviation service signal or life safety service. Considering the demand of high integrity of civil aviation, the satellite navigation signal design of each satellite navigation system in this frequency band tends to interoperate with GPS L5 and Galileo E5 signals. Beidou global satellite navigation system B2 frequency point civil signal design also adhering to this idea, trying to get as close as possible to Galileo AltBOC modulation signal. However, limited by Galileo AltBOC modulation of intellectual property rights, China has to seek a new four signals constant-envelope multiplex modulation technique [1–3]. Under this background, in recent years, two scholars from Huazhong University of Science and Technology and Tsinghua University have proposed two modulation modes: TD-AltBOC [4–6] and ACE-BOC [7–13].

At present, the public papers on the systematic comparative study of the two modulation modes are rare. This paper attempts to compare the performance differences between the two modulation modes and analyze the underlying causes behind them. Considering that the method based on receiver test is limited by the implementation method and parameters of the receiver, this paper uses the theoretical performance analysis method to compare the performance of the two modulation modes. At the same time, because the time domain analysis is related to the specific pseudo-code sequence design, this paper attempts to analyze the causes of the performance

S. Han et al. (Eds.): AICON 2019, LNICST 287, pp. 52–64, 2019.
https://doi.org/10.1007/978-3-030-22971-9_5

difference between the two modulation modes from the angle of power level and power spectral density by using the frequency domain analysis method.

Firstly, the definition and power spectrum of TD-AltBOC modulation signal and ACE-BOC modulation signal are studied, and then the pseudo-code tracking precision, anti-multipath ability, anti-jamming ability and compatibility of these two modulation signals are compared and analyzed. In terms of anti-jamming ability, DME/TACAN pulse interference is the actual interference faced by L5/E5/B2 frequency point signal reception, however, the method of pulse hiding can effectively combat it, so the following two common interference types of matching spectrum interference and single carrier interference are analyzed in this paper. In terms of compatibility, pseudo-code sequence cross-correlation characteristics and spectral separation coefficients are two common analytical methods, the former method is closely related to the specific pseudo-code sequence design, so this paper adopts the latter method.

2 ACE-BOC Modulated Signal and TD-AltBOC Modulated Signal

2.1 ACE-BOC Modulated Signal Definition and Spectrum

ACE-BOC Signal Definition. Asymmetric constant Envelope BOC (Asymmetric Constant Envelop BOC ACE-BOC Multiplexing) is a new dual-frequency multiplexing modulation technique proposed by Tsinghua University, which can modulate four independent spread spectrum codes in two different carrier frequencies with arbitrary power ratio combinations.

Note four different bipolar baseband spread spectrum signals as $S_{UI}(t)$, $S_{UQ}(t)$, $S_{LI}(t)$, $S_{LQ}(t)$. To combine these four baseband signals to a composite signal with constant envelope with splitting spectrum, where $S_{UI}(t)$, $S_{UQ}(t)$ modulated on the upper side with the same phase, orthogonal components, respectively, and $S_{LI}(t)$, $S_{LQ}(t)$ modulated on the lower side with the same phase, orthogonal components, respectively, then the optimal solution is ACE-BOC modulation. If the frequency interval of the upper sideband and lower sideband is $2f_s$, and the central frequency is f_ω, then radiofrequency ACE-BOC modulation can be expressed as

$$S_{ACE,RF}(t) = \mathrm{Re}\{S_{ACE}(t)\exp(j\pi 2f_\omega t)\} \tag{1}$$

Where $S_{ACE}(t)$ is complex baseband ACE-BOC signal, which can be expressed as:

$$S_{ACE}(t) = \frac{\sqrt{2}}{2}\alpha_I\,\mathrm{sgn}[\sin(2\pi f_s t + \varphi_I)] + j\frac{\sqrt{2}}{2}\alpha_Q\,\mathrm{sgn}[\sin(2\pi f_s t + \varphi_Q)] \tag{2}$$

In this equation, the additional phase of real number and imaginary parts is

$$\begin{cases} \phi_I = -\mathrm{atan}\,2(S_{UI} + S_{LI}, S_{UQ} - S_{LQ}) \\ \phi_Q = \mathrm{atan}\,2(S_{UQ} + S_{LQ}, S_{UI} - S_{LI}) \end{cases} \tag{3}$$

Where $\mathrm{atan}\,2(\cdot, \cdot)$ is anti-tangent function.

The four components of the ACE-BOC modulated signal can be combined with arbitrary power ratio, in which the symmetric four-component combination of unequal power is the most feasible. In this power distribution, the same phase and orthogonal components of each edge band have different power, but the total power of the upper and lower side bands is the same, which is

$$P_{UQ} : P_{LQ} : P_{UI} : P_{LI} = 1 : 1 : \beta^2 : \beta^2 \tag{4}$$

Where $P_{UQ}, P_{LQ}, P_{UI}, P_{LI}$ is the power of the signal $S_{UQ}(t), S_{LQ}(t), S_{UI}(t), S_{LI}(t)$ respectively. Without losing its general, suppose $\beta^2 \geq 1$. This type of ACE-BOC signal can provide different power ratios for each side band's data channel and pilot channel. In order to optimize the robustness and measurement accuracy of tracking, it is often hoped that the pilot channel will have higher power. In this paper, the ACE-BOC modulation signal is studied in the following focus, and when the specific sub-carrier frequency and pseudo-code frequency are introduced, the modulation mode can be expressed as ACE-BOC$(f_s, R_c; [1, 1, \beta^2, \beta^2])$ or simplified as $ACE - BOC(m, n, \beta^2)$, where $m = f_s/(1.023 \times 10^6\,\mathrm{MHz})$ and $n = R_c/(1.023 \times 10^6\,\mathrm{MHz})$, R_c represents pseudo-random code rate.

As mentioned above, the advantage of ACE-BOC modulated signal is that on the basis of AltBOC modulated signal, the power ratio between the data channel and the pilot channel is adjusted to obtain better signal performance.

ACE-BOC Signal Spectrum. The spectrum of ACE-BOC modulated signal $G_{ACE-BOC}(f)$ is [14]

$$G_{ACE-BOC}(f) = \frac{R_c \cos^2\left(\frac{\pi f}{R_c}\right)\{1 - \cos(6\varphi)[\sin(5\varphi)\sin\varphi + \cos^2\varphi]\}}{2\pi^2 f^2 \cos^2(6\varphi)} \tag{5}$$

Where $\varphi = \frac{\pi f}{12 f_s}$.

2.2   TD-AltBOC Modulated Signal Definition and Spectrum

TD-AltBOC Signal Definition. The Galileo system uses quadrupole carrier AltBOC modulation at the E5 frequency, and its baseband waveform flip rate is 8 times the subcarrier frequency, and the product is attached to maintain the constant envelope [15]. When four different PN codes are used, there is no doubt that this modulation greatly increases the complexity of the receiver. Time-division multiplexing is another modulation method that joint the constant envelope of four E5 signal components, which uses a code-by-bit multiplexing method, and emits only 2 signal components at any moment, so that the constant envelope can be obtained without the addition of the product item [4]. This modulation method is called time-division AltBOC, which is recorded as TD-AltBOC. When the specific sub-carrier frequency and pseudocode frequency are introduced, the modulation mode can be abbreviated as $TD - AltBOC(m, n)$.

Using TD-AltBOC modulation, the subcarrier is bipolar, and the baseband waveform flip rate is only 4 times the subcarrier frequency. Its signal generation and reception complexity is similar to BOC modulation. In addition, the reuse efficiency is 100%, which makes it feasible to use larger emission and receive bandwidth containing harmonics for further performance improvements.

As mentioned above, the advantage of the TD-AltBOC signal is that the implementation complexity is lower than that of the AltBOC modulation signal.

TD-AltBOC Signal Spetrum. When $2f_s/R_c$ is odd, note the spectrum of TD-AltBOC modulated signal is $G_{TD-AltBOC}^{odd}(f)$, which can be expressed as 4

$$G_{TD-AltBOC}^{odd}(f) = \frac{2R_c}{(\pi f)^2} \cos^2(\frac{\pi f}{R_c}) \frac{\sin^2\left(\frac{\pi f}{4f_s}\right)}{\cos^2\left(\frac{\pi f}{2f_s}\right)} \tag{6}$$

When $2f_s/R_c$ is even, note the spectrum of TD-AltBOC modulated signal is $G_{TD-AltBOC}^{even}(f)$, which can be expressed as 4

$$G_{TD-AltBOC}^{even}(f) = \frac{2R_c}{(\pi f)^2} \sin^2(\frac{\pi f}{R_c}) \frac{\sin^2\left(\frac{\pi f}{4f_s}\right)}{\cos^2\left(\frac{\pi f}{2f_s}\right)} \tag{7}$$

2.3   Comparison of ACE-BOC Modulated Signal Spectrum and TD-AltBOC Modulated Signal Spectrum

Figure 1 shows the power spectral density curve of ACE-BOC(15,10;3) signal and TD-AltBOC(15,10) signal. As can be seen from the graph, the power spectral density of the ACE-BOC (15,10;3) signal and the TD-AltBOC (15,10) signal is very similar, except for the following:

(1)   At the fourth order harmonic (60 MHz), the power spectral density of ACE-BOC is significantly higher than that of TD-AltBOC, because the TD-AltBOC signal has constant envelope and there is no intermodulation, ACE-BOC signal introduced the intermodulation in order to ensure the envelope constant. The effect of intermodulation is as follows: at the same transmitting power P, the useful power of the received ACE-BOC signal is $P\eta$, and $\eta = 82.7\%$ is the power efficiency. However, the useful power of the received TD-AltBOC signal is P.

(2)   The power spectral density of TD-AltBOC at the central frequency is slightly higher than that of ACE-BOC, while the power spectral density curve of TD-AltBOC is slightly converging to the spectrum center at the third order harmonic (45 MHz) than the ACE-BOC power spectral density curve. Because the difference is so small, the impact is completely negligible.

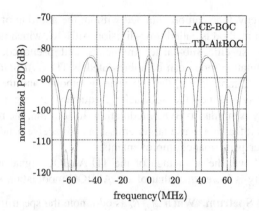

Fig. 1. The power spectral density curve of ACE-BOC and TD-AltBOC

3 Analysis Method of Navigation Performance of Satellite Navigation Signal

3.1 Pseudo-Code Tracking Accuracy

The Cremer-rao lower limit of pseudo-code tracking error is as follow [16]

$$\sigma_{LB}^2 = \frac{B_n(1 - 0.5B_nT)}{(2\pi)^2 \frac{C}{N_0} \beta_{rms}^2} \tag{8}$$

Where σ_{LB}^2 represents the lower bound of the error variance of the pseudo-code tracking. B_n represents the noise bandwidth of the tracking loop. T represents the length of the integral time. C/N_0 represents the carrier-to-noise ratio. β_{rms} represents the mean square root bandwidth.

$$\beta_{rms} = \int_{-B_r/2}^{B_r/2} f^2 G_{S,0}(f) df \tag{9}$$

Where $G_{S,0}(f)$ represents the normalized signal power spectral density. B_r indicates the bilateral band bandwidth of the receiver.

3.2 Anti-multipath Capability

Multipath Error Envelope. For simplicity, it is discussed that there is only one multipath signal, and the multipath error can be expressed in the following equations:

$$[R(\varepsilon - \frac{d}{2}, \gamma) - R(\varepsilon + \frac{d}{2}, \gamma)] + \alpha[R(\varepsilon - \tau - \frac{d}{2}, \gamma) - R(\varepsilon - \tau + \frac{d}{2}, \gamma)] \cos\theta \equiv 0 \tag{10}$$

In the formula, $R(\cdot, \cdot)$ represents the code correlation function, which is related to the delay and signal bandwidth. ε represents the multipath error. d represents the space between the early code and the late code of the code tracking loop discriminator. α, τ and θ represents the amplitude, delay and phase of the multipath signal relative to the direct signal respectively.

Set the multipath amplitude as α, when $\theta = 0°$ and $\theta = 180°$, the multipath error reaches the maximum and minimum values respectively, and the variation curve of multipath error on multipath delay, that is, multipath error envelope curve, is obtained on this condition. The maximum absolute value of the multipath error envelope indicates the worst multipath error.

The Expectation of Multipath Error Envelope. The normalized probability density function of multipath signal with different amplitude and delay can be described as follows [17]

$$p(\tau) = \frac{3e^{-\frac{3\tau}{2\tau_0}}}{2\tau_0}[1/m] \tag{11}$$

Where τ_0 represents the typical multipath delay in a multipath environment, which is related to the type of multipath environment.

Combining the probability of multipath occurrence and multipath error envelope, the multi-path envelope expectation is obtained to describe the typical multipath error by considering the fact that the close-range multipath ratio is more likely to enter the receiver than the long-range multipath signal. Typical multipath errors can be calculated in the (12) formula:

$$E\{e\} = \frac{1}{2}\int_0^\infty \frac{[\|E_{max}(\tau)\| + \|E_{min}(\tau)\|]}{2}p(\tau)d\tau \tag{12}$$

Where $E_{max}(\tau)$ and $E_{min}(\tau)$ are respectively represent the positive and negative multipath envelopes under the condition of multipath delay being τ, and $\|\cdot\|$ represents an absolute value operation.

3.3 Anti-jamming Capability

Carrier Tracking Anti-jamming Quality Factor. Its definition is [18]

$$Q = \frac{1}{\sqrt{\int_\infty^\infty G_{JO}(f)G_{SO}(f)df}} = Q_{CR\_T} = \frac{1}{\int\limits_{-\infty}^{\infty} G_{S,0}(f)G_{I,0}(f)df} \tag{13}$$

In the formula, the normalized signal and the interference power spectral density function are represented as $G_{S,0}(f)$ and $G_{I,0}(f)$ respectively.

Pseudo-Code Tracking Anti-jamming Quality Factor. Its definition is [18]

$$Q_{CD\_T} = \frac{\int\limits_{-\infty}^{\infty} f^2 G_{S,0}(f) df}{\int\limits_{-\infty}^{\infty} f^2 G_{S,0}(f) G_{I,0}(f) df} \tag{14}$$

3.4   Compatibility

Spectral Separation Coefficient. Its definition is [19]

$$\chi_{S,I} = \int\limits_{-\infty}^{\infty} G_{S,0}(f) G_{I,0}(f) df \tag{15}$$

Code Tracking Spectrum Sensitivity Coefficient. Its definition is [19]

$$\eta_{S,I} = \frac{\int\limits_{-\infty}^{\infty} G_{S,0}(f) G_{I,0}(f) \sin^2(\pi f \Delta) df}{\int\limits_{-\infty}^{\infty} G_{S,0}(f) \sin^2(\pi f \Delta) df} \tag{16}$$

In the formula, Δ indicates the interval between the early code correlator and the late code correlator.

4   Analysis of Navigation Performance of the ACE-BOC Modulation Signal and the TD-AltBOC Modulation Signal

The trend of the new generation GNSS receiver processing technology is to use the navigation channel to complete the measurement of the pseudo-distance and the carrier, and the data channel is only used for message demodulation. The following is for comparison of the pseudo-code tracking accuracy, multipath performance, anti-jamming performance and compatibility of the pilot channel of the two modulation signals ACE-BOC(15,10;3) and TD-AltBOC(15,10). If there is no special description below, it refers to the pilot channel signal.

4.1   Pseudo-Code Tracking Accuracy

The pseudo-code tracking accuracy of the two signals are compared under the condition of the same transmitting signal power and receiver loop parameters. Without losing generality, the total carrier-to-noise ratio of the transmitting signal is 45 dB-Hz, considering the power efficiency and the ratio power between the pilot channel and the data channel, the double-sideband received carrier-to-noise ratio of the ACE-BOC pilot signal can be calculated as 45–10 lg (87.2% × 3/4) = 43.2 (dB-Hz), and that of the TD-AltBOC pilot signal is 45–10 lg(1/2) = 42 (dB-Hz). It can be seen that under the same transmission power conditions, the carrier-to-noise ratio of the ACE-BOC pilot signal is 1.2 dB larger than the TD-AltBOC pilot signal. Set the loop noise bandwidth 0.5 Hz, the integration time 5 ms and the signal bandwidth 71.61 MHz, the pseudo-code tracking accuracy of the two signals are calculated according to formula (1) and shown in Table 1.

Table 1. Comparison of pseudo-code tracking accuracy between ACE-BOC(15,10;3) and TD-AltBOC(15,10)

Signal	CNR (dB-Hz)	Mean square root bandwidth (MHz)	Pseudo-code tracking accuracy (m)
ACE-BOC (15,10; 3)	43.2	14.29	0.016
TD-AltBOC (15,10)	42	14.20	0.019
TD-AltBOC (15,10)	43.2	14.20	0.016

As can be seen from the table, the ACE-BOC signal has a higher pseudo-code tracking accuracy than the TD-AltBOC signal for the following reasons:

(1) Under the same transmission power condition, because the pilot channel is allocated a higher power ratio the ACE-BOC(15,10;3) signal can eventually obtain a 1.2 dB higher carrier-to-noise ratio compared with the TD-AltBOC(15,10) signal, even if the power efficiency of ACE-BOC (15,10;3) is lower than that of TD-AltBOC(15,10).

(2) ACE-BOC (15,10;3) signal has a slightly larger mean square root bandwidth compared with the TD-AltBOC(15,10) signal. This is because the power spectrum of the TD-AltBOC modulation is more converging to the central frequency point (seen in Fig. 1), so its mean square root bandwidth is smaller, but the inducing difference of pseudo-code tracking accuracy is negligible. This can be seen from the Table 1 that the pseudo-code tracking accuracy of the two signals are the same under the same carrier-to-noise ratio condition.

4.2 Anti-multipath Capability

Use the coherent early-later delay lock loop, and set the early code and the later code interval 0.5 chip, the signal bandwidth 71.61 MHz. When the amplitude of the multipath signal relative to the direct TD-AltBOC pilot signal is −3 dB, because the level of ACE-BOC pilot signal is 1.2 dB higher than that of the TD-AltBOC pilot signal under the same transmission power condition, the amplitude relative to the direct ACE-BOC pilot signal is −4.2 dB. According to formula (3), the multipath envelope of the TD-AltBOC pilot signal and that of the ACE-BOC pilot signal are obtained as shown in Fig. 2(a). And similarly, when the multipath signal is 10 dB relative to the direct TD-AltBOC pilot signal, its amplitude is −11.2 dB relative to the direct ACE-BOC pilot signal, and according to the formula (3) the multipath envelope of the TD-AltBOC pilot signal and that of the ACE-BOC pilot signal are obtained as shown in Fig. 2(b).

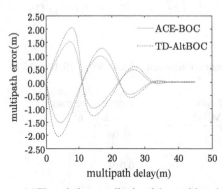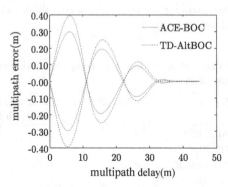

(a)The relative amplitude of the multi-path signals are -3 dB, -4.2 dB respectively

(b)The relative amplitude of the multi-path signals are -10 dB,-11.2 dB respectively

Fig. 2. The multipath Error Envelope curve of two signals TD-AltBOC(15,10) and ACE-BOC (15,10; 3)

Taking the rural or suburban environment as an example, $\tau_0 = 90$ m, in the two cases of the amplitude of the multipath signal relative to the TD-AltBOC signal respectively −3 dB and −10 dB, the multipath error of two signals are calculated according to the formula (4) and shown in Table 2.

Table 2. Comparison of multipath errors between ACE-BOC 15,10;3) and TD-AltBOC (15,10)

Conditions	Case 1		Case 2	
Signal	TD-AltBOC (15,10)	ACE-BOC (15,10;3)	TD-AltBOC (15,10)	ACE-BOC (15,10;3)
Multipath amplitude (dB)	−3	−4.2	−10	−11.2
Worst multipath error (m)	2.05	1.52	0.04	0.03
Typical multipath error (m)	0.18	0.14	0.40	0.30

It can be seen from the above table that the ACE-BOC signal has better anti-multipath capability than the TD-AltBOC signal. And its reasons are analyzed as follows:

(1) The power amplitude factor. The pilot channel power of the ACE-BOC(15,10;3) signal is 1.2 dB higher than that of the TD-AltBOC(15,10) signal, which directly leads to a better anti-multipath capability of the ACE-BOC(15,10;3) signal.

(2) The power spectrum shape factor. In order to separate the influence of power amplitude, the calculation results of −3 dB and −10 dB of multipath signal relative to direct signal show that when the power of received signal is equal, the worst multipath error of the ACE-BOC signal is mm order of magnitude lower than that of the TD-AltBOC signal, And the typical multipath error is 0.1 mm order of magnitude higher. Visibly the multipath error difference caused by the difference in the shape of the power spectrum is negligible.

4.3 Anti-jamming Capability

The anti-jamming quality factor of two signals ACE-BOC and TD-AltBOC are calculated according to the formula (6) and (7), as shown in Table 3.

Table 3. Comparison of anti-jamming quality factors between ACE-BOC(15,10;3) and TD-AltBOC(15,10)

Signal	Carrier tracking anti-jamming quality factor (dB)		Code tracking anti-jamming quality factor (dB)	
	Matched spectral interference	Single carrier interference	Matched spectral interference	Single carrier interference
ACE-BOC (15,10;3)	74.57	72.02	73.89	71.02
TD-AltBOC (15,10)	74.65	72.16	73.95	71.22

It can be seen from Table 3 that:

(1) The anti-jamming quality factor of the TD-AltBOC (15,10) is 0.1 dB–0.2 dB higher than that of the ACE-BOC(15,10;3).
(2) The maximum tolerated interference-signal-ratio is proportional to the anti-jamming quality factor, so the maximum tolerated interference-signal-ratio of the TD-AltBOC(15,10) is 0.1 dB–0.2 dB higher than that of the ACE-BOC(15,10;3).
(3) The signal level of the TD-AltBOC(15,10) is 1.2 dB lower than that of the ACE-BOC(15,10;3), therefore, its maximum tolerated interference signal level can be 1.0 dB–1.1 dB lower than that of the ACE-BOC(15,10; 3), that is, its anti-jamming ability is 1.0 dB–1.1 dB lower than that of the ACE-BOC(15,10; 3).

4.4 Compatibility

The spectral separation coefficients and the code tracking spectral sensitivity coefficients of the two signals ACE-BOC and TD-AltBOC are respectively calculated according to formula (8) and formula (9) and shown in Table 4 and Table 5. The modulation mode of the GPS L5 signal in the table is BPSK (10) with the signal bandwidth of 24 MHz; and that of the Galileo E5 signal is AltBOC (15,10) with the signal bandwidth of 51.150 MHz.

Table 4. Comparison of spectral separation coefficients between ACE-BOC(15,10;3) and TD-AltBOC(15,10)

Signal	Self spectral separation coefficient (dB)	Spectral separation coefficient to GPS L5 (dB)	Spectral separation coefficient to Galileo E5 (dB)
ACE-BOC (15,10;3)	−74.57	−85.06	−74.44
TD-AltBOC (15,10)	−74.65	−84.13	−74.49

Table 5. Comparison of code tracking spectral sensitivity coefficients between ACE-BOC (15,10;3) and TD-AltBOC(15,10)

Signal	Self-spectral sensitivity coefficient(dB)	Spectral sensitivity coefficient to GPS L5 (dB)	Spectral sensitivity coefficient to Galileo E5 (dB)
ACE-BOC (15,10;3)	−74.54	−89.98	−74.43
TD-AltBOC (15,10)	−74.51	−89.43	−74.49

It can be seen from Tables 4 and 5 that:

(1) The spectral separation coefficient of the ACE-BOC(15,10;3) is −0.9 dB–0.1 dB different to that of the TD-AltBOC(15,10).

(2) Because the signal level of the ACE-BOC(15,10;3) is 1.2 dB higher than that of the ACE-BOC(15,10), the carrier-to-noise ratio decreasing caused by its mutual interference is 1.1 dB–2.1 dB less than that of the TD-AltBOC(15,10).

5 Conclusion

The ACE-BOC and the TD-AltBOC are two kinds of four-component signal constant envelope multiplex modulation modes. In this paper, the navigation performance of the ACE-BOC(15,10;3) modulation signal and the that of the TD-AltBOC (15,10) modulation signal are compared, and its mechanisms are studied. Firstly, the power spectral density function and the power level of each channel are analyzed, then the pseudo-code tracking accuracy, anti-multipath capability, anti-jamming capability and compatibility are compared, and the mechanisms of the performance difference between the two signals are analyzed.

The results show that there is little difference between the power spectral density function curve shape of the TD-AltBOC(15,10) modulation signal and that of the ACE-BOC(15,10;3) modulation signal, and the distributed signal level of the ACE-BOC (15,10;3) pilot channel is 1.2 dB higher than that of the TD-AltBOC(15,10) pilot channel. Equivalently to the input signal level, the pseudo-code tracking accuracy and the anti-multipath capability of the ACE-BOC(15,10;3) pilot channel are 1.2 dB superior to that of the TD-AltBOC(15,10) pilot channel. The anti-jamming ability and compatibility of the ACE-BOC(15,10;3) pilot channel are respectively 1.0 dB–1.1 dB and 1.1 dB–2.1 dB superior to that of the TD-AltBOC(15,10) pilot channel. In short, the ACE-BOC(15,10;3) has a 1.0 dB–2.1 dB superior performance than the TD-AltBOC(15,10). The analysis results show that the difference of performance between the two signal is mainly caused by the power spectral density function shape difference and 1.2 dB power level distribution difference.

The research results of this paper can be used as a reference for the optimization of the satellite navigation signal modulation mode.

References

1. Zhu, X., Huang, X., Chengeng, S., et al.: Constant envelope modulation and multiplexing technologies for BDS global navigation signals. J. Nat. Univ. Defense Technol. 39(05), 6–13 (2017)
2. Yan, T., Wang, Y., Qu, B., et al.: Constant envelope multiplexing methods for the modernized GNSS signals. Space Electron. Technol. 14(05), 27–33, 40 (2017)
3. Cai, M., Xie, J., Wang, G.: Study of constant-envelop multiplex algorithm in satellite navigation systems. Electron. Des. Eng. 24(07), 70–72, 75 (2016)
4. Tang, Z., Zhou, H., Wei, J., et al.: TD-AltBOC: a new COMPASS B2 modification. Sci. China Phys. Mech. Astron. 54(6), 1014–1021 (2011)
5. Wang, Y., Meng, Y., Tao, X., et al.: Analysis of 2 order complex FIR filter effects on TD-AltBOC satellite navigation signal. Space Electron. Technol. 12(6), 61–66 (2015)
6. Liu, K., Zhu, S., Wang, Y., et al.: Fast acquisition based on PMF-FFT for TD-AltBOC. In: China Satellite Navigation Conference (CSNC) 2015, China Satellite Navigation System Management Office Academic Exchange Center: Organizing Committee of China Satellite Navigation Conference, Xi'an, China, pp. 66–71 (2015)
7. Zhang, J., Yao, Z., Lu, M.: Applications and low-complex implementations of ACE-BOC multiplexing. In: Proceedings of the 2014 International Technical Meeting of the Institute of Navigation, pp. 781–791. The Institute of Navigation, San Diego (2014)
8. Gao, Y., Li, C., Fu, L., et al.: Overall performance comparison of three dual-frequency constant envelop modulation schemes for GNSS frequency. In: China Satellite Navigation Conference (CSNC) 2016 Proceeding: Volume II, China Satellite Navigation System Management Office Academic Exchange Center: Organizing Committee of China Satellite Navigation Conference, Changsha, China, pp. 47–56 (2016)
9. Yao, Z., Lu, M.: Constant envelope combination for components on different carrier frequencies with unequal power allocation. In: International Technical Meeting of the Institute of Navigation, pp. 629–637. The Institute of Navigation, San Diego (2013)
10. Zhang, X., Zhang, X., Yao, Z., Lu, M.: Implementations of constant envelope multiplexing based on extended interplex and inter-modulation construction method. In: Proceeding of 25th International Technical Meeting of the ION Satellite Division, pp. 893–900. The Institute of Navigation, Nashville (2012)
11. Zhu, L., Yao, Z., Lu, M., Feng, Z.: Non-symmetrical ALTBOC multiplexing for Compass B1 signal design. J. Tsinghua Univ. (Sci. Technol.) 52(6), 869–873 (2012)
12. Guo, F., Yao, Z., Mingquan, L.: BS-ACEBOC: a generalized low-complexity frequency constant-envelop multiplexing modulation for GNSS. GPS Solutions 19(6), 1–15 (2016)

13. Yao, Z., Zhang, J., Mingquan, L.: ACE-BOC: dual-frequency constant envelope multiplexing for satellite navigation. IEEE Trans. Aerosp. Electron. Syst. **52**(2), 1–18 (2016)

14. Yao, Z., Lu, M.: Design, implementation, and performance analysis of ACE-BOC modulation. In: Proceeding of 26th International Technical Meeting of the ION Satellite Division, pp. 361–368. The Institute of Navigation, Nashville, Tennessee (2013)

15. European Union: European GNSS (Galileo) Open Service Signal In Space Interface Control Document, Issue 1.1, pp. 5–6. European Union (2010)

16. Betz, J.W., Kolodziejski, K.R.: Generation theory of code tracking with an early-late discriminator part I: lower bound and coherent processing. IEEE Trans. Aerosp. Electron. Syst. **45**(4), 1538–1564 (2009)

17. Hein, G.W., Avila-Rodriguez, J.-A.: Combined Galileo PRS and GPS M-code. Inside GNSS **1**(1), 48–55 (2006)

18. Li, C., Chu, H., Wang, H.: Analysis of the anti-jamming performance of BOC modulated signal. J. Geomatics Sci. Technol. **29**(6), 414–417 (2012)

19. Soualle, F., Burger, T.: Introduction of an additional radio frequency compatibility criterion for code tracking performance. In: ION GNSS 20th International Technical Meeting of the Satellite Division, pp. 1201–1210. The Institute of Navigation, Forth Worth (2007)

A Video-Selection-Encryption Privacy Protection Scheme Based on Machine Learning in Smart Home Environment

Qingshui Xue[1(✉)], Haozhi Zhu[1], Xingzhong Ju[1], Haojin Zhu[2],
Fengying Li[2], Xiangwei Zheng[3], and Baochuan Zuo[1]

[1] School of Computer Science and Information Engineering,
Shanghai Institute of Technology, Shanghai 201418, China
xue-qsh@sit.edu.cn
[2] Department of Computer Science and Engineering,
Shanghai Jiao Tong University, Shanghai 200240, China
[3] School of Information Science and Engineering,
Shandong Normal University, Jinan 250014, China

Abstract. The Internet of things is a new technological revolution following the computer and Internet. It aims to connect all physical objects existing in the world and forms a network with everything. In recent years, smart home gradually enters into our life. Smart home uses the Internet of things technology to connect all kinds of devices in the home, to achieve a smart home environment. Although the development of smart home has brought a qualitative leap to people's life, there are many problems in security. Privacy security is one of the challenges to the smart home environment. Attackers can intrude various smart devices in the smart home environment, to achieve the purpose of stealing users' personal information and privacy. Among these devices, smart cameras are the most intruded frequently. Since many cameras are installed in users' homes to achieve real-time monitoring of the environment, but the existence of these cameras provides a channel to get information for attackers. In recent years, the leak of video privacy is emerging in an endless stream. According to the researches about privacy protection, this paper proposes a new scheme to selectively encrypt the video captured by the cameras through machine learning technology, so as to protect the personal privacy of users and improve the security of the smart home environment.

Keywords: Internet of things · Smart home · Privacy protection · Machine learning · Video selective encryption

1 Introduction

The Internet of things (IoT) has gradually entered into our lives due to the continuous development of wireless communication technology and brings great changes to our lives [1]. The Internet of things is a new stage in the development of ubiquitous networks based on the Internet. It can be integrated with the Internet over a variety of wired and wireless networks. It integrates the application of a large number of sensors

© ICST Institute for Computer Sciences, Social Informatics and Telecommunications Engineering 2019
Published by Springer Nature Switzerland AG 2019. All Rights Reserved
S. Han et al. (Eds.): AICON 2019, LNICST 287, pp. 65–76, 2019.
https://doi.org/10.1007/978-3-030-22971-9_6

and intelligent processing terminals to achieve the anytime and anywhere connection of objects with objects and objects with people. The Internet of things has led the third wave of the information industry revolution and will become the most important infrastructure for social and economic development, social progress and scientific and technological innovation in the future. By 2020, experts believe that the Internet of things network will contain about 50 billion object entities [2]. By using the Internet of things, everything around us, including computers, mobile phones, cars, etc., will be connected through the wireless network to achieve self-organized communication.

Security is an important factor restricting the rapid development of the Internet of things, which has been mentioned in literature [3–5]. The smart home is one of the best applications of the Internet of things. With the continuous development of the Internet of things technology, the smart home industry is also developing. The smart home is a residential platform, which integrates the facilities related to home life with technologies such as integrated wiring technology, network communication technology, and security prevention technology [6]. A self-organized home network can be formed to share resources and communicate [7], which can build an effective management system of residential facilities and family schedule, improve the safety, convenience, comfort, and artistry of the home, and realize the energy-saving living environment.

The smart camera is an important part of the smart home, which installed in the home to achieve monitoring the home real-time. The video captured by the camera can be transmitted to the storage device via a wireless or wired network, such as a computer or cloud server. The users can view the video when they go home, and can also check the environment of home in real time through the APP terminal on their mobile phone when they are out, so as to ensure that have a grasp of the situation at home. With the continuous development of technology, the smart camera can not only be used for monitor, but also for communication, video, information collection, and other multimedia functions. However, due to the use of these smart cameras, there are also many security issues. Most of the smart cameras on the market are not very secure, and they are easily attacked and exploited by attackers. In recent years, malicious attackers have posted a lot of incidents on the user's video privacy by attacking the cameras, which has brought a lot of troubles and injuries for users. Now, many companies and researchers concerned about the privacy of the home environment and are working hard to improve the security of smart cameras.

In the smart home environment, many places involve the privacy of the user, such as the daily activities of the user at home, the time of the user at home, and the personal preferences of the user [8]. If the attacker obtains information by attacking the cameras, then the users' privacy may be leaked, which will affect the users. It is the most intuitive benefit and the most common attack method for an attacker to obtain the user's personal privacy information by attacking cameras installed at home. Therefore, when users purchase these smart cameras, security is the first consideration for them. Only when the cameras are highly secure, users will be assured to purchase and use them. At the same time, the security of the camera is also the selling point of major companies. Only high-security cameras can survive in the market and bring benefits to the company.

In recent years, researchers have also proposed a lot of video encryption schemes for camera shooting. From these schemes, they can be roughly divided into two categories, one is full encryption and the other is selective encryption [13]. For full encryption, all data in the video stream is directly encrypted by the encryption algorithm. However, this approach leads to high computational complexity and does not meet real-time requirements. Another type of video encryption is selective encryption. This method encrypts part of the video content, or selectively encrypts, encrypts important or sensitive information. On the premise of ensuring security, selective encryption can not only protect users' privacy but also reduce computational complexity and overhead [13]. So, selective encryption has been widely used in recent years.

As the amount of information in the video data is large, the video should be compressed before being transmitted [14]. Therefore, the relationship between encryption and compression should be considered clearly. It can neither make encryption affect the quality and efficiency of video compression nor can video compression increase the complexity of encryption. Therefore, the best way is to combine encryption and compression. The first to consider this combination is the order of encryption and compression, whether it is compressed before encrypted, or compressed after encrypted, or at the same time, and the order used different, the results obtained are different [13].

In recent years, many researchers have conducted in-depth research on the combination of encryption and compression based on H.264 video coding technology. According to this method of combining encryption and compression, we can filter the information in the process of compression, select important information or sensitive information for encryption [15]. In general, the focus of this encryption method is how to choose the location of the encryption during the compression process [13].

Many scholars have conducted in-depth research on video encryption. Radha et al. [14] proposed a security mechanism based on the measurement matrix to generate secret keys to encrypt video information, but the scheme still encrypts the video completely, although it can guarantee the security of video information, the computational complexity is too large and inefficient. Xu et al. [13] proposed an efficient chaotic pseudo-random number generator to encrypt video data. This scheme can also selectively encrypt video, but it is too complicated to select sensitive information. Based on the above-mentioned selective encryption of video and encrypt some important or sensitive information, our team proposed a new video selective encryption scheme, which utilizes machine learning technology and principle to encrypt video selectively.

Due to the development of video technology at present, the new video coding technology HEVC is becoming more and more mature. Our team chooses the HEVC standard to be applied in the camera to obtain high-quality video information. By combining machine learning, video compression technology, and video encryption, we can selectively encrypt video in an efficient, high-quality and comprehensive way, which can greatly reduce the computational complexity and improve efficiency, as well as improve the security and protect the privacy of users.

We will introduce the process of selective encryption of video through machine learning technology. The rest of the paper is organized as follows. Section 2 introduces the related works and knowledge involved in the scheme. Section 3 introduces the whole process of implementation. In Sect. 4, we do performance and security analysis. Finally, the paper is concluded and look forward to in Sect. 5.

2 Related Works and Knowledge

This section introduces some of the related works about video selective encryption, and relevant knowledge used in our program, including machine learning technology and HEVC coding standard.

2.1 Related Works

Selective video encryption has emerged in recent years, considers the coding structure of the video bitstream and encrypts only the most sensitive information in the video bitstream. There are some research discussed:

Authors in [14] proposed an efficient compressed sensing-based security approach for video surveillance. The solution is applied in wireless multimedia sensor networks. The security keys are generated from the measurement matrix elements for protecting the user's identity. The scheme can achieve selective encryption.

Hamidouche et al. [15] proposed a real-time selective video encryption scheme based on the chaos system. And the solution blends High Efficiency Video Coding (HEVC) standard which named SHVC. The SHVC parameters including TCs, TCsign, MV difference sign.

Authors in [16] have investigated the encryption of Region of Interest based on tiles repartition in HEVC through both selective and naive encryption of the tiles within the Region of Interest.

These schemes can achieve selective encryption. However, they cannot achieve encrypt different people with different secret keys. Our scheme can do this.

2.2 Machine Learning

With the continuous development of technology, many popular emerging technologies, such as artificial intelligence, machine learning, and deep learning have emerged in recent years. Machine Learning is a multi-disciplinary subject, which includes probability theory, statistics, approximation theory and algorithm complexity theory [16]. As the technical basis of artificial intelligence, machine learning not only has the ability to process computer data quickly through algorithms, but also has the ability to predict and classify problems in statistical models, and under the current trend of increasing data volume, there is a huge development potential for it [16]. The goal of machine learning is to study how computers simulate or implement human learning behaviors to acquire new knowledge or skills and reorganize existing knowledge structures to continuously improve their performance [17].

Machine learning is a general term for a class of algorithms that attempt to mine the implicit rules from a large amount of historical data and use them for prediction or classification. More specifically, machine learning can be seen as looking for a function, and input is sample data, the output is the desired result, but this function is too complicated to be formally expressed. It is important to note that the goal of machine learning is to make the learned functions work well for "new samples," not just for training samples. The ability of the learned function to apply to new samples is called generalization ability [18].

2.3   HEVC

Our scheme using the coding technology standard is the High-Efficiency Video Coding (HEVC) standard, a new video compression standard used to replace the H.264/AVC coding standard. HEVC has become an international standard officially, and it has many advantages over H.264, as follows:

(1) Better compression
   Compared to the H.264 codec, HEVC offers significant improvements in compression. In fact, HEVC compresses video twice as efficiently as H.264. With HEVC, video of the same visual quality takes up half the space. Or, videos with the same file size and bit rate can exhibit better quality [19].

(2) Improved inter-frame motion prediction
   A major factor in video compression is the prediction of motion between frames. When the pixel remains stationary (solid-state background image), the intelligent video codec can save space by referencing it instead of reproducing it. With improved motion prediction, HEVC can provide smaller file sizes and higher compression quality [19].

(3) Improved inter-frame prediction
   Video compression also benefits from analyzing the "movement" within a single frame, which allows for more efficient compression of a single frame of video. This can be achieved by using a mathematical function instead of the actual pixel value to describe the pixel layout [20]. This feature takes up less space than pixel data, reducing file size. However, the codec must support sufficiently advanced mathematical functions to make the technology really work. HEVC's interframe prediction function is more detailed than H.264, which supports motion prediction in 33 directions, while the latter only supports 9 directions [21].

   HEVC coding technology has many advantages, and it is now more and more widely used. Although the mature of HEVC coding technology may take some time, it is inevitable that it will become the future video coding standard. Therefore, combined with the Internet of things technology in the smart home environment, the use of HEVC coding standard for smart cameras will become popular.

3   The Video-Selection-Encryption Privacy Protection Scheme Based on Machine Learning in a Smart Home Environment

In this section, we will introduce the implementation process of our scheme in detail, which will elaborate on the definition of privacy in the home environment, image classification and character recognition, and privacy protection.

3.1 Definition of Privacy in the Home Environment

Privacy of individual refers to the secrets of citizens who are unwilling to disclose or known for others in their personal lives. In modern society, the quality of citizens is constantly improving, and the requirements for quality of life are constantly improving, the awareness of the protection of personal privacy is also constantly strengthening, and the security of personal privacy is also valued. Personal privacy includes many aspects, including personal data privacy, location privacy, identity privacy, behavioral privacy and environmental privacy [6]. They are inviolable and indispensable for building a happy and harmonious society. Therefore, the protection of personal privacy is very important.

In the smart home environment, the entire home environment belongs privacy category for the user, including all activities of the family's characters, schedules, and personal preferences. These personal privacy screens are captured during the entire surveillance of the camera, so it is necessary to encrypt these video images that involve the user's personal privacy. However, there is more than one person in the home, and everyone has privacy. Hence, the people at home, do not want privacy to be accessed by attackers, also not want privacy to be accessed by the others who at home. So, it is necessary to encrypt each person's video image individually to achieve protect everyone privacy. Besides, an image will include both the character and the background, we just need to encrypt the character in the image to protect the privacy of the person. The problems are how to classify these video images taken by the smart camera and how to recognize the person and select the character area for encryption. The scheme we proposed will achieve this function. This issue is being discussed in detail in succeeding paras.

3.2 Image Classification and Character Recognition

Before the smart cameras are put into use, the first thing what should we do is make the smart cameras to be smarter. We need to design a machine learning algorithm, the function of this algorithm is to distinguish different images. And then, the algorithm will be implanted into the smart cameras when it is mature so that the smart cameras can distinguish different character images. Therefore, the key to achieve this function is how to choose an appropriate algorithm, and how to set different labels, and how to train the algorithm. These issues are being discussed in detail in succeeding paras.

Choose an Appropriate Algorithm. Machine learning has many algorithms, different algorithms achieve different functions. As deep learning is a branch of machine learning, and the convolutional neural network algorithm of deep learning is very suitable for image classification [23]. Therefore, we choose a convolutional neural network (CNN) as an appropriate algorithm. The convolutional neural network is a multi-layer neural network, each layer is composed of multiple two-dimensional planes, and each plane is composed of multiple independent neurons (as shown in Fig. 1). The input image is convolved with three trainable filters and a bias. After the convolution, three feature maps are generated in the C1 layer, and then the four pixels of each group in the feature map are summed, weighted, and offset [23]. The feature maps of the three S2 layers are obtained through a sigmoid function. These maps are then filtered to the C3 layer. This hierarchy then generates S4, just like S2. Finally, these pixel values are rasterized and connected into a vector input to the traditional neural network to obtain the output [24].

Set Different Labels. We assume that there are three people at home, such as user1, user2, user3. The cameras will take abundant images, and these images involve the three people's privacy. It is necessary to distinguish them. Hence, we set the images which involve the user1 as label-1, the images which involve the user2 as label-2, and the images which involve the user3 as label-3. And consider the outsiders, we set outsiders as OS. Then, collect thousands of images of user1, user2 and user3, and use them to train algorithm.

Training Algorithm. For an algorithm to become mature, it must undergo extensive samples training. The training steps of convolutional neural network algorithm are divided into four steps, and the four steps between two stages [24]. The first stage, forward propagation stage: ① take a sample (X, Yp) from the sample set and input X into the network; ② calculate the corresponding actual output Op. The second stage is the backward propagation stage: ① calculate the difference between the actual output Op and the corresponding ideal output Yp; ② the weight matrix is adjusted by back propagation according to the method of minimizing error [25]. So, we according to the steps to train the algorithm that we design. First, give about thousands of images with label-1 to the algorithm, and make the algorithm can tell which image belongs to the label-1 image and recognize the person in the image is user1 and mark the character area. Second, through the same process, make the algorithm can tell which image belongs to the label-2 image, label-3 image, and recognize the person in the image is user2 or user3 and mark the character area. After the algorithm becomes mature, embed it into the smart camera. Hence, the smart camera can classify the three kinds of label images automatically.

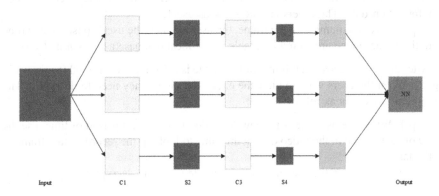

Fig. 1. Structure of the convolutional neural network

3.3   Privacy Protection

After the above introduction, the cameras installed at home have the ability to intelligently recognize and can classify different images that involve different people. Therefore, smart cameras can selectively encrypt images according to classification. So, the key is how to encrypt these images. The issue is being discussed in detail in succeeding paras.

Because video data is huge and it's a real-time stream of data, fast encryption is required, we choose AES (128bits) as the encryption algorithm of our scheme. As mentioned above, we supposed there are three users at home, user1, user2 and user3. And after the camera classification, the camera can identify the users in the image and mark them. In order to be able to encrypt them separately, it is necessary to generate three different secret keys, such as K_1, K_2 and K_3. Besides, the K_1 belongs to user1, and only encrypts the area of images which involve user1. The K_2 belongs to user2, and only encrypts the area of images which involve user2. The K_3 belongs to user3, and only encrypts the area of images which involve user3. And we also need to generate a separate key, such as K. The K used to encrypt the area of images which the camera can't identify, for example, outsiders (OS). When the camera is in the process of shooting, there will be countless frame images. We study on the basis of one frame of the images. Before the camera encrypts the images, it numbers every frame image which it takes. The specific encryption process is as follows.

Step 1: The camera selects a frame image.

Step 2: The camera determines if there are any characters in the image. If there is no one in the image, the camera does nothing to this image and continues to select the next frame image. If there is somebody in the image, go to step 3.

Step 3: The camera determines which the user in the image is, and recognizes the user. After that, confirms the position of the character in the image, and uses the four corners of the rectangle to determine the coordinates of the character in the image. The coordinates are defined as (A_i, B_i, C_i, D_i) (i represents the user of the image). For example, the user is user1.

Step 4: The camera uses the K_1 to encrypt the identified character rectangle area information data. The others are the same as user1.

Step 5: Make the number of the frame, the user number, the user's position and time in the frame image are stored in a table in the local database(as shown in Table 1).

After the above steps, each frame of the image is selectively encrypted (as shown in Fig. 2). When the users want to view the encrypted video, they need to decrypt it. The decryption process is as follows.

Step 1: When the user wants to view the video for a certain period of time, use the ID of each frame in the video during this time to look up the record of that frame in the table.

Step 2: Determines the location to be decrypted and the decryption key to use.

Step 3: Determines the identity of the decryptor and decrypt the encrypted region in the frame image with the decryptor's secret key. For example, the user1 wants to decrypt the video, then uses K_1 to decrypt the video. Besides, the user1 only can view the video about himself. The others are the same as user1.

The above is the whole process of encryption and decryption. The process of encryption can selective encryption exactly and do the record so that the process of decryption can be done quickly.

Table 1. The information recorded in each frame

Frame ID	User ID	Coordinates	Frame Time
1	User1	(A_1, B_1, C_1, D_1)	Time 1
	User2	(A_2, B_2, C_2, D_2)	
	User3	(A_3, B_3, C_3, D_3)	
	OS1	(A, B, C, D)	
	...	...	
2	User1	(A_1, B_1, C_1, D_1)	Time 2
	User2	(A_2, B_2, C_2, D_2)	
	User3	(A_3, B_3, C_3, D_3)	
	OS1	(A, B, C, D)	
	...	...	
...	User1	(A_1, B_1, C_1, D_1)	...
	User2	(A_2, B_2, C_2, D_2)	
	User3	(A_3, B_3, C_3, D_3)	
	OS1	(A, B, C, D)	
	...	....	
n	User1	(A_1, B_1, C_1, D_1)	Time n
	User2	(A_2, B_2, C_2, D_2)	
	User3	(A_3, B_3, C_3, D_3)	
	OS1	(A, B, C, D)	
	...	...	

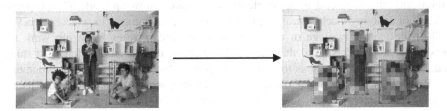

Fig. 2. The result of selective encryption

4 Performance and Security Analysis

In this section, we analyze the performance and security of our scheme. Our scheme aims at implementing selective encryption for video, so that reduces computational complexity and reduces overhead. Compared with other schemes, our scheme incorporates machine learning and HEVC standard to achieve encryption for video. Privacy information in the video can be classified and encrypted quickly, efficiently and with high quality by our scheme. Besides, our scheme also achieves real-time encryption. And our scheme encrypts everyone in the home separately.

Considering security, our scheme is resistant to various passive and active attacks.

① **The cameras' gateway by breached**

In order to make the cameras secure, the first step is authentication security, so that the attacker cannot easily break through the cameras. We assume that the attacker has already broken into the cameras and can check the situation at home. Our scheme is to encrypt the video shot by the camera in real time. Every frame shot by the camera is encrypted for the privacy involved, so the scheme is relatively safe.

② **The attacker obtains the stored video file**

When attacker stole the video file, it's hard to decrypt it, because the video images that involve privacy are encrypted by AES algorithm, which security is very high, and it is hard for attackers to get the key.

③ **The attacker obtains one of the keys of users**

When the attacker obtains one of the keys of users, for example, the user's K_1 is stolen, the attacker just can decrypt the video images which involve user1, the others video images are still secure. So, our scheme can protect privacy well.

5 Conclusions

In this paper, an efficient video-selective encryption scheme is proposed based on machine learning and HEVC. In our scheme, we just propose a new method to achieve selective encryption for video. After theoretical analysis, it indicates that our scheme can encrypt video quickly and efficiently. Due to our goal is not to design a new encryption algorithm, so we choose the traditional encryption algorithm AES as our scheme algorithm.

Although our scheme can improve encryption efficiency and reduce computational complexity, there are still some problems that require follow-up work. The proposed scheme of applying machine learning technology to smart cameras to protect privacy is still in the feasibility stage of theoretical research and requires follow-up work for feasibility experiments. And there are still not many related articles found to study machine learning applications to protect user privacy in the smart home environment.

Besides, there is a problem exist in our scheme, when the people in the image overlap, the camera doesn't mark the area very well, so, need further study. Considering the development of technology and the maturity of IoT technology, these smart cameras will become more and more intelligent, their size will be smaller and smaller, and most of them are in the wireless environment, they are used to collect multimedia information. So, resource limitation is an important issue. Their computing power and storage capacity are not very high. It is necessary to study a more suitable lightweight cryptography to encrypt the video.

At present, our team only applies the research environment of the scheme to the smart home. Considering the superiority of machine learning for selective video encryption, this scheme can continue to be applied in more fields, such as smart cities. Covered with a large number of smart cameras throughout the city, these cameras can monitor well. But due to the presence of these large number of smart cameras, and they are distributed in every corner of the city, most of them are in an unsafe channel and are vulnerable to be attacked, many of the people and environments captured by these cameras are in the privacy category. Once they are used by attackers, it will cause great harm. However, most cameras are in a public environment, most of the information is not in the privacy category. At this time, the video can be selectively encrypted by machine learning technology, and only the video information related to the privacy category can be encrypted, which can improve the privacy security of urban people and reduce the overhead and computational complexity. We will then conduct in-depth research on its application in smart cities to explore better privacy protection options.

Acknowledgments. This paper is supported by NSFC under Grant No. 61672350 and 61373149, NSSFC under Grant No.16BGL003, Ministry of Education Fund under Grant No. 39120K178038 and 14YJA880033, SIT Collaborative innovation platform under Grant No. 3921NH166033, and SIT Foundation for Distinguished Scholars under Grant No. 39120K176049. We are also grateful for the support of the National Natural Science Foundation of China (61170227).

References

1. Xiaolei, D.: Advances of privacy preservation in internet of things. J. Comput. Res. Dev. **52**(10), 2341–2352 (2015)
2. Ping, Q., Meng, W.: Survey on privacy preservation in IoT. Appl. Res. Comput. **30**(01), 1001–1008 (2013)
3. Zhihao, Y., Li, M., Chunping, H.: Internet of Things Security Technology. Tsinghua University Press, Beijing (2016)
4. Masum Sadique, K., Rahmani, R.: Towards security on internet of things: applications and challenges in technology. Procedia Comput. Sci. **141**, 199–206 (2018)
5. Miorandim, D., Sicari, S., De Pellegrini, F.: Internet of things: vision, applications and research challenges. Ad Hoc Netw. **10**(7), 1497–1516 (2012)
6. Yinghui, Z., Robert, H.: Secure smart health with privacy-aware aggregate authentication and access control in internet of things. J. Netw. Comput. Appl. **123**, 89–100 (2018)
7. Lu, Z., Jiguo, Y., Chuanqing, H., Honglu, J.: Fine-grained access control with privacy support and network service optimization in ad hoc networks. Procedia Comput. Sci. **129**, 372–374 (2018)
8. Kevin, A., Katia, O., Leland, M.: Solar-powered, wireless smart camera network: an IoT solution for outdoor video monitoring. Comput. Commun. **118**, 217–233 (2018)
9. Charlie, W., Tom, H., et al.: Benefits and risks of smart home technologies. Energy Policy **103**, 72–83 (2017)
10. Frédéric, B., Kevin, B., Gaboury, S.: Tracking objects within a smart home. Expert Syst. Appl. **113**, 428–442 (2018)

11. Burrows, A., Coyle, D., GoobermanHill, R.: Privacy, boundaries and smart homes for health: an ethnographic study. Health Place **50**, 112–118 (2018)
12. Min, L., Wenbin, G., Wei, C.: Smart home: architecture, technologies and systems. Procedia Comput. Sci. **131**, 393–400 (2018)
13. Hui, X., Xiaojun, T., Xianwen, M.: An efficient chaos pseudo-random number generator applied to video encryption. Optic **127**, 9305–9319 (2016)
14. Aasha Nandhini, S., Radha, S.: Efficient compressed sensing-based security approach for video surveillance application in wireless multimedia sensor network. Comput. Electr. Eng. **60**, 175–192 (2017)
15. Hamidouche, W., Farajallah, M., Sidaty, N.: Real-time selective video encryption based on the chaos system in scalable HEVC extension. Signal Process. Image Commun. **58**, 73–86 (2017)
16. Mousa, F., Wassim, H., Olivier, D.: ROI encryption for the HEVC coded video centents. In: IEEE International Conference on Image Processing, ICIP, Spain, Barchalona, pp. 3096–3100 (2015)
17. Santiago, L., Rafael, M.: Using machine learning to detect and localize concealed objects in passive millimeter-wave image. Eng. Appl. Artif. Intell. **67**, 81–90 (2018)
18. Assem Mahmoud, A., Mai, A.: A time-efficient optimization for robust image watermarking using machine learning. Expert Syst. Appl. **100**, 197–210 (2018)
19. Sheng, H., Lambert, S.: Deep adaptive learning for writer identification based on single handwritten word images. Pattern Recogn. **88**, 64–74 (2019)
20. Shengtao, Y., Cheolkon, J., Qiaozhou, L.: HEVC encoder optimization for HDR video coding based on irregularity concealment effect. Sig. Process. Image Commun. **64**, 68–77 (2018)
21. Sami, J., Mohamed-Chaker, L., Jamel Belhadj, T.: Low complexity intra prediction mode decision for 3D-HEVC depth coding. Signal Process. Image Commun. **67**, 34–47 (2018)
22. Xiaojie, L., Wenpeng, D., Yunhui, S.: Content adaptive interpolation filters based on HEVC framework. J. Vis. Commun. Image R. **56**, 131–138 (2018)
23. Xing, X., Xiaopeng, S., Chunhui, D.: Captcha recognition based on deep learning. J. Test Measur. Technol. **33**(02), 138–142 (2019)
24. Hong, H., Liang, P., Zhongzhi, S.: Image matting in the perception granular deep learning. Knowl.-Based Syst. **102**, 51–63 (2016)
25. Yuan, J., Xingxing, H., Yaoqiang, X., Da, C.: Multi-criteria active deep learning for image classification. Knowl.-Based Syst. **172**, 86–94 (2019)

A Multi-agent Reinforcement Learning Based Power Control Algorithm for D2D Communication Underlaying Cellular Networks

Wentai Chen and Jun Zheng[✉]

National Mobile Communications Research Laboratory, Southeast University,
Nanjing 210096, Jiangsu, People's Republic of China
{wtchen, junzheng}@seu.edu.cn

Abstract. This paper considers the power control problem in device-to-device (D2D) communication underlaying a cellular network and explores the application of the machine learning (ML) approach in power control for improving the system throughput. Two multi-agent reinforcement learning (MARL) based algorithms are proposed for performing power control of D2D users (DUs): centralized Q-learning algorithm and distributed Q-learning algorithm. In the centralized algorithm, all DU pairs sharing the same RB use a common Q table in the learning process, while in the distributed algorithm each DU pair maintains its own Q table. Simulation results show that both the centralized algorithm and the distributed algorithm can converge to the same optimum Q values, and the distributed algorithm can converge faster than the centralized algorithm. Moreover, both the proposed Q-learning algorithms outperform the random power control algorithm in terms of the system throughput and satisfaction ratio.

Keywords: D2D communication · Power control ·
Multi-agent reinforcement learning · MARL · Q learning

1 Introduction

D2D communication has widely been considered as one of the promising technologies for 5G mobile cellular networks and beyond. In device-to-device (D2D) communication, a couple of closely located mobile devices are allowed to build direct connection, and communicate directly with each other with no need to pass through a base station (BS). As a result, D2D communication can effectively offload BS' traffic load, increase spectral efficiency and system throughput, reduce data transmission latency, and extend device battery lifetime [1]. To increase spectral efficiency, D2D users are usually allowed to share the spectrum resources of cellular users for communication. However, reusing spectrum resources would lead to severe interference between D2D users and cellular users. To achieve good system performance, it is critical to effectively mitigate such interference through efficient resource management, including spectrum allocation and power control. In the context of power control, extensive work has been conducted to study the power control problem in D2D communication [2–5]. However, most

S. Han et al. (Eds.): AICON 2019, LNICST 287, pp. 77–90, 2019.
https://doi.org/10.1007/978-3-030-22971-9_7

existing work uses traditional approaches in solving the problem. With recent advances in artificial intelligence (AI), the machine learning (ML) approach is receiving an increasing attention in the area of wireless communication. Even so, the study on the application of the ML approach in resource management for D2D communication is still limited. It is interesting to further explore the advanced ML approach in resource management for improving the performance of D2D communication, which motivated us to conduct this work.

In this paper, we consider the power control problem in D2D communication underlaying a cellular network and explore the application of the ML approach in solving the problem. Two multi-agent reinforcement learning (MARL) based power control algorithms are proposed for D2D communication: centralized Q-learning algorithm and distributed Q-learning algorithm. In the centralized algorithm, all D2D user (DU) pairs sharing the same resource block (RB) use a common Q table in the learning process, which makes the time and space complexity for calculating the value of the Q table exponentially increase as the number of DU pairs grows. To solve the problem, the distributed algorithm allows each DU pair to maintain a Q table of its own, which can dramatically reduce the time and space complexity for calculating the value of the Q table. Simulation results are shown to evaluate the performance of the proposed MARL-based power control algorithms in terms of the system throughput and satisfaction ratio.

The rest of this paper is organized as follows. Section 2 reviews recent related work. Section 3 describes the system model and formulates the power control problem. Section 4 presents the proposed power control algorithms. Section 5 shows simulation results to evaluate the performance of the proposed algorithms. Section 6 concludes this paper.

2 Related Work

The power control problem has been widely studied for D2D communication underlaying cellular networks in the literature [2–5]. In [2], Lee et al. proposed two centralized and distributed power control schemes for a D2D communication system. The former sets a limit on the interference of D2D users to ensure the cellular users to work with sufficient coverage probability; the latter uses an optimal on-off power control strategy, which maximizes the throughput of the D2D links. In [3], Ren et al. considered a vehicle-to-vehicle (V2V) communication system supported by a D2D underlaying cellular system (D2D-V), and introduced a power control framework based on convex function programming to achieve the optimal performance in terms of the system sum rate. In [4], Silva and Fodor proposed a binary power control (BPC) scheme for D2D communications. An objective function is introduced considering the power consumption for BPC, and a sub-optimal BPC solution is obtained to D2D power control problem. In [5], Sun et al. proposed a novel power control scheme based on stochastic channel-state information (CSI), and employed the opportunistic access control to reduce the interference caused by D2D communication and maximize the area energy efficiency, which overcomes the difficulty to acquire real-time CSI.

Recent advances in the ML technology have attracted much interest in using ML in D2D power control and several ML-based power control algorithms have already been proposed in the literature [6–8]. In [6], two centralized and distributed Q-learning algorithms were proposed for a single-cell cellular system with D2D users sharing the same resource blocks. In the proposed algorithms, all the D2D users were treated as different agents and the goal of the algorithms is to select the optimal D2D transmission power to maximize the system throughput by maintaining a two-state Q table. In [7], a cooperative reinforcement learning algorithm was proposed for the adaptive power allocation problem. The state action reward state action (SARSA), one of the on-policy reinforcement learning algorithms, was used to simulate the power control decision process of each D2D agent. The learning process is similar to that in [6], while the system model and state information in SARSA are more sophisticated. In [8], a Q-learning based power control algorithm was proposed for a single cell with a single cellular user. However, the system model is not realistic and the components of Q-learning were not well designed.

3   System Model and Problem Formulation

In this section, we first describe the system model and then formulate the power control problem in D2D communication considered in this paper.

3.1   System Model

We consider a single-cell cellular system consisting of one base station (BS), a set of M cellular users (CUs), and N D2D user (DU) pairs. The set of M CUs is denoted by $\mathcal{C}$ = $\{C_1, C_2, ..., C_M\}$ and the set of N DU pairs is denoted by $\mathcal{D} = \{D_1, D_2, ..., D_N\}$. Here, a DU pair consists of the transmitter (T_x) of one DU and the receiver (R_x) of another DU, which communicate with each other without passing through the BS. The system has K orthogonal resource blocks (RBs), which are denoted by $\mathcal{B} = \{B_1, B_2, ..., B_K\}$. We assume that the DU pairs work in an underlay mode and are allowed to share the uplink spectrum resources (i.e., RBs) of CUs. Each CU occupies one RB which can be shared by multiple DU pairs, and one DU pair can only occupy one RB. The BS is able to obtain the CSI of both CUs and DU pairs. Moreover, we assume that the transmission power of each CU is fixed to p_c and that of each DU is adjustable. Each DU can select a transmission power level from a set of values, which is denoted by $\mathcal{P} = \{p_1, p_2, ..., p_L\}$.

Considering that each DU pair is allowed to share the uplink RBs of CUs, there exist three types of interference in the system, which are illustrated in Fig. 1:

(1) I_1: the interference from the transmitter T_x of a DU pair to the BS;
(2) I_2: the interference from a CU to the receiver R_x of a DU pair, where the CU and the DU pair share the same RB;
(3) I_3: the interference from the transmitter T_x of one DU pair to the receiver R_x of another DU pair, where the two DU pairs share the same RB.

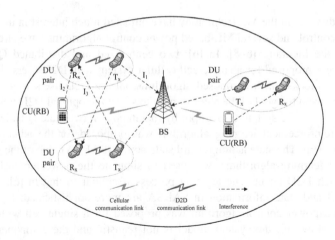

Fig. 1. System model

3.2 Problem Formulation

In this paper, we focus on the power control problem in D2D communication in the single-cell cellular system described in Fig. 1. For simplicity, we assume that the RB allocation is fixed. Specifically, we assume that $M = K$. Each CU is allocated a different RB and each DU pair is randomly allocated one RB.

Before we formulate the power control problem, we first analyze the signal to interference plus noise ratio (SINR) at a CU and at the receiver of a DU, respectively. For a CU that occupies the rth RB, the SINR at the CU is given by

$$SINC_{C_i}^r = \frac{p_{C_i}^r \cdot G_{C_i}^r}{\sigma^2 + \sum\limits_{D_j \in \mathcal{D}^r} p_{D_j}^r \cdot G_{D_j}^r}, i = 1, 2, \ldots, M; j = 1, 2, \ldots, N \qquad (1)$$

where C_i denotes the ith CU, D_j denotes the jth DU pair; $\mathcal{D}^r$ denotes the set of DU pairs that share the rth RB; $p_{C_i}^r$ and $p_{D_j}^r$ denote the transmission power of C_i and D_j which share the rth RB, respectively; $G_{C_i}^r$ and $G_{D_j}^r$ denote the channel gains on the rth RB from the BS to C_i and D_j, respectively; σ^2 is the noise variance.

Similarly, for a DU pair that shares the rth RB, the SINR at the receiver of the DU pair is given by

$$SINC_{D_j}^r = \frac{p_{D_j}^r \cdot G_{D_j D_j}^r}{\sigma^2 + p_{C_i}^r \cdot G_{C_i D_j}^r + \sum\limits_{\substack{D_k \in \mathcal{D}^r \\ k \neq j}} p_{D_k}^r \cdot G_{D_k D_j}^r}, \qquad (2)$$

where $G_{D_j D_j}^r$, $G_{C_i D_j}^r$, and $G_{D_k D_j}^r$ denote the channel gain on the link from the transmitter of D_j to the receiver of D_j, the channel gain from C_i to the receiver of D_j, and the channel gain from the transmitter of D_k to the receiver of D_j, respectively.

Next we formulate the power control problem. Given a set of available power levels $\mathcal{P} = \{p_1, p_2, ..., p_L\}$ and RB allocation for CUs and DU pairs, the power control problem under consideration is to find a set of optimal power levels $\mathcal{P}_D^* = \{p_{D_1}^*, p_{D_2}^*, \cdots, p_{D_N}^*\}$ for all the DU pairs so that the overall system throughput is maximized, i.e.,

$$\text{Objective}: \quad \max \sum_{r=1}^{K} \{\log_2(1 + SINR_{C_i}^r) + \sum_{D_j \in \mathcal{D}^r} \log_2(1 + SINR_{D_j}^r)\} \qquad (3)$$

$$\text{subject to} \quad SINR_{C_i}^r \geq \tau_0, \qquad (4)$$

$$p_1 \leq p_{D_j}^r \leq p_L, \qquad \forall j, r \qquad (5)$$

where τ_0 denotes the minimum SINR requirement of a CU, constraint (4) ensures the SINR requirement of each CU, and constraint (5) ensures that the transmission power of each DU is limited to the range $[p_1, p_L]$.

In the next section, we will present two MARL-based power control algorithms to solve the above power control problem.

4 MARL-Based Power Control Algorithm

In this section, we first introduce the concepts of reinforcement learning and then present two MARL-based power control algorithms: centralized Q-learning and distributed Q-learning.

4.1 Reinforcement Learning

Reinforcement learning is an important branch of machine learning. A standard RL problem can be represented by a tuple $(\mathcal{S}, \mathcal{A}, \mathcal{T}, R)$, where $\mathcal{S}$ denotes a set of states; $\mathcal{A}$ denotes a set of actions that can be selected by an agent; $\mathcal{T}$ denotes a set of transition probabilities from one state to another, and R denotes the reward function. A standard RL process is illustrated in Fig. 2.

In a standard RL process, an agent interacts with the environment in a sequence of episodes, which are denoted by $t = 0, 1, 2, ...$ There are three steps in each episode. In step (1), the agent receives the current state S_t and reward R_t. In step (2), it takes the action A_t. In step (3), the environment transfers to another state S_{t+1}, and gives a new reward R_{t+1}. The agent starts learning from an initial state S_0, and continues the episodes until the learning process converges.

In the above learning process, the agent selects its action in each episode according to a policy π, which is given by

$$\pi_t(a|s) = P(A_t = a | S_t = s), \quad a \in \mathcal{A}, s \in \mathcal{S}, \qquad (6)$$

where $P(A_t = a | S_t = s)$ is the probability of selecting action a at state s. By selecting different actions and updating the current policy in each episode, the agent is able to make a better decision and reaches the optimal policy π^* after a number of episodes.

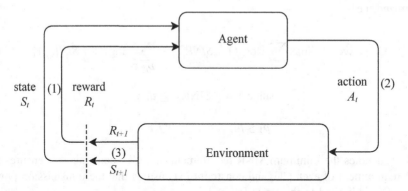

Fig. 2. Standard reinforcement learning process

To find an optimum policy, we introduce a value function $V_\pi(s)$ to determine the value of a state s under a given policy π, which is defined as the expectation of the discounted sum of the rewards in future episodes, i.e.,

$$V_\pi(s) = E_\pi(\sum_{i=1}^{\infty} \eta^{i-1} R_{t+i} | S_t = s), \qquad (7)$$

where $E_\pi(\cdot)$ denotes the expected value of a random variable given that the agent follows the policy π, η is the discount rate, and R_{t+i} is the reward in the $(t+i)$th episode. The discounted sum of rewards in future episodes reflects an important feature of RL: delayed reward, i.e., the action selected by each agent relies on not only the immediate reward, but also all the rewards in subsequent episodes. The value function represents how good it is to perform a given action in a given state, and thus can be used to evaluate the effectiveness of the policy. A higher value of $V_\pi(s)$ means a better policy for the agent. A policy is called an optimal policy if the corresponding value function is higher than any other value functions.

Q learning is a typical form of reinforcement learning. Like all other RL algorithms, Q learning needs no prior knowledge about the environment. In Q learning, an agent learns how to behave based on the previous experience, which is traced by a Q function. The Q function is used to determine the value of an action a under a given state s and is defined as

$$Q_t(s,a) = E_\pi(\sum_{i=1}^{\infty} \eta^{i-1} R_{t+i} | S_t = s, A_t = a). \qquad (8)$$

A Q function is represented by a two-dimensional table, in which each row represents a state of the environment, and each column represents an action of the agent.

The learning process starts from an initial state S_0, and the initial Q table is usually set to all-zero. At each episode, assuming the current state is $S_t = s$, the agent needs to select the best action $A_t = a$ according to the policy. After performing a, the agent receives a reward R_{t+1}, and the environment transfers to the next state S_{t+1}. It can be proved by induction that Q learning is able to converge to the optimal values if all the states can be visited infinitely as the learning process proceeds [9].

As assumed in Sect. 3.2, the RB allocation for CUs and DU pairs is fixed. Thus, the power control for the DU pairs on different RBs is independent. For this reason, the power control problem under consideration can be viewed as K independent power control sub-problems on K RBs. For a particular RB, all the DUs sharing the RB should select a proper power level from $\mathcal{P} = \{p_1, p_2, ..., p_L\}$ to reach the maximum throughput on this RB. To use Q learning to solve the problem, each DU pair can be considered as an individual agent. In this way, it becomes a multi-agent Q-learning problem. In the next two sections, we will present a centralized Q-learning algorithm and a distributed Q-learning algorithm to solve the problem.

4.2 Centralized Q-learning Algorithm for D2D Power Control

In this section, we present the proposed centralized Q-learning algorithm for D2D power control.

A. Component Definitions
We first define the basic components in the centralized Q-learning algorithm: agent, state, action, and reward. In the centralized Q-learning algorithm, an agent is defined as a DU pair in the cellular system. Thus, there are N agents in the whole system. An action of an agent is defined as the action that a DU pair takes to select a power level p from $\mathcal{P} = \{p_1, p_2, ..., p_L\}$. The joint actions for all DUs sharing a particular RB constitute a vector. A reward in the centralized Q-learning algorithm is defined as the conditional overall throughput of an RB in the cellular system. The value of a reward is determined using the following reward function:

$$R = \begin{cases} \log_2(1 + SINR^r_{C_i}) + \sum_{D_j \in \mathcal{D}^r} \log_2(1 + SINR^r_{D_j}), & SINR^r_{C_i} \geq \tau_0 \\ -1 & \text{otherwise} \end{cases}. \tag{9}$$

According to Eq. (9), if the SINR requirement of C_i cannot be satisfied, i.e., $SINR^r_{C_i} < \tau_0$, the reward is set to -1 as a penalty term, which ensures the priority of C_i.

In a standard Q-learning algorithm, an agent needs to transfer between different states by selecting different actions, which usually takes a large number of episodes to converge. Furthermore, it is difficult to define the states in the Q-learning algorithm that matches the physical states in the single-cell cellular system [10]. According to [10], we use a single-state Q table in the centralized Q-learning algorithm and the state formulation is not needed.

B. Algorithm Description
The centralized Q-learning algorithm is an algorithm that is executed at the BS for performing power control for DU pairs. Unlike that in [6], it uses a single state Q table

in the learning process instead of a two-state Q table. In the learning process, the Q table for the rth RB is first set to all zeros. In each episode, all DU pairs on the rth RB select different power levels simultaneously, receive a reward, and update the Q table. The learning process continues until the Q table converges to the optimal values.

In each episode, an action is selected based on an ε-greedy strategy, which is described as follows:

- Select a random action with a probability ε;
- Select an action according to the maximum Q value of the current state with a probability $(1 - \varepsilon)$.

Here, ε is the threshold of the probability, which decays with the number of episodes as

$$\varepsilon = \varepsilon_{\min} + (\varepsilon_{\max} - \varepsilon_{\min}) \cdot \exp(-h \cdot t), \tag{10}$$

where $\varepsilon_{\max}$ and $\varepsilon_{\min}$ denote the upper limit and the lower limit of ε; h is a decay rate within $[0, 1]$; t is the index of the current episode. At the beginning of learning, ε is set to a value close to 1. Thus, the agent is likely to select a random action that it has not selected before to find more new states of the environment. As the learning process continues, the value of ε decreases accordingly, and thus the agent relies more on the learned policy. The ε-greedy strategy helps an agent explore more states and actions at the beginning of the learning process so that the convergence of Q learning can be ensured [9]. After an action is selected, the Q table is updated based on the following function:

$$Q_{t+1}^r(s, a) = Q_t^r(s, a) + \alpha[r_{t+1} + \gamma \max_{a' \in \mathcal{A}} Q_t^r(s', a') - Q_t^r(s, a)], \tag{11}$$

where $Q_{t+1}^r(s, a)$ denotes the Q table in the $(t + 1)$th episode $Q_{t+1}^r(s, a)$; α is the learning rate ranging from 0 to 1, which decides how much the reward contributes in the update of the Q value; γ is the discount factor which varies from 0 to 1. The higher the value, the more the DU pairs rely on the future rewards than the current reward. According to Eq. (11), $Q_{t+1}^r(s, a)$ depends on the current Q value $Q_t^r(s, a)$, the reward for taking the action a under the state s, and the maximum future reward given the new state s' and all possible actions $a' \in \mathcal{A}$ under s'

The pseudo codes of the centralized Q-learning algorithm for D2D power control are given in Algorithm 1.

Algorithm 1 Centralized Q-learning algorithm for D2D power control

---

Input:

$\mathcal{B}= \{B_1, B_2, ..., B_K\}$ {a set of K resource blocks}

$C= \{C_1, C_2, ..., C_M\}$ {a set of M cellular users}

$\mathcal{D}= \{D_1, D_2, ..., D_N\}$ {a set of N D2D users}

$\mathcal{P}= \{p_1, p_2, ..., p_L\}$ {a set of available power levels}

Output:

$\mathcal{P}_D^* = \{p_{D_1}^*, p_{D_2}^*, \Lambda, p_{D_N}^*\}$ {optimal power levels of all DU pairs}

Function:

$Q_t^r(s, a)$ {Q table for the rth RB in the tth episode

                            under state s and action a}

Initialize:

for the rth RB, $r \in \{1,2, ..., K\}$

initialize $Q_t^r(s, a)$, $a \in \mathcal{A}$

Learning:

for:

select the rth RB, $r \in \{1,2, ..., K\}$

for:

select action $a \in \mathcal{A}$ according to the ε greedy strategy

execute a and

calculate the reward

update $Q_t^r(s, a)$ according to Eq. (11)

end for

end for

4.3   Distributed Q-learning Algorithm for D2D Power Control

In the centralized Q-learning algorithm, all DUs on the same RB update a common Q table with the size of $1 \times L^n$, where L is the number of available power levels, and n is the number of DU pairs on the RB. As the number of D2D pairs grows, the complexity increases exponentially and it is intractable to compute the value of the Q table. To solve this problem, we propose a distributed Q-learning algorithm, in which each agent maintains and updates its own Q table with the size of $1 \times L$. This can dramatically reduce the time and space complexity for calculating the value of the Q table.

The definitions of the agent, state, action and reward in the distributed Q-learning algorithm are the same as those in the centralized Q-learning algorithm. It is worth noting that in [6], the throughput of a DU pair is used as the reward, excluding the throughput of CUs and other DU pairs sharing the same RB. However, according to [9], the optimal Q value can be obtained only if the reward function remains the same as that in the centralized Q-learning algorithm. Thus, we keep the same reward function as that in Eq. (9). The update function for the distributed Q-learning algorithm [11] is given by

$$Q_{t+1}^j(s,a) = \max\{Q_t^j(s,a), r_{t+1} + \gamma \max_{a' \in \mathcal{A}} Q_t^j(s',a')\}, \tag{12}$$

where $Q_t^j(s,a)$ denotes the Q value for D_j in the tth episode.

An important problem with the distributed Q-learning algorithm is the coordination between different agents during the learning process. Since each agent selects its own action independently and the change of the action will in turn affect the throughput of other agents, it is not possible for all the agents to select their actions simultaneously. To deal with this problem, a simple heuristic method is used for scheduling the update of the Q tables. Specifically, for the rth RB, the DU pairs update their Q tables by turns in one episode. After all the DU pairs on the rth RB have updated their Q tables, the next episode starts with the first agent until all the Q tables converge to the same optimal value. It can be proved that the optimal Q values for the distributed Q-learning algorithm and the centralized Q-learning algorithm are equal [9].

The pseudo codes of the distributed Q-learning algorithm for D2D power control is given in Algorithm 2.

Algorithm 2   Distributed Q-learning algorithm for D2D power control

---

Input:

    $\mathcal{B}= \{B_1, B_2, ..., B_K\}$ {a set of K resource blocks}

    $\mathcal{C}= \{C_1, C_2, ..., C_M\}$ {a set of M cellular users}

    $\mathcal{D}= \{D_1, D_2, ..., D_N\}$ {a set of N D2D users}

    $\mathcal{P}= \{p_1, p_2, ..., p_L\}$ {a set of available power levels}

Output:

    $\mathcal{B}^* = \{p_{D_1}^*, p_{D_2}^*, \Lambda, p_{D_N}^*\}$ {optimal power levels of all DU pairs}

Function:

    $Q_t^j(s,a)$ {Q table for D_j in the tth episode

                                              under state s and action a}

Initialize:

    for D_j , $j \in\{1,2, ..., N\}$

    initialize $Q_t^j(s,a)$ =0, $a\in\mathcal{A}$

Learning:

    for:

    select the rth RB, $r \in\{1, 2,..., K\}$

    for:

    select D_j, for all the DUs on the rth RB.

    for:

    select action $a \in\mathcal{A}$ according to the ε greedy strategy

    execute a and

    calculate the reward r_{t+1}

    update $Q_t^j(s,a)$ according to Eq. (12)

    end for

    end for

    end for

---

5 Simulation Results

In this section, we evaluate the performance of the proposed centralized and distributed Q-learning algorithms through simulation results. The simulation experiments were conducted on a simulator developed using python. We consider a single cell cellular system where the CUs and DU pairs are uniformly distributed. The parameters used in the simulation experiment are listed in Table 1.

In the performance evaluation, we compare the proposed centralized and distributed Q-learning algorithms with a random allocation algorithm. The random algorithm randomly selects a power level from $\mathcal{P}$ for each DU pair. Moreover, we use the system throughput and satisfaction ratio as the performance metrics. The system throughput is defined as the throughput of all CUs and DU pairs in the system. The satisfaction ratio is defined as the number of CUs whose SINR requirements are satisfied over the total number of CUs in the system.

Table 1. Simulation parameters

Parameter	Value
M	20
N	10–100
K	20
L	5
Cell radius	500 m
p_1, p_2, p_3, p_4, p_5	{1, 6.5, 12, 17.5, 23}dBm
p_c	24 dBm
Noise power	−116 dBm/Hz
Resource block bandwidth	180 kHz
Gain model between user and BS	$15.3 + 37.6\lg(d(km))$ dB
Gain model between two users	$128 + 40\lg(d(km))$ dB
Learning rate α	0.9
Discount factor γ	0.9
τ_0	6 dB

Figure 3 compares the convergence of the optimal Q values with the centralized Q-learning algorithm and the distributed Q-learning algorithm under $M = 1$, $N = 5$, respectively. It can be observed that both the centralized algorithm and the distributed algorithm converge to the same Q value, which conforms to the conclusion in [9]. Meanwhile, it takes more episodes for the centralized algorithm to converge than for the distributed algorithm. This is because the centralized algorithm uses a larger Q table than the distributed algorithm.

According to Fig. 3, the centralized Q-learning algorithm and the distributed Q-learning algorithm converge to the same optimal Q value. Thus, the optimal power levels of the DU pairs with the two algorithms are equal, which results in the equal system throughput and satisfaction ratios. Therefore, we will only show the simulation results with the distributed Q-learning algorithm in the following figures.

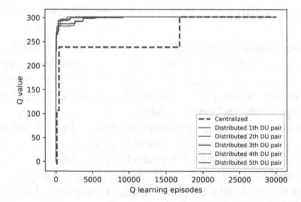

Fig. 3. Comparison of the convergence with the two algorithms ($M = 1$, $N = 5$)

Figure 4 shows the system throughput with the distributed Q-learning algorithm and a random algorithm, respectively. It is observed that the system throughput increases as the number of DU pairs increases. On the other hand, the system throughput with the distributed algorithm is larger than that with the random algorithm.

Figure 5 shows the satisfaction ratios of CUs with the distributed Q-learning algorithm and the random algorithm, respectively. It can be observed that the satisfaction ratio with the distributed algorithm is larger than that with the random algorithm. Moreover, as the number of DU pairs increases, the distributed algorithm can keep relatively stable at a higher value ($>=0.9$), while the satisfaction ratio with the random algorithm decreases dramatically.

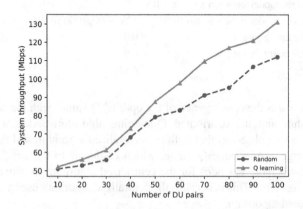

Fig. 4. System throughput with the distributed Q-learning algorithm

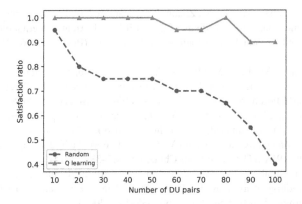

Fig. 5. Satisfaction ratio with the distributed Q-learning algorithm

6 Conclusions

In this paper, we considered the power control problem in D2D communication underlaying a cellular network and proposed two MARL-based algorithms for performing power control of D2D users: centralized Q-learning algorithm and distributed Q-learning algorithm. In the centralized algorithm, all D2D user (DU) pairs sharing the same RB use a common Q table in the learning process, while in the distributed algorithm each DU pair maintains its own Q table. Simulation results show that both the centralized algorithm and the distributed algorithm can converge to the same Q value, and the distributed algorithm can converge faster than the centralized algorithm. Moreover, both the proposed Q-learning algorithms outperform the random power control algorithm in terms of the system throughput and satisfaction ratio. In future work, we will explore to use the ML approach in joint spectrum allocation and power control for D2D communication underlaying cellular networks.

References

1. Asadi, A., Wang, Q., Mancuso, V.: A survey on device-to-device communication in cellular networks. IEEE Commun. Surv. Tutorials **16**(4), 1801–1819 (2014)
2. Lee, N., Lin, X., Andrews, J.G., Heath, R.W.: Power control for D2D underlaid cellular networks: modeling, algorithms, and analysis. IEEE J. Sel. Areas Commun. **33**(1), 1–13 (2015)
3. Ren, Y., Liu, F., Liu, Z., Wang, C., Ji, Y.: Power control in D2D-based vehicular communication networks. IEEE Trans. Veh. Technol. **64**(12), 5547–5562 (2015)
4. da Silva, J., Fodor, G.: A binary power control scheme for D2D communications. IEEE Wireless Commun. Lett. **4**(6), 669–672 (2015)
5. Sun, P., Shin, K.G., Zhang, H., He, L.: Transmit power control for D2D-underlaid cellular networks based on statistical features. IEEE Trans. Veh. Technol. **66**(5), 4110–4119 (2017)

6. Nie, S., Fan, Z., Zhao, M., Gu, X., Zhang, L.: Q-learning based power control algorithm for D2D communication. In: Proceedings of 2016 IEEE 27th Annual International Symposium on Personal, Indoor, and Mobile Radio Communications (PIMRC 2016), Valencia, Spain, pp. 1–6 (2016)
7. Khan, M.I., Alam, M.M., Le Moullec, Y., Yaacoub, E.: Cooperative reinforcement learning for adaptive power allocation in device-to-device communication. In: Proceedings of 2018 IEEE 4th World Forum on Internet of Things (WF-IoT), Singapore (2018)
8. Luo, Y., Shi, Z., Zhou, X., Liu, Q., Yi, Q.: Dynamic resource allocations based on Q-learning for D2D communication in cellular networks. In: Proceedings of 2014 11th International Computer Conference on Wavelet Active Media Technology and Information Processing (ICCWAMTIP), Chengdu, China, pp. 385–388 (2014)
9. Lauer, M., Riedmiller, M.: An algorithm for distributed reinforcement learning in cooperative multi-gent aystems. In: Proceedings of the 17th International Conference on Machine Learning, San Francisco, CA, pp. 535–542 (2000)
10. Jiang, T., Zhao, Q., David, G., Burr, A.G., Clarke, T.: Single-state Q-learning for self-organized radio resource management in dual-hop 5G high capacity density networks. Trans. Emerg. Telecommun. Technol. **27**, 1628–1640 (2016). https://doi.org/10.1002/ett.3019
11. Sutton, R.S., Barto, A.G.: Reinforcement learning: an introduction. IEEE Trans. Neural Networks **9**(5), 1054 (1998)

An Adaptive Window Time-Frequency Analysis Method Based on Short-Time Fourier Transform

Zhiqiang Li[1,2(✉)], Xiao Wang[1], Ming Li[2], and Shuai Han[1]

[1] Communication Research Center,
Harbin Institute of Technology, Harbin, China
1084298918@qq.com, {hitwx,hanshuai}@hit.edu.cn
[2] Institute of Telecommunication Satellite, CAST, Beijing, China
liminghit@163.com

Abstract. Frequency hopping signal has the advantages of strong anti-jamming ability and low probability of interception. It can effectively improve communication quality and security. Therefore, frequency hopping technology is widely used in the field of information countermeasures, and has become one of the main anti-jamming technologies adopted by various countries. As a non-partner, how to quickly obtain the main parameters of frequency hopping signal in order to implement effective and timely interference is particularly important. In this paper, a blind estimation algorithm based on short-time Fourier transform (STFT) is proposed. STFT is a time-frequency analysis method with low complexity. The performance of this method depends largely on the length of the Fourier transform window. The algorithm in this paper roughly estimates the period of frequency hopping signal according to the Frequency domain characteristics of input signal, and uses this information to determine the length of local window. The obtained time-frequency distribution is purified by setting a reasonable threshold, and the purified time-frequency distribution is used to extract information and estimate the main parameters of frequency hopping signal. The results show that this method can roughly estimate the length of Fourier transform window in very low SNR environment, and fine estimation method has higher accuracy in estimating the Frequency hopping period of frequency hopping signal.

Keywords: Frequency hopping communication · Time-frequency analysis · Parameter estimation

1 Introduction

Frequency hopping communication systems are widely used in military communications and civil mobile communications due to their low interception rate, anti-fading and strong networking capabilities. In the field of communication countermeasures and radio monitoring, the analysis of frequency hopping signals is extremely significant in the study of parametric detection techniques. The analysis of FHSS signals required a method suitable for representing time-varying signals. Time–frequency (TF) analysis is suitable since it produces a representation for time varying signals jointly in both time and frequency.

S. Han et al. (Eds.): AICON 2019, LNICST 287, pp. 91–106, 2019.
https://doi.org/10.1007/978-3-030-22971-9_8

In paper [1], compressed sensing technology is applied to time-frequency analysis of frequency hopping signals. According to the model of frequency hopping signal, the sparse characteristics of frequency hopping signal are analyzed and a sparse dictionary is constructed. Then, a time-frequency analysis algorithm of frequency hopping signal is proposed by using partial reconstruction algorithm. For the spectrum estimation problem of multi-hop frequency hopping signals existing in random frequency hopping observation, paper [2] uses the signal structure inherent in the frequency hopping signal to design the corresponding time-frequency core, and represents the nucleation result in the instantaneous autocorrelation function domain, using redesign. The structure-aware Bayesian compressed sensing algorithm processes signals. Based on the basic approximation theory of scaling function, a new method for constructing the basis pairs of Hilbert transform (HT) wavelets is proposed in [3]. A kind of Bayesian algorithm based on sparse Bayesian reconstruction for approximate blind estimation is proposed to estimate multi-hopping signal parameters in [4]. For the non-stationary character-istics of frequency hopping signals, paper [5] proposes a blind detection and parameter estimation algorithm for single-hop signals in complex electromagnetic environment based on STFT. The frequency hopping signal can be identified by the same duration of the signal components on different frequencies, and the interference signal and noise can be effectively removed to achieve the purpose of blind detection. The fast Fourier transform can then be used to estimate the frequency hopping and frequency hopping periods. A kind of frequency hopping duration estimation algorithm for frequency hopping signals based on multi-window partially overlapping reallocation smoothing Pseudo-WVD and adaptive threshold detection technology is proposed in [6]. It divides the signal into several segments according to an analysis window, analyses each segment with connects the maximum values of all segments of each sampling time with multi-window partial overlap method, and estimates the hopping time of frequency hopping signal with adaptive threshold detection. A kind of resolution metrics for objective evaluation of secondary time-frequency distribution performance are given in [7]. This criterion considers key attributes of time-frequency distribution, such as main and side lobes and cross terms. And apply the defined criteria to analyze the advantages and disadvantages of different time-frequency distributions. An advanced time-frequency distribution of the extended modified-B distributions (EMBD) is given in [8]. The time-frequency distribution is designed with a variable Time-Frequency core, and an independent tightly supported hyperbolic cosine function is used as a kernel function to filter the fuzzy function to obtain a time-frequency diagram. Based on the traditional STFT, a new algorithm for extracting the frequency characteristics of fre-quency diversity signals is proposed. The algorithm combines STFT with false posi-tives and detection probabilities to make full use of frequency domain information in [9]. The paper [10] proposes a globally adaptive optimal kernel smooth-windowed Wigner-Ville distribution. The autocorrelation function envelope of the signal and the localized weighted regression (LOWESS) is used to obtain the frequency hopping signal period. The power spectrum is obtained from the autocorrelation function. The information sets the length of the window function added to the Wigner transform. Based on the time-frequency diagrams of EMBD [8] and SWWVD [10], the paper [11] proposes a quadratic-based accurate FHSS signal parameter estimation method: TF moments method (TF moments method) and instantaneous frequency method

(IF method). Linear TFD like short time Fourier transform suffers from time–frequency resolution trade off. On the other hand, QTFDs like Wigner–Ville distribution provides a good time–frequency resolution at the drawback of cross terms [12]. Thus, a variety of TFDs which is much application dependent have been introduced. However, if the kernel function is chosen properly, the QTFD can provide an accurate representation.

The above literature mainly studies the performance of methods and often ignores the complexity of the algorithm. Although the quadratic time-frequency distribution solves the problem that the time-frequency resolution cannot be improved at the same time, it also brings the interference of the cross-term, and the complexity of the algorithm is also greatly improved. This method is no longer applicable in the case of rapid frequency hopping. When we are in a non-partner, there is no a priori information, and the performance of some methods is difficult to guarantee. In this paper, the complexity of the algorithm is considered, and a low-complexity hopping period blind estimation method based on STFT is proposed. The method utilizes the frequency domain characteristics of the received signal, first roughly estimates the frequency hopping period, and then appropriately sets the Fourier transform window length according to the obtained information. At the same time, this paper also makes full use of the obtained information to optimize the frequency hopping period estimation method and obtain better performance.

2 Problem Definition

Frequency hopping system only adds carrier frequency hopping ability in conventional communication system, which widens the whole working frequency band greatly, and improves the anti-interference and anti-fading ability of communication system. The anti-jamming ability of frequency hopping system is "evasive", which is different from DSSS system. DSSS system improves anti-jamming ability by spectrum expansion and de-spreading processing. Obviously, the frequency hopping signal is non-stationary, and the time-frequency analysis method is a powerful tool for frequency hopping analysis and estimating the parameters of frequency hopping signal.

2.1 Signal Mode

Frequency hopping communication is a kind of communication mode that periodically changes the carrier of transmitting signal under the control of frequency hopping sequence. Frequency hopping sequence is a pseudo-random sequence. The function of frequency hopping sequence is to control carrier frequency hopping, which is generally a multi-valued pseudo-random sequence. For this paper, prime frequency hopping sequence is used. Frequency hopping modulation is secondary modulation and primary modulation can be any common modulation mode, such as phase shift key (PSK), quadrature phase shift key (QPSK), frequency shift key (4FSK) and so on. This paper adopts 4FSK modulation mode. The expression of frequency hopping signal is as follows.

$$S_i(t) = S_d(t) \sum_{-\infty}^{\infty} 2P(t - nT_c) \cos(w_n t + \phi_n) \tag{1}$$

Where $S_d(t)$ is 4FSK signal, P is a rectangular pulse, T_c is the duration of each hop frequency, w_n is the hopping frequency within a kth hopping duration, ϕ_n is phase at the beginning of a kth hopping duration.

The signal parameters of the signals used in this paper are given as follows.

(1) 4FSK: $[f_1 \ f_2 \ f_3 \ f_4] = [500 \, \text{Hz} \quad 1 \, \text{kHz} \quad 1.5 \, \text{kHz} \quad 2 \, \text{kHz}]$
(2) Frequency hopping duration: 0.004 s
(3) Frequency hopping set: Taking 10 FH points at equal intervals from 3 kHz to 30 kHz

2.2 Analytical Form of Signal

In the signal spectrum analysis method, people often prefer to choose the analytical form of signal to eliminate the negative frequency effect of signal. Assuming that the signal $s(t)$ to be processed is a real signal, its corresponding spectrum is given as.

$$S(f) = \int_{-\infty}^{+\infty} s(t) e^{-j2\pi ft} dt \tag{2}$$

Signal spectrum is conjugate

$$S^*(f) = \int_{-\infty}^{+\infty} s(t) e^{j2\pi ft} dt = S(-f) \tag{3}$$

From the perspective of effective bandwidth utilization of information, the negative frequency spectrum of real signal is redundant, because the negative frequency component can be obtained from the positive frequency part of the spectrum. Therefore, the negative frequency spectrum of the real signal is removed and the positive frequency spectrum is retained, which can reduce the bandwidth of the signal and improve the bandwidth utilization. However, if only the positive frequency spectrum part of the signal is retained, the receiver spectrum will no longer have conjugate symmetry, and the corresponding time-domain signal is complex. If we want to remove the negative frequency component of the signal and keep the total energy of the signal unchanged, the spectrum of the analytic form $z(t)$ of the signal should be given as.

$$Z(f) = \begin{cases} 2S(f), & f > 0 \\ S(f), & f = 0 \\ 0, & f < 0 \end{cases} \tag{4}$$

The complex analytic signal satisfying the above formula is composed of two signals, real part and imaginary part. The analytic signal $z(t)$ corresponding to real signal $s(t)$ can be defined as.

$$z(t) = s(t) + jHilbert[s(t)] \tag{5}$$

Compared with the narrowband stationary signal, the spectrum obtained by traditional Fourier transform can well describe its physical characteristics. However, for non-stationary signals, the frequency is time-varying. In this case, the concept of frequency and Fourier analysis method cannot achieve good analysis results, so the concept of instantaneous frequency is introduced. From the physical point of view, signals can be divided into single and multi-component signals. Multicomponent signal means that the signal has several different instantaneous frequencies at some time; single component signal has only one frequency at any time. Vile gives a generally accepted definition of instantaneous frequency:

For real signals.

$$s(t) = a(t)e^{j\theta(t)} \tag{6}$$

Where $\theta(t)$ is the instantaneous phase and $a(t)$ is the instantaneous amplitude, the analytic signal can be expressed.

$$z(t) = a(t)\cos[\theta(t)] \tag{7}$$

The derivative of the phase of the analytic signal is the instantaneous frequency.

$$f_i(t) = \frac{d[\arg z(t)]}{dt} \tag{8}$$

Vile also proposed that since the instantaneous frequency is time-varying, the corresponding instantaneous spectrum should also exist. The instantaneous frequency is the average frequency of the instantaneous spectrum.

$$Z(f) = \int_{-\infty}^{+\infty} z(t)e^{-j2\pi ft}dt = \int_{-\infty}^{+\infty} a(t)e^{j[\theta(t)-2\pi ft]} \tag{9}$$

The characteristic of signal energy concentration along instantaneous frequency plays an important role in signal reconstruction, identification, parameter estimation, target tracking and modeling.

3 Time–Frequency Analysis

Traditional Fourier transform is a commonly used spectrum analysis tool, which has great significance in the analysis and processing of stationary signals. But Fourier transform has one obvious disadvantage, that is, Fourier transform decomposes the whole signal into different frequency components. This is to observe the signal from a global perspective, lacking local information, and any part of the signal change or loss will have a huge impact on the entire spectrum. It can't tell us which time period the various frequency components occur, and we can't establish the time-frequency domain joint relationship. Therefore, the Fourier transform is only applicable to the stationary signal whose statistics do not change with time. However, in reality, signals are confidential, anti-interference, etc., and many of them are non-stationary signals, such as frequency hopping signals. For such signals, the traditional Fourier transform is no longer adapted, and its local performance requires a two-dimensional joint representation of the time domain and the frequency domain in order to obtain an accurate description. Therefore, non-stationary signals usually use a two-dimensional function with two-dimensional variables of time and frequency.

3.1 Short-Time Fourier

Based on the traditional Fourier transform, STFT is proposed based on the non-stationary signal characteristics [9]. Add different window functions to the signal, propose local information, and then perform Fourier transform. The STFT uses a linear transformation method of signals. When analyzing a signal containing multiple components, there is no interference of cross terms, and it also has a small amount of calculation.

For non-stationary signals, people usually pay more attention to the instantaneous frequency of signals. Thus, the concept of "local spectrum" is introduced. The signal is extracted with a very narrow window function, and the signal outside the window is suppressed. Then, the signal is Fourier transformed in the window. The basic idea is to divide the signal into many small intervals and then use the Fourier transform for each small interval. In order to study the local characteristics of the signal at time t, it is necessary to strengthen the signal at time t, compress or filter the others. This is equivalent to extracting the signal with a finite length window.

$$s_t(\tau) = s(\tau)h(\tau - t) \tag{10}$$

Moving the window function continuously, this processing is used for all moments, and the result is STFT, defined as.

$$STFT_s(t,f) = \int_{-\infty}^{+\infty} s(\tau)h(\tau - t)e^{-j2\pi f\tau}d\tau \tag{11}$$

Where $h(t)$ is Hamming window
The corresponding STFT inverse transform is.

$$s(t) = \int_{-\infty}^{\infty}\int_{-\infty}^{\infty} STFT_s(u,f)h(u - t)e^{j2\pi ft}dudf \tag{12}$$

In the STFT process, the length of the window determines the time resolution and frequency resolution of the spectrogram. The longer the length of the window function, the higher the frequency resolution after Fourier transform and the worse the time resolution. Conversely, the shorter the intercepted signal, the worse the frequency resolution, and the better the corresponding time resolution. Therefore, we should consider the time resolution and frequency domain resolution together. For non-stationary signals, the width of the selected window is preferably close to the length of each hop of the frequency hopping signal, and is compatible with local stationarity.

3.2 Adaptive Window

By analyzing the spectrum characteristics of frequency hopping signals, this paper proposes a kind of method for estimating window length in frequency domain. This method can still work in low SNR environment.

In frequency hopping communication, no matter which pseudo-random sequence is adopted, the carrier frequency will not be repeated in a short time. In this way, the frequency hopping period can be roughly estimated according to the spectrum characteristics of some intercepted signals, and the window length can be designed according to this information (Fig. 1).

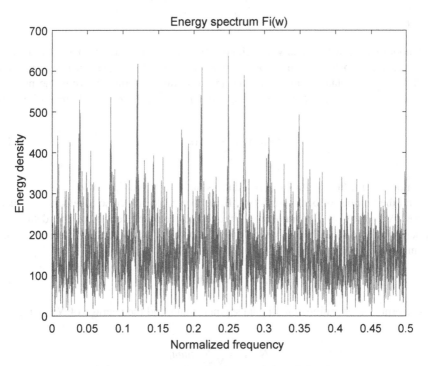

Fig. 1. Frequency domain characteristics of signals.

The specific steps are as follows.

Assuming that the received radio signal has completed the down conversion operation, and is an intermediate frequency signal. Divide the signal into N segments.

Select a fragment of data $x_i(n)$ and find the analytical form $z_i(n)$ of this data fragment, then DFT transform for segment of data and Get frequency domain Information of Signal $F_i(w)$.

$$z_i(n) = x_i(n) + jHilbert[x_i(n)] \tag{13}$$

$$F_i(w) = DFT[z_i(n)] = \sum_{n=0}^{N-1} z_i(n) W_N^{kn} \tag{14}$$

Choose half of the maximum value of $F_i(w)$ as the threshold λ to filter the noise. The value greater than λ in $F_i(w)$ is retained and the value less than λ is set to zero, and then get $G_i(w)$.

$$G_i(w) = \begin{cases} 0, & F_i(w) < \lambda \\ F_i(w), & F_i(w) > \lambda \end{cases} \tag{14}$$

Smooth $G_i(w)$ with Locally Weighted Regression, which is discussed in detail in [10]. According to the instantaneous frequency theory, the signal energy is concentrated along the instantaneous frequency in the frequency domain, while the noise is relatively dispersed. Sum $G_i(w)$ every few data points on frequency domain direction.

$$S_i(w_1) = \sum_{j=1}^{a-1} G_i(aw + j) \tag{15}$$

Among them, the length of $G_i(w)$ data is an integer multiple of a.

Find the number of peaks for $S_i(w)$, If the two peaks are close together, treat them as one. According to the number of frequencies and the length of the data, each frequency duration can be derived. You can set the window length N based on this information.

$$num_i = findpeaks(S_i(w)) \tag{16}$$

Perform 2–7 operations on all data segments and find the average of N_{aver} (Fig. 2).

$$N_{aver} = \frac{1}{N} \sum_i^{N} num_i \tag{17}$$

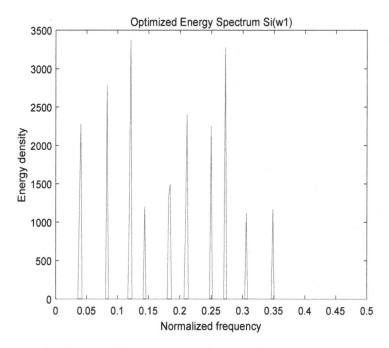

Fig. 2. Rough estimation of frequency number based on frequency domain characteristics

4 Hopping Parameters Estimation

Once the Time-frequency distribution of the signal is obtained, the next step is to estimate the FHSS signal parameters: hopping frequencies, hopping duration and hopping sequence.

Two methods for estimating parameters of frequency hopping signals have been proposed which are instantaneous frequency method [23] and maximum curve method [21]. Furthermore, according to the rough estimation information of frequency hopping period and the maximum curve method, the frequency hopping period estimation method is optimized (Fig. 3).

4.1 Instantaneous Frequency Method

The use of IF estimation is to characterize time-varying signals and estimate the signal parameters [11]. Extending its use for FHSS signals, the IF estimation from the peaks of the TFD

$$f_i(t) = \arg\{\max_f[\rho_z(t,f)]\} \quad 0 \leq t \leq T \tag{18}$$

Find the histogram of the instantaneous frequency and estimate the frequency hopping frequency set from the histogram.

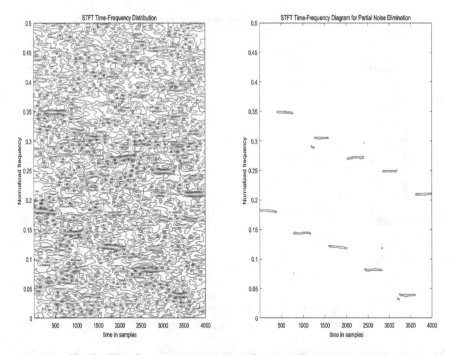

Fig. 3. Time-frequency distribution before and after noise removal

$$\hat{f_h} = \arg\{\max_f[hist(\hat{f_i})]\} \quad 1 \leq h \leq M_h \tag{19}$$

Estimate the transition time by finding the reciprocal of $f_i(t)$.

$$\frac{df_i(t)}{dt} \simeq |f_i(t) - f_i(t + \Delta t)|, \quad 0 \leq t \leq T, \tag{20}$$

Where Δt is the adjacent instantaneous frequency difference. It changes immediately within each hop interval, so the reciprocal value of this instantaneous frequency will appear at the maximum value at the time of the transition.

$$\hat{t_{h,k}} = \arg\{\max_t[\frac{df_i(t)}{dt}]\}, \quad 0 \leq k \leq N_h - 1, \tag{21}$$

The hopping carrier duration of the Kth hop is obtained by finding the time difference between the signal hopping times.

$$\hat{T_{h,k}} = \hat{t_{h,k}} - \hat{t_{h,k-1}}, \quad 0 \leq k \leq N_h - 1, \tag{22}$$

The averaging of $\hat{T_h}$ for all hops Nh results in the estimate of the hopping duration.

$$\hat{T_h} = \frac{1}{Nh} \sum_{k=0}^{Nh-1} \hat{T}_{h,k} \tag{23}$$

Once this frequency hopping frequency set F and frequency hopping period t are estimated, the average power is first calculated in one hop period.

$$f_{IF,avg,k} = \frac{1}{\hat{T}_{h,k}} \int_{t=\hat{t}_{h,k-1}}^{\hat{t}_{h,k}} \hat{f_i}(t)dt \tag{24}$$

Find the absolute value of the difference between the average frequency and the sum of each hop period.

$$D_{h,k} = |f_{IF,avg,k} - \hat{f_h}| \tag{25}$$

The instantaneous frequency during each hop period is as follows (Fig. 4).

$$\hat{f}_{h,k} = \arg\min_{k}(D_{h,k}) \tag{26}$$

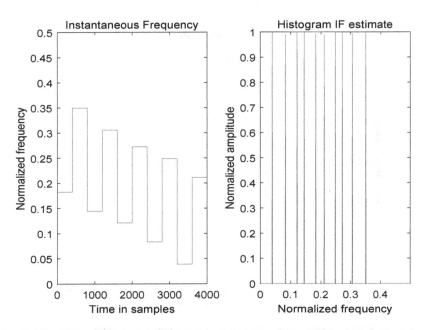

Fig. 4. IF estimation method: IF estimation from the peaks of TFD and Histogram of frequencies derived from the IF

4.2   Maximum Curve Method

The average power of additive Gauss noise may be much higher than that of signal. However, the noise is uniformly distributed on the time-frequency plane and the value of noise power distribution to every point on the time-frequency plane is very small. According to this characteristic, the maximum curve method is proposed [13].

Detailed steps are as follows:

Search for maximum amplitude at each time along the frequency axis and obtain the function between time and maximum amplitude as shown in Fig. 5.

$$y(n) = \max_{k} STFT(n, k) \tag{27}$$

Then the $y(n)$ is transformed by FFT to get $w(k)$. The abscissa k_f corresponding to the maximum value of $w(k)$ is the frequency hopping frequency, and its reciprocal is the frequency hopping period (Fig. 6)

$$w(k) = DFT[y(n)] = \sum_{n=0}^{N-1} y(n) W_N^{kn} \tag{28}$$

$$k_f = \arg \max w(k) \tag{29}$$

$$\hat{T} = 1/k_f \tag{30}$$

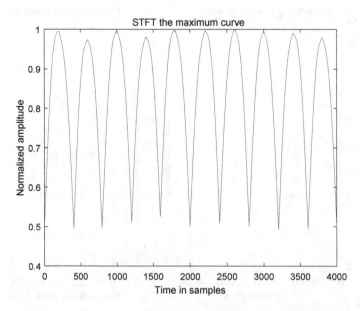

Fig. 5. Maximum curve method: the law of maximum signal amplitude conversion

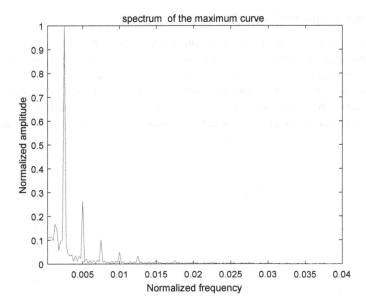

Fig. 6. Maximum curve method: frequency domain characteristics of maximum curve

Because the time-frequency diagram shows the local spectrum of the signal, the spectrum energy of the signal is larger than the noise energy near the instantaneous frequency of the signal at each moment. Therefore, the maximum curve $y(n)$ represents the law of the spectrum maximum changing with time, and equals to the component of the spectrum of the signal passing through the moving window. The period of the curve change is the frequency hopping period of the frequency hopping signal, and the corresponding time at the curve trough point is the time of carrier frequency hopping.

4.3   Optimizing Maximum Curve Method

According to the roughly estimated frequency hopping period, the method of estimating frequency hopping period by maximum curve can be optimized. After obtaining the maximum curve, Fourier transform is applied to the curve to obtain the frequency domain information. The frequency hopping period of the signal corresponds to the maximum amplitude in the frequency domain. Therefore, according to the number of roughly estimated frequencies, the searching range of maximum amplitude can be greatly reduced, and the accuracy of estimation can be improved.

5   Result

The performance of the method has been evaluated by simulation in the presence of additive white Gaussian noise.

5.1 Rough Estimation Method

Figure 7 is a rough estimate of the frequency hopping period using the frequency domain characteristics of the received signal. From the error curve, it can be known that when the signal-to-noise ratio is −15 dB, the error is less than 15%. Since this estimate is to design the window length and optimize and correct the subsequent methods, there is a large allowable error range, and the 15% error ratio meets the required requirements. It can be concluded that the adaptive window design method can work in a very low signal to noise ratio environment.

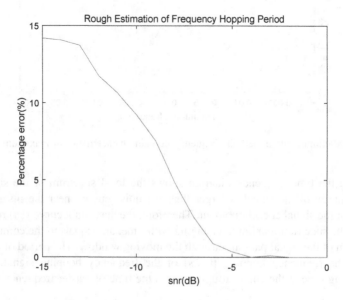

Fig. 7. Rough estimation error curve of frequency hopping signal period

5.2 Fine Estimation Method

After obtaining the STFT distribution, the maximum value curve method, the instantaneous frequency method and the improved maximum curve method are used to accurately estimate the frequency hopping period. As can be seen from Fig. 8, the improved method has a better performance improvement than the maximum curve method. Although the instantaneous frequency method performs better than the maximum curve method, the complexity is greater than it. The improved maximum curve method has the best performance and the complexity is lower than the instantaneous frequency method. As can be seen from Fig. 8, the improved method can achieve an error of zero at −8 dB.

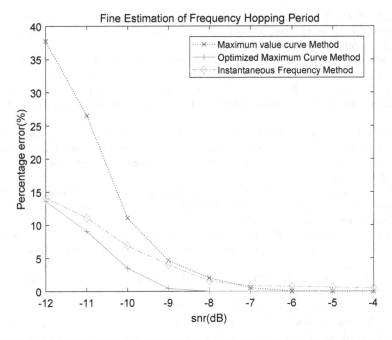

Fig. 8. Fine estimation error curve of frequency hopping signal period

6   Conclusion

In this article, we make full use of the frequency domain information of the received frequency hopping signal to design an adaptive window. At the same time, we use the rough estimation information to improve the frequency hopping period estimation method and obtain better estimation accuracy. Compared to other time-frequency analysis tools, such as the quadratic time-frequency distribution method, short-time Fourier changes have a very low complexity. And because the complexity of adaptive window design is also low, the overall complexity of the algorithm is low, and it has good performance. However, since the simulation environment is only an additive Gaussian channel, we also need to consider a more complex and realistic environment, such as Rayleigh channel, to fully estimate the feasibility of the method.

Acknowledgements. This work is supported by the National Natural Science Foundation of China (No. 41861134010 and No. 91438205).

References

1. Zhang, Y., Jia, X., Yin, C.: Time-frequency analysis of frequency hopping signal based on partial reconstruction. In: International Conference on Signal Processing, Communications and Computing (ICSPCC), pp. 1–5 (2017)

2. Liu, S., Zhang, Y.D., Shan, T., Tao, R.: Structure-aware bayesian compressive sensing for frequency-hopping spectrum estimation with missing observations. IEEE Trans. Signal Process. **66**(8), 2153–2166 (2018)
3. Chaudhury, K.N., Unser, M.: Construction of hilbert transform pairs of wavelet bases and gabor-like transforms. IEEE Trans. Signal Process. **57**(9), 3411–3425 (2009)
4. Zhao, L., Wang, L., Bi, G., Zhang, L., Zhang, H.: Robust frequency-hopping spectrum estimation based on sparse bayesian method. IEEE Trans. Wireless Commun. **14**(2), 781–793 (2015)
5. Ma, Y., Yan, Y.: Blind detection and parameter estimation of single frequency-hopping signal in complex electromagnetic environment. In: Sixth International Conference on Instrumentation & Measurement, Computer, Communication and Control (IMCCC), pp. 370–374 (2016)
6. Lei, Y., Zhong, Z., Wu, Y.: A new hop duration blind estimation algorithm for frequency-hopping signals. In: IEEE Pacific-Asia Workshop on Computational Intelligence and Industrial Application, pp. 695–699 (2008)
7. Boashash, B., Sucic, V.: Resolution measure criteria for the objective assessment of the performance of quadratic time-frequency distributions. IEEE Trans. Signal Process. **51**(5), 1253–1263 (2003)
8. Boashash, B., Azemi, G., O'Toole, J.M.: Time-frequency processing of nonstationary signals: advanced TFD design to aid diagnosis with highlights from medical applications. IEEE Signal Process. Mag. **30**(6), 108–119 (2013)
9. Zhao, Y., Zou, Z., Wu, L., Li, Y.: Frequency detection algorithm for frequency diversity signal based on STFT. In: Fifth International Conference on Instrumentation and Measurement, Computer, Communication and Control (IMCCC), pp. 790–793 (2015)
10. Tan, J.L., Sha'ameri, A.: Adaptive smooth-windowed wigner-ville distribution for digital communication signal. In: Telecommunication Technologies & Malaysia Conference on Photonics NCTT-MCP National Conference on. IEEE, pp. 254–259 (2009)
11. Kanaa, A., Sha'ameri, A.Z.: A robust parameter estimation of FHSS signals using time–frequency analysis in a non-cooperative environment. Phys. Commun. **26**, 9–20 (2018)
12. Li. N., Dong, S., Yang, D., Hao, Z.: The research on frequency-hopping signals analysis methods based on adaptive optimal kernel time-frequency representation. In: International Conference on Measuring Technology and Mechatronics Automation, pp. 544–547 (2009)
13. Barbarossa, S., Scaglione, A.: Parameter estimation of spread spectrum frequency-hopping signals using time-frequency distributions. In: First IEEE Signal Processing, Workshop on Signal Processing Advances in Wireless Communications, pp. 213–216 (1997)

Research on the Security of Personal Information in the Era of Big Data

Cheng Chi[1(✉)], Tengyu Liu[2], Xiaochen Yu[1], Shuo Zhang[3], and Shuo Shi[3]

[1] People's Procuratorate of Heilongjiang Province,
Harbin 150001, Heilongjiang, China
13904614111@139.com
[2] Higher Court of Heilongjiang Province, Harbin 150001, Heilongjiang, China
[3] Harbin Institute of Technology, Harbin 150001, Heilongjiang, China

Abstract. The advent of the era of big data has made people's lives more intelligent and convenient, and has brought enormous value to human beings. At the same time, it has brought about a lot of challenges. Personal information security is one of them. In the big data era, massive amounts of personal information are continuously input, simultaneously, the means of illegally acquiring, disseminating, and applying personal information are emerging in endlessly, Raising human thinking about information security. Therefore, the personal information security problem caused by big data should not be underestimated. Firstly, it introduces the related concepts of personal information, discusses the sources of risks faced by personal information in the process of implantation, dissemination and application. Secondly, it discusses the existing problems and solutions in China. Finally, the application difficulties and coping strategies of information security technology are analyzed, which provides theoretical support for personal information security in the era of big data.

Keywords: Personal information security · Source of risk · Legal protection · Information security technology

1 Introduction

With the vigorous development of network and information technology, the amount of data generated by human beings using the Internet is growing exponentially. In the era of information explosion, the concept of "big data" came into being. Nowadays, this concept is applied to almost all areas of human intelligence and development, such as advertising, finance, medical care, travel, artificial intelligence, etc., which not only promotes the digital transformation of government, enterprises, and social organizations, but also makes people's lives become more intelligent and convenient.

According to statistics, there are 2.9 million emails being sent every second in the world. If you read one article in a minute, it is enough for one person to read 5.5 years day and night. 28,800 h of video will be uploaded to YouTube every day, enough for one person to watch it day and night for 3.3 years. Amazon generates 6.3 million orders a day. Google processes 24 petabytes of data per day.

S. Han et al. (Eds.): AICON 2019, LNICST 287, pp. 107–114, 2019.
https://doi.org/10.1007/978-3-030-22971-9_9

The era of big data has come quietly. Whether people use "Internet +", "Industry 4.0" or "Cloud Computing" to describe the current world, they are inseparable from the extensive use of "big data". While the era of big data has brought about tremendous changes in human production and lifestyle, personal information security is facing serious threats and challenges, such as various fraudulent calls and harassing text messages. Our personal information is inadvertently being used illegally. The issue of personal information security brought about by the era of big data cannot be ignored.

As a product of the information age, big data aims to explore the potential value between data and serve the economic and social development through the storage and analysis of massive data. However, with the further development of the industry, the resulting problems have attracted more and more public attention. The world's leading companies are caught up in the scandal of user information leakage, which poses a serious threat to the information security of citizens. In the era of big data, the market initiative lies in the hands of those who have the most data. Therefore, the demand for data including personal information is expanding, which further increases the importance of protecting personal information in the era of big data. In this context, this paper introduces the definition of personal information in the era of big data, the legal protection of personal information and Internet technology, and finally puts forward the protection countermeasures. It is hoped that the research in this paper can enlighten this subject.

2 Personal Information Security in the Era of Big Data

In a broad sense, personal information refers to the sum of all the content that can be transmitted related to a natural person. In the context of big data, personal information is often associated with personal information on the Internet. Therefore, personal information should be divided into two categories: the first category is the personal information that appears on the Internet with the birth of the Internet, such as e-mail addresses, online records, etc.; the second category is the personal information that existed before the birth of the Internet. Such as name, gender, age, ethnicity, occupational status, etc., after the birth of the Internet, this personal information becomes personal information on the Internet according to the needs of life or obeying social management.

Gemalto, a research company of digital security, released a report of Breach Level Index for the year of 2015. It pointed out that 2015 witnessed serious incidents of data breach. During the 12 months, security staff of the company collected and categorized 1673 cases of data breach, resulting in the breach of 707 million data records. The major forms include the attack of personal information and identity theft (Fig. 1). According to the report about the Protection of the Rights of Chinese Netizens 2015 released by Internet Society of China, the personal identity information of nearly 80% netizens had been breached. The information about personal online activities of over 60% netizens had been breached. In this case, the analysis of the means of obtaining information and the sources of risk is the first step to protect personal information.

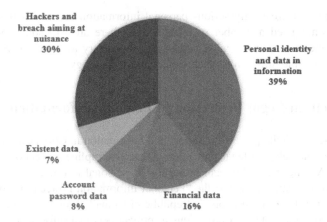

Fig. 1. The forms of data breach in 2015 (released by Gemalto)

With the implantation, dissemination and application of personal information, personal information faces three risks: access to information by network service providers, hackers and Trojans, and illegal circulation of information.

The first source of risk is the access of personal information to network service providers. Nowadays, the premise of people enjoying the services of various computers and mobile phone software and service platforms is registration, which inevitably involves personal information such as name, mobile phone number and e-mail address. In September 2017, Beijing police arrested illegal criminal suspects on 26 illegal websites and seized more than 1 million citizen information, involving information security of hundreds of thousands of people.

The second source of risk is that the means of obtaining personal information is itself an offence. Hackers and Trojans are products of the Internet era. In the era of big data, hackers and Trojans have become more rampant and embarrassing on the Internet. In September 2018, the information of 500 million users of China Lodging Group was leaked due to a hacker attack and turned to overseas websites for selling. In October 2018, online fashion retailer SHEIN was hit by a massive hack that resulted in a data breach for 6.5 million users.

The third source of risk is the subsequent disposal of the data after obtaining personal information. In the first case, the personal information is illegally transferred to the other people, and thus the personal data is "shared" between different subjects. The second case is that the Internet platform analyzes and infers the legally acquired personal information using big data technology to obtain the user's personal preferences. Such information mining may violate the conventions originally used for a specific purpose or within a specific scope. On December 28, 2017, the People's Court of Chang jiang Li Autonomous County of Hainan Province publicly pronounced a large- scale crime of infringing citizens' personal information. The defendant obtained a large amount of personal information from the hands of two people in the same village, deposited in Baidu's network disk, and send QQ information on the Internet sells more than 100 million citizens' personal information online and draws huge profits from it.

In the face of increasingly serious personal information security issues, although China has promulgated a number of related laws, there are still some loopholes in legislation, supervision, and legal remedies. It is necessary to protect personal information from multiple dimensions such as law and technology.

3 Research on Legal Protection of Personal Information

At present, the key to the protection of personal information in China can be expressed in two aspects, namely the legal protection and self-discipline protection of personal information. Among them, the legal protection of personal information is in the relevant laws and regulations, such as the "Personal Information Protection Law" and the "Internet Security Law of the People's Republic of China", through the formulation of personal information protection provisions to protect personal information, which can be mainly divided into legal Direct protection and indirect protection. The former is a law and regulation that explicitly proposes the protection of personal information, while the latter is a category that laws and regulations have proposed to protect personal dignity and personal privacy and personal information, thereby extending the protection of personal information. Compared with other countries, the protection of personal information in China is in a relatively backward position, and there are mainly three problems.

3.1 Lack of Clear Personal Information Protection Objects

In China's relevant laws and regulations, a big problem is the object of personal information protection, although the concept of "personal information" has been formed in relevant laws, its specific scope has not been clearly defined, such as personal information terms, personal data and personal information rights. If only according to the definition of personal information in law, the object of personal information protection is identified as all identifiable information related to individuals, then its extension will be very broad.

3.2 The Personal Information Protection Law Enforcement System Is Relatively Lagging Behind

There is a certain lag in the personal information protection law enforcement system. Although many departments in China currently supervise the network information security, there is no supervision responsibility for the actual processing of enterprise data. The current relevant laws and regulations have not yet reached a relatively perfect state, an effective regulatory system has not yet been formed. And law enforcement agencies lack a strong regulatory system. The law enforcement agencies did not construct the cyber security review mechanism and the threshold access system. Therefore, the information security threshold of the industry is very low, and all enterprises are mixed together, which creates great difficulties in management.

3.3 Improve the Existing Model Litigation System

In the era of big data, the infringement of personal information usually involves many groups, and the specific scope is widely dispersed. Therefore, compared with the past, the benefits of participating in litigation and efficiency cost considerations during this period are even more critical. We can study from foreign demonstration cases and parallel actions of group litigation to fully liberate the infringed information subject, and at the same time, the litigation is replaced by professional institutions and related personnel to reduce the individual's rights protection costs to a certain extent. In this way, the actual capacity of rights relief is effectively improved.

The protection of personal information is not only a simple legal issue, but also involves many factors such as the public's right to know and public opinion supervision. Therefore, both the criminal law and the judicial system need to be further improved. Of course, the protection of personal information is closely related to information technology, and technically improving the level of information security of big data helps to strengthen the level of information protection.

4 Research on Personal Information Security Technology

In order to implement the relevant requirements of the "Network Security Law" for the protection of personal information, the Central Network Information Office, the Ministry of Industry and Information Technology, the Ministry of Public Security, the National Standards Committee and other departments form an expert working group, and privacy provisions for 10 network products and services such as WeChat and Taobao. A review was conducted to regulate the collection, storage, use, and transfer of user personal information. In this special review of privacy protection, the transparency of privacy provisions and the increase of user choices have become highlights. However, efficient and streamlined data management is a higher requirement of enterprise practice. This includes establishing privacy management, planning data protection strategies, developing privacy policy procedures and guidelines. From the perspective of information technology, considering privacy protection in system and program design, and conducting privacy impact assessment, privacy protection can be placed at the "front end. "In the early stage of the product, the concept of privacy protection was added, and the whole life cycle management strategy was consolidated through continuous supervision and evaluation. But to achieve this goal, there are still some difficulties in the technical level.

4.1 Technical Level Application Difficulties

Big data is the product of the full development of information technology. The information form of big data is essentially different from the original information form. Therefore, it is difficult to analyze the existing information security technology from the information.

Mass and Diversification of Information. Smart devices record our personal information all the time, such as browsing records, online platform purchase records, geographical location records, etc. Once we connect to the Internet, the service provider will collect and record the generated data, resulting in a huge amount of data. And the structure of these data is very confusing. When extracting data, it often adopts a non-differentiated way, which may expose some personal privacy information, or out of the actual information and incomplete information, thus affecting the confidentiality, authenticity and integrity of information security.

Information Can Be Digitized. Now, the information can be digitized, can be expressed by different combinations of binary numbers "0" and "1", which will make the data more easily obtained and transmitted, and data can make the stealing method more concealed, giving some information theft means provides convenience and makes information security more difficult.

Information Can Be Transmitted. After the information is digitized, it can be transmitted arbitrarily. There is no geographical or time limit on the transmission of information on the Internet, such features undoubtedly provide great convenience to those who anonymously collect information about netizens, distorted facts, and make a living. Due to the limitations of existing technologies, we cannot determine the information of collectors at present, so our information security protection has fallen into a very passive situation.

4.2 Technical Level Response Strategy

The threats to personal information in the era of big data come from the abuse of technology. Therefore, using advanced technology to prevent and control and counter the use of networks to invade personal information security is the most direct and efficient way.

Do a Good Job of Data Encryption Protection. The development of computer networks has greatly improved the efficiency of data transmission and circulation. In the era of big data, the transmission speed of data information is accelerated, and the effectiveness of data transmission is closely related to the security of computer networks. We must pay attention to the encryption protection of data, and use existing file encryption technology to protect the security of personal information. For enterprises, when conducting relevant enterprise information exchange, it is necessary to set relevant authority settings, and standardize the use of the internal network module information by the personnel of each work module to improve the effectiveness of personal information protection.

Data Technology for Real-Time Monitoring. In the protection of computer network security, it is of great significance to do relevant real-time monitoring. Doing relevant monitoring and intrusion detection is also an effective supplement to the existing personal information security protection measures. With the help of big data technology, the task of snooping information security threats can be completed, that is, a flexible predictive of the threat of attacks is completed. And a comprehensive test of the unknown danger, timely identify the phenomenon of violation of information security use, and do the relevant protection work. Through a series of data screening and other classification of abnormal phenomena, it is possible to perform alarm processing, which can reduce the probability of information leakage in the shortest time and ensure the security of personal information.

Data Anonymization. The so-called anonymization is to erase the personal identity information from the database. These personally identifiable information includes name, address, credit card number, date of birth, and social security number. The remaining data can be used and shared. Although this measure does not completely eliminate the risk of personal information disclosure, it helps to maintain the security of personal information data, which is a feasible protective measure at this stage.

Strengthen Data Security Protection. At present, the more popular anti-virus software, security guards, computer butlers and other software are typical examples. Software engineers have fully developed Internet software to prevent and control viruses, Trojans, and malicious programs, and protect personal information from illegal attacks. Intelligent firewalls, access control technologies, data encryption technologies, and vulnerability scanning technologies are all common techniques used in big data Internet to prevent personal information from being attacked. In addition, using big data technology to address the information security challenges of the big data era is a useful attempt. For example, in response to harassing calls and text messages, some Internet technology companies have launched information interception service software based on large databases. This type of software effectively selects and identifies malicious calls and spam and intercepts them by creating a "call blacklist" database. Similar information technology tools can not only effectively respond to new data security threats, but more importantly, show us new ideas for dealing with information security threats.

5 Future Work

The development of computer network technology has brought about big data changes, but also brought the risk of information leakage. Computer network plays an important role in the development of modern society. It is related to people's daily life, business development and social harmony and stability. It is necessary to correctly recognize the development of computer network technology, attach importance to relevant information protection, and improve its own. Concept awareness, strengthen investment in relevant information protection, improve relevant legal and legal systems, do a good job in computer information security, and improve the use of computer networks. Only by continuously improving technology and improving the legal system, personal information will be protected.

6 Summary

In the context of the development of big data, data information has become an important asset of the state and enterprises, and information security has become a major strategic issue for the development of the country and society. However, due to improper management, hacker attacks and network system security vulnerabilities, personal information always faces the possibility of being leaked. Strengthening the research on information technology has important practical value in the case that information leakage cannot be completely eliminated.

Big data has brought us great convenience, promoted the rapid development of the economy, the continuous improvement of the society, and it also brought us some unexpected troubles. We enjoyed the big data for us. Convenient and fast personalized life, while being troubled by these problems. There are many reasons for the security of personal information. To solve this problem, we need the joint efforts of the whole society. We also need to take corresponding measures at the legal level, technical level and personal level to coordinate the harmonious development of big data and information security based on the actual situation of today's society.

References

1. Huang, C.: Personal privacy in the era of big data. Huazhong Normal University, Wuhan (2015)
2. Zhang, M.: Risks and countermeasures of citizens' personal information data in the age of big Data. Inf. Stud. Theory Appl. **6**, 57–70 (2015)
3. Wang, Z., Yu, Q.: Privacy trust crisis of personal data in china in the era of big data: the survey and countermeasures. Comput. Law Secur. Rev. **31**(6), 782–792 (2015)
4. Chen, K.: The research of Open-sensitive data security. Zhejiang University, Hangzhou (2007)
5. Zou, H.: Protection of personal information security in the age of big data. In: International Conference on Computational Intelligence and Security 2016, CIS. IEEE, Wuxi (2016)
6. Ruixiang, W.: Research on the Legal dilemma and countermeasures of personal information protection in big data age. J. Inf. Secur. Res. **12**, 1097–1101 (2017)
7. Hao, X.: A preliminary study on the legal issues of citizen personal information security in the era of big data. Knowl. Base **12**, 9–10 (2017)
8. Li, F.: Analysis of personal information legal protection in the age of big data. Glob. Market Inf. Guide **25**, 30 (2017)
9. Dekker, M., Karsberg, C.: Technical guidance on the security measures in Paper 13a, Version 2.0. European Union Agency for Network and Information Security (ENISA) (2014)
10. Kshetri, N.: Big data's impact on privacy. Secur. Consum. Welf. **38**(11), 1134–1145 (2014)
11. Wang, L.: Privacy system in the United States and its impact on the development of China's Legislation (2007)

Secure Access and Routing Scheme for Maritime Communication Network

Yuzhou Fu[1,3], Chuanao Jiang[2,3], Yurong Qin[1], and Liuguo Yin[2,3(✉)]

[1] School of Computer and Electronics Information, Guangxi University,
Nanning 530004, China
[2] School of Information Science and Technology, Tsinghua University,
Beijing 100084, China
[3] Key Laboratory of EDA, Research Institute of Tsinghua University in Shenzhen,
Shenzhen 518057, China
yinlg@tsinghua.edu.cn

Abstract. This paper proposes a transmission scheme to ensure the maritime communication security, which includes access rules, routing selection scheme, and power allocation mechanisms. The access rules and the routing selection utilize the automatic identification system (AIS) information to choose the secure access points and routing links to prevent eavesdropping, and the power allocation limits the leaked information by means of reducing the received signal power of the eavesdroppers. The simulation results show that the intercept probability of the proposed scheme decreases by about ten to the negative two power compared with that of the contrastive scheme, and the recovering proportion for eavesdropper is less than 0.2. In addition to above, the secrecy capacity of the proposed scheme achieves about 6.8% improvement compared with the baseline scheme.

Keywords: Security · Access rules · Routing ·
Maritime Communication Network · Cooperative communication

1 Introduction

With the increase of maritime economic activities, the security of maritime communication network (MCN) is becoming increasingly important. Nowadays, the MCN mainly depends on the satellite and shore-based station, which cannot satisfy the increasing communication need. There have been some researches about

This work was supported by the National Natural Science Foundation of China (91538203 and 61871257), the new strategic industries development projects of Shenzhen City (JCYJ20170307145820484), the Joint Research Foundation of the General Armaments Department and the Ministry of Education (6141A02033322), and the Beijing Innovation Center for Future Chips, Tsinghua University.

S. Han et al. (Eds.): AICON 2019, LNICST 287, pp. 115–126, 2019.
https://doi.org/10.1007/978-3-030-22971-9_10

the high-speed and long-distance MCN, which mostly depend on the relay networks [1–3]. However, these schemes cannot effectively prevent the eavesdropping. Therefore, an effective transmission scheme for the maritime scenario is in urge need.

In the MCN, all the ships are mandatory to install AIS. Therefore, the location information of the ships is easy to obtain for the operators via the AIS. In the MCN, the shipborne base stations are used to provide access points for the user ships. In addition, the device-to-device (D2D) communication is enabled among the users in the scenario [4], which constitutes a flexible relay network. The physical layer security (PLS) enhances the secrecy of wireless communications by the characteristics of wireless channels, without using complex encryption/decryption algorithms [5]. Therefore, the relay-aided PLS is suited for MCN. In [6], the authors used relay selection technique to enhance the communication security and the formula of the intercept probability of the multi-relay network was derived. In [7], the technique of fountain code and relay-aided PLS were used in the wireless sensor networks. Also, the secrecy outage probability (SOP) of the DF relay network with joint multiple users and full-duplex (FD) relays was examined in [8]. In the literature [9], the author considered PLS of D2D communications and developed a Stackelberg game framework to analyze the communication rate of cellular users and secrecy rate of D2D links.

In this paper, we present a location information assisted secure access and routing scheme in the MCN, the MCN ensures the security by means of selecting the access point and the routing. To compensate high path loss in maritime network, the technique of directional antennas, narrow beam and LDPC code [10,11] are employed. With the aid of location information, the shipborne base stations can provide the secure wideband access for the user ships. If intercepting by the eavesdropper is unavoidable, the user ship can send a random sequence to shipborne base stations by D2D communication. And then, the shipborne base station uses these random sequences as the keys to encrypt original data by means of simple XOR operation. After the shipborne base station encoding the original data, the encoded data are transmitted back to the user ship. With the aid of location information and D2D communications, the eavesdropper can hardly intercept sufficient data to recover the original data. In addition to the aforementioned method, the proposed scheme can also limit the received information of eavesdroppers by power optimization, which reduces the amount of the received data packets of eavesdroppers.

The rest of this paper is organized as follows. In Sect. 2, the system model and the problem formulation are presented. Section 3 introduces the proposed transmission scheme as well as the resource allocation process in detail. Then Sect. 4 presents the simulation setup and simulation results among the proposed scheme. Finally, conclusions are drawn in Sect. 5.

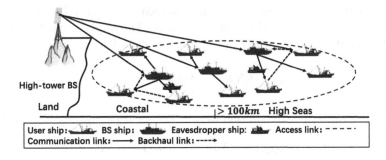

Fig. 1. Maritime Communications Network (MCN) Architecture

2 System Model and Problem Formulation

2.1 System Model

As shown in Fig. 1, the proposed scenario includes one high-tower base station (HBS), shipborne base stations (SBSs), user ships (USs) and eavesdropper ships (ESs). The HBS provides down-link transmission for the SBS. In maritime, the maritime satellite can provide the backhaul for the SBS and is connected to the HBS, so the SBSs can connect to the HBS through the satellite. The satellite backhaul can transmit the secret key to ensure security of the down-link data. Therefore, we assume that the down-link is secure. If two USs are close enough, they can communicate with each other by D2D communication. All the ESs are close to the USs. The SBS is denoted as $B = \{B_i | i = 1, 2, 3..., I\}$ and is equipped with N directional antennas to forward data to user ships. The USs denoted as $U = \{U_j | j = 1, 2, 3..., J\}$ are equipped with one directional antenna. The ESs denoted as $E = \{E_s | s = 1, 2, 3..., S\}$ are equipped with one omnidirectional antenna. The SBSs and USs can accurately receive the signal by directional antenna with the help of the AIS location information. Therefore, we assume that the interference is not considered in this paper. In this paper, we assume that the ES and the US have same antenna gain.

In the MCN scenario, the large-scale fading caused by the two-ray reflection model is modeled as [12]

$$L_{i,j} = \left(\frac{\lambda}{4\pi d_{i,j}} \right)^2 \left[2sin \left(\frac{2\pi h_i h_j}{\lambda d_{i,j}} \right) \right]. \tag{1}$$

where λ is the carrier frequency wavelength, h_i and h_j represent the heights of transmitter and receiver, and $d_{i,j}$ is the distance between transmitter and receiver. Besides, the channel coefficients of small-scale fading remain constant during one data packet and change independently among different data packet. The channel coefficient is a circularly symmetric complex Gaussian random variable, namely $\mathcal{CN}(0, 1)$. Therefore, the received signal can be written as:

$$y_{i,j} = \sqrt{p_{i,j} L_{i,j}} h_{i,j} s_k + n_{i,j}. \tag{2}$$

where $n_{i,j}$ is the additive white Gaussian noise (AWGN); s_k is the k th data symbol of stream and $p_{i,j}$ is the power of transmitter; The $h_{i,j}$ is channel coefficient. Then the signal noise ratio (SNR) of received is given by:

$$SNR_{i,j} = \frac{p_{i,j}H_{i,j}}{\sigma_{n_{i,j}}}. \tag{3}$$

where $H_{i,j} = L_{i,j}|h_{i,j}|^2$. In addition to this, the security capacity is given by:

$$C_{i,j} = log_2(1 + SNR_{i,j}) - log_2(1 + SNR_{i,s}). \tag{4}$$

2.2   Problem Formulation

The problem formulation can be divided into two parts: the user ships access (USsA) phase and the User ships backhaul (USsB) phase. In the USsA phase, the user association and power allocation are related to the channel gain and the security capacity. In addition, we define some threshold values to determine the security of USsA link. If the USsA link cannot ensure security, we will encode the data of the SBS in the USsB phase. The optimization problems are formulated as:

$$USsA(P1): \max_{\mathbf{X}, \mathbf{P}_{I,J}} \sum_{i=1}^{I} \sum_{j=1}^{J} x_{i,j}C_{i,j}. \tag{5}$$

$$P1C1: \sum_{j=1}^{J} x_{i,j}p_{i,j} \le P_{B,th}, \forall i, \qquad P1C2: \sum_{j=1}^{J} x_{i,j} \le N, \forall i,$$

$$P1C3: \sum_{i=1}^{I} x_{i,j} \le 1, \forall j, \qquad P1C4: x_{i,j}\left(\frac{p_{i,j}H_{i,s}}{\sigma_{n_{i,s}}} \le \gamma_{th}^{E}\right), \forall i, j,$$

$$P1C5: x_{i,j}(C_{i,j} \ge C_{th}), \forall i, j, \quad P1C6: x_{i,j} \in \{0,1\}, \forall i, j, \quad P1C7: \mathbf{P}_{I,J} \ge 0.$$

where P1C1 is the maximum transmission power constraint for the SBS. P1C2 represents the maximum downlink data stream constraint for SBS; P1C3 means that the users can access no more than one SBS; P1C4 presents maximum SNR of ES, where γ_{th}^{E} is maximum SNR for Eve; P1C5 is the minimum security capacity constraint for the SBS; P1C6 and P1C7 constrain the value of variables, where $x_{i,j} = 1$ means that the user ship (U_j) selects BS (B_i) as the access point.

$$USsB(P2): \max_{\mathbf{X}, \mathbf{P}_{J,M}, \mathbf{P}_{M,I}} \sum_{i=1}^{I} \sum_{\substack{m=1 \\ m \ne j}}^{J} Q_{m,i} \tag{6}$$

$$Q_{m,i} = \min\left\{x_{m,i}C_{m,i}, x_{m,i}C_{j,m}\right\}. \tag{7}$$

$$P2C1: \sum_{i=1}^{I}\sum_{\substack{m=1 \\ m \neq j}}^{J} x_{m,i}p_{j,m} \leq P_{U,th}, \qquad P2C2: \sum_{i=1}^{I}\sum_{\substack{m=1 \\ m \neq j}}^{J} x_{m,i}p_{m,i} \leq P_{U,th},$$

$$P2C3: \sum_{i=1}^{I} x_{m,i} \leq 1, \forall m, \qquad P2C4: \sum_{\substack{m=1 \\ m \neq j}}^{J} x_{m,i} \leq 1, \forall j,$$

$$P2C5: x_{m,i}C_{m,i} \geq Q_{m,i}\forall m, i, \qquad P2C6: x_{m,i}C_{j,m} \geq Q_{m,i}\forall m, i,$$

$$P2C7: x_{m,i}\left(\frac{p_{j,m}H_{j,s}}{\sigma_{n_{j,s}}}\right) \leq \gamma_{th}^{E}, \forall i, m, \qquad P2C8: x_{m,i}\left(\frac{p_{m,i}H_{m,s}}{\sigma_{n_{m,s}}}\right) \leq \gamma_{th}^{E}, \forall i, m,$$

$$P2C9: x_{m,i} \in \{0,1\}\forall m, i, \qquad P2C10: \boldsymbol{P}_{J,M} \geq 0, \boldsymbol{P}_{M,I} \geq 0.$$

where P2C1 and P2C2 are the maximum transmission power constraint for the user ship; P2C3 and P2C4 mean that the users can select no more than one user ship to backhaul; P2C5 and P2C6 are the minimum security capacity constraint for the D2D link; P2C7 and P2C8 present maximum SNR of ES, where γ_{th}^{E} is maximum SNR for Eve; P2C9 and P2C10 constrain the value of variables.

3   Algorithm Development

In the previous section, we know that the problem (5) and (6) are non-convex. Therefore, We should transform the non-convex problem into a series of convex subproblems with logarithmic approximation [13], and then we use the Lagrangian dual method to solve. Finally, we can get the original problem solution by the successive convex approximation (SCA) approach proposed in [14]. We will make use of the following lower bound:

$$\theta \log_2(SNR) + \beta \geq \log_2(1 + SNR). \tag{8}$$

that is tight at $SNR = \overline{SNR}$ when the approximation constants are chosen as

$$\theta = \frac{\overline{SNR}}{1 + \overline{SNR}}. \tag{9}$$

$$\beta = \ln\left(1 + \overline{SNR}\right) - \frac{\overline{SNR}}{1 + \overline{SNR}}\ln\left(\overline{SNR}\right). \tag{10}$$

By applying the logarithmic approximation and changing the variables by $\hat{\mathbf{P}}_{I,J} = \ln \mathbf{P}_{I,J}$, $\hat{\mathbf{P}}_{J,M} = \ln \mathbf{P}_{J,M}$, $\hat{\mathbf{P}}_{M,I} = \ln \mathbf{P}_{M,I}$. The lower bound of the objective function is obtained as follows:

$$C_{i,j} \geq \hat{C}_{i,j} = \frac{1}{\ln 2}\left(\theta_{i,j} \ln\left(SNR_{i,j}\right) + \beta_{i,j}\right) - \log_2\left(1 + \gamma_{th}^E\right). \tag{11}$$

$$Q_{m,i} \geq \hat{Q}_{m,i} = \min\left\{x_{m,i}\hat{C}_{m,i}, x_{m,i}\hat{C}_{j,m}\right\}. \tag{12}$$

For solving the aforementioned questions, we introduce the Lagrangian dual method. The Lagrangian functions are given as

$$L_{P1}(e^{\hat{\mathbf{P}}_{I,J}}, X, \mu, \kappa, \zeta, \omega, \tau)$$

$$= -\sum_{i=1}^{I}\sum_{j=1}^{J} x_{i,j}\hat{C}_{i,j} - \sum_{i=1}^{I}\mu_i(P_{B,th} - \sum_{j=1}^{J} x_{i,j}e^{\hat{p}_{i,j}})$$

$$-\sum_{i=1}^{I}\kappa_i(N - \sum_{j=1}^{J} x_{i,j}) - \sum_{j=1}^{J}\zeta_j(1 - \sum_{i=1}^{I} x_{i,j})$$

$$-\sum_{i=1}^{I}\sum_{j=1}^{J}\omega_{i,j}x_{i,j}\left(\gamma_{th}^E - \frac{e^{\hat{p}_{i,j}}H_{i,s}}{\sigma_{n_{i,s}}}\right)$$

$$-\sum_{i=1}^{I}\sum_{j=1}^{J}\tau_{i,j}x_{i,j}(\hat{C}_{i,j} - C_{th}). \tag{13}$$

$$L_{P2}(e^{\hat{\mathbf{P}}_{J,M}}, e^{\hat{\mathbf{P}}_{M,I}}, X, \lambda, \eta, \epsilon, \rho, \varphi, \phi, \xi, \partial)$$

$$= -\sum_{i=1}^{I}\sum_{\substack{m=1 \\ m \neq j}}^{J}\hat{Q}_{m,i} - \lambda\left(P_{U,th} - \sum_{i=1}^{I}\sum_{\substack{m=1 \\ m \neq j}}^{J} x_{m,i}e^{\hat{p}_{j,m}}\right) - \eta\left(P_{U,th} - \sum_{i=1}^{I}\sum_{\substack{m=1 \\ m \neq j}}^{J} x_{m,i}e^{\hat{p}_{m,i}}\right)$$

$$-\sum_{\substack{m=1 \\ m \neq j}}^{J}\epsilon_m(1 - \sum_{i=1}^{I} x_{m,i}) - \sum_{i=1}^{I}\rho_j(1 - \sum_{\substack{m=1 \\ m \neq j}}^{J} x_{m,i})$$

$$-\sum_{i=1}^{I}\sum_{\substack{m=1 \\ m \neq j}}^{J}\varphi_{m,i}(x_{m,i}\hat{C}_{m,i} - \hat{Q}_{m,i}) - \sum_{i=1}^{I}\sum_{\substack{m=1 \\ m \neq j}}^{J}\phi_{m,i}(x_{m,i}\hat{C}_{j,m} - \hat{Q}_{m,i})$$

$$-\sum_{i=1}^{I}\sum_{\substack{m=1 \\ m \neq j}}^{J}\xi_{m,i}x_{m,i}\left(\gamma_{th}^E - \frac{e^{\hat{p}_{j,m}}H_{j,s}}{\sigma_{n_{j,s}}}\right) - \sum_{i=1}^{I}\sum_{\substack{m=1 \\ m \neq j}}^{J}\partial_{m,i}x_{m,i}\left(\gamma_{th}^E - \frac{e^{\hat{p}_{m,i}}H_{m,s}}{\sigma_{n_{m,s}}}\right). \tag{14}$$

where the parameters $\mu, \delta, \zeta, \omega, \tau, \lambda, \eta, \epsilon, \rho, \varphi, \phi, \xi, \partial$ are the Lagrangian multipliers. By solving $\frac{\partial L_{P1}}{\partial e^{\hat{p}_{i,j}}} = 0$, $\frac{\partial L_{P1}}{\partial x_{i,j}} = 0$, $\frac{\partial L_{P2}}{\partial e^{\hat{p}_{j,m}}} = 0$, $\frac{\partial L_{P2}}{\partial e^{\hat{p}_{m,i}}} = 0$, $\frac{\partial L_{P2}}{\partial x_{m,i}} = 0$, we can obtain the optimal solutions as

$$p_{i,j} = \left[\frac{\theta_{i,j}x_{i,j}(1 + \tau_{i,j})}{\ln 2\left(\mu_i + \frac{\omega_{i,j}H_{i,s}}{\sigma_{n_{i,s}}}\right)}\right]^+. \tag{15}$$

$$x_{i,j} = 1|_{i,j=\max \tau_{i,j}\hat{C}_{i,j}}. \tag{16}$$

$$p_{j,m} = \left[\sum_{i=1}^{I} \frac{\theta_{m,i}\varphi_{m,i}x_{m,i}}{\ln 2 \left(\lambda + \frac{\xi_{j,m}H_{j,s}}{\sigma_{n_{j,s}}} \right)} \right]^{+}. \tag{17}$$

$$p_{m,i} = \left[\frac{\theta_{m,i}\phi_{m,i}x_{m,i}}{\ln 2 \left(\eta + \frac{\partial_{m,i}H_{m,s}}{\sigma_{n_{m,s}}} \right)} \right]^{+}. \tag{18}$$

$$x_{m,i} = 1|_{m,i=\max \min \{\varphi_{j,m}\hat{C}_{j,m}, \phi_{m,i}\hat{C}_{m,i}\}}. \tag{19}$$

Where (x^{+}) is min $\{0, x\}$. Note that the user ships tend to access the SBS and select user ship with the largest security link rate. While the USsB phase should consider two links of security rate. Finally, we calculate the Lagrange multipliers using the subgradient method.

$$\mu_i[t+1] = \left[\mu_i[t] - \delta_{\mu_i}[t+1] \left(P_{B,th} - \sum_{j=1}^{J} x_{i,j}e^{\hat{p}_{i,j}} \right) \right]^{+},$$

$$\omega_{i,j}[t+1] = \left[\omega_{i,j}[t] - \delta_{\omega_{i,j}}[t+1] \left\{ x_{i,j} \left(\gamma_{th}^{E} - \frac{p_{i,j}H_{i,s}}{\sigma_{n_{i,s}}} \right) \right\} \right]^{+},$$

$$\tau_{i,j}[t+1] = \left[\tau_{i,j}[t] - \delta_{\tau_{i,j}}[t+1] \left\{ x_{i,j}(C_{i,j} - C_{th}) \right\} \right]^{+},$$

$$\lambda[t+1] = \left[\lambda[t] - \delta_{\lambda}[t+1] \left(P_{U,th} - \sum_{i=1}^{I} \sum_{\substack{m=1 \\ m \neq j}}^{J} x_{m,i}p_{j,m} \right) \right]^{+},$$

$$\eta[t+1] = \left[\eta[t] - \delta_{\eta}[t+1] \left(P_{U,th} - \sum_{i=1}^{I} \sum_{\substack{m=1 \\ m \neq j}}^{J} x_{m,i}p_{m,i} \right) \right]^{+},$$

$$\varphi_{m,i}[t+1] = \left[\varphi_{m,i}[t] - \delta_{\varphi_{m,i}}[t+1] (x_{m,i}C_{m,i} - Q_{m,i}) \right]^{+},$$

$$\phi_{m,i}[t+1] = \left[\phi_{m,i}[t] - \delta_{\phi_{m,i}}[t+1] (x_{m,i}C_{j,m} - Q_{m,i}) \right]^{+},$$

$$\xi_{m,i}[t+1] = \left[\xi_{m,i}[t] - \delta_{\xi_{m,i}}[t+1] \left\{ x_{m,i} \left(\gamma_{th}^{E} - \frac{p_{j,m}H_{j,s}}{\sigma_{n_{j,s}}} \right) \right\} \right]^{+},$$

$$\partial_{m,i}[t+1] = \left[\partial_{m,i}[t] - \delta_{\partial_{m,i}}[t+1] \left\{ x_{m,i} \left(\gamma_{th}^{E} - \frac{p_{m,i}H_{m,s}}{\sigma_{n_{m,s}}} \right) \right\} \right]^{+}. \tag{20}$$

In the Algorithm 1, we defined a threshold value (C_{th}^{Min}). If the security capacity of SBS link is less than threshold value, the SBS link is not security. Therefore, we use Algorithm 2 to replan route. And then, the Algorithm 1 will be performed based on the access scheme of algorithm 2 until the results converge.

Algorithm 1

1: **Input:** the user set U
2: **while** U is not empty **do**
3:     **Initialize:** $t = 1, \theta_{i,j} = 1, \beta_{i,j} = 0, p_{i,j} = 1, \forall i, j.$ $\mu, \omega, \tau \geq 0$
4:     **while** $x_{i,j}, p_{i,j}$ converge and $C_{i,j} \geq C_{th}^{Min}, \forall i, j$ **do**
5:         **Update** $x_{i,j}, H_{i,s}$ calculated by (16) and **Algorithm 2**
6:         **while** $p_{i,j}$ converge, $\forall i, j$ **do**
7:             **for** $i = 1$ to I **do**
8:                 **for** $j = 1$ to J **do**
9:                     **Update** $p_{i,j}$ calculated by (15)
10:                **end for**
11:            **end for**
12:            **Update** μ, ω, τ calculated by (20) and $t = t + 1$
13:        **end while**
14:        **for** $i = 1$ to I **do**
15:            **for** $j = 1$ to J **do**
16:                **Update** $\theta_{i,j}, \beta_{i,j}$ calculated by (9) and (10)
17:            **end for**
18:        **end for**
19:        **Update** $C_{i,j}$ calculated by (4)
20:        **if** $C_{i,j} \leq C_{th}^{Min}$ **then**
21:            **Loading** the **Algorithm 2**
22:        **end if**
23:    **end while**
24:    **Set:** $U = U - U_j$
25: **end while**

---

4   Performance Evaluation

In this section, the simulation setup and simulation results are presented for evaluating the performance of proposed scheme. We choose the DFbORS scheme in [6] as the compared scheme, and the power of SBS is equal allocated. The carrier frequency is set as 2 GHz and the available bandwidth B is 10 MHz. The AWGN power is defined as $\sigma_n = BN_0$, where N_0 is the AWGN spectral efficiency, and $N_0 = -174$ dBm/Hz. We set $P_{B,th} = 43$ dBm and $P_{U,th} = 40$ dBm. The heights of SBS antennas, user ship antennas and ES antennas are 30 m, 15 m and 15 m respectively. The maximum data streams of SBS number N is set to 6. The number of user ships is also a variable which ranges from 20 to 80. The number of ESs is set to 3. We emulate the transmission for 10^5 times. Moreover, the total number of data packets is denoted as K, which is assumed to be 128. If the eavesdropper are successfully recovering 80% of original data in one transmission time, the total confidential file is successfully intercepted by ES. The packet error rate (PER) can be defined as [15]:

$$FER_n(\gamma) = \begin{cases} 1, & \text{if } 0 < \gamma < \gamma_{pn}; \\ a_n exp(-g_n \gamma), & \text{if } \gamma \geq \gamma_{pn}. \end{cases} \quad (21)$$

Algorithm 2

1: **Initialize:** $t = 1, \theta_{j,m} = \theta_{m,i} = 1, \beta_{j,m} = \beta_{m,i} = 0, p_{j,m} = p_{m,i} = 1, \forall m, i.\ \lambda, \eta, \varphi, \phi, \xi, \partial \geq 0$
2: **while** $x_{m,i}, p_{j,m}, p_{m,i}$ converge, $\forall i, j$ **do**
3:     **Update** $x_{m,i}$ calculated by (19)
4:     **while** $p_{j,m}, p_{m,i}$ converge,$\forall m, i, j$ **do**
5:         **for** $m = 1$ to J **do**
6:             **Update** $p_{j,m}$ calculated by (17)
7:             **for** $i = 1$ to I **do**
8:                 **Update** $p_{m,i}$ calculated by (18)
9:             **end for**
10:         **end for**
11:         **Update** $\lambda, \eta, \varphi, \phi, \xi, \partial$ and $t = t + 1$ calculated by (20)
12:     **end while**
13:     **for** $m = 1$ to J **do**
14:         **Update** $\theta_{j,m}, \beta_{j,m}$ calculated by (9) and (10)
15:         **for** $i = 1$ to I **do**
16:             **Update** $\theta_{m,i}, \beta_{m,i}$ calculated by (9) and (10)
17:         **end for**
18:     **end for**
19: **end while**
20: **Update** $x_{i,j} = 1$ and $H_{i,s} = 0$

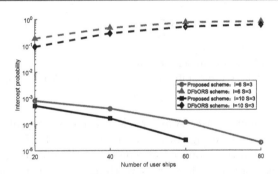

Fig. 2. Comparison of intercept probability between the proposed scheme and the baseline scheme, where the number of user ships varies from 20 to 80.

Where γ is received SNR and n denotes mode index. The fitting parameters of different transmission modes can be found in [16]. The fitting parameters are listed as follows [16]:

$$a_n = 50.1222,$$
$$g_n = 0.6644,$$
$$\gamma_{pn} = 7.7021. \tag{22}$$

In the simulation, we set a situation, namely different number of SBSs. In Fig. 2, the intercept probabilities of the proposed scheme decline with the

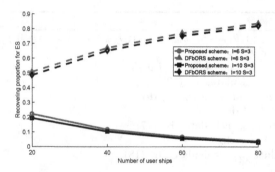

Fig. 3. Comparison of recovering proportion for Eve between the proposed scheme and the baseline scheme, where the number of user ships varies from 20 to 80.

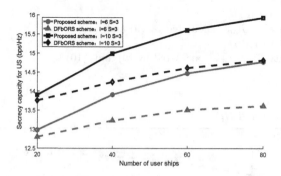

Fig. 4. Comparison of secrecy capacity for user ship between the proposed scheme and the baseline scheme, where the number of user ships varies from 20 to 80.

increase of the number of user ships, while the intercept probabilities of the DFbORS scheme are increasing. In this situation (namely, $I = 10, S = 3$), the intercept probability of the proposed scheme is less than ten to the negative five power if the number of user ships is more than 60. With the increase of the number of user ships, the proposed scheme can be more flexible to select routing with D2D communication. While, the contrastive scheme is opposite. The intercept probability of the proposed scheme at least decreases by about ten to the negative two power compared with that of the DFbORS scheme. Hence, the proposed scheme achieves a better communication security than the DFbORS scheme. From Fig. 3, the recovering probability of the proposed scheme is lower than the baseline scheme. The recovering probability for EB is less than 0.2, because the eavesdropper can receive sufficient original data and the random sequences. In Fig. 4, the secrecy capacity of the proposed scheme achieves about 6.8% improvement compared with the baseline scheme. Namely, the proposed scheme can securely transmit more data in one transmission process.

5   Conclusions

This paper proposes an access and routing transmission scheme in the maritime communication networks. According to the location information from AIS, the scheme can select access point and routing flexibly to avoid eavesdropping. In addition, the power allocation can limit the leaked information by means of reducing the received signal power of the eavesdroppers. The simulation results show that the proposed scheme achieves a better performance in security. The proposed scheme can at least decrease intercept probability by about ten to the negative two power compared with the contrastive scheme, and the recovering proportion for EB is less than 0.2. The secrecy capacity of the proposed scheme achieves about 6.8% improvement compared with the baseline scheme. Namely, the proposed scheme can securely transmit more data in one transmission process. In conclusion, the proposed scheme can securely transmit more data in one transmission process.

References

1. Li, Y.: Efficient coastal communications with sparse network coding. IEEE Netw. **32**(4), 122–128 (2018)
2. Rao, S.N., Raj, D., Parthasarathy, V.: A novel solution for high speed internet over the oceans. In: Proceedings of IEEE INFOCOM 2018 - IEEE Conference on Computer Communications Workshops, Honolulu, pp. 906–912 (2018)
3. Singh, D., Kimbahune, S., Singh, V.V.: Mobile signal extension in deep sea - towards a safe and sustainable fisheries. In: Proceeding of 2016 ITU Kaleidoscope: ICTs for a Sustainable World, Bangkok, pp. 1–8 (2016)
4. Liu, J.: Device-to-device communication in LTE-advanced networks. A survey. IEEE Commun. Surv. Tutorials **17**(4), 1923–1940 (2015)
5. Hong, Y.W.P.: Enhancing physical-layer secrecy in multiantenna wireless systems: an overview of signal processing approaches. IEEE Signal Process. Mag. **30**(5), 29–40 (2013)
6. Zou, Y.: Optimal relay selection for physical-layer security in cooperative wireless networks. IEEE J. Sel. Areas Commun. **31**(10), 2099–2111 (2013)
7. Sun, L.: Fountain-coding aided strategy for secure cooperative transmission in industrial wireless sensor networks. IEEE Trans. Ind. Inf. **12**(1), 291–300 (2016)
8. Feng, Y., Yang, D.Z., Yan, S.: Physical layer security enhancement in multi-user multi-full-duplex-relay networks. In: Proceedings of 2017 IEEE International Conference on Communications, Paris, pp. 1–7 (2017)
9. Luo, Y., Cui, L., Yang, Y.: Power control and channel access for physical-layer security of D2D underlay communication. In: 2015 International Conference on Wireless Communications and Signal Processing, Nanjing, pp. 1–5 (2015)
10. Chen, Z.: CodeHop: physical layer error correction and encryption with LDPC-based code hopping. Sci. China Inf. Sci. **59**, 102309:1C–102309:15 (2016)
11. Ping, W.: An efficient helicopter-satellite communication scheme based on check-hybrid LDPC coding. Tsinghua Science and Technology **10**(26599), TST.9010038 (2018)
12. Zhao, Y., Ren, J., Chi, X.: Maritime mobile channel transmission model based on ITM. In: 2nd International Symposium on Computer, Communication, Control and Automation. Atlantis Press (2013)

13. Papandriopoulos, J., Evans, J.S.: SCALE: a low-complexity distributed protocol for spectrum balancing in multiuser DSL networks. IEEE Trans. Inf. Theor. **55**(8), 3711–3724 (2009)
14. Marks, B.R.: A general inner approximation algorithm for nonconvex mathematical programs. Oper. Res. **26**(4), 681–683 (1978)
15. Liu, Q.: Queuing with adaptive modulation and coding over wireless links: cross-Layer analysis and design. IEEE Trans. Wireless Commun. **4**(3), 1142–1153 (2005)
16. Qinghe, D., Ying, X., Wanyu, L., et al.: Security enhancement for multicast over internet of things by dynamically constructed fountain codes. Wireless Commun. Mob. Comput. **2018**, 1–11 (2018)

Multipath Based Privacy Protection Method for Data Transmission in SDN

Na Dong[1,2], Zhigeng Han[2,3], and Liangmin Wang[1,2(✉)]

[1] School of Computer Science and Communication Engineering, Jiangsu University,
Zhenjiang 212013, China
`wanglm@ujs.edu.cn`
[2] Jiangsu Key Laboratory of Security Technology for Industrial Cyberspace,
Zhenjiang, China
[3] School of Information Engineering, Nanjing Audit University,
Nanjing 211815, China

Abstract. With the development of Software-Defined Networking (SDN), privacy and security issues have become an urgent problem to be solved. Although there are many ways to solve these problems, the existing technology represented by encryption cannot effectively deal with traffic analysis attacks, and there are also key management problems. For this reason, we propose a privacy protection method for SDN data transmission based on multipath, including path searching procedure for searching for all paths between the sender and the receiver, and path filtering procedure for filtering out paths to reduce path correlation, and path selection procedure for randomly selecting one path to disturbed the traffic similarity between multiple transmission. The experiment results show that our method is more effective, less similarity of traffic compared with Multipath-Floyd method and single-path method, respectively. Moreover, it is difficult for attackers to capture the traffic feature and do not need key management, which reduces the cost of the controller.

Keywords: Software-Defined Networking · Multipath filtering · Privacy protection · Traffic analysis attack

1 Introduction

Software-Defined Network (SDN) is defined as a novel network architecture, which consists of application layer, physical layer, and especially control layer. SDN has the ability to decouple data plane and control plane, and it gives the opportunity to solve the control limitations of other infrastructures. In SDN, network resources can be effectively utilized by using the centralized controller for different business requirements [11]. Moreover, it provides an overview of whole underlying network, allowing more flexible and complex management. Recently, SDN architecture has been applied in various scenarios such as data centers and enterprise.

© ICST Institute for Computer Sciences, Social Informatics and Telecommunications Engineering 2019
Published by Springer Nature Switzerland AG 2019. All Rights Reserved
S. Han et al. (Eds.): AICON 2019, LNICST 287, pp. 127–138, 2019.
https://doi.org/10.1007/978-3-030-22971-9_11

With the development of SDN, privacy and security issues have become an urgent problem to be solved. Especially, network programmability and control logical centralization introduce new privacy threats and attack planes. Recently, considerable researchers pay attention to these problems. Kreutz, D. et al. analyzed the potential threat vectors and presented the information about its specificity for SDN [6]. Some of them are specific to SDN as they arise from a new entity introduced subsequently-the centralized controller. And the impact of threats presented in traditional networks may be potentially augmented or expressed differently [13]. Focusing on the security and privacy preservation, the solutions have already been presented in [9,12,13]. Sha et al. [12] designed a method to measure the sensitivity-degree of information and detected the sensitive information covert channel based on the OpenFlow in SDN. There are also some methods [14] using the encryption to solve information disclosure problem. Attackers can still obtain traffic features by traffic analysis attack. At the same time, the security of encryption method highly depends on the secure and reliable key management system.

Multipath has been used to solve privacy and security problems, especially in Mobile Ad-hoc Networks (MANET) [8,10]. In the proposed multipath protocol, messages are split into multiple pieces that sent out via multiple independent paths. Attackers have to collect all pieces of the message. To enhance the communication efficiency, [5,7,15,16] researched the topology-hiding to obscure the traffic features. Multipath transmission is a useful method to improve network service performance, especially in SDN. [1,2,4,11] support routing flows through different paths to overcome the traffic congestion and physical impairment. But there are few studies that use multipath to implement SDN privacy protection.

Compared with the purpose of multipath in the above literature, the method we proposed uses multipath filtering to instead of data partition, which randomly select one trusted paths for data transmission. This avoids traffic analysis attacks that exploit the similarity between multiple transmissions in SDN. Our contributions are as follows.

- We proposed a privacy protection method for SDN data transmission. In the proposed method, the optimal transmission path can be computed and selected by the SDN controller, which resists traffic analysis attack effectively.
- We set constraints and established a novel model to filter multiple paths. Based on this model, we discussed the tradeoff between privacy protection and path correlation degree.
- Experimental results show that numerical results of path correlation degree can be obtained from the tradeoff model. Our method reduces similarity of traffic compared with single-path scenario.

The rest of this paper is organized as follows: In the next section, we introduce the system architecture and attack assumption. Description of method is presented in Sect. 3. In Sect. 4, we discuss the performance and experiment results. Finally, we conclude this paper in the last section.

2 System Description and Assumption

In this section, we introduce the system architecture, network model and attack assumption.

As shown in Fig. 1, the system consists of four entities, i.e., SDN controller, hosts, switches and attacker. Multiple switches are included in underlying network, wherein the switches connected to Host1 and Host2 are sender and receiver, respectively. In SDN controller, the global overview is provided in order to compute the different paths between Host1 and Host2.

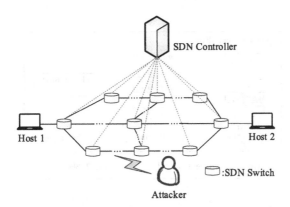

Fig. 1. Architecture, which consist of SDN controller, hosts, switches and attacker.

We formalize our target network problem. Given a graph $G = (V, E)$, where V is set of nodes in the network and E is the set of links. Each $v_i \in V$, and each link $e = (v_i, v_j) \in E$. A path is defined as a list of node $path_i = (v_1, v_2, v_3...v_N), \forall i, 1 \leq i \leq N$, where N is the number of nodes. The set of multiple paths is defined as $Path = (path_1, path_2...path_M)$, where M is the number of paths. Denoted the source node as v_s, and the destination node as v_d.

In our network model, we assume that:

- Attackers launch traffic analysis attacks by eavesdropping nodes. Attackers can attack on vulnerabilities in controller or switches. But cost of proactive attack is higher than that of reactive attack. Therefore, we assume that attacker is more inclined to reactive attack.
- SDN controller is trusted. If the controller, as the core of the whole network, conspire with the attacker, the whole network will be threatened. So, we assume that SDN controller will not disclose the path information or sensitive data to the attacker.
- The source and destination nodes are both reliable. Others are honest that not expose flow table to attacker.

If sensitive information is transmitted through a single path, attacker can break any switch in the path to cause link failure, or eavesdrop switch to analyze traffic features. While in a multipath scenario, multiple disjoint paths are allowed to be established between source node and destination node and one disjoint path is randomly selected for each transmission. If attackers want to analyze the traffic features by eavesdropping, he must simultaneously listen on all of paths. The question is how to find the multiple disjoint paths in SDN. However, fully disjoint paths are not possible, finding maximally disjoint paths are preferred, wherein it is allowed for paths to share common edges or nodes, as long as the number is minimum [4].

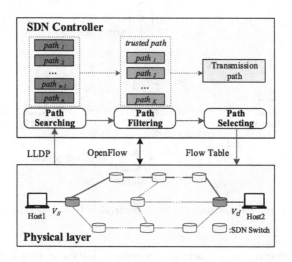

Fig. 2. Proposed method for multipath, where SDN controller focuses on obtaining transmission path and physical layer concentrates on data transmission.

3   Proposed Privacy Protection Method

The idea behind our method is to decrease the correlation between paths then randomly choose one path. Then, we exploit the randomization of multiple transmission paths to resist traffic analysis attack. Even if an attack succeeds to eavesdrop one path, the probability that the next transmission path can be analyzed is low. As shown in Fig. 2, the method is divided into three steps: (1) **Path Searching**, (2) **Path Filtering** and (3) **Path Selection**.

3.1   Path Searching

Based on the idea of Depth-First, SDN controller searches for all paths between the sender v_s and the receiver v_d. Path Searching is implemented in adjacent matrix.

We use a simple topology to describe the searching method as shown in Fig. 3. Let source and destination node be v_1 and v_9, respectively.

We search the first neighbor of v_1, i.e., v_2 as shown in Fig. 4(a), and put v_1 into the stack. Then, we do the same procedure from v_2. Until we come to the destination node, the first path, i.e., $path_1 = (v_1, v_2, v_4, v_6, v_7, v_9)$ can be obtained. Before the second path, we put out the node v_9 at the top of the stack. We start with the node v_7 as shown in Fig. 4(b), repeat the searching method. The whole searching process will be terminated until the stack is empty. Algorithm 1 describes the Path Searching process, which complexity is $O(n^2)$.

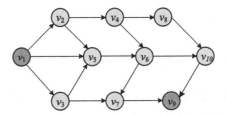

Fig. 3. A network topology with 10 nodes, where v_1 is the source node and v_9 is the destination node.

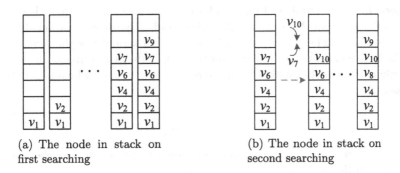

(a) The node in stack on first searching

(b) The node in stack on second searching

Fig. 4. Nodes in the stack during path searching

3.2 Path Filtering

All paths computed in the previous process need to be filtered to decrease the correlation between paths. And the paths satisfied the conditions are defined as the trusted paths. Detailed filtering conditions as follows:

Algorithm 1. Depth-First Path Searching.

Input: Adjacent matrix $M(n_{dimensionality})$, Start of path V_S, Destination of path V_D.

Output: Set of path list S.

1: **while** $destination of S_i \neq V_D$ **do**
2:    set start of S_i: tmp
3:    **for** i in [tmp+1: n] **do**
4:      **if** $M[tmp][i] \neq 0$ **then**
5:        tmp = i
6:        Add $M[tmp][i]$ to weight of S_i
7:        Add i to path of S_i
8:      **end if**
9:      **return** S_i
10:   **end for**
11: **end while**

---

(1) **Path Correlation Degree.** We use the number of joint nodes to evaluate path correlation degree $(d(path_i))$.

$$d(path_i) = \sum_{i=1,j\leq n,i\neq n}^{N} \frac{J_{ir}}{N_i} + \frac{J_{ir}}{N_r} \tag{1}$$

where J_{ir} is the number of joint nodes between $path_i$ and $path_r$, whose number of nodes are N_i and N_r. The threshold of path correlation degree is denoted as $maxD$ that $d(path_i)$ of trusted path should less than $maxD$.

(2) **Path Cost.** To reduce the consumption of network resources, the cost of a single path must be smaller than the average path costs, which is denoted as $c(path_i)$.

$$c(path_i) = \sum_{i=1}^{N} c_i \tag{2}$$

where c_i presents the cost of one node when transmitting a packet. So, the average of link costs is

$$C_{average} = \frac{\sum_{i=1}^{N} c(path_i)}{n} \tag{3}$$

(3) **Path Weight.** After being filtered by the above conditions, if the number of paths is still large, we select the first K paths in ascending order of weights. The link weight represents delay and is denoted by w, so a path weight is

$$w(path) = \sum_{i=1}^{N} w(v_i, v_{i+1}) \tag{4}$$

3.3   Path Selection

SDN controller randomly selects one path from the set of trusted paths by generating random numbers, whose range is $[1, W]$, where

$$W = \sum_{k=1}^{K} w(path_j) \tag{5}$$

Algorithm 2 describes the Path Selection process, which complexity is $O(n^2)$. This process guarantees that each transmission path is randomized and different. Therefore the similarity between multiple transmission is effectively disturbed.

Algorithm 2. Path Random Selection.

Input: Path weight $T(path_i)$, Sum of path weight W, Account of path K.
Output: The path list L.
1: **while** $i < K$ **do**
2:　　Set the random number interval$[1,W]$
3:　　**for** i in range (len(T) **do**
4:　　　if W-$T[i] < 0$ **then**
5:　　　　Set the current path i
6:　　　　Add i to L
7:　　　　**if** current path = previous path **then**
8:　　　　　$i++$
9:　　　　**end if**
10:　　　　**return** L
11:　　　**end if**
12:　　**end for**
13: **end while**

3.4   Tradeoff Model Between Privacy and $maxD$

In our scenario, the probability of path-attacked represents privacy protection performance, which related to the change of $maxD$. Therefore, we take some considerations: (1) enough number of paths to ensure random selection. (2) less number of joint nodes to reduce the correlation of multiple paths. (3) the more paths, the more joint nodes.

Let the probability of joint nodes and disjoint nodes being attacked be p_a and p_b, $p_b<p_a$, excluding the source and destination. If one node is compromised, the link is attacked. We assume that there are K trusted path, whose probability is denoted as

$$p(path_i) = 1 - (1 - p_a)^Q (1 - p_b)^{S-Q} \tag{6}$$

then,

$$p(path_i) = 1 - (1 - p_b)^S (\frac{1 - p_a}{1 - p_b})^Q \tag{7}$$

$$\frac{1 - p_a}{1 - p_b} < 1 \tag{8}$$

where the intermediate nodes number of $path_i$ is S, and the joint number excepted the source and destination is Q.

Under the constraints of paths weight and cost, the total number of nodes S in each path has little difference. So, the number of joint nodes will affect $p(path_i)$ from Eqs. (7) and (8).

The average probability of k paths is

$$P_{average} = \frac{\sum_{k=1}^{K} p(path_k)}{K} \tag{9}$$

We note that the less $p_{average}$ is, the more security paths we use to transmit sensitive information. When we set $maxD$ in Path Selection larger, the K increases, which results the correlation of filtered paths $d(path_i)$ increases. However, if the $maxD$ decreases, correlation of each path decreases, the performance degrades in terms of privacy protection.

In order to minimize $p_{average}$, we propose a tradeoff model as a flowchart illustrated in Fig. 5, which can obtain the optimal threshold $maxD$. First, the p_a and p_b are given, and $maxD$ is set the minimum initially. Then, we filter paths that be searched in Path Searching process and calculate the $p_{average}$. If the $p_{average}$ decreases as threshold $maxD$ increases, the step is repeated. Finally, $maxD$ is determined and the tradeoff is balanced.

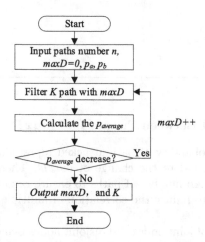

Fig. 5. Tradeoff model between $maxD$ and $p_{average}$

4   Evaluation and Result

In this section, we show the numerical results to discuss the performance of our method. We tested the implementation on mininet that deployed topologies with different number of nodes; RYU as the SDN controller. The experiments were conducted using the virtual machine running 64-bit Ubuntu 14.04, with 4 Gb of RAM. And we configured networks at 200, 300, 400, 500 nodes, with a random topologies.

We evaluated performance of the proposed method from two aspects: (1) the probability of path being attacked $p_{averagw}$ when threshold $maxD$ increases. (2) performance of multipath method with the optimal threshold $maxD$.

4.1 Tradeoff Results

Figure 6 indicates the effect of threshold $maxD$ on the number of paths and the probability of path being attacked under different scale network. We assumed p_a and p_b mentioned in Sect. 3.4 is 0.8 and 0.2, respectively. The trend we observed in Fig. 6(a) is, as the $maxD$ is strictly limited, the path number K become large. But the probability $p_{average}$ can be minimized when $maxD$ takes the appropriate value in Fig. 6(b). Combining both figures, we observed the optimal $maxD$ and K that the path are trust. For example, when we set $maxD$ 6, the probability $p_{average}$ is minimum in the network size of 500 nodes and the average number of paths is 8.3.

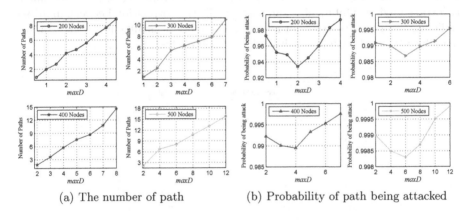

(a) The number of path   (b) Probability of path being attacked

Fig. 6. Tradeoff model of $maxD$ with different number of nodes

4.2 Performance of Multipath

We confirmed the effect of our proposed method by comparing it with the existing method Multipath-Floyd [3]. Figure 7 shows an average of the number of paths. As the size of network increases, the number of paths in our method are greater than Multipath-Floyd. Meanwhile, the correlation between multiple paths decrease relatively. We allow paths to share nodes or edges, while fully disjoint paths are obtained in Multipath-Floyd.

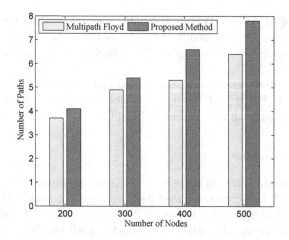

Fig. 7. Comparison between Multipath-Floyd and our method

We also discussed ability to resist traffic analysis attacks. We simulated the a communication between hosts in the different scenarios. Dijkstra algorithm are used to calculate path in single path scenario. From Fig. 8, traffic of single path transmission exhibits high similarity, while the correlation between multiple traffic has been disturbed by our method. Therefore, it is difficult for an attacker to analyze the real path of sensitive data based on traffic similarity.

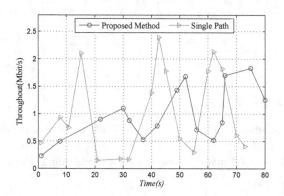

Fig. 8. Comparison between single path and proposed method

5   Conclusion

In this paper, we presented a multipath filtering method to enhance privacy of SDN data transmission, which has the ability to effectively resist traffic attack. First, Depth-First path searching algorithm was adopted to compute each path from the transmitter to the receiver. Then, we set conditions to filter all paths to obtain the set of trusted paths. Moreover, we established a novel model to discuss privacy protection and $maxD$. The experiments results show that our method obtained optimal $maxD$, which reduces the correlation of paths. Compared with single path scenario, privacy protection can be improved in proposed method. The situation that the probability of nodes being attacked is a variable will be an open topic. We will pay more attention in the future.

Acknowledgments. This work was supported by the National Natural Science Foundation of China (U1736216), the natural science foundation of Jiangsu Province (BK20151460) and the University Natural Science Foundation of Jiangsu Province (16KJB520021).

References

1. Duan, J., Wang, Z., Wu, C.: Responsive multipath TCP in SDN-based datacenters. In: 2015 IEEE International Conference on Communications (ICC), London, UK, pp. 5296–5301, June 2015. https://doi.org/10.1109/ICC.2015.7249165
2. Dulinski, Z., Rzym, G., Cholda, P.: MPLS-based reduction of flow table entries in SDN switches supporting multipath transmission. Networking and Internet Architecture arXiv:1805.07993 (2018)
3. Guan, Y., Lei, W., Zhang, W., Liu, S., Li, H.: Scalable orchestration of software defined service overlay network for multipath transmission. Comput. Netw. **137**, 132–146 (2018)
4. Guillen, L., Izumi, S., Abe, T., Suganuma, T., Muraoka, H.: SDN implementation of multipath discovery to improve network performance in distributed storage systems. In: 2017 13th International Conference on Network and Service Management (CNSM), vol. 1, pp. 1–4. IEEE Computer Society, Tokyo, November 2017. https://doi.org/10.23919/CNSM.2017.8256054
5. Jose, J., Rigi, R.C.: A comparative study of topology enabled and topology hiding multipath routing protocols in MANETs. In: 2015 International Conference on Electrical, Electronics, Signals, Communication and Optimization (EESCO), Visakhapatnam, India, pp. 1–4, January 2015. https://doi.org/10.1109/EESCO.2015.7254001
6. Kreutz, D., Ramos, F.M., Verissimo, P.: Towards secure and dependable Software-Defined Networks. In: Proceedings of the Second ACM SIGCOMM Workshop on Hot Topics in Software Defined Networking, HotSDN 2013, pp. 55–60. ACM, New York (2013). https://doi.org/10.1145/2491185.2491199
7. Liu, H., Wang, Z., Miao, F.: Concurrent multipath traffic impersonating for enhancing communication privacy. Int. J. Commun. Syst. **27**(11), 2985–2996 (2014)
8. Lou, W., Liu, W., Zhang, Y., Fang, Y.: SPREAD: improving network security by multipath routing in mobile ad hoc networks. Wireless Netw. **15**(3), 279–294 (2009)
9. Nakahara, M., Shinkuma, R., Yamaguchi, K., Yamaguchi, K.: Tradeoff between privacy protection and network resource in community associated network virtualization. In: 2015 IEEE 26th Annual International Symposium on Personal, Indoor, and Mobile Radio Communications (PIMRC), Hong Kong, China, pp. 2143–2148, August 2015. https://doi.org/10.1109/PIMRC.2015.7343652

10. Othman, J.B., Mokdad, L.: Enhancing data security in ad hoc networks based on multipath routing. J. Parallel Distrib. Comput. **70**(3), 309–316 (2010)
11. Pasca, S.T.V., Kodali, S.S.P., Kataoka, K.: AMPS: application aware multipath flow routing using machine learning in SDN. In: 2017 Twenty-Third National Conference on Communications, Chennai, India (NCC), pp. 1–6, March 2017. https://doi.org/10.1109/NCC.2017.8077095
12. Sha, L., He, L., Fu, J., Sun, J., Li, P.: SDN-based sensitive information SI protection: sensitivity-degree measurement in software and data lifetime supervisor in Software Defined Network. Sec. Commun. Netw. **9**(13), 1944–1957 (2016)
13. Wang, Y., Chau, P., Chen, F.: Towards a secured network virtualization. Comput. Netw. **104**(C), 55–65 (2016)
14. Zeng, T., Meng, S., Wang, M., Zhu, L., Fan, L.: Self-adaptive anonymous communication scheme under SDN architecture. In: 2015 IEEE 34th International Performance Computing and Communications Conference (IPCCC), Nanjing, China, pp. 1–8. December 2015. https://doi.org/10.1109/PCCC.2015.7410337
15. Zhang, Y., Tan, Y., Jie, T., Qi, H., Wang, G., Li, Z.: TOHIP: a topology-hiding multipath routing protocol in mobile ad hoc networks. Ad Hoc Netw. **21**(5), 109–122 (2014)
16. Zhang, Y., Wang, G., Hu, Q., Li, Z., Tian, J.: Design and performance study of a topology-hiding multipath routing protocol for mobile ad hoc networks. In: 2012 Proceedings IEEE INFOCOM, Orlando, FL, USA, pp. 10–18, March 2012. https://doi.org/10.1109/INFCOM.2012.6195468

A Biometric-Based IoT Device Identity Authentication Scheme

Qingshui Xue[1(⊠)], Xingzhong Ju[1], Haozhi Zhu[1], Haojin Zhu[2], Fengying Li[2], and Xiangwei Zheng[3,4]

[1] School of Computer Science and Information Engineering,
Shanghai Institute of Technology, Shanghai 201418, China
xue-qsh@sit.edu.cn
[2] Department of Computer Science and Engineering,
Shanghai Jiao Tong University, Shanghai 200240, China
[3] School of Information Science and Engineering,
Shandong Normal University, Jinan 250014, China
[4] Shandong Provincial Key Laboratory for Distributed Computer Software
Novel Technology, Jinan 250014, China

Abstract. IoT is an important part of the new generation of information technologies and the next big thing in the IT industry after the computer and the internet. The IoT has great development potential and a wide range of possible applications, especially commercial applications. And information security of the IoT is the key to the long-term development of the whole industry. Currently, the two most significant factors in the development of the IoT are user identity authentication and privacy protection. This paper contains an analysis on the current picture of inter-device user identity authentication in the IoT and proposes an inter-device biometric authentication solution for the IoT that's designed to work with larger devices, addressing the shortcomings of the traditional user identity authentication technologies including security and efficiency problems. A strategy for further solution optimization is also included. This paper elaborates on the specific process of user identity authentication carried out by users on devices and between devices making use of fingerprints. We'll demonstrate the security of this solution against existing attack methods and in the last part, we enumerate various possible applications of this solution in smart homes.

Keywords: IoT technologies · User identity authentication · Biometrics · Fingerprint recognition · Information security

1 Introduction

IoT is an important part of the new generation of information technologies and the next big thing in the IT industry after the computer and the internet. The definition of the IoT is simply an Internet network connected to objects. It refers to the connection with devices, users, systems, information resources and intelligent services, and information exchange and communication through the Internet to achieve intelligent identification, control, and intelligent services that are managed or monitored. The IoT can be

S. Han et al. (Eds.): AICON 2019, LNICST 287, pp. 139–149, 2019.
https://doi.org/10.1007/978-3-030-22971-9_12

integrated with the Internet through various wired and wireless networks, integrating a large number of sensors, intelligent processing terminals, global positioning systems, etc., to achieve inter-devices and human-and-devices connectivity anytime, anywhere, to achieve intelligent management and control [1].

The IoT technology is widely used in all aspects of our lives, from smart home, smart medical to intelligent transportation, smart city, the IoT is everywhere [20]. At present, the IoT technology is in the stage of rapid development, and it will have a wider impact and change our lives in the future. It is worth noting that while we enjoy the convenience of IoT technology for our lives, the development of the IoT is also faced with various challenges such as market fragmentation, lacking uniform access standards and inadequate equipment security [15]. Especially in terms of safety, this can directly harm the user's personal safety when a security problem occurs [8]. Therefore, reliable and effective security is the prerequisite for the continuous and stable operation of the IoT system [9]. User identity authentication and data privacy disclosure of IoT devices are the two main factors that constrain the rapid development of the IoT [19].

In smart home scenarios, smart door locks, smart cameras, and other devices all have strong user identity authentication security requirements, involving users in the life cycle of binding devices, using devices, and unbinding devices [7]. Currently, various authentication operations for these devices are usually based on account system services provided by the device manufacturer (for example, access to log in the mobile APP, the operating authority is obtained after the cloud user identity authentication). Due to the limitations of the username/password authentication method, the diversity of smart home device manufacturers, and the security of the produced devices, there are some security risks in the process of user identity authentication in some scenarios.

The hierarchical structure of the IoT system can be divided into three layers from bottom to top, namely the sensing layer, the network layer, and the application layer. The sensing layer is mainly composed of sensors, cameras, and other devices. Its main task is to collect and to identify static and dynamic information of objects by means of different types of sensors. The network layer mainly plays the role of transmitting and processing information about the IoT. The application layer is mainly responsible for the intelligent management and control of devices in the IoT.

Combined with the architecture of the IoT, scholars have proposed dynamic cryptography and static cryptography in authentication technology. Ke [2] proposed to solve the user identity authentication problem by using USB cryptography in the literature; Lin proposed to use the static cryptography to achieve Internet authentication in the literature [3]. However, the use of static passwords in the IoT environment can easily lead to low security of the system. In addition, as the main authentication method, digital certificates will increase the delay and reduce efficiency [4]. In order to solve the above problems, we propose a fingerprint-based inter-device biometric authentication solution for the IoT. At present, the fingerprint-based biometric authentication solution has been widely used for user identity authentication by users on devices [11], but it is rarely used in user identity authentication between devices. This article will focus on the research and application of fingerprint recognition in user identity authentication between devices.

2 Two Fingerprint-Based Inter-device Biometric Authentication Systems for the IoT

2.1 The Proposed Basic System

When we study the fingerprint-based inter-device biometric authentication solution for the IoT, we assume that all IoT devices have fingerprint information collection modules and the communication links are secure and reliable. Simultaneously, it is assumed that the communication key M1 between devices is secure and can't be stolen. Based on the schematic diagram of the IoT device user identity authentication process shown in Fig. 1, we develop a method based on fingerprint identification with IoT device identity authentication.

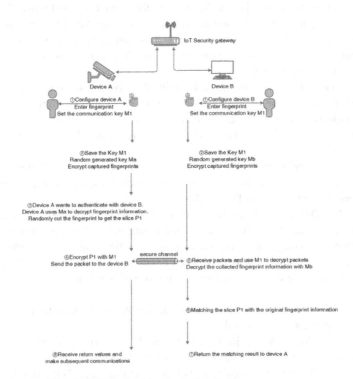

Fig. 1. IoT device identity authentication process map

Step1. The user logs in to the device configuration interface through the initial configuration account password of Device A and modifies the device management password. The device-related information is configured to enable the device to connect to the IoT security gateway. The fingerprint collection module enters fingerprint information and sets the device-to-device communication key M1 (Device B operates as above).

Step2. After Device A collects the fingerprint information of the user, Device A randomly generates a key Ma and uses a symmetric encryption algorithm to encrypt and store the fingerprint information to ensure the security of the collected fingerprint information. At the same time, the device communication key M1 and the key is saved. Communication key M1 acts as a public key to encryption and decryption between devices (Device B operates as above).

Step3. Device A decrypts the stored fingerprint information with the secret key Ma firstly, When Device A wants to authenticate with Device B. After the fingerprint information is decrypted, Device A randomly cuts the fingerprint image to get a fingerprint slice P1 and ensures that the area of the slice P1 is not less than α % of the original fingerprint area.

Step4. Device A uses a symmetric encryption algorithm, uses the communication key M1 as an encryption key, encrypts slice P1, and transmits the encrypted data packet to Device B through trusted network channels.

Step5. After receiving the data packet sent by the Device A, the Device B decrypts the received data packet by using the stored communication key M1, and restores the plaintext information about the slice P1, and simultaneously decrypts the encrypted stored fingerprint information by using the secret key Mb to obtain the plaintext information of the fingerprint.

Step6. Device B matches the slice P1 with the original fingerprint information. When the similarity reaches β, the matching is successful, and the user identity of the sending method is confirmed. When the matching result does not meet the requirement, the user identity authentication fails. At the same time, the decrypted fingerprint is encrypted back.

Step7. When Device B matches successfully, the return value of the successful authentication is sent to Device A. When the match fails, the return value of the authentication failure is sent to Device A.

Step8. After Device A successfully receives the matching value of Device B and confirms the user identity of the sender of the return value, the user identity authentication process is completed, and subsequent operations such as communication, management, control or data sharing between devices can be performed. When device A receives the message of authentication failure, it will return to the step3–8 to restart authentication.

The participants in this system are: user, Device A, and Device B. The functional tasks for each participant are as follows:

Users: (1) Configure the device to connect the IoT security gateway normally and set the communication key of devices. (2) Input the fingerprint.

Device A: (1) Save the user-configured communication key. (2) Randomly generate the key Ma, encrypt and store the collected fingerprint information. (3) Decrypt the fingerprint information and randomly cut the fingerprint picture to obtain the fingerprint slice P1. (4) Encrypt fingerprint slice P1 with communication key M1 and send it to Device B. (5) Receive the return result of Device B for subsequent communication.

Device B: (1) Save the user-configured communication key M1. (2) Randomly generate the secret key Mb to encrypt and store the collected fingerprint information. (3) Receive the encrypted data packet sent by Device A. (4) Decrypt the data packet to obtain the slice P1. (5) Decrypt the original fingerprint information to get the complete fingerprint. (6) The fingerprint slice is matched with the original fingerprint information. (7) The matching result is returned to Device A.

The specific information interaction process is shown in Fig. 2.

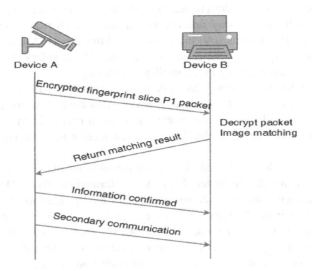

Fig. 2. Information exchange in the basic inter-device biometric authentication system

2.2   The Improved System

In the above solution, the premise of our research is that each IoT device has a module for collecting fingerprint information of the user. Considering the actual situation and equipment production cost, some devices may not have a fingerprint collection module. In order to solve this problem and optimize user experience, we further improved the solution. We also assume that the communication link is secure and trustworthy and that the communication key M1 between the devices is secure and cannot be stolen.

In the improved system, we design the task of fingerprint collection and encryption by the IoT security gateway. The specific steps are as follows:

Step1. The user logs in the device configuration interface through the initial configuration account and password of the IoT security gateway, and modifies the device management password; configures device related information; inputs the fingerprint through the fingerprint collection module, and sets the communication key M1 among devices.

Step2. The IoT security gateway stores the communication key M1 and uses M1 to encrypt the collected fingerprint information. When the user completes the first configuration, the password and fingerprint matching is needed for the second configuration modification to enter the gateway configuration interface and modify the gateway configuration. This will prevent an attacker from a malicious attack on the security gateway device.

Step3. When a new Device A needs to join the network, the user logs in to the device configuration interface through the initial configuration account password of Device A, and modifies the device management password; configures device-related information to enable the device to connect to the IoT security gateway normally and set the communication key M1 between devices.

Step4. After the gateway detects that the new device is normally connected to the network, the intelligent gateway first encrypts a string of characters with the communication key M1and sends it to the Device A. After Device A receives the data packet of the gateway, it uses the communication key M1 to unlock the data packet. And send the unwrapped string to the intelligent gateway.

Step5. After the smart gateway receives the decrypted information of Device A, it compares with the string sent by the smart gateway. After the comparison is successful, the smart gateway will send the fingerprint information encrypted by the communication key M1 to Device A, so that Device A can receive the encrypted fingerprint information.

Similarly, when Device B needs to join the network, the above steps will also be performed to obtain the encrypted fingerprint information. When Device A and Device B are authenticated, the subsequent authentication process will be the same as that of step3–step8 in the 2.1 basic solutions, except that in step 3 and step 5, the secret key Ma and Mb are no longer needed to decrypt the fingerprint information and only the communication key M1 is needed to decrypt fingerprint information.

Of course, for some devices with fingerprint collection module, we can manually select whether the input of fingerprint information needs to be obtained from the intelligent gateway in the configuration interface. If necessary, the fingerprint collection will be sent from the gateway to the device. If not, the above steps will not be performed.

The participants in this solution are: user, intelligent gateway, Device A and Device B. The tasks that participants need to accomplish are as follows:

User: (1) Configure the device communication key M1. (2) Enter the fingerprint and complete the fingerprint collection.

Intelligent gateway: (1) Save the user-configured communication key M1. (2) Encrypt and store fingerprint information. (3) Use the communication key M1 to encrypt random string to verify Device A. (4) After receiving the correct return value of Device A, send the encrypted fingerprint information to Device A.

Device A: (1) Save the user-configured communication key M1. (2) Receive and decrypt the encrypted data packets sent by the intelligent gateway and result to the intelligent gateway. (3) Receive and store the fingerprint information encrypted data packets sent by the intelligent gateway. (4) Decrypt the fingerprint information and randomly cut fingerprint pictures to get the fingerprint slice P1. (5) Encrypt fingerprint slice P1 with the communication key M1 and send it to Device B (6) receive the return result of Device B for subsequent communication.

Devices B: (1) Save the user-configured communication key. (2) Receive and decrypt the encrypted data packet sent by the intelligent gateway and return the result to the intelligent gateway. (3) Receive and store the encrypted data packets sent by the intelligent gateway. (4) Receive the encrypted data packets from Device A and decrypt the data packets to get slice P1. (5) Decrypt the original fingerprint information and get the complete fingerprint. (6) Match the fingerprint slice with the original fingerprint information. (7) Return the matching result to Device A. The specific information interaction process is shown in Fig. 3.

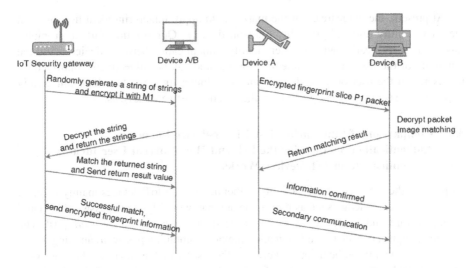

Fig. 3. Information exchange in the improved inter-device biometric authentication system

3 Performance Analysis of the Fingerprint-Based Inter-device Biometric Authentication Solution for the IoT

IoT technology integrates the Internet, mobile Internet, wireless communication network and various wireless sensor network technologies [14]. The complex structure and rich application scenarios make IoT security more serious than traditional network security [16]. Specifically, on the issue of user identity authentication, the challenge of user identity authentication faced by the IoT is far greater than that of traditional networks.

In order to consider the feasibility and security of fingerprint-based inter-device biometric authentication solution for the IoT comprehensively, we will analyze and demonstrate this solution form the following aspects.

3.1 Feasibility Analysis of the Fingerprint-Based Inter-device Biometric Authentication Solution for the IoT

Fingerprints have become a synonym of biometric recognition because of its lifetime invariance, uniqueness and convenience [17]. At present, fingerprint recognition is quite mature as an identification technology and has a solid market backing [13]. Fingerprint recognition technology can extract the feature values extracted from fingerprints by analyzing the global features of fingerprints and local feature points such as ridge, valley and end points, bifurcation points or divergence points, so as to reliably identify a user's identity through fingerprints [18]. On average, each fingerprint has several unique and measurable feature points, each feature point has about seven features, and our ten fingers produce a minimum of 4,900 independently measurable features, which is sufficient to prove that fingerprint recognition is a more reliable identification method [5].

At present, the mainstream of the market is to apply fingerprint identification with the user identity authentication by users on devices. Our solution further promotes fingerprint identification with the user identity authentication between devices. And the reliability of the user identity authentication method can be subjectively controlled by the user, and the user only needs to input more finger fingerprints, which can greatly improve the security of user identity authentication between devices.

3.2 Comparison of Fingerprint-Based Inter-device Biometric Authentication Solution for the IoT and How Current User Identity Authentication on IoT Devices Works

At present, the methods of user identity authentication on IoT devices mainly include: based on user knowledge such as user name and password, dynamic password [12] and other software and hardware devices such as smart cards owned by users [10]. The solution adopts a two-factor authentication method combining password and fingerprint in the user identity authentication between the user and the device, which is more secure than the single-factor or two-factor authentication methods of the traditional password and the dynamic password. Similarly, compared with smart cards and other authentication methods, this solution is more convenient and fast, and the fingerprint recognition is extended to the user identity authentication between devices. Due to the unique and complex characteristics of fingerprints, the security of the solution is guaranteed in user identity authentication between devices.

3.3 Performance Comparisons Between the Basic and Improved Systems

The main difference between the basic system and the improved system is that the basic system requires each device to have a fingerprint collection function, and the improved system only requires the intelligent gateway to have a fingerprint collection function. Compared with the basic system, the improved system has the following advantages: (1) it does not need the fingerprint acquisition module on each device to reduce the cost of equipment production. (2) The user does not need to perform fingerprint collection of each device, thereby reducing user intervention. The operation is more convenient. (3) It is difficult to ensure that the collected information is consistent because each fingerprint is collected, so the success rate is higher when the fingerprint is matched.

3.4 Security Analysis of the Fingerprint-Based Inter-device Biometric Authentication Solution for the IoT

The main security threats currently faced by IoT authentication included user identity-based forgery, eavesdropping-based attacks, user identity-based forgery, and eavesdropping combined attacks, data manipulation-based attacks, and service availability attacks [6].

In order to prevent attackers from illegally registering Device And stealing the communication key M1 and user fingerprinted information between the devices, the solution adopts this method: in the basic system, we assume that each device has a fingerprint collection function, after completing the first configuration, users need to use double authentication of account password and fingerprint to log in normally in the second time you log in again. When viewing or modifying important parameters (such as communication keys), the current device needs to verify the fingerprint information again and requires the smart gateway to authorize the changes. For the collected fingerprint information, the smart device randomly generates a key for encrypted storage and ensures that the stored fingerprint information is secure again. In the improved system, we do not require each IoT device to have a fingerprint acquisition module. However, in order to ensure the security of the device, you need to log in to other devices to view the configuration information after you log in to the smart gateway for the second time. Also, when viewing or modifying important parameters (such as communication keys), you need to verify the fingerprint information on the smart gateway, and you can view the changes after authorization.

In the solution, we assume that the communication key to devices is not stolen, and the transmission channel is safe and reliable. In order to prevent the attacker from intercepting the intercepted fingerprint information about the transmission, we take the form of fingerprint random cutting (Random cutting means that the shape of the slice is arbitrary, and the ratio of the cut area is larger than the programmed value α %). Only randomly cut fingerprint slices are transmitted during each verification process, and the slices are encrypted using a symmetric encryption algorithm. This ensures that even if the packet is intercepted, the attacker cannot obtain the complete fingerprint information.

4   Application Scenarios of Fingerprint-Based Inter-device Biometric Authentication Solution for the IoT

In the fingerprint-based inter-device biometric authentication solution for the IoT, the device needs to perform image encryption and decryption, image segmentation and image comparison, which have certain requirements on the performance and computing processing capability of the device. At present, we only consider the system to be applied to an inter-device biometric authentication system with a relatively large device size and relatively strong computing processing capability. We will use this program to do application scenario analysis in a smart home.

Suppose Andy ends his busy day's work and prepares to go home. He plans to go home and have a hot bath. Andy opens the IoT device client installed on the mobile phone. After successful login through fingerprint matching, the mobile phone client randomly encrypts the fingerprint information and sends it to the smart water heater at home. The smart water heater decrypts the fingerprint slice sent by the mobile phone to perform fingerprint image matching. After the matching is successful, the device is in a controlled state, and Andy remotely turns on the smart water heater, and the water will be heated to a suitable temperature. At the same time, after the smart gateway communicates with the mobile APP, the APP will obtain the location of Andy, and estimate the time required for Andy to arrive at the smart gateway through the cloud service. When it is calculated that Andy will arrive home after about 20 min, the intelligent gateway will perform device authentication with the air conditioner, encrypt the randomly segmented fingerprint slice and send it to the smart air conditioner. After the smart air conditioner receives the information and decrypts it successfully, the air conditioner controls the air conditioner according to the temperature sensor. To the temperature data, the automatic opening adjusts the indoor temperature to a comfortable range. After Andy arrives at the door of the house, the door is opened by the fingerprint lock. At the same time, after the fingerprint lock receives the door opening command from Andy, the command to automatically turn on the light is sent to the smart light fixture. The smart light fixture automatically determines whether the light needs to be turned on according to the data of the light sensor. When Andy arrives home, the Bluetooth speaker will play Andy's favorite songs according to Andy's daily hobbies, so Andy can soak in a hot bath in a comfortable room.

5 Conclusions

This paper presents a fingerprint-based authentication solution for IoT devices. This solution not only applies fingerprint recognition by users on devices but also extends it to devices. Through a series of steps such as random cutting of fingerprints, encrypted transmission of slices, decryption and image matching, the process of user identity authentication between devices through fingerprints is completed. And for the possible existence of IoT identity authentication attacks, corresponding solutions are proposed, which greatly improves the security and reliability of user identity authentication between devices as well as users and devices. It is also noteworthy that this solution requires that the device must be able to perform image segmentation, encryption and decryption, image matching and other operations, so it has certain requirements for the operating performance of the device, and is more suitable for the relatively large equipment, relatively strong computing capacity, and relatively centralized equipment distribution scenarios. At the same time, how to continue to optimize the solution so that it can be applied to more relatively small computing capacity of relatively weak equipment is the direction of future research.

Acknowledgments. This paper is supported by NSFC under Grant No. 61672350 and 61373 149, NSSFC under Grant No. 16BGL003, Ministry of Education Fund under Grant No. 39120 K178038 and 14YJA880033, SIT Collaborative innovation platform under Grant No. 3921NH 166033, and SIT Foundation for Distinguished Scholars under Grant No. 39120K176049. We are also grateful for the support of the National Natural Science Foundation of China (61170227).

References

1. Chuankun, W.: An overview on the security techniques and challenges of the Internet of things. J. Cryptologic Res. **2**(1), 40–53 (2015)
2. Ke, J., Zhou, P., Jing, X.: Mixed parameters of differential and weighted mel cepstrum used in speaker recognition. Microelectronics Comput. **31**(9), 89–91 (2014)
3. Lin, W., Wang, X.: One-time password authentication protocol based on non-homogeneous linear equations. Comput. Eng. **36**(13), 154–155 (2010)
4. Zhang, M., Ma, Z., Zhang, X., Gao, F.: An identity authentication scheme on IoT. Designing Tech. Posts Telecommun. 19–22 (2017)

5. Wang, A., Guo, Y., Wang, X.: An introduction to identification and authentication technology. Comput. Appl. Softw. (2002)
6. Internet Finance Authentication Alliance. https://ifaa.org.cn/whitebook. Accessed Sept 2018
7. IoT Security Guidelines for IoT Endpoint Ecosystem. http://www.gsma.com/connectedliving. Accessed 23 May 2017
8. Chuankun, W.: Security Fundamentals for Internet of Things. Science Press, Beijing (2013)
9. IoT Security Guidelines Overview Document. http://www.gsma.com/connectedliving. Accessed 23 May 2017
10. Lee, S., Ong, I., Lim, H., et al.: Two factor authentication for cloud computing. J. Inf. Commun. Convergence Eng. 8(4), 427–432 (2010)
11. Yuan, J., Jiang, C.: A biometric-based user authentication for wireless sensor networks. Wuhan Univ. J. Nat. Sci. 15(3), 272–276 (2010)
12. Das, A.K., Chatterjee, S., Sing, J.K.: Formal security verification of a dynamic password-based user authentication scheme for hierarchical wireless sensor networks. Commun. Comput. Inf. Sci. 2(1), 78–102 (2013)
13. Periaswamy, S.C.G., Thompson, D.R., Di, J.: Fingerprinting RFID tags. IEEE Trans. Dependable and Secure Comput. 8(6), 938–943 (2011)
14. Ai, Y.X., Mei, L.X.: Security characteristic and technology in the Internet of Things. Network Secur. Technol. Appl. 30(4), 20–29 (2013)
15. National Internet Emergency Response Center: China Internet Network Security Report 2016. People's Posts and Telecommunications Publishing House, Beijing (2017)
16. Bertino, E., Islam, N.: Botnets and Internet of Things security. Computer 50(2), 76–79 (2017)
17. Zhang, N., Zang, Y.-L., Tian, J.: The integration of biometrics and cryptography—a new solution for secure identity authentication. J. Cryptologic Res. 2, 159–176 (2015)
18. Long, W., Sun, D.: Research on security and user privacy of biometric authentication solution. Secret Sci. Technol. (2014)
19. Li, C., Xin, Y., Niu, X., et al.: Identity authentication scheme based on biometric certificate. Comput. Eng. 33(20), 165–167 (2007)
20. Xiao, W.U., Jian-Ping, Z., Chu-Hua, L., et al.: Application of Internet of Things in smart home. Internet Things Technol. (2012)

A Physical and Verbal Bullying Detecting Algorithm Based on K-NN for School Bullying Prevention

Shangbin Gao[1,2] and Liang Ye[2(✉)]

[1] Harbin Institute of Technology, Weihai, China
1270565172@qq.com
[2] Harbin Institute of Technology, Harbin, China
yeliang@hit.edu.cn

Abstract. School bullying is a common social problem around the world which affects teenagers, and physical violence is considered to be the most harmful while verbal bullying is the most frequent. This paper proposes an automatic physical and verbal bullying detecting method in the field of artificial intelligence. Dozens of features were extracted from acceleration and gyro data to train the physical bullying recognition while the mean value of each frame of samples was calculated for verbal bullying detection. The authors used the k-NN algorithm as the classifier. The final test accuracies of physical and verbal bullying detecting were 70.4% and 78.0%, respectively, indicating that activity recognition and speech emotion recognition can be used for detecting bullying behaviors as an artificial intelligence technique, and speech emotion recognition appeared to be better than activity recognition.

Keywords: Physical bullying · Verbal bullying · k-NN ·
Artificial Intelligence · School bullying

1 Introduction

School bullying is a common social problem among teenagers. It affects the victims both mentally and physically and is considered as one of the main reasons for depression, dropping out of school and adolescent suicide [1, 2]. In view of this, anti-bullying is a significant as well as timeless topic. New approaches for preventing school bullying become available as classification methods develop. School bullying can take various forms, such as cursing, physical violence, and so on. Physical violence is considered to be the most harmful to teenagers while the verbal bullying is the most frequent. Consequently, this paper will focus on detecting both physical and verbal bullying.

Following the popularity of smartphones, several anti-bullying applications can be found on Internet. Nevertheless, the victim or a witness needs to take out a smartphone, run the application and press a button to send an alarm message. To photograph the event, they must hold the camera toward the bullies. However, this is not convenient for the victim, especially when bullied physically. Therefore, Alasaarela [3] and his

© ICST Institute for Computer Sciences, Social Informatics and Telecommunications Engineering 2019
Published by Springer Nature Switzerland AG 2019. All Rights Reserved
S. Han et al. (Eds.): AICON 2019, LNICST 287, pp. 150–157, 2019.
https://doi.org/10.1007/978-3-030-22971-9_13

team proposed some algorithms to detect physical bullying by using a 3D accelerometer and a 3D gyroscope. Once activated, it could run in the background and detect physical bullying automatically.

There are also some experiments focusing on emotion recognition and daily-life activity recognition. For instance, Ferdinando had found a method that was able to recognize emotions indicative of bullying incidents with ECG and Heart Rate Variability (HRV), reaching an average accuracy of 47.69% for arousal and 42.55% for valence [4]. Zalluhoglu and Ikizler-Cinbis had reached the accuracy of 72.4% [5]. Moreover, Seyed Ali and Rokni got an accuracy of 82.2% in activity recognition [6].

This paper applied an algorithm for detecting physical and verbal bullying—the k-Nearest Neighbor (k-NN) algorithm. It is a non-parametric method used for classification and regression in pattern recognition. In both cases, the input consists of k closest training examples in the feature space. And the output depends on whether k-NN is used for classification or regression.

The remainder of this paper is constructed as follows: Sect. 2 shows the process of activity recognition; Sect. 3 shows the process of speech emotion recognition; Sect. 4 gives out the classification results by simulation; and Sect. 5 draws a conclusion.

2 Activity Recognition

Nowadays activity recognition with various sensors is a very popular topic. For the convenience of life, many researchers try to use this technique to assist people with their daily life, e.g. elder care [1, 2], smart home [7, 8], and other artificial intelligence (AI) environments. As a matter of fact, there are quite a number of classifiers as well as feature selection methods for activity recognition. However, it is nearly impossible to draw a conclusion which activity recognition algorithm is absolutely the best, considering the differences of databases used by different researches, as well as the difference sources of activities provided by different actors/actresses. This paper focuses on the activity recognition by accelerometers and gyroscopes.

The following is the concrete procedures in activity recognition.

The data were collected by Ye, *et al.* in Finland. A movement sensor (integrated accelerometer and gyroscope) was fixed on the subjects' waist in order to collect 3D accelerations and 3D gyros at 50 Hz. All experiments were video-recorded for synchronization. Each activity was repeated several times by different actors or actresses.

The authors had finally gathered more than 250 fragments of movement in total and then selected 221 of them as samples. The data were the acceleration in x-axis, y-axis and z-axis, and the gyro in x-axis, y-axis and z-axis. The y-axis was a vertical vector, while the x-axis and the z-axis were horizontal vectors. Classified by movement, it can be divided into 9 kinds, i.e. falling down, jumping, playing, pushing, pushing down, running, shoulder-hit, standing and walking.

The authors firstly loaded these data from Excel to documents ending with ".mat". These data were equally and randomly divided into 2 groups, namely the training group and the testing group (if one certain kind of movement cannot be divided equally, let the training set contain one more sample than the testing group) (Table 1).

Table 1. The exact number of each movement in the training group and the testing group.

	Training group	Testing group
Falling down	8	7
Jumping	6	6
Playing	16	15
Pushing	30	29
Pushing down	22	21
Running	5	4
Shoulder-hit	15	15
Standing	6	5
Walking	6	5
Sum	114	107

Then the authors calculated the maximum, minimum, median absolute deviation, mean value, variance, sum and energy of each movement in both two groups. Each feature value concluded 6 sections, e.g. the maximum concluded the maximum acceleration in x-axis, y-axis, and z-axis, and the maximum gyro in x-axis, y-axis, and z-axis. Table 2 shows the extracted features.

Table 2. All the 42 features that should be calculated.

Maximum from accelerations in x-axis	Maximum from accelerations in y-axis	Maximum from accelerations in z-axis	Maximum from gyros in x-axis	Maximum from gyros in y-axis	Maximum from gyros in z-axis
Minimum from accelerations in x-axis	Minimum from accelerations in y-axis	Minimum from accelerations in z-axis	Minimum from gyros in x-axis	Minimum from gyros in y-axis	Minimum from gyros in z-axis
Median absolute deviation from accelerations in x-axis	Median absolute deviation from accelerations in y-axis	Median absolute deviation from accelerations in z-axis	Median absolute deviation from gyros in x-axis	Median absolute deviation from gyros in y-axis	Median absolute deviation from gyros in z-axis
Mean value from accelerations in x-axis	Mean value from accelerations in y-axis	Mean value from accelerations in z-axis	Mean value from gyros in x-axis	Mean value from gyros in y-axis	Mean value from gyros in z-axis
Variance from accelerations in x-axis	Variance from accelerations in y-axis	Variance from accelerations in z-axis	Variance from gyros in x-axis	Variance from gyros in y-axis	Variance from gyros in z-axis

(*continued*)

Table 2. (*continued*)

Sum from accelerations in x-axis	Sum from accelerations in y-axis	Sum from accelerations in z-axis	Sum from gyros in x-axis	Sum from gyros in y-axis	Sum from gyros in z-axis
Energy from accelerations in x-axis	Energy from accelerations in y-axis	Energy from accelerations in z-axis	Energy from gyros in x-axis	Energy from gyros in y-axis	Energy from gyros in z-axis

All values from the maximum to the energy were extracted and finally formed a 1 row by 42 column matrix (Table 3).

Table 3. The features extracted in each document

Maximum (*1* row by 6 column)	Minimum (*1* row by 6 column)	Median absolute deviation (*1* row by 6 column)	Mean value (*1* row by 6 column)	Variance (*1* row by 6 column)	Sum (*1* row by 6 column)	Energy (*1* row by 6 column)

Next, the authors used the same procedure to calculate the values mentioned above in others documents.

Add up all 1 row by 42 column matrices in each kind of movement in each group. For example, in the training group, the number of documents of falling down is 8, so add up that 81 row by 42 column matrices to form an 8 row by 42 column matrix. Table 4 shows the exact number of row and column of all movements.

Table 4. The number of row and column of all movements

Movement	Training group		Testing group	
	Number of rows	Number of columns	Number of rows	Number of columns
Falling down	8	42	7	42
Jumping	6	42	6	42
Playing	16	42	15	42
Pushing	30	42	29	42
Pushing down	22	42	21	42
Running	5	42	4	42
Shoulder-hit	15	42	15	42
Standing	6	42	5	42
Walking	6	42	5	42

Add all the 9 matrices in the training group into one sum-up matrix, as well as all the 9 matrices in testing group. Then, a 114 row by 42 column matrix $\mathbf{A}_{144\times42}$ and a 107 row by 42 column matrix $\mathbf{A}_{107\times42}$ were built.

Two transition matrices T_1 and T_2 were produced by using PCA (Principal Component Analysis).

The matrix after dimensionality reduction was created by multiplying the sum-up matrix and the transition matrix, written as M_1 and M_2.

$$M_1 = A_{144 \times 42} \times T_1 \tag{1}$$

$$M_2 = A_{107 \times 42} \times T_2 \tag{2}$$

The authors then constructed two n row by 2 column matrices which referred to the two sum-up matrices M_1 and M_2, respectively. Bullying behaviors (pushing, pushing down and shoulder-hit) matched matrix [1 0] while non-bullying behaviors (falling down, jumping, playing, running, shaking, standing and walking) matched matrix [0 1]. Two 0-1 matrices were got (written as Z_1 and Z_2, respectively).

A k-NN model NET was created with input dimension NIN, output dimension NOUT and k neighbours where k is a user-defined constant.

Took a matrix X of input vectors (one vector per row) and uses the k-NN rule on the training data contained in NET to produce a matrix Y of outputs and a matrix L of classification labels.

Two-fold cross validation was used to calculate the accuracy, i.e., in the first round, the training group was used to train the classifier and the testing group was used to test the classifier, but in the second round, the testing group was used to train the classifier and the training group was used to test the classifier. The accuracies of the two rounds were recorded as Accuracy$_1$ and Accuracy$_2$, respectively. Then the final accuracy was calculated as

$$\text{Accuracy} = \frac{1}{2}(\text{Accuracy}_1 + \text{Accuracy}_2) \tag{3}$$

Change the value of k, and repeat the steps above. The simulation results are given in Sect. 4.

Compared with Seyed Ali's team [6] and other teams [9, 10], the accuracies achieved were not better, so the authors decided to add 2 kinds of features into the features aggregation. The 2 features were the sum vectors of the absolute value of acceleration and the angle of gyroscope. The simulation results are also given in Sect. 4 as a comparison.

3 Speech Emotion Recognition

Nowadays, speech emotion recognition is a very popular topic. In the field of artificial intelligence, a system that is able to recognize the voice of a consumer and to control a robot's movements with verbal instructions has been developed [11]. However, most of the speech emotion recognition has not been used in detecting bullying behaviors. Considering that it is significant to prevent bullying as soon as possible, the authors also used k-NN to detect verbal bullying.

The following is the concrete procedure in speech emotion recognition.

(1) The data were collected by Ye in Finland, too. Several pupils provided the sound recording in 4 kinds, namely, bullying, cry, happy and normal. The pupils were asked to pretend that they were under these circumstances so that the data were divided by class in advance.

(2) The authors finally gathered hundreds of seconds of sound recordings, and cut them equally into hundreds of parts. These data were divided into 4 classes— bullying, cry, happy and normal. Bullying and cry were classified into bullying while happy and normal were classified into non-bullying for convenience. These data were in form of mp4.

(3) These two groups of data were equally and randomly divided into 2 groups (the training group and the testing group), and in each of them there were 80 s bullying recordings and 81 s non-bullying recordings.

(4) The authors then extracted the feature parameters from the selected voice sequences by using the MFCC (Mel Frequency Cepstral Coefficients).

$$\text{Mel}(f) = 2595 \times \lg\left(1 + \frac{f}{700}\right) \tag{4}$$

12 MFCC parameters, 12 first-order differential MFCCs and 12 second-order differential MFCCs were extracted and classified by k-NN. The classification results are also given in Sect. 4.

4   Classification Results

Table 5 shows the first activity recognition accuracy ($k = 1$). Table 6 shows the average accuracy of physical bullying detection ($k = 1$–6), indicating that the accuracy was the highest when k equaled to 1. Nevertheless, the highest average accuracy ass 52.8%, which is not high enough.

Table 5. Accuracy of physical bullying detection ($k = 1$)

	Bullying	Non-bullying
Bullying (real)	55.5%	45.5%
Non-bullying (real)	50.0%	50.0%

Table 6. Average accuracy of physical bullying detection (k = 1–6)

The value of k	1	2	3	4	5	6
Accuracy	52.8%	32.9%	20.0%	16.2%	8.7%	4.8%

Table 7 shows the activity recognition accuracy after adding 2 kinds of sum vectors ($k = 1$). And Table 8 shows the average activity recognition accuracy after adding 2 kinds of sum vectors ($k = 1$–6). Similarly, when k equaled to 1, the accuracy was the highest, which is 70.4%, higher than the first one.

Table 7. Accuracy of physical bullying detection after adding 2 kinds of sum vectors ($k = 1$)

	Bullying	Non-bullying
Bullying (real)	72.4%	31.6%
Non-bullying (real)	27.6%	68.4%

Table 8. Average accuracy of physical bullying detection after adding 2 sum vectors ($k = 1$–6)

The value of k	1	2	3	4	5	6
Accuracy	70.4%	50.5%	35.5%	19.0%	12.1%	7.8%

Table 9 shows the accuracy of speech emotion recognition ($k = 1$). Table 10 shows the average accuracy of speech emotion recognition ($k = 1$–6). The highest average accuracy is 78.0%, a bit higher than that of the activity detection.

Table 9. The accuracy of speech emotion recognition ($k = 1$)

	Bullying	Non-bullying
Bullying (real)	74.5%	18.5%
Non-bullying (real)	35.5%	81.5%

Table 10. The average accuracy of speech emotion recognition ($k = 1$–6)

The value of k	1	2	3	4	5	6
Accuracy	78.0%	62.5%	47.6%	34.7%	16.8%	8.5%

5   Discussion and Conclusion

Considering that physical bullying and verbal bullying have the worst impact on teenagers among all school bullying types but most of the existing anti-bullying methods are unrealistic and inconvenient, this paper applied an algorithm to detect physical bullying and verbal bullying events automatically. Time domain features and frequency domain features of activities and MFCC features of speeches were extracted to describe the characteristics of bullying events. k-NN was used as the classifier. A preliminary result of 52.8% of activity recognition was achieved, which was not satisfying. After adding the sum of the absolute value of acceleration and the angle of gyroscope, the accuracy was increased to 70.4%, indicating that the sum of the absolute value have a great impact on recognition. Additionally, the authors thought that speech emotion recognition could play a better role in bullying detection since the accuracy of speech emotion recognition was higher than that of the activity recognition. Gathering more samples to train the classifier might be helpful for improving recognition accuracy in future work.

Acknowledgements. This work was supported by the National Natural Science Foundation of China (61602127). The authors would like to thank the pupils from the second and the sixth grades who acted in the school bullying experiments.

References

1. Kim, Y.S., Leventhal, B.: Bullying and suicide. A review. Int. J. Adolesc. Med. Health **20**(2), 133–154 (2008)
2. Hinduja, S., Patchin, J.W.: Bullying, cyberbullying, and suicide. Arch. Suicide Res. **14**(3), 206–221 (2010)
3. Ye, L., Ferdinando, H., Seppänen, T., Alasaarela, E.: Physical violence detection for preventing school bullying. Adv. Artif. Intell. **2014**, f1–f9 (2014)
4. Ferdinando, H., Ye, L., Seppänen, T., et al.: Emotion recognition by heart rate variability. Aus. J. Basic Appl. Sci. Special **8**(14), 50–55 (2014)
5. Zalluhoglu, C., Ikizler-Cinbis, N.: Region based multi-stream convolutional neural networks for collective activity recognition. J. Vis. Commun. Image Represent. **60**, 170–179 (2019)
6. Rokni, S.A., Ghasemzadeh, H.: Autonomous training of activity recognition algorithms in mobile sensors: a transfer learning approach in context-invariant views. Hassan Source IEEE Trans. Mob. Comput. **17**(8), 1764–1777 (2018)
7. Chen, L.M., Nugent, C.D., Wang, H.: A knowledge-driven approach to activity recognition in smart homes. IEEE Trans. Knowl. Data Eng. **24**(6), 961–974 (2012)
8. Wongpatikaseree, K., Ikeda, M., Buranarach, M., Supnithi, T., Lim, A.O., Tan, Y.: Activity recognition using context-aware infrastructure ontology in smart home domain. KICSS **2012**, 50–57 (2012)
9. Liangying, P., Ling, C., Menghan, W., et al.: Complex activity recognition using acceleration, vital sign, and location data. Gencai Source IEEE Trans. Mob. Comput. **18**(7), 1488–1498 (2019)
10. Uddin, M.Z., Kim, J.: Human activity recognition using spatiotemporal 3-D body joint features with hidden markov models. KSII Trans. Internet Inf. Syst. **10**(6), 2767–2780 (2016)
11. Shuaibu, A.N., Abdullahi, Z.H., Buhari, M.D.: Mobile robot voice recognition in control movements. Int. J. Comput. Sci. Electron. (IJCSEE) **3**(1) (2015). ISSN: 2320–4028

Speech Bullying Vocabulary Recognition Algorithm in Artificial Intelligent Child Protecting System

Tong Liu[1,2,3], Liang Ye[1,4(✉)], Tian Han[2,4], Yue Li[3,5],
and Esko Alasaarela[4]

[1] Department of Information and Communication Engineering,
Harbin Institute of Technology, Harbin 150080, China
yeliang@hit.edu.cn
[2] School of Software and Micro Electronics,
Harbin University of Science and Technology, Harbin 150080, China
[3] Key Laboratory of Police Wireless Digital Communication,
Ministry of Public Security, Harbin 150080, China
[4] Health and Wellness Measurement Research Group, OPEM Unit,
University of Oulu, 90014 Oulu, Finland
[5] Electrical Engineering School, Heilongjiang University, Harbin 150080, China

Abstract. With the continuous breakthrough of various technologies, speech recognition technology has become a research hotspot. It is a way to find out the phenomenon of bullying in time by detecting whether the voice contains campus bullying vocabulary. In practical applications, an infinite network is established through sensors to transmit information, and the occurrence of campus bullying events is prevented in time. This paper studies the theory of support vector machine and its application in speech recognition. In order to identify bullying vocabulary, this paper firstly built a voice library with 250 voice audios, including 125 campus bullying word audios and 125 non-bullying audios. The first sub-frame of the speech signal was used for endpoint detection. Then mode decomposition and Fourier transform were applied. The maximum value of the primary frequency spectrum was extracted as the acoustic feature. Finally, 200 audios in the database were used for training, and 50 audios were used for speech recognition testing. The average recognition accuracy was 94%, indicating that the support vector machine theory showed a good advantage in the case of small samples for speech recognition.

Keywords: Support vector machine · Empirical mode decomposition · Intrinsic mode function component

1 Introduction

With the continuous breakthrough of various technologies, speech recognition technology has become a research hotspot, and the methods of speech recognition technology are also very rich [1]. In this paper, the application of support vector machine theory in speech recognition is studied. Firstly, the speech signal is preprocessed, and

S. Han et al. (Eds.): AICON 2019, LNICST 287, pp. 158–164, 2019.
https://doi.org/10.1007/978-3-030-22971-9_14

then the acoustic features are extracted. The support vector machine hyper-plane and kernel function are optimized for speech recognition. The voice features are used for the training of the model, and finally the speech recognition system was identified and tested.

The remainder of this paper is organized as follow: Sect. 2 describes the procedures of 2 speech signal preprocessing and feature extraction; Sect. 3 analyzes the Support Vector Machine; Sect. 4 shows the simulation results; Sect. 5 draws a conclusion.

2 Speech Signal Preprocessing and Feature Extraction

2.1 Voice Signal Preprocessing

Firstly, the speech signal is pre-emphasized by a high-pass filter to improve the high-frequency part of the speech, reduce the amplitude range of the gene line, and reduce the dynamic range of the spectrum.

Secondly, the Hanning window is used to frame and window the speech signal. Finally, endpoint detection is performed on the speech signal. In order to solve the problem that the energy curve and the zero-crossing rate curve will fluctuate in the non-speech area, the data are subjected to median smoothing in the endpoint detection. The number of wild spots in the processed speech waveform is significantly reduced (Fig. 1).

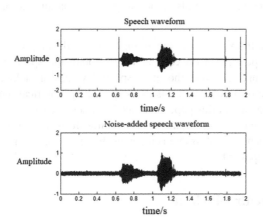

Fig. 1. Endpoint detection map for the "stupid" audio.

2.2 Speech Signal Feature Extraction

The Basic Principle of EMD. Treat the original signal $x(t)$ as a signal to be processed. Firstly, determine all the extreme points of the signal, and connect all the maxima and all the minima points with a cubic spline curve. The upper and lower envelopes of the original signal are obtained. The mean of the upper and lower envelopes is called as $m(t)$.

Subtract the upper and lower envelope mean values $m(t)$ from the pending signal $x(t)$:

$$h_1(t) = x(t) - m(t) \tag{1}$$

Verify that it is a basic mode component. If the two basic conditions are not met, it repeats the above operation as a signal to be processed until it is a basic mode weight.

$$c_1(t) = h_1(t) \tag{2}$$

After the first basic mode component is decomposed from the original signal, Subtract $c_1(t)$ from $x(t)$. The sequence of residual values is as follows:

$$r_1(t) = x(t) - c_1(t) \tag{3}$$

The $r_1(t)$ acts as a new raw signal. Repeat the above process for $r_1(t)$, and get n basic mode weights. Thus, the original signal is decomposed into the sum of several basic mode components and a remainder.

$$x(t) = \sum_{i=1}^{n} c_1(t) + r_n(t) \tag{4}$$

If the last basic mode component $c_n(t)$ is less than the threshold, the procedure will stop. In addition, the procedure also stops when the remaining component becomes a monotonic function.

Feature Selection. In this scheme, the empirical mode decomposition and the Fourier transform are first performed on each audio to obtain the spectrum of the intrinsic modal function component, and the main spectral values are taken for training and testing. Each frame of a voice audio is decomposed by empirical mode to resolve six basic mode components. In this paper, the first 7 frames in each audio are selected, and the basic mode weight in each frame is Fourier transformed. The maximum value of each mode component in each frame is taken as the main spectrum value of the natural mode function component.

3   Support Vector Machine

3.1   Support Vector Machine and Kernel Function

In the state where the training samples are linearly separable, a classification hyperplane can be found. The convex quadratic programming at this time can be transformed by (5) [2]:

$$\begin{cases} \left\{ \max_{\alpha} \sum_{i=1}^{n} \alpha_i - \frac{1}{2} \sum_{i,j=1}^{n} \alpha_i \alpha_j x_i x_j \langle x_i, x_j \rangle \right. \\ s.t. \\ \sum_{i=1}^{n} \alpha_i y_i = 0, \alpha_i \geq 0, i = 1, 2, \ldots, n \end{cases} \tag{5}$$

where α_i is the Lagrange multiplier.

$$f(x, w, b) = sign(<w, x> + b) = sign\left(\sum_{i=1}^{n} \alpha_i y_i \langle x_i, x \rangle + b \right) \tag{6}$$

where x_i is called Support Vector.

Some sample data are linearly separable in the input space, but some are not. After the dimensionally indistinguishable sample data is subjected to dimensionality reduction, it can be transformed into linearly separable sample data [3]. However, dimensionality reduction also has some shortcomings, such as losing useful information. Compared with the dimension reduction method, the kernel function method is much better. The kernel function is to map these linearly inseparable sample data into a high-dimensional space through a kernel function. In this high-dimensional space, these linearly inseparable samples are converted into linearly separable samples.

The main types of kernel functions are: linear kernel function, polynomial kernel function, S-type growth curve kernel function, and tensor product kernel function [4].

3.2 Sequence Minimum Optimization Algorithm

In the support vector machine theory, the problem to be optimized is [5]:

$$\begin{cases} \max_{\alpha} W(\alpha) = \sum_{i}^{m} \alpha_i - \frac{1}{2} \sum_{i,j=1}^{m} y^i y^j \alpha_i \alpha_j \langle x^i, x^j \rangle \\ s.t.\ 0 \leq \alpha_i \leq C, i = 1, \ldots, m \\ \sum_{i=1}^{m} \alpha_i y^i = 0 \end{cases} \tag{7}$$

Constraints can be obtained from Eq. (7):

$$\alpha_1 y^1 = -\sum_{i=2}^{m} \alpha_i y^i \tag{8}$$

Because $y \in \{-1, 1\}$, the formula (8) can be written as:

$$\alpha_1 = -y^1 \sum_{i=2}^{m} \alpha_i y^i \tag{9}$$

It can be known from Eq. (9) that α_1 and $\alpha_2, \ldots, \alpha_m$ are associated, so at least two variables must be selected at a time to satisfy the constraint [6]. Choose the best pair of combinations α_i, α_j based on experience, then all parameters except the α_i, α_j are fixed and optimized. Therefore, the efficiency of the SMO (Sequence Minimum Optimization) algorithm is relatively high [7].

Figure 2 shows the value of α_i, α_j and the relationship between them.

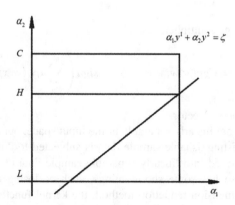

Fig. 2. The relationship of α_i, α_j

4   Classification Result

4.1   Influence of Different Kernel Functions on Training Accuracy

K-fold cross-validation solves the problem of generating more test samples [8]. Using the K-fold cross-validation method, the original data set was equally divided into 5 parts, each with 50 audio samples, and a total of 5 rounds of model training and testing were performed.

The effect of using three different kernel functions on training is shown in Table 1.

Table 1. Influence of different kernel functions on training accuracy

Kernel function type	1	2	3	4	5	Training accuracy
Polynomial kernel function	75.3%	76.2%	80.5%	78.2%	75.5%	77.1%
Two-layer neural network kernel function	84.4%	85.3%	86.2%	87%	89.4%	86.5%
Radial kernel function	93.8%	96%	94.7%	93%	94.3%	94.4%

It can be seen from Table 1 that the training accuracy with the radial kernel function is significantly higher than those with the other two kernel functions.

4.2   Simulation Results

The training samples still use the data in Table 1. The testing accuracies of the training samples and the testing samples are shown in Table 2.

Table 2. Simulation results

Data set	1	2	3	4	5	Testing accuracy
Training samples	96.2%	95.9%	97.3%	95.2%	96%	96.1%
Testing samples	93.8%	96%	94.7%	93%	94.3%	94.4%

As can be seen from Table 2, the accuracy of the testing samples reached 94.4%. This is a good illustration of the fact that in the case of small samples, the use of support vector machine theory to solve the two-class problem is a very suitable method. The support vector machine successfully found the optimal classification hyper-plane to classify the samples.

The testing accuracy after SMO optimization is shown in Table 3.

Table 3. Simulation results

	1	2	3	4	5	Accuracy
Before optimization	93.8%	96%	94.7%	93%	94.3%	94.4%
After optimization	94.5%	96.2%	95.2%	94.1%	95.0%	95.0%

It can be seen from Table 3 that after parameter optimization, the accuracy of speech recognition is increased by 0.6%.

5   Conclusion

This paper proposed a speech bullying vocabulary recognition algorithm in artificial intelligent child protecting system. After preprocessing the speech signal, the empirical mode decomposition method is used to extract the IMF of each order mode component, and then the main frequency value of the IMF is separated by Fourier transformation as the feature vector.

Through the K-fold cross-validation method, more training data were generated in the case of a small sample, and a total of five recognition tests were performed. The effects of three different kernel functions on the recognition accuracy rate were tested. The recognition rate of the radial kernel function was the highest, and the recognition accuracy reached 94.4%.

Finally, the model is optimized and the sequence minimum optimization algorithm is adopted. The SMO optimization algorithm not only improves the efficiency, but also improves the accuracy of the recognition test by 0.6%. The optimized recognition accuracy reached 95%.

Acknowledgement. This work was supported by the National Natural Science Foundation of China (61602127), the Basic scientific research project of Heilongjiang Province (KJCXZD201704), the Key Laboratory of Police Wireless Digital Communication, Ministry of Public Security (2018JYWXTX01), and partly by the Harbin research found for technological innovation (2013RFQXJ104) national education and the science program during the twelfth five-year plan (FCB150518). The authors would like to thank all the people who participated in the project.

References

1. Weidang, L., Yi, G., Xin, L., Jiaying, W., Hong, P.: Collaborative energy and information transfer in green wireless sensor networks for smart cities. IEEE Trans. Ind. Inform. **14**(4), 1585–1593 (2017)
2. Zhiyuan, T., Lantian, L., Dong, W., Ravichan-der, V.: Collaborative joint training with multitask recurrent model for speech and speaker recognition. IEEE/ACM Trans. Audio Speech Lang. Process. **25**(3), 493–504 (2017)
3. Shu-sen, Z., Qing-cai, C., Xiao-long, W.: Convolutional deep networks for visual data classification. Neural Process. Lett. **38**(20), 17–27 (2013)
4. Mrazova, I., Kukacka, M.: Image classification with growing neural networks. Int. J. Comput. Theory Eng. **5**(3), 422–427 (2013)
5. Han, B., Davis, L.S.: Intelligent video surveillance systems and technology, pp. 79–103 (2010)
6. Geoffery, E.H., Salakhutdinov, R.R.: Reducing the dimensionality of data with neural networks. Science **313**(5786), 504–507 (2006)
7. Vapnik V.N.: The Nature of Statistical Learning Theory, pp. 131–145. Springer (2000)
8. Larochelle, H., Mandel, M., Pascanu, R., et al.: Learning algorithm for the classification restricted Boltzmann machine. J. Mach. Learn. Res. **13**, 643–669 (2012)

Cross Station-Voltage-Level Route Planning Algorithm for System Protection Services in UHV Grid

Danyang Xu[✉], Peng Yu, Wenjing Li, Xuesong Qiu,
and Luoming Meng

State Key Laboratory of Networking and Switching Technology,
Beijing University of Posts and Telecommunications,
Beijing 100876, People's Republic of China
623094588@qq.com

Abstract. Since the current route planning algorithms for system protection service in communication network fail to consider the situation of station voltage level crossing in ultra-high voltage grid, based on immune algorithm, a planning algorithm is proposed in this paper to lower the network operational risk by ensuring the voltage level balance degree and main-backup route similarity are both as small as possible. Firstly, the risk of node and link is analyzed to derive the network risk balance degree index, and secondly, the cross station-voltage-level planning problem model is established with the consideration of impact brought by station voltage level crossing and route similarity, and then it is solved utilizing IA. Finally, the experimental result shows that the planning algorithm proposed in this paper can lower the network risk, station voltage level balance degree and the route similarity effectively, which provides a useful reference while planning service routing.

Keywords: Service route planning · Immune algorithm ·
UHV grid · Risk balance

1 Introduction

Due to the construction and expansion of UHV grid in China, traditional power system protection strategies and methods have gradually failed to meet the needs. Thus system protection using the latest information communication and protection control technologies is proposed based on profound characteristics changes of the transitional power grid, and its high reliability is built by strengthening the first defense line, expanding the second defense line, and connecting the third defense line to achieve high-security new generation of large-scale UHV grid defense system.

In order to realize this kind of intelligent protection for UHV power transmit grid, the dedicated real-time high-speed power communication network supporting system protection services, such as relay protection services and stability control services etc.,

S. Han et al. (Eds.): AICON 2019, LNICST 287, pp. 165–180, 2019.
https://doi.org/10.1007/978-3-030-22971-9_15

is constructed. The most striking feature of the system protection service is that its source and terminal stations are almost high-voltage level. It should be aware that the station in this paper does not mean substation but network equipment in it, which is used for communication. There are main and backup routes for each system protection service, and it will not change readily once set up to ensure the stability of the system, thus, reasonable planning of service routes is the key to not only achieve fast and reliable transmission of services but also improve the utilization of communication resources and reduce the risk of the communication networks.

There are some researches on the routing planning problem of power communication networks at present. Liu et al. proposes a non-uniform service routing energy model for the typical structure of power communication network, which considering the service importance and its configuration method [1], but it does not consider the importance of nodes and links. Huang et al. combines the pressure of service transmission channels and the special constraints of power communication network and proposes a maximum disjoint main-backup routing mechanism based on multi-condition constraints [2], however it does not consider the delay characteristics of the services, and its consideration of service risk is insufficient. He et al. adopts the improved maximum disjoint dual routing algorithm for planning [3], but neither the reliability nor the time domain was considered, what's more, it is ineffective while more factors appear.

It is necessary to transmit services through the low voltage level station while there is no direct communication line laid between the high voltage level stations in most of UVH grid scenarios in China, thereby causes station-voltage-level crossing. In general, the lower the voltage level, the weaker the protection measures, and the greater the risk of carrying critical services on it. But these above-mentioned power communication network routing researches rarely have a consideration for this situation. Therefore, an in-depth cross station-voltage-level route planning approach is needed to strengthen the system operational security and reliability.

In view of the shortcomings of the existing research and the needs of system protection services, an intelligent cross station-voltage-level route planning algorithm considering the UHV's roundabout risk for system protection services in UHV grid is proposed in this paper. As a new type of artificial intelligence algorithm, immune algorithm, which is suitable for dealing with complex problems, has a big advantage over global search and has a good application prospect in optimization problems [4]. The follow-up structure of this paper is organized as follows: Sect. 2 derives the network risk balance degree index considering node and link risk, designs the voltage level balance degree and routing similarity index, and further establish the mathematical model of route planning. Section 3 proposes a main-backup route planning algorithm based on the immune algorithm to solve the problem. Section 4 utilizes the proposed algorithm to plan the service routes in a specific scenario and compares the optimal main-backup routes obtained by the proposed algorithm with the k-shortest path (KSP) algorithm and the maximum disjoint routing (Bhandari) algorithm. The scenario is excerpted from a partial communication topology in China. Section 5 concludes this paper and points out the future work.

2 Modeling of Planning Problem

In UHV grid, the higher the voltage level of the station, the farther the transmission distance is. The UHV DC transmission distance is about 1000 km [5]. Source and terminal stations of the system protection service are high-voltage levels, but sometimes communication with each other requires low voltage level stations for transit. The lower the voltage level of the passing station, the shorter the distance of transmission, the more stations will be needed. Relatively speaking, stations with high voltage level are better protected. Due to a large number of services transmitted by low voltage level stations and high risks, once a fault occurs, the impact is also greater. Therefore, it is necessary to select stations with similar voltage levels to transmit long-distance system protection services. In this paper, considering the factors of network risk, voltage level balance degree, and similarity of main and backup routes, a cross station-voltage-level route planning algorithm for UHV system protection service is proposed, which is the max disjoint main and backup routes for all services in the system protection communication network to ensure the safe and stable operation of the communication network and the power grid.

In the system protection communication network, the nodes are generally various stations of the power grid, and the links are generally communication optical cables between the stations. In order to facilitate the research, the power communication network is abstracted into an undirected connectivity graph $G(V, E)$ according to the graph theory method, where V represents the node set, E represents the link set, and the number of links is $|E| = M$, the number of nodes is $|V| = N$. The service set $S = \{s_1, ..., s_k\}$ represents all the power communication network services carried on the network G, and the route of the service is the node and the link set passed by the source node v_s to the terminal node v_d.

2.1 Network Risk Model

Node Risk and Link Risk. The node and link, which are the basis for assessing the network risk, play a vital role to guarantee the stability running of service in power communication network. Their respective risk indexes contain the probability of failure and the risk impact on the network after a failure [6]. According to the risk definition, the risk index of node v_i and link e_{ij} can be expressed as

$$R_i^V(t) = P_i^V(t)I(v_i) \tag{1}$$

$$R_{ij}^E(t) = P_{ij}^E(t)I(e_{ij}) \tag{2}$$

Where $P_i^V(t)$ and $P_{ij}^E(t)$ are the probabilities of node and link failure, respectively. $I(v_i)$ and $I(e_{ij})$ are risk impact of link and node failure, respectively. We utilize the service pressure and importance of node and link to reflect impact.

Failure Risk Impaction. In the power communication network, since each node and link carry different types and different numbers of services, it is necessary to consider the service distribution influence on network risks. Besides, there are differences of importance degree between different nodes and links. The severity of the fault events is different, and the impact degree on the network operational level is also different. To analyze the impact of failure, we will evaluate the impact from two aspects: service pressure and communication equipment importance degree. The formulas are as follows.

$$I(v_i) = D(v_i)NP(v_i) \tag{3}$$

$$I(e_{ij}) = D(e_{ij})NP(e_{ij}) \tag{4}$$

Where $D(v_i)$, $D(e_{ij})$ are the importance degree of node and link, respectively. $NP(v_i)$, $NP(e_{ij})$ are the service pressure of node and link, respectively.

Service Pressure. Various power communication services have different influences on the safe and stable operation of the power system, and the security requirements are also different [7]. Service importance degree is a vital evaluation index for analyzing the impact of power communication services on the power grid [8], which can be quantified with the type of business. For example, if the relay protection service and the security and stability control service only lose a small flow, it may bring huge troubles to the power system. So, the higher the importance degree of service the more serious impact on the power grid its interruption.

The service pressure of node/link is introduced to indicate the impact while fault occurs. The node's service pressure index $NP(v_i)$ and the link's service pressure index $NP(e_{ij})$ are concerned with the number of services carried on each node and each link as well as the importance of the service. If the index is higher, the service carried on each node and each link is more important, the distribution of the service is more unevenly, the failure consequence is worse, and the risk is higher. They can be expressed as:

$$NP(v_i) = \sum\nolimits_{s_k \in V_{S_i}} n_i^V(s_k) \cdot Z_k \tag{5}$$

$$NP(e_{ij}) = \sum\nolimits_{s_k \in E_{S_{ij}}} n_{ij}^E(s_k) \cdot Z_k \tag{6}$$

Z_k is the service importance of the service type k, $n_i^V(s_k)$ and $n_{ij}^E(s_k)$ are the services number of the service type k carried on the node v_i and link e_{ij}, and V_{S_i} and $E_{S_{ij}}$ are the service types carried on the node v_i and link e_{ij}, respectively.

The pressure indexes consider the difference of the service importance and the service number carried on the nodes and links, which evaluates the risk impacts of the services reasonably.

Communication Equipment Importance Degree. Studies have shown that it often leads to the collapse of the entire power communication network after some important nodes and links are attacked and failed in the power communication network [9]. The higher the position of the nodes or links in the network topology, the greater the impact of the fault. Therefore, we utilize node importance degree and link importance degree to assess the critical degree of nodes and links, which can reasonably reflect their position in the network.

The stations with different voltage levels may have different ranking and different importance degree. For example, a 500 kV station that has a higher voltage level than a 220 kV station, has a higher importance degree, because the service's security running on the 500 kV station has larger impact on the stable operation of power system. So, node importance degree is concerned with the node voltage level, and link importance degree is also concerned with the node voltage level at both ends.

In addition, the betweenness of node $B(v_i)$ is defined as the proportion of the number of shortest paths through vi relative to the number of the all shortest paths in the network [10]. It is more accurate and reasonable that node utilizes the betweenness as an important index to reflect its importance degree. Link utilizes $B(e_{ij})$ to reflect its importance degree as well.

Based on the above analysis, we evaluate node importance degree from two aspects: the voltage level of the node and the betweenness of node.

Since the betweenness of node and voltage level belong to different dimensions, normalization is required. Suppose that there are stations with different voltage levels in the network, record as a set $L = \{l_1, l_2 \ldots l_z\}$, and $l_i \in L$ is different voltage values (unit: kV). In this paper, the Min-Max standardization method is used to normalize different levels of stations, as follows:

$$w_i = \frac{l_i - l_{\min}}{l_{\max} - l_{\min}} \tag{7}$$

Where, $l_{\min}$ and $l_{\max}$ are the minimum and maximum values of the station voltage, respectively, and w_i is the normalized value for l_i.

Combined with the analysis of the node importance impact indexes, the node importance $D(v_i)$ can be obtained as follows:

$$D(v_i) = \sum_{i=1}^{N} w_i B(v_i) \tag{8}$$

Where N is the node number, w_i is the voltage level, and $B(v_i)$ is the betweenness of node.

We evaluate link importance degree from two aspects: (1) the voltage level at both ends of the link, (2) the betweenness of link. Normalization processing is described in the same Eq. (7), and the link importance degree $D(e_{ij})$ can be obtained as follows:

$$D(e_{ij}) = \sum_{i=1}^{M} \max\{w_i, w_j\} B(e_{ij}) \tag{9}$$

Where M is link number, w_i and w_j are the voltage level at both ends of the link, $B(e_{ij})$ is the betweenness of link.

The node and link importance indexes consider the betweenness and voltage level which can reasonably describe their importance.

Network Risk Balance Degree. The balance degree of risk distribution of node and link in the network can reflect the relative rationality of the network configuration. The large value of the network risk balance degree indicates the risk are distributed unevenly, that is, the risk is excessively concentrated. If the node or link with high-risk faults, it will have a major impact on the services in the network. Therefore, we evaluate the overall network risk $RBD(t)$ at time t with the risk balance degree of nodes and links, which is defined as follows.

$$RBD(t) = \sqrt{\frac{1}{N}\sum_{v_i \in V}\left(R_i^V(t) - \overline{R_i^V(t)}\right)^2} + \sqrt{\frac{1}{M}\sum_{e_{ij} \in E}\left(R_{ij}^E(t) - \overline{R_{ij}^E(t)}\right)^2} \quad (10)$$

$$\overline{R_i^V(t)} = \frac{1}{N}\sum_{i=1}^{n}R_i^V(t) \quad (11)$$

$$\overline{R_{ij}^E(t)} = \frac{1}{M}\sum_{i=1}^{M}R_{ij}^E(t) \quad (12)$$

Where $\overline{R_i^V(t)}$ and $\overline{R_{ij}^E(t)}$ are the average cost value of the nodes and links risk balance degree, respectively. N is the number of nodes, and M is the number of links.

2.2   Voltage Level Balance Degree

According to the characteristics of cross station-voltage-level of the system protection services, we select stations with same voltage level for each service as much as possible in the route planning. In this paper, the sum of the voltage level's standard deviations of nodes that each service passes through is regarded as the measure of the cross-impact of the node's voltage level. This index called the routing voltage level balance degree $VBD(t)$, has the following formula:

$$VBD(t) = \sum_{s_k \in S}\sqrt{\frac{1}{n}\sum_{i=1}^{n}(w_i - \overline{w_i})^2} \quad (13)$$

Where w_i is the normalized voltage level of the node that each service passes through, $\overline{w_i}$ is the average of the normalized voltage levels of the node that each service passes through, and n is the number of nodes that each service passes through.

2.3   Similarity Between Main and Backup Routes

The dual-route configuration is to further ensure the reliability of the service. When the main route fails, the system can quickly switch to the backup route, rising the ability to tackle emergencies and ensure the network security and reliability running. If the main route and backup route are dissimilar or approximately dissimilar, the above advantages can be maximized [11]. The main and backup routes may contain the same nodes and links that cannot be avoided, we try to select the most different main and backup route. We utilize similarity to represent the relationship between the main and backup routes. Because main and backup routes with higher similarity have more common elements, failure probability at the same time is extremely higher and the service risk is higher as well. The similarity of main and backup routes is determined by the link similarity and the node similarity. In reality, the probability of link failure is much higher than the probability of node failure [12], so we only consider the link similarity. The formula is as follows:

$$SD_k = \frac{2 \times ol_k}{l_k} \tag{14}$$

Where SD_k is the routing similarity of the service type k, ol_k is the number of overlapping links of main and backup routes, and l_k is the total number of links of the main and backup routes.

2.4 Objective Functions

In order to reduce the operational risk of the network, we propose a route planning algorithm. For main route, we consider the impact of service pressure and node and link importance degree. Besides, the characteristics of voltage level crossing of the node are considered as well. Then, the minimum weighted sum of the network risk balance degree and voltage level balance degree is formulated as the objective functions of the main route:

$$P(m) = \frac{\min[\alpha RBD + (1 - \alpha)VBD]}{s.t. \; \forall s_k, t_k^\gamma \leq T_{\max}^k} \tag{15}$$

t_k^γ is the main route time delay of the service s_k, $T_{\max}^k$ is the max time delay of service s_k. For backup route, besides considering the same objective of the main route, it is necessary to take additional consideration for the relationship between main and backup routes, and select the backup route with the lowest similarity to the main route. The objective function of the backup route is as follows:

$$P(b) = \min \left\{ [\alpha RBD + (1 - \alpha)VBD] \times e^{\sum\limits_{s_k \in S} SD_k} \right\} \\ s.t \; \forall s_k, t_k^\varphi \leq T_{\max}^k \tag{16}$$

t_k^φ is the backup route time delay of service s_k.

3 Route Planning Algorithm

3.1 Description of Planning Algorithm

The analysis shows that the main and backup routing planning is an NP-Hard problem [13]. For such problems, the shortest path algorithm cannot give an effective planning scheme in the limited time, but the artificial intelligence algorithm performs well. Among them, the immune algorithm, as an artificial intelligence algorithm, has advantages in time convergence and stability [14]. Therefore, we propose a main and backup route planning algorithm based on immune algorithm. Because main and backup route planning objectives are different, we utilize the immune algorithm to plan the main route for all services firstly, map the main route of the service to the graph G secondly, and then utilize the immune algorithm to plan the backup route of all services again. The procedure of cross station-voltage-level main and backup route algorithm is:

Step 1. Abstract the power communication network as $G(V, E)$ utilizing graph theory, where V is a set of nodes and E is a set of communication links.

Step 2. Set the service list $S(v_s, v_d, p_1, p_2)$, where v_s, v_d are the source and terminal node respectively; p_1, p_2 are the main and backup routes respectively.

Step 3. Take $P(m)$ as the planning objective, the service time delay does not exceed the upper limit as constraint, the optimal main route for each service in S is selected through immune algorithm.

Step 4. Output the main route for each service, as well as the $RRD(t)$ and $VBD(t)$, and get a new topology G'.

Step 5. For G', takes $P(b)$ as the planning objective, the latency of service does not exceed the upper limit as the constraint, and the IA is utilized again to select the optimal backup route for each service in S.

Step 6. Output the backup route for each service, as well as the $RRD(t)$ and $VBD(t)$.

3.2 Procedure of Immune Algorithm

The procedure of the immune algorithm utilized in this paper is described as follows.

Step 1: Set the algorithm parameters. The antibody population size is set to N_q and the number of memory cells is set to N_m, and the maximum iteration is max.

Step 2: Initialize the antibody population. The data of the system protection communication network to be planned is imported, and N_q antibodies are generated as the initial antibody group $A(t)$, and the index of iterations t is set to 0. At this time, the memory is empty and needs to be generated randomly.

Step 3: Calculate the affinity and similarity between each antibody and the antigen in the above antibody population, and then calculate the antibody concentration Con and the selection probability P_a. The N_m antibodies with the best affinity were stored in the memory antibodies.

Step 4: Immunization. The selection probability of each antibody in the antibody group $A(t)$ is calculated and ranked in descending order of the selection probability P_a, and the first N_x antibodies were taken as the parent population $F(t)$. Then the parent antibody group is cloned, mutated, and then the local vaccine is injected proportionally to generate a new antibody population. Finally, the memory antibody in the memory library is added to form a new antibody group $A(t + 1)$.

Step 5: Evaluation. If $t = $ max, output the optimal solution $A(t)$; otherwise, set $t = t+1$, and then back to step 3.

3.3 Antibody Encoding

The antibody is encoded by natural number coding, and each service route is regarded as a gene of the antibody. The length of the antibody is the number of the service, and each possible optimization strategy corresponds to one antibody. Since the number of nodes and links included in the main and backup routes is unknown, the variable length antibody coding method is utilized in this paper. The first of the antibody gene is encoded as the source node of the service, and the next code is randomly selected from the nodes connected to it, and the process is repeated until the terminal node of the service is reached. For example, the antibody gene of a certain service from the source node S to the terminal node D is encoded as $SN_1N_2N_3...N_i D$.

3.4 Antibody Evaluation

Affinity. The affinity between antibody and antigen is used to evaluate the superiority of the antibody. In this problem, affinity functions of antibody in main and backup routes are different based on their optimization objective.

The affinity function S_a in main route is determined by the network risk and the voltage level balance degree, which is defined as follows:

$$f(S_a) = \frac{1}{P(m)} = \frac{1}{\alpha RBD(S_a) + (1 - \alpha)VBD(S_a)} \tag{17}$$

Similarly, the affinity function S_a in backup route is determined by the network risk, voltage level balance degree and routing similarity, which is defined as follows:

$$f(S_a) = \frac{1}{P(b)} = \frac{1}{[\alpha RBD(S_a) + (1 - \alpha)VBD(S_a)] \times e^{\sum_{k \in S} SD_k}} \tag{18}$$

Antibody Concentration. In order to avoid the algorithm to select the antibody with high similarity and fall into local optimization, this paper introduces the antibody concentration function [15]. The similarity between antibody S_a and antibody S_b is as follows:

$$Ratio(S_a, S_b) = \frac{f(S_a)}{f(S_b)} \tag{19}$$

The concentration $Con(S_a)$ of antibody S_a indicates the ratio of the antibody similar to S_a in antibody population and reflects the diversity of the antibody population. The formula is as follows.

$$Con(S_a) = \frac{\sum_{b=1}^{N_q} Sim(S_a, S_b)}{N_q} \tag{20}$$

$$Sim(S_a, S_b) = \begin{cases} 1, 1 - \gamma \leq Ratio(S_a, S_b) \leq 1 + \gamma \\ 0, Otherwise \end{cases} \tag{21}$$

Where N_q is the total number of antibodies, and $Sim(S_a, S_b)$ indicating whether the antibody S_a and the antibody S_b are similar. When there is any positive number γ such that $1 - \gamma \leq Ratio(S_a, S_b) \leq 1 + \gamma$ is satisfied, the antibody S_a is treated as similar with S_b, and thus $Sim(S_a, S_b)$ is 1, otherwise, it is 0.

3.5 Details of Immune Algorithm Solver

Clone. Clone the parent antibody population $P(t)$, and each antibody produces h copies to form a new population.

Variation. After cloning operation, some genes on the antibody are randomly altered with a small probability of mutation. The variation process designed in this paper is that a node from a certain antibody gene is regarded as a mutation point, but the source node and the terminal node of the service route are not regarded as mutation points. Then the route from the source node to the mutation point is guaranteed to be unchanged. The nodes connected with the mutation point are randomly selected till the terminal node.

Selection. It is necessary to ensure that antibodies with higher affinity are selected with greater probability when selecting antibodies, and the diversity of the progeny population should be ensured to avoid premature convergence. The selection operator is determined by the affinity between the antibody and the antigen and the antibody concentration. The greater the affinity of the antibody, the smaller the concentration, the greater the probability of being selected. Therefore, the selection probability of the antibody S_a is defined as follows:

$$P_a(S_a) = \frac{f(S_a)}{Con(S_a)} \tag{22}$$

Vaccine Extraction and Injection. The extraction and injection of the vaccine is carried out after each iteration. Extract the fixed gene sequence of the optimal antibody, and then inject into the antibody population in proportion, which can effectively suppress the degradation phenomenon in the mutation process and speed up the algorithm convergence.

4 Experimental Details

In order to verify the effectiveness of the proposed planning algorithm, we utilize the topology of the communication network in a certain region of China to conduct simulation experiments. Plan the main and backup routes for each service, and the network topology is shown in Fig. 1. There are three types of stations in the network, namely 1000 kV station, 750 kV station and 500 kV station, 33 nodes and 45 communication links. The network carries eight services, its specific data is shown in Table 1, and service importance degree is set according to [15].

Table 1. Service details

Service	Source	Terminal	Service importance
1	1	18	3
2	3	25	10
3	29	16	6
4	29	19	5
5	4	12	5
6	5	20	3
7	8	26	6
8	15	18	1

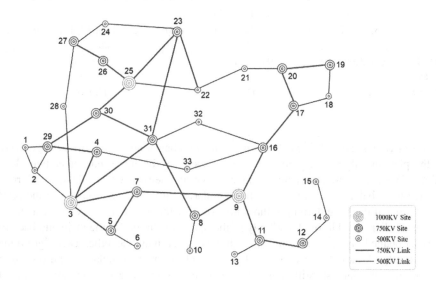

Fig. 1. Partial communication network topology in China

We collect various data from the network management equipment of the system protection communication network, including the time delay, the related fault records, etc. With the data, the failure probability of each node and link can be obtained according to the method in [16]. The planning algorithm proposed above is used to perform service routing planning for the foregoing services. In the immune algorithm, the antibody length is 8, the initial antibody population is set to 200, the number of memory cells is set to 20, the number of iterations is set to 300, the crossover rate is set to 0.8, and the mutation rate is set to 0.2, α is set to 0.5 while calculating affinity.

Compare the optimal main and backup routes obtained in this operation with the routes generated through the k-shortest path (KSP) algorithm [17] and the maximum disjoint routing (Bhandari) algorithm [3]. The main routing results are shown in Table 2, and the backup routing results are shown in Table 3.

Table 2. Main route planning result comparison of three different algorithms

S_i	KSP	IA	Bhandari
1	1, 29, 4, 33, 16, 17, 18	1, 29, 4, 33, 16, 17, 18	1, 29, 4, 33, 16, 17, 18
2	3, 2, 29, 30, 25	3, 31, 23, 25	3, 2, 29, 30, 25
3	29, 4, 33, 16	29, 30, 31, 32, 16	29, 4, 33, 16
4	29, 30, 25, 22, 21, 20, 19	29, 4, 33, 16, 17, 20, 19	29, 30, 25, 22, 21, 20, 19
5	4, 33, 16, 9, 11, 12	4, 29, 30, 31, 8, 9, 11, 12	4, 33, 16, 9, 11, 12
6	5, 7, 9, 16, 17, 20	5, 7, 3, 28, 27, 24, 23, 22, 21, 20	5, 7, 9, 16, 17, 20
7	8, 31, 30, 25, 26	8, 31, 23, 24, 27, 26	8, 31, 30, 25, 26
8	15, 14, 12, 11, 9, 7, 3, 28	15, 14, 12, 11, 9, 8, 31, 23, 24, 27, 28	15, 14, 12, 11, 9, 7, 3, 28
AVG delay	0.382 ms	0.415 ms	0.382 ms
Affinity	0.0026	0.0039	0.0026

From Tables 2 and 3, it can be seen that the number of nodes and the average delay of the planning algorithm proposed in this paper may be more than other two algorithms. This is because the planning algorithm comprehensively takes the network risk, voltage level balance degree and routing similarity into consideration, while the KSP algorithm and the Bhandari algorithm only consider the time delay so that the average time is smaller. In addition, the affinity of the optimal solution for the main and backup routes obtained by the planning algorithm is better than the other two algorithms significantly. Although the number of nodes and the average delay of the proposed algorithm is the largest, still satisfy the delay constraint. The indexes are compared among our algorithm and other two algorithms, as shown in Figs. 2 and 3.

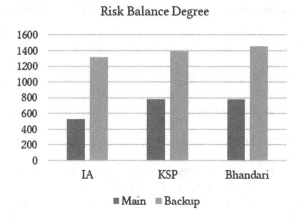

Fig. 2. Main-backup routing indexes (*RBD*)

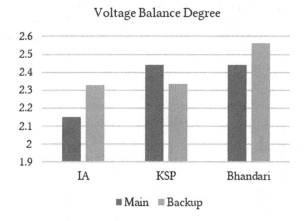

Fig. 3. Main-backup routing indexes (*VBD*)

The risk balance degree figure is a comparison of the *RBD* utilizing three algorithms. As for network risk, that of planning algorithm is the smallest and is decreased by 27% and 29% compared with the KSP algorithm and the Bhandari algorithm, which reflects the effectiveness of this algorithm. The figure on the right is a comparison of the *VBD* utilizing three algorithms. As for voltage level balance degree, it is reduced by 6% and 9% compared with the KSP algorithm and the Bhandari algorithm, which is also superior to the other two algorithms. Comparison of the similarity of main and backup routes of each service generated utilizing three algorithms is shown in Fig. 4.

From Fig. 4, it can be seen that the routing similarity of the 1st, 2nd, 3rd, and 7th services obtained by the planning algorithm are 0, and the similarities of the 4th, 5th, 6th, and 8th services are 0.11, 0.15, and 0.11, 0.29, respectively, which guarantee the maximum dissimilarity of the main and backup routes basically. The sum of the similarity of each service obtained by the planning algorithm, KSP algorithm, and

Table 3. Backup route planning result comparison of three different algorithms

S_i	KSP	IA	Bhandari
1	1, 29, 30, 31, 32, 16, 17, 18	1, 2, 29, 30, 31, 23, 22, 21, 20, 19, 18	1, 2, 29, 30, 25, 22, 21, 20, 19, 18
2	3, 2, 1, 29, 30, 25	3, 4, 29, 30, 25	3, 28, 27, 26, 25
3	29, 30, 31, 32, 16	29, 4, 33, 16	29, 30, 31, 32, 16
4	29, 4, 33, 16, 17, 18, 19	29, 30, 31, 23, 24, 27, 26, 25, 22, 21, 20, 17, 18, 19	29, 4, 33, 16, 17, 18, 19
5	4, 3, 7, 9, 11, 12	4, 29, 1, 2, 3, 28, 27, 24, 23, 22, 21, 20, 19, 18, 17, 16, 32, 31, 8, 9, 11, 12	4, 3, 7, 9, 11, 12
6	5, 3, 31, 32, 16, 17, 20	5, 7, 9, 8, 31, 32, 16, 17, 18, 19, 20	5, 3, 2, 29, 30, 25, 22, 21, 20
7	8, 31, 23, 25, 26	8, 9, 16, 17, 18, 19, 20, 21, 22, 23, 25, 26	8, 9, 7, 3, 28, 27, 26
8	15, 14, 12, 11, 9, 7, 5, 3, 28	15, 14, 12, 11, 9, 7, 5, 3, 2, 1, 29, 4, 33, 16, 17, 18, 19, 20, 21, 22, 23, 25, 26, 27, 28	15, 14, 12, 11, 9, 8, 31, 30, 25, 26, 27, 28
AVG delay	0.408 ms	0.533 ms	0.447 ms
Affinity	0.00059	0.0024	0.00059

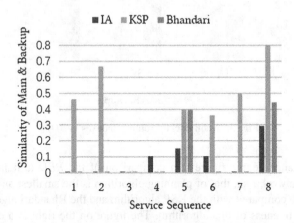

Fig. 4. Main-backup routing similarity

Bhandari algorithm is 0.65849, 3.1918, and 0.84444, respectively, which reflects the similarity of planning algorithm is greatly decreased compared with the KSP algorithm and is also better than the Bhandari algorithm. Although the KSP algorithm and the Bhandari algorithm have the smaller average delay, they can't plan the optimal main and backup routes from multiple aspects. Therefore, there is a large gap between the planning algorithm and other two algorithms.

Figure 5 shows the optimal solution in the antibody population after each iteration in this simulation. In this case study, the max number of the iteration is 300. And when the number of the iteration is around 50 and 250, the optimal solutions of main and backup routes is almost stable, which shows the planning algorithm has good convergence.

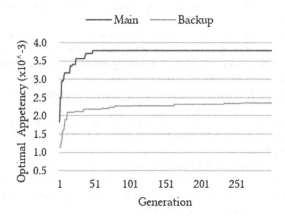

Fig. 5. Convergence graph of our algorithm

In summary, after the above analysis, the cross station-voltage-level planning algorithm can select main and backup routes with minimized risk and routing similarity under the constraint of delay, so as to reduce the overall operational risk of the network and provide a useful reference for network resource allocation optimization and service routing planning.

5 Conclusion and Future Works

Considering the UHV's roundabout risk level, this paper proposes a route planning algorithm based on immune algorithm for UHV communication network. Through considering the three major influencing factors, including network risk, voltage level balance degree and routing similarity, and constraint of the service delay, construct the cross station-voltage-level planning model and verify the effectiveness of it by simulation experiments. It has strong application value in routing planning and risk management of power communication network.

However, there are some imperfections in this paper. In the simulation experiment, it only considers that the source node and the terminal node are the same voltage level, and ignore the voltage level difference between them. Besides, the index lacks a unified evaluation scale. It is difficult to directly quantify and compare the evaluation results of different networks. The next step will be to consider the communication network routing planning problem with service endpoints at different voltage levels and establish a reasonable and standardized risk standard.

References

1. Liu, J., Huang, H., Zhang, Y., et al.: A route allocation method for power communication networks based on non-uniform service equalization. Electr. Power Inf. Commun. Technol. **15**, 103–108 (2017)
2. Huang, H., Tang, Y., Jiang, W.: Maximum disjoint routing mechanism of power communication network based on multiple constraints. Wirel. Interconnect Technol. **23**, 7–10+33 (2017)
3. He, Y., Chen, W., Zhang, W., et al.: A maximum disjoint dual routing configuration method for power communication network. Power Syst. Prot. Control **44**, 60–68 (2016)
4. Wang, W.: Application of artificial intelligence algorithm in elevator group control system. Electromech. Technol. **02**, 130–132 (2015)
5. Shu, Y., Chen, W.: Research and application of UHV power transmission in China. High Voltage **3**, 1–13 (2018)
6. Chen, X., Zhao, P., Yu, P., et al.: Risk analysis and optimization for communication transmission link interruption in Smart grid cyber-physical system. Int. J. Distrib. Sens. Netw. **14**(2), 1 (2018)
7. Wei, Z.: Design and application of power communication network planning algorithm based on service reliability. Beijing University of Posts and Telecommunications (2015)
8. Zheng, R., Zhao, Z., Liu, Z.: Route assignment algorithm for power communication services based on importance. Electr. Power Inf. **10**, 23–28 (2012)
9. Xie, Q., Deng, C.: Evaluation of importance of power network nodes based on right network model. Autom. Electr. Power Syst. **33**, 21–24 (2009)
10. Wang, L., Liu, Y., Gu, X., et al.: Network reconstruction considering node importance and line betweenness. Autom. Electr. Power Syst. **34**, 29–33 (2010)
11. Ni, M., Wang, W., Wu, X., et al.: Multi-constrained optimal routing and disjoint routing problems. Mil. Commun. Technol. **31**, 71–76 (2010)
12. Cai, W., Yang, H., Xiong, F., et al.: Service route optimization allocation method considering the reliability of power communication network. Power Grid Technol. **37**, 3541–3545 (2013)
13. Cao, H.: Summary of the "12th Five-Year" communication network planning of state grid corporation of China. Power Syst. Commun. **32**, 1–6 (2011)
14. Shi, Y.: Communication network planning and optimization method in smart grid. Beijing University of Posts and Telecommunications (2015)
15. Ji, C., Yu, P., Li, W., et al.: Comprehensive vulnerability assessment and optimization method of power communication network. In: The 2016 International Conference on Smart X, July 2016
16. Zhao, P., Yu, P., Ji, C., et al.: A routing optimization method based on risk prediction for communication services in smart grid. In: 2016 12th International Conference on Network and Service Management (CNSM), pp. 377–382 (2016)
17. Aggarwal, A., Schieber, B., Tokuyama, T.: Finding a minimum weight K-link path in graphs with Monge property and applications. In: 9th Symposium Computational Geometry, pp. 189–197 (1993)

An Efficient Implementation of Multi-interface SSD Controller on SoC

Yifei Niu⑩, Hai Cheng, Songyan Liu$^{(\boxtimes)}$, Huan Liu, Xiaowen Wang,
and Yanlin Chen

Heilongjiang University, Harbin 150076, China
{2171304, 2171309, 2171414, 2161359}@s.hlju.edu.cn,
{2002066, liusongyan}@hlju.edu.cn

Abstract. This paper designs a high-performance multi-interface SSD controller built on Xilinx SoC. An efficient firmware is also implemented, which is elaborate to cooperate with the hardware. Parallelism techniques, such as plane-level, die-level, chip-level and channel-level, are used for improving performance. The system has hard real-time performance of sequential writing, with the minimum bad block management and wear-leveling policy to balance performance and lifetime. A transparent encryption is proposed to guarantee high security storage, that is, connecting an AES-256 core and a RAID core with DMA engine in series. Performance evaluation of physical hardware shows that writing speed can exceed 100 MiB/sec for every logical channel which combines 8 NAND Flash chips.

Keywords: SSD · Pipeline · SoC · NAND Flash · Security · AES

1 Introduction

Solid state disk (SSD) has been favored not only by consumer electronics but also by enterprise, industry and military due to its high performance. The design of SSD needs to be extensible and optimizable for domain specific requirements [1]. Moreover, NAND flash needs to be carefully managed to extend lifetime and improve performance, which is the challenges of designing high-performance SSD for a special purpose [2]. System on Chip (SoC) is an excellent solution for SSD controller due to its well extensibility and programmability.

We will focus on two points in this SSD system. One is to design a high-performance SSD which gives full play to modern NAND Flash parallelism characters. There are many discussions about improving SSD performance by using various level parallel resources in the NAND Flash. Yan [3] and Kao [4] exploits to maximize effect of parallelism technologies by out-of-order commands schedule. Mao [5] proposes a new scheduler and exploits the high-level request characteristics and low-level parallelism of flash chips. Some research also analyze and contrast the performance and scalability of parallelism technologies in various levels [6]. For the architecture of this paper, processor and FPGA both work on different levels of parallelism resources to play their own advantages.

The other is to enhance the security of data. Transparent AES and RAID functions are built-in mechanisms to achieve this. At a more basic level, enhanced ECC, wear

© ICST Institute for Computer Sciences, Social Informatics and Telecommunications Engineering 2019
Published by Springer Nature Switzerland AG 2019. All Rights Reserved
S. Han et al. (Eds.): AICON 2019, LNICST 287, pp. 181–189, 2019.
https://doi.org/10.1007/978-3-030-22971-9_16

leveling and bad block management are implemented to against the restricted endurance of NAND Flash. Park [7] presents a dynamic wear leveling method based on circular queue and a hardware driven 2-channel 4-wafahuiy interleaving model. Chang [8] proposes a hierarchical block management method to reduce RAM space. Other various excellent approaches of this topic have also been proposed by experts.

The rest of this paper is organized as follows. System hardware architecture is described in Sect. 2. Software techniques such as bad block management and pipeline operations are detailed in Sect. 3. In Sect. 4, we analyze the performance under different configurations. Finally, Sect. 5 concludes this paper.

2 System Hardware Architecture

This system is designed to receive data from upper computer and store them to SSD via a high speed GTX bus, and download the data by a download board which provides multi-interface for reading data. The download board is also a test platform for the SSD to avoid connecting to real dedicated upper computer.

2.1 SSD Controller

The SSD controller uses Xilinx Kintex-7 series SoC. FPGA can interconnect multiple NAND chips and provide hardware acceleration. 4 ARM Cortex-M1 soft cores are built, which suits for doing the scheduling and management work. To guarantee optimum performance, all MCUs run at the frequency of 100 MHz, and tightly coupled memory (TCM) is used to minimize memory access latency. The architecture of SSD controller can be partitioned as Fig. 1, contents are described on below.

- GTX Bus Interface. It uses Xilinx IP core to implement a high-speed differential IO and a scheme of 8b/10b coding. Both data and commands transferred on the bus are driven by DMA.
- Master Control MCU. It is responsible for bad block and wear-leveling management, parallel dispatching commands and handling upper computer commands. An MRAM is connected to Master Control MCU via general SPI bus. It is used to store some software management and runtime information. And when the power is shut down by accident, it is also used to store some last words to ease power failure recovery when the next boot. Master Control MCU also manages a packet buffer that receives packets from upper computer. The ping-pong access operation is implemented to maximize the bandwidth, details of which are described in the next section.
- NAND Array Controller (NAC). It is responsible for connecting flash chips as an array and translating upper computer commands into low level flash operations. The array means that 8 chips are tightly bound together by FPGA so that they can work in parallel. There are two parts in NAC: The FPGA handles data interface which is compliant with the ONFI 3.0 standard and provides ECC correction. An ARM Cortex-M1 core schedules flash operations, notifies DMA Controller to transfer data and reports status to Message Unit finally. The number of NAC is decided by requirements of capacity and performance.

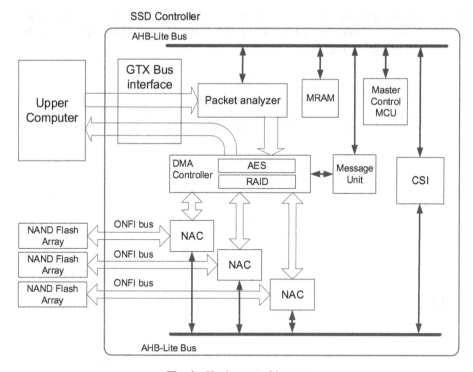

Fig. 1. Hardware architecture

- DMA Controller. The DMA controller has two separate channels for sending and receiving data, and provides an interface in the form of a request queue for each NAC. The deep of request queue is 16 levels, so some requests can be buffered. DMA completes most of work on data transfer, improving overall performance and reducing MCU burden. It also provides the transparent RAID and AES function.
- Message Unit. It is a memory pool with synchronization mechanism for exchanging commands and status between master control MCU and NACs. Message Unit can buffer commands in a first-in-first-out way, which contributes to pipeline and parallel commands dispatching.

2.2 Inside Pipelined AES Core

The AES algorithm is widely used for protecting the user data, which has the advantage of good safety, high efficiency, practicability and high flexibility [9]. AES can also contribute to suppress the bit error rate in MLC/TLC NAND Flash due to its homogeneous function [10]. To provide transparent encryption in the controller, we propose an implementation to connect an AES-256 core and a RAID core with DMA engine in series. In this scheme, when data are transmitted from packet buffer to NAC, encryption and RAID are also done with no performance loss but a little delay. To achieve this, the AES engine is implemented as pipeline structure. We choose CTR (CounTeR) block cipher mode of operation, so only encryption need to be implemented. It is better for saving resources to build the pipeline. The DMA controller with inside AES and RAID engine is illustrated in Fig. 2.

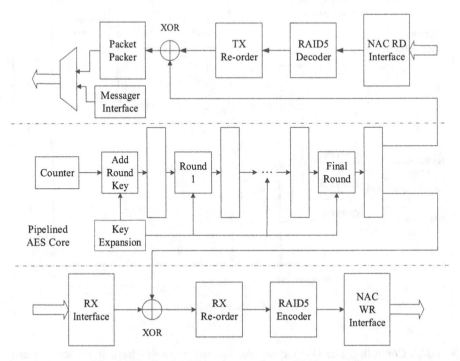

Fig. 2. Pipelined AES implementation in DMA controller

As shown in Fig. 2, all 14 rounds in AES-256 are expand into independent units, and cascaded as a 10-stage pipeline. Each independent unit takes only one cycle. For each round, we use 2 S-box in block RAM, one is for encryption process, the other is for key expansion. The transfer bandwidth of DMA controller is 128-bit, which matches AES cipher block size.

2.3   Download Board

Download board uses a Xilinx Zynq-7000 series SoC which integrates a dual-core ARM Cortex-A9 processor and FPGAs. A GTX interface is also equipped for simulating upper computer of SSD, so download board can also be a test platform when there is no upper computer. General USB 3.0 and gigabit Ethernet interface are equipped for reading data in different usage scenarios.

3   Software Design

3.1   Bad Block Management

3.1.1   Organization of Bad Block Table

As we all know, there may be bad blocks even factory, or may arise during the lifetime of the device. A bad block table is usually built for managing them [11]. For a new device, firmware will do the initialization of bad block checking. Good and bad blocks marked by the manufacturer will be separately. Each entry of the bad block table contains physical addresses of channel, logical unit (LUN) and block. And the index of entry becomes the logical block address (LBA). LBA is always used for communicating with the download board. A bad block table is divided into 3 parts. The top of it is user zone, which saves good blocks in the initial checking. Reserved zone also saves good blocks under the user zone. The different point is that blocks in the reserved zone are used to replace bad blocks, and they are not addressed by user-visible capacity. The third part is bad block zone, partly overlapping with reserved zone, in fact, it grows up from the bottom of the reserved zone. There is not just one bad block table, the number of table is corresponding to parallel resources of the system. For example, if there are 3 NAND flash arrays and 2 LUNs on a chip, there should be 6 tables.

3.1.2   Block Replacement Without Speed Loss

When a bad block appears, a good block must be selected to replace it immediately for later operations. And written data in bad block must be kept and transferred to a new block at the suitable time. Since this system is implemented to have a hard real-time writing performance, the internal data transfer which takes a long time must not happen when data is inputting. The solution is to divide block replacement and data transfer into two parts (top half and bottom half). The top half will be executed immediately when bad block appears, and the bottom half will be executed when system synchronization command is received.

The Fig. 3 shows the work method of block replacement, sN means the state of bad block table, B_N means Nth bad block, R_N means Nth reserved good block, and C_N means Nth temporary block for transferring data.

1. Top half (on the fly)

   - s1. Bad block B_1 is founded.
   - s2. Getting the good block R_1 from bottom of the reserved zone (close to bad block zone), and swapping the address of R_1 and B_1 in bad block table.
     If other bad blocks are founded, s1 and s2 will repeat in order.

2. Bottom half (on synchronization)

   - s3. Getting a good block C_1 from bottom of the reserved zone. Firstly, copying the written data in corresponding bad block B_1 to C_1, then copying remain data in R_1 to C_1. If the process of copying from B_1 to C_1 is faulty, it means block C_1 is also bad. Moving up the top pointer of bad block zone to put C_1 into bad block zone, and getting another one from the reserved zone.
   - s4. Swapping the address of R_1 and C_1 in bad block table. Erasing the block R_1 to be used as a reserved block.

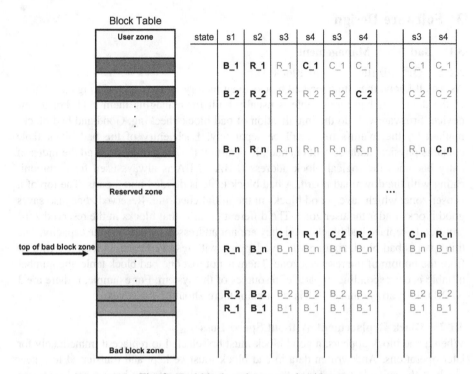

Fig. 3. Bad block replacement algorithm

If there are multiple bad blocks in previous steps, repeating s3 and s4 until all bad blocks are handled.

The written data in bad block B_N cannot be copied directly into reserved block R_N, because the programming order of pages in a block is limited to have a sequential order in many NAND flash chips.

3.2 Pipeline Operation

3.2.1 Die Interleaving

Every LUN (Die) which can independently execute commands and report status is considered as a parallelizable resource. So the MCU does not need to wait for completion of one die, it can send commands to another die until all dies in all channels are accessed, the MCU must wait for completion of the die that has been issued the command this time.

As shown in Fig. 4, the time of writing data is mostly spent on internal program operations of NAND chip, the time of I/O transfer is short and should be counted. Obviously, for writing bandwidth, internal program operations will be the bottleneck, and the time of MCU scheduling and DMA transferring can be hidden behind that. To estimate the performance of this pipeline, we can imagine splicing program operation on one die at the synchronization point, and we can see all dies are paralleled with only

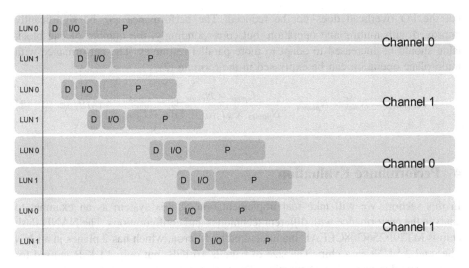

Fig. 4. Die-interleaving

a short delay for I/O overhead in one time. So, if we only consider the contribution of die interleaving, the performance can be expressed in Eq. (1).

$$P_{time \to \infty} = N_{dies} \times \frac{C_{page} \times N_{chips\_per\_channel}}{T_{DMA} + T_{I/O} + T_{program}} (MB/\sec) \qquad (1)$$

It should be noted that this is an idealized analysis, an additional time should be counted because the difference of time of each program can cause a gap on the synchronization point.

3.2.2 Cached Write/Read Operation

To further improve the performance, internal buffer of NAND chip can be used. Vendors usually called it cache register and they provide special instructions to do cached write and read operations. In program operation, firstly, the data go through cache register. The process of copying data from cache register to NAND is handled by chip automatically. Otherwise, data are read out to cache register and are automatically sent out of the chip in reading operation. This means that MCU does not need to wait for completion of the program operation before issuing a new command to the same die, it only waits for cache register that is available to receive new data. So the $T_{program}$ in formula (1) could be shortened. The local buffer in NAND array controller (NAC) is equivalent to provide a 1-stage pipeline, and cache register increase it to 2 stages.

3.2.3 Multi-plane Operation

Planes in a LUN are also parallel resources but with more limits [12]. Each plane is equipped with cache register. And controller input data to every addressed plane cache register and execute a command to do the program operation for all planes together in parallel. That means the program time of planes can be pared down to that of one plane, but the I/O overhead does not be reduced. The performance can be significantly improved with multi-plane operation, but correspondingly, the number of bad block table should be increased to adapt to more parallel resources. The performance with multi-plane operation can be expressed in the formula (2).

$$P_{time \to \infty} = N_{dies} \times N_{planes} \times \frac{C_{page} \times N_{chips\_per\_channel}}{N_{planes} \times (T_{DMA} + T_{I/O} + T_{program})} (MB/\sec) \quad (2)$$

4 Performance Evaluation

In this section, we will take real implementation of this system as an example to analyze the performance with different techniques and configurations. The NAND flash chip is MT29F256G08CEEAB manufactured by Micron, which has 2 planes in a LUN (die) and 2 LUNs in a chip. The size of page is 16 KiB, but only 14 KiB is used for storing data due to the RAID function. The typical time of program page and reading page are 1.6 ms and 115 us, and the time of I/O transfer is about 300 us in Single Data Rate (SDR) mode at 50 MHz. 8 NAND flash chips combine together to work in parallel by hardware, called a logical channel.

For only using die-interleaving technique, for example, we can substitute below parameters into formula (1), the writing performance of one channel, that is, $2 \times 14\,\text{KB} \times 8 \div (0.3 + 1.6)\,\text{ms} \approx 117.9\,\text{MB/s}$. In our solution, the 8 NAND flash chips do program operation in parallel, so the maximum program time of these chips will be used as the actual program time. Results of different configurations are illustrated in Fig. 5.

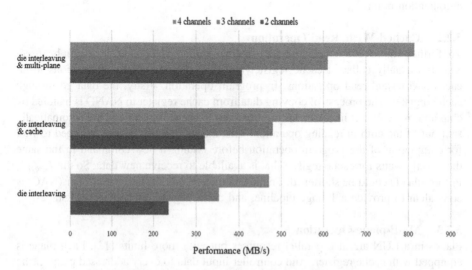

Fig. 5. Performance of using various channels and techniques

5 Conclusion

In this paper, we present a high performance SSD controller based on SoC, it provides multiple interfaces, low power consumption, high reliability and security. The well programmability of FPGA helps us to build AES and RAID functions inside to give well security of data. We use various parallel and pipeline techniques to enhance the performance.

For future work, 3D NAND Flash are considered to incorporate into our system since their high storage density. But characters of those architectures like less endurance cycle, longer program time and big block size will be challenging issues to flash management and power-off recovery.

References

1. Alsalibi, A.I., Mittal, S., Al-Betar, M.A., Sumari, P.B.: A survey of techniques for architecting SLC/MLC/TLC hybrid flash memory–based SSDs. Concurrency Comput. Pract. Experience **30**(6), 4420–4421 (2018)
2. Mielke, N.R., Frickey, R.E., Kalastirsky, I., Quan, M., Ustinov, D., Vasudevan, V.J.: A survey of techniques for architecting SLC/MLC/TLC hybrid flash memory–based SSDs. Concurrency Comput. Pract. Experience **105**(9), 19–53 (2017)
3. Yan, W., Liu, Y., Wang, X.: An efficient parallel executing command scheduler for nand flash storage systems. In: 4th International Conference on Electronics Information and Emergency Communication (ICEIEC), pp. 20–24. IEEE, Beijing (2013)
4. Kao, Y.H., Huang, J.D.: High-performance nand flash controller exploiting parallel out-of-order command execution. In: Proceedings of 2010 International Symposium on VLSI Design, Automation and Test, pp. 160–163. IEEE, Taiwan (2010)
5. Mao, B., Wu, S., Duan, L.: Improving the SSD performance by exploiting request characteristics and internal parallelism. IEEE Trans. Comput. Aided Des. Integr. Circuits Syst. **37**(2), 472–473 (2018)
6. Tavakkol, A., Arjomand, M., Sarbazi-Azad, H.: Design for scalability in enterprise SSDs. In: Proceedings of the 23rd International Conference on Parallel Architectures and Compilation, pp. 417–430. ACM, Edmonton (2014)
7. Park, C., et al.: A high performance controller for nand flash-based solid state disk (NSSD). In: Non-Volatile Semiconductor Memory Workshop, pp. 17–20. IEEE (2006)
8. Chang, L.P., Kuo, T.W.: Efficient management for large-scale flash-memory storage systems resource conservation. ACM Trans. Storage (TOS) **1**(4), 381–418 (2005)
9. Xie, M., Li, S., Glova, A.O., Xie, Y., Hu, J.: Securing emerging nonvolatile main memory with fast and energy-efficient AES in-memory implementation. IEEE Trans. Very Large Scale Integr. (VLSI) Syst. **26**(11), 2443–2455 (2018)
10. Fan, L., Luo, J., Liu, H., Geng, X.: Data security concurrent with homogeneous by AES algorithm in SSD controller. IEICE Electron. Express **11**(13), 20140535 (2014)
11. Pan, Y., Li, Y., Zhang, H., Xu, Y.: Lifetime-aware FTL to improve the lifetime and performance of solid-state drives. Future Gener. Comput. Syst. **93**(4), 138–163 (2019)
12. Winata, Y., Kim, S., Shin, I.: Enhancing internal parallelism of solid-state drives while balancing write loads across dies. Electron. Lett. **51**(24), 1978–1980 (2015)

Joint BP and RNN for Resilient GPS Timing Against Spoofing Attacks

Sriramya Bhamidipati[1], Kyeong Jin Kim[2($\boxtimes$)], Hongbo Sun[2], Philip Orlik[2], and Jinyun Zhang[2]

[1] University of Illinois at Urbana-Champaign, Urbana, IL 61801, USA
sbhamid2@illinois.edu
[2] Mitsubishi Electric Research Labs (MERL), Cambridge, MA 02139, USA
{kkim,hongbosun,porlik,jzhang}@merl.com

Abstract. In this paper, we propose a new wide-area algorithm to secure the Global Positioning System (GPS) timing from spoofing attack. To achieve a trusted GPS timing, belief propagation (BP), recognized as one of the Artificial Intelligence (AI) approaches, and the recurrent neural network (RNN) are jointly integrated. BP is employed to authenticate each GPS receiving system in the wide-area network from malicious spoofing attacks and estimate the corresponding spoofing-induced timing error. To evaluate the spoofing status at each of the GPS receiving system, RNN is utilized to evaluate similarity in spoofing-induced errors across the antennas within the GPS receiving system. Having applied a proper training stage, simulation results show that the proposed joint BP-RNN algorithms can quickly detect the spoofed receiving system comparing with existing work.

Keywords: GPS spoofing · Artificial Intelligence ·
Belief Propagation · Recurrent Neural Network

1 Introduction

Now-a-days, Artificial Intelligence (AI) has been emerging as an important tool for revolutionizing different safety-critical infrastructures, such as, banking, electrical grids and communication networks. In electrical grids, AI offers unique solutions [1] to improve the overall grid resilience and localize the power disruptions caused by the increasing complexity of interconnected grids, high power demand and distributed generation with the usage of renewable sources.

AI techniques are already being incorporated in the power plants to increase the production and also by grid operators to optimize the energy consumption [2]. Recently, GE developed an AI related technology [3] for wind turbines in Japan that is expected to lower the overall maintenance costs by 20% and increase the power output by 5%. Similarly, Google's DeepMind is in discussion with the UK's National Grid to develop AI solutions [4] that balance the requirements of supply and demand in Britain. Also, IBM showed an improvement of 30% in solar forecasting while working with the U.S. Department of Energy SunShot Initiative [5].

© ICST Institute for Computer Sciences, Social Informatics and Telecommunications Engineering 2019
Published by Springer Nature Switzerland AG 2019. All Rights Reserved
S. Han et al. (Eds.): AICON 2019, LNICST 287, pp. 190–209, 2019.
https://doi.org/10.1007/978-3-030-22971-9_17

In addition to efficient energy production and consumption, another critical research area is related to improving the grid resilience against power disruptions that can potentially destabilize the grid [6]. A few notable incidents that occurred in the recent past are the Northeastern blackout in 2003 [7], which is caused due to the shutdown of a high-voltage power line and power outrage of Ukraine [8] in 2015, which caused by the malicious cyber attacks. Recently, there has been a world-wide effort to modernize the grid, coined as *Smart Grid*, which refers to a fully automated power network that monitors and controls every node as well as ensures a steady flow of electricity and exchange of information [9].

Smart grids utilize the concept of microgrids [10] in power distribution networks, which possess the capability to function both when connected to a traditional grid as well as an independent electrical island. However, unlimited power consumption causes the microgrid to be vulnerable to voltage collapse, which needs to accurately monitored. Therefore, smart grids rely on advanced devices, namely, Phasor Measurement Units (PMUs), which provide better insights into the state of the smart grid and in turn help optimize the grid efficiency. PMUs require precise time-keeping sources, such as GPS, to obtain global timing for synchronization [11]. However, GPS civilian signals are unencrypted and their power is as low as -160 dBW, which makes them vulnerable to external spoofing attacks [12]. Based on the IEEE C37.118.1-2011 standard for synchrophasors [13], in this work, we consider 1% TVE equivalent to a timing error of $26.5\,\mu s$, as a benchmark in our power grid stability analysis.

In this paper we mainly focus on a sophisticated type of spoofing attack, known as signal-level spoofing [14]. However, our proposed algorithm is also directly applicable for the detection and mitigation of other spoofing attacks [15, 16]. One scenario of a sophisticated signal-level spoofing is a three-stage attack during which, a spoofer simulates and broadcasts malicious look-alike GPS signals identical to the authentic signals received at the target receiver and thereafter, increases the power of these malicious signals. Once the target receiver locks onto the malicious signals, the spoofed manipulates the receiver time to deviate slowly from its authentic value. Given there are no abrupt changes in GPS timing, this attack is harder to detect and more dangerous as compared to other attacks.

AI has immense potential to serve as a *automated brain* that can analyzes the GNSS measurements to tackle these malicious spoofing attacks [17, 18]. In [19], spoofing detection has been performed by computing the wavelet transformation coefficients of both spoofing and authentic signal, which are later fed into support vector machines, the probabilistic neural networks and the decision tree. In our prior work [20], to isolate spoofing attacks, we proposed a geographically Distributed Multiple Directional Antennas (DMDA) setup, with each antenna facing a different part of the sky, thereby, each receiving signals from only a subset of the total visible GPS satellites. In particular, we designed a Belief Propagation (BP)-based Extended Kalman Filter (EKF) algorithm for single power substation that utilizes the proposed DMDA setup to detect timing anomalies caused due to spoofing. Next, in [21], we extended our work to develop a wide-area-based BP-EKF algorithm that reduces the overall sensitivity of the prior distribution of timing error at each antenna.

To improve the resilience of the grid during sophisticated spoofing attacks, we further extend our work to develop an innovative wide-area joint BP and Recurrent Neural Network (RNN) algorithm, which is based on two powerful tools used in the AI community, namely, BP [22] that isolates the timing errors observed at each antenna and RNN [23] that adaptively analyzes the timing errors to authenticate the spoofing status of each power substation in the wide-area network. Using our joint BP-RNN algorithm, we can not only detect and isolate these malicious attacks but also mitigate the corresponding spoofing-induced timing errors.

2   Joint BP and RNN Algorithm

In this section, we first briefly outline the details of our DMDA setup [20] and later explain the proposed wide-area communication structure. Next, we describe the algorithm details of our wide-area joint BP-RNN algorithm.

2.1   DMDA Setup

Several advantages of the employed DMDA setup in [20] are summarized as follows:

- During a spoofing attack, an attacked antenna may see more satellites in its section of the sky than expected, whereas each of the directional antennas in authentic conditions sees the expected number of satellites in its section of the sky.
- Due to a limited height of physical location of a directed attack, all the directional antennas are not in the line of sight from the attacker. Thus, a geographical diversity can be achievable from malicious spoofing attacks.
- All the antennas are triggered by the same clock, so that a metric, which distinguish an authentic condition from a non-authentic spoofing condition, can be developed (Fig. 1).

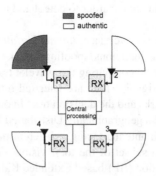

Fig. 1. Configuration of the DMDA setup [20]. Each directional antenna is provided with selective visibility by pointing it towards a different section of the sky, such that, not all the directional antennas can be spoofed simultaneously. Sector of circle represents the field-of-view of each antenna.

2.2 Proposed Wide-Area Communication Structure

To perform a wide-area authentication of GPS timing against spoofing attacks, we consider a network of N power substations, as seen in Fig. 2. We assume the system configuration as follows:

- Any ath infrastructure, with $\forall a \in \{1, \cdots, N\}$, is equipped with a single DMDA based GPS receiving system that includes a common clock and a DMDA setup composed of M_a antennas. For the ath infrastructure, we define S_a as the set of *neighboring infrastructures*. Note that bth infrastructure is included in S_a only when a communication link, π_{ab}, between ath and bth infrastructure exists, that is, $b \in S_a$, if $\pi_{ab} = 1, \forall b \in \{1, \cdots, N\}, b \neq a$.
- For any kth antenna in the ath receiving system, with $k \in \{1, \cdots, M_a\}$, its *neighboring antennas* $\mathcal{B}_k^a$ represents the set of antennas in its infrastructure excluding itself, as well as the antennas belong to its neighboring infrastructures S_a,

$$\mathcal{B}_k^a = \Big\{\{1, \cdots, M_a\} - k\Big\} \bigcup_{b \in \{1, \cdots, |S_a|\}} \{1, \cdots, M_b\}.$$

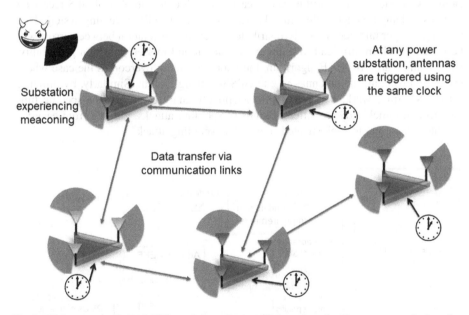

Fig. 2. Wide-area network of GPS receiving systems, each equipped with a common clock and a DMDA setup.

The overall framework of the proposed wide-area joint BP-RNN algorithm, illustrated Fig. 3, is described as follows:

- Across the infrastructures, pseudoranges are measured at each directional antenna, in each of the receiving systems. Based on the communication structure, the *system data* is exchanged across the receiving systems.

- At each of the receiving systems, we form $\mathcal{B}_k^a$. Then, we compute the *single difference pseudorange residual vector* by considering one satellite visible to the first antenna and the another satellite visible to the second antenna in $\mathcal{B}_k^a$.
- At each antenna, *belief* is computed according to the marginal Gaussian distribution of the antenna-specific timing error.
- Using the BP estimates of antenna-specific timing errors, at each GPS receiving system, the pseudoranges are corrected, which are utilized by EKF in the CP unit. The CP unit provides the trustworthy GPS timing, which is given to the infrastructures for a time synchronization.
- A Bidirectional LSTM-based RNN [24] utilizes the BP estimates of the antenna-specific timing errors to compute a test statistic, which authenticates the spoofing status of each GPS receiving system.

Across the wide-area network, by implementing a distributed architecture, it is possible to efficiently utilize the already in-place communication platform. Highly computational extensive calculation of marginal distribution is simplified through the distributed AI algorithm, namely, BP. BP plays a pivotal role in maintaining accuracy while reducing the latency involved in spoofing detection, which is critical for timing-related applications. Our wide-area algorithm can be easily scaled to any number of GPS receiving systems and any number of directional antennas within the GPS receiving system. Due to using a larger number of widely-distributed antennas, correlation between errors will be lower, which in-turn lead to a lower false alarm and missed detection probability. Unlike single area BP-EKF algorithm, the wide-area setup overcomes the case where spoofing affects all the antennas in one GPS receiving system. Similarly, by utilizing a BP-RNN framework, it is possible to adaptively analyze the antenna-specific timing errors to quickly detect different kinds of spoofing attacks, ranging from easy-to-execute meaconing to sophisticated signal-level spoofing attack.

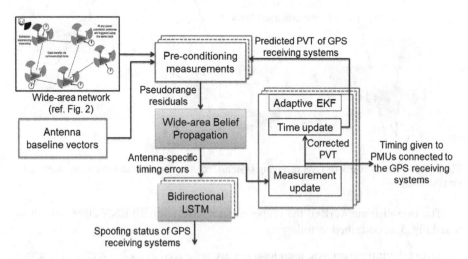

Fig. 3. Flowchart of the wide-area joint BP-RNN algorithm.

2.3 Detailed Descriptions of the Proposed Algorithm

By utilizing the GPS signals received at multiple infrastructures geographically distributed, we describe the proposed wide-area joint BP-RNN algorithm as follows:

Pre-conditioning the GPS Measurements

Considering a wide-area network of N GPS receiving systems, the baseline vectors between the antennas installed at the ath receiving system are computed as b_{kn}^a, $k, n \in \{1, \ldots, M_a\}$. The three-dimensional (3D) position and 3D velocity of the kth antenna at tth time are respectively defined as $x_{k,t}^a \triangleq [x, y, z]_k$ and $v_{k,t}^a \triangleq [\dot{x}, \dot{y}, \dot{z}]_k$. At the ath receiving system, the pseudorange observed at the kth antenna corresponding to the ith satellite is given by

$$
\begin{aligned}
\rho_k^i &= \|x_1^a - b_{1k}^a - y^i\| + (c\delta t_t^a + \alpha_k^a - c\delta t^i) + I^i + \omega_k^i, \\
&= h_k^a(x_1, T^a, y_t^i) + \alpha_k^a,
\end{aligned} \tag{1}
$$

where $i \in L_{k,t}$ denotes the ith satellite among the $L_{k,t}$ visible satellites at the kth antenna in the ath receiving system. In addition, y_t^i and $c\delta t^i$ respectively denote the 3D position and clock corrections of the ith visible satellite. Note that since all the antennas installed at the ath receiving system is triggered by the same clock, the clock bias, $c\delta t_t^a$, is independent of k. The antenna-specific timing errors in pseudorange are denoted by α_k^a. For a proper processing, the antenna, specified by $k = 1$, is recognized as the reference antenna. Furthermore, $h_k^a(\cdot, \cdot, \cdot)$ denotes the measurement model of the kth antenna of the ath receiving system, which depends on the reference antenna's 3D position, $x_{1,t}^a$, receiver clock bias, $c\delta t_t^a$, baseline vector, b_{1k}^a, and the satellite position, y_t^i. The atmospheric errors I_t^i related to ionosphere and troposphere are estimated using existing models [25]. The additive Gaussian white noise in the satellite measurements is represented by ω_k^i.

Having utilized the predicted state vector $\hat{\beta}_t^a \triangleq [\hat{x}_1, c\hat{\delta t}, \hat{v}_1, c\dot{\hat{\delta t}}]_t^T$ obtained from the EKF time update at time t, the known baseline vector, b_{1k}^a, with respect to the reference antenna, the satellite 3D position, y_t^i, and clock corrections, $c\delta t^i$, the pseudorange residuals at tth time can be computed as follows:

$$
\Delta \rho_{k,t}^i \triangleq \rho_{k,t}^i - \|\hat{x}_{k,t} - y^i\| - (c\hat{\delta t} - c\delta t^i) - I^i, \tag{2}
$$

where $\hat{x}_{k,t} \triangleq \hat{x}_1 - b_{1k}^a$.

System Data Exchange and Measurement Likelihood

Based on the communication structure of the wide-area network, the *system data* is exchanged across different GPS receiving systems. In particular, system data transmitted from the ath receiving system comprises of the following: number of antennas M_a, pseudorange residuals, $\Delta \rho_{k,t}^i$, and beliefs at the kth antenna of the receiving system, $b_{t-1}(\alpha_k^a)$. At the ath receiving system, we collect the system data from all the receiving systems that belong to its neighboring system, S_a. Thereafter, we form all the possible pairs of antennas, by considering the first antenna, $k \in \{1, \cdots, M_a\}$, and the second antenna, $n \in \mathcal{B}_k^a$. After then, the single difference pseudorange residuals between the ith satellite visible to the kth antenna and that of the jth satellite visible to the nth antenna as follows:

$$
\begin{aligned}
\gamma_{kn,t}^{ij} &\triangleq \Delta \rho_{k,t}^i - \Delta \rho_{n,t}^j \\
&= \alpha_k^a - \alpha_n^b + \omega_{kn}^{ij} \\
&= \begin{cases} 0 & k, n \in \{1, \ldots, M_a\}, \; k \neq n \\ \eta_{ab} & k \in \{1, \ldots, M_a\}, \; n \in \{1, \ldots, M_b\}, a \neq b, \end{cases}
\end{aligned}
\tag{3}
$$

where in authentic conditions, $\gamma_{kn}^{ij} \approx 0$ across any two antennas that belong to the same receiving system. However, across antennas that belong to two different receiving systems, that is, $a \neq b$, γ_{kn}^{ij} is a non-zero value η_{ab} due to the error in predicted clock bias estimates and the receiver noise. Thereafter, we calculate the measurement metric vector, denoted by $\gamma_{kn,t} \triangleq \{\gamma_{kn,t}^{ij}, i \in L_{k,t}, j \in L_{n,t}\}$ across all the pairs of antennas and the corresponding satellites observed at the respective antennas. Across a pair of antennas, the corresponding measurement likelihood probability is calculated as

$$
p(\gamma_{kn,t} | \alpha_k^a, \alpha_n^b) = \frac{1}{\sqrt{(2\pi\nu^2)^{L_{k,t}L_{n,t}}}}
$$
$$
\exp\left\{\frac{-L_{k,t}L_{n,t}}{2\nu_{kn}^2}\left(\frac{\mathbf{1}^T \gamma_{kn,t}}{L_{k,t}L_{n,t}} + (\alpha_k^a - \alpha_n^b)\right)^2\right\} \; \forall \, n \in \mathcal{B}_k^a, \tag{4}
$$

where ν_{kn}^2 denotes the measurement variance of the summation of single difference residual components which comprises errors observed from pseudoranges, and errors in satellite ephemeris, predicted position and velocity of the antenna.

Belief Propagation (BP)
To authenticate each receiving system against spoofing attacks and estimate the corresponding spoofing-induced timing errors at each antenna, the marginal distribution using a factor graph-based BP framework is used as an AI approach. BP [22] is a sum-product message passing algorithm to make inferences on graphical models, such as the factor graphs. Factor graph is a probabilistic graphical model [26], which consists of two nodes: variable nodes that represent the unknowns to be estimated and factor nodes that represent the relationship between different variable nodes. At the ath receiving system, given the joint posterior distribution, $p(\alpha_1, \ldots, \alpha_{M_a} | \gamma_{kn})$, the marginal distribution, $g(\cdot)$, is formulated as follows:

$$
g(\alpha_k^a) = \int_{\alpha_1^a, \ldots, \alpha_{k-1}^a} \int_{\alpha_{k+1}^a, \ldots, \alpha_M^a} p(\alpha_1^a, \ldots, \alpha_{M_a}^a | \{\gamma_{kn}\}_{k=1,\ldots,M_a, n \in \mathcal{B}_k^a})
$$
$$
d\alpha_1^a \ldots d\alpha_{k-1}^a \, d\alpha_{k+1}^a \ldots d\alpha_{M_a}^a, \tag{5}
$$

where $\mathcal{B}_k^a$ denotes the neighboring antennas of the kth antenna in the ath receiving system. With an increased total number of antennas, that is, $\sum_{a=1}^N M_a$ in the wide-area network, (5) becomes computationally intractable. Thus, a factor graph-based BP is formulated to approximate the marginal distribution in a computationally-efficient manner, which is termed as belief, $b_t(\alpha_k^a)$. Belief at the kth antenna, $b_t(\alpha_k^a)$, is computed as the product of its prior distribution and all the incoming messages from all the neighboring antennas $\mathcal{B}_k^a$. Given that the attacker transmits counterfeit GPS signals, the corresponding spoofing-induced timing errors follow a Gaussian distribution $\mathcal{N}(:,\cdot,\cdot)$. Therefore, belief can be represented by Gaussian process [27] with mean, $\mu_{k,t}^a$, and variance, $(\sigma_{k,t}^a)^2$, as follows:

$$b_t(\alpha_k^a) = m_{f_k^a \to \alpha_k^a} \prod_{n \in \mathcal{B}_k^a} m_{f_{kn}^a \to \alpha_k^a}(\alpha_k^a),$$

$$= \mathcal{N}\left(\alpha_k^a : \mu_{k,t}^a, (\sigma_{k,t}^a)^2\right), \tag{6}$$

where the factor node, f_{kn}^a, connects two variable nodes, α_k^a and α_n^b, based on the likelihood probability, $p(\gamma_{kn}|\alpha_k^a, \alpha_n^b)$, and the other factor node, f_k^a, connects to its corresponding variable node, α_k^a, and indicates the prior distribution of α_k^a.

As seen from (6), at the kth antenna of the ath receiving system, belief, $b_t(\alpha_k^a)$, is updated by computing two kinds of messages, namely, measurement-related messages, $m_{f_{kn}^a \to \alpha_k^a}$, and prior-related message, $m_{f_k^a \to \alpha_k^a}$, as follows:

- The message, $m_{f_{kn}^a \to \alpha_k^a}$, is based on the factor node, f_{kn}^a, and represents the belief of the nth neighboring antenna, $n \in \mathcal{B}_k^a$, on the variable node, α_k^a. From (4) and (6), we derive the message, $m_{f_{kn}^a \to \alpha_k^a}$, as follows:

$$m_{f_{kn}^a \to \alpha_k^a}(\alpha_k^a) = \int_{n \in \mathcal{B}_k^a} p(\gamma_{kn}|\alpha_k^a, \alpha_n^b)\, b_{t-1}(\alpha_n^b) d\alpha_n^b,$$

$$= \int \frac{1}{\sqrt{(2\pi\nu^2)^{L_k L_n}}} \exp\left\{ \frac{-L_k L_n}{2\nu^2}\left(\frac{1^T \gamma_{kn,t}}{L_k L_n} - (\alpha_k^a - \alpha_n^b)\right)^2\right\}$$

$$\exp\left\{ \frac{-(\alpha_n^b - \mu_{n,t-1}^b)^2}{2(\sigma_{n,t-1}^b)^2}\right\} d\alpha_n^b,$$

$$= \mathcal{N}\left(\alpha_k^a : \mu_{kn,t}^a, (\sigma_{kn,t}^a)^2\right), \tag{7}$$

where $\mu_{kn,t}^a = \mu_{n,t-1}^b - \dfrac{1^T \gamma_{kn,t}}{L_{k,t} L_{n,t}}$ and $(\sigma_{kn,t}^a)^2 = \dfrac{\nu_{kn}^2}{2 L_{k,t} L_{n,t}} + (\sigma_{n,t-1}^a)^2$.

- The message, $m_{f_k^a \to \alpha_k^a}$, represents the prior distribution formulated as a Gaussian; that is,

$$m_{f_k^a \to \alpha_k^a} = p(\alpha_k^a) \int b(\alpha_k^a) d\alpha_k^a = p(\alpha_k^a) = \mathcal{N}\left(\alpha_k^a : \mu_{pk,t}^a, (\sigma_{pk,t}^a)^2\right). \tag{8}$$

Based on (7) and (8), the updated belief at time instant t is computed as follows:

$$b_t(\alpha_k^a) = \mathcal{N}\left(\alpha_k^a : \mu_{pk,t}^a, (\sigma_{pk,t}^a)^2\right) \prod_{n \in \mathcal{B}_k^a} \mathcal{N}\left(\alpha_k^a : \mu_{kn,t}^a, (\sigma_{kn,t}^a)^2\right),$$

$$= \mathcal{N}\left(\alpha_k^a : \mu_{k,t}^a, (\sigma_{k,t}^a)^2\right), \tag{9}$$

where

$$(\sigma_{k,t}^a)^2 = \left(\frac{1}{(\sigma_{pk,t}^a)^2} + \sum_{n \in \mathcal{B}_k^a} \frac{1}{(\sigma_{kn,t}^a)^2} \right)^{-1}, \text{ and}$$

$$\mu_{k,t}^a = (\sigma_{k,t}^a)^2 \left(\frac{\mu_{pk,t}^a}{(\sigma_{pk,t}^a)^2} + \sum_{n \in \mathcal{B}_k^a} \frac{\mu_{kn,t}^a}{(\sigma_{kn,t}^a)^2} \right). \tag{10}$$

Dependency of Wide-Area BP on Prior Distribution

Note that (8) specifies the prior distribution of the antenna-specific timing error. In our prior work [20], if the mismatch between the observed and the expected set of satellites is ≥ 2, then we assumed that $\mu_{pk,t}^a = 0$ and $(\sigma_{pk,t}^a)^2 = \infty$, thereby representing an approximated uniform distribution. However, by utilizing a wide-area network of antennas, we significantly reduce the dependency of the attack-resilience of the GPS timing on this prior distribution. To achieve this, among the N widely-dispersed infrastructures, we choose the GPS receiving system with the least spoofing risk, that is,

$$a_m = \underset{a \in \{1, \cdots, N\}}{\arg \min} \ r_t^a,$$

where $r_t^a, \forall a \in \{1, \cdots, N\}$, is computed later in Sect. 2.3. Except the a_mth receiving system, we assign the prior distribution of GPS receiving system, such that, $\mu_{pk,t}^a = 0$ and $(\sigma_{pk,t}^a)^2 = \infty, \forall a \in \{1, \cdots, N\} - a_m$. However, for the a_mth receiving system, $\mu_{pk,t}$ and $\sigma_{pk,t}^2$ are computed from the empirical distribution calculated on-the fly by considering the most recent W timing errors; that is, $\alpha_{k,t-W:t}^{a_m}, \forall k = \{1, \cdots, M\}$.

RNN-based Authentication of GPS Receiving Systems

Based on the belief estimates of the timing error at each antenna, we design an AI-based RNN framework to authenticate each GPS receiving system in the wide-area network. To evaluate the spoofing status at each ath receiving system, we need to monitor the values of the BP estimates of antenna-specific timing error as well as their similarity across the antennas within the GPS receiving system. By utilizing the vast amounts of available GPS data, we initially train a coarse RNN-based framework offline that we later finely train during the initialization stage, to adaptively estimate the spoofing status of each ath receiving system, which is denoted by $r_t^a \in \{0, 1\}$, such that, 0 indicates authentic and 1 indicates spoofed.

The architecture of our RNN framework is such that, at any time instant, the shape of the input features $\theta_t^a \triangleq [\alpha_1^a, \cdots, \alpha_{M_a}^a]_t^T$ is a $M_a \times 1$ vector that stacks the estimated antenna-specific timing errors across all antennas in each ath receiving system. This captures the spatial similarity in the antenna-specific timing errors. We also consider multiple time instants of input features as input to our RNN, so as to capture the temporal variations in the absolute values of these input features. In particular, we utilize Long Short Term Memory (LSTM) [24], a special kind of RNN, for training our data, given its capability to retain the information learned from long time sequences. This is especially useful during signal-level spoofing attacks, described in Sect. 1, where the

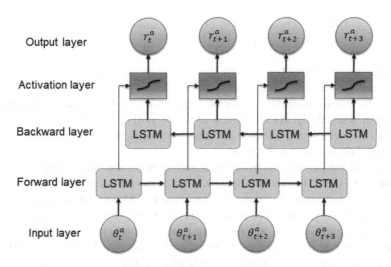

Fig. 4. Overall architecture of our Bidirectional-LSTM, which takes the antenna-specific timing errors of all antennas within the ath GPS receiving system, denoted by θ_t^a and estimates the spoofing status, denoted by r_t^a.

rate of change in timing errors are not abrupt but increases gradually over time. The overall architecture of our multivariate time-series-based Bidirectional-LSTM [28], as seen in Fig. 4, consists of an input layer, forward layer, backward layer, activation layer and finally an output layer. In the input layer, we consider W^a time instants of *input nodes* denoted by $\theta_{t-W^a:t}$. In the output layer, we consider one *output node* at each instant, which either takes the value 0 or 1, thereby indicating the spoofing status r_t^a of the ath receiving system. The input to the final output layer is obtained by combining the outputs from the forward and backward layers in a activation layer, which is governed by a softmax function [29].

The forward and backward layers are comprised of *LSTM units*, which consists of a *cell* that analyzes the dependencies between elements in our multivariate time sequence. Within each cell, we consider regulators called *gates*, which control the information that is passed through the LSTM unit. The equations related to the processing within each LSTM unit are provided in (11). Our LSTM network utilizes three kinds of gates: an input gate, an output gate, and a forget gate. The input gate controls the extent to which a new value flows into the cell, the forget gate controls the extent to which a value remains in the cell and the output gate controls the extent to which the value in the cell is used to compute the output activation of the LSTM unit. We implement a logistic activation function [30], denoted by σ_g at each gate. The associated unknown weights and biases at these connections are estimated during the training stage.

$$
\begin{aligned}
f_t &= \sigma_g \left(W_f \theta_t^a + U_f h_{t-1} + b_f \right), \\
i_t &= \sigma_g \left(W_i \theta_t^a + U_i h_{t-1} + b_i \right), \\
o_t &= \sigma_g \left(W_o \theta_t^a + U_o h_{t-1} + b_o \right),
\end{aligned}
\tag{11}
$$

$$c_t = f_t \circ c_{t-1} + i_t \circ \sigma_c \left(W_c \theta_t^a + U_c h_{t-1} + b_c \right), \text{ and}$$
$$h_t = o_t \circ \sigma_h \left(c_t \right),$$

where θ_t^a denotes the input feature at tth time instant given as an input to the LSTM network, h_t denotes the hidden state vector, and c_t denotes the cell state vector. Similarly, f_t, i_t, o_t denotes the activation vector associated with the forget gate, input gate and output gate, respectively. As mentioned above, $W_f, W_i, W_o, U_f, U_i, U_o, b_f, b_i, b_o$ represents the weights and biases in different layers indicated by their subscripts, and are estimated during the training stage.

During our training stage, considering same number of antennas in each GPS receiving system, we utilize the antenna-specific timing errors obtained from different GPS receiving systems to train our coarse Bidirectional-LSTM network. Using a GPS simulator, we generate various cases of authentic and simulated spoofing attacks. Thereafter, during an initialization, by processing several minutes of received data, we further finely train our Bidirectional-LSTM network to account for the individual GPS receiving system-based noise distribution related to timing.

Adaptive EKF

According to [20], we summarize the adaptive EKF as follows:

- Define corrected psedoranges: $\zeta_t^a \triangleq [\rho_c^1, \ldots, \rho_c^{L_a}]$, $\forall a$, with $\rho_c^i \triangleq \rho_k^i - \alpha_k^a$ and $L^a \triangleq L_1 + \cdots + L_{M_a}$.
- Define required quantities: the measurement noise covariance matrix, R_t^a, measurement model, H_t^a, predicted state vector, $\hat{\beta}^a$, predicted state covariance matrix, $\hat{P}_t^a$, state transition matrix, F, and static process noise covariance, Q_t^a.
- Perform measurement update:

$$\bar{\beta}_t^a = \left(I_8 - K_t H_t^a \right) \hat{\beta}_t^a + K_t \zeta_t^a,$$
$$\bar{P}_t^a = \left(I_8 - K_t H_t^a \right) \hat{P}_t^a,$$
$$K_t = \hat{P}_t^a (H_t^a)^T \left(H_t^a \hat{P}_t^a (H_t^a)^T + R_t^a \right)^{-1},$$

$$h_t^a(\beta_t) = \begin{bmatrix} h_{1,t}(x_{1,t}, T_t, b_{1k}) \\ \vdots \\ h_{L,t}(x_{1,t}, T_t, b_{1L}) \end{bmatrix}, \tag{12}$$

$$H_t = \left. \frac{\partial h_t^a(\beta_t^a)}{\partial \beta_t^a} \right|_{\hat{\beta}_t^a},$$
$$\epsilon_t = \zeta_t - h_t(\bar{\beta}_t^a), \text{ and}$$
$$R_{t+1}^a = R_t^a d + (\epsilon_t^T \epsilon_t + H_t^a \hat{P}_t^a (H_t^a)^T)(1 - d),$$

where K_t represents the Kalman gain and I_8 denotes the 8×8 identity matrix. According to [31], a forgetting factor fixed by $d = 0.3$.

– Perform time update:

$$\hat{\beta}^a_{t+1} = F \bar{\beta}^a_t, \text{ and } \hat{P}^a_{t+1} = F \bar{P}^a_t F^T + Q^a_t, \tag{13}$$

where

$$F = \begin{bmatrix} I_4 & \delta t I_4 \\ 0_{4 \times 4} & I_4 \end{bmatrix}, Q^a_t = F \begin{bmatrix} 0_{4 \times 4} & \delta t I_4 \\ 0_{4 \times 4} & \kappa^a \end{bmatrix} F^T \quad, \text{ and } \kappa^a = \begin{bmatrix} 0_{3 \times 3} & 0 \\ 0 & c\tau^a \end{bmatrix}$$

with τ^a representing allan deviation of the front-end oscillator, δt representing the update interval of our adaptive EKF step, I_4 denotes the identity matrix of size 4×4 and $0_{4 \times 4}$ denotes the zero matrix of size 4×4.

3 Experiments

In this section, we validate our wide-area joint BP-RNN algorithm via two experimental scenarios, to detect and mitigate the timing error caused by simulated signal-level spoofing attacks. We demonstrate the capability of our BP algorithm to accurately estimate the associated timing errors and our RNN-framework to adaptively authenticate the spoofing status of the GPS receiving systems in the wide-area network.

3.1 Experimental Setup and Implementation Details

As seen in Fig. 5, we consider four GPS receiving systems, such that, the DMDA setup in each GPS receiving system comprises of three antennas. In our wide-area network, we consider the GPS receiving systems to be located in Austin, Boston, Chicago, and Pasadena, denoted by A, B, C, and D, respectively. We considered realistic pre-computed baseline vectors across the antennas in each DMDA setup, marked in the Fig. 5, to mimic the setup of actual power substations.

For a given stationary configuration of the antenna and an associated ephemeris file, we simulated the GPS signals received at each antenna and at each receiving system, using a C++-based software-defined GPS simulator known as GPS-SIM-SDR [32]. We collected the simulated GPS signals at a sampling rate of 2.5 MHz, where each raw sample is a 16-bit complex. At each DMDA setup, the corresponding antennas are provided with selective visibility of the sky, such that, the field of view are $150 - 270°$, $270 - 30°$, and $30 - 150°$, respectively, in reference to geographic north.

Utilizing this setup, we simulated the authentic GPS signals received at each antenna in the three GPS receiving systems, i.e., Austin, Chicago, and Pasadena for the first experiment and Austin, Boston, and Chicago for the second experiment. Based on the signal-level spoofing attack explained in Sect. 1, we generated the spoofed GPS signals at the attacked GPS receiving system, i.e., Boston for the first experiment and Pasadena for the second experiment, by adding high-powered and simulated malicious samples to the generated authentic simulated GPS samples. We post-processed the simulated GPS signals using a MATLAB-based software-defined radio known as SoftGNSS [33]. We utilized the external ephemeris to extract authentic satellite positions, which are provided as input to the algorithm.

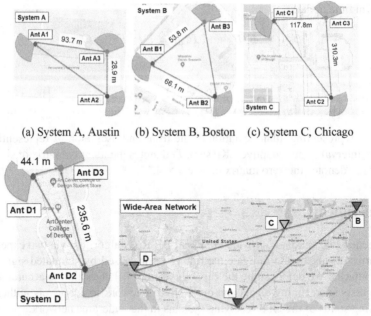

(a) System A, Austin   (b) System B, Boston   (c) System C, Chicago

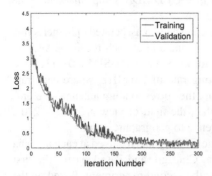

(d) System D, Pasadena   (e) Wide-area network and communication links

Fig. 5. The simulated experimental setup consists of four GPS receiving systems in the wide-area network, with three antenna-based DMDA setup in each. In the first experiment case, the GPS receiving system in Boston is attacked by simulated signal-level spoofing, such that, the B1 antenna of the DMDA setup experiences spoofing. In the second experiment case, the GPS receiving station in Pasadena is attacked by a different simulated signal-level spoofing, during which the D3 antenna is affected.

Fig. 6. Loss function obtained for training and validation of Bidirectional-LSTM, which consists of 50 hidden nodes and a batch size of 1028.

Table 1. Training and validation accuracy for different hyper-parameter settings

Hyper-parameters			Accuracy (%)	
Hidden nodes	Batch size	Iterations	Training	Validation
50	**1028**	**300**	**83.4**	**84.1**
100	1028	300	76.9	71.3
50	512	300	72.6	73.7

For training and validating our Bidirectional-LSTM, we considered 1000000 data samples of input features, that is, antenna specific timing error-based vector $\theta_t^a, \forall a$, obtained from different GPS receiving systems. Out of the 1000000 data samples of input features considered, 99% of the data is used for training our Bidirectional-LSTM, while rest is used for validating the neural network at the end of each epoch. The total considered data samples consists of 65% authentic data, which is obtained from real-world GPS signals collected using a GPS receiver as well as simulated GPS signals obtained from a GPS simulator. In addition, rest of the 40% of the training data comprises of simulated GPS signals affected by different configurations and types of simulated spoofing attacks. We executed back propagation by considering the cost function to be mean squared error and utilized an Adam optimizer [34]. We considered $W^a = 60, \forall a$ time instants of the past antenna-specific timing errors at each ath GPS receiving system to estimate the spoofing status r_t^a at each time instant. Based on the training and validation accuracy for different hyper-parameter settings, as seen in Table 1, during testing, we utilize our trained RNN that is initialized with 50 hidden nodes and a batch size of 1028. The training and validating loss for the chosen hyper-parameters is seen in Fig. 6.

3.2 Under Simulated Signal-Level Spoofing Attack - Only Timing

In the simulated authentic GPS signals received at the Bth GPS receiving system, during the time duration $t = 25 - 60$ s we induced simulated signal-level spoofing that causes an increasing timing error from $0 - 28\,\mu$s in a span of 35 s. Due to the DMDA configuration at the GPS receiving system, the attacker can only affect B1 antenna, thereby, causing it to receive malicious GPS signals from 9 satellites instead of the expected 3 satellites. At the B1 antenna, the attacker causes the pseudoranges to show an increasing time error during $t = 25 - 60$ s. For $t \geq 60$ s these errors further continue to grow due to the destabilization of receiver tracking loops.

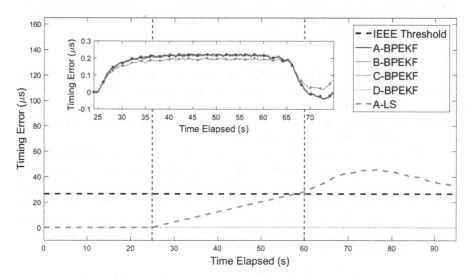

Fig. 7. Timing error estimated using our wide-area joint BP-RNN algorithm, indicated by dotted-solid line, as compared to least-squares, indicated by the dashed line. (Color figure online)

As seen in Fig. 7, the conventional least-squares approach with one omni-directional antenna, showed an RMS timing error of $29.8\,\mu s$ as indicated by the red-dashed line. After the spoofing starts at $t = 25\,s$, we observed that the timing error computed via least-squares increases with time, even after spoofing ends, thereby, exceeding beyond $26.5\,\mu s$ and violating the IEEE C37.118-1 standards. However, our proposed joint BP and RNN algorithm, which is executed for $t \geq 12\,s$, showed steady convergence and demonstrated significantly lower RMS timing errors of $0.13\,\mu s$, $0.14\,\mu s$, $0.13\,\mu s$ and $0.13\,\mu s$ at A, B, C, and D GPS receiving systems, respectively, during the simulated signal-level spoofing.

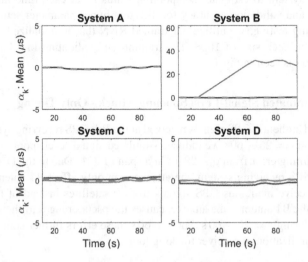

Fig. 8. Antenna-specific timing errors μ_k^a estimated during BP step at all the GPS receiving systems. The different antennas in the DMDA setup of each receiving system are indicated by red, blue and magenta lines. (Color figure online)

As seen in Fig. 8, the wide-area BP-RNN algorithm not only isolates the presence of spoofing attacks to B1 antenna but also accurately estimates the increasing timing error as $\alpha_{k,t}^a - \alpha_{k,t-1}^a \approx 0.4\,\mu s/s$ induced during the spoofing attack, that is, $t = 25 - 60\,s$. This can be observed by the red solid line at the Bth GPS receiving system whereas the timing error in other antennas is close to zero.

In addition, we also analyzed the spoofing status associated with each GPS receiving system, based on the Bidirectional-LSTM. We compared the performance of our RNN approach, seen in Fig. 9(a) with that of a KL-divergence approach [35], seen in Fig. 9(b) with pre-determined threshold manually set as $\Pi = 25$. When the KL-test statistic $m_{KL,t}^a > \Pi$, the KL-based metric $r_{KL,t}^a = 1$ indicating spoofed GPS receiving system and $r_{KL,t}^a = 0$ otherwise, indicating authentic conditions. The KL-test statistics, $m_{KL,t}^a$, are calculated as follows:

$$m_{KL,t}^a = \sum_{\nu=0}^{W} \sum_{i=1}^{M_a} \sum_{j=1, j\neq i}^{M_a} \left(\alpha_{i,t-\nu}^a \ln \left(\frac{\alpha_{i,t-\nu}^a}{\alpha_{j,t-\nu}^a} \right) \right). \tag{14}$$

In Fig. 9, we observed that while demonstrating similar consistency in performance as that of the KL-divergence-based metric, our RNN-based metric quickly detects that the Bth receiving system is being spoofed at $t = 25.7$ s, that is, 0.7 s after the spoofing starts, as compared to the KL-based metric that first detects spoofing at a later time $t = 34.6$ s. Therefore, even though the simulated signal-level spoofing does not cause abrupt changes in the timing errors, by analyzing the multivariate time-series of antenna-specific timing errors, our trained RNN-based metric quickly as well as accurately detects spoofing attacks at the Bth GPS receiving system.

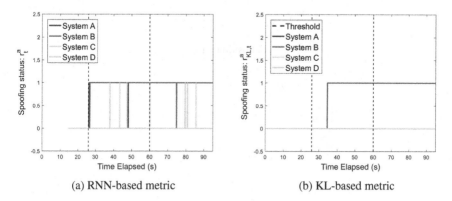

(a) RNN-based metric   (b) KL-based metric

Fig. 9. Spoofing status estimated using (a) RNN-based metric; (b) KL-based metric. RNN-based metric detects the presence of spoofing at the Bth receiving system 0.7 s after the spoofing starts at $t = 25$ s, whereas KL-divergence first detects spoofing 9.6 s after the spoofing starts.

3.3   Under Simulated Signal-Level Spoofing Attack - Both Positioning and Timing

In the next set of experiments, we generated a simulated signal-level spoofing attack that induces both a constant change in position of 55 m and an increasing timing error of 33 μs in a span of 25 s. During a time duration of $t = 25 - 50$ s, these simulated spoofing signals are added to the simulated authentic GPS signals received at the Dth GPS receiving system are induced with spoofing signals. Due to our DMDA setup, the attacker only successfully spoofs the satellite signals received at the D3 antenna. Similar to Sect. 3.2, due to the destabilization of receiver tracking loops caused during the attack, the pseudorange errors continue to grow unbounded.

Due to unbounded increase in pseudorange errors, the error in both position and timing obtained via conventional least-squares approach diverged, which is indicated by the green dashed line in the Fig. 10(a) and (b), respectively. In particular, we observed that the IEEE C37.118-1 standards related to the timing error obtained via least-squares approach is violated within 10 s after the start of spoofing attack. However, as seen in Fig. 10(b), our proposed joint BP and RNN algorithm, which is initialized at $t = 12$ s, similar to the Sect. 3.2, showed a convergence trend with RMS timing errors of 0.14 μs, 0.16 μs, 0.15 μs and 0.15 μs at A, B, C, and Dth GPS receiving systems respectively.

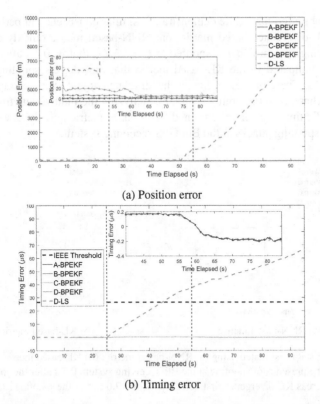

(a) Position error

(b) Timing error

Fig. 10. Position and timing errors estimated using the proposed wide-area joint BP-RNN algorithm, indicated by the dotted-solid lines, as compared to the conventional least squares approach, indicated by the dashed line. In particular, green represents the Dth GPS receiving system. Due to spoofing, the least squares solution in both position and timing diverged, whereas our wide-area BP-RNN showed steady convergence. (Color figure online)

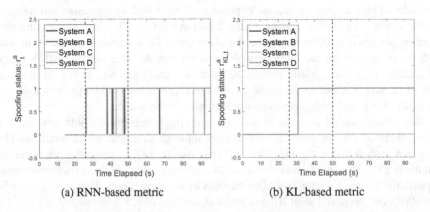

(a) RNN-based metric

(b) KL-based metric

Fig. 11. Spoofing status estimated using (a) RNN-based metric; (b) KL-based metric. RNN-based metric detects the presence of spoofing at the Bth receiving system 0.7 s after the spoofing starts at $t = 25$ s, whereas KL-divergence first detects spoofing 9.6 s after the spoofing starts.

Similarly, as seen in Fig. 10(a), the RMS position errors computed using BP-RNN algorithm are 5.11 m, 19.28 m, 1.38 m, 0.77 m at A, B, C, and Dth GPS receiving systems, respectively, whereas least-squares approach showed an RMS position error of 2410.71 m.

Based on the Bidirectional LSTM, explained in Sect. 3.1, we analyzed the spoofing status computed using our BP-RNN algorithm, as seen in Fig. 11(a) and compared its performance with that of the KL-divergence approach, as seen in Fig. 11(b) and described in (14). The KL-divergence approach detected the spoofing attack for the first time at $t = 31.2$ s, whereas our BP-RNN approach quickly detected the spoofing attack at $t = 25.4$ s, while simultaneously demonstrating low false alarms and misdetections. Therefore, we validated the improved performance of the proposed wide-area joint BP and RNN algorithm even during more sophisticated attacks that involve both position and timing being spoofed.

4   Conclusions

To summarize, we have proposed a wide-area joint Belief Propagation and Recurrent Neural Network (BP-RNN) algorithm to detect and mitigate the spoofing attacks as well as estimate the attack-resilient GPS timing that is given to the geographically distributed infrastructures, which are monitored by PMUs. By considering a wide-area network of GPS receiving systems, we have estimated the marginal distribution of the spoofing-induced timing errors at each antenna using distributed BP algorithm. In addition, based on the BP-estimated timing errors, we have adaptively evaluated the spoofing status of each GPS receiving system using an RNN framework.

Table 2. Summarizing the RMS timing errors of the attacked GPS receiving system estimated via the proposed wide-area BP-RNN and conventional least-squares approach

Spoofing attack	RMS timing error of attacked GPS receiving system	
	BP-RNN	Least-Squares
Timing error of 28 μs in a span of 35 s	0.14 μs	29.8 μs
Position error of 55 m and timing error of 33 μs in a span of 25 s	0.16 μs	37.94 μs

We have validated the proposed wide-area BP-RNN using four GPS receiving systems, with three-antenna-based DMDA setup each and subjecting one GPS receiving system to a simulated signal-level spoofing attack. For two cases of simulated spoofing attacks, the RMS timing errors obtained via the proposed wide-area BP-RNN algorithm and conventional least squares approach are listed in Table 2. While one omni-directional antenna-based least squares has shown large RMS timing errors that violated the IEEE-C37.118 standards, the wide-area BP-RNN algorithm has demonstrated low RMS timing errors of less than 0.16 μs. Also, as compared to the existing works, we have assessed the improved performance of our RNN-based metric, which has shown a quick detection of spoofing, that is, 0.7 s after the spoofing attack starts in the first experiment and 0.4 after spoofing attack starts in the second experiment.

References

1. Raza, M.Q., Khosravi, A.: A review on artificial intelligence based load demand forecasting techniques for smart grid and buildings. Renew. Sustain. Energy Rev. **50**, 1352–1372 (2015)
2. Venayagamoorthy, G.K.: Potentials and promises of computational intelligence for smart grids. In: Power & Energy Society General Meeting PES 2009, pp. 1–6. IEEE (2009)
3. Li, B.-H., Hou, B.-C., Yu, W.-T., Lu, X.-B., Yang, C.-W.: Applications of artificial intelligence in intelligent manufacturing: a review. Front. Inf. Technol. Electron. Eng. **18**(1), 86–96 (2017)
4. Edwin, R.: Community energy consumption management. US Patent App. 10/59,294, 9 Jan 2003
5. Tuohy, A., et al.: Solar forecasting: methods, challenges, and performance. IEEE Power Energy Mag. **13**(6), 50–59 (2015)
6. Fernandez, S.J., et al.: Real-time simulation of power grid disruption. US Patent App. 13/747,779, 25 July 2013
7. Lin, S., Fletcher, B.A., Luo, M., Chinery, R., Hwang, S.-A.: Health impact in New York city during the Northeastern blackout of 2003. Public Health Rep. **126**(3), 384–393 (2011)
8. Liang, G., Weller, S.R., Zhao, J., Luo, F., Dong, Z.Y.: The 2015 ukraine blackout: Implications for false data injection attacks. IEEE Trans. Power Syst. **32**(4), 3317–3318 (2017)
9. McDaniel, P., McLaughlin, S.: Security and privacy challenges in the smart grid. IEEE Secur. Priv. **3**, 75–77 (2009)
10. Wang, Z., Sun, H., Nikovski, D.: Static voltage stability detection using local measurement for microgrids in a power distribution network. In: 2015 IEEE 54th Annual Conference on Decision and Control (CDC), pp. 3254–3259. IEEE (2015)
11. De La Ree, J., Centeno, V., Thorp, J.S., Phadke, A.G.: Synchronized phasor measurement applications in power systems. IEEE Trans. Smart Grid **1**(1), 20–27 (2010)
12. Shepard, D.P., Humphreys, T.E., Fansler, A.A.: Evaluation of the vulnerability of phasor measurement units to GPS spoofing attacks. Int. J. Crit. Infrastruct. Prot. **5**(3–4), 146–153 (2012)
13. Martin, K., et al.: Exploring the IEEE standard c37. 118–2005 synchrophasors for power systems. IEEE Trans. Power Del. **23**(4), 1805–1811 (2008)
14. Bhamidipati, S., Mina, T.Y., Gao, G.X.: GPS time authentication against spoofing via a network of receivers for power systems. In: 2018 IEEE/ION Position, Location and Navigation Symposium (PLANS), pp. 1485–1491 (2018)
15. Bhamidipati, S., Gao, G.X.: GPS multi-receiver joint direct time estimation and spoofer localization. IEEE Trans. Aerosp. Electron. Syst. (2018). https://doi.org/10.1109/TAES.2018.2879532
16. Margaria, D., Motella, B., Anghileri, M., Floch, J.-J., Fernandez-Hernandez, I., Paonni, M.: Signal structure-based authentication for civil GNSSs: recent solutions and perspectives. IEEE Signal Process. Mag. **34**(5), 27–37 (2017)
17. Shafiee, E., Mosavi, M., Moazedi, M.: Detection of spoofing attack using machine learning based on multi-layer neural network in single-frequency GPS receivers. J. Navig. **71**(1), 169–188 (2018)
18. LaST, D.: GNSS: the present imperfect. Inside GNSS **5**(3), 60–64 (2010)
19. Mosavi, M.R., Zebarjad, R., Moazedi, M.: Novel anti-spoofing methods based on discrete wavelet transform in the acquisition and tracking stages of civil GPS receiver. Int. J. Wirel. Inf. Netw. **25**, 449–460 (2018)
20. Bhamidipati, S., Kim, K.J., Sun, H., Orlik, P.V.: GPS spoofing detection and mitigation in PMUs using distributed multiple directional antennas. In: IEEE International Conference on Communications (ICC), pp. 1–7 (2019)

21. Bhamidipati, S., Kim, K.J., Sun, H., Orlik, P.V.: Wide-area GPS time monitoring against spoofing using belief propagation. In: IEEE International Conference on Sensing, Communication, and Networking (SECON), pp. 1–8 (2019)
22. Yedidia, J.S., Freeman, W.T., Weiss, Y.: Understanding belief propagation and its generalizations. Exploring Artif. Intell. New Millennium **8**, 236–239 (2003)
23. Mikolov, T., Karafiát, M., Burget, L., Černockỳ, J., Khudanpur, S.: Recurrent neural network based language model. In: Eleventh Annual Conference of the International Speech Communication Association (2010)
24. Hochreiter, S., Schmidhuber, J.: Long short-term memory. Neural Comput. **9**(8), 1735–1780 (1997)
25. Misra, P., Enge, P.: Global Positioning System Signals, Measurements, and Performance. Ganga Jamuna Press, Lincoln (2006)
26. Kschischang, F.R., Frey, B.J., Loeliger, H.-A.: Factor graphs and the sum-product algorithm. IEEE Trans. Inf. Theory **47**(2), 498–519 (2001)
27. Leng, M., Wu, Y.-C.: Distributed clock synchronization for wireless sensor networks using belief propagation. IEEE Trans. Signal Process. **59**, 5404–5414 (2011)
28. Graves, A., Schmidhuber, J.: Framewise phoneme classification with bidirectional LSTM and other neural network architectures. Neural Networks **18**(5–6), 602–610 (2005)
29. Gimpel, K., Smith,N.A.: Softmax-margin CRFs: training log-linear models with cost functions. In: Human Language Technologies: The 2010 Annual Conference of the North American Chapter of the Association for Computational Linguistics, pp. 733–736. Association for Computational Linguistics (2010)
30. Harrell, F.E.: Ordinal logistic regression. In: Regression Modeling Strategies, pp. 311–325. Springer, Cham (2015). https://doi.org/10.1007/978-3-319-19425-7
31. Akhlaghi, S., Zhou, N., Huang, Z.: Adaptive adjustment of noise covariance in Kalman filter for dynamic state estimation. In: IEEE Power & Energy Society General Meeting 2017, pp. 1–5. IEEE (2017)
32. Ebinuma, T.: Gps-sdr-sim. https://github.com/osqzss/gps-sdr-sim
33. Paul, K.: Soft GNSS. https://github.com/kristianpaul/SoftGNSS
34. Bello, I., Zoph, B., Vasudevan, V., Le, Q.V.: Neural optimizer search with reinforcement learning. In: Proceedings of the 34th International Conference on Machine Learning-Volume 70, pp. 459–468 (2017). www.JMLR.org
35. Eguchi, S., Copas, J.: Interpreting kullback-leibler divergence with the neyman-pearson lemma. J. Multivar. Anal. **97**(9), 2034–2040 (2006)

Cloud and Big Data of AI-Enabled Networks

Regional Landslide Sensitivity Analysis Based on CPSO-LSSVM

Yanze Li[1(✉)], Zhenjian Yang[1,2], Yunjie Zhang[1], and Zhou Jin[1]

[1] School of Computer and Information Engineering,
Tianjin Chengjian University, Tianjin 300384, China
1341485766@qq.com
[2] Tianjin Key Laboratory of Soft Soil Characteristics and Engineering
Environment, Tianjin, China

Abstract. Landslide sensitivity analysis is of great significance for predicting landslide hazards. Taking the landslide in the hilly area of Sichuan Province as an example, through the interpretation of high spatial resolution remote sensing images and the analysis of the occurrence mechanism of landslides in the low hilly areas of Sichuan Province, eight landslide susceptibility evaluation factors were obtained. (elevation, slope, terrain relief, rivers, roads, geotechnical types, NDVI, fault structures). Then, using the neighborhood statistical analysis, ArcGIS technology and other methods to obtain training sample data and regional sample data. According to the characteristics of the landslide development, the Chao Particle Swarm Optimization (cpso) is used to optimize the parameters of the Least Square Support Vector Machine (lssvm), the cpso-lssvm landslide sensitivity prediction model was formed. The experimental results show that cpso-lssvm has obtained good prediction results in landslide sensitivity evaluation, and the prediction accuracy has increased to 70.5%.

Keywords: Landslide · CPSO · LSSVM · ArcGIS

1 Introduction

The Sichuan Province of China is a region with frequent geological disasters of landslides. There are 2,664 landslides caused by rainfall, and the disaster density is as high as $1/100 \text{ km}^2$, ranking first in the country. Moreover, the population density of the region is relatively high, and the level of regional economic development is relatively high, which makes the region one of the areas where the landslide geological disasters in China are concentrated and the damage is extremely high. Therefore, the scientific and rigorous analysis of landslide sensitivity in this area is of great practical significance for disaster mitigation and disaster risk management [1].

There are two reasons for the difficulty in accurately assessing the sensitivity of regional landslides [2]. One of them is the predisposing factor, which includes internal factors, fundamental factors such as lithology, stratigraphic structure, topography, etc.; external factors are direct Factors such as rainfall, vegetation, and human activities, and the uncertainty, high latitude, and nonlinearity of these factors make it difficult to identify the landslides and their connections. Secondly, compared with evaluating

S. Han et al. (Eds.): AICON 2019, LNICST 287, pp. 213–223, 2019.
https://doi.org/10.1007/978-3-030-22971-9_18

single landslides, the sensitivity of landslides in the evaluation area is not only the need to find the sensitivities of landslides in a certain area statistically, but also the participation of other disciplines. From a practical point of view, it is also more research significance. So far, no better way to evaluate the landslide susceptibility has been found, which is why many scholars are keen to study this topic.

Advances in human scientific research in geological exploration, GIS, and AI have catalyzed more scientific research results in evaluating landslide susceptibility, such as Artificial Neural Network models, grey system models, logistic regression prediction models, and support vector machines (SVM). Applied to the sensitivity evaluation of landslides. Among them, support vector machine (SVM) [3] has higher prediction accuracy and has been successfully applied in landslide sensitivity. SVM is a small sample learning method and can effectively solve the problem of low input space dimension. Least Square Support Vector Machine (LSSVM) [4, 5] is a derivative of support vector machine, which is suitable for solving small sample problems and solves the "big sample" required by BP neural network. The convergence speed is slow, and the shortcomings of SVM operation time are overcome. Based on this, this paper proposes to use the LSSVM model to evaluate the landslide sensitivity. However, due to the problem of premature ripening when LSSVM model parameters are optimized, the Chao Particle Swarm Optimization (CPSO) algorithm is used to optimize the LSSVM model. The CPSO has the characteristics of ergodicity and strong searching ability. Applying it to the optimization parameter process, when the LSSVM algorithm falls into the premature phenomenon, the chaotic sequence method is used to chase the LSSVM model, and the optimal solution is quickly found, which improves the accuracy and convergence speed of the solution and improves the landslide. The accuracy of prediction of sensitivity evaluation is of great significance [6, 7].

2   Model Principle

LSSVM is an algorithm for improving SVM. It replaces the inequality constraint in SVM with equality constraint, and uses the loss function to change the quadratic programming problem of SVM into solving linear equation and set input n-dimensional vector. $\{(x_1, y_1), (x_2, y_2)...(x_l, y_l)\} \subset R^n \times R$, Linear function set to

$$f(x) = w^T - x + b \tag{1}$$

Optimization problem is

$$\min\left(\frac{1}{2}||w||^2 + \frac{1}{2}\gamma\sum_{i=1}^{l}\xi_i^2\right) \tag{2}$$

Constrained to

$$y_i = w^T x_i + b + \xi_i, \ i = 1, 2, ..., l \tag{3}$$

Define the Lagrangian function as

$$L = \frac{1}{2}\|w\|^2 + \frac{1}{2}\gamma\sum_{i=1}^{l}\xi_i^2 - \sum_{i=1}^{l}\alpha_i\left(w^T x_i + b + \xi_i - y_i\right) \tag{4}$$

Seeking partial derivatives for each parameter

$$\frac{\partial L}{\partial w} = 0 \rightarrow w = \sum_{i=1}^{l}\alpha_i x_i \tag{5}$$

$$\frac{\partial L}{\partial b} = 0 \rightarrow \sum_{i=1}^{l}\partial_i = 0 \tag{6}$$

$$\frac{\partial L}{\partial \xi_i} = 0 \rightarrow \alpha_i = \gamma\xi_i, \ i = 1, 2, \ldots, l \tag{7}$$

$$\frac{\partial L}{\partial \alpha_i} = 0 \rightarrow w^T + b + \xi_i - y_i = 0, \ i = 1, 2, \ldots, l \tag{8}$$

Equations (5)-formula (8) is expressed as a matrix form

$$\begin{bmatrix} I & 0 & 0 & -x \\ 0 & 0 & 0 & -1 \\ 0 & 0 & \gamma I & -I \\ x^T & 1 & I & 0 \end{bmatrix}\begin{bmatrix} w \\ b \\ \xi \\ \alpha \end{bmatrix} = \begin{bmatrix} 0 \\ 0 \\ 0 \\ y \end{bmatrix} \tag{9}$$

where I is a unit matrix; $x = [x_1 \ldots x_l]; y = [y_1 \ldots y_l]; \mathbf{1} = [1 \ldots 1]^T; \xi = [\xi_1 \ldots \xi_l];$ $\alpha = [\alpha_1 \ldots \alpha_l]];$
The solution of the formula (9) is determined by the formula (10).

$$\begin{bmatrix} 0 & \mathbf{1}^T \\ \mathbf{1} & x^T x + \gamma^{-1}I \end{bmatrix}\begin{bmatrix} b \\ a \end{bmatrix} = \begin{bmatrix} 0 \\ y \end{bmatrix} \tag{10}$$

By choosing the best kernel function K(x, y), we can get linear regression to

$$f(x) = \sum_{i=1}^{l}\alpha_i K(x_i, x) + b \tag{11}$$

This paper selects the radial basis kernel function and the expression is

$$K(x_i, x_j) = \exp\left(\frac{-\|x_i - x_j\|^2}{\sigma^2}\right) \tag{12}$$

where, σ is the perceived variable, and this paper needs to optimize (γ, σ) parameters.

2.1   CPSO-LSSVM Model

The PSO algorithm is an evolutionary algorithm that imitates the foraging process of the bird group. Compared with other algorithms, the PSO algorithm has the advantages of simple algorithm implementation and few parameters, but it is easy to fall into local extremum and cause premature convergence. In this paper, in order to make the group jump out of the local optimum quickly, the chaos idea and the PSO algorithm are combined, and the chaotic sequence is used to optimize the search of the PSO algorithm, which improves the accuracy and convergence speed of the PSO algorithm.

The position and velocity of the particles are updated using Eqs. (13) and (14).

$$v_j^{k+1} = w v_j^k + c_1 r_1 \left(p_{j-}^k x_j^k \right) + c_2 r_2 (p_g^k - x_j^k) \tag{13}$$

$$x_j^{k+1} = x_j^k + v_i^{k+1} \tag{14}$$

where, v_j is particle velocity; w is the weight; c_1 and c_2 are acceleration coefficients; r_1 and r_2 are random Numbers within the range of [0,1]. p_j is the individual optimal solution; p_g is the overall optimal solution; x_j^k is the decision variable.

Its iterative formula is

$$z_{i+1} = \mu z_i (1 - z_i), i = 1, 2, 3 \ldots, \mu \subset (2, 4] \tag{15}$$

at $\mu = 4$ and $0 \leq z_i \leq 1$, the system is completely chaotic.

The CPSO algorithm is mainly used to optimize the regularization parameter γ and kernel function σ of LSSVM. I'm going to use $x_j = (\gamma_j, \sigma_j)$ for the position of the JTH particle. The fitness function is

$$\text{fitness} = \sum_{i=1}^{N} |y_i - \widehat{y}_l| / N \tag{16}$$

where, N is the sample number; y_i is the actual sample value and $\widehat{y}_l$ is the predicted sample value.

The flow chart of cpso-lssvm is shown in Fig. 1.

3   Regional Landslide Data Acquisition and Feature Extraction Were Studied

3.1   Study the Geology of the Area

The overall terrain of Sichuan Province is high in the west and low in the east, with high and low disparity, complex landforms, rich soil types, plateaus and mountains in the west, more than 3,000 m above sea level, basins and hills in the east, and altitudes between 500 and 2000 m. The experimental observation area is 112,000 km^2 and is located in the hilly area of eastern Sichuan Province, accounting for 23% of the total area of Sichuan Province, as shown in Fig. 2.

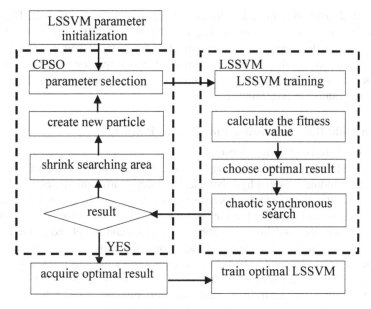

Fig. 1. CPSO-LSSVM flow chart

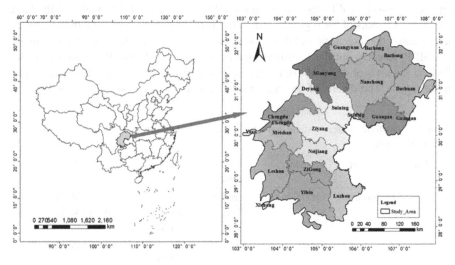

Fig. 2. Distribution of hilly areas in Sichuan Province

The administrative units included in the study area include: Chengdu, Zigong City, Zhangzhou City, Deyang City, Mianyang City, Guangyuan City, Suining City, Neijiang City, Leshan City, Nanchong City, Meishan City, Yibin City, Guang'an City, Da 18 cities (autonomous prefectures) including Chuan City, Ya'an City, Bazhong City, Ziyang City, and Liangshan Yi Autonomous Prefecture. From the perspective of world geography, Sichuan is located in the Asia-Europe earthquake zone. From the geographical division of China, it is located in the southwest seismic belt. The crustal movement is active, the earthquake is frequent, the mountain structure is unstable, and some areas are in the monsoon climate zone. The dry rainy season is distinct and the precipitation is concentrated. In the summer, there are many heavy rains, and there are many types of meteorological disasters, and the frequency of occurrence is high, so it is easy to cause landslide phenomenon.

3.2 Landslide Data Acquisition and Feature Extraction

3.2.1 Landslide Data Acquisition

The various influencing factors leading to landslides are called landslide susceptibility factors [8], including topography, geological lithology, artificial slopes (roads, reservoirs, etc.), natural slopes (rivers, lakes, etc.), vegetation cover, geological structures. Wait. Whether it can be selected as the landslide susceptibility factor has the following two criteria: First, the landslide susceptibility factor should be related to the landslide activity, that is, whether it is the root cause or direct cause of the landslide phenomenon; secondly, landslide sensitivity factor is obtainable and quantifiable. Under the analysis of the observation of Sichuan hilly area, firstly, considering the disaster-causing mechanism of landslides, landslides are mainly affected by topography, lithology, geological structure, slope cutting and underlying surface conditions. Second, consider to the availability of data, select elevation, slope, terrain relief, fault structure, geotechnical types, rivers, roads, NDVI. Wang et al. [9] analyzed the landslide impact factors of the region based on the variable dimension fractal theory and the deterministic coefficient probability model, and used the multi-layer perceptron model (CF-MLP) to carry out the landslide susceptibility in the region. Evaluation [10] verified the importance of the above eight landslide impact factors on the landslide impact in the region. The details of the eight landslide impact factors are shown in Table 1.

Table 1. Sensitivity index system construction table of low-mountain and hilly landslide in Sichuan Province

Number	The main class	The class	The data format	Access	Scale
1	Topography	Elevation	GeoTiff	DEM	30 m × 30 m
		Slope	GeoTiff	Extraction based on DEM	30 m × 30 m
		Relief	GeoTiff	Extraction based on DEM	30 m × 30 m
2	Cut slope	The river	Shape File	River network map	1:250,000
		The road	Shape File	Dart map	1:250,000
3	The lithology	Rock and soil types	Shape File	Geological map extraction	1:500,00
4	Vegetation coverage	NDVI	GeoTiff	MODIS offers products	30 m × 30 m
5	Geological structure	Fracture structure	Shape File	Geological map extraction	1:500,000

3.2.2   Landslide Data Preprocessing

The eight landslide impact factors mentioned in Sect. 3.2.1 of this paper constitute the conditional attributes of the LSSVM model. The state of the landslide (landslide state: 1; non-landslide state: 0) constitutes the decision attributes of the model. In order to achieve data standardization, different hierarchical quantization methods are used for different factors. For numerical factors, if the classification has a clear geographical significance, it is graded according to its geographical significance (including: slope, terrain relief); if its classification has no clear geologic significance, it is graded at equal intervals (Including: elevation, distance from the fault structure, distance from the river, distance from the road and vegetation cover). For type value factors, no classification is required, such as geotechnical types. The grading of each factor is shown in Table 2.

Table 2. Classification of landslide impact factors in hilly areas of Sichuan Province

The main class	Factor	Grading\class	Area (%)	Factor	Classification	Area (%)
Topography	Slope	0–3°	20.57	Elevation	0–400 m	37.2
		3–5°	17.09		400–600 m	45.84
		5–15°	43.01		600–800 m	11.31
		15–25°	14.42		800–1000 m	3.41
		25–30°	2.55		1000–1200 m	1.18
		30–45°	2.13		>1200 m	1.06
		>45°	0.24			
The geological structure	Distance from fault	0–2 km	5.83	Distance from fault	10–12 km	8.84
		2–4 km	14.36		12–14 km	7.54
		4–6 km	13.68		14–16 km	6.26
		6–8 km	12.09		>16 km	5.04
		8–10 km	10.23			
Cut slope	Distance from river	0–2 km	10.14	Distance from road	0–2 km	13.6
		2–4 km	33.49		2–4 km	11.65
		4–6 km	22.16		4–6 km	10.43
		6–8 km	16.01		6–8 km	9.16
		8–10 km	11.17		8–10 km	8.38
		>10 km	7.02		10–12 km	7.48
		0–200 m	71.81		12–14 km	6.36
		200–600 m	25.96		>14 km	32.93
		>600 m	2.23			
Geological lithology	The lithology	1(loose deposits)	9.96	The lithology	6 (conglomerate)	37.7
		2 (mudstone)	16.78		7 (dolomite)	
		3 (limestone)	3.35		8 (carbonate rock)	
		4 (basalt)	0.84		9 (granite)	0.54
		5 (sandstone)	20.83		10 (shale)	
Vegetation coverage	NDVI	[−1, 1]				

When there is abnormal data or missing data when acquiring sample data, mainly due to meshing or boundary value, the ignore value method is used for such data, that is, the missing attribute values are ignored, the purpose is to keep Enter the integrity of the data. In addition, in order to reduce the computational difficulty, this paper normalizes and normalizes the attributes. The normalization formula is as follows:

$$x' = (x - x_{min})/(x_{max} - x_{min}) \tag{17}$$

where, $x(x \in [x_{min}, x_{max}])$ is the real attribute value, x_{min} and x_{max} are the minimum and maximum values of this attribute respectively, and $x' \in (0, -1)$ is the normalized attribute value.

4   Simulation Research

In order to verify the validity of the algorithm model in this paper, the training sample data are arranged, the training set samples are taken from the odd items of the sample data, and the test set samples are taken from the even items of the data. Set the total number of particle swarm to 100, because the fitness converges rapidly with the number of iterations, so set the number of iterations to 100, the learning factor $c_1 = 1$, $c_2 = 5.9$, and the inertia weight $W = 0.5$. The optimal parameters obtained in the end $\gamma = 25$, $\sigma = 2.76$. In order to compare the map-making effect of ArcGis [11] predicted by cpso-lssvm model, this paper also uses PSO-LSSVM for experiments. The results are shown in Fig. 3. In this paper, the research area is divided into five grades by natural breakpoint method, which are extremely low sensitivity, low sensitivity, medium sensitivity, high sensitivity and extremely high sensitivity. That is, the more sensitive the part of the landslide is, the closer it is to red. In the CPSO-LSSVM (Fig. 3A), most of the areas where the landslide points fall are highly sensitive areas, and the sensitive areas of each level are more accurately divided. In the PSO-LSSVM (Fig. 3B), some areas with dense landslide sites are not highly sensitive, which is inconsistent with the characteristics of the landslide development in the study area. Therefore, CPSO-LSSVM is more in line with the actual landslide distribution law than PSO-LSSVM.

And using the ROC curve [12], the CPSO-LSSVM model PSO-LSSVM model was compared and analyzed. The ROC curve is a comprehensive indicator of the sensitivity (Sensitivity) and specificity (1-Specificity) continuous variables. Sensitivity refers to the proportion of all positive categories that are predicted to be positive, and specificity refers to the proportion of all negative classes that are predicted to be positive. Then, the ROC curve is plotted with the sensitivity as the ordinate and the specificity as the abscissa. The ROC is calculated as follows:

$$\text{Sensitivity} = \frac{TP}{TP + FN} \tag{18}$$

$$1 - \text{Specificity} = \frac{FP}{FP + TN} \tag{19}$$

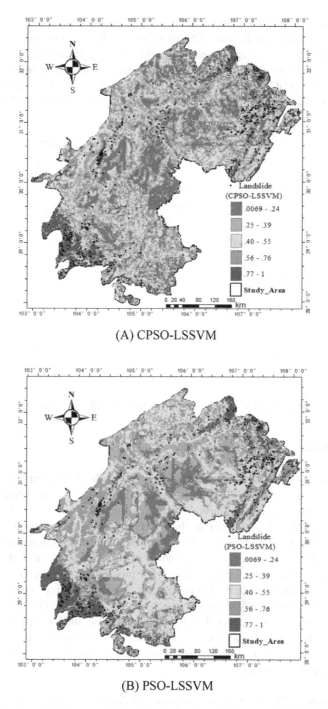

(A) CPSO-LSSVM

(B) PSO-LSSVM

Fig. 3. Landslide sensitivity areas obtained by different prediction models (Color figure online)

where TP refers to positive samples with positive predictions, FP refers to positive samples with negative predictions, TN refers to negative samples with positive predictions, and FN refers to negative samples with negative predictions.

Figure 4 shows the ROC curves formed by two prediction models. As shown, CPSO – LSSVM(AUC) = 0.716, PSO – LSSVM(AUC) = 0.708. It can be seen that the prediction accuracy of CPSO-LSSVM is better than that of PSO-LSSVM.

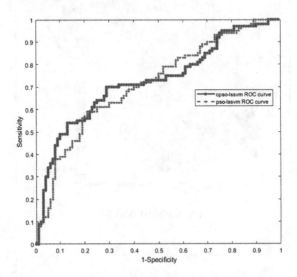

Fig. 4. ROC curves of relative ratios of different models

5   Conclusion

In view of the problem that the landslide sensitivity is difficult to accurately predict, the LSSVM is used to predict the landslide in Sichuan Province, and the hyperparameter of the model is optimized by the particle swarm optimization algorithm. Aiming at the problem of insufficient optimization ability of typical particle swarm optimization algorithm, an improved particle swarm optimization algorithm is proposed. The cpso-lssvm landslide sensitivity evaluation model was constructed, and the defect of LSSVM easily falling into the local minimum problem was overcome. In order to verify the effect of the model, the landslide point density renderings were drawn using ArcGis, and the CPSO-LSSVM model was compared with the PSO-LSSVM model in combination with the ROC curve. Finally, both evaluation methods show that CPSO-LSSVM is more suitable for landslide susceptibility evaluation, and the prediction effect is better than PSO-LSSVM, which provides a new way of thinking in the direction of landslide sensitivity prediction.

Acknowledgments. This research was supported by Tianjin Key Laboratory of Soft Soil Characteristics and Engineering Environment.

References

1. Huang, F., Yin, K., Jiang, S.: Evaluation of landslide vulnerability based on clustering analysis and support vector machine. J. Rock Mech. Eng. **37**(1), 156–167 (2008)
2. Wang, Z., Hu, Z., Zhao, W.: Determining the best statistical unit of topographic relief by using cumulative and analytical algorithm. Surv. Mapp. Sci. **39**(6), 59–64 (2014)
3. Niu, R., Peng, L., Ye, R.: Landslide susceptibility assessment based on rough sets and support vector machine. J. Jilin Univ.: Earth Sci. **42**(2), 430–439 (2012)
4. Suykens, J., Vandevalle, J.: Least squares support vector machine classifiers. Neural Process. Lett. **9**(3), 293–300 (1999)
5. Li, X., Xu, J.: Landslide deformation prediction based on wavelet analysis and LSSVM. Geodesy Geodyn. **29**(04), 127–130 (2009)
6. Liu, Q., Sun, J., Chen, X., Liu, J., Zhang, Q.: Application of CPSO-LSSVM in autoregressive clock difference forecasting. J. Jilin Univ. (Eng. Ed.) **44**(03), 807–811 (2014)
7. Liu, M.: Network intrusion detection based on CPSO-LSSVM. Comput. Eng. **39**(11), 131–135 (2013)
8. Nie, J., Lian, J., Hu, Z.: Analysis of landslide spatial characteristics in wenchuan earthquake-stricken area. Geogr. Res. **33**(2), 214–224 (2014)
9. Wang, Z., Hu, Z., Zhao, W.: Sensitivity analysis of environmental factors for rainfall-induced landslides based on probability model of deterministic coefficients-taking the low mountain and hilly areas of Sichuan Province as an example. Disaster Sci. **29**(2), 109–115 (2014)
10. Wang, Z., Hu, Z., Zhao, W.: Regional landslide sensitivity assessment based on multilayer perceptron model district as an example. J. Disaster Prev. Mitig. Eng. **35**(5), 691–698 (2015)
11. Saadatkhah, N., Kassim, A., Lee, L.M.: Qualitative and quantitative landslide susceptibility assessments in Hulu Kelang area, Malaysia. Electron. J. Geotech. Eng. **19**, 545–563 (2014)
12. Feng, F., Wu, X., Niu, R.: Landslide sensitivity evaluation of BP neural network based on particle swarm optimization. Sci. Surv. Mapp. **42**(10), 170–175 (2017)

Multitasks Scheduling in Delay-Bounded Mobile Edge Computing

Longyu Zhou[✉], Supeng Leng, Ning Yang, and Ke Zhang

University of Electronic Science and Technology of China,
Chengdu, Sichuan, China
zhoulyfuture@outlook.com

Abstract. The Mobile Edge Computing (MEC) is a very novel technology in the social network. In order to satisfy the users' delay and enhance data security and reduce energy consumption of the system. In this paper, we design an optimized strategy of edge servers chosen by reinforcement learning (AI algorithm) for resource consumption of multi-edge server. We transform the objective function into a convex optimization problem for the single edge server, and give proofs. In this scenario, it is made up of multi-users with multi-tasks and the same type of edge servers deployed on the edge of the base stations, the edge servers allocate computing resources to users. Meanwhile, the users send different tasks to the edge servers to complete computing tasks. In order to complete users' requirements under their delay-bounded, we design an optimal path algorithm named Betweenness Centrality Algorithm (BCA) to reduce the transmission delay and we use Fuzzy Logical algorithm to classify computing tasks. We propose a resource allocation mechanism under satisfying delay-bounded. Finally, comparing to the random selected strategy and other schemes, we prove the effectiveness of the introduced algorithm, which reduces the energy consumption by 20% approximately for the single edge server, and the simulation proves that the Double Deep Q-learning (Double DQN) algorithm shows better performance than Random Selected Strategy for the multi-edge servers.

Keywords: Mobile edge computing · Energy consumption ·
Reinforcement learning · Convex approximation · Tasking scheduling

1 Introduction

With the development of 5G technology and the popularity of the intelligent terminals, kinds of application services come into being. Meanwhile, users are stricter in the service quality and delay for requesting. In the case of smart devices with AI, Cartner predicts that the number of smart devices supporting AI will increase from 10% in 2017 to 80% in 2020, it is obvious that smart mobile devices will become the one of the most popular artificial intelligence platform in the world [1]. In December 2017, Google launched android 8.1 which support the Neural Network API(NNAPI), it provides faster hardware computing ability for machine learning [2]. To serve the delay-sensitive applications, the Mobile Edge Computing (MEC) architecture has been proposed. In MEC, edge servers will be addressed locally, and are consequently more efficient in delay-sensitive applications.

© ICST Institute for Computer Sciences, Social Informatics and Telecommunications Engineering 2019
Published by Springer Nature Switzerland AG 2019. All Rights Reserved
S. Han et al. (Eds.): AICON 2019, LNICST 287, pp. 224–237, 2019.
https://doi.org/10.1007/978-3-030-22971-9_19

MEC is a distributed cloud system, which refers to the deployment of computing resources at the edge network [3]. Because mobile devices are short in the resource computing, the terminal device hands over some or all computing tasks to the cloud, the mobile device decides how to offload, how much to offload and what to offload. The resource allocation focuses on how to allocate resources after offloading. In fact, the MEC can be regarded as a cloud service platform which is running on the edge network. By deploying resources such as computing, storage, networking and communications at the edge of the mobile network [4]. To better satisfy the users' delay, we get the lower energy consumption, the link selection and computing cost are suggested to be jointly scheduled [5].

There are some recent papers about the optimization of the computing cost in the MEC system. In [6], the authors study ways to minimum the delay of users in the MEC system by joint optimization of tasks scheduling and resource allocation. In [7], authors propose an online algorithm that decides the local execution and computation offloading policy is developed based on Lyapunov optimization. This method optimizes the power consumption of edge servers. In [8], the authors consider a scenario of Vehicular Edge Computing (VEC), they adopt a Stackelberg game theoretic approach to design an optimal multilevel offloading scheme, which maximizes the utilities of both the vehicles and the computing servers. In [9], the authors study the offloading and auto-scaling in MEC system. They propose an efficient reinforcement learning-based resource management algorithm, which learns on-the-fly the optimal policy of dynamic workload to minimize the long-term system cost. In [10], the authors present a novel framework for offloading computation tasks, from a user device to a server hosted in the mobile edge (ME) with highest CPU availability. In [11] and [12], in order to jointly computation offloading and content caching strategies, the authors transform the original problem into a convex problem and find the optimal solution of approximated problem. In [13], the authors provide an architecture of centralized cloud and distributed MEC over hybrid fiber-wireless network in MEC system, which has the features of supporting diverse network techniques, easy expansibility, high capacity and reliability, low latency and energy consumption. They solve the question by an approximation collaborative computation offloading scheme. They consider the shortcomings of single networking mode, high congestion, high latency and energy consumption, but the proposed algorithms are hard to be implemented.

In this paper, we study into how the tasks route to destinations and how the computation resource in the edge server is allocated to users. Considering the limited resource utilization of edge servers and the data-offloaded with bounded delay requirements, so how to utilize the resource of edge servers needs to be paid attention. If an edge server's tasks are too much in a period of time, it will perform a terrible effectiveness. We propose the data route scheme that users can chose a better path to upload data and the chosen edge server offloads data through the same path, this scheme undoubtedly produces collision, so we solve this problem by RTS/CTS scheme. When a user wants to upload data to an edge server through several base stations, the user sends RTS to the first base station, if the base station is idle, it will send CTS to user, if not, it will not send. If a base station sends RTS to another, if it doesn't receive the ACK, data will be stored in the cache. In fact, collision is an event with probability, so we use Free Path Distribution to minimum the collision in a period of time [14]. However, if all the edge servers are available, the edge servers allocate more computing resources to the tasks with delay bounds, and users can upload more data to edge servers. Meanwhile, other users maybe have the same result that this user want to get, the base station is only as a forwarding role without edge server, through this way, we can save computing consumptions. It is obvious that computing consumption is much than link consumption. We assume that this method obeys an exponential distribution. So far, we solve the link consumption successfully. As for the computing cost, for an edge server, different users with different sizes of data associate the edge server, we can analogy a M/M/1 queuing system. The computing ability of an edge server is directly related to the performance of CPU, we assume that every edge server has the same CPU ability. The MEC system includes multiple users, multiple base stations with edge servers and same base stations without edge servers. Our goal is to minimum the energy cost for the all MEC system [12].

The rest of paper is organized as follows. Section 2 introduces the system model and formulation. In Sect. 3, we study the multiple tasks scheduling schemes for single edge server. In Sect. 4, we study the multiple tasks scheduling for the MEC system. In Sect. 5, we express the Double Deep Q-learning algorithm. In Sect. 6, we show the numerical result through our analysis, and we display the relationship between bounded delay and energy consumption. We conclude in Sect. 7.

2 System Model and Formulation

We consider that a MEC system include multiple users, base stations with computing ability and base stations without computing ability, users communicate with base stations by wireless, in other words, the MEC system is a wireless network. When the computing task is done, the results are sent to users. The MEC system is shown in Fig. 1.

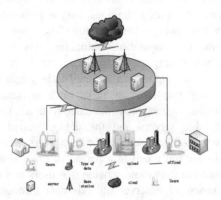

Fig. 1. System model includes that users, base stations with edge servers and base station without edge servers.

2.1 Deployment Model

In this paper, there are M base stations which make up a set $\mathbf{a} = \{1, 2, \ldots M\}$, we assume that the number of base stations is larger than the number of edge servers, there are K edge servers in MEC system, which make up a set $\mathbf{b} = \{1, 2, \ldots K\}$, and there are N users in a MEC system, which make up a set $\mathbf{c} = \{1, 2, \ldots N\}$. We apply the optimal path algorithm to help user find destination. During transmission, if path only has one hop, we use direct transmission strategy. As long as the count of hop is greater than 1, we take Betweenness centrality algorithm to get the better path routing.

The scheme can be displayed through connected undirected graph $G(V, E)$. For all the base station network, we assume that b_i is the i-th sensor, $P(b_i)$ denoted the probability of graph.

$$P(b_i) = \frac{1}{z} \prod_{i \in c_G} \phi_i(b_i) \tag{1}$$

Through the **Hammersley-Clifford Theorem**, the probability of graph can be expressed as the product of the potential functions, which defined on all the largest group for a graph. c_G denotes the set of the largest group, $z = \sum b \prod_{i \in c_G} \phi_i(b_i)$ denotes normalized constant. ϕ_i denotes the potential function of graph.

Proof: Because the sensors are dynamic in a graph, and the path selection only related to the previous path, so this scenario satisfies Markov random field model, so we use BCA to select a node named observation vertex, other two nodes are independent in a condition. In other words, anyone node in a graph satisfy:

$$P(X_i | X_{G \setminus i}) = P(X_i | X_{N_i}) \tag{2}$$

$X_{G \setminus i}$ denotes all the nodes except for i, X_{N_i} denotes all vertices connected to X_i. The formulation is another definition.

2.2 Transmission Model

For an edge server, we assume that l_i bits are transferred in a period of time, and we assume that $X_{t,i}$ denotes that the i-th base station delivers data to the next base station or user in a period of time. We assume that collision obeys Free Path Distribution. The probability of a collision between $X_{t,i}$ and $X_{t,i} + dX_{t,i}$ is as follows.

$$P_{t,i}(X) = \exp(-\frac{X}{\bar{\lambda}}) \tag{3}$$

$\bar{\lambda}$ denotes the average time between two collisions. We can get a conclusion that the probability obeys the exponential distribution.

As for a MEC system, the smaller probability of collision, the better. From the perspective of the edge servers, we assume the energy consumption of receiving data in a period of time is as follows:

$$r_i = \varepsilon_{elec} \times l_i \tag{4}$$

and the energy consumption of sending data in a period of time is as follows:

$$s_i = r_i + \varepsilon_{amp} \times l_i \times T^{\alpha} \tag{5}$$

In formulation (4) and (5), ε_{elec} denotes electric consumption for every bit, and ε_{amp} denotes amplifier's gain consumption while sending a single bit, and T denotes that the distance from the users to the edge server, α denotes that the index of path loss.

During the data transmission, we assume N tasks will be sent in a slot time, so the SINR (Signal to Interference plus Noise Ratio) of the i-th task is as follows:

$$r_i(t) = \frac{p_i g_i(t)}{\sum\limits_{m=1,m\neq i}^{M} p_m g_m(t) + \delta_t} \tag{6}$$

In formulation (6), p_i denotes the power of i-th task, $g_i(t)$ denotes the i-th task's power gain in the t slot time, p_m denotes the m-th task's power, and $g_m(t)$ denotes the m-th task's power gain in the t slot time, δ_t denotes white Gaussian noise. So the i-th task's transmission rate is as follows:

$$v_i(t) = \omega_i \log_2(1 + r_i(t)), \forall i \in c, j \in b \tag{7}$$

In formulation (7), ω_i denotes the i-th task's bandwidth.

2.3   Edge Computing Model

In computing tasks of edge servers, the most consumed is resource of CPU [15]. The processing ability for each CPU is directly related to the efficiency. In other words, the more resource of CPU, the faster processing efficiency, and the more users satisfy the minimum delay. However, the resource for every CPU is limited, and the size of data is usually different. We assume that an edge server receives π tasks in a period of time, which makes up a set $\pi = \{1, 2 \ldots N\}$, and every edge server receives different size of task because of the size of task is rand, so we introduce Fuzzy logical algorithm to help solve. There are K edge servers, every edge server has bounded resource, we assume the bounded resource is c_{max} for every edge server. The energy consumption for the i-th edge server follows the model:

$$c_j = \sum_{i=1}^{N} fuzzy(\pi_{i,j}) \times c_{i,j} \tag{8}$$

In formulation (8), $c_{i,j}$ denotes the unit resource consumption of the i-th task from the i-th user to the j-th base station. So the i-th task's transmission rate is as follows:

$$t_i^{trans} = \frac{\pi_i}{v_i(t)} \tag{9}$$

Except for the transmission delay, the computing delay and the waiting time are also not ignored, we assume the concurrency value of one server is ϑ, the computing delay is as follows:

$$t_i^{copt} = \frac{\pi_i}{\vartheta \times QPS} \tag{10}$$

In the above formulation, QPS denotes the unit computing ability.

We assume that the arrival rate of tasks is $e_i(t)$, the unit computing ability is $c_j(t)$, so we can get the average waiting time by Queue theory:

$$t_i^{wait} = \frac{e_i(t)}{c_j(t)(c_j(t) - e_i(t))} \tag{11}$$

After discussing the delay of users, we can define the delay-bounded:

$$t_{c,k} = 2 \times t_k^{trans} + t_k^{copt} + t_k^{wait}, \forall k \in c \tag{12}$$

2.4 Problem Formulation

We assume that consumption among base stations is the same, $l_{\cos t}$ denotes the link consumption, $t_{k,\max}$ denotes the maximum delay tolerance. The link consumption for every segment is the same, in other words, we ignore the subtle difference about different link distance, our optimized goal can be written in the following form, which minimizes the cost in MEC system.

$$\begin{aligned} \min \ & \sum_{i \in b} c_i + \sum_{j \in a} l_{\cos t_j} \\ s.t. \ & c_i \le c_{\max}, \forall i \in b \\ & t_{c,k} \le t_{k,\max}, \forall k \in c \end{aligned} \tag{13}$$

3 Tasks Scheduling for the Single-Server

For the i-th base station with edge server, the optimization objective is $\sum_{i \in b} c_i + \sum_{j \in a} l_{\cos t_j}$.

In this part, we study into how the tasks of users should be scheduled so that the object is minimized.

3.1　Data Transmission

In this scenario, a user transfer data to edge server through several base stations. In other words, data is sent from one base station to another base station. Under this circumstance, probability of no collision is $1-P_{t,i}$, we assume that the delay-bounded is T_i, the number of total segments is $n = \frac{T_i}{X_{t,i}}$. To guarantee to transfer successfully, the probability of transfer successfully can be written exponential distribution:

$$P_{su} = (1 - P(X_{t,i})) \times \exp(n) \tag{14}$$

Proof: In order to ensure that data is transferred successfully between base stations, it is necessary to ensure that data is transferred successfully in each segment.

$$
\begin{aligned}
P_{su} &= (1 - P(X_{t,i}))^n \\
&= \exp(\log(1 - P(X_{t,i}))^n) \\
&= (1 - P(X_{t,i})) \times \exp(n)
\end{aligned}
$$

3.2　Computing Consumption

Through our analysis, as for the computing consumption, the size of data is not suitable by Fuzzy algorithm [16]. We introduce the computing time of queuing theory (M/M/1), we assume that the computing time obeys the exponential distribution. The energy consumption for computing is as follows:

$$c_j = \sum_{i=1}^{N} fuzzy(\pi_{i,j}) \times c_{i,j} \tag{15}$$

We convert data capacity to computing time, in other words, $\omega_{t,i}$ denotes that i-th base station's unit computing consumption in a t slot time.

Proof: according to the queuing theory, processing time obeys exponential distribution, so the time is as follows:

$$F(\omega_{t,i}) = 1 - \exp(-(\pi_{i,j} - \lambda_{i,j})\omega_{t,i})$$

$\Rightarrow \omega_{t,i} = \frac{\ln(1-F(\omega_{i,j}))}{\lambda_{i,j}-\pi_{i,j}}$, because $F(\omega_{t,i}) > 1$, we can get $\omega_{t,i} > 0$.

Because $F(\omega_{t,i})$ obeys the exponential distribution, it is obvious that $F(\omega_{t,i}) > 1$ is always established.

3.3　Optimization Energy Consumption

In a MEC system, if a user requires data to an edge server, it is likely that the edge server gets data from other users [17]. We assume that not all data is computed by edge server, in a period of time, we can optimize the energy consumption.

$$\min \lambda_{i,j} \times c_i + (\lambda_i - \lambda_{i,j}) \times l_{\cos t} \qquad (16)$$

In formulation (16), we can get a conclusion that when data from users is too big, edge server can get some advice from other users, and it is a concave optimization problem.

Proof: as for the formulation (11), we can get the derivative of the $\lambda_{i,j}$. If we want to get the solution of derivation.

$$\frac{\partial F}{\partial \lambda_{i,j}} = 0$$

From computing consumption and link cost, the equation has a solution or not is related to the probability P_{su}, so we can find a suitable probability to change into a concave problem.

4   Tasks Scheduling for Multi-servers

In a MEC system, multi-edge servers need to jointly schedule to complete the computing tasks [18]. By our analysis and the model of the queuing theory, some data needs to be computed by edge servers and others can be got from other users, this is our goal to get the optimization of this problem.

4.1   Computing Consumption Analysis

For the multi-edge servers and multi-tasks, we can't get a valid scheme by transforming concave function. Thanking of the delay-bounded of users and the computing capacity of edge servers, we design an edge server selected scheme. We import a binary variance to complete the work of selecting which edge server to compute and define $f_i = \{0, 1\}$. When an edge server is chosen, the tasks will be offloaded through the path designed by BCA to the edge server. The mathematic model is defined as follows:

$$\min_{f(j)} \sum_{j=1}^{M} f_j \times c_j, \forall j \in a \qquad (17)$$

4.2   Bounded Delay for Users

In the actual MEC network, some important data usually be stored in the cache or the remote cloud, when the amount of data is increasing, the early data in the cache will be deleted because the space of cache is limited, we assume that the base stations with edge server or not is a probability event [19]. We can see it that this probability obeys Gaussian distribution, and it is very likely that users can obtain data through other users within a certain period of time, so the delay-bounded of users is redefined as follows:

$$t_{c,k} = 2 \times t_k^{trans} + \kappa_t(t_k^{copt} + t_k^{wait}), \forall k \in c \tag{18}$$

In the above formulation, κ_t denotes Gaussian distribution in t slot time.

4.3   Energy Consumption for MEC System

In this paper, our final optimized goal is minimizing energy consumption for all the MEC system. However, we should satisfy the bounded delay of users, so for all the MEC system, we assume the number of edge servers is K, the number of base stations is M. we define that all the energy consumption includes the computing consumption and link consumption. After receiving inspiration from queuing theory, we get the final option of energy consumption.

$$\min \sum_{i \in b} \sum_{j \in a} f_j \times (c_i + l_{\cos t_j})$$
$$s.t. f_j \in \{0, 1\} \tag{19}$$
$$c_i \le c_{\max}, \forall i \in b$$
$$t_{c,k} \le t_{k,\max}, \forall k \in c$$

For the above formulation, it is a non-linear math model, so we can't get a good result within limited time, so we use AI algorithm to solve this model and get a good strategy. Because we can't get any information about transport channel, so we use the Double Deep Q-learning algorithm that no need training sample.

5   Double DQN Analysis

In this paper, we use the Double DQN algorithm to solve the non-linear mathematic model. The core of this algorithm is that agent interact with environment, by learning Y_t^Q value to update the last true value to get the optimized result. the Y_t^Q is defined as follows:

$$Y_t^Q = R_{t+1}(s, a) + \gamma Q(s_{t+1}, \arg\min_a Q(s_{t+1}, a; \theta_t); \theta_t) \tag{20}$$

The double Q-learning error can be written as:

$$Y_t^{DQ} = R_{t+1}(s, a) + \gamma Q(s_{t+1}, \arg\min_a Q(s_{t+1}, a; \theta_t); \theta_t') \tag{21}$$

In above formulation, $R_{t+1}(s, a)$ denotes that when adapting action a and state s, the system's reward, γ denotes penalty factor, θ_t denotes a parameter updating the main network, and θ_t' denotes a parameter updating the target network. The algorithm flow chart is as follows (Table 1):

Table 1. Algorithm flow chart

input number of iteration, dimension of state, action, step, penalty factor, target and main network, frequency updating.
output: Q value
for i,..T, do:
get the state's eigenvector $\phi(s)$;
get Q-value of all the state, using greedy algorithm to choose action A;
execute action A, get new state s' 's eigenvector $\phi(s')$ and reward R;
update the state set;
calculating target Q-value using samples ;
updating all the parameters in Q-network;
updating the target parameters every C steps;
end for;

6 Numerical Results

In this part, the numerical results are simulated to show the optimization, we consider the data about some people's behaviors from RAWDAD, which is a community resource for archiving wireless data at Dartmouth. In Fig. 2, the x-axis denotes the bounded delay of people from RAWDAD, and y-axis denotes satisfied requirement, in other words, the number or rate of the satisfied people in a period of time, from Fig. 1, we can get that the delay between 0.1 s and 3 s. So we set the range of bounded delay from 0.1 s to 3 s. For the base station, the arrival rates of data $\lambda_i \in [0, 30]$, the range of tasks from 10 to 50, and the sizes of the tasks obeys the Gaussian Fuzzy, the mean value is 0, and the variance is 0.1.

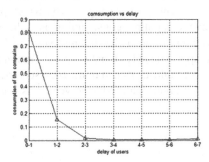

Fig. 2. The satisfied requirement under different delays

In Fig. 2, the relationship between the satisfied requirement that the satisfied or successful rate of requirement and the delay of the users. We can get some conclusions from it, the data is from the RAWDAD, and the most delays of the users are under 3 s, so we assume that the delay between 0.1 s and 3 s can get better results. If the delay is bigger than 3 s, we assume that the high rate of people cannot stand. And we can learn that the satisfied rate focus on under 2 s. The data of MEC can help us the work for the simulation, and we can make the goal well done under the conference of the data.

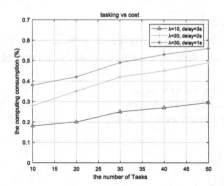

Fig. 3. The computing consumption under the number of tasks, which is compared in different delay and the Poisson stream.

In Fig. 3, the performance of four sides are compared in single-edge server. In the figure, x-axis denotes the number of tasks, which stand for the size of the queue, and y-axis denotes the rate of the computing consumption for the edge servers, which is set that the total rate is 1. When the data is required firstly, we assume that the most results should be got from the edge servers, and when the Poisson stream is large, we assume that some data can be got from edge servers and others can be got from other users. On the whole, the different side with different size is linear growth but multiple growth approximately, which proves that the optimization has a better performance. Under the bounded delay for users, we can get several conclusions from the figure. Firstly, for every trend of curve, the gradient is decreasing slowly, which proves that as the tasks are increasing, the relative computing consumption is reduced. Secondly, we can compare computing consumption under the different sides, we can get result that the algorithm improves 20% approximately. Finally, the algorithm can give us the better results from our analysis. For multi-tasks and multi-edge servers, we design the DDQN algorithm to solve, the result about multi-edge servers is as follows.

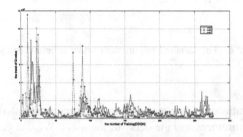

Fig. 4. Under different penalty factor, the trend of the Q-value.

In Fig. 4, the penalty factor is from 0.7 to 0.9, the x-axis denotes the step of training and the y-axis denotes the trend of the Q-value, the Q-value can be convergent in a range, but different penalty factor has different speed of convergence. From Fig. 4, we can get when the penalty factor is 0.7, Q-value has a better convergence.

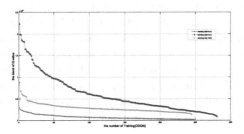

Fig. 5. Under different learning rate, the trend of the Q-value.

In Fig. 5, the learning rates we chosen are 1e–2, 1e–4 and 1e–6, the performance for the trend of Q-value is easily gotten that the good convergence. Comparing to the three learning rates, when equaling with 1e–2, the performance of convergence is best. We confirmed validation by comparing with Random Selection Scheme. the Fig. 6 is showed as follows.

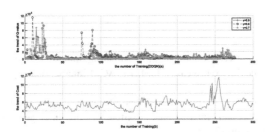

Fig. 6. Under different scheme, different scheme shows different validation and confirms Double DQN's effectiveness in this paper.

In Fig. 6, the DDQN algorithm is compared with Random Selection Algorithm (RSA), the two algorithm respectively corresponds Fig. 6(a) and (b). The x-axis denotes the number of training, and y-axis denotes the different cost between the two algorithms. From above results, Firstly, we add the number of the base stations with the edge servers, the average computing consumption will decrease. Secondly, from the performance, we can get that the speed of the DDQN's convergence is obviously better than RSA. Finally, the energy consumption of DDQN is one magnitude lower than RSA, which based on the energy analysis.

7 Conclusions

In this work, we consider the mobile computing for edge servers and the delay of users in a scenario in which some base stations with edge servers and others without edge servers. By jointly scheduling tasks to the base stations with edge servers, we optimize a MEC system so that the cost of link and computing resource. By solving the problems, we can get several conclusions. Firstly, in the MEC system, we should consider the users who are strict with the bounded delay. Secondly, we should choose the near neighbors to communicate and transfer what a user need. Thirdly, when the time of communication is larger, the edge servers should first find data from other users. Finally, for a certain MEC system, the number of the tasks scheduling is related to the number of the edge servers, but not absolutely. If we consider the number of the edge servers, we believe that the result will be better.

Acknowledgment. This work is supported by the National Key R&D Program of China (No. 2018YFC0807101).

This work is supported by the National Natural Science Foundation of China (No. 61374189), the joint fund of the Ministry of Education of China and China Mobile (MCM 20160304).

This work is supported by fundamental research funds for the central universities, China, under Grant No. 2672018ZYGX2018J001.

This work was supported by the Science & Technology Department of Sichuan Province under Grant 2018GZ0092.

References

1. Reiter, A., Zefferer, T.: Hybrid mobile edge computing: unleashing the full potential of edge computing in mobile device use cases. In: IEEE/ACM International Symposium on Cluster. IEEE (2017)
2. Wang, X., Liu, Z.: An energy-aware VMs placement algorithm in cloud computing environment. In: Second International Conference on Intelligent System Design & Engineering Application (2012)
3. Hung, C.H., Hsieh, Y.C., Wang, L.C.: Control plane latency reduction for service chaining in mobile edge computing system. In: International Conference on Network & Service Management. IEEE Computer Society (2017)
4. Abbas, N., Zhang, Y., Taherkordi, A., et al.: Mobile edge computing: a survey. IEEE Internet Things J. **99**, 1 (2017)
5. Bellavista, P., Chessa, S., Foschini, L., et al.: Human-enabled edge computing: exploiting the crowd as a dynamic extension of mobile edge computing. IEEE Commun. Mag. **56**(1), 145–155 (2018)
6. Zhao, T., Zhou, S., Guo, X., et al.: Tasks scheduling and resource allocation in heterogeneous cloud for delay-bounded mobile edge computing. In: IEEE International Conference on Communications. IEEE (2017)
7. Mao, Y., Zhang, J., Song, S.H, et al.: Power-delay tradeoff in multi-user mobile-edge computing systems (2016)
8. Zhang, K., Mao, Y., Leng, S., et al.: Optimal delay constrained offloading for vehicular edge computing networks. In: ICC 2017 - 2017 IEEE International Conference on Communications. IEEE (2017)

9. Xu, J., Ren, S.: Online learning for offloading and autoscaling in renewable-powered mobile edge computing. In: 2016 IEEE Global Communications Conference (GLOBECOM). IEEE (2017)
10. Wang, Y., Min, S., Wang, X., et al.: Mobile-edge computing: partial computation offloading using dynamic voltage scaling. IEEE Trans. Commun. **64**(10), 4268–4282 (2016)
11. Yu, Y., Zhang, J., Letaief, K.B.: 2016 IEEE Global Communications Conference (GLOBECOM) - Joint Subcarrier and CPU Time Allocation for Mobile Edge Computing, Washington, DC, USA, pp. 1–6, 4–8 December 2016
12. Wang, C., Liang, C., Yu, F.R., et al.: Computation offloading and resource allocation in wireless cellular networks with mobile edge computing. IEEE Trans. Wirel. Commun. **16**(8), 4924–4938 (2017)
13. Wang, C., Yu, F.R., Chen, Q., et al.: Joint computation and radio resource management for cellular networks with mobile edge computing. In: IEEE International Conference on Communications. IEEE (2017)
14. Ti, N.T., Le, L.B., Ti, N.T., et al.: Computation offloading leveraging computing resources from edge cloud and mobile peers. In: IEEE International Conference on Communications. IEEE (2017)
15. Corcoran, P.: Mobile-edge computing and internet of things for consumers: part II: energy efficiency, connectivity, and economic development. IEEE Consum. Electron. Mag. **6**(1), 51–52 (2016)
16. Ma, L., Liu, X., Pei, Q., et al.: Privacy-preserving reputation management for edge computing enhanced mobile crowdsensing. IEEE Trans. Serv. Comput. **99**, 1 (1939)
17. Liai, W., Xudong, Z., Chengyi, S., et al.: Studying parameter of MEC used to multi-modal optimization by two-level MEC. In: International Conference on Artificial Intelligence & Computational Intelligence. IEEE Computer Society (2009)
18. Xiang, S., Ansari, N.: EdgeIoT: Mobile Edge Computing for the Internet of Things (2016)
19. Lee, S.Q., Kim, J.U.: Local breakout of mobile access network traffic by mobile edge computing. In: International Conference on Information & Communication Technology Convergence. IEEE (2016)

Edge Computing Based Traffic Analysis System Using Broad Learning

Xiting Peng, Kaoru Ota, and Mianxiong Dong

Department of Information and Electronic Engineering,
Muroran Institute of Technology, Muroran, Japan
{17096505,ota,mxdong}@mmm.muroran-it.ac.jp

Abstract. Current traffic analysis methods are executed on the cloud, which need to upload the traffic data and consume precious bandwidth resources. Edge computing is a more promising way to save the bandwidth resources and improve users' privacy by offloading these tasks to the edge node. However, traffic analysis methods based on traditional machine learning need to retrain all traffic data when updating the trained model, which are not suitable for edge computing due to the poor computing power and low storage capacity of edge nodes. In this paper, we propose a novel edge computing based traffic analysis system using broad learning. For one thing, edge computing can provide a distributed architecture for saving the bandwidth resources and protecting users' privacy. For another, we use broad learning to incrementally train the traffic data, which is more suitable for edge computing because it can support incremental updates of models on the edge nodes without retraining all data. We implement our system on the Raspberry Pi, and experimental results show that we have 98% probability to accurately identify these traffic data. Moreover, our method has the faster training speed compared with Convolutional Neural Network (CNN).

Keywords: Traffic analysis · Edge computing · Broad learning system

1 Introduction

With the rapid development of Internet services, traffic types become diverse. In the complex network environment, traffic analysis is regarded as an important approach to ensure the security of network. It can effectively deal with many security issues, such as intrusion detection [3]. Moreover, network traffic analysis also plays an important role in modern network management systems, such as quality of service (QoS) [26]. Accurate identification of network traffic types is the basis for providing better services. By executing accurate traffic analysis, service providers can monitor the operation of the entire network. By analyzing users' traffic, service providers can realize their behaviors, which can provide the personalized services. Therefore, how to provide accurate traffic classification method is crucial.

© ICST Institute for Computer Sciences, Social Informatics and Telecommunications Engineering 2019
Published by Springer Nature Switzerland AG 2019. All Rights Reserved
S. Han et al. (Eds.): AICON 2019, LNICST 287, pp. 238–251, 2019.
https://doi.org/10.1007/978-3-030-22971-9_20

Current classification methods for traffic types are executed on the cloud, which need to upload all users' traffic to the cloud [19]. However, many applications, such as video applications, can generate large amounts of traffic in a short amount of time, and it will consume a lot of precious bandwidth resources if all traffic data is uploaded to the server [5]. Therefore, current cloud-based traffic analysis system does not apply to traffic-intensive applications. Moreover, service providers only need the classification results for monitoring the network operation and providing better services, rather than all traffic data. Therefore, it is better to propose a novel distributed traffic analysis architecture, which only needs to upload the classification results to the cloud.

Edge computing is a promising way to achieve the distributed traffic analysis architecture by offloading this task to the edge node close to user devices [2,9,17]. We can deploy the traffic classification models on the edge node, such as WiFi access points. In one hand, this method only needs to send the classification results to the cloud, rather than uploading all traffic data, which can analyze users' traffic in real time and save the precious bandwidth resources. In the other hand, users' traffic may contain many private information, such as location, gender, or education background, which can be inferred by the malicious service providers [22]. Compared with the cloud based traffic analysis architecture, edge computing can better protect the privacy of users.

Current traffic classification models are mainly based on traditional machine learning, including SVM, random forest and decision tree. However, these traditional methods cannot be directly used at edge computing based traffic analysis architecture due to the low computing and storage capabilities of edge nodes. In order to maintain the classification accuracy, it is better to regularly update the trained model. Traditional methods require retraining all data when performing model updates, which consume large amounts of computing power. Usually, the edge node has these characteristics: poor computing power and low storage capacity [20], which cannot support frequent retraining of all data. To address the above challenges, we use a novel and lightweight neural network structure, broad learning system (BLS) [4], which has the faster training speed due to its flat network structure. More importantly, BLS can use incremental learning to constantly update the trained model when new data enters, and no retraining process is needed.

In this paper, we propose a novel edge computing based traffic analysis system using broad learning. The proposed system is composed of two major modules: basic training on the cloud and incremental training (model updating) on the edge node. Firstly, we use some traffic data to train a basic model and send the basic model to the edge node. Secondly, when the accuracy of the trained model is not enough to provide better services, model updating will be executed on the edge node by the incremental way. We implement the edge computing based traffic analysis system on the Raspberry Pi, and the experimental results show that our method has the faster training speed compared with Convolutional Neural Network (CNN).

The main contributions of this paper are summarized as follows:

- We propose a distributed traffic analysis architecture, edge computing based traffic analysis system, which can save the bandwidth resources and protect users' privacy from being inferred by malicious service providers.
- In order to solve the problem of poor computing power and low storage capacities of edge nodes, we use a novel and lightweight neural network structure (broad learning system) to analyze traffic data, which has fast training speed and can support incremental learning.
- We implement our system on the Raspberry Pi and perform comprehensive experiments using real-world dataset to validate its performance.

The rest of this paper is organized as follows. Related work about the traffic analysis and the edge computing is introduced in Sect. 2. We briefly introduce the broad learning system in Sect. 3. Section 4 presents the proposed edge computing based traffic analysis system. We discuss the experimental evaluation in Sect. 5. We conclude this paper in Sect. 6.

2   Related Work

In this section, we will introduce the existing works with respect to the traffic analysis and explain their disadvantages under the environment with diverse traffic-intensive applications in detail.

2.1   Traffic Analysis

Traffic analysis plays an important role in providing better services by service providers. Nowadays, traffic analysis has received wide attention from both the academia and the industry [10,15]. Researchers have proposed many methods for traffic classification, which can be classified as follows: port-based identification, deep packet inspection, and machine learning. With the rapid development of Internet services, the first two technologies have strong limitations, which has the low accuracy when identifying varied traffic types. Therefore, machine learning based methods have been widely used by the academia and the industry.

Machine learning based traffic classification methods [14] have a wide range of applications in different fields. In [11], the authors proposed a traffic classification method based on semi-supervised support vector machine (S-SVM) to accurately identify a variety of network traffic. In [24], random forest was used to identify smartphone apps by fingerprinting the network traffic. Besides, many machine learning based methods are available for traffic classification. For instance, in [1], the authors used six common algorithms, such as Linear Regression, Decision Tree, and Multi-layer Perceptron, for malware traffic classification and compared their performances when confronted with real network data.

However, these methods are executed on the cloud, which need to upload all traffic to the server and consume large amounts of precious bandwidth resources.

In addition to wasting resources, uploading traffic to the cloud will also cause the leakage of users' privacy. In [7], the authors pointed out that users' privacy can be inferred by executing traffic analysis even in the case of encryption. Therefore, in this paper, we propose a novel distributed architecture with the help of edge computing to ensure that traffic data is analyzed at the edge node which is trustworthy to users. Furthermore, edge node always has the poor computing power and low storage capacity, which cannot directly deploy traditional machine learning based methods because these methods need to retrain all data when model updating. Deep learning based traffic analysis methods [23] can save and update the trained model in an incremental way. However, due to the complexity of the deep structure, it costs more time. Therefore, we use a lightweight neural network structure, broad learning system, to train the traffic data on the edge node in this paper.

2.2 Edge Computing

As users have higher requirements for lower latency, lower bandwidth consumption, and higher security and privacy, cloud services cannot meet their requirements. Therefore, edge computing is proposed as a promising way to assist cloud to achieve these requirements [13,20,25]. Generally speaking, edge computing means offloading some tasks that are previously carried out on the cloud to the devices that are close to the user side [21]. In some classic edge computing scenarios, such as Vehicular Network, Smart Home, Body Things, and other IoT scenarios, the edge nodes refer to the Road Side Unit (RSU), Hub (Gateway), smartphone, and WiFi access point, which always have little computing and storage capacities. By combining edge computing and cloud computing, service providers not only can meet the requirements of large-scale data processing, but also meet the needs of real-time [12].

The classic edge computing based architecture is comprised of the following three layers [8]: Cloud layer, Edge layer, and User layer. In this architecture, the users send the data to the edge node, rather than the cloud. And the edge node performs data processing tasks, which can provide the real-time services and reduce the burden of the server. After completing the data processing, the edge node sends the results to the cloud.

3 Preliminary Knowledge

In order to meet the characteristics of the poor computing power and low storage capacity of the edge node, we utilize broad learning system [4], a novel and lightweight neural network structure, which has fast training speed and does not need to retrain all data when regularly updating the trained model.

Broad learning system (BLS) is developed with fewer parameters and the training speed can be faster due to its flat network structure, which is composed of input layer, feature nodes/enhancement nodes, and output layer. The standard structure of BLS is shown in Fig. 1: Firstly, the mapped features are

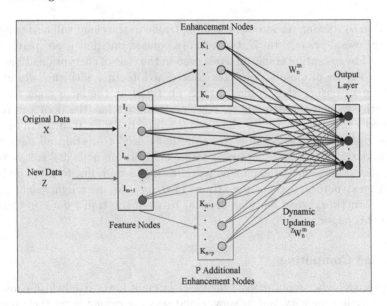

Fig. 1. The architecture of the broad learning system

extracted from the original data to generate the feature nodes. Then through the activation functions which can be either nonlinear or linear, the feature nodes are enhanced into enhancement nodes. The connections of all the feature nodes and the enhancement nodes are used to generate the output through the pseudoinverse.

We set I_X^m and K_X^n as the m groups of feature mapping nodes and n groups of enhancement nodes of the initial network respectively, where X represents the initial input. These nodes can be generated by the following way:

$$I_X^m = \left[\varphi(XA_{e1} + \theta_{e1}), ..., \varphi(XA_{em} + \theta_{em})\right] \tag{1}$$

$$K_X^n = \left[\chi(I_X^m A_{h1} + \theta_{h1}), ..., \chi(I_X^m A_{hn} + \theta_{hn})\right] \tag{2}$$

where $A_{ei}, \theta_{ei}, \varphi$ are the random weights, bias and activation function of feature nodes, and $A_{hi}, \theta_{hi}, \chi$ are corresponding parameters of enhancement nodes. According to these generated nodes, we can compute the weights $W_n^m = (I_X^m|K_X^n)^+ Y$, where $(I_X^m|K_X^n)^+$ is the pseudoinverse of the matrix $(I_X^m|K_X^n)$ and Y is the label of the input data.

In traffic analysis scenarios, we need to update traffic classification model frequently. BLS with incremental learning can meet this requirement in a resource-saving way. Introducing incremental learning into BLS is a good option which can avoid retaining all traffic data. When new traffic data comes into the trained model, the output-layer weights of the network can be updated without retraining the network model. What's more, how to update the network model is illustrated as follows.

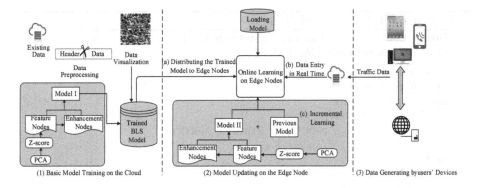

Fig. 2. Edge computing based traffic analysis system

When new data Z inputs, the corresponding feature nodes I_Z^m and enhancement nodes K_Z^n can be calculated using the same way as the Eqs. (1) and (2). The new weights of the BLS model can be updated by the dynamic stepwise updating algorithm based on the previous weights W_n^m:

$$^Z W_n^m = \left[W_n^m + B(Y_z - (I_Z^m | K_Z^n) W_n^m) \right] \tag{3}$$

where Y_z is the label of the new data Z. Note that,

$$B = \begin{cases} (C^T)^+, & \text{if } C \neq 0 \\ (I_X^m | K_X^n)^+ D(I + D^T D)^{-1}, & \text{if } C = 0 \end{cases} \tag{4}$$

where $C^T = (I_Z^m | K_Z^n) - D^T (I_X^m | K_X^n)$, and $D^T = (I_Z^m | K_Z^n)(I_X^m | K_X^n)^+$.

4 System Design and Implementation

In this section, we will introduce the proposed edge computing based traffic analysis system from the perspective of its architecture and the concrete training process.

4.1 System Design

To thwart the problems that cannot be solved by the cloud computing (saving bandwidth resources) and protect users' data privacy, we propose a distributed traffic analysis system with the help of edge computing and use a novel and lightweight network structure to train the traffic data, which can better fit the edge computing based architecture. As shown in Fig. 2, the proposed edge computing based traffic analysis system is mainly composed of two stages: basic classification model training on the cloud and the model updating on the edge node, which are designed to reduce the bandwidth resources and protect users' privacy from being inferred by malicious service providers without affecting the classification results.

Algorithm 1. Basic Model Training

Input: Traffic Data X, Label $Y_{a,c}$, maptimes t_1, enhencetimes t_2, Batchsize g
Output: Trained Basic Model $\mathcal{M}$

$X^{'} \leftarrow$ PCA (X); $X^{''}_{a,b} \leftarrow$ Z-score $(X^{'})$;
// Feature Nodes I
for *each* $i \in [1, t_1]$ **do**
    $A_{b,g}, \theta \leftarrow$ Random ();
    $I^i_{a,g} \leftarrow \varphi(X^{''}_{a,b}A_{b,g} + \theta)$; //$\varphi$ is activation function
    $I_{a,m} \leftarrow$ Add $I^i_{a,g}$; // $m = t_1 * g$
end
// Enhancement Nodes K
for *each* $i \in [1, t_2]$ **do**
    $A^{'}_{m,g}, \theta^{'} \leftarrow$ Random ();
    $K^i_{a,g} \leftarrow \chi(I_{a,m}A^{'}_{m,g} + \theta^{'})$; //$\chi$ is activation function
    $K_{a,n} \leftarrow$ Add $K^i_{a,g}$; // $n = t_2 * g$
end
// Updating weight W
$P_{m+n,a} \leftarrow$ Pseuedoinverse $(I_{a,m}, K_{a,n})$;
$W_{m+n,c} \leftarrow P_{m+n,a}Y_{a,c}$;
$\mathcal{M} \leftarrow$ Save the Model $(W_{m+n,c}, P_{m+n,a}, I_{a,m}, K_{a,n})$
return $\mathcal{M}$

Basic Model Training on the Cloud. Considering that the edge node usually has poor computing power and low storage capacity, it is impossible to process large amounts of traffic data for basic model training. Therefore, we use the cloud to perform this task, which is the same as the current architecture. After the basic model training, the cloud sends the basic model to the edge node, and the edge node updates the trained model using the incremental learning, which does not need to interact with the cloud.

In order to make broad learning system more suitable for the proposed architecture, we modify the basic broad learning algorithm. In our system, the cloud performs the following two steps as shown in Algorithm 1: (1) Analyzing the existing traffic data and generating the basic model. Our approach is not to completely abandon the previous architecture, but to further optimize on the basis of the existing architecture. Since the cloud has collected many traffic data, we can reuse these data for basic model training instead of recollecting the data, which can further save the bandwidth resources. Firstly, we use data reduction method, principal component analysis (PCA), to process these traffic data and extract the important feature data (input data). Then feature nodes and enhancement nodes can be generated based on the input data, random weights and bias, and the activation function. By computing the pseudoinverse of the feature nodes and enhancement nodes, we can obtain the final weights, which constitute the trained model. (2) Saving the trained model and distributing it to the edge nodes. In order to obtain the trained model which has a certain precision, the cloud can set the checkpoint. When the training accuracy reaches a threshold (the checkpoint), the training process is over. Then this model will be distributed to the edge nodes. Note that, the training process on the cloud only needs to be done once in an offline way when the traffic types do not change. If the traffic types increase, the basic model needs to be retrained on the cloud. However, the traffic types will not change for a long time and the retraining process can be completed in an offline way, which has a negligible impact on the system's performance.

Algorithm 2. Incremental Learning on the Edge Node

Input: Basic Model $\mathcal{M}$, New Traffic Z, Label $Y'_{a',c}$
Output: The Updated Model $\mathcal{M}'$

$W_{m+n,c}$, $P_{m+n,a}$, $I_{a,m}$, $K_{a,n}$ $\leftarrow$ Load Basic Model $\mathcal{M}$
$Z' \leftarrow$ PCA (Z); $Z''_{a',b} \leftarrow$ Z-score (Z');
// Feature Nodes I'
$I'_{a',m} \leftarrow$ Use the same method as Algorithm 1
// Enhancement Nodes K'
$K'_{a',n} \leftarrow$ Use the same method as Algorithm 1
// Calculate $B_{m+n,a'}$
$D^T_{a',a} \leftarrow (I'_{a',m}|K'_{a',n})P_{m+n,a}$;
$C^T_{a',m+n} \leftarrow (I'_{a',m}|K'_{a',n}) - D^T_{a',a}(I_{a,m}|K_{a,n})$;
if $C_{m+n,a'}$ $!= 0$ **then**
| $B_{m+n,a'} \leftarrow$ Pseuedoinverse ($C^T_{a',m+n}$);
end
else
| $B_{m+n,a'} \leftarrow P_{m+n,a}D_{a,a'}((D^T_{a',a}D_{a,a'} + diag(a')).I)$
end
// Updating weight W
$W_{m+n,c} \leftarrow W_{m+n,c} + B_{m+n,a'}(Y'_{a',c} - (I'_{a',m}|K'_{a',n})W_{m+n,c})$;
$P_{m+n,a+a'} \leftarrow ((P_{m+n,a} - B_{m+n,a'}D^T_{a',a})|B_{m+n,a'})$;
return $\mathcal{M}'$

Model Updating on the Edge Node. To save the precious bandwidth resources and protect users' data privacy, we change the current system and adopt the edge computing based traffic analysis system. In our system, the edge nodes refer to the devices between the user side and the cloud, which are close to the users' device and can be controlled by the users instead of the service providers. In our scenario, the common edge nodes refer to the WiFi access point, router, hub, and switch devices. Usually, the edge nodes have poor computing power and lower storage capacity. Therefore, it is reasonable to deploy the lightweight machine learning on the edge node.

After receiving the trained model from the cloud, the edge node loads this model and continues to train the model by the way of incremental learning. The concrete algorithm is shown in Algorithm 2. The edge node does not need to process previous data, and it only needs to generate additional feature nodes and enhancement nodes for the new input data. Data preprocessing is completed by principal component analysis and the generated method of the additional feature nodes and enhancement nodes is the same as the Algorithm 1. These newly generated nodes will be used to update the BLS model by the dynamic stepwise updating algorithm. Through incremental learning, we can constantly update the model and maintain the accuracy of the trained model.

Moreover, we use a specific scenario to show the operational process: The network operator wants to block some types of traffic (e.g., video traffic) going through their networks. Firstly, they construct the classification model based on the broad learning algorithm on the server (Step 1: Basic model training on the cloud). Then this model will be distributed to the edge nodes (such as gateway in this scenario), which can be used to continue training on the edge node based on the real-time incoming data (Step 2: Model updating on the edge node). This model can be deployed on the edge nodes, and special types of data will be blocked when they go through these edge nodes based on the classification results.

4.2   Principal Component Analysis for Data Reduction

Although broad learning system can efficiently reduce the training time due to its simple network structure, it is difficult to directly deploy the broad learning algorithm on the devices with the limited performance. Fortunately, it can be realized with the following step: Since the input data always has higher dimension, it will inevitably take up a lot of training time if we directly input high-dimensional data into the training algorithm. Therefore, instead of inputting all traffic data into the training algorithm, we use data reduction method to process these traffic data and extract the important features. Principal component analysis is a common method for data reduction. It uses an orthogonal transformation to convert the high-dimensional data, which can convert the correlated variables into a set of linearly uncorrelated variables. We can set the suitable parameters for principal component analysis, which will have a negligible influence to the classification accuracy.

5   Evaluation

To evaluate the performance of the edge computing based traffic analysis system, we implement our system on the classic devices, Raspberry Pi, and compare its performance with other machine learning based method. In this paper, we use a similar metric to other works on traffic analysis to evaluate the performance of our system, which selects several classic traffic types [11]. We use massive data packets which mainly contain the following traffic: Twitter, Youtube, Gmail, Http, Instagram, Samba, and so on. The traffic data used in this paper is collected by Wireshark, a classic network packet capture, which is saved as the packet capture (pcap) file and can be analyzed by the standard libpcap library. The pcap file is consist of the pcap header, a series of the packet header and the corresponding packet data. Especially, the packet header contains some meta-data about the packet, including the packet length, timestamp, and a 32-bit link layer type field, which needs to be removed when preprocessing data [10]. Note that we only use the packet data for traffic classification.

In our experiment, we use 40% of traffic data for training the basic model on the cloud. After the basic training, the trained model will be distributed to the edge node for further training. Moreover, 40% of traffic data is used for incremental learning on the edge node. In the process of incremental training, we will assign these data to four training steps to evaluate the effectiveness of the incremental learning. The model will be saved when each training step is completed. Finally, the remaining 20% of the data is the test set.

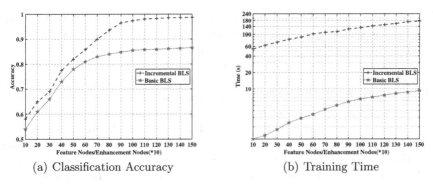

(a) Classification Accuracy   (b) Training Time

Fig. 3. Accuracy and time under different number of nodes

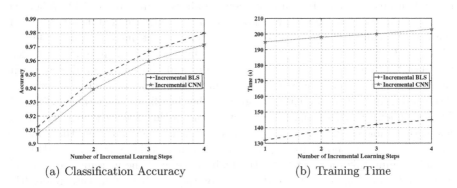

(a) Classification Accuracy   (b) Training Time

Fig. 4. Accuracy and efficiency comparison with CNN

5.1 Prototype

For evaluating the effectiveness/efficiency of our proposed scheme, we have deployed our scheme on the Raspberry Pi 3 Model B with a 64-bit quad-core ARM-v8 CPU at 1.2 GHz and 1 GB of ARM memory. As a classic device, Raspberry Pi has the similar computing and storage capabilities with the edge node that is defined in the paper [6,16,18]. Therefore, it is reasonable to evaluate the proposed edge computing based traffic analysis system using this device.

The performance metrics in the experiments include training accuracy and training time, which can be affected by the number of feature/enhancement nodes. In our experiment, we evaluate the effect of the number of feature nodes and the enhancement nodes by varying their numbers from 100 to 1500. For comparison with other methods, we fix the number of feature nodes and the enhancement nodes at 1000. The activation function is the commonly used functions in machine learning, including sigmoid, tanh, relu, and orth.

5.2   Classification Performance

We deploy the proposed broad learning system model on the edge nodes, Raspberry Pi 3 Model B, to evaluate its performance. Firstly, we will use the classification accuracy as the evaluation parameter. The number of the feature nodes and enhancement nodes are the important factors affecting the classification accuracy, which can be adjusted for obtaining accurate results. Note that, the training time will grow with the increase of the number of these nodes. Therefore, we should find a tradeoff between the training time and the accuracy by choosing suitable number of nodes. Figure 3(a) shows the classification accuracy of the basic model and the incremental model under different number of nodes. From this figure, we can see that the accuracy of the trained model is significantly improved on the basis of the basic model by incremental training of new data.

In our experiment, we evaluate the effect of the number of feature nodes and the enhancement nodes by varying their numbers from 100 to 1500. When we set the value of both the feature nodes and the enhancement nodes to 1000, the classification accuracy of the basic model and the incremental model are 85.5% and 98%. We can see that with the increase of the number of nodes, the classification accuracy of the basic model and the incremental model will significantly grow when these nodes are small. However, in the later stage, even if the nodes continue to increase, the grow of the classification accuracy is limited. That is, when the classification accuracy reaches a threshold, the increase of the nodes does not work. Moreover, the increase of the nodes means the training time will grow, as shown in Fig. 3(b). As shown in this figure, although basic model training takes a short time, the training time of the incremental learning will significantly increase with the grow of the number of feature nodes/the enhancement nodes. Therefore, we need set a reasonable parameter (such as 1000 or 1100) instead of increasing these nodes as many as possible.

5.3   Performance Comparison with Deep Learning

We compare the broad learning system based traffic classification model with the deep learning based model, which is the most popular machine learning method. Note that, in this paper we use the classic deep structure, Convolutional Neural Network, which includes multiple convolutional layers and full-connected layers. Like the Broad learning system, CNN can also save the trained model and continue to train the model by the way of incremental learning. Therefore, we can use the same dataset and set the same parameters as the broad learning system, which can provide a consistent environment for performance comparison.

In our setting, we construct a CNN model which contains four convolutional layers and two full-connected layers. Data pre-processing uses the same steps as the broad learning system, including the data visualization (38×38). When the accuracy of the basic CNN model is consistent with the basic model of the broad learning system, the basic CNN model is distributed to the same Raspberry Pi for incremental learning. The training results are shown in Fig. 4(a), where $i = 1, 2, 3, 4$ represents each incremental stage. This figure shows that these two models have the similar training accuracy in each incremental stage. Then we evaluate the training time of each incremental stage, and the results are shown in Fig. 4(b). From this figure we can see that our scheme only needs about 70% of the training time of the CNN model, which can show the superiority of the proposed model.

6   Conclusion

We propose a novel edge computing based traffic analysis system using broad learning. In one hand, edge computing can provide a distributed architecture, which can save the precious bandwidth resources and provide the safer service environment. In the other hand, we use broad learning system to incrementally train the traffic data, which is more suitable for the edge computing because it can support incremental updates of models on the edge nodes without retraining all data. We implement the edge computing based traffic analysis system on the Raspberry Pi, and the experimental results show that our method has the faster training speed compared with other neural network architecture.

Acknowledgments. This work is partially supported by JSPS KAKENHI Grant Number JP16K00117, JP19K20250, KDDI Foundation and the China Scholarship Council (201808050016). Mianxiong Dong is the corresponding author.

References

1. Anderson, B., McGrew, D.: Machine learning for encrypted malware traffic classification: accounting for noisy labels and non-stationarity. In: Proceedings of the 23rd ACM SIGKDD International Conference on Knowledge Discovery and Data Mining KDD 2017, pp. 1723–1732. ACM, New York (2017). https://doi.org/10.1145/3097983.3098163
2. Baktir, A.C., Ozgovde, A., Ersoy, C.: How can edge computing benefit from software-defined networking: a survey, use cases, and future directions. IEEE Commun. Surv. Tutorials **19**(4), 2359–2391 (2017). https://doi.org/10.1109/COMST.2017.2717482

3. Buczak, A.L., Guven, E.: A survey of data mining and machine learning methods for cyber security intrusion detection. IEEE Commun. Surv. Tutorials **18**(2), 1153–1176 (2016). https://doi.org/10.1109/COMST.2015.2494502

4. Chen, C.L.P., Liu, Z.: Broad learning system: an effective and efficient incremental learning system without the need for deep architecture. IEEE Trans. Neural Networks Learn. Syst. **29**(1), 10–24 (2018). https://doi.org/10.1109/TNNLS.2017.2716952

5. Han, S., Xu, S., Meng, W., Li, C.: Dense-device-enabled cooperative networks for efficient and secure transmission. IEEE Network **32**(2), 100–106 (2018). https://doi.org/10.1109/MNET.2018.1700292

6. Jalali, F., Hinton, K., Ayre, R., Alpcan, T., Tucker, R.S.: Fog computing may help to save energy in cloud computing. IEEE J. Sel. Areas Commun. **34**(5), 1728–1739 (2016). https://doi.org/10.1109/JSAC.2016.2545559

7. Korczyński, M., Duda, A.: Markov chain fingerprinting to classify encrypted traffic. In: IEEE INFOCOM 2014 - IEEE Conference on Computer Communications, pp. 781–789, April 2014. https://doi.org/10.1109/INFOCOM.2014.6848005

8. Li, H., Ota, K., Dong, M.: Learning IoT in edge: deep learning for the internet of things with edge computing. IEEE Network **32**(1), 96–101 (2018). https://doi.org/10.1109/MNET.2018.1700202

9. Li, H., Ota, K., Dong, M.: ECCN: orchestration of edge-centric computing and content-centric networking in the 5G radio access network. IEEE Wirel. Commun. **25**(3), 88–93 (2018). https://doi.org/10.1109/MWC.2018.1700315

10. Li, L., Ota, K., Dong, M.: DeepNFV: a light-weight framework for intelligent edge network functions virtualization. IEEE Network **99**, 1–6 (2018). https://doi.org/10.1109/MNET.2018.1700394

11. Li, X., Qi, F., Xu, D., Qiu, X.: An internet traffic classification method based on semi-supervised support vector machine. In: 2011 IEEE International Conference on Communications (ICC), pp. 1–5, June 2011. https://doi.org/10.1109/icc.2011.5962736

12. Liu, J., Wan, J., Zeng, B., Wang, Q., Song, H., Qiu, M.: A scalable and quick-response software defined vehicular network assisted by mobile edge computing. IEEE Commun. Mag. **55**(7), 94–100 (2017). https://doi.org/10.1109/MCOM.2017.1601150

13. Mao, Y., You, C., Zhang, J., Huang, K., Letaief, K.B.: A survey on mobile edge computing: the communication perspective. IEEE Commun. Surv. Tutorials **19**(4), 2322–2358 (2017). https://doi.org/10.1109/COMST.2017.2745201

14. Meidan, Y., et al.: Profiliot: a machine learning approach for IoT device identification based on network traffic analysis. In: Proceedings of the Symposium on Applied Computing SAC 2017, pp. 506–509. ACM, New York (2017). https://doi.org/10.1145/3019612.3019878

15. Naboulsi, D., Fiore, M., Ribot, S., Stanica, R.: Large-scale mobile traffic analysis: a survey. IEEE Commun. Surv. Tutorials **18**(1), 124–161 (2016). https://doi.org/10.1109/COMST.2015.2491361

16. Patel, P., Intizar Ali, M., Sheth, A.: On using the intelligent edge for IoT analytics. IEEE Intell. Syst. **32**(5), 64–69 (2017). https://doi.org/10.1109/MIS.2017.3711653

17. Peng, M., Yan, S., Zhang, K., Wang, C.: Fog-computing-based radio access networks: issues and challenges. IEEE Network **30**(4), 46–53 (2016). https://doi.org/10.1109/MNET.2016.7513863

18. Roman, R., Lopez, J., Mambo, M.: Mobile edge computing, fog et al.: a survey and analysis of security threats and challenges. Future Gener. Comput. Syst. **78**, 680–698 (2018). https://doi.org/10.1016/j.future.2016.11.009

19. Sankari, S., Varalakshmi, P., Divya, B.: Network traffic analysis of cloud data centre. In: 2015 International Conference on Computing and Communications Technologies (ICCCT), pp. 408–413, February 2015. https://doi.org/10.1109/ICCCT2. 2015.7292785

20. Shi, W., Cao, J., Zhang, Q., Li, Y., Xu, L.: Edge computing: vision and challenges. IEEE Internet Things J. **3**(5), 637–646 (2016). https://doi.org/10.1109/JIOT.2016. 2579198

21. Shi, W., Dustdar, S.: The promise of edge computing. Computer **49**(5), 78–81 (2016). https://doi.org/10.1109/MC.2016.145

22. Sung, K.Y., Biswas, J., Learned-Miller, E.G., Levine, B.N., Liberatore, M.: Server-side traffic analysis reveals mobile location information over the internet. IEEE Trans. Mobile Comput. 1 (2018). https://doi.org/10.1109/TMC.2018.2857777

23. Tang, T.A., Mhamdi, L., McLernon, D., Zaidi, S.A.R., Ghogho, M.: Deep learning approach for network intrusion detection in software defined networking. In: 2016 International Conference on Wireless Networks and Mobile Communications (WINCOM), pp. 258–263, October 2016. https://doi.org/10.1109/WINCOM.2016. 7777224

24. Taylor, V.F., Spolaor, R., Conti, M., Martinovic, I.: Robust smartphone app identification via encrypted network traffic analysis. IEEE Trans. Inf. Forensics Secur. **13**(1), 63–78 (2018). https://doi.org/10.1109/TIFS.2017.2737970

25. Xu, J., Ota, K., Dong, M.: Saving energy on the edge: in-memory caching for multi-tier heterogeneous networks. IEEE Commun. Mag. **56**(5), 102–107 (2018). https://doi.org/10.1109/MCOM.2018.1700909

26. Zhang, J., Chen, C., Xiang, Y., Zhou, W., Xiang, Y.: Internet traffic classification by aggregating correlated naive bayes predictions. IEEE Trans. Inf. Forensics Secur. **8**(1), 5–15 (2013). https://doi.org/10.1109/TIFS.2012.2223675

The Performance of DF Relaying System Based on Energy Harvesting and Dual-Media Channels

Zhixiong Chen, Lijiao Wang, Cong Ye[(✉)], and Dongsheng Han

North China Electric Power University, Baoding 071003, China
{zxchen,handongsheng}@ncepu.edu.cn,
18831633659@163.com, 739693695@qq.com

Abstract. In recent years, energy efficiency in multi-hop cooperative power-line communication (PLC) and wireless systems has recently received considerable attention. This paper considers the dual-hop PLC/wireless parallel communication system based on decode and forward (DF), where the relay harvests the high noise inherent in PLC channels to further enhance energy efficiency. In this paper, we derive the exact analytic expression of energy efficiency and the closed expression of outage probability. In order to compare and highlight the achievable gain, we also analyzed the related performances of DF relaying PLC system with energy harvesting (DF-EH). Then based on the theoretical calculation and simulation results, the influence of energy-harvesting time factor and other parameters on the system performance is analyzed. The result shows that energy-harvesting time factor and power allocation are the key factors affecting system performance. Relevant conclusions provide necessary theoretical support for the application of energy harvest technology in mixed media cooperative communication.

Keywords: Decode and forward · Energy harvesting · Outage probability · Energy efficiency

1 Introduction

Smart-grid techniques have attracted growing attention in recent years due to their inherent capacity to realize future energy-management system [1]. Power line communication has been deployed in the existing network structure [2, 3], where no new circuit installation is required and the construction cost is low. And wireless communication has the advantages of access flexible and simple networking, therefore, wireless relay technology has been widely used in the transmission field with wide coverage, and maintains good communication link quality in the PLC network.

To enhance robustness and link quality, a PLC network can collaborate with wireless network. Literature [4] and [5] put forward a new communication architecture, which allows signals to be transmitted simultaneously on PLC and wireless channels. The results show that the cooperation between PLC and wireless networks can ensure good communication quality and reduce the bit error rate and outage probability of the system. The study in [6] also presents a hybrid architecture of wireless and PLC

© ICST Institute for Computer Sciences, Social Informatics and Telecommunications Engineering 2019
Published by Springer Nature Switzerland AG 2019. All Rights Reserved
S. Han et al. (Eds.): AICON 2019, LNICST 287, pp. 252–260, 2019.
https://doi.org/10.1007/978-3-030-22971-9_21

networks which has been installed in rural and sparsely populated environments to provide broadband services and smart-grid services. Leonardo et al. [7] analyzed contrastively the characteristics and advantages of PLC/wireless hybrid data communication technology in smart grid and IoT. The results show that the mixed data communication method can effectively improve the performance of the system.

Very recently, power consumption in multi-hop PLC systems has attracted a large amount of research attention. For instance, D'Alessandro et al. proposed opportunistic decode and forward (ODF) and opportunistic amplify and forward (OAF) relaying for PLC systems [8, 9]. The authors showed that the scheme can effectively reduce transmission power. But that the two studies above considered only minimizing the transmit power of PLC modems. All the aforementioned studies have focused on only optimizing system parameters to reduce transmit power of PLC modems. In contrast, in reference [10], it is proposed for the first time to harvest energy of impulsive noise present over PLC channels and then forward the source signal with it to improve the energy efficiency of PLC systems. In the latest study, the author proposed a dual-hop PLC system based with energy harvesting (DF-EH) [11], and derived the analytical expressions of energy efficiency and outage probability. However, this paper only considers the PLC transmission medium, which has poor reliability.

In this paper, we present a PLC/Wireless parallel DF system based on energy harvesting (P/W-DF-EH). Firstly, we derive accurate analytical expressions for the energy efficiency (EE) and average outage probability of P/W-DF-EH and DF-EH systems, which are then validated with Monte Carlo simulations. Secondly, the effects of energy-harvesting time factor and impulse noise parameters on energy efficiency of the system are studied. Finally, a feasible scheme is proposed to balance the reliability and effectiveness of the system.

2 System Model

The model of PLC/W-DF-EH and DF-EH systems are shown in Fig. 1, which consists of source (S), relay (R) and destination (D). Relay installing Energy Harvesting (EH) device collects the inherent high noise energy in a PLC channel.

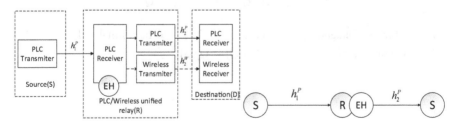

Fig. 1. System model for PLC/wireless-DF-EH and DF-EH system.

In the first time slot, the signal received by the power-line at the relay is given as:

$$y_r = \sqrt{P_s} h_1^P x_s + n_r^P \tag{1}$$

where P_s and x_s is the source transmit power and information signal normalized as $E\{|x_s|^2\} = 1$, and n_r^P is the PLC noise signal with variance N_{Pl}. h_1^P is the PLC channel fading coefficient, following the Lognormal (LogN) [12] with a probability density function (PDF) is:

$$f_{h_n^P} = \frac{\varsigma}{\sqrt{2\pi}\sigma_P Z} exp\left[-\frac{(10log_{10}(z) - \mu_P)^2}{2\sigma_P^2}\right], n \in \{1, 2\} \tag{2}$$

where $\varsigma = 10/ln\,10$ is a scaling constant, μ_P and σ_P^2 are the mean and the variance of $10log_{10}(h_n^P)$, respectively, the fading envelope is normalized, making $E[(h_n^P)^2] = exp(2\mu_P + 2\sigma_P^2) = 1$, namely $\mu_P = -\sigma_P^2$.

In the energy-harvesting part, we adopt the time-switching relaying energy-harvesting protocol. The total time needed to transmit information is T, and the EH time in the relay is defined as τT, where $0 \leq \tau \leq 1$ being the energy-harvesting time factor. The energy harvested by relay is $E_H = \kappa \tau T N_{Pl}$, where $0 < \kappa < 1$ is the energy-harvesting efficiency determined by the circuitry of the energy harvester at R.

In the second time slot, relay R with power P_r will transmit the signal x_r to D, then the signals received at node D are respectively:

$$y_d^P = \sqrt{\rho P_r} h_2^P x_r + n_d^P \tag{3a}$$

$$y_d^W = \sqrt{(1 - \rho)P_r} h_2^W x_r + n_d^W \tag{3b}$$

where n_d^w is the noise signal of wireless at D with variance N_W, h_2^W is the wireless channel fading coefficient, following the Nakagami distribution with a PDF is:

$$f_{h_2^W}(z) = \frac{2}{\Gamma(m)}\left(\frac{m}{\Omega}\right)^m z^{2m-1} exp\left(-\frac{mz^2}{\Omega}\right) \tag{4}$$

where $m \geq 0.5$ is Nakagami parameter, $\Omega = E[(h_2^W)^2]$, to be normalized $\Omega = 1$, then $(h_2^W)^2$ following the Gamma distribution $G(m, \Omega/m)$.

3   Performance Analysis

3.1   System Energy Efficiency

The total transmitted power of the relay is $P_r = P_{rh} + P_{re}$, where P_{re} is the power provided by the external power at the relay, and P_{rh} is the power harvested by the relay, as shown in [11]:

$$P_{rh} = \frac{E_H}{(1 - \tau)T/2} = \frac{\tau}{(1 - \tau)} 2\kappa N_{Pl} \tag{5}$$

Maximal Ratio Combining (MRC) is used at the destination. The signal-noise ratio (SNR) of relay R(γ_r) and the SNR of target node D(γ_d) can be obtained as $\gamma_r = P_s \left(h_1^P \right)^2 / N_{pl}$ and $\gamma_d = \rho P_r \left(h_2^h \right)^2 / N_{Pl} + (1 - \rho) P_r \left(h_2^W \right)^2 / N_W$.

The Energy Efficiency (EE, η) of the dual-hop DF system is the minimum EE of the SR and RD links. The EE is defined as the ratio of spectral efficiency (ξ) to transmitted power. Then the EE of R and D is respectively:

$$\eta_r = \xi_r / P_{t,1}^{P/W-DF-EH}, \eta_d = \xi_d / P_{t,2}^{P/W-DF-EH} \tag{6}$$

Referencing [11], we can write the total energy consumption for the proposed system during phase I and phase II, respectively, as

$$E_{t,1}^{P/W-DF-EH} = \frac{(1 - \tau)T}{2} (P_{dyn} + 2P_{stc} + 2P_{idl}) \tag{7a}$$

$$E_{t,2}^{P/W-DF-EH} = \frac{(1 - \tau)T}{2} (P_{dyn} + 3P_{stc} + P_{idl}) \tag{7b}$$

where P_{dyn} is dynamic power, P_{stc} is static power and P_{idl} is idle power.

The PLC noise is modeled as the Bernoulli–Gaussian noise model, where the probability of impulse noise is p. Therefore, the total noise power is $N_{Pl} = N_G + pN_I$, where N_G and N_I are the variance of background noise and impulse noise respectively. For non-Gaussian impulsive noise channels, the instantaneous spectral efficiency is determined as $\xi_i = p_0 log_2 \left(1 + \gamma_{j,0} \right) + p_1 log_2 \left(1 + \gamma_{j,1} \right), i \in \{r, d\}$, where $\gamma_{i,0}$ and $\gamma_{i,1}$ are the SNR of the receiver when probability is $p_0 = 1 - p$ and $p_1 = p$. In order to obtain the end-to-end Energy Efficiency of the P/W-DF-EH system, we first need to derive the EE for the SR and RD links as follows.

(a)   SR link: the average spectral efficiency of SR link can be expressed as

$$\xi_r = \frac{(1 - \tau)}{2} \sum_{j=0}^{1} p_j \int_0^\infty log_2(1 + \gamma) f_{\gamma_{r,j}}(\gamma) d\gamma \tag{8}$$

where $f_{\gamma_{r,0}}(\cdot)$ and $f_{\gamma_{r,1}}(\cdot)$ are the PDFs of $\gamma_{r,0}$ and $\gamma_{r,1}$, respectively, $\gamma_{r,0} = P_s(h_1^P)^2/N_G$, $\gamma_{r,1} = P_s(h_1^P)^2/(N_G + N_I)$. Considering the SNR obey the LogN, the PDF of $\gamma_{r,j}$ can be expressed as:

$$f_{\gamma_{r,j}}(\gamma) = \frac{\varsigma}{\gamma\sqrt{8\pi}\sigma_P} exp\left[-\frac{(\varsigma \ln(\gamma) - (2\mu_P + \varsigma \ln(a_j)))^2}{8\sigma_P^2}\right], j \in \{0,1\} \tag{9}$$

where $a_0 = P_s/N_G$, $a_1 = P_s/(N_G + N_I)$. We use the Hermite-Gauss quadrative method to obtain the approximate analytical expression of (8). To do this, we first let $x = \varsigma \ln(\gamma) - 2\mu_P - \varsigma ln(a_j)/\sqrt{8\sigma_P^2}$, we can get:

$$\xi_r = \frac{(1-\tau)}{2}\sum_{j=0}^{1}\int_{-\infty}^{\infty}\frac{p_j}{\sqrt{\pi}}h(x)exp\left[-x^2\right]dx \tag{10}$$

Average spectral efficiency of the relay can consequently be calculated as

$$\xi_r \simeq \frac{(1-\tau)}{2}\sum_{j=0}^{1}\sum_{n=1}^{N}\frac{p_j}{\sqrt{\pi}}w_n h(x_n) \tag{11}$$

where $h(x_n) = log_2(1 + exp[\frac{\sqrt{8}\sigma_P x_n + 2\mu_P + \varsigma ln(a_j)}{\varsigma}])$, $\{w_n\}_{n=1}^{N}$ and $\{x_n\}_{n=1}^{N}$ are the weights and abscissas of the N-point Hermite–Gauss quadrature. According to Eqs. (7a) and (11), the EE of the relay is

$$\eta_r = \frac{(1-\tau)}{2(P_{dyn} + 2P_{stc} + 2P_{idl})}$$
$$\times \sum_{j=0}^{1}\sum_{n=1}^{N}\left\{\frac{p_j w_n}{\sqrt{\pi}} \times log_2\left(1 + exp\left[\frac{\sqrt{8}\sigma_P x_n + 2\mu_P + \varsigma ln(a_j)}{\varsigma}\right]\right)\right\} \tag{12}$$

(b) RD Link: the average spectral efficiency of RD link is

$$\xi_d = \frac{(1-\tau)}{2}\sum_{j=0}^{1}p_j\int_{0}^{\infty}log_2(1+\gamma)f_{\gamma_{d,j}}(\gamma)d\gamma \tag{13}$$

We need to analyze the PDF of SNR at the node D. It is known that Gamma distribution is similar to the specific LogN, the SNR of the PLC follows the LogN distribution, and the sum of the LogN variables still follows the LogN. Therefore, we will approximate the $(h_2^w)^2$ to LogN using Moment Generating Function (MGF) approximation algorithm, which makes it converte into the performance analysis problem under the same distribution of LogN-LogN.

Known $(h_2^W)^2$ meets the Gamma distribution, its MGF is $M_W(s) = (1 + \Omega/m)^{-m}$. First of all, we approximate $(h_2^W)^2$ to LogN, namely $(h_2^W)^2 \sim Log N(\mu_W, \sigma_W^2)$. By using

Hermite–Gauss quadrature method, we can get the MGF of the LogN variable, $M_{LN}(s) = \sum_{n=1}^{N} \omega_n \cdot exp\left(-s \cdot exp\left(\sqrt{2}\sigma_W a_n - \mu_W\right)\right)/\sqrt{\pi}$.

By the simultaneous MGF above, we can get

$$(1 + \Omega/m)^{-m} = \sum_{n=1}^{N} \frac{\omega_n}{\sqrt{\pi}} exp\left(-s \cdot exp\left(\sqrt{2}\sigma_W a_n - \mu_W\right)\right) \tag{14}$$

Choose two fixed s values, we can obtaine the equations about μ_W and σ_W^2, then we can get $\gamma_{d,W} \sim Log N(\mu_A, \sigma_A^2)$, where $\mu_A = \mu_W + ln((1 - \rho)P_r/N_W), \sigma_A^2 = \sigma_W^2$.

Knowing $\gamma_{d,P} \sim Log N(\mu_B, \sigma_B^2)$, where $\mu_B = \mu_P + ln(\rho P_r/N_{Pl}), \sigma_B^2 = 4\sigma_P^2$, the sum of the LogN variables follows the LogN $\gamma_d = [\gamma_{d,W} + \gamma_{d,P}] \sim LogN(\mu_D, \sigma_D^2)$. Denote the MGF respectively of $\gamma_{d,W}$, $\gamma_{d,P}$ and γ_d as $M_{d,W}(s)$, $M_{d,P}(s)$ and $M_d(s)$. Because the MGF of the sum of the two variables is equal to the product of the two MGF, the MGF of the γ_d is equal to $M_d(s) = M_{d,W}(s) \times M_{d,P}(s)$. Choosing fixed values of s, we can get the distribution of the SNR at D as $\gamma_d = LogN(\mu_D, \sigma_D^2)$.

Considering that the noise of power line is impulse noise, the SNR of destination node under fixed probability can be obtained:

$$f_{\gamma_{d_j}}(\gamma) = \frac{1}{\gamma \sigma_{D,j}\sqrt{2\pi}} exp\left[-\frac{(ln\gamma - \mu_{D,j})^2}{2\sigma_{D,j}^2}\right], j \in \{0, 1\} \tag{15}$$

Therefore, the spectral efficiency of the RD link can be written as

$$\xi_d = \frac{(1 - \tau)}{2} \sum_{j=0}^{1} \int_{-\infty}^{\infty} \frac{p_j}{\sqrt{\pi}} h(x) exp\left[-x^2\right] dx \tag{16}$$

where $h(x) = log_2\left[1 + exp\left(\sqrt{2\sigma_{D,j}^2}x + \mu_{D,j}\right)\right]$. The EE derivation of the relay-destination link can be obtained:

$$\eta_d = \frac{(1 - \tau)}{2(P_{dyn} + 3P_{stc} + P_{idl})}$$
$$\times \sum_{j=0}^{1} \sum_{n=1}^{N} \left\{\frac{p_j w_n}{\sqrt{\pi}} \times log_2\left(1 + exp\left[\sqrt{2\sigma_{D,j}^2}x + \mu_{D,j}\right]\right)\right\} \tag{17}$$

Finally, choosing the minimum of η_r and η_d, we can yield the overall EE of the proposed P/W-DF-EH system. The EE of DF-EH system is shown in literature [11].

3.2 System Outage Probability

When the system information rate R is less than the required minimum rate threshold R_{th}, the normal communication of the system will be interrupted. Let the threshold be R_{th} and $\gamma = \exp(2R_{th}) - 1$. Then the outage probability of the system is as follows:

$$P_{out} = P_r(I < R_{th}) = 1 - [1 - P_r(\gamma_r < \gamma)] \times [1 - P_r(\gamma_d < \gamma)] \qquad (18)$$

Substituting the cumulative distribution function (CDF) of γ_r and γ_d into the above equation, we can obtain the outage probability:

$$P_{out} = 1 - \left[1 - \sum_{j=0}^{1} p_j Q\left(\frac{ln\gamma - \mu_{Rj}}{\sigma_{Rj}^2}\right)\right] \times \left[1 - \sum_{j=0}^{1} p_j Q\left(\frac{ln\gamma - \mu_{Dj}}{\delta_{Dj}^2}\right)\right] \qquad (19)$$

where $\mu_{R0} = 2\mu_P + ln(P_s/N_G)$, $\mu_{R1} = 2\mu_P + ln(P_s/(N_G + N_I))$, $\sigma_{R0}^2 = \sigma_{R1}^2 = 4\sigma_P^2$, the outage probability of the DF-EH system can be straightforwardly obtained from (19) by making the following substitutions: $\mu_{D0} = 2\mu_P + ln(P_r/N_G)$, $\mu_{D1} = 2\mu_P + ln(P_r/ (N_G + N_I))$.

4 Numerical Results and Discussions

In this section, we carried out Monte Carlo simulation experiment, which compared with the theoretical results, and analyzed the influence of system parameters on the EE and average outage probability of the two systems. Unless clearly stated otherwise, we will be using: $P_s = P_{re} = 1$ W, $P_{stc} = 0.9$ W, $P_{idl} = 0.1$ W, $\sigma_P^2 = 4dB$, m=3.5, $\kappa = 1$, $\rho = 0.5$, $K = N_I/N_G = 3 \times 10^3$. Let S_{SNR} represents the average SNR of the channel, so $N_W = N_{PI} = 1/S_{SNR}$.

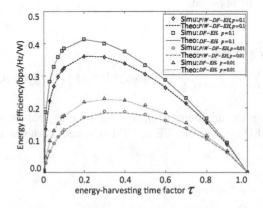

Fig. 2. EE of P/W-DF-EH and DF-EH system versus the energy-harvesting time factor.

We first analyzed the influence of energy-harvesting time factor τ and impulse noise probability on the energy efficiency performance of the two systems, where $P_{re} = 0$, then the relay forwards signal completely depends on the harvested energy. From the analysis of Fig. 2, the following conclusions can be drawn: (1) The theoretical performance of the system is basically consistent with the simulation results, which verifies the accuracy of the theoretical analysis. (2) For a given τ, higher noise pulse probability leads to better energy efficiency performance. That is because increasing the noise probability implies more energy can be harvested. (3) In these two systems, we can observe that the system becomes energy inefficient when τ is either too small or too large, so there exists an optimal energy-harvesting time that maximizes the system performance in the different values of p. This is basically because when τ is too small, there is not enough time to collect energy, when τ is too large, unnecessary energy is harvested at the cost of less information transmission time, which both reduce EE. (4) The EE of P/W-DF-EH system is lower than that of DF-EH system, which is because adding the wireless parallel communication will increase the power consumption of the system.

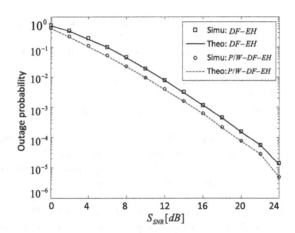

Fig. 3. The average outage probability of P/W-DF-EH and DF-EH system versus S_{SNR}

Through the analysis of Fig. 2, we know that there is an optimal energy-harvesting time factor in each system. Optimal energy harvesting time τ^* can be obtained according to $\partial\eta(\tau)/\partial\tau = 0$. Figure 3 shows the relationship between the two system outage probabilities and the average SNR of the channel based on the optimal energy-harvesting time factor. System parameters are set as follows: $p = 0.1$, $K = 10$. As can be seen from the results, with the increase of the S_{SNR}, P/W-DF-EH system has a lower average outage probability than the DF-EH system. The reliability of the system can be improved by adding wireless parallel channels. We can select the appropriate time factor and power split ting coefficient in the P/W-DF-EH system, so that the effectiveness and reliability of the system can be optimized at the same time.

5 Conclusions

This paper studies the performance of the dual-hop PLC/wireless parallel communication system. In order to improve the energy efficiency of the system, we proposed energy-harvesting at the relay, adopting the time-switching relaying protocol. The results show that the EE of the proposed system is lower than that of the DF-EH system due to the increase of power consumption, but the outage performance is better than that of the DF-EH because of adding the wireless channel. The optimization of energy-harvesting time is the key to achieve the highest energy efficiency.

Acknowledgments. The research is supported by the National Natural Science Foundation of China (Nos. 61601182 and 61771195), Natural Science Foundation of Hebei Province (F2017502059 and F2018502047), and Fundamental Research Funds for the Central Universities (No. 2019MS088).

References

1. Ahmad, A.: Optimization for emerging wireless networks: IoT, 5G, and smart grid communication networks. IEEE Access **5**, 2096–2100 (2017)
2. Galli, S.: The role of power line communications in the smart grid. Proc. IEEE **99**(6), 998–1027 (2011)
3. Jianqi, L.I.: On (power-) line defined power line communication solution based on channel sensing. Proc. CSEE **35**(20), 5235–5243 (2015)
4. Lai, S.W.: Using the wireless and PLC channels for diversity. IEEE Trans. Commun. **60**(12), 3865–3875 (2012)
5. Qian, Y., Yan, J.: Design of hybrid wireless and power line sensor networks with dual-interface relay in IoT. IEEE Internet Things J. **6**(1), 239–249 (2019)
6. Kuhn, M., Berger, S.: Power line enhanced cooperative wireless communications. IEEE J. Sel. Areas Commun. **24**(7), 1401–1410 (2006)
7. Leonardo, D.M.B.A.D., Fernandes, V.: Hybrid PLC/wireless communication for smart grids and internet of things applications. IEEE Internet Things J. **5**(2), 655–667 (2018)
8. D'Alessandro, S., Tonello, A.M.: Power savings with opportunistic decode and forward over in-home PLC networks. In: IEEE International Symposium on Power Line Communications & Its Applications. IEEE (2011)
9. Salvatore, D.: On rate improvements and power saving with opportunistic relaying in home power line networks. EURASIP J. Adv. Signal Process. **2012**(1), 1–17 (2012)
10. Rabie, K.M., Adebisi, B.: Improving energy efficiency in dual-hop cooperative PLC relaying systems. In: International Symposium on Power Line Communications & Its Applications. IEEE (2016)
11. Rabie, K.M., Tonello, A.M.: For more energy-efficient dual-hop df relaying power-line communication systems. IEEE Syst. J. **12**(2), 2005–2016 (2018)
12. Dubey, F.: Performance analysis of a power line communication system employing selection combining in correlated log-normal channels and impulsive noise. IET Commun. **8**(7), 1072–1082 (2014)

School Violence Detection Based on Multi-sensor Fusion and Improved Relief-F Algorithms

Liang Ye[1,2(✉)], Jifu Shi[1], Hany Ferdinando[2,3], Tapio Seppänen[4], and Esko Alasaarela[2]

[1] Department of Information and Communication Engineering,
Harbin Institute of Technology, No. 2 Yikuang Street, Harbin 150080, China
yeliang@hit.edu.cn
[2] Health and Wellness Measurement Research Group, OPEM Unit,
University of Oulu, Pentti Kaiteran katu 1, 90014 Oulu, Finland
[3] Department of Electrical Engineering, Petra Christian University,
Siwalankerto 121-131, Surabaya 60236, Indonesia
[4] Physiological Signal Analysis Team, University of Oulu,
Pentti Kaiteran katu 1, 90014 Oulu, Finland

Abstract. School bullying is a common social problem around the world, and school violence is considered to be the most harmful form of school bullying. This paper proposes a school violence detecting method based on multi-sensor fusion and improved Relief-F algorithms. Data are gathered with two movement sensors by role playing of school violence and daily-life activities. Altogether 9 kinds of activities are recorded. Time domain features and frequency domain features are extracted and filtered by an improved Relief-F algorithm. Then the authors build a two-level classifier. The first level is a Decision Tree classifier which separates the activity of jump from the others, and the second level is a Radial Basis Function neural network which classifies the remainder 8 kinds of activities. Finally a decision layer fusion algorithm combines the recognition results of the two sensors together. The average recognition accuracy of school violence reaches 84.4%, and that of daily-life reaches 97.3%.

Keywords: Improved Relief-F · Activity recognition · School violence · Artificial intelligence · Pattern recognition

1 Introduction

Activity recognition has become a popular topic in the fields of machine learning and artificial intelligence (AI) as movement sensor techniques become more and more mature. Activity recognition has a wide application prospect, e.g. smart home, smart city [1]. On the other hand, as scientific techniques develop, the human society also develops. However, an undesired problem has also grown, namely school bullying. School bullying is a kind of offensive behavior which hurt another person physically and/or mentally. School bullying can happen in various forms, e.g. physical violence, verbal bullying, destroying personal properties, among which physical violence is

S. Han et al. (Eds.): AICON 2019, LNICST 287, pp. 261–269, 2019.
https://doi.org/10.1007/978-3-030-22971-9_22

considered to be the most harmful to teenagers. Traditional anti-bullying methods are passive and man-driven. For example, *Stop Bullies* and *TipOff* are two anti-bullying smartphone applications. The user needs to operate the smartphone to send an alarm when he/she is being bullied, which is obviously very difficult for him/her.

Fortunately, as mentioned above, since activity recognition is already available, an active and information-driven bullying detecting method comes to people's mind. The authors' research group has started this research work ever since 2013. Alasaarela [2] firstly argued that a smartphone embedded with a 3D accelerometer and a 3D gyroscope was able to detect school bullying events automatically. Then Ye in 2014 [3] developed an experimental classifier FMT (Fuzzy Multi-Threshold) and recognized some typical violent activities and daily-life ones with an average accuracy of 92%. However, as the number of activity types increased and players of different ages were involved, FMT failed to work because it was difficult to find unified thresholds. Later in 2015 [4], Ye developed an instance-based classifier named PKNN (Proportional K-Nearest Neighbor) which could deal with players of different ages and more activity types. However, the average accuracy dropped to 80%. On the other hand, besides movement data, physiological characteristics can also be used for bullying detection. Ferdinando [5] in this group focused on HRV (Heart Rate Variability) and ECG (Electrocardiography) signals, and improved the average accuracy from 70% [6] to 88% [7]. Of course it is also possible to combine multiple models together for bullying detection, e.g. Ye in 2018 [8] combined motion features and acoustic features together, and precision = 92.2% whereas recall = 85.8%.

In the authors' previous work, they only used one single movement sensor fixed on the player's waist. In this paper, the authors are going to apply multiple movement sensors fixed on the player's waist and leg. Simulation results will show that the proposed method outperforms single sensor methods, even better than the multi-model one.

The remainder of this paper is organized as follows: Sect. 2 describes how the authors gathered data with multiple movement sensors; Sect. 3 describes the extracted features and proposes an improved Relief-F feature selecting method; Sect. 4 proposes a DT-RBF two-layer classifier; Sect. 5 shows the simulation results; and Sect. 6 finally draws a conclusion.

2   Data Acquisition

Activity recognition with a single motion sensor of the authors' research work has hit a bottleneck when they tried to improve the recognition accuracy, so this paper chooses to use multiple motion sensors for activity recognition. The numbers and positions of the motion sensors affect recognition accuracy [9, 10]. For a single motion sensor, the best position is the waist [11], whereas for multiple sensors, there are several possible positions for the sensor, e.g. the waist, the chest, the wrist, the arm, and the leg. However, in daily-life activities, the motions of wrists and arms are very random, and are difficult for recognition. Therefore, the authors consider the waist, the chest, and the leg. Chowdhury [12] has given a comparison of the recognition performance of the three positions as shown in Table 1.

Table 1. Recognition performance of different positions.

Position(s)	Average accuracy
Leg	83.6%
Waist	84.1%
Chest	79.6%
Leg+chest	81.7%
Leg+waist	91.6%
Chest+waist	90.5%
Waist+leg+chest	88.6%

It can be seen from Table 1 that the combination of the leg and the waist outperformed the others. Therefore, the authors chose to use two motion sensors to collect motion data, i.e. one on the leg and the other on the waist.

Motion data were gathered by role playing of school violence and daily life. Eight people of different ages participated in the role playing, and they acted three kinds of school violence activities, namely beat, push, and push down, and six kinds of daily life activities, namely stand, walk, run, jump, play, and fall down. These people took turns to act different roles, e.g. the bullied and the bullies. During the role playing, the authors used a camera to record every action and made fine synchronization with the motion sensors. After the role playing, the authors extracted the activity samples according to the video recording, and the total number of activity samples was 1,160.

3   Feature Extraction and Feature Selection

As the authors did in their previous work [8], both time domain features and frequency domain features are considered, but more features have been extracted in this experiment. All the features are extracted from the following three items:

(1) Combined horizontal vector of acceleration: As mentioned above, two motion sensors are used in this experiment, one of which is fixed on the waist whereas the other on the leg. The x-axes and z-axes of the motion sensors point to two orthogonal horizontal directions, and this paper combines them together, i.e.

$$ACC_{Hori}(i) = \sqrt{(ACC_{x-axis}(i)^2 + ACC_{z-axis}(i)^2)} \tag{1}$$

(2) Vertical vector of acceleration: The y-axes of the motion sensors are the vertical vectors.

(3) Combined vector of gyro: This paper combines all the three axes of gyro together, i.e.

$$Gyro = \sqrt{(Gyro_{x-axis}(i)^2 + Gyro_{y-axis}(i)^2 + Gyro_{z-axis}(i)^2)} \tag{2}$$

For example, when the authors extract the *Mean* feature, they extract $Mean_{AccHori}$ (the mean of the combined horizontal vector of acceleration), $Mean_{AccVert}$ (the mean of the vertical vector of acceleration), and $Mean_{Gyro}$ (the mean of the combined vector of gyro).

3.1 Time Domain Features

Table 2 lists the extracted time domain features.

Table 2. Time domain features.

Feature	Meaning
Mean	Mean
MAD	Median absolute deviation
Var	Variance
Max_{diff}	Maximum of differential
$Mean_{diff}$	Mean of differential
Max	Maximum of amplitude
Min	Minimum of amplitude
PCC	Pearson's Correlation Coefficient
Kurtosis	Kurtosis
Skewness	Skewness
$Quan^{25th}$	1/4 Quantile
$Quan^{75th}$	3/4 Quantile
ZCR	Zero Cross Ratio

PCC (Pearson's Correlation Coefficient) here is used to describe the correlationship between two axes, and calculated as

$$PCC_{xy} = \frac{n \sum x_i y_i - \sum x_i \sum y_i}{\sqrt{n \sum x_i^2 - (\sum x_i)^2} \sqrt{n \sum y_i^2 - (\sum y_i)^2}} \tag{3}$$

Kurtosis is a measure of the flatness of the data distribution, and calculated as

$$Kurtosis = \frac{\frac{1}{n} \sum_{i=1}^{n} (x_i - \bar{x})^4}{(\frac{1}{n} \sum_{i=1}^{n} (x_i - \bar{x})^2)^2} \tag{4}$$

Skewness is a measure of data symmetry, and calculated as

$$Skewness = \frac{\frac{1}{n}\sum_{i=1}^{n}(x_i - \bar{x})^3}{(\frac{1}{n}\sum_{i=1}^{n}(x_i - \bar{x})^2)^{\frac{3}{2}}} \tag{5}$$

3.2 Frequency Domain Features

Table 3 lists the extracted frequency domain features.

Table 3. Frequency domain features.

Feature	Meaning
$Mean_{FFT}$	Mean
MAD_{FFT}	Median absolute deviation
$Energy_{FFT}$	Energy
Max_{FFT}	Maximum

All the frequency domain features are extracted with FFT (Fast Fourier Transformation) from the 3 items (i.e. the combined horizontal vector of acceleration, the vertical vector of acceleration, and the combined vector of gyro). Features like main lob center frequency [8] have proven to be useless, so this paper does not take them into consideration.

3.3 Improved Relief-F Feature Selecting Algorithm

The authors used a Wrapper method for feature selection in their previous work [8]. However, Wrapper is very time-consuming, especially when the number of features is large. Therefore, this paper chooses to use a Filter-based feature selecting algorithm.

The Relief algorithm selects features according to the inter-class distances and intra-class distances. Relief itself is designed for 2-class classification, and Relief-F is an improvement on Relief for multi-class classification. Relief-F selects feature sets in the same way as Relief, i.e. it only considers the discrimination of the samples, but ignores the redundancy of similar features. Therefore, this paper proposes am improved

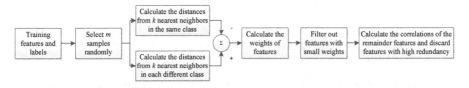

Fig. 1. Framework of the improved Relief-F algorithm.

Relief-F algorithm which eliminates the redundancy of similar features during the feature selection procedure. Figure 1 shows the framework of the improved Relief-F algorithm.

After feature selection, the dimensionality of the feature vector is reduced from 51 (39 time domain features and 12 frequency domain features) to 23.

4 Classifier Design

In the authors' previous work [8], BPNN (Back Propagation Neural Network) was used for classification. However, the learning speed of BPNN is very slow because of global approximation, so BPNN is not suitable for practical use when re-training is needed. Deep learning based classifiers such as CNN (Convolutional Neural Network) need quite a lot of training samples and thus are also unsuitable for practical use for the same reason. As for other classifiers such as DT (Decision Tree) based [3] and KNN (K-Nearest Neighbor) based [4], the authors had made a comparison [8] and found that they were not even as good as BPNN in terms of accuracy.

Therefore, this paper chooses the RBF (Radial Basis Function) Neural Network as the basic classifier. The RBF Neural Network has several advantages compared with the authors' previously used classifier BPNN. Firstly, the generalization ability of RBF is superior to that of BPNN in many aspects. Secondly, the approximation accuracy of RBF is higher than that of BPNN. It can almost achieve complete approximation, and it is extremely convenient to design. The network can automatically increase neurons until it meets the accuracy requirements. RBF is a kind of feedforward neural network with excellent performance. RBF can approximate any nonlinear function with arbitrary accuracy and has the ability of global approximation. It solves the local optimum problem of BPNN. Moreover, its topological structure is compact, and its convergence speed is fast.

In an RBF network, the number of neurons in the hidden layer can be smaller than that of the training samples, which will reduce the time cost. Add training samples into the hidden until the error meets the demand. The built RBF neural network is given in Fig. 2.

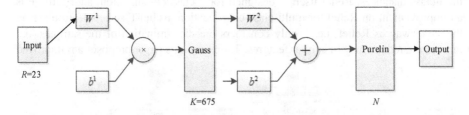

Fig. 2. The built RBF neural network.

The number of inputs $R = 23$ which is the dimensionality of the feature vector. The number of neurons in the hidden layer $K = 675$, and the radial basis function of the hidden layer is Gauss. The transfer function of the output layer is Purelin, and the number of outputs N equals to the kinds of activities, i.e. if the activities are to be classified into 9 classes, $N = 9$.

Among all the remainder features after feature selection, the authors find that the energy of the y-axis of acceleration in frequency domain can distinguish "jump" from other activities quite well. Therefore, the authors design a two-level classifier. The first level is a DT classifier which separates "jump" from other activities, and the second level is an RBF classifier which classifies the remainder 8 kinds of activities.

The authors use two separate movement sensors for activity recognition, so a decision-layer fusion algorithm is needed to combine the recognition results together. The Dempster-Shafe theory is used in this paper as the decision-layer fusion algorithm.

5 Experiments

The authors gathered 1,160 sections of activities which are classified into 9 kinds. Feature filtering by the improved Relief-F algorithm were performed after feature extraction. Then the proposed two-layer DT-RBF classifier tried to classify the samples with 5-fold cross-validation. The recognition results are given in Table 4.

Table 4. Confusion matrix of school violence detection (unit: %, classified into 9 kinds)

	Beat	Jump	Play	Push	Run	Stand	Walk	Push down	Fall down
Beat	**85.2**	0.0	3.0	0.7	3.7	1.5	2.2	1.5	2.2
Jump	0.0	**100.0**	0.0	0.0	0.0	0.0	0.0	0.0	0.0
Play	1.1	0.0	**88.9**	2.2	0.0	2.2	4.4	0.0	1.1
Push	12.9	0.0	5.7	**71.4**	2.9	0.0	7.1	0.0	0.0
Run	0.0	0.0	0.0	0.0	**100.0**	0.0	0.0	0.0	0.0
Stand	1.3	0.0	2.7	0.0	0.0	**95.3**	0.7	0.0	0.0
Walk	0.7	0.0	2.1	0.0	0.0	0.0	**97.1**	0.0	0.0
Push down	35.6	0.0	2.2	0.0	4.4	4.4	0.0	**40.0**	13.3
Fall down	10.0	0.0	4.0	0.0	12.0	0.0	0.0	12.0	**62.0**

Since the aim of this paper is to recognize school violence, then the authors classify the activities into 2 kinds, i.e., school violence and non-violence. The confusion matrix is given in Table 5.

Table 5. Confusion matrix of school violence detection (unit: %, classified into 2 kinds)

	Violence	Non-violence
Violence	84.4	15.6
Non-violence	2.7	97.3

The average accuracy of violence recognition is 84.4%, and that of non-violence is 97.3%. Moreover, *Accuracy* = 93.7%, *Precision* = 92.6%, *Recall* = 84.4%, and F_1_score = 88.3%, which shows an improvement compared with the authors' previous work in the aspect of activity recognition [8].

6 Conclusion

This paper proposed a school violence detecting method based on multi-sensor fusion and improved Relief-F algorithms. The authors gathered 9 kinds of activities including school violence and daily-life activities and extracted time domain features and frequency domain features. Then the authors proposed a feature selecting algorithm – improved Relief-F, which takes the redundancy of similar features into consideration. Different features fit different classifiers, so the authors proposed a two-level classifier DT-RBF. The first level DT separated "jump" from the other activities, and the second level RBF classified the remainder. The Dempster-Shafe theory was used as the decision-layer fusion algorithm. The final recognition accuracy of violence recognition is 84.4%, and that of non-violence is 97.3%, which showed an improvement compared with the authors' previous work.

Acknowledgements. This work was supported by the National Natural Science Foundation of China (61602127), the Directorate General of Higher Education, Indonesia (2142/E4.4/K/2013) and the North Ostrobothnia Regional Fund of the Finnish Cultural Foundation.

References

1. Weidang, L., Yi, G., Xin, L., et al.: Collaborative energy and information transfer in green wireless sensor networks for smart cities. IEEE Trans. Industr. Inf. **14**(4), 1585–1593 (2018)
2. Liang, Y., Hany, F., Esko, A.: Techniques in pattern recognition for school bullying prevention: review and outlook. J. Pattern Recogn. Res. **9**, 50–63 (2014)
3. Liang, Y., Hany, F., Tapio, S., et al.: Physical violence detection for preventing school bullying. Adv. Artif. Intell. **2014**, 1–9 (2014)
4. Liang, Y., Hany, F., Tapio, S., et al.: An instance-based physical violence detection algorithm for school bullying prevention. In: 2015 International Wireless Communications and Mobile Computing Conference (IWCMC), pp. 1384–1388 (2015)
5. Hany, F., Liang, Y., Seppänen, T., et al.: Emotion recognition by heart rate variability. Aust. J. Basic Appl. Sci. **8**(14), 50–55 (2014)
6. Hany, F., Seppänen, T., Esko, A.: Enhancing emotion recognition from ECG signals using supervised dimensionality reduction. In: Proceeding of 6th International Conference on Pattern Recognition Applications and Methods (ICPRAM), pp. 112–118 (2017)
7. Hany, F., Liang, Y., Tian, H., et al.: Violence detection from ECG signals: a preliminary study. J. Pattern Recogn. Res. **12**(1), 7–18 (2017)
8. Liang, Y., Peng, W., Le, W., et al.: A combined motion-audio school bullying detection algorithm. Int. J. Pattern Recogn. Artif. Intell. **32**, 1850046 (2018)
9. Coskun, D., Incel, O.D., Ozgovde, A.: Phone position/placement detection using accelerometer: impact on activity recognition. In: IEEE Tenth International Conference on Intelligent Sensors, Sensor Networks and Information Processing, pp. 1–6. IEEE (2015)

10. Mannini, A., Intille, S.S., Rosenberger, M., et al.: Activity recognition using a single accelerometer placed at the wrist or ankle. Med. Sci. Sports Exerc. **45**, 2193 (2013)
11. Yang, C.C., Hsu, Y.L.: A review of accelerometry-based wearable motion detectors for physical activity monitoring. Sensors **10**, 7772–7788 (2010)
12. Chowdhury, A., Tjondronegoro, D., Chandran, V., et al.: Physical activity recognition using posterior-adapted class-based fusion of multi-accelerometers data. IEEE J. Biomed. Health Inform. **99**, 1 (2017)

A UAV Based Multi-object Detection Scheme to Enhance Road Condition Monitoring and Control for Future Smart Transportation

Jian Yang[1], Jielun Zhang[2] (ID), Feng Ye[2]([✉]) (ID), and Xiaohui Cheng[1]

[1] Nanjing University of Posts and Telecommunications, Nanjing, China
{yangj,chengxh}@njupt.edu.cn
[2] University of Dayton, Dayton, OH 45469, USA
{zhangj46,fye001}@udayton.edu

Abstract. Road condition monitoring and control is essential for smart transportation in the era of autonomous driving. In this paper, we propose to apply unmanned aerial vehicle (UAV), wireless communications and artificial intelligence (AI) to achieve multi-object detection for smart road monitoring and control. In particular, the application of UAV enables real-time image view to monitor road condition, such as traffic flow and on-road objects, in an efficient way without disturbing normal traffic. Those raw image data are first offloaded to a road side unit through wireless communications. A computing platform connected to the road side unit can execute the AI based scheme for road condition monitoring and control. The AI based scheme is developed around convolutional neural network (CNN). For demonstration, the objects of interest considered in this work include advertisement billboards, junctions, traffic signs and unsafe objects. Other objects can be extended to the developed system with more collected data. To evaluate the proposed scheme, we launched a UAV to collect real-life road images from multiple road sections of a highway. The AI based scheme is then developed using portion of the raw data. Test of the AI scheme is conducted using the rest of the dataset. The evaluation results have demonstrated that the proposed UAV based multi-object detection scheme can provide accurate results to support efficient road condition monitoring and control in future smart transportation.

Keywords: Artificial Intelligence · Unmanned Ariel Vehicle · Object detection · Traffic monitoring · Internet of Things

1 Introduction

Enabled with advanced information and communications technologies, Smart Cities are a future reality for municipalities around the world, which will significantly transform the way people live, enhance the quality of life, and contribute

Published by Springer Nature Switzerland AG 2019. All Rights Reserved
S. Han et al. (Eds.): AICON 2019, LNICST 287, pp. 270–282, 2019.
https://doi.org/10.1007/978-3-030-22971-9_23

to the solutions to key challenges in society, economy, and environment [3,27,29]. As one of the basic components of Smart Cities, smart transportation have received increased attentions and have been translating from a vision into reality. Real-time road condition monitoring is essential to ensure driving safety. The World Health Organization (WHO) recently estimated that road injuries are the 8th leading cause of death worldwide, with 1.4 million deaths all around the world [26]. In the U.S., 37,461 people died on roadways in 2016, a 5.6% increase from 2015 [16]. This increase is significant [1] since the number of motor vehicle fatalities remained virtually unchanged varying between 32,479, and 37,461 over the 2010–2016 time period [22]. In the new era of autonomous driving, the advancement in the next-generation mobile networks (also known as 5G), vehicular networks, and Internet-of-Things (IoT) shall be part of a smart road infrastructure to achieve road condition monitoring and control for both safety and efficiency.

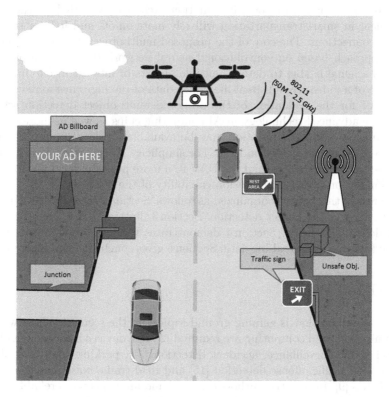

Fig. 1. Overview of the UAV based multi-object detection framework.

As a preliminary work to enhance the smart traffic, in this paper, we propose to apply unmanned aerial vehicle (UAV), wireless communications and artificial intelligence (AI) based schemes to assist road condition monitoring. An overview of the proposed UAV based multi-object detection framework is shown in Fig. 1. Particularly in this work, objects of interest for road monitoring are advertisement billboards, junctions, traffic signs and unsafe objects. Other objects of interest can be easily extended to the proposed framework if required. Those objects need to be monitored and shared by drivers and autonomous driving systems. For example, traffic signs provide important information and instructions for drives, and they need to be maintained and updated when necessary to ensure a safe driving environment. View to junctions may be blocked which would cause safety issues to driving, especially autonomous driving. Unsafe objects on the road side also challenge the drivers. For instance, the glare reflected by some of them can be extremely dangerous to drivers, over-size objects can block traffic signs, etc. To tackle the issues caused by these objects, we propose to use UAV as image data acquisition equipment for objects in our interest to be detected from the collected images. Meanwhile, the UAV is designed to be connected with a road side unit through wireless communications. In the current implementation, IEEE 802.11 is applied for local information exchange. Nonetheless, the future deployment in smart transportation will rely more on 5G and IoT for seamless network connections. The core of the proposed multi-object detection scheme is an AI approach based on convolutional neural network (CNN). The proposed AI based scheme is able to detect multiple objects of interest in one image, or one frame of a video stream. Real-life image data of the highways were collected using UAV for the evaluation of the proposed multi-object detection scheme. With more advanced technology in AI computing chips as well as more efficient algorithms, on-board computation may be available for data pre-processing or even the multi-object detection itself. For simplicity, in this work, it is assumed to offload the computation from the UAV to a more powerful local platform due to the limited on-board computation capability of the testbed.

The rest of this paper is organized as follows. Section 2 introduces the related works that cover the object detection. Section 3 illustrates the proposed multi-object detection scheme. Section 4 demonstrates the evaluation results of the proposed scheme using real-life data. Section 5 gives conclusion and future works.

2   Related Work

IoT is a paradigm that is gaining ground rapidly in the scenario where wireless communications and computing are required [2]. IoT devices have been deployed for road traffic surveillance, accident detection [21], parking spots availability detection [7], traffic offense detection [15] and road traffic noise management in Smart Cities [9]. In [17], the authors designed and implemented a reliable intelligent framework to monitor vehicle traffic condition with a low cost by applying IoT devices. The processed data are transferred to the server through Wi-Fi for the further traffic control. To keep up with the transition towards smart transportation, next generation mobile networks will support the communication requirements for IoT and smart transportation. Thanks to the ultra-reliable low latency communications, 5G transport network is expected to provide the satisfactory capacity, required latency, for real-time road monitoring and control in smart transportation [18,20], which is promising to promote smart drive-assistant services, cooperative driving services, as well as fully autonomous driving services. In this work, we leverage the advancement in the next-generation mobile network and IoT to support the data transmission for the proposed multi-object detection scheme.

Raw data collection is critical to multi-object detection for road monitoring. Traditionally, special utility vehicles are deployed in field to collect data. For example, researchers developed a special vehicle named as S.T.I.E.R. for data collection [5]. A high-speed camera is installed at the tail of the vehicle to collect image data of road surfaces for pavement distress detection in the driving lane. However, such data collection method is limited in coverage as it only monitors one driving lane at a time. Moreover, operating such a vehicle on highways may affect normal traffics. Using UAV is an alternative way to address those issues and collect data [10]. For example, due to the wider field of view from a UAV, a larger area can be covered. Thus more objects besides road surface can be included in the object of interests, such as traffic signs, road junctions, etc. Moreover, the operational cost of deploying UAV for data collection is much cheaper than deploying a specific vehicle.

AI has been widely adopted in the recent years for object detection in images and videos [11,23,24]. Object detection approaches can be mainly classified into three types: classic, two-stage, and one-stage approaches [10]. One of the widely adopted classic object detection algorithm is the CNN used for digits recognition that proposed by LeCun in [11]. The classical detectors conduct the detection by operating like a sliding window, where a classifier is applied every time over a image grid that is predefined. Two-stage detection approaches, e.g. region-based convolutional neural network (R-CNN) is being developed over the last few years with several improvements [6,25] and extensions [8,13]. In R-CNN and its extensions, region proposal methods are first applied to generate a sparse set of candidate proposals which contain all objects. The process would filter out the majority of negative locations in an image. The second stage is to perform classifications on these proposals to separate them into foreground classes and background classes. One-stage approach has been adopted more recently. For example, SSD [14], YOLO [23,24] are two main approaches that assume a single detection stage that is closer to the way human beings detect objects. The two approaches both enhance the efficiency as well as detection precision. For instance, the latest YOLO can achieve almost the same detection precision compared with other two-stage detection approaches [4]. In this work, we develop an AI based multi-object detection scheme around a CNN structure.

3   Multi-object Detection Scheme for Road Condition Monitoring

Without loss of generality, the proposed multi-object detection scheme is designed and implemented in two steps. In the first step, we establish a database by collecting raw images from a UAV along the highway in Jiangsu province, China. With the established database, in the second step, we develop a multi-object detection scheme around a CNN based deep learning algorithm. Detailed illustration is given in the rest of this section.

3.1 UAV Based Raw Data Collection

The UAV used for data collection is shown in Fig. 2. For practical monitoring, a UAV is required to cruise at a relatively high speed between 40 km/h to 80 km/h for a long duration. The actual implementation has a hovering height at 40 meter. Meanwhile, the UAV must be able to resist strong wind, e.g. below the level Beaufort 6. Reasonable payload capacity is also required to mount a high-resolution camera, data communication modules, and possible on-board computing devices for data acquisition, transmission and processing, respectively. The communication module in the applied UAV needs to be energy efficiency, high bandwidth, low latency, and secure. Currently, the raw data captured from the on-board camera is beyond 4K resolution. Transmission of raw data in real-time causes a challenge to the current implementation that relies on the IEEE 802.11. A better transmission module, e.g., based on 5G, must be developed for the actual system in future smart transportation. An on-board computing device is yet to be developed so that data pre-processing can be conducted in real-time to reduce the transmission overhead. For simplicity, the specifications of the deployed UAV are listed in Table 1.

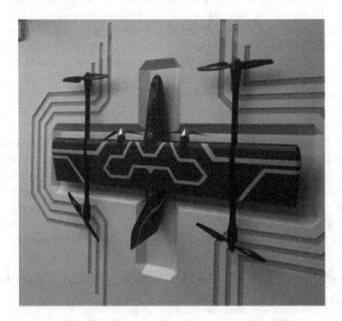

Fig. 2. SwapImagine - the UAV used for data collection.

Table 1. Specifications of the deployed UAV.

UAV specification	Value
Cruise duration (min)	70
Wind-resistance (Beaufort)	>6
Payload (kg)	6–8
Cruising speed (km/h)	40–80
Com. specification	Value
Modulation	COFDM, 16QAM
Frequency (Hz)	50M–2.5G
Bandwidth (Mbps)	2–8
Output power (W)	0.5–2
Encryption	AES 128
Range (km)	8 (40 for the directional)

3.2 AI Based Multi-object Detection Scheme for Road Monitoring

Our proposed AI based multi-object detection scheme is built around the core structure of a CNN. A typical CNN has the architectures designed for processing grid-like data [12]. Compared with a traditional feedforward neural network where each weight is used only once, a typical CNN uses kernels at all positions of the input data. A well developed CNN would capture the features for every location in the data, especially for image data [4].

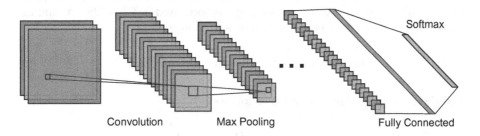

Fig. 3. CNN standard architecture.

As shown in Fig. 3, convolutional layers are the core components of a CNN. The key function of the convolutional layers is to perform feature extraction from the input image data. They are composed of a set of spatial filters which are usually known as convolutional kernels. Each convolutional layer in a CNN is followed by an activation layer which gives nonlinear transformation to the previously obtained feature map. The activation function enhances computational efficiency and helps to eliminate gradient vanishing in the training progress [19].

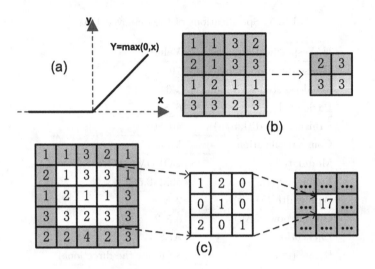

Fig. 4. Operations in CNN layers.

Rectified linear unit (ReLU) expressed in Eq. (1) is usually used as the activation function, which is illustrated in Fig. 4(a).

$$f(x) = \max(0, x) = \begin{cases} x, & \text{if } x \geq 0, \\ 0, & \text{else.} \end{cases} \tag{1}$$

A pooling layer also follows the convolutional layer to reduce the dimension of the extracted feature map without losing essential information. Max pooling and average pooling are two common pooling methods used in CNN [28]. Assuming a filter of 2×2, the max pooling computes as follows:

$$\text{max pooling} \begin{bmatrix} x_1 & x_2 \\ x_3 & x_4 \end{bmatrix} = \max(x_1, x_2, x_3, x_4). \tag{2}$$

And the average pooling computes as follows:

$$\text{average pooling} \begin{bmatrix} x_1 & x_2 \\ x_3 & x_4 \end{bmatrix} = \frac{1}{4} \sum_{i=1}^{4} x_i. \tag{3}$$

In comparison, max pooling reduces the feature map size by picking the maximum value within a sliding window, while average pooling takes the average value in the sliding window to streamline the feature map. Figure 4(b) demonstrates a max pooling process with a 2-by-2 filter and stride equals 2. An example of a completed convolution operation is given in Fig. 4(c). In this example, an input image data with a size of 5-by-5 is convoluted by a 3-by-3 filter. The stride, a hyper-parameter that determines the sliding interval of the kernel, is set to be 1. The convolution operation produces a two-dimension feature map.

A fully connected layer and a softmax layer are the final layers of a CNN architecture. The fully connected layer is known as multilayer perceptron where neural nodes are fully connected to the output of the previous layer. The softmax layer is used to normalize the probability value for classification decision. The softmax computes an output as follows:

$$S_j = \frac{e^{a_j}}{\sum_{k=1}^{T} e^{a_k}}, \tag{4}$$

where S_j is the probability of the j_{th} class to be the classification result among all T possible classes. a_i are the output of the former fully connected layer. The cross entropy is further calculated for classification.

$$E = -\sum_{j=1}^{T} y_i \log(S_j), \tag{5}$$

where $y_i = 1$ only if the i_{th} class it the true class matching the classification result, otherwise $y_i = 0$.

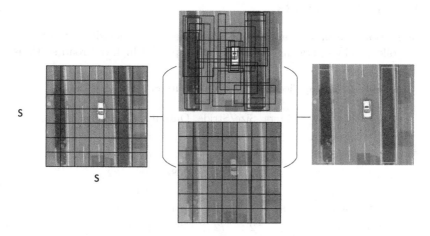

Fig. 5. Work flow of the AI based multi-object detection scheme.

The proposed AI based scheme is built around the CNN structure described above to achieve multi-object detection in one image. For simplicity, the work flow of the implemented AI scheme is illustrated in Fig. 5. An input image is first divided into $S \times S$ grid cells. Boundary boxes and probabilities will be calculated to make detection on the relevant objects. Each of the grid cells is composed of $(\mathbf{x}, \mathbf{y}, \mathbf{w}, \mathbf{h}, \mathbf{c})$, where $(\mathbf{x}, \mathbf{y})$ is the coordinates stands for the centers of the position of B detection boundary boxes of the corresponding grid cell; $\mathbf{w}$ is the width of the detection boundary boxes; $\mathbf{h}$ stands for the height; and $\mathbf{c}$ is the confidence score which is a column vector represents the predicted probabilities of respective C categories. Success of a detection is computed as follows:

$$\mathbf{o} = \frac{1}{2} + \frac{1}{2}\frac{pI - \eta}{|pI - \eta|}, \tag{6}$$

where $\mathbf{o}$ is either 1 or 0 indicates a successful detection of targeted objects or object detection failure respectively. In Eq. (6), p reflects the probability of a targeted object existing in the grid cell, I is the value of the term as Intersection over Union (IOU) which is defined as the overlapping rate of the predicated bound and the ground truth bound. The production pI is the confidence score of the prediction and η is the threshold to filter out low confidence scores. The remaining boundary boxes will be processed by non-maximum suppression to finalize the object detection. Finally, IOU is computed as follows:

$$I = \frac{A_p \cap A_t}{A_p \cup A_t}, \tag{7}$$

where A_p and A_t are the area of predicted bounding box and the ground-truth bounding box respectively.

4   Evaluation Results

In this section, we first establish our database which includes sets of sample images collected by operating the UAV above partial highway road sections in

Table 2. The applied network architecture in the scheme design.

Layer		Filters	Size/Stride	Output data dimension
1	conv	16	$3 \times 3/1$	$416 \times 416 \times 16$
2	max		$2 \times 2/2$	$208 \times 208 \times 16$
3	conv	32	$3 \times 3/1$	$208 \times 208 \times 32$
4	max		$2 \times 2/2$	$104 \times 104 \times 32$
5	conv	64	$3 \times 3/1$	$104 \times 104 \times 64$
6	max		$2 \times 2/2$	$52 \times 52 \times 64$
7	conv	128	$3 \times 3/1$	$52 \times 52 \times 128$
8	max		$2 \times 2/2$	$26 \times 26 \times 128$
9	conv	256	$3 \times 3/1$	$26 \times 26 \times 256$
10	max		$2 \times 2/2$	$13 \times 13 \times 256$
11	conv	512	$3 \times 3/1$	$13 \times 13 \times 512$
12	max		$2 \times 2/1$	$13 \times 13 \times 512$
13	conv	1024	$3 \times 3/1$	$13 \times 13 \times 1024$
14	conv	1024	$3 \times 3/1$	$13 \times 13 \times 1024$
15	conv	30	$1 \times 1/1$	$13 \times 13 \times 30$
16	detection			

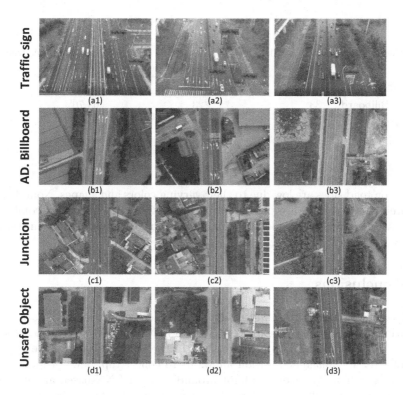

Fig. 6. Examples of the multi-object detection results.

Jiangsu, China. The operating height of the UAV is fixed at 40 m. The captured videos are in 4K resolution, which is 4608×3456 in specific. Each image extracted from each frame has a file size around 25 Megabytes. The applied dataset includes multiple video clips collected from 25 different road sections of the monitored highway. The raw data is captured and stored from the UAV in the current implementation, and processed in an offline computing platform. In order to achieve real-time monitoring and control, data pre-processing and filtering will be further investigated in the future work.

The AI based multi-object detection scheme first extracts a single frame of from a raw video clip. The extracted image is then resized to a fixed size of 416×416, which is used as the input to the multi-object detection scheme. The architecture of the proposed AI scheme in the current implementation is illustrated in Table 2. The current AI scheme is evaluated based on $1,457$ images extracted from multiple raw video clips captured from the UAV described earlier. Figure 6 shows some results of the multi-object detection scheme.

For better illustration, the overall performance of the proposed scheme is provided in Table 3. The evaluation results show that the detection accuracy is higher when the detection objects are traffic signs or junctions connected to the highway. The detection accuracy of advertisement billboards and unsafe

Table 3. Evaluated detection performance

Object class	Number of labeled objects	Number of successful detection	Detection accuracy
Traffic sign	978	818	83.64%
AD. Billboard	33	23	69.70%
Junction	2571	2212	86.04%
Unsafe object	733	506	69.03%

objects on road sides are low due to their varying colors and shapes. Nonetheless, the preliminary results are presented to demonstrate the efficacy of combining UAV, AI, next-generation mobile networks and IoT to support the future smart transportation.

5 Conclusions

Road condition monitoring and control will be critical in future smart transportation. In this paper, we explored the possibility to apply UAV and AI based scheme for on-road multi-object detection. In the studied scenario, the application of UAV for image acquisition allows us to collect top views of roads in an efficient way. The AI scheme is built around modern CNN-based architectures that can achieve multi-object detection in an image. Evaluation of the studied work was conducted using real-life data collected by a UAV. The evaluation results demonstrated that our proposed AI based scheme, together with UAV, wireless communications and IoT can provide a good solution to future road condition monitoring and control in smart transportation. In future work, we will further explore the schemes for accurate and efficient multi-object detection for road monitoring. For example, different objects of interest should be detected simultaneously in the AI based scheme. Moreover, we will also validate the schemes in various road monitoring techniques such as the live web-cam along the highway and on-board dash-cam.

References

1. Essex, A., Shinkle, D., Miller, A., Pula, K.: Traffic safety trends—state legislative action 2017. In: National Conference of State Legislatures (2018)
2. Atzori, L., Iera, A., Morabito, G.: The Internet of Things: a survey. Comput. Netw. **54**(15), 2787–2805 (2010)
3. Clarke, R.Y.: Smart cities and the internet of everything: the foundation for delivering next-generation citizen services. IDC Government Insights (2013)
4. Ćorović, A., Ilić, V., Durić, S., Marijan, M., Pavković, B.: The real-time detection of traffic participants using yolo algorithm. In: 26th Telecommunications Forum (TELFOR), pp. 1–4. IEEE (2018)

5. Eisenbach, M., et al.: How to get pavement distress detection ready for deep learning? A systematic approach. In: International Joint Conference on Neural Networks (IJCNN), pp. 2039–2047, May 2017. https://doi.org/10.1109/IJCNN.2017.7966101
6. Girshick, R., Donahue, J., Darrell, T., Malik, J.: Rich feature hierarchies for accurate object detection and semantic segmentation. In: IEEE Conference on Computer Vision and Pattern Recognition, pp. 580–587, June 2014. https://doi.org/10.1109/CVPR.2014.81
7. Goyal, R., Kumari, A., Shubham, K., Kumar, N.: IoT and XBee based smart traffic management system. J. Commun. Eng. Syst. **8**(1), 8–14 (2018)
8. He, K., Zhang, X., Ren, S., Sun, J.: Deep residual learning for image recognition. In: Proceedings of the IEEE Conference on Computer Vision and Pattern Recognition, pp. 770–778 (2016)
9. Kazmi, A., Tragos, E., Serrano, M.: Underpinning IoT for road traffic noise management in smart cities. In: IEEE International Conference on Pervasive Computing and Communications Workshops (PerCom Workshops), pp. 765–769, March 2018. https://doi.org/10.1109/PERCOMW.2018.8480142
10. Kharchenko, V., Chyrka, I.: Detection of airplanes on the ground using YOLO neural network. In: IEEE 17th International Conference on Mathematical Methods in Electromagnetic Theory (MMET), pp. 294–297, July 2018. https://doi.org/10.1109/MMET.2018.8460392
11. LeCun, Y., et al.: Backpropagation applied to handwritten zip code recognition. Neural Comput. **1**(4), 541–551 (1989). https://doi.org/10.1162/neco.1989.1.4.541
12. LeCun, Y., Bengio, Y., Hinton, G.: Deep learning. Nature **521**(7553), 436 (2015)
13. Lin, T.Y., Dollár, P., Girshick, R., He, K., Hariharan, B., Belongie, S.: Feature pyramid networks for object detection. In: CVPR, vol. 1, p. 4 (2017)
14. Liu, W., et al.: SSD: single shot multibox detector. In: Leibe, B., Matas, J., Sebe, N., Welling, M. (eds.) ECCV 2016. LNCS, vol. 9905, pp. 21–37. Springer, Cham (2016). https://doi.org/10.1007/978-3-319-46448-0_2
15. Mihelj, J., Kos, A., Sedlar, U.: Source reputation assessment in an IoT-based vehicular traffic monitoring system. Procedia Comput. Sci. **147**, 295–299 (2019)
16. Moore, W., et al.: Transportation statistics annual report, 2016. United States, Bureau of Transportation Statistics (2017)
17. Nagmode, V.S., Rajbhoj, S.: An intelligent framework for vehicle traffic monitoring system using IoT. In: International Conference on Intelligent Computing and Control (I2C2), pp. 1–4. IEEE (2017)
18. Nakao, A., et al.: End-to-end network slicing for 5G mobile networks. J. Inf. Process. **25**, 153–163 (2017)
19. Nwankpa, C., Ijomah, W., Gachagan, A., Marshall, S.: Activation functions: comparison of trends in practice and research for deep learning. arXiv preprint arXiv:1811.03378 (2018)
20. Öhlén, P., et al.: Data plane and control architectures for 5G transport networks. J. Lightwave Technol. **34**(6), 1501–1508 (2016)
21. Patel, R., Dabhi, V.K., Prajapati, H.B.: A survey on IoT based road traffic surveillance and accident detection system (a smart way to handle traffic and concerned problems). In: Innovations in Power and Advanced Computing Technologies (i-PACT), pp. 1–7, April 2017. https://doi.org/10.1109/IPACT.2017.8245066
22. Patil, D., Rosekind, M.: Traffic fatalities data has just been released: a call to action to download and analyze. US Department of Transportation (2015)
23. Redmon, J., Divvala, S., Girshick, R., Farhadi, A.: You only look once: unified, real-time object detection. In: Proceedings of the IEEE Conference on Computer Vision and Pattern Recognition, pp. 779–788 (2016)

24. Redmon, J., Farhadi, A.: Yolo9000: better, faster, stronger. arXiv preprint (2017)
25. Ren, S., He, K., Girshick, R., Sun, J.: Faster R-CNN: towards real-time object detection with region proposal networks. In: Advances in Neural Information Processing Systems, pp. 91–99 (2015)
26. World Health Organization, et al.: The top 10 causes of death (2016). https://www. who.int/en/news-room/fact-sheets/detail/the-top-10-causes-of-death. May 2018
27. Ye, F., Qian, Y., Hu, R.Q.: Smart service-aware wireless mixed-area networks. IEEE Netw. **33**(1), 84–91 (2019). https://doi.org/10.1109/MNET.2018.1700399
28. Yi, Z.: Evaluation and implementation of convolutional neural networks in image recognition. In: Journal of Physics: Conference Series, vol. 1087, p. 062018. IOP Publishing (2018)
29. Zhang, J., Ye, F., Qian, Y.: A distributed network QoE measurement framework for smart networks in smart cities. In: IEEE International Smart Cities Conference (ISC2), pp. 1–7, September 2018. https://doi.org/10.1109/ISC2.2018.8656854

Sentiment Analysis for Tang Poetry Based on Imagery Aided and Classifier Fusion

Yabo Shen[1], Yong Ma[1], Chunguo Li[2], Shidang Li[1],
Mingliang Gu[1(✉)], Chaojin Zhang[1], Yun Jin[1,3], and Yingli Shen[1]

[1] School of Physics and Electronic Engineering,
Jiangsu Normal University, Xuzhou, China
shenyabohpu@163.com, mlgu@jsnu.edu.cn
[2] School of Information Science and Engineering,
Southeast University, Nanjing, China
[3] Kewen College, Jiangsu Normal University, Xuzhou, Jiangsu, China

Abstract. This paper aims to do sentiment analysis for Tang poetry from the perspective of text mining. Most previous works just focus on the literariness of Chinese poetry or establish language models statistically, which ignore the features of sentiment and specific applications. We propose a sentiment analysis system for Tang poetry based on imagery aided and classifier fusion. Especially, we extract sentimental imageries at two levels: character and word, and bring them into sentiment analysis. In addition, classifier fusion is adopted in this paper to improve classification performance. Experiments show the effectiveness of our model and our method is superior to the traditional method.

Keywords: Sentiment analysis · Tang poetry · Imagery aided ·
Classifier fusion

1 Introduction

As a kind of classical Chinese poetry, Tang poetry is precious spirit wealth of human being [1]. Nowadays, with the rise of artificial intelligence, it becomes a hot trend to process and analyze various data through machine learning or natural language processing (NLP) [2]. However, for classical Chinese poetry, most related works just focus on its literariness or establish language models locally while ignoring the global features of statistics and the applications in NLP.

In order to apply NLP to classical Chinese poetry, Fang [3] addressed the issue of machine-aided analysis and understanding of classical Chinese poetry and proposed a computational framework. Nevertheless, it suffered from high model complexity and focused more on the imagery itself. He [4] used general methods of machine learning, and established a SVM-based poetry style classification system while there was too little detailed study.

Besides, Liu [5] studied colors in Tang poetry and the social networks of the Tang poets. Wang [6] proposed a novel two-stage poetry generating method and Zhang [7] introduced a model for Chinese poetry generation based on recurrent neural networks.

S. Han et al. (Eds.): AICON 2019, LNICST 287, pp. 283–290, 2019.
https://doi.org/10.1007/978-3-030-22971-9_24

Peng [8] studied the multi-grained Chinese text representation for Chinese sentiment analysis. Actually, all these studies give us great inspiration and help.

In this paper, we select fine-grained Tang poetry texts, which have been manually marked, and then perform sentiment analysis task. In addition to the general framework of sentiment analysis, we also make statistical analysis of the Complete Tang Poems (CTP) and extract sentimental imageries at character and word levels to help us implement the task. Furthermore, classifier fusion is used in this paper to optimize the performance. The contributions of our work can be summarized as follows:

(1) This paper makes statistical analysis of the CTP (about 43000 poems) from the character and word levels to extract the sentimental imageries and brings them into classification model.
(2) The idea of sentiment analysis for short text is transferred to the Tang poetry, and classifier fusion is adopted to obtain better experimental results.

The remainder of the paper is organized as follows. Section 2 presents our model and corresponding analysis in detail. Section 3 describes the experimental settings and results. In Sect. 4, the conclusion is drawn.

2   Our Proposed Method

In this section, we present the details of our sentiment analysis system for Tang poetry. An overall framework is shown in Fig. 1.

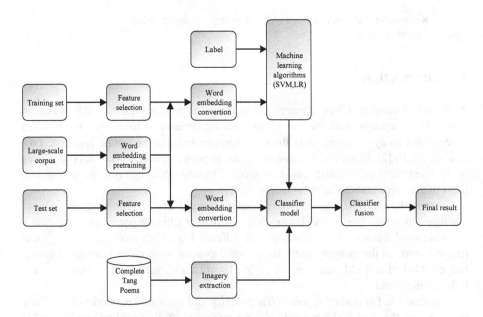

Fig. 1. The framework of sentiment analysis system for Tang poetry

2.1 Sentiment Analysis for Tang Poetry

Text sentiment analysis refers to the process of detecting, analyzing and mining subjective texts including views, preferences and emotions expressed by users [9]. Actually, it is a specific functional implementation of text classification.

As shown in Fig. 1, the sentiment analysis system for Tang poetry consists of training and testing part. For the labeled training set, we extract the features by information gain (IG) and mutual information (MI).

Information gain is used to calculate the amount of information contributed to the text classification by the presence or absence of features, and the formula is as follows:

$$Gain(w_i) = Entropy(S) - Entropy(S_i) \qquad (1)$$

Entropy(S) indicates the information entropy when the feature w_i does not appear, and *Entropy(S_i)* indicates the information entropy after the appearance of the feature w_i.

Mutual information is used in text classification to measure how much a feature is dependent on a category, as follows:

$$MI(w_i, c_j) = \log \frac{p(w_i, c_j)}{p(w_i)p(c_j)} \qquad (2)$$

$p(w_i, c_j)$ indicates the probability that a document containing feature w_i belongs to class c_j, and $p(w_i)$ indicates the probability that feature w_i will appear in the document, and similarly $p(c_j)$ indicates the probability that a document belongs to class c_j.

Then according to the pretrained word embeddings, we convert the features extracted to word embeddings of corresponding dimensions. Next, what we do is establishing the classifier model using machine learning algorithms (i.e. SVM, LR).

In the same way, for the test set, feature extraction and word embedding convertion are implemented, and when we give a testing sample, the classifier model will return a label as "1" or "0" (positive = 1, negative = 0).

2.2 Word Segmentation for Tang Poetry

Word segmentation is the basis of Chinese Natural Language Processing and has considerable importance [10]. If word segmentation is not good, the following result is probably not good either.

For example, if we make word segmentation for the poem "烽火连三月，家书抵万金 (feng huo lian san yue, jia shu di wan jin)". The correct segmentation should be "烽火 连 三月, 家书 抵 万金", which shows the cruelty and persistence of the war, as well as the eagerness to get family news. But if divided into "烽火 连 三月, 家书 抵 万 金", it will make people very confused about the meaning of its expression.

In this paper, we use THULAC [11] to make word segmentation.

2.3 Imagery Aided Classification

Imagery in poetry refers to a meaningful image, that is, an artistic image created through the unique emotional activities of the creative subject. And if we know the imagery well, we can easily judge the sentiment of the poetry.

As shown in Fig. 2, text preprocessing is the first step because the text contains ordinal numbers, titles, authors and contents. So it is segmented and preliminarily screened out. At the same time, special symbols should be eliminated. We only keep commas and periods, and the rest of symbols are regarded as invalid symbols. Then, for the preprocessed text, we make statistical analysis at two levels. For character level, we count character frequency and find some characters that can be imageries. And for word level, we make word segmentation and statistical analysis. By these steps, we can get the sentimental imageries we need.

Thus we can use the sentimental imageries to construct a classifier for Tang poetry according to the imageries included in the poems.

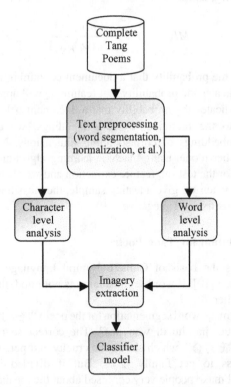

Fig. 2. The detailed process of imagery aided classification

2.4   Classifier Fusion

In order to improve the performance of the proposed method, the classifier fusion method is adopted [12], and the detail is shown in Fig. 3.

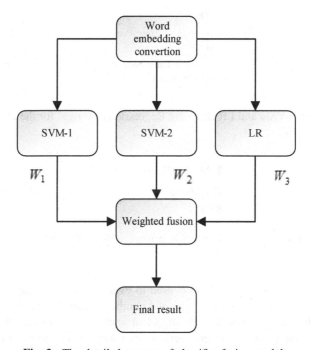

Fig. 3. The detailed process of classifier fusion module

As shown in Fig. 3, three independent classifiers are used. The formula is as follows:

$$P = \sum_{i=1}^{3} W_i * P_i \tag{3}$$

The weight of each classifier W_i(i = 1, 2, 3) is determined by grid search algorithm. Then the weights are multiplied by corresponding probability P_i and sum to obtain the final probability p.

3   Experiments Analysis

3.1   Experiment Setting

As shown in Table 1, the experimental data in this paper are the untagged Complete Tang Poems (a text of 42974 poems) and the labeled 5598 lines of Tang poems. We label 5598 lines of poems manually, among which 3,403 are negative and 2,195 are positive.

The experiments in this paper are all carried out in python environment of Linux system.

Table 1. Experimental data and environment

	Data
1	Complete Tang Poems (42974 poems)
2	labeled Tang poems (5598 lines)

In this paper, SVMs and LR (Logistic Regression) are used for the classifier fusion (Table 2).

Table 2. Classifier setting

Classifier 1	Classifier 2	Classifier 3
SVM-1 (kernel = 'rbf', degree = 2, gamma = 1, coef0 = 10)	SVM-2 (kernel = 'poly', degree = 2, gamma = 10, coef0 = 10)	LR (penalty = '12')

In this paper, the accuracy (Acc) is used to evaluate the performance of the classifiers. It represents the proportion of the total number of correctly predicted samples in the test samples to the total number of actual samples. In general, the higher the accuracy is, the better the classifier's performance will be. The formula is as follows:

$$Acc = \frac{TP + TN}{TP + FP + FN + TN} \tag{4}$$

TP means that the predicted results are consistent with the actual results and are positive samples. TN means that the predicted results and actual samples both are negative. FP means that the predicted results are positive but the actual samples are negative. Similarly, FN means the opposite of FP.

3.2 Result Analysis

As can be seen from Table 3, through the statistical analysis of Tang poetry at the character and word level, we find some sentimental imageries that can be used to identify the sentiment polarity (not all listed).

Table 3. Sentimental imageries

	Positive Imageries		Negative Imageries	
	Chinese	*English*	*Chinese*	*English*
Character level	松	pine	柳	willow
	竹	bamboo	猿	ape
	梅	plum	秋	autumn
	兰	orchid	坟	tomb
Word level	春风	Spring breeze	白发	white hair
	朝阳	the rising sun	白骨	bones of the dead
	高山	high mountain	夕阳	the setting sun
	青天	blue sky	孤城	lonely town
	青云	high official position	落花	falling flowers
	碧水	blue water	琵琶	Chinese lute

Table 4. Tang poetry's sentiment analysis results (dimension = 100)

Method		Acc
No classifier fusion	Imagery-aided classifier	52.4%
	SVM-1	58.6%
	SVM-2	54.8%
	LR	59.0%
With classifier fusion		**67.2%**

As can be seen in Table 4, the accuracy of sentiment classification with classifier fusion is obviously higher than that without classifier fusion.

Table 5. The results when word embedding dimensions change

Dimension	Acc
100	67.2%
200	**67.9%**
300	67.5%
400	66.9%

Besides, we also explore the influence of the word embedding dimension. From Table 5, it doesn't make much difference due to the characteristic of short text.

4 Conclusion

This paper proposes a sentiment analysis system for Tang poetry based on imagery aided and classifier fusion. The results show the effectiveness of the system, which is of certain significance to the research on the sentiment analysis for Tang poetry and other literary short texts. There are still some problems in this paper, such as the low accuracy. All in all, the method in this paper is worth further research in the future.

Acknowledgement. This work is supported by the National Natural Science Foundation of China (Grant No. 61708061, 6167114, and 61673108), Xuzhou Science and technology project (KC18015), Industry-University-Research collaboration project of Jiangsu Province (BY2018077), Research Fund for the Doctoral Program of New Teachers of Jiangsu Normal University (Grant No. 17XLR029), Natural Science Foundation of Jiangsu Higher Education Institutions of China (Grant No. 17KJB510016, 17KJB510018, and 18KJB510013), and Jiangsu Normal University School Funding Project (2018YXJ611).

References

1. Hou, Y., Frank, A.: Analyzing sentiment in classical chinese poetry. In: Proceedings of the 9th SIGHUM Workshop on Language Technology for Cultural Heritage, Social Sciences, and Humanities, pp. 15–24 (2015)
2. Zheng, Y.: Affective computing applied in chinese classical poetry study. E-sci. Technol. Appl. **3**(4), 59–66 (2012)
3. Fang, A.C., Lo, F., Chinn, C.K.: Adapting NLP and corpus analysis techniques to structured imagery analysis in classical chinese poetry. In: Workshop Adaptation of Language Resources and Technology to New Domains, pp. 27–34 (2009)
4. He, Z., Liang, W., Li, L., et al.: SVM-based classification method for poetry style. In: the Proceedings of ICMLC06, pp. 1588–1591 (2007)
5. Liu, C., Wang, H., Cheng, W., et al.: Color aesthetics and social networks in complete tang poems: explorations and discoveries. Comput. Sci. (2015)
6. Wang, Z., He, W., Wu, H., et al.: Chinese poetry generation with planning based neural network. In: Proceedings of the 26th International Conference on Computational Linguistics: Technical Papers, pp. 1051–1060 (2016)
7. Zhang, X., Lapata, M.: Chinese poetry generation with recurrent neural networks. In: Proceedings of the 2014 Conference of Empirical Methods in Natural Language Processing (EMNLP), pp. 670–680 (2014)
8. Peng, H., Ma, Y., Li, Y., Cambria, E.: Learning multi-grained aspect target sequence for Chinese sentiment analysis. Knowl.-Based Syst. **148**, 167–176 (2018)
9. Poria, S., Cambria, E., Bajpai, R., et al.: A review of affective computing: from unimodal analysis to multimodal fusion. Inf. Fusion **37**, 98–125 (2017)
10. Li, Y., Pan, Q., Yang, T., et al.: Learning word representations for sentiment analysis. Cogn. Comput. **9**, 843–851 (2017)
11. Sun, M., Chen, X., Zhang, K., Guo, Z., Liu, Z.: THULAC: an efficient lexical analyzer for Chinese (2016)
12. Zhao, D., Shen, Y., Shen, Y., et al.: Short text sentiment analysis based on windowed word vector. In: The 7th International Conference on Communication Signal Processing and Systems, p. 346 (2018)

Detection of Insulator Defects Based on YOLO V3

Fei Guo[1], Kun Hao[1(✉)], Mengqi Xia[1], Lu Zhao[1], Li Wang[1], and Qi Liu[2]

[1] School of Computer and Information Engineering,
Tianjin Chengjian University, Tianjin 300384, China
1641693948@qq.com, Kunhao@tcu.edu.cn,
1437098867@qq.com, zhaolu6892@163.com,
liwang_tjcj@qq.com
[2] Computation Center, Tianjin Chengjian University, Tianjin 300384, China
liuqicj@126.com

Abstract. The power system of China is still composed of power generation, transmission, substation, power distribution and other links. To ensure the safety and stability of transmission lines is an important part of large-scale transmission process, and the insulators are important in the transmission line. The existing parts, such as surface contamination, cracks, damage and other surface defects seriously threaten the operation safety of the power grid. Faults caused by insulator defects are currently the highest proportion of power system faults, so the surface defects of insulators are detected and timely completion of fault repair becomes more important. In this regard, this paper proposes a target detection algorithm based on YOLO V3 (You Only Look Once: Real-Time Object Detection), which utilizes the powerful learning ability of deep convolutional neural networks and a large number of data annotation samples. The image of the insulator photo-graphed by the machine is detected and classified, finally the intelligent detection of the intact insulator and the defective insulator is realized. The experimental results show that the YOLO V3 based insulator defect detection method can effectively identify the defective insulator strings from the aerial image of the drone. Compared with the previous insulator defect identification method, the accuracy and detection time are significantly improved, and it can realize the intelligent detection of intact insulators and defective insulators.

Keywords: Insulator · YOLO V3 · Target detection · Defect detection · Target classification

1 Introduction

The invention and widespread use of electricity have brought convenience to human beings. Electrical equipment such as computers, mobile phones, and smart appliances have made us more dependent on electricity, which has become a necessity in people's life [1]. At present, the transmission lines most commonly used are overhead transmission lines, which are mainly composed of wires, overhead ground wires, insulator strings, poles, grounding devices, etc. The insulator is a large number of components in

S. Han et al. (Eds.): AICON 2019, LNICST 287, pp. 291–299, 2019.
https://doi.org/10.1007/978-3-030-22971-9_25

the transmission lines, playing the role of electrical insulation and mechanical support, and is also a fault multiple component. Therefore, it is necessary to carry out regular inspection on the transmission lines and timely replace and maintain the insulators that have failed or are about to fail.

At present, the physical methods for on-line detection mainly include the following methods: observation method, ultraviolet imaging method and infrared imaging method, laser Doppler vibration method, ultrasonic flaw detection method, etc. [2]. The above have played a certain role, but mainly rely on manual monitoring, artificial vision consumes a lot of manpower and material resources, low efficiency, but also due to differences in personnel experience and personal qualities, the detection effect is difficult to standardize [3].

Along with the continuous advancement of technology, there has been a transmission line inspection platform based on a helicopter and unmanned aerial vehicle. The inspection platform is characterized by high efficiency, accuracy and safety, has become the main method of transmission line inspection in recent years. In order to understand the operation of and the potential hidden dangers of the transmission line, the power department used the drone inspection instead of the manual inspection [4, 5], by loading the camera on the platform to obtain a large number of aerial images, including effective insulator targets. If only by manpower for visual judgment without automatic image analysis, it is easy to cause missed or misjudged phenomenon, resulting in major safety hazards in transmission lines [6].

At present, there are related researches on the detection methods of insulators. The commonly used detection methods include: Aerial image detection method based on skeleton extraction [6]; Insulator string automatic state recognition based on infrared image [7]; Color matrix based Insulator single-chip infrared image fault diagnosis [8]; In literature [9] proposed a method for detecting internal defects of composite insulators based on misaligned speckle interference. It is used to eliminate the unqualified insulators in production and the concealed defects of composite insulators in diagnostic operation. These methods require manual feature extraction, with a heavy workload and a low recognition rate, which is likely to lead to the misdetection or omission of insulators due to the loss of subjective information [10]. In response to this phenomenon, researchers have proposed an image segmentation method based on deep learning [11, 12]. Literature [8] uses infrared imaging technology to acquire imaging, and the process of image treatment is as follow: image segmentation, data regularization, homomorphic filtering and data randomization, and BP neural network algorithm (The back propagation neural network algorithm is a multi-layer feed forward network trained according to error back propagation algorithm and is one of the most widely applied neural network models. BP network can be used to learn and store a great deal of mapping relations of input-output model, and no need to disclose in advance the mathematical equation that describes these mapping relations. Its learning rule is to adopt the steepest descent method in which the back propagation is used to regulate the weight value and threshold value of the network to achieve the minimum error sum of square) to extract insulator single-chip center. The RGB (The RGB color model is an additive color model in which red, green, and blue light are added together in various ways to reproduce a broad array of colors. The name of the model comes from the initials of the three additive primary colors, red, green, and blue) color matrix of the line is trained and analyzed as characteristic parameters, and an infrared diagnostic model of the insulator single chip based on the center line color matrix in the fault condition is constructed. In the literature [13], the six-rotor electric drone was introduced, and the manual inspection and the drone inspection were combined. Based on the threshold segmentation, morphology and edge detection techniques, the connected domain characteristics and shape characteristics of the insulator were designed. It can adapt to the complex background of aerial photography and multi-angle insulator self-explosion defect recognition algorithm to realize automatic detection of insulator defects and reduce manual intervention. For example, power inspection insulator detection based on convolutional neural network; it can automatically be compared with traditional detection methods. Compared with the traditional algorithm, improve the recognition accuracy under the complex background. However, in the case of image classification of insulators by convolutional neural network, an image classification block is required for each pixel. For insulator images with complex background, the classification block of adjacent pixels has high similarity which leads to slow and accurate network training [10]. Aiming at this problem, this paper based on the defect detection method of insulator in YOLO V3, using the powerful YOLO V3 real-time target detection algorithm, an end-to-end insulator defect detection method based on deep learning detection algorithm is proposed. Insulators are detected and automatically distinguish between defective insulators and intact insulators. Therefore, the automatic identification of insulator faults has practical significance for the inspection of transmission lines. Since most of the methods for detecting insulator defects based on aerial photographs are carried out in the laboratory environment, which has great limitations and does not take into account the complex background images of insulators and other factors, it is very important to use the YOLO V3 algorithm to study the automatic detection method for insulator surface defects.

The organization of the paper is as follows. In Sect. 2, the advantages of YOLO V1 and YOLO V2 relative to other target detection algorithms are summarized. In Sect. 3, the main algorithm part of YOLO V3 is introduced: basic method and network model design. In Sect. 4, a brief analysis of the experimental results and data. In Sect. 5 presents the conclusions.

2 Related Work

In this section, we review the advantages of YOLO V1 [14] and YOLO V2 [15] relative to other target detection algorithms, and give a brief overview of their advantages. The most important point is to point out that YOLO V3 is relatively inspecting small objects in relation to V1. And V2 speed and accuracy improvements. Object detection systems before YOLO (You Only Look Once: Unified, Real-Time Object Detection and YOLO9000: Better, Faster, Stronger) used classifiers to perform physical detection tasks, The method is to use a classifier to evaluate the presence or absence of the object on the boundary boxes of different positions and sizes of a test graph. For example, in the DPM system (Deformable Part Model System), a sliding window is used to evenly slide the whole image, and a classifier is used to evaluate whether there is an object. Other methods proposed after DPM, such as the R-CNN

(Region-Convolutional Neural Networks) method, use region proposal to generate possible bounding boxes of the entire image that may contain objects to be detected. And then use classifiers to evaluate the meshes, improve the bounding boxes by preprocessing, eliminate duplicate detection targets, and re-predict the grid based on other objects in the entire scene. The entire process is slow to execute, and because these links are trained separately, detection performance is difficult to optimize. Unlike these object detection methods, YOLO treats the object detection task as a regression problem, using a neural network to directly predict the coordinates of the boundary box, the confidence of the object contained in the target grid and the probability of the object from a whole image. YOLO's object detection process is done in a neural network, so end-to-end optimization of object detection performance is achieved, while YOLO detection of objects is extremely fast, the standard version of YOLO can reach 45 frames per second on Titan X GPU (A graphics processing unit, also occasionally called visual processing unit, is a specialized electronic circuit designed to rapidly manipulate and alter memory to accelerate the creation of images in a frame buffer intended for output to a display). The smaller version of the network Fast YOLO can maintain a detection speed of 155 frames per second while keeping the mAP (Mean Average Precision is the standard single-number measure for comparing search algorithms) twice as fast as other real-time object detectors. However, since the YOLO V1 training model only supports input of the same resolution image as the training image, and the target detection effect is relatively poor for relatively small targets, YOLO V2 provides power. YOLO V2 solves the problem that V1 can only input fixed size. The problem, but still not good at detecting small objects, is easy to produce object positioning errors, especially for dense objects. So this article uses YOLO V3 as the insulator defect detection algorithm.

3   Defect Detection of Insulator Based on YOLO V3

In the traditional power transmission line insulator target detection task can be divided into two aspects. First check for the target. That is, the target of the insulator is positioned in the image, where in the unfavorable factors such as complex background and image resolution are overcome. The insulators classified as intact insulators and defective insulators are classified according to the state characteristics of the insulators. Extracting features that adequately identify defective insulators is currently the most critical.

3.1   Basic Methods

Firstly, the feature extraction network is used to extract the features of insulator image, and a feature map of a certain size is obtained. For example, see (Fig. 2), the input insulator image is divided into S * S grids. The grid is responsible for detecting the insulator in which grid the center coordinates of the insulator fall. Since a fixed number of bounding boxes are predicted in each grid, the bounding box with the highest confidence value of the bounding box and the real insulator is selected and Ground Truth is the union of them, which is the IOU (Intersection over Union is an evaluation metric used to measure the accuracy of an object detector on a particular dataset. We often see this evaluation metric used in object detection challenges). The optimal situation is that IOU = 1 (that is, the predicted bounding box completely coincides with the bounding box of the real insulator) (Fig. 1).

$$IOU = \frac{DectionResult \cap GroundTruth}{DectionResult \cup GroundTruth} \tag{1}$$

The neural network predicts the bounding box by 4 coordinates: t_x, t_y, t_w, t_h. t_x, t_y represents the central coordinate of the predicted bounding box; t_w, t_h represents the width and height of the predicted bounding box, if the cell deviates from the upper left of the insulator image by (c_x, c_y), and the bounding box prior has width and height p_w, p_h, then the final grid predictions value correspond to

$$\begin{aligned} b_x &= \sigma(t_x) + cx \\ b_y &= \sigma(t_y) + cy \\ b_w &= p_w e^{tw} \\ b_h &= p_h e^{th} \end{aligned} \tag{2}$$

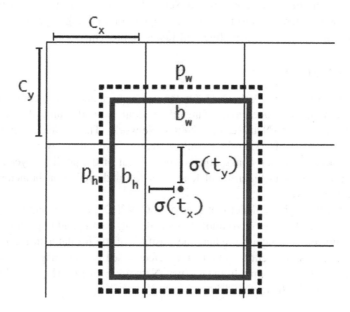

Fig. 1. Bounding boxes with dimension priors and location prediction.

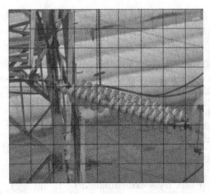

Fig. 2. Model schematic (Color figure online)

While predicting the bounding box, each grid also needs to predict the probability of three conditional categories, that is, the probability that each grid belongs to the background, the complete insulator, and the missing insulator. When an insulator is included in a mesh, it belongs to a complete insulator or missing insulator should be maximized. When the mesh does not contain an insulator, belong to the background should be the greatest. See (Fig. 2, the light red grid belongs to the missing insulator, the light green grid belongs to the complete insulator, and the yellow grid indicates the predicted background. To enhance the accuracy of the detection of small insulators, YOLO V3 uses an FPN (Feature Pyramid Networks for Object Detection. A top-down architecture with lateral connections is developed for building high-level semantic feature maps at all scales) upsampling and fusion approach.

3.2 Network Model

The whole network adopts Darknet-53. On the one hand, it adopts full convolution. On the other hand, it introduces a newfangled residual network stuff. Profit from the Residual structure of ResNet (Residual Neural Network). The model has improved its accuracy significantly. Darknet-53 is only a feature extraction layer. In the implementation process, only the convolution layer in front of the pooling layer is used to extract features, so multi-dimensional feature fusion and prediction branches are not reflected in the network.

YOLO V3 is a hybrid model that uses YOLO V2, Darknet-19, and Reset. It uses successive 3 * 3 and 1 * 1 convolutional layers during training, adding some shortcuts later. The connection structure predicts the position of the insulator in the image and the class probability prediction value of the defect based on the image features of the features extracted by the convolutional layer. Network Structure (Fig. 3). (From You Only Look Once: An Incremental Improvement).

Type	Filters	Size	Output
Convolutional	32	3 × 3	256 × 256
Convolutional	64	3 × 3 / 2	128 × 128

	Type	Filters	Size	Output
1×	Convolutional	32	1 × 1	
	Convolutional	64	3 × 3	
	Residual			128 × 128

Convolutional	128	3 × 3 / 2	64 × 64

	Type	Filters	Size	Output
2×	Convolutional	64	1 × 1	
	Convolutional	128	3 × 3	
	Residual			64 × 64

Convolutional	256	3 × 3 / 2	32 × 32

	Type	Filters	Size	Output
8×	Convolutional	128	1 × 1	
	Convolutional	256	3 × 3	
	Residual			32 × 32

Convolutional	512	3 × 3 / 2	16 × 16

	Type	Filters	Size	Output
8×	Convolutional	256	1 × 1	
	Convolutional	512	3 × 3	
	Residual			16 × 16

Convolutional	1024	3 × 3 / 2	8 × 8

	Type	Filters	Size	Output
4×	Convolutional	512	1 × 1	
	Convolutional	1024	3 × 3	
	Residual			8 × 8

Avgpool		Global	
Connected		1000	
Softmax			

Fig. 3. Darknet-53

3.3   How It Works

Prior detection systems repurpose classifiers or localizers to perform detection. They apply the model to an image at multiple locations and scales. High scoring regions of the image are considered detections. YOLO V3 uses totally different approach, which apply a Darknet-53 network to the entire insulator image. The network divides the image into different regions and predicts bounding boxes and probabilities for each region.

4   Experimental Results and Analysis

4.1   Dataset

In the process of deep neural network learning, we usually need a large amount of tagged data to train the model. Through the BP (Back Propagation) algorithm, the model learns better parameters to fit the mapping from input to output [7]. Therefore, we used a hand-labeled image of approximately 1,400 drones to train the model.

4.2 Experimental Results

The experimental test results are shown in (Fig. 4), and the box shows the defective insulator. The results show that the insulator defect detection algorithm based on YOLO V3 can quickly and accurately detect defective insulators in aerial photographs. Although it can't guarantee 100%, it solves the problem of correct distinction between intact insulators and defective insulators to some extent.

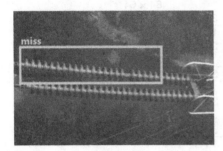

Fig. 4. Test results

In this paper, only more than 100 aerial insulator images are used for testing. The results are shown in Table 1. The average image of each insulator is only 0.55 s, which is faster, because there are fewer aerial images and some parts during the training. The insulators in the photo are the same, resulting in insufficient generalization.

Table 1. Insulator detection statistics

	Total	Positive identification	Error identification
Perfect insulator	118	112	6
Miss insulator	30	29	1

5 Conclusion

In the circuit inspection process, the accuracy and time of insulator defect detection are related to the safety of the entire transmission lines. This paper proposes an insulator defect detection algorithm based on YOLO V3 for the insulator photo taken by the drone, which can accurately detect the position of the defective insulator. For the insulator image of the complex background, the influence of the occlusion can be effectively eliminated. The missed detection rate and the false detection rate are greatly reduced. The higher accuracy rate can effectively reducing the insulation fault and safety issues, but due to the complex natural background of aerial insulators, all the training sets in this paper are limited, resulting in insufficient generalization features, but can meet the basic engineering application requirements. Next, we continue to collect images of composite insulator strings in various backgrounds. Propose more accurate defect detection algorithms as future research hotspots, providing new concepts and technical means for the detection of defective insulators in smart grids in China.

Acknowledgements. This research was supported by Tianjin Enterprise Science and Technology Commissioner Project 18JCTPJC60500, Tianjin Natural Science Fund Project 18JCYBJC85600, Qinghai Key Laboratory of Internet of Things Project (2017-ZJ-Y21), Infrared Radiation Heating Intelligent Control and Basic Ventilation Auxiliary Engineering System Development of No. 2 Section of Changchun Metro Line 2 (hx 2018-37).

References

1. Wang, L.J.: Research on insulator fault detection algorithm based on deep convolutional neural network. Tianjin University of Technology (2018)
2. Wang, J., Jiao, X.X.: Common faults and troubleshooting methods of insulator. Electr. Drive Autom. **36**(06), 50–53 (2014)
3. Li, L.X.: The UAV intelligent inspection of transmission lines. In: Proceedings of 2015 International Conference on Advances in Mechanical Engineering and Industrial Informatics (AMEII 2015), p. 4. Computer Science and Electronic Technology International Society (2015)
4. Li, X., et al.: Application and demand analysis of UAV in power industry. Electr. Appl. **34**(S2), 773–775 (2015)
5. Peng, X.Y., Liu, Z.J., Mai, X.M., Luo, Z.B., Wang, K., Xie, X.W.: A transmission line inspection system based on remote sensing: system and its key technologies. Remote Sens. Inform. **30**(01), 51–57 (2015)
6. Zhai, Y.J., Wang, D., Wu, Y., Cheng, H.Y.: Two-stage recognition method of aerial insulator images based on skeleton extraction. J. North China Electr. Power Univ. **42**(03), 105–110 (2015)
7. Yao, J.G., et al.: Algorithm research of automatically extracting the area of insulator from infrared image and state identification. J. Hunan Univ. (Nat. Sci.) **42**(02), 74–80 (2015)
8. Fu, W.P., Shi, F.X., Wang, W., Liu, Y.P., Ji, X.X., Pei, S.T.: Single insulator fault diagnosis method based on color matrix. Insul. Surge Arresters **285**(05), 226–232+240 (2018)
9. Liu, L.S., Wang, L.M., Mei, H.W., Guo, C.J.: Defects detection method for composite insulator based on shearing speckle interferometry. In: Proceedings of the CSEE, pp. 1–8 (2019)
10. Chen, J.W., Zhou, X., Zhang, R., Zhang, D.: Aerial insulator detection based on U-net network. J. Shaanxi Univ. Sci. Technol. **36**(04), 153–157 (2018)
11. Silver, D., Huang, A., Maddison, C.J., et al.: Mastering the game of Go with deep neural networks and tree search. Nature **529**(7587), 484–489 (2016)
12. Murthy, V.S., Gupta, S., Mohanta, D.K.: Digital image processing approach using combined wavelet hidden markov model for well-being analysis of insulators. IET Image Process. **5**(2), 171–183 (2011)
13. Wang, M., Du, Y., Zhang, Z.R.: Study on power transmission lines inspection using unmanned aerial vehicle and image recognition of insulator defect. J. Eelectron. Meas. Instrum. **29**(12), 1862–1869 (2015)
14. You Only Look Once: Unified, Real-Time Object Detection. http://pjreddie.com/yolo/. Accessed 09 May 2016
15. YOLO9000: Better, Faster, Stronger. http://pjreddie.com/yolo/. Accessed 25 Dec 2016

MCU-Based Isolated Appealing Words Detecting Method with AI Techniques

Liang Ye[1,2,3(✉)], Yue Li[3,4], Wenjing Dong[1], Tapio Seppänen[5], and Esko Alasaarela[2]

[1] Department of Information and Communication Engineering,
Harbin Institute of Technology, Harbin 150080, China
yeliang@hit.edu.cn
[2] Health and Wellness Measurement Research Group, OPEM Unit,
University of Oulu, 90014 Oulu, Finland
[3] Key Laboratory of Police Wireless Digital Communication,
Ministry of Public Security, Harbin 150080, China
[4] Electrical Engineering School, Heilongjiang University, Harbin 150080, China
[5] Physiological Signal Analysis Team, University of Oulu, 90014 Oulu, Finland

Abstract. Bullying in campus has attracted more and more attention in recent years. By analyzing typical campus bullying events, it can be found that the victims often use the words "help" and some other appealing or begging words, that is to say, by using the artificial intelligence of speech recognition, we can find the occurrence of campus bullying events in time, and take measures to avoid further harm. The main purpose of this study is to help the guardians discover the occurrence of campus bullying in time by real-time monitoring of the keywords of campus bullying, and take corresponding measures in the first time to minimize the harm of campus bullying. On the basis of Sunplus MCU and speech recognition technology, by using the MFCC acoustic features and an efficient DTW classifier, we were able to realize the detection of common vocabulary of campus bullying for the specific human voice. After repeated experiments, and finally combining the voice signal processing functions of Sunplus MCU, the recognition procedure of specific isolated words was completed. On the basis of realizing the isolated word detection of specific human voice, we got an average accuracy of 99% of appealing words for the dedicated speaker and the misrecognition rate of other words and other speakers was very low.

Keywords: Appealing words detection · Speech recognition · MCU · AI

1 Introduction

In recent years, more and more bullying events have been reported in middle school campus or primary school campus. Slight campus bullying includes curse and push, and serious campus bullying includes beat and abuse. A survey in China reported that, over 40% of students had suffered from various campus bullying [1], which showed a different campus life from people's mind in which campus should be a safe place. In USA, a survey by *USA Today* reported that about 50% of the surveyed high school students had bullied others in the past one year, whereas 47% of them said that they had

S. Han et al. (Eds.): AICON 2019, LNICST 287, pp. 300–308, 2019.
https://doi.org/10.1007/978-3-030-22971-9_26

been bullied, ridiculed, or mocked. 44% of the surveyed boys and 50% of the girls said that they had ever been victims of campus bullying [2]. Obviously, campus bullying has become a very common and serious problem in all societies. Campus bullying seriously endangers the normal study and life of the victims, and more seriously, it will affect the establishment of their world outlook and outlook on life in the growing stage. However, after being hurt by violence, the bullied often do not dare to give timely feedback to teachers or parents because of fear, self-esteem and other reasons. On one hand, the bullied children cannot be comforted and protected; on the other hand, the bullies are not timely educated and monitored, and eventually the phenomenon of bullying on campus becomes more and more serious.

Fortunately, campus bullying can be monitored by many indicators with artificial intelligence (AI) [3], and the acoustic characteristics of voice are one of them. With the rapid development of speech recognition technology in recent years, it has become a hot research field to monitor campus bullying events through speech keywords. Different types of campus bullying incidents are more or less accompanied by verbal bullying, and equally, in such circumstances, there are also appealing words or begging words from the victims. Therefore, through real-time monitoring of specific common words of campus bullying, teachers and parents can be informed of the occurrence of campus bullying incidents in the first time, so as to take timely measures to minimize the impact of campus bullying. In addition, due to the development of large-scale integrated circuit technology, these complex speech recognition systems can also be made into dedicated chips. Speech keyword recognition technology and embedded systems are combined, which is convenient to students who are not allowed to carry mobile phones. Hand rings, watches and other portable devices play a monitoring role for teenagers.

The remainder of this paper is organized as follows: Sect. 2 talked about some related work; Sect. 3 describes the proposed campus bullying word detecting method; Sect. 4 displays the experiment result; and Sect. 5 finally draws a conclusion.

2   Related Work

Nordic countries were the first to study campus bullying, but most of these studies were from the perspectives of pedagogy, analysis of students' psychology, and giving students the right teaching. However, many students who suffer from bullying dare not report their own experiences to their parents, so it seems that the prevention and control of campus bullying from the perspective of education alone is weak. With the popularity of smartphones, some researchers have developed campus bullying prevention programs based on smartphones, such as Stop Bullies, Campus Safety, ICE BlackBox, TipOff, Back Off Bully and so on. "Stop Bullies": When bullying occurs, the user presses a key on the mobile phone, and the mobile phone can send live video, photos or text messages along with the user's GPS information to the designated recipient. Receiver can find the user's location and take corresponding measures according to the site information to stop bullying. TipOff: Users can upload bullying or crime scene data (such as photos) recorded on their mobile phones to a secure server, and only the administrator of that server can view the evidence. Other bullying detection technologies work similarly. These methods are passive and need to be triggered manually by the user. In the process of bullying, it is very difficult for the victim, and even invites further aggression from the perpetrator. Bystanders may be afraid of being retaliated by the perpetrator, and not dare to operate mobile phones to alarm in the process.

Therefore, there should be an automatic method to detect campus bullying in an artificial intelligence way [4], and speech recognition is a possible one. In recent years, with the development of computer technology and microelectronics technology, the research of speech recognition technology in the AI field has moved from laboratory to application field, and has achieved breakthrough results. Many enterprises in developed countries, such as BIM, APPLE, AT&T, Microsoft and other well-known companies in the United States, Japan and Korea, have done a lot of research in the field of speech recognition technology. The technology of Speaker-Independent and continuous speech recognition is becoming more and more mature, and the research of speaker-specific recognition has also made some achievements in embedded applications. China has also invested a lot of energy in speech recognition research. The Chinese Academy of Sciences, Tsinghua University, Northeast University, Beijing University of Technology, Shanghai Jiaotong University, Huazhong University of Science and Technology, and Harbin Institute of Technology are all engaged in the research and development of speech recognition.

In speech feature recognition of isolated words, linear prediction coefficient has the lowest complexity, and the combination of linear prediction coefficient and piecewise linear matching method is one of the mainstream methods of speech keyword recognition in China. Linear prediction coefficients are the basic features of speech. In order to reduce the complexity of the algorithm, we can use fixed coefficients with constant prediction coefficients for a long time. In order to improve the recognition accuracy, we can use the adaptive prediction in which each frame recalculates the prediction coefficients and predicts the average energy of the remaining signals. In addition, there are single-level prediction, multi-level prediction and other ways [5, 6]. In this paper, a fixed coefficient prediction scheme is adopted. Linear predictive coding with fixed coefficients can analyze speech signals by estimating the formant of speech signals, eliminating the role of formant in speech signals, and estimating the strength and frequency of retained speech signals. In the training process, the digital signals describing the strength and frequency of speech signals, common peaks and residual signals are stored in a Microcontroller Unit (MCU) and ready to be called at any time.

In speech recognition, the piecewise linear dynamic time matching recognition method based on time series eigenvalue difference has the least computation and is suitable for short-term speech recognition. The basic idea of this method is to find out the relative quantities of phonological features (consonants, vowels, transitional tones, *etc.*) of speech signals for distance comparison. The specific method is to find out the difference of frame features according to the time sequence, and then divide the difference of phonological features by the total difference of phonological features to get the relative accumulated difference of features. In this way, although the pronunciation speed is different, the relative cumulative difference of phonological features is basically unchanged [7]. Through the analysis of speech data, it is found that although the spectrum of the end segment changes dramatically, the semantics of the end segment are few, and it has little effect on distinguishing speech. The feature of the end segment is deleted in this recognition method.

3 Isolated Word Recognition for Specific Voice

Considering the practical application scene, it is the victim who carries the bullying detecting device, so the voice of the victim is clearer than that of the bullies. Therefore, this paper focuses on the detection of appealing words and begging words by the victims.

The isolated word recognition system consists of the following steps: data sampling, data pre-processing, feature extraction, feature selection, classifier training, and classifier testing (or practical use).

3.1 Data Sampling and Pre-processing

Students in most primary schools and middle schools in China are not allowed to take mobile phones at school, so this paper considers applying the campus bullying detecting system in a MCU. This paper chooses the Sunplus for this purpose because it has the following advantages:

(1) Small size, high integration, good reliability and easy expansion.
(2) Strong interrupt handling ability. The Sunplus MCU interrupt system supports 14 interrupt vectors and more than 10 interrupt sources, which is suitable for real-time applications.
(3) ROM, static RAM and multi-functional I/O ports with high addressing capability.
(4) The instruction system with strong function and high efficiency has compact format and fast execution.
(5) Low energy consumption.

The Sumplus MCU provides a microphone input with automatic gain control (AGC). Voice data were gathered by the embedded microphone. Because voice is affected by oronasal radiation, the high frequency part of voice attenuates more seriously than the low frequency part. Therefore, pre-emphasis is essential in the pre-processing procedure. Since voice is short-term stationary stochastic processes, faming is needed to cut long-term voice into short-term segments. In order to avoid spectrum leakage, the frames should be windowed. Normally the Hamming window is used because its sidelobe attenuation is large. In a complete utterance, there are always blank segments, so voice activity detection (VAD) is used to detect the valid part in a speech in speech recognition. Usually, VAD is judged by short-time energy and zero crossing ratio (ZCR).

3.2 Acoustic Features

After pre-processing, acoustic features can be extracted from the speech. Commonly used features include pitch, fomant, Linear Predictive Cepstral Coefficient (LPCC), Mel Frequency Cepstrum Coefficient (MFCC), *etc*. MFCC has been proved to be a good set of acoustic features for speech recognition as well as speech emotion recognition.

MFCC is based on human auditory model. Mel is pitch unit. Pitch is a subjective psychological quantity, and it is the sense of human auditory system to sound frequency [8]. Through years of research on human ear auditory system, scholars have found that the sensitivity of human ear auditory system to different frequencies of signals is different. Generally speaking, the treble is easily concealed by the bass, and vice versa. In frequency domain, the critical bandwidth of high frequency speech signal masking is larger than that of low frequency speech signal masking. Therefore, band-pass filters can be arranged densely to sparsely according to the critical bandwidth from low frequency to high frequency, and the input speech signal can be filtered. The energy of the speech signal after the filter is used as the characteristic parameter of the speech signal. Because the modified feature parameters take into account the particularity of human ear auditory system and make use of some research achievements in the field of human ear auditory system research, the feature parameters are more in line with human ear auditory characteristics. The corresponding relationship between Mel frequency and actual frequency is shown as,

$$Mel(f) = 2595 \times \lg\left(1 + \frac{f}{700}\right) \tag{1}$$

Transform the time domain signals into frequency domain signals by FFT (Fast Fourier Transform), and calculate the energy of the frequency domain signals after passing the Mel filters as,

$$S(i, m) = \sum_{k=0}^{N-1} E(i, k) H_m(k), \qquad 0 \le m \le M \tag{2}$$

where $E(i, k)$ is the energy spectrum before the filters and $H_m(k)$ is the frequency response of the filter and calculated as,

$$H_m(k) = \begin{cases} 0 & (k < f(m-1)) \\ \frac{k - f(m-1)}{f(m) - f(m-1)} & (f(m-1) \le k \le f(m)) \\ \frac{f(m+1) - k}{f(m+1) - f(m)} & (f(m) \le k \le f(m+1)) \\ 0 & (k > f(m+1)) \end{cases} \tag{3}$$

Then MFCC can be got by DCT (Discrete Cosine Transform),

$$mfcc(i, n) = \sqrt{\frac{2}{M}} \sum_{m=0}^{M-1} \log[S(i, m)] \cos\left(\frac{\pi n(2m-1)}{2M}\right) \tag{4}$$

3.3 Classifier Design

There are normally many kinds of classifiers that can be used for speech recognition. Considering that the classification is to be applied on a MCU in which the resources are limited, the authors chose an efficient DTW (Dynamic Time Warp) classifier with small computational cost.

Different voice signals produced by different people have different modes. Even the same person will produce different speeds and other changes in speech characteristic parameters at different times due to different methods of voice production. Thus, speeches can be recognized by means of template matching.

Assume that the test and reference templates are represented by T and R, respectively. The smaller the distance $D[T, R]$ between them is, the higher the similarity is. In order to calculate the distortion distance, the distance between the corresponding frames in T and R should be calculated. Let n and m be arbitrarily selected frame numbers in T and R, respectively. $D[T(n), R(m)]$ denotes the distance between the two frame feature vectors. Distance function is executed by the distance measure actually adopted, and Euclidean distance is usually used in DWT algorithm. If $N = M$, it can be calculated directly. Otherwise, $T(n)$ should be aligned with $R(m)$. Alignment is mainly based on dynamic time warping. Each frame number $n = 1{:}N$ of the test template is marked on the horizontal axis in a two-dimensional rectangular coordinate system, and the frame number $m = 1{:}M$ of the reference template is marked on the vertical axis. By drawing some vertical and horizontal lines from the integer coordinates representing the frame number, a grid can be formed. Each intersection point (n, m) in the grid represents the intersection point between a frame in the test mode and a frame in the training mode.

The DTW algorithm is to find a path through a number of grid points in this grid, which is the frame number of distance calculation in the test and reference templates. The path is not optional. First of all, the pronunciation speed of any kind of voice may change, but the order of each part cannot change. Therefore, the chosen path must start from the lower left corner and end at the upper right corner.

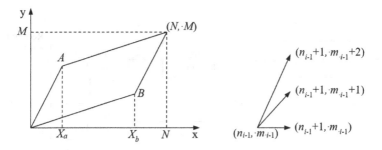

Fig. 1. Efficient DTW searching path

However, because the slope of bending is limited in the matching process, many lattices cannot actually be reached. Therefore, it is not necessary to calculate the matching distance of the lattice points outside the diamond. In addition, it is not necessary to save all the frame matching distance matrices and cumulative distance matrices, because only three grids of the previous column are used for matching calculation at each grid point in each column, making full use of these two characteristics can reduce the computational load and storage space requirements. This procedure is given in Fig. 1.

If the actual dynamic bending is divided into three sections, namely $(1, X_a)$, $(X_a + 1, X_b)$, (X_b, N), where $X_a = 1/(6M - 3N))$, and $X_b = 2/(6N - 3M)$, one can get the restrictive conditions as,

$$2M - N \geq 3 \qquad (5)$$

$$2N - M \geq 3 \qquad (6)$$

When each frame on the x-axis no longer needs to be compared with each frame on the y-axis, but only with the frames on the y-axis (y_{min}, y_{max}), the calculations of y_{min} and y_{max} are given as follows,

$$y_{min} = \begin{cases} 0.5x, & 0 \leq x \leq X_b \\ 2x + (M - 2N), & X_b \leq x \leq N \end{cases} \qquad (7)$$

$$y_{max} = \begin{cases} 2x, & 0 \leq x \leq X_a \\ \frac{1}{2x} + (M - \frac{1}{2N}), & X_a \leq x \leq N \end{cases} \qquad (8)$$

4 Experiments and Results

The algorithms mentioned above were implemented on a Sunplus MCU, and the system flow chart is given in Fig. 2.

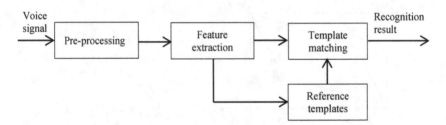

Fig. 2. Speech recognition system on a Sunplus MCU

The Sunplus MCU provided a microphone with 8kNz sampling rate. The voice signal then passed a low-pass filter and A/D converter. Pre-emphasis was used to enhance the high frequency part. The components of MFCC extraction and DTW classifier were programed on the MCU.

Totally 4 girls and 2 boys were invited to say the appealing or begging words, and each of them said 1000 words, including 500 appealing or begging words and 500 other words. The recognition result is given in Table 1. The aim of this experiment was to recognize the appealing or begging words (known as keywords in Table 1) of the dedicated speaker (Girl 1 in this experiment) but ignore other words of that speaker or appealing or begging words of the other speakers.

Table 1. Recognition results of different speakers

Speaker	Keywords	Recognized	Non-keywords	Recognized
Girl 1	500	497	500	0
Girl 2	500	3	500	0
Girl 3	500	5	500	1
Girl 4	500	0	500	0
Boy 1	500	0	500	0
Boy 2	500	0	500	0

It can be seen from Table 1 that for the dedicated speaker, the keywords can be recognized with an average accuracy of 99.4%, none of the non-keywords were misrecognized. For the other speakers, only 9 out of 5000 words were misrecognized. It shows that the implemented system can recognize the appealing or begging words of the dedicated speaker with a high accuracy.

5 Conclusions

This paper implemented an isolated appealing words detecting method on a Sunplus MCU. The voice of the speakers was gathered by a microphone embedded on the MCU and passed a low-pass filter and A/D converter. Then pre-processing was performed to enhance the speech signal and MFCC features were extracted. An efficient DTW algorithm acted as the classifier. In the experiments, the keywords of the dedicated speaker could be recognized with an average accuracy of 99.4%, while only very few of the other words of the dedicated speaker and speeches of the other speaker were misrecognized.

Acknowledgement. This work was supported by the National Natural Science Foundation of China under Grant No. 61602127, the Basic scientific research project of Heilongjiang Province under Grant No. KJCXZD201704, and the Key Laboratory of Police Wireless Digital Communication, Ministry of Public Security under Grant No. 2018JYWXTX01. The authors would like to thank those people who have helped with these experiments.

References

1. Dawei, W., Hongmei, Y.: The alarming sound of campus alarm bells. People's Public Secur. **10**, 19–21 (2004)
2. Sharon, J.: Bullying survey: most teens have hit someone out of anger. USA Today **26** (2010)
3. Lu, W., Gong, Y., Liu, X., et al.: Collaborative energy and information transfer in green wireless sensor networks for smart cities. IEEE Trans. Industr. Inf. **14**(4), 1585–1593 (2017)
4. Ye, L., Wang, P., Wang, L., et al.: A combined motion-audio school bullying detection algorithm. Int. J. Pattern Recogn. Artif. Intell. **32**(12), 1850046 (2018)
5. Liu, J., Zhang, W.: Research progress on key technologies of low resource speech recognition. J. Data Acquisit. Process. **32**(2), 205–220 (2017)

6. Zhang, P., Ji, Z., Hou, W., et al.: Design and optimization of a low resource speech recognition system. J. Tsinghua Univ. (Sci. Technol.) **57**(2), 147–152 (2017)
7. Wang, J., Zhang, J., Lu, W., et al.: Automatic speech recognition with robot noise. J. Tsinghua Univ. (Sci. Technol.) **57**(2), 153–157 (2017)
8. Remesa, U., Lópeza, A.R., Juvela, L., et al.: Comparing human and automatic speech recognition in a perceptual restoration experiment. Comput. Speech Lang. **34**, 450–457 (2016)

Performance Analysis Based on MGF Fading Approximation in Hybrid Cooperative Communication

Cong Ye[(✉)], Zhixiong Chen, Jinsha Yuan, and Lijiao Wang

North China Electric Power University, Baoding 071003, China
739693695@qq.com, zxchen@ncepu.edu.cn,
yuanjinsha@126.com, 18831633659@163.com

Abstract. Wireless communications and power line communications (PLC) are essential components for smart grid communications. In this study, the performance of dual-hop wireless/power line hybrid fading system is analyzed from two aspects of outage probability and bit error rate (BER). The system adopts a hybrid fading model based on the general Nakagami-m wireless and lognormal (LogN) power line fading based on amplify and forward (AF) relay protocol, and the Bernoulli Gaussian noise model attached to the PLC channel. Since the LogN distribution has a certain similarity with the Gamma, the key parameters of PDF with approximated LogN distribution from Gamma distribution are determined by using the moment generating function (MGF) equation and the approximation of LogN variable sum. Then the exact closed-form expression of the system outage probability and BER are obtained by integral variation. Finally, Monte Carlo simulation is used to verify the correctness of the theory and analyze the influence of different system parameters on the performance.

Keywords: Cooperative communication · Nakagami-m distribution · Log-normal distribution · PDF approximate · MGF

1 Introduction

With the development of power supply network, the coverage area of power lines is becoming wider and wider. How to make full use of the existing power supply network resources to achieve reliable information transmission on power lines is gradually attracting extensive attention and research [1]. Therefore, the combined PLC and wireless dual-media cooperative communication technology can integrate resources, optimize and complement each other. The latest research results include multipath transmission [2, 3], relay forwarding [5, 6, 10], parallel communication [12, 14], and multimedia collaboration [10, 13] and other PLC collaboration technologies.

For the Cooperative technology of wireless and PLC, many works such as the literature [4, 5] have utilized the relay-assisted scheme of PLC and wireless communication, which has been proved to improve reliability and expand communication range. The research of relay is mainly divided into double hop [6, 7] and multi hop [8, 9], both of which are mainly concentrated on the decoding and forwarding protocol. Mathur analyzed the average error rate performance of power line and wireless hybrid

© ICST Institute for Computer Sciences, Social Informatics and Telecommunications Engineering 2019
Published by Springer Nature Switzerland AG 2019. All Rights Reserved
S. Han et al. (Eds.): AICON 2019, LNICST 287, pp. 309–317, 2019.
https://doi.org/10.1007/978-3-030-22971-9_27

cooperative communication systems using dual-hop parallel communication and decode and forward (DF) protocols in [11]. In [12], the indoor wireless and power line channel models of LogN distribution are used to study the reliability of indoor wireless and power line dual-media cooperative communication systems based on AF and DF protocols. In addition, DF protocol using hard decision will lose useful information and may cause error codes, and its performance is obviously worse than AF protocol [14]. Thus, these ideas have inspired us to study the wireless-power line mixed system model.

Contribution: Most of the works in the literature focus on the performance of a dual-hop wireless system or a dual-hop PLC system, performance analysis in such systems is simple due to the symmetry of the system model. In order to solve the problem that there is no closed expression in the communication theory performance under the Nakagami-m/LogN hybrid fading condition, which leads to the key technical performance analysis is overly dependent on computer simulation. We apply approximation of the sum of LogN distribution variables, integral variation, Mehta algorithms and MGF equation to determine the PDF parameters of approximated distribution. Finally, Monte Carlo simulation is used to verify the versatility and accuracy of the proposed method, which provides a new perspective and necessary theoretical support for dual-media cooperative communication applications.

2   System Model

We consider a dual-hop, two-medium hybrid communication system, as shown in Fig. 1. The source (S) conducts wireless communication with the relay (R) using transmitting power P_S, R is used to amplify and forward (AF) the received data and transmit the data to destination (D) through power line communication (PLC) with power P_R.

In the first time slot, the signal received by R is

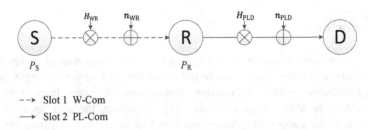

Fig. 1. System model for a dual-hop wireless-power line hybrid communication system with AF relay.

$$y_{GR} = H_{GR}\sqrt{P_S}X_S + n_{GR} \tag{1}$$

where noise n_{GR} satisfies normal distribution $N(0, N_W)$; H_{GR} is the wireless fading coefficient, subject to Nakagami-m distribution. $\Omega_R = E(|H_{GR}|^2)$ is the variance of the fading amplitude, and $\Omega_R = 1$ is used to ensure that the fading does not change the average power of the received signal.

Let $\Delta_{GR} = P_S/N_W$ denote the channel average signal to noise ratio. Then, the instantaneous signal to noise ratio of the wireless channel relay R is

$$\gamma_{GR} = H_{GR}^2 \Delta_{GR} = \frac{P_S |H_{GR}|^2}{N_W} \tag{2}$$

It is known that $|H_{GR}|^2$ satisfies the Gamma distribution $G(\alpha_R, \beta_R)$ and has the following form [14]:

$$G(H_{GR}, \alpha_R, \beta_R) = \frac{(H_{GR})^{\alpha_R - 1}}{\beta_R^{\alpha_R} \Gamma(\alpha_R)} \exp(-\frac{H_{GR}}{\beta_R}) \tag{3}$$

The parameter relationship between $G(\alpha_R, \beta_R)$ and Nakagami-m distribution in the formula satisfies $\alpha_R = m_R$, $\beta_R = \Omega_R/m_R$.

In the second time slot the signal received by the receiver is

$$y_{LD} = H_{LD}\sqrt{P_R}X_R + n_{LD} \tag{4}$$

where H_{LD} is the power line fading coefficient, which satisfies the LogN(μ_D, σ_D^2) distribution [14]:

$$f_{H_{LD}}(H_{LD}, \mu_D, \sigma_D) = \frac{1}{H_{LD}\sigma_D\sqrt{2\pi}} \exp(-\frac{(\ln H_{LD} - \mu_D)^2}{2}) \tag{5}$$

where μ_D and σ_D are the mean and mean variance of ln, respectively. The $E(|H_{LD}|^2) = \exp(2\mu_D + 2\sigma_D^2) = 1$, that is $\mu_D = -\sigma_D^2$. The noise types are modeled using the two-term Bernoulli Gaussian noise model.

Let $\Delta_{LD} = P_R/N_P$, the instantaneous SNR of the power line receiving end can be expressed as

$$\gamma_{LD} = |H_{LD}|^2 \Delta_{LD} \tag{6}$$

Therefore, the total SNR of the dual-hop AF relay protocol communication system is

$$\gamma_{GL} = \frac{\gamma_{GR}\gamma_{LD}}{\gamma_{GR} + \gamma_{LD} + 1} \tag{7}$$

In the case of high SNR (P_S/N_W, P_R/N_P), Formula (7) can be approximate to

$$\gamma_{GL} \approx \frac{\gamma_{GR}\gamma_{LD}}{\gamma_{GR} + \gamma_{LD}} = \frac{1}{1/\gamma_{GR} + 1/\gamma_{LD}} \tag{8}$$

3 Performance Analysis

3.1 System Fading Approximation Based on PDF and MGF Equation

Because the PDF of the hybrid fading system D cannot be known, it increases the difficulty of system performance analysis. Therefore, there is a certain similarity between the Gamma distribution and the LogN distribution [15], this study proposes a PDF approximation algorithm based on the MGF equation, which can approximate the $|H_{GR}|^2$ of the $G(\alpha_R, \beta_R)$ to distribution $LogN(2\mu_R, 4\sigma_R^2)$ distribution.

It is known that $|H_{GR}|^2$ satisfies the $G(\alpha_R, \beta_R)$ distribution. Then, the parameters μ_R and σ_R after the approximation can be solved:

$$(1 + \beta_R s_i)^{-\alpha_R} = \sum_{n=1}^{N} \frac{w_n}{\sqrt{\pi}} \exp(-s_i \exp(\sqrt{2}2\sigma_R a_n + 2\mu_R)) \tag{9}$$

Under the condition of channel fading normalization $(E(|H_{GR}|^2) = 1)$. Figure 2 shows the PDF curve comparison before and after channel distribution approximation when $m_R = 2.8$.

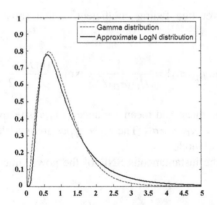

Fig. 2. The PDF of for different approximations

Since $\gamma_{GR} = H_{GR}^2 \Delta_{GR}$, the variable γ_{GR} can be approximately expressed as the key parameter of $LogN(\mu_R', (\sigma_R')^2)$ according to Δ_{GR}

$$(\sigma_R')^2 = 4\sigma_R^2 \tag{10}$$

$$\mu_R' = \ln \Delta_{GR} + 2\mu_R \tag{11}$$

3.2 Performance Analysis of LogN-LogN System

We convert the system performance analysis under hybrid fading conditions into the performance analysis problem under the same LogN distribution condition, and the instantaneous mutual information I of the system is

$$I = \frac{1}{2}\log(1 + \gamma_{LL}) \tag{12}$$

Since $P_S|H_{LR}|^2/N_W$ and $P_R|H_{LD}|^2/N_P$ are satisfied LogN distribution when P_S/N_W and P_R/N_P are constant. Since the reciprocal of the LogN variable still satisfies LogN distribution, $1/(P_S|H_{LR}|^2/N_W)$ and $1/(P_R|H_{LD}|^2/N_P)$ also satisfy LogN distribution. Therefore, the inverse of the variable sum of LgN distribution.

Let $G = 1/(P_S|H_{LR}|^2/N_W) + 1/(P_R|H_{LD}|^2/N_P)$, then $\gamma_{LL} \sim \text{LogN}(-\mu_G, \sigma_G^2)$. When using the Mehta algorithm, the following relations are used for the parameters μ_G and σ_G of the variable G:

$$\sum_{n=1}^{N} \frac{w_n}{\sqrt{\pi}} \exp(-s_i \exp(\sqrt{2}\sigma_G a_n + \mu_G)) =$$
$$\sum_{n=1}^{N} \frac{w_n}{\sqrt{\pi}} \exp(-s_i \exp(\sqrt{2}\sigma_A a_n + \mu_A)) \cdot \sum_{n=1}^{N} \frac{w_n}{\sqrt{\pi}} \exp(-s_i \exp(\sqrt{2}\sigma_B a_n + \mu_B)) \tag{13}$$

$P_S|H_{LR}|^2/N_W \sim \log N(\mu_A, \sigma_A^2)$, $P_R|H_{LD}|^2/N_P \sim \log N(\mu_B, \sigma_B^2)$. The two equations in the simultaneous Eq. (13) can be solved by fsolve function of MATLAB to obtain μ_G and σ_G.

Let the threshold be R_{th} and $\gamma = \exp(2R_{th}) - 1$, then the system's outage probability P_{out}^{LL} is

$$P_{out}^{LL} = \sum_{j=0}^{1} p_j Q(-\frac{\ln \gamma + \mu_{Gj}}{\sigma_{Gj}}) \tag{14}$$

where $p_0 = 1-p$, $p_1 = p$, which represent the probability of whether impulse noise exists in power line channel respectively. The BER of the system has the following expression:

$$P_{BER}^{LL} = -\sum_{j=0}^{1} \sum_{k=1}^{4} p_j \frac{Z_{kj}}{X_{kj}} Q(\frac{Y_{kj}}{\sqrt{1 + X_{kj}^2}}) \tag{15}$$

which includes

$$X_{kj} = \sqrt{2\sigma_{Gj}^2/R_{3k}^2}$$

$$Y_{kj} = \frac{4\sigma_{Gj}(\mu_{Gj} + \ln 0.5 - R_{2k}) - \mu_{Gj}R_{3k}^2}{2X_k R_{3k}^2} \qquad (16)$$

$$Z_{kj} = 0.5R_{1k}\sigma_{Gj}\exp(\frac{-\mu_{Gj} + Y_k^2}{2})\exp[-(\frac{-\mu_{Gj} + \ln 0.5 - R_{2k}}{R_{3k}})^2]$$

4 Numerical Results and Discussions

In this section, we performed Monte Carlo computer simulation experiments with MATLAB software to verify the reliability and accuracy of the theoretical formula. In all simulations, unless it mentioned otherwise, the simulation process adopts the following default settings: (1) the total system power is 2, $P_S = P_R = 1$. (2) In order to highlight the influence of channel fading and noise on performance, assume that the average SNR of the system channel is Δ, $N_W = N_p = 1/\Delta$, i.e. $\Delta_{GR} = \Delta_{LD} = \Delta$. (3) System interruption threshold $R_{th} = 0.2$. (4) Bernoulli Gaussian noise parameter: $p = 0.1$, $T = 10$.

Figure 3 compares the outage and BER performance of the simulated and theoretical calculations for two different fading parameters. The fading parameters are set to $\{m_R, \sigma_D\} = \{2.8, 2.6\}$ and $\{2.2, 2.8\}$. As we see, the outage probability and BER of the two sets of parameters decrease with increasing SNR of the system, and theory curves match well with Monte Carlo simulations in wider range of SNR at the low SNR, implying the validity of the derived analytical expressions, and the choice of s_1 and s_2 will also affect the approximation accuracy when determining the approximate parameters.

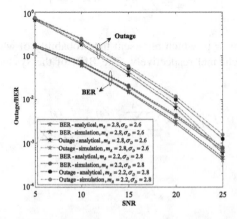

Fig. 3. System outage probability and BER against per hop average SNR with different Fading factors.

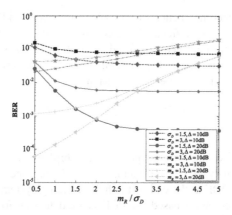

Fig. 4. Impact of parameters m_R/σ_D on theory BER performance

Figure 4 compares the relationship between the system BER and another fading parameter m_R (σ_D) under different fading parameters σ_D (m_R) and the average signal to noise ratio Δ. We assume that m_R and σ_D are 1.5 and 3 respectively, and the Δ is 10 dB and 20 dB. For vertical and horizontal analysis of Fig. 4, we can draw the following conclusions: (1) Fixing arbitrary fading parameters, it can be obviously seen that increasing Δ then system BER will decrease. (2) At the same m_R and Δ, the system BER will decrease as σ_D decreases, the system BER will decrease as m_R increases when the same σ_D and Δ. (3) The four downward curves of the fixed σ_D have no obvious trend of the four upward curves of the fixed m_R, that is to say the influence of σ_D on the system BER is higher than the influence of m_R on the BER.

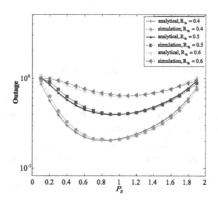

Fig. 5. Impact of transmitting power on outage performance

Figure 5 compares the relationship between outage probability and power for different thresholds. Here, only one set of fading parameters is set in order to more clearly show the effect of R_{th} on outage, which is 0.4, 0.5, 0.6. The point to be emphasized is that the total system power is 2. It can be seen from the figure that the system performance becomes better as the outage decrease, and the theoretical performance of the system under different R_{th} is consistent with the simulation results. The optimal power transmission factor is used to optimize the system performance. Therefore, the system can design the optimal transmit power according to different interrupt thresholds to achieve green energy saving.

5 Conclusions

In this study, a novel dual-hop wireless/power line hybrid communication system based on AF protocol is analyzed. The difficulty in analyzing the system performance increases because the PDF at the end of the hybrid-fading system is difficult to solve. Therefore, the MGF equation based on PDF is used to transform the performance analysis of the hybrid-fading system into the performance analysis of the LogN-LogN system. Furthermore, the exact closed expressions of system outage probability and BER are obtained by synthesizing the approximation of logarithmic normal distribution variable sum and Mehta algorithm. As can be seen from the numerical figure, the fading parameters of each link affect the system performance to varying degrees, so that the LogN link plays a dominant role in the whole system. In addition, for the purpose of green energy-saving communication, there exists an optimal ratio of source transmission power to relay transmission power, which makes the system performance optimal.

Acknowledgments. The research is supported by the National Natural Science Foundation of China (Nos. 61601182 and 61771195), Natural Science Foundation of Hebei Province (F2017502059 and F2018502047), and Fundamental Research Funds for the Central Universities (No. 2019MS088).

References

1. Dubey, A., Mallik, R.K.: PLC system performance with AF relaying. IEEE Trans. Commun. **63**(6), 2337–2345 (2015)
2. Papaleonidopoulos, I.C., et al.: Statistical analysis and simulation of indoor single-phase low voltage power-line communication channels on the basis of multipath propagation. IEEE Trans. Consum. Electron. **49**(1), 89–99 (2003)
3. Guzelgoz, S., Celebi, H.B., Arslan, H.: Statistical characterization of the paths in multipath PLC channels. IEEE Trans. Power Delivery **26**(1), 181–187 (2010)
4. Cho, W., Cao, R., Yang, L.: Optimum resource allocation for amplify-and-forward relay networks with differential modulation. IEEE Trans. Signal Process. **56**(11), 5680–5691 (2008)
5. Hong, Y.W., Huang, W.J., Kuo, C.C.J.: Cooperative Communications and Networking. Technologies and System Design. Springer, New York (2010). https://doi.org/10.1007/978-1-4419-7194-4
6. Zou, H., Chowdhery, A., Jagannathan, S., Cioffi, J.M., Masson, J.L.: Multi-user joint subchannel and power resource-allocation for power line relay networks. In: Proceedings of the International Conference on Communications, pp. 1–5 (2009)

7. Tan, B., Thompson, J.: Relay transmission protocols for in-door powerline communications networks. In: Proceedings of the International Conference on Communications, pp. 1–5 (2011)
8. Balakirsky, V.B., Han Vinck, A.J.: Potential performance of PLC systems composed of several communication links. In: Proceedings of the International Symposium on Power Line Communications, Vancouver, Canada, pp. 12–16 (2005)
9. Lampe, L., Schober, R., Yiu, S.: Distributed space-time coding for multihop transmission in power line communication networks. IEEEJ. Sel. Areas Commun. 24(7), 1389–1400 (2006)
10. Cheng, X., Cao, R., Yang, L.: Relay-aided amplify-and-forward power line communications. IEEE Trans. Smart Grid 4(1), 265–272 (2013)
11. Mathur, A., Bhatnagar, M.R., Panigrahi, B.K.: Performance of a dual-hop wireless-power line mixed cooperative system. In: International Conference on Advanced Technologies for Communications, pp. 401–406 (2016)
12. Zhixiong, C., Dongsheng, H., Lijun, Q.: Research on performance of indoor wireless and power line dual media cooperative communication system. Proc. CSEE 37(9), 2589–2598 (2017)
13. Stephen, W.L., Geoffrey, G.M.: Using the wireless and PLC channels for diversity. IEEE Trans. Commun. 60(12), 3865–3875 (2012)
14. Zhixiong, C., Yifang, J., Dongsheng, H.: Optimal power allocation based on the approximation of the moment generation function in a two-media cooperative communication. Autom. Electr. Power Syst. 42, 159–167 (2018)
15. Guzelgoz, S., Celebi, H.B., Arsian, H.: Analysis of a multi-channel receiver: wireless and PLC reception. In: European Signal Processing Conference, pp. 1106–1110. IEEE (2010)

Age and Gender Classification for Permission Control of Mobile Devices in Tracking Systems

Merahi Choukri$^{(\boxtimes)}$ and Shaochuan Wu

Harbin Institute of Technology, Harbin, China
merahichoukri1991@yahoo.com, scwu@hit.edu.cn

Abstract. Not only does the human voice provide the semantics of the spoken words but also it contains the speaker-dependent characteristics, such as the gender, the age, and the emotional state of the speaker. In the last decade, speech recognition gained a great interest in identifying and tracking systems. According to the speech length of ten to thirty seconds, this paper proposes an age and gender classification method for permission control of mobile devices. Each speech signal is firstly extracted to 40 features by Mel Frequency cepstral Coefficients (MFCC). After that, the Support Vector Machine (SVM) is used to finish the age and gender classification. This paper studies six kernel models of SVM and concludes that cubic, quadratic, and medium Gaussian kernel models could improve the recognition rate up to 93.75%, 91.25% and 93.75% respectively. Therefore, it is promising for permission control of a mobile in tracking systems.

Keywords: Classification · Permission control ·
Mel Frequency cepstral Coefficients (MFCC) · Support Vector Machine (SVM)

1 Introduction

For permission control of mobile devices based on speech recognition, several features must be extracted from humans' voices, such as the gender, the age, and the emotional state of the speaker. Although currently there are some available approaches to identify certain information about callers or speakers and classify them according to their emotion [1–3], age [4, 5] and gender [6, 7], the performance of classification is still need to be improved.

Support Vector Machine (SVM) is one of the most popular machine learning algorithms which have been widely used for the recognition of speech. Controlling the error level and improving the efficiency of speech recognition is still a big challenge. Several speech recognition methods have been proposed based on the SVM approach [8, 9]. Depending on the models used in SVM, the recognition accuracy changes in the range from 60% to 75% [10] which it too low to be used in permission control of mobiles.

In this work, the SVM approach with six kernel models (linear, cubic, quadratic, medium Gaussian, fine Gaussian and coarse Gaussian) has been used. As our best knowledge, cubic, quadratic, and medium Gaussian kernel models have not been used in previous literatures. Three main steps are adopted in this work. The first step is the signal preprocessing at which the noisy speech is preprocessed into noise-free speech.

© ICST Institute for Computer Sciences, Social Informatics and Telecommunications Engineering 2019
Published by Springer Nature Switzerland AG 2019. All Rights Reserved
S. Han et al. (Eds.): AICON 2019, LNICST 287, pp. 318–324, 2019.
https://doi.org/10.1007/978-3-030-22971-9_28

At the same time, the silence epoch of speech will be removed by voice activity detection. The second step is the speech features extraction realized by Mel frequency cepstral coefficients method. The final step is the age and gender classification based on features by the SVM classifier. By simulation analysis, the recognition rate of cubic, quadratic, and medium Gaussian kernel models is 93.75%, 91.25% and 93.75% respectively, which is obviously high than previous methods. Since the recognition rate is higher than 90%, our methods can be efficiently used for the permission control of mobile devices in tracking systems.

2   Methods

2.1   Database

This work was based on ELSDSR database, developed by the Department of Informatics and Mathematical Modeling (IMM) at Technical University of Denmark [11]. In this database, 22 speakers of different ages, genders (12 males and 10 females), and nationalities (no native speakers) were selected randomly. It is worth mentioning that there was no rehearsal when creating the database. Each speaker read seven sentences in training and two sentences in testing. The duration of each speech was between 10 and 30 s. The age structure was balanced between 20 years and 60 years with different labels for training and testing. The different speakers have been classified as follow:

- Class one (Medium female): age 20–39.
- Class two (Old female): age 40–60.
- Class three (Medium male): age 20–39.
- Class four (Old male): age 40–60.

2.2   Feature Extraction

The feature extraction method, Mel Frequency cepstral Coefficients (MFCC), was introduced in the 1980s by Davis and Mermelstein [12]. They considered a time window of 30 ms with a time shift of 10 ms and 40 coefficients. Based on this method, we can obtain a vector with 40 components to be further used in the classification procedure. MFCC is a well-known feature extraction method used to recognize speech, speakers and even emotion. One of the most vital advantages of MFCCs is that it is a more effective method in terms of noise and spectral estimation errors compared to other methods [14].

2.3   Algorithm

In this part, an effective age and gender recognition scheme will be introduced. In order to obtain better results, some pre-processing techniques were applied to the training data. The first pre-processing method was spectral subtraction method, which was applied to remove the background noise such as white noise or musical noise. After spectral subtraction method, voice activity detection was used to training data in order to remove the silence epoch in the speech [13]. Due to its reliability, the MFCC was used as a potential spectral subtraction method for this scheme. At the end, we used SVM for training and testing (Figs. 1 and 2).

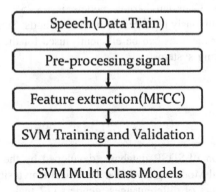

Fig. 1. Process of the training data.

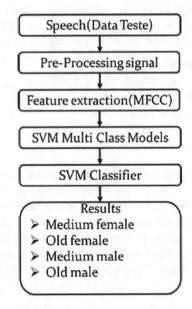

Fig. 2. Process of the testing data.

2.4   Training

Age and gender recognition is a multi-class classification task. After the previous pre-processing and MFCC feature extraction steps, an SVM was used for training both genders and age groups. Six kernel models were used for comparison. The four generated classes are already mentioned at Sect. 2.1. The training labels included medium males and medium females whose ages range between 20 and 39 years old, and also old males and old females whose ages range between 40 and 60 years old for SVM training. The training was selected by cross-validation, and the SVM parameters were selected randomly.

3 Support Vector Machines

3.1 SVM Classification

The optimization objective function of Support Vector Machines can be described as Below [8]:

$$\min_\theta c \sum_{i=1}^{m} \left[y^{(i)} \cos t_1(\theta^T x^{(i)}) + (1 - y^{(i)}) \cos t_0(\theta^T x^{(i)}) \right] + \frac{1}{2} \sum_{i=1}^{n} \theta_j^2 \qquad (1)$$

where the idea is to try to minimize this objective function. If the parameter vector θ transpose times x is greater or equal than zero, it will be classified as 1 and otherwise, it will be classified as zero:

$$h_\theta(x) = \begin{cases} 1, & if \ \theta^T x \geq 0 \\ 0, & otherwise \end{cases}$$

A binary classification $y \in \{-1, 1\}$ based on hyperplane separation was performed by Support Vector Machine SVM. In order to maximize the distance between the hyperplane and the closest training vectors, a support vector was chosen using the Kernel functions $K(x_i, x_j)$, these functions must satisfy the Mercer condition. As a result, the SVM can be extended to non-linear boundaries. Where y_i and x_i are target values and the support vectors respectively. λ_i must be determined during the training process. L represents the number of support vectors, and d is a (learned) constant:

$$f(x) = \sum_{i=1}^{L} \lambda_i y_i K(x, x_i) + d \qquad (2)$$

The aim of our work is four-class identification, which allows us to extend the binary SVM. In order to extend the binary SVM, the simplest way is to take each class as an independent class. Therefore, a classifier has to be created for each class. The class of the speaker is determined according to the largest score of the classifier:

$$\arg \max \frac{1}{N} \sum_{K=1}^{N} \left(\sum_{i=1}^{L} \lambda_i y_i K(x, x_i) + d \right) \qquad (3)$$

With $j \in \{1, ..., N\}$.

3.2   SVM Models

Trying different models on the training and testing data for comparison will be very benefiting for future works, i.e. the optimized models can be used in future works in order to get optimum results. SVM has several types of kernel models, each model gives different results of training and classification, Herein, six kernel models were carried out, the results and the comparison between them will be introduced in the sequel.

4   Results and Discussion

In this paper, age and gender recognition was carried out in six experiments. Each experiment contains two steps to use ELSDER database. In the first step, the training was performed with all SVM models in order to get the best-trained models of SVM. In the second step, we performed testing with the trained models in order to get significant result of classification, which allows us to conclude the best model.

The computation of SVM models with training and classification are illustrated in Table 1.

Table 1. Training and classification of the database ELSEDER using six SVM models.

SVM models	Class 1	Class 2	Class 3	Class 4	Overall accuracy
Linear	40%	80%	100%	00%	55%
Cubic	100%	100%	100%	75%	93.75%
Quadratic	90%	100%	100%	75%	91.25%
Medium Gaussian	100%	100%	100%	75%	93.75%
Fine Gaussian	00%	00%	100%	00%	25%
Coarse Gaussian	70%	100%	100%	00%	68.75%

According to Table 1, the overall accuracy varied between 25% and 93.75%. The best results were given by the cubic model and medium Gaussian model (93.75%), in these two models three classes had a successful recognition rate of 100% for testing, and the fourth class had a successful recognition rate of 75%, which also can be considered acceptable.

The quadratic model also gave a significant overall accuracy (91.25%), two classes had a 100% successful recognition rate, class one had 90%, and class four had 75%.

The linear and coarse Gaussian models obtained poor testing results (55% and 68.75% successful recognition rate, respectively). Fine Gaussian model is the worst one with successful recognition rate 25%.

By comparison with polynomial and radial basis function kernel models proposed in [10], the cubic, the medium Gaussian and the quadratic models utilized in this paper are better for age and gender recognition.

5   Conclusion

This work performed an age and gender recognition and classification according to speech signals for permission control of mobile. The SVM approach based on six kernel models was carried out. By speech signal preprocessing technique, speech feature extraction and classification, we found that three models (the cubic model, the medium Gaussian model and the quadratic model) achieved overwhelming performance advantages. With above 90% successful recognition ratio, the new classification method can be useful for the permission control of mobile devices.

Acknowledgements. This work was supported by the National Key R&D Program of China under grant 2018YFC0806803.

References

1. Patel, P., et al.: Emotion recognition from speech with Gaussian mixture models & via boosted GMM. Int. J. Res. Sci. Eng. **3** (2017)
2. Adeyanju, I.A., Omidiora, E.O., Oyedokun, O.F.: Performance evaluation of different support vector machine kernels for face emotion recognition. In: SAI Intelligent Systems Conference (IntelliSys). IEEE (2015)
3. Sokolov, D., Patkin, M.: Real-time emotion recognition on mobile devices. In: 2018 13th IEEE International Conference on Automatic Face and Gesture Recognition (FG 2018). IEEE (2018)
4. Qawaqneh, Z., Mallouh, A.A., Barkana, B.D.: Age and gender classification from speech and face images by jointly fine-tuned deep neural networks. Expert Syst. Appl. **85**, 76–86 (2017)
5. Wang, S., Tao, D., Yang, J.: Relative attribute SVM+ learning for age estimation. IEEE trans. Cybern. **46**(3), 827–839 (2016)
6. Akbulut, Y., Şengür, A., Ekici, S.: Gender recognition from face images with deep learning. In: 2017 International Artificial Intelligence and Data Processing Symposium (IDAP). IEEE (2017)
7. Kaya, K., et al.: Emotion, age, and gender classification in children's speech by humans and machines. Comput. Speech Lang. **46**, 268–283 (2017)
8. Chang, C.C., Lin, C.J.: LIBSVM: a library for support vector machines. ACM trans. Intell. Syst. Technol. (TIST) **2**(3), 27 (2011)
9. Burges, C.J.C.: A tutorial on support vector machines for pattern recognition. Data min. Knowl. Discov. **2**(2), 121–167 (1998)
10. Bocklet, T., et al.: Age and gender recognition for telephone applications based on GMM supervectors and support vector machines. In: ICASSP (2008)
11. Feng, L.: Speaker recognition, informatics and mathematical modelling. Technical University of Denmark (2004)

12. Davis, S., Mermelstein, P.: Comparison of parametric representations for monosyllabic word recognition in continuously spoken sentences. IEEE trans. Acoust. Speech Signal Process. **28**(4), 357–366 (1980)
13. Sohn, J., Kim, N.S., Sung, W.: A statistical model-based voice activity detection. IEEE Signal Process. Lett. **6**(1), 1–3 (1999)
14. Kim, H.-J., Bae, K., Yoon, H.-S.: Age and gender classification for a home-robot service. In: The 16th IEEE International Symposium on Robot and Human interactive Communication, RO-MAN 2007. IEEE (2007)

Research on Fusion of Multiple Positioning Algorithms Based on Visual Indoor Positioning

Guangchao Xu, Danyang Qin$^{(\boxtimes)}$ (ID), Min Zhao, and Ruolin Guo

Key Lab of Electronic and Communication Engineering,
Heilongjiang University, Harbin 150080, People's Republic of China
qindanyang@hlju.edu.cn

Abstract. Due to the limited penetration ability of GPS signal to buildings, indoor high-precision positioning combined with a variety of technologies has been paid more and more attention by researchers. Based on the traditional indoor positioning technology, a new indoor positioning method is proposed in this paper, which combines vision and inertial sensor. In this paper, we will first independently evaluate the quality of inertial positioning and visual positioning results, and then integrate them with complementary advantages to achieve the effect of high-precision positioning.

Keywords: Inertial positioning · Visual positioning ·
Multi-source positioning · Data fusion

1 Introduction

In recent years, due to the continuous development of wireless communication networks and wireless sensor networks, people have higher and higher requirements for location services in complex indoor environments. Researchers have proposed a series of indoor location technology, known as WI-FI location, Radio Frequency Identification (RFID) location, Ultra Wideband (UWB) location and so on. In comparison, various technologies have both advantages and disadvantages.

At present, the focus of high precision indoor positioning research is to combine the advantages of different technologies. [1] describes the HiMLoc solution, which focuses on the advantages of Pedestrian Dead Reckoning (PDR) and WIFI fingerprint technology, that is, the solution only relies on the parameters of some buildings, as well as the accelerometer, WIFI card and compass in smart phones for positioning. However, the inertial sensor is unable to accurately extract the corresponding motion trajectory due to the constant checking of the mobile phone in the room. What is described in [2] is to evaluate the effectiveness of PDR in the corresponding camera through the change rate of pixels, which can effectively improve the positioning accuracy of PDR. In [3],

This work is supported by the National Natural Science Foundation of China (61771186), University Nursing Program for Young Scholars with Creative Talents in Heilongjiang Province (UNPYSCT-2017125), Distinguished Young Scholars Fund of Heilongjiang University, and postdoctoral Research Foundation of Heilongjiang Province (LBH-Q15121).

S. Han et al. (Eds.): AICON 2019, LNICST 287, pp. 325–334, 2019.
https://doi.org/10.1007/978-3-030-22971-9_29

Ashish Gupa and Alper Yilmaz showed that their proposed indoor positioning method is to install a plane building information model and multi-directional sensor suite in the mobile phone. The above research improves the accuracy of indoor positioning system to a certain extent.

Visual indoor positioning and PDR indoor positioning are two common indoor positioning methods. [4–6] describe the use of visual indoor positioning, which has the advantages of low power consumption and low cost. However, some disadvantages of the smart phone itself, such as the resolution of the camera itself, as well as external lighting, will affect its imaging. In 2016, Google came up with Tango and launched the first Tango smartphone with Lenovo. Tango is known for its regional learning, a feature that, when combined with a smartphone, allows it to capture and remember architectural features of interior Spaces quickly and efficiently, such as corners, walls and bumps. Tango has its own coordinate system and its own method of extracting feature points, which makes Tango's positioning system more accurate. But in indoor the place with darker light, the accuracy of this certain bit method is about to discount greatly.

By contrast, Tango visual positioning is highly reliable in indoor positioning accuracy, except that it has certain shortcomings in light. Therefore, we need to use other indoor positioning techniques to make up for Tango's shortcomings. The smart phone inertial sensor described in [8] is similar to Tango visual positioning in that it USES PDR and Tango visual positioning, because both of them are relative positioning technologies that estimate walking direction and walking distance from known positions. [9] describes the main problems existing in PDR: its positioning accuracy will gradually decrease with the passage of time, and the error will accumulate more and more.

This paper presents an indoor positioning algorithm based on the combination of visual positioning and inertial sensor. The algorithm combines the advantages of the two methods and achieves better precision and robustness. The algorithm will be described in the next section. The third part is the experimental results and the fourth part is the conclusion.

2   System Description

The system block diagram of the indoor positioning system proposed in this paper is shown in Fig. 1. Tango is used for visual location measurement. The inertial sensor is located using the accelerometer and gyroscope inside the smartphone. These two parts of the system do not affect each other and work independently. Then the accuracy of the positioning results will be evaluated, and the loose coupling method is taken to achieve the fusion.

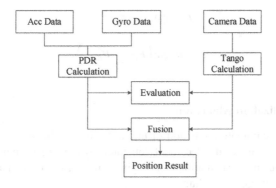

Fig. 1. System architecture

2.1 Tango Visual Interior Location Algorithm

The cyclic process of Tango device positioning is screening, identifying feature points, matching feature points, filtering error matches, and coordinate transformation. In Tango positioning, the motion and acceleration direction of the smartphone are measured by the accelerometer and gyroscope in the device, and the measured sensor data are fused to solve the accumulated errors in the motion through regional learning, so as to achieve the effect of three-dimensional motion tracking. The coordinates Tango uses for its location are in a custom virtual framework, so the coordinate transformations must be made to integrate with PDR. The expression to convert the coordinates in the PDR frame into the coordinates in the Tango visual frame is:

$$x_T = (x_P - x_0) \times \cos\theta - (y_P - y_0) \times \sin\theta \tag{1}$$

$$y_T = (y_P - y_0) \times \cos\theta + (x_P - x_0) \times \sin\theta \tag{2}$$

Instead, the expression for converting coordinates in Tango visual frames to coordinates in PDR frames is will be as (3) and (4).

$$x_P = x_0 + y_T \times \sin\theta + x_T \times \cos\theta \tag{3}$$

$$y_P = y_0 + y_T \times \cos\theta - x_T \times \sin\theta \tag{4}$$

where (x_0, y_0) is the origin coordinate of Tango visual frame in PDR positioning frame. θ is the angle between Tango visual frame y axis. (x_P, y_P) is the coordinate in PDR positioning frame. (x_T, y_T) is the coordinate in Tango visual framework.

The sampling frequency of Tango is 100 Hz, and the output is a continuous sample value. We need to find the zero velocity point from the coordinates of the output value, and use this point to estimate the coordinates of step size and heading. Where, the step size and heading can be calculated by (5) and (6):

$$L = \|P_{K_N} - P_{K_{N-1}}\| \tag{5}$$

$$\Psi = angle\left(\vec{P}_{K_N} - \vec{P}_{K_{N-1}}\right) \tag{6}$$

2.2 PDR Localization Algorithm

PDR is a relative, cumulative position of the navigation technology. Namely, starting from a known position, the displacement generated by the target's motion trajectory is added. The displacement calculation can be given in the form of a change in Cartesian coordinates or a change in heading.

According to the inverted pendulum model described in [11], the vertical distance can be converted into the horizontal step length. The inverted pendulum model is shown in Fig. 2.

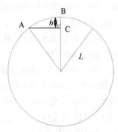

Fig. 2. Inverted pendulum model

where L is the radius of the model, indicating the target step; h is the vertical displacement, and the time interval of this displacement is from the moment of landing on the heel to the moment of standing firm. H can be obtained by (7). Step length D can also be obtained through Pythagorean Theorem with the first half D_1 and the last half D_2 as (8):

$$h = \iint a(t)\mathrm{d}t \tag{7}$$

$$D = D_1 + D_2 = \sqrt{2Lh_1 - h_1^2} + \sqrt{2Lh_2 - h_2^2} \tag{8}$$

Using the angular information and quaternion algorithm in the 6-axis inertial sensor, we can transform the coordinates in the pedestrian coordinate system into the coordinates in the navigation coordinate system by using the coordinate transformation matrix as in (9).

$$c_b^n = \begin{bmatrix} T_{11} & T_{12} & T_{13} \\ T_{21} & T_{22} & T_{23} \\ T_{31} & T_{32} & T_{33} \end{bmatrix} \tag{9}$$

The direction of pedestrian can be calculated from (10):

$$\Psi = \tan^{-1}\left(\frac{T_{12}}{T_{22}}\right) \tag{10}$$

where Ψ is defined between 0 and 360°.

2.3 Fusion Algorithm of Tango and PDR

Compared with PDR localization, Tango can achieve relatively accurate indoor positioning result with a good lighting condition. The lighting sensitivity, however, may be the weakness for Tango, because if the lighting conditions change, such as too much reflection on the indoor floor or too much white on the surrounding walls, it will affect Tango's positioning effect. And PDR positioning although will over time to produce the error affecting the positioning accuracy of the system, but the IMU (Inertial Measurement Unit) in each point estimation error is reliable, so the IMU is used to determine the effectiveness of the Tango dots: if the dots in the range of error, the output is valid, otherwise is invalid. The error range ε is shown in Fig. 3.

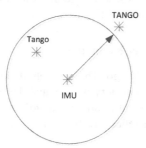

Fig. 3. Judging the validity of Tango output

The validity of step size and heading observed in Tango can be expressed as (11) and (12):

$$\left\|\vec{L}^V\right\| \in \left(\left\|\vec{L}^I\right\| - \varepsilon_1, \left\|\vec{L}^I\right\| + \varepsilon_1\right) \tag{11}$$

$$\left\|\vec{\theta}^V\right\| \in \left(\left\|\vec{\theta}^I\right\| - \varepsilon_2, \left\|\vec{\theta}^I\right\| + \varepsilon_2\right) \tag{12}$$

L^V and L^I are the step size estimation of tango visual positioning and PDR positioning, respectively. θ^V and θ^I are the course observed by tango visual positioning system and PDR positioning system respectively. Kalman filter is part of inertial navigation system. In this paper, Kalman filter and heading are used for fusion: once the inertial navigation system detects the zero velocity value point, it will trigger the Kalman filter to change the vertical velocity to zero. Then the optimal estimation is obtained from the measured value of the current state:

$$X(k|k) = X(k|k-1) + Kg(k) \times (Z(k) - HX(k|k-1)) \tag{13}$$

(13) above can be expanded as (14):

$$X(k|k) \approx X(k|k-1) + Kg(k) \times (Z(k-1) - HX(k-1|k-2)) \tag{14}$$

where $Z(k-1)$ is the course observation detected by Tango at the previous moment. $X(k-1|k-2)$ is the course information estimated by PDR positioning system in the previous moment. The previous non-zero vertical velocity is fed back to the Kalman filter as compensation so that the cumulative error can be eliminated.

3 Performance Analysis

The accuracy of the proposed method is evaluated and analyzed by conducting field positioning experiments. The experiments are performed by Tango smart phone jointly launched by Google and Lenovo: Lenovo PHAB 2 Pro. The location was located on the 7th floor of the physical experiment building of Heilongjiang University. We will use the verification point to represent the ground truth value, carry out error analysis, and compare with the traditional positioning method.

3.1 Tango Visual Positioning Evaluation

Figure 4 shows the results of Tango. The red dots indicate that we are at the preset checkpoint, the Tango output trajectory is blue, and the red lines indicate the walls of the floor plan of the experimental building. Tango's output jumps, as shown in the black circle, because the floor reflects light at that point.

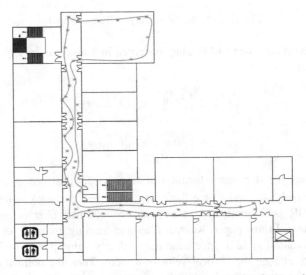

Fig. 4. Results of Tango positioning experiments (Color figure online)

3.2 PDR Positioning Evaluation

Figure 5 shows the results of PDR positioning. The results of PDR positioning deviated greatly from the areas we specified. As mentioned above, the error gradually increases with time, which leads to the black point in Fig. 5 moving from $(-2.6, 1.1)$ to $(-0.8, 3.8)$.

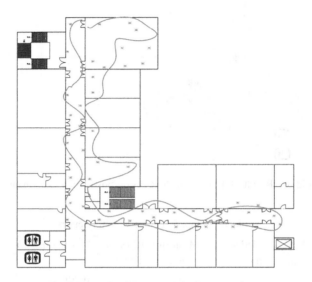

Fig. 5. Result of PDR positioning experiment

3.3 Analysis of Fusion Positioning System

Figure 6 intuitively shows that the output trajectory of Tango and PDR fusion positioning system is very similar to that of Tango visual positioning system. However, it can be seen from Fig. 6 that when the light ray changes significantly, Tango displacement is inconsistent with the normal displacement, especially with the merging system.

The accuracy of the three positioning systems are compared, and the median, mean, root-mean-square and three-fourths of the positioning errors of all the markers are calculated. As it can be seen from Table 1, the accuracy of the three positioning systems is higher than that of Tango visual positioning system and higher than that of PDR positioning system from high to low. The median error of all markers was similar. The mean error of all markers in the fusion system is lower than that of Tango positioning system.

Figure 7 shows the error distribution of the two typical positioning methods. The X-axis is the positioning error and the Y-axis is the cumulative probability. The significance of any point on the curve is that 90% of the positioning error is below (assuming y is less than 0.9) x meters. When $y = 1$, its corresponding X-axis value is the maximum error of this experiment. On the contrary, when $y = 0$, the corresponding X-axis value is the minimum error of this experiment.

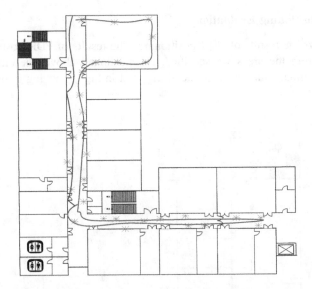

Fig. 6. Result of Tango and PDR fusion positioning experiment

Table 1. Comparison of positioning errors

Method	Median (m)	Mean (m)	RMS (m)	3rd Quartile (m)
Tango	0.62	2.58	4.98	1.32
PDR	5.68	7.56	9.83	10.85

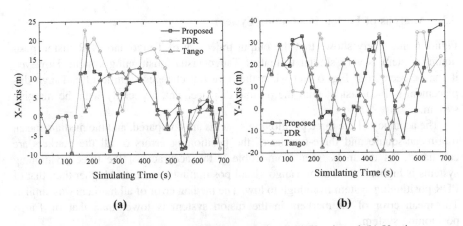

Fig. 7. Coordinate structure and error analysis on (a) X-axis and (b) Y-axis

Moreover, the error accumulating percentage of the two simulated positioning methods is shown in Fig. 8, which indicates that the error of Tango positioning system is 80% the same as that of fusion positioning system, but the error of Tango will increase greatly once the light changes. In conclusion, the accuracy of fusion positioning system is higher.

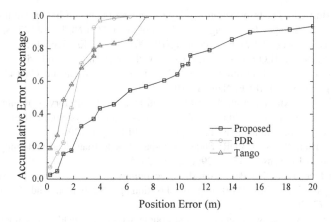

Fig. 8. Accumulating error percentage comparison

4 Conclusion

In this paper, a kind of indoor positioning system is proposed, which integrates the visual positioning system and inertia-based positioning system in a loosely coupled architecture. The measurements obtained by Tango are evaluated using the PDR output. If the step size given by Tango is reliable, it will be directly used in the fusion system; otherwise, the step size will be derived from the inverted pendulum model. The fusion system also uses a Kalman filter for course fusion. Data from the inertial sensor is used for prediction, and Tango provides measurements. Experimental results show that, compared with the traditional PDR or Tango positioning method, we achieve a more accurate indoor positioning system.

References

1. Radu, V., Marina, M.K.H.: Indoor smartphone localization via activity aware pedestrian dead reckoning with selective crowdsourced WiFi fingerprinting. In: International Conference on Indoor Positioning and Indoor Navigation (IPIN), pp. 1–10. IEEE, Montbeliard-Belfort (2013)
2. Li, Y., He, Z., Nielsen, J.: Enhancing Wi-Fi based indoor pedestrian dead reckoning with security cameras. In: Fourth International Conference on Ubiquitous Positioning, Indoor Navigation and Location Based Services (UPINLBS), pp. 107–112. IEEE, Shanghai (2016)
3. Yilmaz, A., Gupta, A.: Indoor positioning using visual and inertial sensors. In: SENSORS, pp. 1–3. IEEE, Orlando (2016)
4. Werner, M., Hahn, C., Schauer, L:. DeepMoVIPS: visual indoor positioning using transfer learning. In: International Conference on Indoor Positioning and Indoor Navigation (IPIN), pp. 1–7. IEEE, Alcala de Henares (2016)
5. Werner, M., Kessel, M., Marouane, C.: Indoor positioning using smartphone camera. In: International Conference on Indoor Positioning and Indoor Navigation (IPIN), pp. 1–6. IEEE, Portugal (2011)

6. Hile, H., Borriello, G.: Information overlay for camera phones in indoor environments. In: Hightower, J., Schiele, B., Strang, T. (eds.) LoCA 2007. LNCS, vol. 4718, pp. 68–84. Springer, Heidelberg (2007). https://doi.org/10.1007/978-3-540-75160-1_5

7. Kao, W.W., Huy, B.Q.: Indoor navigation with smartphone-based visual SLAM and bluetooth-connected wheel-robot. In: CACS International Automatic Control Conference (CACS), pp. 395–400. IEEE, Nantou (2013)

8. Ma, L., Fan, Y., Xu, Y., et al.: Pedestrian dead reckoning trajectory matching method for radio map crowdsourcing building in WiFi indoor positioning system. In: IEEE International Conference on Communications (ICC), pp. 1–6. IEEE, Paris (2017)

9. Kang, W., Han, Y.: SmartPDR: Smartphone-based pedestrian dead reckoning for indoor localization. IEEE Sens. J. **15**(5), 2906–2916 (2015)

10. Beauregard, S., Haas, H.: Pedestrian dead reckoning: a basis for personal positioning. In: Proceedings of the 3rd Workshop on Positioning, Navigation and Communication, pp. 27–35 (2006)

11. Wu, D., Peng, A., Zheng, L., et al.: A smart-phone based hand-held indoor tracking system. In: International Conference on Indoor Positioning and Indoor Navigation (IPIN), pp. 1–7. IEEE, Sapporo (2017)

Social Aware Edge Caching in D2D Enabled Communication

Jingyi Chen[1,2,3(✉)] (iD)

[1] School of Communication and Information Engineering,
Chongqing University of Posts and Telecommunications,
Chongqing 400065, China
chenjytree@163.com
[2] Key Laboratory of Optical Communication and Network in Chongqing,
Chongqing 400065, China
[3] Key Laboratory of Ubiquitous Sensing and Networking in Chongqing,
Chongqing 400065, China

Abstract. As a promising architecture, mobile edge networks can effectively mitigate the load on backhaul links and reduce the transmission delay simultaneously. With the development of artificial intelligence (AI) and machine learning, how to reasonably combine AI as well as machine learning with communication is a hot topic. In this paper, considering the content features and user preference jointly, the projective adaptive resonance theory neural network (PART NN) is used to design the community architecture. After that, we can obtain the status table of communities. In order to reduce the redundant caching, the popular contents will be cached in the user equipment (UE) of center user in advance. The cache scheme of center user is adjusted according to the status table. Two transmission links are considered, i.e., cellular link and device-to-device (D2D) link, to reduce the transmission delay. Since the content preference of UE is time-varying and the migration patterns are various, the community architecture will be updated dynamically to further improve the cache hit rate. The migration patterns of UEs are affected by social factors as well as geographical factors. The simulation results show that the community construction scheme and cache scheme effectively improve the cache hit rate and reduce the transmission delay simultaneously.

Keywords: Device-to-Device (D2D) · Edge caching ·
Projective adaptive resonance theory neural network (PART NN) ·
Social attributes

This work was supported in part by the National Natural Science Foundation of China under Grants 61771082 and 61871062, and in part by the Program for Innovation Team Building at the Institutions of Higher Education in Chongqing under Grant CXTDX201601020.

S. Han et al. (Eds.): AICON 2019, LNICST 287, pp. 335–349, 2019.
https://doi.org/10.1007/978-3-030-22971-9_30

1   Introduction

According to the data released by Cisco in August 2017, the amount of data traffic will continue growing exponentially year by year [1]. The rapid development of data traffic has leaded to stringent requirements in not only communications but also computations, which will cost a mass of resources [2–6]. Compared to traditional centralized network architecture, the mobile edge networks utilize low-cost resources to provide computing and caching capabilities at the edge of cellular networks, which brings better performances in various aspects, i.e., the transmission delay, proximity services and so on [7]. Furthermore, edge caching is widely considered to effectively solve the large-scale content interaction of future networks and mitigate the backhaul loads.

Researches indicate that the data requested by user equipments (UEs) mainly conform to the Paretos principle, which means most of data requests result from less contents [8]. As a consequence, there may be a plenty of redundant repeated requests, which will cause ever-increasing backhaul loads. In order to reduce the backhaul loads, the consumption of community energy, and the request delay, the contents are cached on edge, i.e., the base station (BS) and the UE [9,10]. However, as a widely agreement, the caching capacities of BSs and UEs are limited. Hence, how to select the most useful or valuable data, which will be cached proactively, is critical to guarantee the quality of service (QoS) of different UEs. With the introduction of social attributes, the combination of social attributes and caching has stimulated growing interests. Generally, the social relationship, social trust, user mobility and other features are considered to build communities and select caching strategy [7,11–13]. However, the importance of content characteristic is ignored and the migration patterns of user are not fully considered. In addition, the communities are built based on the offline data and the community structure is fixed. Hence, the contents cached may not always meet the user demands, which will cause the decline of cache hit rate and the growth of the waste of resources.

With the developments of artificial intelligence (AI) and machine learning, many researches consider to incorporate them into communication systems and networks. Typically, to solve the problem mentioned above, part of researches preprocess the cached data using neural network, which can obtain the popular contents to improve the cache hit rate [14–16]. In [14], the preference list of each cache entity is derived from the data analysis of tweets during the 2016 U.S. presidential election using deep learning long short-term memory (LSTM) neural network. In [15], the convolutional neural network (CNN) is used to analyze the sentence and extract the features. In [16], the features of contents are analyzed using the extreme learning machine, and then the popularity of contents can be obtained. Generally, the popularity of content is defined as the requested ratio of particular content [13], and the data analysis is usually applied to offline data ignoring the fact that the data are updated constantly. The research in [17] shows the user preference is not always stable. On the contrary, it may change periodically according to different factors.

In addition, device-to-device (D2D) technology, which is one of the key technologies of 5G, has been validated to be able to guarantee the data forwarding performance well for short distance communications from the social point of view [18]. Hence, caching data in UEs and delivering data through D2D are promising ideas to further reduce the transmission delay.

Taking above situations into consideration, in this paper, a D2D enabled system model is shown where the UE of center user can cache contents. Under the system model, the requested contents can be delivered efficiently and fast to the UEs. A projective adaptive resonance theory neural network (PART NN) based community construction scheme is proposed considering social characteristics and content preferences of each UE. With such scheme, the content characteristics of each community become more and more distinct as the number of UEs increases, which will guide the caching of the center UE. Considering the case that the content preferences of the UEs may change varying with time and the migration patterns of UEs, the community architecture will be updated dynamically. The cache scheme of center UE will be adjusted accordingly.

The remaining of this paper is organized as follows. Section 2 introduces the system model environment. Section 3 illustrates the social aware community construction scheme. Section 4 studies D2D enabled caching scheme. In Sect. 5, simulation results are presented and discussed. Section 6 finally concludes the paper.

2   System Model

The system model considered in this paper is depicted in Fig. 1, which contains three layers, i.e., the cloud layer, the access layer and the terminal layer. The whole network resources are controlled by the cloud servers in the cloud layer. Due to the long distances between the cloud servers and the UEs, the transmission delay is very high. Besides, the redundant requests cause huge traffic burden at the cloud servers and the resources can not be utilized rationally and efficiently. As a result, the computing and caching capabilities on the edge are used. In this paper, the BSs provide the network access and computing capabilities for UEs. However, in the hot spot region there are mass UEs within the coverage of a specific BS, which will cause vast repeated requests of the popular contents. Hence the construction of communities in the terminal layer is vital to improve the resource utilization rate. Furthermore, D2D technology can be used to reduce the transmission delay.

In detail, the communities are denoted by $C = \{C_1, C_2, \cdots, C_i, \cdots, C_{N_C}\}$, where N_C represents the number of communities. In each community, there are two types of UEs, i.e., one center UE and several normal UEs, which have similar content requests considering the social factors. The center UE will cache the popular contents in the community it belongs to in advance. The normal UEs will firstly build the D2D links with the center UE to obtain the contents. Due to the constraint of trust, normal UEs can not directly transmit data with each other via D2D links. Hence, if the center UE has not cached the contents

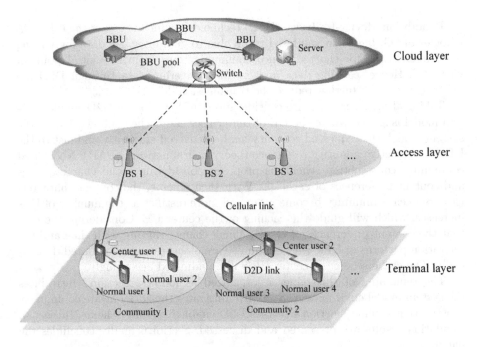

Fig. 1. System model.

requested by normal UE, the cellular link will be built between the normal UE and the corresponding BS to obtain the data. In this paper, UEs of both types are simply referred as UEs. Therefore, in an initial hot spot area, UEs served by the same BS are denoted by $U = \{u_1, u_2, \cdots, u_j, \cdots, u_{N_u}\}$, where N_u represents the number of UEs. Note that the belonging community of a particular UE may change dynamically due to the mobility as well as the time-varying content preference of UE. As a result, the community members are varying which will affect the contents cached in the center UE.

As mentioned above, the data delivery performance of the considered system model is dominated by the construction of community. Hence, how to build and update the community construction in real time, considering the social attributes, the content characteristics, and the migration patterns simultaneously, is critical to guarantee the content delivery performance.

3   Social Aware Community Construction Scheme

Generally, UEs in the same hot spot area may request similar popular contents at the same time period. To reduce the redundant data requests, the community should be built and the popular contents of community should be cached in the center UE in advance. However, most of existing community construction schemes just consider the effects of social attributes and geographical locations, ignoring the importance of content characteristics. Considering that the content

OUTPUT

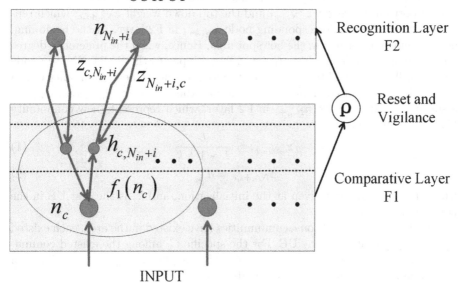

Recognition Layer
F2

Reset and
Vigilance

Comparative Layer
F1

INPUT

Fig. 2. PART NN model.

characteristics of UEs are different and change dynamically, the PART NN is used to construct and update the community dynamically.

Evolved from the adaptive resonance theory neural network (ART NN), which is a representative of competitive learning, the PART NN is proposed to solve the problem that the subspace formed by clustering can not be determined in advance [19,20]. The traditional PART NN architecture is shown in Fig. 2, including the comparison layer (F1 layer) and the cluster layer (F2 layer). Furthermore, the actual implementation of PART NN includes five states, i.e., initialization stage, cognition stage, comparison stage, search stage and adjustment stage. The community construction scheme will be discussed in detail based on the PART NN.

The set $M = \{m_1, m_2, \cdots, m_c, \cdots, m_k\}$ denotes the contents considered in this paper, where k represents the number of content types. The preference degree set about contents M of UE u_j is denoted by $D^{u_j} = \{d_{m_1}^{u_j}, d_{m_2}^{u_j}, \cdots, d_{m_k}^{u_j}\}$. Since various contents have different effects on UE u_j and the effects are varying with time, the value of preference degree $d_{m_c}^{u_j}$ in D^{u_j} varies continuously and may be different. The value of $d_{m_c}^{u_j}$ is an average value during a time period, and is standardized in the range of $[0,1]$.

The input of PART NN is D^{u_j}. The nodes in F1 layer are denoted by $N_1 = \{n_1, n_2, \cdots, n_{N_{in}}\}$. That is, the input value of the node n_c is $d_{m_c}^{u_j}$, where $c \in [1,k]$, and $N_{in} = k$. Additionally, the nodes in F2 layer, i.e., the output nodes are denoted by $N_2 = \{n_{N_{in}+1}, n_{N_{in}+2}, \cdots, n_{N_{in}+N_{out}}\}$, where the output node $n_{N_{in}+i}$ represents the community C_i.

In the PART NN, two weights are critical to construct the communities named bottom-up weight $z_{c,N_{in}+i}$ and the top-down weight $z_{N_{in}+i,c}$, which represent the features of corresponding node $n_{N_{in}+i}$ in F2 layer. At the beginning, no community is formed in the hot spot area. Hence, when the preference degree set of the first UE denoted by u_1, i.e., D^{u_1}, is input to the PART NN, the node $n_{N_{in}+1}$ will be assigned to u_1. That is, the u_1 is belong to new community C_1. In the whole process of community construction, the weights $z_{c,N_{in}+i}$ and $z_{N_{in}+i,c}$ associated with the node $n_{N_{in}+i}$ in F2 layer, which represents new community C_i, are calculated as

$$z_{c,N_{in}+i} = \frac{L}{L-1+k} \tag{1}$$

$$z_{N_{in}+i,c} = d^{u_j}_{m_c} \tag{2}$$

where L is the constant given at the initialization, and u_j is the first UE in the new community C_i.

On the other hand, if some communities have existed in the area, each existed community has at least one UE. For the specific C_i among the existed communities, after the current u_j is put in C_i, the weights $z_{c,N_{in}+i}$ and $z_{N_{in}+i,c}$ of corresponding node $n_{N_{in}+i}$ are calculated as

$$z_{c,N_{in}+i} = \begin{cases} \frac{L}{L-1+|x|} & if \ h_{c,N_{in}+i} = 1 \\ 0 & if \ h_{c,N_{in}+i} = 0 \end{cases} \tag{3}$$

$$z_{N_{in}+i,c} = (1-\alpha) z^{old}_{N_{in}+i,c} + \alpha d^{u_j}_{m_c} \tag{4}$$

where x is the current number of cached contents in C_i and α is the learning rate given at the initialization. $h_{c,N_{in}+i}$ is the selectable output signal which will be discussed later.

Based on $z_{c,N_{in}+i}$ and $z_{N_{in}+i,c}$, the communities are constructed as follows. As mentioned before, when the preference degree set D^{u_1} of the first UE u_1 is input to the PART NN, the first community C_1 will form and the corresponding weights are set as (1) and (2).

When the preference degree set of the jth $(j > 1)$ UE, i.e., D^{u_j}, is input to the PART NN, since some communities already exist, each existing community will be determined whether it is the most appropriate to u_j or not. If so, the u_j will be put in the most appropriate community. If not, a new community will be assigned to the u_j. To this end, for the input D^{u_j} of u_j, the selectable output signal should be calculated considering the weights of each node of N_2 as follows:

$$h_{c,N_{in}+i} = h_\sigma \left(f\left(n_c\right), z_{N_{in}+i,c} \right) l\left(z_{c,N_{in}+i} \right) \tag{5}$$

where $l\left(z_{c,N_{in}+i} \right)$ is a threshold function, and h_σ denotes whether the condition of similarity is satisfied. There holds

$$h_\sigma \left(f\left(n_c\right), z_{N_{in}+i,c} \right) = \begin{cases} 1 & if \ d\left(f\left(n_c\right), z_{N_{in}+i,c}\right) \le \sigma \\ 0 & otherwise \end{cases} \tag{6}$$

where the signal equation $f\left(n_c\right)$ is generated at n_c, $d\left(f\left(n_c\right), z_{N_{in}+i,c}\right)$ means the quasi-distance, and σ is the distance parameter, which controls the degree of similarity between the input UE and current community. And then the forward output filter parameter $T_{N_{in}+i}$ can be calculated for all the nodes in F2 layer:

$$T_{N_{in}+i} = \sum_{n_c \in N_1} z_{c,N_{in}+i} h_{c,N_{in}+i} \tag{7}$$

Furthermore, the matching degree of content similarity between u_j and C_i needs to be calculated. The node whose matching degree $Mat_{N_{in}+i}$ is less than the vigilance parameter ρ is considered as a candidate, i.e.,

$$Mat_{N_{in}+i} = \sum_c h_{c,N_{in}+i} \le \rho \tag{8}$$

Finally, the most appropriate C_i corresponding to u_j should satisfy the following expression:

$$i = \arg\max_{\text{s.t.} \quad (8)} T_{N_{in}+i} \tag{9}$$

When the most appropriate community C_i is found, the weights of corresponding node $n_{N_{in}+i}$ should be updated according to (3) and (4). If the optimal community is not existing, i.e., the constraint of vigilance parameter is not satisfied, a new community will be assigned to the current UE, and the weights associated with the node in the layer F2, which represents the new community will be updated according to (1) and (2).

When all the UEs' preference degree sets are put into the PART NN, the initial community construction is completed. The content characteristics of community C_i and UE u_j are denoted as $G^{C_i} = \{g_{m_1}^{C_i}, g_{m_2}^{C_i}, \cdots, g_{m_k}^{C_i}\}$ and $G^{u_j} = \{g_{m_1}^{u_j}, g_{m_2}^{u_j}, \cdots, g_{m_k}^{u_j}\}$, where

$$g_{m_c}^{C_i} = \begin{cases} 1 & \text{If } C_i \text{ has } m_c \\ 0 & \text{otherwise} \end{cases},$$

$$g_{m_c}^{u_j} = \begin{cases} 1 & \text{If } u_j \text{ has } m_c \\ 0 & \text{otherwise} \end{cases}.$$

The preference degree of content m_c in the community C_i is denoted as $d_{m_c}^{C_i}$ and defined as

$$d_{m_c}^{C_i} = \frac{\sum\limits_{\{j|u_j \in C_i\}} d_{m_c}^{u_j} \cdot w_{u_j}}{|C_i|} = \frac{\sum\limits_{\{j|u_j \in C_i\}} d_{m_c}^{u_j} \cdot \frac{1-E_j}{|C_i| - \sum\limits_{\{j|u_j \in C_i\}} E_j}}{|C_i|} \tag{10}$$

where $|C_i|$, w_{u_j}, and E_i denote the number of UEs in C_i, the weight and the information entropy of u_j, respectively. For the specific community, the less number of interests is, the smaller the E_j is, and the greater effect on the content feature of the community is. And there holds

$$E_j = -\ln(|C_i|)^{-1} \sum_{\{j|u_j \in C_i\}} \frac{sd_{m_c}^{u_j}}{\sum\limits_{\{j|u_j \in C_i\}} sd_{m_c}^{u_j}} \ln \frac{sd_{m_c}^{u_j}}{\sum\limits_{\{j|u_j \in C_i\}} sd_{m_c}^{u_j}} \tag{11}$$

where $sd_{m_c}^{u_j}$ is the standardized value of preference degree of the specific content m_c about u_j, which holds as

$$sd_{m_c}^{u_j} = \frac{d_{m_c}^{u_j} - \min D^{u_j}}{\max D^{u_j} - \min D^{u_j}} \tag{12}$$

Therefore, all the preference degrees of contents $d_{m_c}^{C_i}$ and the corresponding preference degree set $D^{C_i} = \left\{ d_{m_1}^{C_i}, d_{m_2}^{C_i}, \cdots, d_{m_k}^{C_i} \right\}$ in C_i can be obtained. In detail, the status table of communities is shown as an example in Table 1. Besides, the status table of communities can be updated dynamically to represent the content preferences of the current users in each community, which may be affected by the changes of preferences and the migrations of UEs, and then the cache strategy of center UE will be updated correspondingly which will be introduced in the following.

Table 1. Status table of communities.

i	C_i	G^{C_i}	D^{C_i}
1	$(u_1, u_3, \cdots)$	$(0, 0, \cdots, 1, 1, 1)$	$(0, 0, \cdots, 0.1, 0.3, 0.04)$
2	$(u_2, u_7, \cdots)$	$(1, 1, \cdots, 0, 0, 1)$	$(0.03, 0.1, \cdots, 0, 0, 0.2)$
3	$(u_4, u_5, \cdots)$	$(1, 0, \cdots, 1, 0, 0)$	$(0.5, 0, \cdots, 0.1, 0, 0)$
...	...	...	...

4 D2D Enabled Caching Scheme

In order to fully utilize the resources on the edge, the caching capacity of UE is considered in this paper to decrease redundant data requests and transmission delay. Hence, for each community, the UE which is outgoing as well as reliable is selected as the center UE considering the duration of stay simultaneously. The center UE in the community C_i is denoted by cu^i and will cache the popular contents in advance. The remaining UEs in C_i are normal UEs denoted by nu_s^i which represents the sth normal UE. Because the incentive mechanisms have been considered in many literature to motivate users to cache content for others [21, 22], we assume that the center UE cu^i is selfless. Hence the entire caching space of cu^i will be used to cache the popular contents of C_i.

Due to the limited caching capacity of cu^i, not all the popular contents whose $g_{m_c}^{C_i}$ equals to one in the content characteristics G^{C_i} of C_i can be put in the caching space of cu^i. Hence the preference degree of content $d_{m_c}^{C_i}$ is crucial to determine whether the content will be cached by cu^i or not. As a result, the content m_c in G^{C_i} will be put into the caching space of cu^i according to the descending order of $d_{m_c}^{C_i}$. And the constraint of caching capacity should be satisfied simultaneously as follow

$$\sum_{c=1}^{k} I \cdot g_{m_c}^{cu^i} \le Q_i \tag{13}$$

where

$$g_{m_c}^{cu^i} = \begin{cases} 1 & \text{if } cu^i \text{ caches } m_c \\ 0 & \text{otherwise} \end{cases}$$

The set $G^{cu^i} = \left\{ g_{m_1}^{cu^i}, g_{m_2}^{cu^i}, \cdots, g_{m_c}^{cu^i}, \cdots, g_{m_k}^{cu^i} \right\}$ denotes popular contents set of cu^i and Q_i is the caching capacity of center UE cu^i. The content size of each type is assumed to be the same size denoted by I.

Since the content preference of UE is time-varying and the caching capacity of the center UE is limited, the contents cached on cu^i in advance may not always be consistent with the contents requested by normal UEs in the same community. Hence, the contents cached on the cu^i should be updated to guarantee the cache hit rate. Impelled by the contents desired, social trust, and time, the normal UEs may migrate to other communities. The migration of normal UEs will change the status table of communities. Furthermore, the caching scheme of cu^i will be changed accordingly. In order to improve the cache hit rate and decrease the transmission delay, as a important factor, the migration patterns of UEs deserve to be discussed in this section.

The migration patterns are divided into two categories, i.e., purposeful migration and purposeless migration. The purposeful migration means the purpose of migration is impelled by the content preferences or social relationship. For the first case, the popular contents requested by nu_b^i are known and not included in the current community C_i. Hence, nu_b^i will migrate to another community in terms of the similarity between the updated content characteristic set $G^{nu_b^i}$ of nu_b^i and G^{cu^x} of the center UE cu^x. And then the nu_b^i belongs to the community C_{win} which has the maximal similarity, i.e.,

$$\text{win} = \arg\max_x \left(sim \left(G^{nu_b^i}, G^{cu^x} \right) \right)$$

$$= \max \left(\frac{\sum\limits_{c=1}^{k} \left(g_{m_c}^{nu_b^i} - \overline{g_{m_c}^{nu_b^i}} \right) \left(g_{m_c}^{cu^x} - \overline{g_{m_c}^{cu^x}} \right)}{\sqrt{\sum\limits_{c=1}^{k} \left(g_{m_c}^{nu_b^i} - \overline{g_{m_c}^{nu_b^i}} \right)^2} \sqrt{\sum\limits_{c=1}^{k} \left(g_{m_c}^{cu^x} - \overline{g_{m_c}^{cu^x}} \right)^2}} \right) \tag{14}$$

where x is an integer and $x \in [1, |C|]$. $|C|$ denotes the number of communities. The set $G^{nu_b^i} = \left\{ g_{m_1}^{nu_b^i}, g_{m_2}^{nu_b^i}, \cdots, g_{m_c}^{nu_b^i}, \cdots, g_{m_k}^{nu_b^i} \right\}$ denotes the content characteristic set of nu_b^i, and

$$g_{m_c}^{nu_b^i} = \begin{cases} 1 & \text{if } nu_b^i \text{ wants } m_c \\ 0 & \text{otherwise} \end{cases}.$$

For the second case, we suppose there is a social relationship between the normal UE nu_a^x and the particular center UE cu^i, i.e., classmate relations, colleague relations and so on. In order to exchange data with cu^i, nu_a^x will migrate to C_i directly where cu^i belongs to. Due to the selflessness of cu^i, the contents are cached for the normal UEs in the community C_i. Hence the purposeful migration will not affect the caching scheme of center UE.

The purposeless migration means the migration of normal UE is impelled by the time. For example, the preference content set $G^{nu_s^i}$ of normal UE nu_s^i is changing with varying time or caused by the change of location. In this case, the attribution community of normal UE and the preference content set of community should be adjusted dynamically. Hence, the new preference content sets of normal UEs should be input into the PART NN which is discussed in the 3th section. Under the construction and update of communities, the center UE can cache data in a highly efficient way. The data transmission is mainly resorted to the D2D links, which not only reduces the traffic load but also improves the content delivery performance.

In this paper, since the caching capacity of the center UE is limited, the desired data of normal user may not be cached in the caching space of the center UE in advance. Therefore, there are two kinds of links for data transmission, i.e., D2D link and cellular link. When the center UE cu^i has the data requested by the user nu_s^i, and the D2D link constraints are satisfied, a D2D link will be built for data transmission between cu^i and nu_s^i. The transmission rate R_{cu^i,nu_s^i} is

$$R_{cu^i,nu_s^i} = B_{dl}\log_2\left(1 + \frac{P_{cu^i}h_{cu^i,nu_s^i}}{N_0}\right) \tag{15}$$

where B is the channel bandwidth, P_{cu^i} denotes the transmitting power of cu^i and h_{cu^i,nu_s^i} denotes the channel gain, N_0 denotes the additive Gaussian white noise.

When the all the center UEs within the BS do not have the data required by nu_s^i, the cellular link is built to transmit data, and also the cu^i obtain the data from the BS through the cellular link. The corresponding transition rate $R_{BS,UE}$ holds as

$$R_{BS,UE} = B_{cl}\log_2\left(1 + \frac{P_{BS}h_{BS,UE}}{N_0}\right) \tag{16}$$

where P_{BS} denotes the transmission power of the BS, $h_{BS,UE}$ denotes the channel gain.

Furthermore, the minimum total content delivery delay holds as

$$T_{total} = \frac{\sum\limits_{\left\{m_c \left| g_{m_c}^{cu^j}=1 \ \& \ g_{m_c}^{nu_s^j}=1, \ j=1,2,\cdots,N_C\right.\right\}} I_{m_c}}{R_{cu^j,nu_s^j}} + \frac{\sum\limits_{\left\{m_c \left| g_{m_c}^{cu^j}=0 \ \& \ g_{m_c}^{nu_s^j}=1, \ j=1,2,\cdots,N_C\right.\right\}} I_{m_c}}{R_{BS,nu_s^j}} \tag{17}$$

5 Performance Analysis

In this section, we evaluate the performance of the PART NN based community construction scheme (PNCCS) and that of the social aware caching scheme (SACS) with the help of MATLAB. The PNCCS in this paper is compared with two related strategies. The first one uses the two-step coalitional game

(2SCG) to build the community architecture considering the payoff [23]. The second one mainly considers the mobility and localization of users in both geographical and virtual communities (MLGVC) to obtain the community architecture [24]. Besides, two caching schemes are compared with the SACS. The first one caches the most popular contents in the world on the UEs which is called as most popular caching scheme (MPCS). The second one caches the content on the UEs randomly which is called as random caching scheme (RCS). In this section, the transmission bandwidth is 10 MHZ and the noise spectral density is −174 dbm/Hz. The transmit power of D2D user and cellular user are 17 dbm and 23 dbm respectively. Besides, the max D2D transmission distance is 50 m and the radius of cell is 500 m.

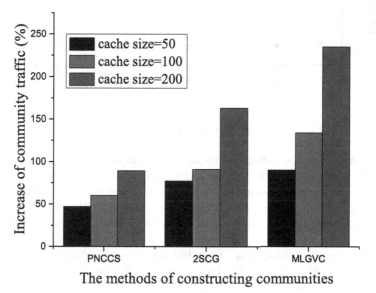

Fig. 3. Increase of community traffic.

Figure 3 depicts the increases of community traffic of different community construction strategies. For the specific cache size of center UE, the increase of community traffic in PNCCS is the minimum compared to other strategies. The reason is that the PNCCS fully utilizes the content characteristics by PART NN. Furthermore, considering the social characteristics and migration patterns, community architecture is updated dynamically to guarantee the cache hit rate of center UEs and efficiently decreases the similar requests simultaneously. Differently, the 2SCG ignores the importance of content characteristics and the MLGVC only considers the location and mobility. Since the factors are not considered completely, the performances of 2SCG and MLGVC are both not optimal. Additionally, Fig. 3 also shows that with the rise of cache size, the increase of community traffic increases accordingly. In detail, the increase of community traffic of PNCCS compared with 2SCG and MLGVC is decreased by 40.7% and 57.2% on average.

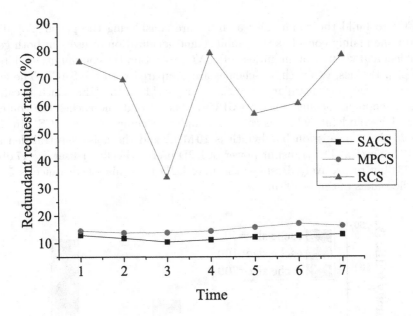

Fig. 4. Redundant request ratio.

Figure 4 depicts the redundant request ratio varying with the period of time under different caching schemes. In RCS, due to the randomness of contents cached, the contents cached in the center UE in advance may not always satisfy the demands of normal UEs within the same community. Hence, the redundant request ratio changes irregularly. Besides, the contents cached in MPCS are globally popular which may not be the popular contents in local area. Hence, normal UEs need to obtain data from the BS. Since the popular contents in a particular area are similar, redundant requests will exist. Considering different factors jointly to accurately build and update the community architecture, Fig. 4 validates that the performance of SACS is the best.

Figures 5 and 6 exhibit the variation trends of the cache hit rate and the average total delay of UEs in different number of UEs. The cache hit rate is positively correlated with the number of UEs. In SACS, as the number of people increases, the community characters will be more and more obvious based on PART NN. Compared with MPCS and RCS, the contents cached on center UE in SACS are more targeted. Considering the social characteristics and migration patterns of UEs, the community architecture is adjusted dynamically to better meet the data requests of UEs. Hence, Fig. 5 shows that the cache hit rate of SACS is always higher than that in MPCS and RCS. In detail, numerical results show that the cache hit rate of SACS is improved by 31.7% compared with MPCS on average. Besides, Fig. 6 shows that as the number of people increases, all the average total delays of three schemes decrease. Moreover, the average total delay of UEs in SACS is the lowest. In addition to the factors considered above, another reason is that the popular contents are cached on center UE in advance, and normal UEs can directly build D2D links with center UE for data transmission. Hence the transmission delay can be reduced effectively.

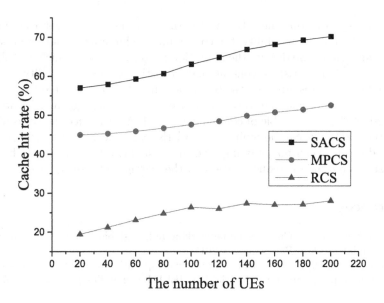

Fig. 5. Cache hit rate.

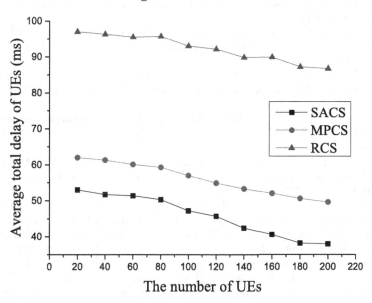

Fig. 6. Average total delay of UEs.

6 Conclusions

In this paper, we first propose a social-aware community construction scheme based on PART NN to improve the cache efficiency. Considering the content preferences, the initial community architecture is built and the status table of communities can be obtained. Due to the time-varying characteristics of users's data requests and user mobility, the community architecture should be updated dynamically. Hence we discuss the migration patterns of users which are affected by the social characteristics, content characteristics as well as mobility. In order to make full use of resources on the edge, the center UEs are selected to cache the popular contents of communities in advance. The caching scheme of center UE is guided by the status table of communities. To further reduce the transmission delay, the D2D links can be built between UEs. Numerical results show that the proposed schemes can not only improve the cache hit rate significantly but also decrease the redundant request ratio and the average total delay of UEs.

References

1. Cisco Systems Inc.: Cisco visual networking index: global mobile data traffic forecast update, White Paper, March 2017
2. Zhou, L., Wu, D., Chen, J., Dong, Z.: When computation hugs intelligence: content-aware data processing for industrial IoT. IEEE Internet Things J. 5(3), 1657–1666 (2018)
3. Wu, J., Wu, J., Cui, H., Luo, C., Sun, X., Wu, F.: DAC-Mobi: data assisted communications of mobile images with cloud computing support. IEEE Trans. Multimedia 18(5), 893–904 (2016)
4. He, C., Wang, H., Hu, Y., Chen, Y., Fan, X.: MCast: high-quality linear video transmission with time and frequency diversities. IEEE Trans. Image Process. 27(7), 3599–3610 (2018)
5. Wu, D., Shi, H., Wang, H., Wang, R., Fang, H.: A feature-based learning system for Internet of Things applications. IEEE Internet Things J. https://doi.org/10.1109/JIOT.2018.2884485
6. Tan, B., Lu, J., Wu, J., Zhang, D., Zhang, Z.: Toward a network slice design for ultra high definition video broadcasting in 5G. IEEE Wirel. Commun. 25(4), 88–94 (2018)
7. Wang, S., Zhang, X., Zhang, Y., Wang, L., Yang, J., Wang, W.: A survey on mobile edge networks: convergence of computing, caching and communications. IEEE Access 5, 6757–6779 (2017)
8. Bastug, E., Bennis, M., Debbah, M.: Living on the edge: the role of proactive caching in 5G wireless networks. IEEE Commun. Mag. 52(8), 82–89 (2016)
9. Gregori, M., Gomez-Vilardeb, J., Matamoros, J.: Wireless content caching for small cell and D2D networks. IEEE J. Sel. Areas Commun. 34(5), 1222–1234 (2016)
10. Liu, A., Lau, V.K.: Asymptotic scaling laws of wireless ad hoc network with physical layer caching. IEEE Trans. Wireless Commun. 15(3), 1657–1664 (2016)
11. Li, Y., Wu, T., Hui, P., Jin, D., Chen, S.: Social-aware D2D communications: qualitative insights and quantitative analysis. IEEE Commun. Mag. 52(6), 150–158 (2014)
12. Li, Y., Su, S., Chen, S.: Social-aware resource allocation for device-to-device communications underlaying cellular networks. IEEE Wirel. Commun. Lett. 4(3), 293–296 (2015)
13. Wang, Z., Sun, L., Zhang, M., et al.: Propagation- and mobility-aware D2D social content replication. IEEE Trans. Mob. Comput. 16(4), 1107–1120 (2017)
14. Tsai, K.C., Li, W., Zhu, H.: Caching for mobile social networks with deep learning: Twitter analysis for 2016 U.S. election. IEEE Trans. Netw. Sci. Eng. (2018)

15. Tsai, K.C., Li, W., Zhu, H.: Mobile social media networks caching with convolutional neural network. In: IEEE Wireless Communications and Networking Conference Workshops (WCNCW), Barcelona (2018). https://doi.org/10.1109/WCNCW.2018.8368988
16. Tanzil, S.M.S., Hoiles, W., Krishnamurthy, V.: Adaptive scheme for caching YouTube content in a cellular network: machine learning approach. IEEE Access **5**, 5870–5881 (2017)
17. Golder, S.A., Wilkinson, D.M., Huberman, B.A.: Rhythms of social interaction: messaging within a massive online network. Chaos Interdisc. J. Nonlinear Sci. **93**(10), 098701–66 (2015)
18. Mach, P., Becvar, Z., Vanek, T.: In-band device-to-device communication in OFDMA cellular networks: a survey and challenges. IEEE Commun. Surv. Tutor. **17**(4), 1885–1922 (2015)
19. Cao, Y., Wu, J.: Projective ART for clustering data sets in high dimensional spaces. Neural Netw. **15**(2), 105–120 (2002). The Official Journal of the International Neural Network Society
20. Cao, Y., Wu, J.: Dynamics of projective adaptive resonance theory model: the foundation of PART algorithm. IEEE Trans. Neural Networks **15**(2), 245–260 (2004)
21. Yi, C., Huang, S., Cai, J.: An incentive mechanism integrating joint power, channel and link management for social-aware D2D content sharing and proactive caching. IEEE Trans. Mob. Comput. **17**(4), 789–802 (2017)
22. Shi, L., Zhao, L., Zheng, G., Zhu, H.: Incentive design for cache-enabled D2D underlaid cellular networks using stackelberg game. IEEE Trans. Veh. Technol. **68**(1), 765–779 (2019)
23. Wang, F., Li, Y., Wang, Z., et al.: Social-community-aware resource allocation for D2D communications underlaying cellular networks. IEEE Trans. Veh. Technol. **65**(5), 3628–3640 (2016)
24. Filiposka, S., Mishev, A., Gilly, K.: Community-based allocation and migration strategies for fog computing. In: IEEE Wireless Communications and Networking Conference (WCNC), Barcelona (2018). https://doi.org/10.1109/WCNC.2018.8377095

AI-Based Network Intelligence for IoT

An Emergency Resource Scheduling Model Based on Edge Computing

Songyan Zhong[1], Tao He[1], Mengyu Li[2(✉)], Lanlan Rui[2],
Guoxin Xia[2], and Yu Zhu[2]

[1] Network Information Department, China Aerospace Science and Industry
Corporation Limited, Beijing, China
`576678349@qq.com`, `541629067@qq.com`
[2] State Key Laboratory of Networking and Switching Technology, Beijing
University of Posts and Telecommunications, Beijing, China
`1006564282@qq.com`, `1912696398@qq.com`,
`736070995@qq.com`, `915808818@qq.com`

Abstract. In recent years, more and more researches are focusing on the field
of disaster emergency management, especially in emergency resource dispatching. In a disaster scenario, a control center needs to obtain a large amount
of real-time information at the scene to make decisions timely and accurately.
Traditional Cloud Computing has many shortcomings in terms of delay and
bandwidth, and Edge Computing (EC) will be more suitable for this scenario.
We apply EC to the emergency rescue to cope with the problem of latency
needs. First, we propose an edge-based emergency rescue architecture that
consists of three layers: Cloud Layer, Edge Layer, and Resource Layer. Based
on this, we give a resource scheduling model that requires the collaboration of
Cloud and Edge Layers. The Cloud Layer gives a partition for these tasks, and
all sub-tasks are assigning to the edge servers to get a locally optimal solution.
Finally, these solutions from different edge servers are summarized to the Cloud
Layer to get a globally optimal solution. We compare our algorithm with CS-
GA and VRP. The simulation results show that RSE has good performance in
scheduling time and cost.

Keywords: Resource scheduling · Edge Computing · Cooperation model

1 Introduction

Frequent disasters like earthquakes have caused serious losses to lives and properties,
and it is the reason why more and more attention being paid to the field of disaster
emergency management [1], especially the emergency resource dispatching. Emergency resource scheduling is the core of emergency management, it mainly studies how
to use intelligent decision theory and computer as aided tools to quickly and effectively
get an optimal emergency resource allocation plan. Through this scheduling, the
emergency resources can reach the destination as soon as possible, and the emergency
rescue can be carried out as soon as possible, thus minimizing economic losses and
casualties caused by disasters.

© ICST Institute for Computer Sciences, Social Informatics and Telecommunications Engineering 2019
Published by Springer Nature Switzerland AG 2019. All Rights Reserved
S. Han et al. (Eds.): AICON 2019, LNICST 287, pp. 353–366, 2019.
https://doi.org/10.1007/978-3-030-22971-9_31

With the development of information technology, emergency resource dispatching is gradually combined with advanced communication technologies to achieve better scheduling. Amounts of information exist in the disaster scene, such as road blockage, collapse, temperature, and humidity. The significant information should be collected and analyzed to avoid blind scheduling, thus saving the rescue time and effect. Therefore, constructing a real-time, high-speed information transmission system is of critical importance in emergency resource scheduling.

In a disaster scenario, it is still difficult to achieve high-bandwidth and real-time communication between the disaster scene and the rescue center with the current communication technology. As an emerging model, Edge Computing (EC) brings a new idea for reducing latency and bandwidth cost, that is deploying the server at the edge of the network. The emergence of EC realizes the decentralization of Cloud Computing, which can effectively avoid the time and bandwidth waste caused by the long-distance transmission, and also reduce the computing load of the cloud center. In this paper, we apply the idea of Edge Computing to the emergency rescue. This scene requires a quick response time and large amounts of data for making decisions. In this way, the efficiency of emergency rescue can be improved.

The contributions of the paper are as follows.

(1) Basing on the disaster scenario, we proposed a cooperating layered architecture which consists of the cloud layer, the edge layer, and the resource layer. In this architecture, a task can be divided and assigned to the edge layers for calculation.
(2) We propose an emergency resource scheduling model basing on latency and cost, which requires the collaboration of cloud and edge layers. The cloud layer receives tasks and divides them, then the divided sub-tasks can be assigned to the edge layer. The edge layer searches for a locally optimal solution for these sub-tasks within its service scope. After all locally optimal solutions are summarized to the cloud layer, the globally optimal solution is calculated, and the resource scheduling plan is completed.

The rest of this paper is organized as follows. Section 2 discusses some related work about Edge Computing, disaster rescue, and allocation algorithm. Section 3 describes the disaster rescue scene and introduces the Cooperating Layered Architecture for an emergency. Moreover, an emergency resource scheduling model is also detailed described. Section 4 gives the simulation of the mechanism we proposed and the effectiveness of the proposed method is demonstrated by simulation results. Section 5 draws our conclusions and portrayed the directions of ongoing work.

2   Related Work

There are many types of research focusing on resource scheduling and give solutions to it. Based on the single material scheduling model and multi-material scheduling model [2], a multi-rescue and multi-material emergency scheduling algorithm that satisfies the continuous emergency material consumption is proposed, and the shortest path is used in this solution. By introducing disaster emergency management [1], a different algorithm based on non-dominated sorting is proposed to solve multiple emergency point multi-resource scheduling problems. It also proposes a CS-GA-based algorithm to minimize transportation costs and demand costs of emergency supplies. In order to minimize disaster losses, [7] proposes a scheduling model of emergency materials under uncertain travel time conditions, and the fuzzy set method is used to select the maximum satisfactory path in the fuzzy network.

Edge Computing has been applied in many fields because of its significant advantages. The typical model is Mobile Edge Computing (MEC) [8]. MEC model stresses setting up edge server between cloud center and edge devices, and the computing tasks are performed on the edge server. However, terminals are regarded as the devices with little computing capabilities, thus edge server undertakes this responsibility. Some studies [9–13] concentrate on the migration of intensive mobile computing task to the edge server of the network. Moreover, MEC is deemed to be a promising solution for handling video streaming services in the context of smart cities [14]. The valuable data can be transmitted to the application server to reduce core network traffic. Augmented Reality (AR) mobile applications can also combine the MEC because these applications have inherent collaborative properties in terms of data collection in the uplink, computing at the edge, and data delivery in the downlink [15]. Besides, in [16, 17], authors give an integration of MEC and 5G to meet the need of 5G in extensibility and latency.

Edge Computing can effectively solve the problems of delay and bandwidth, which are the outstanding problems in emergency resource scheduling. Therefore, we will discuss how to have a combination of them.

3   The Edge-Based Resources Scheduling Model

3.1   Architecture

In an emergency scene, there is an emergency center which needs a large amount of real-time information to make accurate decisions and coordinate operations. However, the transmission of road video surveillance and traffic information requires high bandwidth, and the limited conditions will slow down the decisions. Therefore, we propose an edge-based architecture to improve the performance of emergency command.

As is shown in Fig. 1, the architecture includes three layers: Cloud Layer, Edge Layer, and Resource Layer. The Cloud Layer is the emergency command and data center. Commanders in cloud center make higher-level decisions such as rescue plan, give remote training for on-site rescuers. Besides, multi-screen recording helps commanders get ongoing real-time information. Edge Layer is set at the edge of the network. For example, with Edge Computing server deployed on the base stations, some work such as video management and analysis can be handled in the Edge Layer. In this way, we can get a better exploitation of communication bandwidth. Resource Layer is the actual resources in the disaster scene. We list some parts such as road video surveillance, traffic information, and mobile emergency, in fact, disaster rescue is a complex process and not restricted to these parts. How to allocate these resources will influence the progress of rescue work. In the following part, we describe this issue and propose our method.

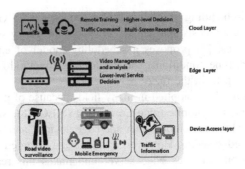

Fig. 1. Edge-based layered emergency architecture

3.2   Problem Model

The proposed emergency architecture can be seen as a typical use case of Mobile Ad hoc Network (MANET). The sensors, wireless devices, and rescuers with smart devices can communicate with each other which are not relying on a preexisting infrastructure, such as routers in wired networks or access points in managed (infrastructure) wireless networks.

We give a resource scheduling model of our scenario first. Variety of services exist in emergency rescue scenarios, such as emergency rescue, material dispatch. We define the service as a set $S = \{S_1, S_2, \ldots S_m\}$, where m is the total number of services. Resources/Devices at the rescue scene are defined as $D = \{d_1, d_2, \ldots d_r\}$, where r is the total number of resource types. Each service has various resource demands. For example, emergency services require rescuers, search and rescue tools, communication equipment, and environmental information. Therefore, a service S_i can be divided into multiple sub-services. It can be expressed as: S_i is composed of many sub-services such as $s_1, s_2, \ldots, s_n$, and each sub-service can be regarded as an atom, and its demand for resources will be single. For example, the above rescue task can be divided into 6 sub-tasks, acquiring environment information (s_1), dispatching rescuers (s_2), dispatching vehicles (s_3), scheduling search and rescue tool (s_4), scheduling communication device (s_5), and on-site rescue (s_6). Each sub-service corresponds to 0 or 1 resources, such as sub-service s_1 requires resource d_1, d_1 represents sensor information, sub-service s_2 requires resource d_2, and d_2 represents rescuer. The serial number of sub-service and resource does not need to be one-to-one. We only need to find the best resource among the multiple resources to complete the scheduling, which will be our next task.

As is shown in Fig. 2, the top level is the Service Layer, which describes all the services S in a rescue scenario. The middle layer is the Atomic Service Layer, which can be expressed as a set $s = \{s_1, s_2, \ldots s_n\}$. This layer is a division of top-level service. A node in a top layer is corresponded to one or more Atomic Service Layer nodes, and there is a certain order of execution among these atomic services. For example, the environmental inspection task s_1 needs to be executed first to ensure that the rescue can be performed, and resource scheduling can be performed after s_1 has been completed. We can use topological sorting to find the execution order of these atomic services, ensuring the normal interaction between subservices. The bottom layer is the Resource

Layer, which displays all the resources that can be scheduled at the rescue site, including rescue team, materials, intelligent terminals, sensors, and rescue equipment.

Our aim is to find the best combination of resources that can work together to support a service and ensure the quality of service, and next, we will elaborate on how to find the mapping from Service Layer node to a Resource Layer node group.

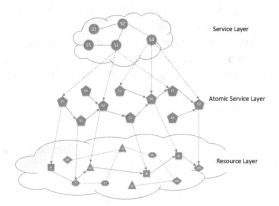

Fig. 2. Three-layer service model

3.3 Resource Scheduling Algorithm

Main Idea

We propose a resource scheduling model that requires the collaboration of cloud and edge layers. When a task arriving at the command center in the cloud layer, the task will be divided into sub-tasks, and the division is expressed in Fig. 2. And then, these sun-tasks are assigning to the edge servers to search for the Locally Optimal Solution (LOS). Finally, these solutions from different edge servers are summarized to the cloud center to get a Globally Optimal Solution (GOS). The process of our algorithm is shown in Fig. 3.

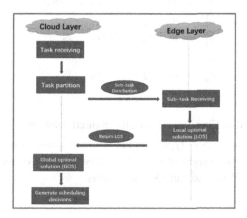

Fig. 3. The process of scheduling strategy making

Service Layer—Atomic Service Layer

From the Service Layer to the Atomic Service Layer is a division of a complete task, which is mainly determined by the control center located in the cloud layer. The principle of division is the independence of tasks. We need to ensure that the requirements for resources/equipment of each sub-task are single after dividing. Each service can be expressed as $S_i(P_i, D, L_i, C_i)$: service location P, resource requirement D, delay demand L, cost requirement C. The mapping from Si to a set of atomic services $\{s_j(P_i, d_j, L_i, C_i)\}$ is done by a set of defined partitioning rules, $R_i = \{r_1, r_2, \ldots r_n\}$. R_i is a set of n-dimensional vectors, where n is the total number of atomic services, and R_i is Boolean, indicating whether the partition contains the sub-service. For example, service S_1 consists of atomic services s_2, s_3, s_4, then $R_i = \{0, 1, 1, 1, 0 \ldots 0\}$.

$$S_i(P_i, D, L_i, C_i) \xrightarrow{R_i(r_1, r_2 \ldots r_n)} \{s_j(P_i, d_j, L_i, C_i)\} \tag{1}$$

After the cloud center completes the task partition, the sub-task set $\{s_j(P_i, d_j, L_i, C_i)\}$ will be dispatched to the edge servers to find the corresponding resources and devices. Due to the limited coverage of edge servers, each edge server can only find the optimal resources for the tasks within the corresponding service scope. Therefore, each edge server can provide a LOS for the sub-task set $\{s_j(P_i, d_j, L_i, C_i)\}$, and solve the GOS by summing the LOS to the cloud center.

Atomic Service Layer—Resource Layer

Works on the Cloud Layer

Servers at the edge layer each maintain a table named res_tab, which counts for the resources within the service scope, including sensors, videos, personal information, and materials. After the sub-service collection $\{s_j(P_i, d_j, L_i, C_i)\}$ arrives at the edge server, each server looks for the best resource combination for these sub-services in the current scope (Table 1).

Table 1. An example of res_tab.

res_id	Type	Position	Cost	Speed
d_1^1	d_1	p_1	c_1	v_1
d_1^2	d_1	p_2	c_2	v_2
...	...	...	...	...
d_n^1	d_n	p_n	c_n	v_n

A formula defined in (2) gives the locally optimal solution $F(s_j)$ of the sub-service s_j. d_j^k represents all resources of type d_j in the scope, $\rho_{i,m}$ is the mth quality indicator of service s_j, and $\alpha_{i,m}$ is the weight of the mth quality indicator of service s_j. We choose scheduling latency and cost as our QoS indicators.

$$F(s_j) = \min\left\{ d_j^k * \sum_m \alpha_{j,m} * \rho_{j,m} \right\} \qquad (2)$$

The formula (2) can be redefined as formula (3):

$$s.t. \begin{cases} F(s_j) = \min\{\rho_{j,1} * (dis|P_i - sp_k|)/sv_k + \rho_{j,2} * sc_k\} \\ |P_i - sp_k|/sv_k \leq L_i \\ \frac{|P_i - sp_k|}{sv_k} * sc_k \leq C_i \end{cases} \qquad (3)$$

Where $dis|P_i - p_k|$ calculates the distance between the target point and the current resource point, c_k is the unit transportation cost of s_j, v_k is the moving speed of s_j, L_i is the highest delay that can be tolerated, and C_i is the highest cost.

For each task s_j in the sub-task set $\{s_j(P_i, d_j, L_i, C_i)\}$, we find an optimal solution in the current server scope. LOS of all edge servers are summarized in the cloud layer to find the GOS.

Works on the Edge Layer

It is mentioned in the problem model that there are certain interactions between these sub-tasks. Therefore, when we look for GOS in the cloud layer, the scheduling sequence we find needs to satisfy the sequential execution relationship of the sub-tasks. We present a solution based on topological sorting.

We can obtain an adjacency matrix of the logical graph $G_i(s, e)$ of these sub-services at the Atomic Service Layer, and we need to find a solution that meets the task constraints from the start to the end of the critical path.

$$G_i(s, e) = \begin{bmatrix} 0 & 1 & 1 & 0 \\ 1 & 0 & 0 & 1 \\ 1 & 0 & 0 & 1 \\ 0 & 1 & 1 & 0 \end{bmatrix} \qquad (4)$$

According to the logic diagram $G_i(s, e)$, we obtain the topological sorting sequence $Q_i(s_{j-1}, s_j)$ derived from the graph $G_i(s, e)$, and Q_i records each node and its corresponding precursor node. Based on this sequence and the quality parameter requirements, we can generate a resource set $D_i = \{V, Gbit\}$ of the execution service. V is a set defined as $V = (d_1, d_2, \ldots d_j)$. d_j is the resource of the service s_j, and the corresponding Gbit is used for identification.

For example, we get an execution sequence (S_1, S_2, S_3, S_4), where the starting node for topological sorting is S_1. If $V = (d_1, d_2, d_3, NULL)$ and $Gbit = 1110$, it means that there are three resources $d_{k_1}, d_{k_2}, d_{k_3}$ satisfy the services S_1, S_2, S_3, and the service S_4 is not found yet. Resources. Therefore, at the beginning, D_i is set to the initial value, such as $V = (NULL, \ldots, NULL)$ and $Gbit = 0 \ldots 0$.

The selection process of resources is as follows. The locally optimal solution $d_j \in U$, d_j returned by the edge server has three parameters, and each resource item $d_j(p_j, l_j, c_j)$ records its position parameter, delay parameter and cost parameter. The selected GOS node is stored in the set V, and the record type is $d_j(p_j, L_i^j, C_i^j)$. Starting from the initial service of the topological sorting sequence, each type of service uses the formula (5) to select the best resource among the currently available resources, selects it and puts it into the set V, and updates the current residual delay L_i^j and the remaining cost C_i^j. The non-first node taken from the topological ordering will refer to the remaining resource status of its predecessor node, and use its updated L_i and C_i as thresholds. This iterative calculation is terminated until the entire topology sorting sequence is completed, or the constraints are not met. If the optimal scheduling is not found during the execution of the algorithm, according to the scenario set in this paper, the algorithm will find a relatively optimal resource scheduling scheme without setting the cost and delay threshold. We use the following algorithm to describe how the cloud layer looks for the optimal set of resources (Table 2).

$$\begin{cases} E(s_j) = \min\{\rho_{j,1} * l_j + \rho_{j,2} * c_j\} \\ l_j \leq L_i^{j-1} \\ l_j * c_j \leq C_i^{j-1} \end{cases} \tag{5}$$

Table 2. Algorithm of scheduling.

Algorithm
Input U, Q_i, L_i, C_i
Output V
While $Q_i \neq$ null
take out s_j at the head of Q_i.
find the best d_j in set U using (3)
update: $L_i^j = L_i^{j-1} - l_j$
$C_i^j = C_i^{j-1} - c_j$
add $d_j (p_j, L_i^j, C_i^j)$ to set V.
If $L_i^j < 0$ or $C_i^j < 0$
Break
If $Q_i \neq$ null
For s_j in Q_i
Find the best d_j in set U using
$E(s_j) = \min\{\rho_{j,1} * l_j + \rho_{j,2} * c_j\}$
Add $d_j (p_j)$ to set V
Return V

Finally, we find the mapping from the task set $\{s_j(P_i, d_j, L_i, C_i)\}$ of the Atomic Service Layer s to the resource set $\{d_j(p_j, l_j, c_j)\}$, completing the resource scheduling from Service Layer S to Resource Layer D.

4 Evaluation

In this section, we give a simulation scenario according to [3, 4]. The experiment uses MATLAB R2017b as experiment platform, which is suitable for Windows 10, CPU Intel 2.5 GHz, 8 GB. The simulation runs for 30 min. We give three times experiments to avoid errors.

We construct a simulation area as 10 * 10 (km^2). There are two emergency rescue centers in the area with coordinates (0, 0) and (10000, 10000). The rescue center has full kind of resources, but it is far away from the rescue point; the coordinates and resources of the rescue center are shown in Table 3. There are scattered resource distributions in other locations throughout the region. We use a random function to distribute periodically. The random function is shown in Eq. (6), and the distribution period is set to 5 min, and 5 resources are distributed each time. We set up a rescue zone with a center (5000, 5000) and a radius of 4000, in which a service request will be generated. The task is generated every 3 min and 10 task requests will be generated during the simulation time. The random function that generates the task satisfies Eq. (7) (Fig. 4).

Table 3. Settings for the resource center.

Name	X-coordinate	Y-coordinate	Resources
res_center1	0	0	$s_1, s_2, s_3, s_4, s_5, s_6, s_7$
res_center2	10000	10000	$s_1, s_2, s_3, s_4, s_5, s_6, s_7$

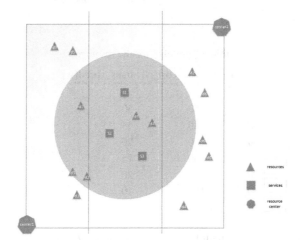

Fig. 4. Simulation area explanation

$$\begin{cases} res\_type = rand\_1()\%7 + 1 \\ \quad x = rand\_2()\%10000 \\ \quad y = rand\_3()\%10000 \end{cases} \tag{6}$$

$$\begin{cases} ser\_type = rand\_4()\%3 + 1 \\ \quad x = rand\_5()\%10000 \\ \quad y = rand\_6()\%10000 \\ (x - 5000)^2 + (y - 5000)^2 \le 4000^2 \end{cases} \tag{7}$$

In the experiment, three edge servers and one central server are set. The edge server has an ideal service range and is divided into three areas. The corresponding x-axis range is (0, 3333), (3333, 6666), (6666, 1000), the edge server can count all resources in the area, maintain a resource table and update periodically. There are three types of rescue services in the simulation scenario. Each type of service, sub-service, resource requirement, delay threshold, and cost requirement setting are shown in Table 4. (Note: v_j and c_j are 0, indicating that the service is a network service. For example, scheduling sensor information), the scheduling cost information of specific resources is shown in Table 5.

Table 4. Settings for the services.

service_type	sub_service	res_type	L_i(h)	C_i
S_1	s_1, s_2, s_3, s_4	d_1, d_2, d_3, d_4	0.5	20
S_2	s_2, s_3, s_5, s_6	d_2, d_{36}, d_5, d_6	1	15
S_3	s_1, s_4, s_5, s_6, s_7	d_1, d_4, d_5, d_6, d_7	0.3	30

Table 5. Settings for the resources.

res_type	trans_cost(c_j)	trans_speed(v_j)
d_1	0	0
d_2	50	30
d_3	80	35
d_4	40	20
d_5	60	15
d_6	90	20
d_7	130	10

We calculate the actual scheduling time of all tasks LL_i, and record the ratio of LL_i to the task's threshold time L_i as $P_L = L_i/LL_i$, which is a parameter of our comparison experiment. On the other hand, we calculate the actual scheduling cost of all tasks CC_i, and record the ratio of CC_i to the threshold cost C_i of the task as $P_C = C_i/CC_i$, which is another parameter. We calculated data for different tasks in three experiments and recorded them in Table 6. In order to avoid the randomness of the experiment, we will use the random letter to generate the data needed for the experiment in advance, and use the same value for the three experiments.

Table 6. Result of resource scheduling.

Index	S_1	S_3	S_1	S_2	S_2	S_3	S_1	S_2	S_3	S_3
P_L	1.32	1.21	1.37	1.16	1.10	1.16	1.28	1.18	1.15	1.08
P_C	1.35	1.31	1.41	1.20	1.14	1.20	1.30	1.24	1.23	1.12

From the data, it can be found that two service requests with the same type are too concentrated in a time, the optimal schedule may have been used by the previous schedule, and the performance of the second schedule will be significantly lower. For example, the last two columns of data in Table 6, the same type of request S_3, the former is numerically superior to the latter.

We apply the same environmental settings to the algorithms proposed in [3, 4] and give a comparison of these results. [3] identified as CS-GA proposed a decision-making algorithm based on CS-GA to minimize the transportation cost and demand cost of emergency materials. Another genetic algorithm optimization path based on an emergency distribution VRP model in [4], we identify it as VRP. Our algorithm is identified as RSE in the comparison chart.

In comparison, it can be found that P_L and P_C values of the RSE are relatively high, which shows that the actual scheduling time LL_i and the actual scheduling cost CC_i of RSE are lower, which is due to the distributed edge cloud can quickly sense the resource update status within the service scope and obtain more accurate resource status, thus achieving a more accurate scheduling scheme than the remote centralized control of the cloud (Figs. 5 and 6).

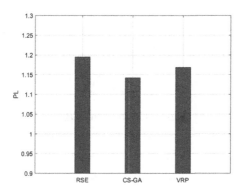

Fig. 5. Comparison of P_L

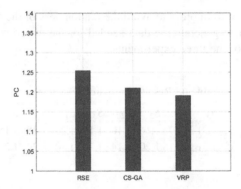

Fig. 6. Comparison of P_C

We adjust the service request rate and give a comparison again. The above results are basing on a service request rate of 1/3 (10 requests every 30 min), and then we give a comparison with changing rates from 1/6 to 1. From Fig. 7, it can be found that three algorithms have a decreasing P_L in the case of increased rate, and the drop is obvious at 0.0667, but the performance of RSE is still better than the other two. In Fig. 8, P_C of the three algorithms also decrease with increasing rate, but the decrease of P_C is not particularly obvious, because the transportation cost does not fluctuate too much within the limited range determined. The performance of RSE is still the best among them.

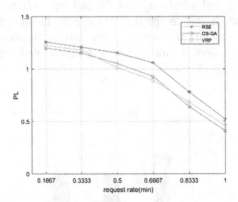

Fig. 7. Comparison of P_L

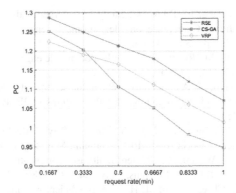

Fig. 8. Comparison of P_C

5 Conclusion

Current emergency communication systems are facing multiple challenges, such as insufficient bandwidth and delayed response, which seriously slow down the emergency scheduling and rescue. The idea of Edge Computing is suitable for these problems. We propose an edge-based architecture to realize an emergency system which can assign some process from the cloud center to the edge of the network. Then, based on this architecture, we give a resource scheduling model which takes latency and cost into consideration. Through the collaboration of cloud and edge layers, the algorithm can achieve a significant performance on scheduling time and transmission cost. However, this model is focusing on a single-service scenario, when it comes to multi-service and multi-resource scenarios, the algorithm should be improved to adopt these factors. The following work is to optimize RSE to fix the scenario of multi-service. Further, we will enrich the content of our architecture in more situations.

References

1. Zhang, T.: Research on emergency resource scheduling in disaster emergency management. Hefei University of Technology (2015)
2. Chai, X.R.: Research on disaster emergency rescue material dispatching system. University of Science and Technology of China (2009)
3. Cai, J.M.: Research on time-varying and reliability related issues of earthquake disaster emergency logistics. Central South University (2012)
4. Zhao, T.: Research on optimization of emergency disaster material distribution system for sudden natural disasters in China. Dalian Maritime University (2011)
5. Xue, H., Cai, B., Jiang, C., Yuan, Y.: Research on the robust decision of emergency material distribution for chain retail supply chain. In: Chinese Control and Decision Conference (CCDC), Shenyang, pp. 1922–1927 (2018)
6. Gu, Y.: Study on scheduling model of emergency materials distribution after natural disaster. In: 2nd International Workshop on Intelligent Systems and Applications, Wuhan, pp. 1–4 (2010)

7. Sun, Q., Kong, F., Zhang, L., Dang, X.: Study on emergency distribution route decision making. In: International Conference on Mechatronic Science, Electric Engineering and Computer (MEC), Jilin, pp. 338–341 (2011)

8. Satria, D., Park, D., Jo, M.: Recovery for overloaded mobile edge computing. Future Gener. Comput. Syst. **70**, 138–147 (2017)

9. Zhao, T., Zhou, S., Guo, X.: A cooperative scheduling scheme of l cloud and Internet cloud for delay-aware mobile cloud computing. In: Proceedings of IEEE GLOBECOM Workshops, pp. 1–6 (2015)

10. Flores, H., Hui, P., Tarkoma, S., Li, Y., Srirama, S., Buyya, R.: Mobile code offloading: from concept to practice and beyond. IEEE Commun. Mag. **53**, 80–88 (2015)

11. Chen, X., Jiao, L., Li, W., Fu, X.: Efficient multi-user computation offloading for mobile-edge cloud computing. IEEE/ACM Trans. Netw. **24**, 2795–2808 (2016)

12. You, C., Huang, K., Chae, H., Kim, B.H.: Energy-efficient resource allocation for mobile-edge computation offloading. IEEE Trans. Wirel. Commun. **16**, 1397–1411 (2017)

13. Sardellitti, S., Scutari, G., Barbarossa, S.: Joint optimization of radio and computational resources for multicell mobile-edge computing. IEEE Trans. Signal Inf. Process. Over Netw. **1**, 89–103 (2015)

14. Taleb, T., Dutta, S., Ksentini, A., Iqbal, M., Flinck, H.: Mobile edge computing potential in making cities smarter. IEEE Commun. Mag. **55**, 38–43 (2017)

15. Lin, S., Cheng, H.F., Li, W., Huang, Z., Hui, P., Peylo, C.: Ubii: physical world interaction through augmented reality. IEEE Trans. Mob. Comput. **16**, 872–885 (2017)

16. Hu, Y., Patel, M., Sabella, D., et al.: Mobile edge computing: a key technology towards 5G. ETSI White Paper (2015)

17. Zhang, K., et al.: Energy-efficient offloading for mobile edge computing in 5G heterogeneous networks. IEEE Access J. **4**, 5896–5907 (2016)

Mobility-Aware Task Parallel Offloading for Vehicle Fog Computing

Jindou Xie, Yunjian Jia$^{(\boxtimes)}$, Zhengchuan Chen, and Liang Liang

School of Microelectronics and Communication Engineering, Chongqing University,
Chongqing 400044, People's Republic of China
{xjd,yunjian,czc,liangliang}@cqu.edu.cn

Abstract. When applying fog computing paradigm into Internet of vehicle, vehicles are regarded as intelligent devices with computation and communication capability. These moving intelligent devices are often employed to assist various computation-intensive task offloading in vehicle fog computing, which brings real-time responses. However, vehicles mobility and network dynamics make it challenging to offload tasks to ideal target nodes for user-vehicle. In this paper, leveraging the result of vehicle mobility-awareness, we investigate the task offloading problem in vehicle fog computing aiming to minimize service time. Specifically, we consider that a task can be decomposed into subtasks in any proportion and offloaded from user-vehicle to multi service vehicles in parallel via vehicle-to-vehicle (V2V) links. Mobility information of vehicles collected by RSU is modeled to predicted the states of V2V links based on hidden Markov model (HMM). Then, we refine a rule to select target service-vehicles and the size of each subtask according to predicted results. Comparing with random and single-point task offloading, the proposed approach indicates a better performance on amount of finished task and service time in vehicle dense area.

Keywords: Mobility · Task offloading · HMM ·
Vehicle fog computing · Parallel offloading

1 Introduction

With the development of wireless multimedia service, increasing more mobile applications such as immersive gaming, video streaming and human-computer interaction services demand intensive computation resource for real-time processing and high network bandwidth for data exchange [1]. Fog computing also known as mobile edge computing [2], is regarded as a promising solution for

Supported by the National Key Research and Development Program of China (Grant No. 2016YFE0121100); and the Program for Innovation Team Building at colleges and Universities in Chongqing, China (Grant No. CXTDX201601006); and National Natural Science Foundation of China(Grant No. 61601067).

S. Han et al. (Eds.): AICON 2019, LNICST 287, pp. 367–379, 2019.
https://doi.org/10.1007/978-3-030-22971-9_32

those challenges by sinking cloud function to edge nodes [3]. To this end, various service tasks generated in user side can be offloaded to target edge servers, taking advantage of sufficient resources on edge servers when mobile users suffer from limited device resource [4].

The development of autonomous driving technology illustrates that the future vehicles are equipped with advanced computational resources to facilitate sophisticated artificial intelligence (AI) based on multi-dimension data collected by on-board-unit [5]. The idea of vehicle-as-a-resource has been proposed, which exploits the enormous resources of vehicular network to facilitate new types of services, such as mobile crowd sensing [6] and cooperative caching [7]. Thus it is a good way to share resource that applying fog computing in vehicle-based settings, to form vehicle fog computing [8]. In vehicle fog computing system, the role of vehicle can be a user or a edge server that is named as user-vehicle (User-V) and service-vehicle (Service-V) respectively in this work. Task offloaded from User-V to Service-V relies on successful transmission via vehicle-to-everything (V2X), including vehicle-to-vehicle (V2V) and vehicle-to-infrastructure (V2I) over different protocols [9].

In the literature, there are some recent efforts dedicating to task offloading in vehicle fog computing. In [10], the authors pointed to exploiting parked cars for task offloading and cooperative sensing. On the contrary, since parked cars can be regarded as static cloud servers, the moving vehicles produce more opportunities to share resources but also high dynamics of vehicle network, which increase the complexity of offloading decision. Some researches focus on utilizing vehicles on the move endowed with ample computation resources. The authors in [8] extended the fog computing paradigm to conventional vehicular networks, and presented a viewpoint of vehicles as infrastructures, discussing the structure in four types of application scenarios. Authors in [11] concentrated on various types tasks offloading in mobile-edge cloud-based vehicular networks. And optimal strategies for mobile edge server selection and task transmission management are proposed. However, they all consider single service node provides resources for computation-intensive task.

In this paper, we consider multi moving vehicles provide service for user-vehicle in parallel processing different parts of one task to meet low-latency demand. To improve the offloading efficiency, we estimate the states of V2V links based hidden Markov model (HMM) modeling the mobility information collected by RSU. After that, we refine a task parallel offloading scheme considering transmission delay, computation delay, as well as task decomposition and handover cost.

The rest of the paper is organized as follows. Section 2 introduces the system scenario; Sect. 3 gives an account of mobility awareness based on V2V links states prediction with HMM. Section 4 analyzes the task parallel offloading policy for service delay reduction. Then simulations are implemented in Sect. 5 and conclusions are provided in Sect. 6.

2 System Overview

As illustrated in Fig. 1, User-V has little computation resource for remained intensive and delay-sensitive task but sufficient communication resource to establish V2I or V2V links. There are several neighbor vehicles with available computation and communication resource in the same RSU coverage area as User-V, such as vehicles A-E in Fig. 1. These vehicles are denoted as $\mathcal{N} = \{1, 2, \cdots n\}$ with different computation capabilities f_n, and regarded as moving intelligent devices. The RSU can collect mobility information from them and control links between vehicles according to offloading decision.

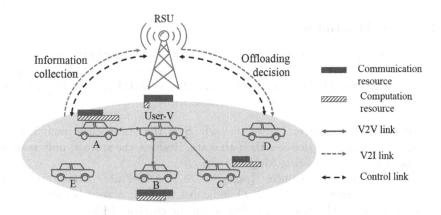

Fig. 1. Illustration of vehicle fog computing system.

We focus on a scenario where User-V with unknown trajectory tends to offload subtasks (parts of task derived from task decomposition in any proportion) to several service vehicles (Service-Vs) for computation resource sharing gain. The objective is to complete more tasks in short service time. At the beginning of offloading process, User-V sends the offloading requests and reports its mobility information to RSU. After received the messages, RSU analyzes all the current and historical mobility information in the coverage area to forecast the states of V2V links between User-V and Service-Vs in the residence time of User-V. Then, RSU selects appropriate vehicles as target edge nodes, formed as set $\boldsymbol{V}_s$ based on available resources. Vehicles in $\boldsymbol{V}_s$ are able to provide service for User-V simultaneously. Afterwards, V2V links between User-V and Service-Vs are established with RSU's assistance and the task is decomposed according to available resources on Service-Vs. User-V transmits different subtasks to the selected nodes with the assistance of RSU. Upon the nodes finishing the corresponding subtasks in parallel, they send the results back to User-V. If task has not been finished by Service-Vs during the time user stayed in the coverage, additional handover cost will be accounted for service time t_f. According to these steps, the task parallel offloading scheme is based on the estimation of states of V2V links that are dynamic due to vehicle mobility. So we address the challenge of mobility awareness firstly based on HMM.

3   HMM-Based Mobility Awareness

We resort to the tool of HMM to characterize the mobility information of vehicles and predict the states of V2V links, which influence component of V_s and transmission rate. Afterwards, we take into account transmission, computation, as well as task decomposition and handover cost to refine a task parallel offloading approach.

3.1   HMM Description

HMM is a typically dynamic Bayesian Network, and a sequential probability model [12]. It is good at describing a process of observable states sequence generated by a hidden Markov chain. The variables in HMM can be divided into two sets, hidden states and observable states.

- Hidden states sequence: $\{s_1, s_2, \cdots, s_t\}$. S is the state space including S elements, and $s_t \in S$ denotes the t-th state. Besides, the state s_t only relates to the state s_{t-1}, following Markov rules.
- Observable states sequence: $\{o_1, o_2, \cdots, o_t\}$. Observable state space O includes O elements, and $o_t \in O$ indicates the t-th observable state. The values of observable states only depend on the current hidden states value.

An HMM can be defined by three parameters:

- $\mathbf{A}$: transmission matrix $\mathbf{A} = [a_{ij}]_{S \times S}$, where a_{ij} is the transmission probability of taking transmission from state s_i to s_j,

$$a_{ij} = P(s_{t+1} = s_j | s_t = s_i), 1 \leq i, j \leq S. \tag{1}$$

- $\mathbf{B}$: confusion matrix. According to the model, the probabilities of observable states are obtained from current states values, denoted as $\mathbf{B} = [b_{ij}]_{S \times O}$. b_{ij} indicates the probability of observation o_j when state s_i is at time t,

$$b_{ij} = P(o_t = o_j | s_t = s_i), 1 \leq i \leq S, 1 \leq j \leq O. \tag{2}$$

- $\boldsymbol{\pi}$: Initial state probability $\boldsymbol{\pi} = (\pi_1, \pi_2, \cdots, \pi_S)$ indicates the probability of initial state,

$$\pi_i = P(s_1 = s_i), 1 \leq i \leq S. \tag{3}$$

The HMM can be written in a compact notation $\theta = (\mathbf{A}, \mathbf{B}, \boldsymbol{\pi})$.

3.2 HMM-Based V2V-Link States Prediction

We predict the states of V2V links between User-V and Service-Vs based on the mobility information collected by RSU, i.e. the relative distance across User-V and Service-Vs. V2V links states contain main two variables, the connectivity between User-V and Service-Vs and relative distance between them.

There are many uncertain impact factors in state of connectivity except relative distance because of sophisticated network environment, such as Service-V authorization and transmission obstacle. Therefore, we apply HMM to estimate the fuzzy relationship between relative distance and connectivity according to historical mobility information, and to predict both of them in the following period, which helps amount of available resource estimation and transmission delay prediction. In the process, the residence time of User-V in the coverage area is divided into T isometric slots, and the length of each slot is T_0. The hidden states value of Service-Vs is $s_t = \{1,0\}, 0 < t \leq T$, describing whether the vehicle could communicate with User-V via V2V links in the slot t. The observable values in slot t are one of O levels of relative distance noted as $o_t \in O = \{o_1, o_2, \cdots o_O\}$, as shown in Fig. 2.

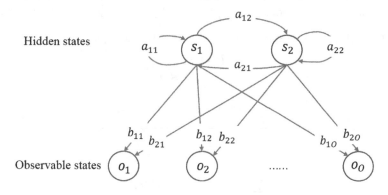

Fig. 2. Framework of the HMM with hidden states $\{s_1 = 0, s_2 = 1\}$, observable values include O levels of relative distance.

In this way, we can learn the transmission matrix $\mathbf{A}$, confusion matrix $\mathbf{B}$, initial state probability $\boldsymbol{\pi}$ from the historical relative distance information in the coverage area using Baum-Welch algorithm in HMM. Then, we can find the most possible hidden states value and observable states value of Service-Vs in every slot based on the derived HMM model parameters $\theta = (\mathbf{A}, \mathbf{B}, \boldsymbol{\pi})$ through forward algorithm. To this end, it is easy to know the transmission rate according to the sequence of relative distance (observable states) $\mathbf{O}$. Then we can choose appropriate vehicles as edge servers who can communicate with User-V via V2V links and offer abundant communication resource (high transmission rate). A solution scheme of HMM model based on the Baum-Welch algorithm and forward algorithm is represented as follows.

Baum-Welch algorithm starts from initial mode parameters, adjusting them based on the given sequence of observation to maximize probability of the sequence. Firstly, we definite Q-function $Q(\theta, \bar{\theta})$ based on the log likelihood function of HMM $\log P(\mathbf{O}, \mathbf{S}|\theta)$, where $\mathbf{O}$ is the observable states sequence, $\mathbf{S}$ denotes the hidden states sequence, and $\log P(\mathbf{O}, \mathbf{S}|\theta) = \pi_{s_1} b_{s_1}(o_1) a_{s_1 s_2} b_{s_2}(o_2) \cdots a_{s_{T-1} s_T} b_{s_T}(o_T)$.

$$Q(\theta, \bar{\theta}) = \sum_S \log P(\mathbf{O}, \mathbf{S}|\theta) P(\mathbf{O}, \mathbf{S}|\bar{\theta})$$
$$= \sum_S \log \pi_{s_1} P(\mathbf{O}, \mathbf{S}|\bar{\theta})$$
$$+ \sum_S \left(\sum_{t=1}^{T-1} \log a_{s_t s_{t+1}} \right) P(\mathbf{O}, \mathbf{S}|\bar{\theta}) \tag{4}$$
$$+ \sum_S \left(\sum_{t=1}^{T} \log b_{s_t}(o_t) \right) P(\mathbf{O}, \mathbf{S}|\bar{\theta}),$$

where $\bar{\theta}$ is current estimated mode parameters, and θ is the goal of parameters. We can obtain $\theta = (\mathbf{A}, \mathbf{B}, \boldsymbol{\pi})$ by maximizing Q-function. Specifically, we can use Lagrange multiplier subjected to $\sum_i \pi_{s_i} = 1, \sum_j a_{ij} = 1, \sum_i b_{ij} = 1$ to maximize three items [13] in (4) respectively to estimate the goal parameters:

$$\pi_{s_i} = \frac{P(\mathbf{O}, s_1 = s_i|\bar{\theta})}{P(\mathbf{O}, \mathbf{S}|\bar{\theta})}, \tag{5}$$

$$a_{ij} = \frac{\sum\limits_{t=1}^{T-1} P(\mathbf{O}, s_t = s_i, s_{t+1} = s_j|\bar{\theta})}{\sum\limits_{t=1}^{T-1} P(\mathbf{O}, s_t = s_i|\bar{\theta})}, \tag{6}$$

$$b_{ij} = \frac{\sum\limits_{t=1}^{T-1} P(\mathbf{O}, s_t = s_j|\bar{\theta}) L(o_t = o_i)}{\sum\limits_{t=1}^{T-1} P(\mathbf{O}, s_t = s_j|\bar{\theta})}. \tag{7}$$

Given the mode $\theta = (\mathbf{A}, \mathbf{B}, \boldsymbol{\pi})$, the likelihood of V2V links connectivity (hidden states) and relative distance (observable states) are calculated with forward algorithm as soon as the User-V steps into the RSU coverage. Forward likelihood means the possibility of a condition where observation sequence is $o_1, o_1, \cdots o_t$, the state value is s_i at slot t in the HMM θ, noted as

$$\alpha_t(s_i) = P(o_1, o_2, \cdots o_t, s_t = s_i|\theta). \tag{8}$$

Possibility of all the possible observation sequence during the residence time will be calculated iteratively while possibilities of hidden states are available from the hidden Markov chain. We choose the most possible hidden state $\boldsymbol{S}$ and observation sequence $\boldsymbol{O}$ as the predicted results to help target Service-Vs selection.

4   Proposed Task Parallel Offloading Scheme

Based on the results of connectivity and relative distance prediction with HMM, we can start task parallel offloading aiming to reduce service time which is defined as follows.

4.1   Service Time Model

In the procedure of task parallel offloading, the service time introduces task transmission delay, computation delay, as well as task decomposition and handover cost.

- **Transmission Delay via V2V Link**
  The task data is transmitted from User-V to the Service-Vs through the wireless V2V channel, let $H_n(o_n^t)$ describe the channel gain between the User-V and Service-V n at slot t. Given the transmission power of User-V P_{tx}, the maximum achievable transmission rate is given by:

$$r(n,t) = W \log_2 \left(1 + \frac{H_n(o_n^t)P_{\text{tx}}}{\sigma^2 + I_n} \right), \qquad (9)$$

  where W is the channel bandwidth, σ^2 is the noise power and I_n is the intra-cell interference power. Then, λ_t is the subtask size. The transmission delay for sending the subtask to selected node n is

$$d_t(n,t) = \frac{\lambda_t}{r(n,t)}. \qquad (10)$$

  In addition, result-return transmission delay, packet loss and control data transmission are not considered in this work. And the following analysis and the proposed solutions are still applicable with the consideration.
- **Computation Delay**
  In slot t, we employ computation capabilities f_t^n to describe the CPU frequency of Service-V n. If Service-V n is allocated to compute a subtask of size λ_c and computation intensity γ, given the allocated CPU frequency f_t^n, the computation delay is

$$d_c(n,t) = \frac{\lambda_c \gamma}{f_n^t}. \qquad (11)$$

  We assume there is no change on Service-Vs computation capabilities during the residence time, recorded as $f_n^t = f_n, t = 1, 2, \cdots, T$.
- **Task Decomposition Cost**
  Because task offloading can be parallelized, task has to be decomposed into several subtasks, which produces decomposition cost related with the number of target Service-Vs. Each additional new target Service-V brings extra decomposition delay c_d. We can cumulate the whole task decomposition cost by

$$C_d = c_d \sum_n z(n), \qquad (12)$$

where $z(x)$ is an indicator function with $z(x) = 1$ if event $x \in V_s$ is true and $z(x) = 0$ otherwise. c_d is a constant that expresses decomposition cost brought by every new target Service-V.

- **Handover Cost**
  If the task is not completed during the residence time, User-V leaving this coverage area switches to a different RSU. The rest of task has to offload to other vehicles via V2V links assisted by another RSU, which brings handover procedure and task migration cost

$$C_h = c_h(\lambda - \sum_{n \in V_s} \lambda_n), \tag{13}$$

where λ is the size of initial task, λ_n is the size of accomplished by Service-V n, and c_h is a constant, the handover cost per task volume.

Thus, the service time can be derived from $t_f = d_t + d_c + C_d + C_h$.

4.2 Task Parallel Offloading Scheme

Up to now, we can refine an offloading approach for task service time t_f reduction. Connectivity of V2V links between User-V and Service-Vs in every slot is obtained, recorded as

$$S_{n \times T} = \begin{bmatrix} s_{11} & s_{12} & \cdots & s_{1T} \\ s_{21} & s_{22} & \cdots & s_{2T} \\ \vdots & & & \\ s_{n1} & s_{n2} & \cdots & s_{nT} \end{bmatrix}.$$

The value of s_{ij} is 0 or 1. $s_{ij} = 1$ means Service-V i can communicate with User-V in slot j, otherwise there is no connectivity between them. Similarly, we can get the relative distance from User-V to Service-Vs $O_{n \times T}$. Thus, the transmission rate matrix according to (9), denoted as

$$r_{n \times T} = \begin{bmatrix} r_{11} & \cdots & r_{1T} \\ r_{21} & \cdots & r_{2T} \\ \vdots & & \\ r_{n1} & \cdots & r_{nT} \end{bmatrix},$$

where r_{ij} expresses the transmission rate between User-V and Service-V i in j-th slot. The available transmission resources can be derived as

$$R_{n \times T}^{tr} = S \circ r \triangleq \begin{bmatrix} s_{11} \times r_{11} & \cdots & s_{1T} \times r_{1T} \\ \vdots & & \\ s_{n1} \times r_{n1} & \cdots & s_{nT} \times r_{nT} \end{bmatrix}. \tag{14}$$

Meanwhile, Service-Vs are equipped with diversity computation capabilities those keep steady during the residence time, so we write $f_{n \times 1} = (f_1, f_2, \cdots, f_n)^T$.

Algorithm 1. HMM-based task parallel offloading algorithm

1: Baum-Welch algorithm mode initial $\theta^{(0)} = (\mathbf{A}^{(0)}, \mathbf{B}^{(0)}, \boldsymbol{\pi}^{(0)})$;

2: iteratively cumulate a_{ij}, b_{ij}, π_i, based on (5), (6) and (7);

3: up on convergency, get the goal parameters $\theta = \theta^{(n)} = (\mathbf{A}^{(n)}, \mathbf{B}^{(n)}, \boldsymbol{\pi}^{(n)})$;

4: forward algorithm value initial $\alpha_1(s_i) = \pi_i b_i(o_1)$

5: **for** each $n \in \mathcal{N}$ **do**

6:    **for** each $t \in [1, T-1]$ **do**

7:       iteratively compute $\alpha_{t+1}(s_i)$ based on (8);

8:       $P(\mathbf{O}|\theta) = \sum_i \alpha_T(s_i)$;

9:       $\boldsymbol{\pi}(t) = \boldsymbol{\pi}(0) \times \mathbf{A}^t$;

10:    **end for**

11: **end for**

12: $\mathbf{O}_{n \times T} = \arg\max_{\mathbf{O}} P(\mathbf{O}|\theta)$;

13: $\mathbf{S}_{n \times T} = \arg\max_i \boldsymbol{\pi}(t)$;

14: Compute $\mathbf{r}_{n \times T}, \mathbf{R}^{tr}_{n \times T}$ based on (9), (14) respectively;

15: **for** each $t \in [1, T]$ **do**

16:    **if** $\max_n \lambda_s(n, t) > f_u \times T_0$ **then**

17:       **for** each $n \in \mathcal{N}$ **do**

18:          **if** $\lambda_f < \lambda$ **then**

19:             compute $\lambda_s(n, t)$ based on (16);

20:             accumulate λ_f based on (17);

21:             update target node set $\mathbf{V}_s$;

22:          **else**

23:             record the time of traverse stop $T_f = t$;

24:             break;

25:          **end if**

26:       **end for**

27:    **end if**

28: **end for**

29: **if** $\lambda_f < \lambda$ **then**

30:    compute handover cost C_h based on (13);

31:    considering handover cost, service time $t_f = t + C_h$;

32: **else**

33:    service time $t_f = T_f$;

34: **end if**

35: **return** service time t_f, amount of finished-task λ_f.

In slot t, if amount of task finished by Service-Vs is less than that of local computation, it is unnecessary to offload for User-V. Considering this condition, we select offloading-slots based on the local computation capability f_u and the maximum available Service-Vs resource in specific slot. The length of one slot is fixed recorded as T_0, so for $\{(n,t)|R^{\text{tr}}(n,t) > 0\}$ we can write

$$T_0 - c_d z(n) = \frac{\lambda_s(n,t)}{R^{\text{tr}}(n,t)} + \frac{\lambda_s(n,t)\gamma}{f_n}. \tag{15}$$

To simplify the cumulation, let $\lambda_t = \lambda_c = \lambda_s$. According to (15), the amount of task finished by Service-V n in slot t can be obtained by

$$\lambda_s(n,t) = \frac{[T_0 - c_d z(n)]\, R^{\text{tr}}(n,t) f_n}{R^{\text{tr}}(n,t)\gamma + f_n}. \tag{16}$$

When we meet a new slot t, we can decide whether to offload in the slot based on $\max_n \lambda_s(n,t)$ and $f_u T_0$. If $\max_n \lambda_s(n,t) > f_u T_0$, subtasks will be offloaded to Service-Vs in this slot; if not, they will be computed by User-V.

Obviously, Eq. (16) presents that greater $R(n,t) = R^{\text{tr}}(n,t) f_n$ lead more finished task by Service-Vs. Thus, we choose target Service-Vs following the declining order list of $R(n,t)$ until T_f when task is finished or User-V leaves the RSU coverage. $R(n,t) = 0$ means that Service-V n has no chance to be picked into the target node set in slot t. So far, we can accumulate the amount of finished task λ_f and total service time t_f through traversing available resources in each slot,

$$\lambda_f = \sum_{t=1}^{T_f} \sum_{n \in V_s} \lambda_s(n,t). \tag{17}$$

If $\lambda_f < \lambda$, C_h should be taken into total service time; otherwise $C_h = 0$,

$$t_f = d_t + d_c + C_d + C_h = T_f + C_h. \tag{18}$$

For clarity, the detailed steps of HMM-based task parallel offloading algorithm (HMM-P) at the beginning of residence time are summarized as Algorithm 1.

5   Simulation Results

In this section, we evaluate the proposed task parallel offloading algorithm by comparing its performances with two algorithms, i.e., random offloading algorithm and HMM-S algorithm. In the random offloading algorithm, User-V selects a Service-V randomly in each slot to offload subtasks. In the HMM-S algorithm, User-V selects only one Service-V in each available slot based on the prediction of V2V links states according to HMM.

RSU coverage area is assumed as a circle with 200 m radius. The vehicles' trajectory are generated randomly. Wireless channel gain is modeled as

$H_n o_n^t = 127 + 30\log(o_n{}^t)$. Besides, channel bandwidth $W = 20\,\mathrm{MHz}$, noise power $\sigma^2 = 10^{-8}\,\mathrm{W}$, intra-interface $I_n \propto d_0^{-4}$ (d_0 is the average distance between vehicles and neighbouring small base station.), and transmission power $P_{\mathrm{tx}} = 200\,\mathrm{mW}$. Computation intensity is $\gamma = 3000$ (cycle/bit) and vehicles' CPU frequency are uniformly distributed $f_n \in [1,2]\,\mathrm{GHz}$. Similarly, the data size of task is $\lambda \in [0.5, 2]\mathrm{Mb}$. Moreover, we set a observable state every 40m, so there is $O = 10$.

The number of vehicles in the same RSU coverage area with User-V is referred to vehicle density n. The resident time of User-V is divided into 8 slots, written as $T = 8$, and length of each slot is $T_0 = 1$ to simplify calculation. We formulate 1000 times for average value of λ_f and t_f.

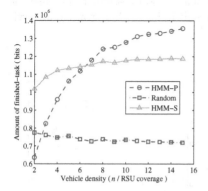

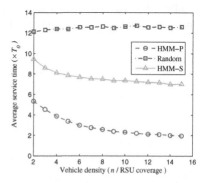

Fig. 3. The amount of finished-task in different vehicle density conditions.

Fig. 4. The service time in different vehicle density conditions.

We discuss amount of task finished by Service-Vs in different vehicle density condition, and more vehicles in the coverage means the area is more dense. Figure 3 compares the amount of task finished by HMM-P, random, and HMM-S. As can be seen, the proposed approach finishes most task than other two methods in vehicle dense area. And the amount of task finished by HMM-S is most when vehicle density is small, while the figure of random algorithm keeps the least in all conditions. The amount of task finished by HMM-P and HMM-S both increase, and the figure for HMM-P takeovers that of HMM-S at $n = 7$. Because in HMM-P there are few vehicles not constrained with inequality $\max\limits_{n} \lambda_s(n, t) > f_u T_0$, and task is most likely to be computed locally in vehicle sparse area. Meanwhile, service time of three methods in diversity conditions is analysed in Fig. 4 that shows opposite situations compared with Fig. 3. Although the service time of HMM-P and HMM-S both decrease, greater changes occur in that of HMM-P with the increase of vehicle density. Service time of random algorithm remains largest around $12T_0$, while that of HMM-P remains lowest and it is less than $6T_0$. Moreover, the data of HMM-S starts from approximately $10T_0$ and decrease to $8T_0$ at $n = 5$. The simulation results show advantages of

HMM-P in vehicle dense condition since User-V can finished more task in less service time assisted by Service-Vs.

Figure 5 shows the effect of slot granularity on amount of finished task. During the fixed residence time, the more slots, the smaller T_0 is, which means the analysis process is more fine-grained. Amount of finished task with HMM-P maintain steady at most, while that of random algorithm experience a significant increase. And the figure for HMM-S remains steady after increasing dramatically. At the same time, the effect of slot granularity on service time is discussed in Fig. 6. Service time of three schemes are in decrease, but in different degrees. That figure of HMM-P shows a modest decrease from approximately $8T_0$ between $T = 2$ and $T = 15$, while average service time for random algorithm and HMM-S decreased dramatically. We can infer the reason is more fine-grained analysis gives more chances to change Service-V and share resources which increase the possibility of ideal target node finding. This result indicates fine-grained analysis is more suitable for dynamic network.

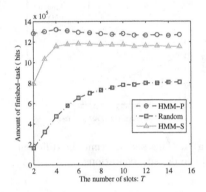
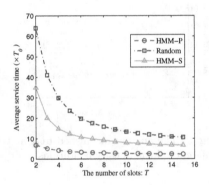

Fig. 5. The effect of slot length on amount of finished-task.

Fig. 6. The effect of slot length on service time.

6 Conclusion

In this paper, the task parallel offloading approach is proposed in vehicle fog computing system through HMM predicting V2V link states between vehicles. We consider the scenario where multi service-vehicles provide resources for User-V in parallel based on task decomposition, and refine an offloading node selection rule for minimizing the task service time. The proposed approach presents good performance on service time and finished-task amount compared with random-selection and HMM-S in vehicle dense area. Besides, the effect of model parameters on results is discussed, and it indicates appropriate value of number of slots can result in better performance.

References

1. Han, S., Xu, S., Meng, W., Li, C.: Dense-device-enabled cooperative networks for efficient and secure transmission. IEEE Netw. **32**(2), 100–106 (2018)
2. Shirazi, S.N., Gouglidis, A., Farshad, A., Hutchison, D.: The extended cloud: review and analysis of mobile edge computing and fog from a security and resilience perspective. IEEE J. Sel. Areas Commun. **35**(11), 2586–2595 (2017)
3. Peng, M., Yan, M., Zhang, K., Wang, C.: Fog-computing-based radio access networks: issues and challenges. IEEE Netw. **30**(4), 46–53 (2016)
4. Zhou, Z., Liao, H., Gu, B., Huq, K.M.S., Mumtaz, S., Rodriguez, J.: Robust mobile crowd sensing: when deep learning meets edge computing. IEEE Netw. **32**(4), 54–60 (2018)
5. Zhou, Z., Gao, C., Xu, C., Zhang, Y., Mumtaz, S., Rodriguez, J.: Social big-data-based content dissemination in Internet of vehicles. IEEE Trans. Ind. Inf. **14**(2), 768–777 (2018)
6. Zhou, Z., et al.: When mobile crowd sensing meets UAV: energy-efficient task assignment and route planning. IEEE Trans. Commun. **66**(11), 5526–5538 (2018)
7. Duan, P., Jia, Y., Liang, L., Rodriguez, J., Huq, K.M.S., Li, G.: Space-reserved cooperative caching in 5G heterogeneous networks for industrial IoT. IEEE Trans. Ind. Inform. **14**(6), 2715–2724 (2018)
8. Hou, X., Li, Y., Chen, M., Wu, D., Jin, D., Chen, S.: Vehicular fog computing: a viewpoint of vehicles as the infrastructures. IEEE Trans. Veh. Tech. **65**(6), 3860–3873 (2016)
9. Zhou, Z., Yu, H., Xu, C., Zhang, Y., Mumtaz, S., Rodriguez, J.: Dependable content distribution in D2D-based cooperative vehicular networks: a big data-integrated coalition game approach. IEEE Trans. Intell. Transp. Syst. **19**(3), 953–964 (2018)
10. Eckhoff, D., Sommer, C., German, R., Dressler, F.: Cooperative awareness at low vehicle densities: how parked cars can help see through buildings. In: Proceedings IEEE GLOBECOM, pp. 1–6, December 2011
11. Zhang, K., Mao, Y., Leng, S., He, Y., Zhang, Y.: Mobile-edge computing for vehicular networks: a promising network paradigm with predictive off-loading. IEEE Veh. Tech. Mag. **12**(2), 36–44 (2017)
12. Yang, J., Xu, Y., Chen, C.S.: Hidden Markov model approach to skill learning and its application to telerobotics. IEEE Trans. Robot. Autom. **10**(5), 621–631 (1994)
13. Qiao, S., Shen, D., Wang, X., Han, N., Zhu, W.: A self-adaptive parameter selection trajectory prediction approach via hidden Markov models. IEEE Trans. Intell. Transp. **16**(1), 284–296 (2015)

A Floor Distinction Method Based on Recurrent Neural Network in Cellular Network

Yongliang Zhang[1,3], Lin Ma[1,3(✉)], Danyang Qin[2], and Miao Yu[3]

[1] School of Electronics and Information Engineering,
Harbin Institute of Technology, Harbin, China
malin@hit.edu.cn
[2] School of Electronic Engineering, Heilongjiang University, Harbin, China
[3] Key Laboratory of Police Wireless Digital Communication,
Ministry of Public Security, Harbin, China

Abstract. Indoor localization is nowadays becoming a hot topic and research trend for future large-scale location-aware services, particularly in high-rise buildings with complex structures. However, the indoor positioning methods existing are just with high interests of two-dimensional planar information, and the crucial height information for accurate position result is awfully neglected. Furthermore, without considering the shadow effect caused by indoor constant changing impact on the terminal to be located, positioning methods cannot achieve a desirable localization accuracy for building environment. In this paper, we proposed a fast and reliable method using deep neural network for floor-level distinction and position estimation based on ubiquitous radio waves in mobile communication system. The framework composed of autoencoder to extract the effective feature vectors and recurrent neural network classifier to solve the misclassification caused by timing-discontinuity of received signal. It is shown that the accuracy of floor distinction is over 90.2% in different structural construction environments, which can provide comparable to current top-performing floor localization methods.

Keywords: Floor distinction · Autoencoder · Recurrent neural network · LTE

1 Introduction

By growing the demand for location-based services (LBS) in indoor environments, covering more detailed and multivariate information localization object is becoming the research interest at the present stage [1]. The emphasis of the solution is shifting from higher accuracy to more robust and lower costs, especially in 3D urban environment. One of the most popular and promising technology for indoor environment is fingerprint-based method, which uses received signal strengths (RSS) from installed wireless equipment to estimate users' location [2]. In general, cellular networks are usually not considered as a choice for indoor location due to its shadow attenuation and its uncontrollable environmental changes. However, with the widely covered by Long Term Evolution (LTE), this trend has been changing. The collaboration of macrocells

© ICST Institute for Computer Sciences, Social Informatics and Telecommunications Engineering 2019
Published by Springer Nature Switzerland AG 2019. All Rights Reserved
S. Han et al. (Eds.): AICON 2019, LNICST 287, pp. 380–392, 2019.
https://doi.org/10.1007/978-3-030-22971-9_33

and femtocells, which are placed in the signal blind zone, can achieve a satisfactory performance. Furthermore, LTE protocol defines specific reference signals and position protocols to support indoor location methods [3, 4].

Fingerprint-based methods usually include two steps, an offline step at which constructed databases by collecting signal parameter transmitted by APs and online step at which UEs are located by matching parameter values [5]. The fingerprint can be images, acoustic waves, visible light, radio signals, and other movement characteristics [6]. But with more and more high-rise buildings rising, the labor-intensive and time-consumed is becoming an important factor which confines the development of fingerprinting methods, especially in complex large-scale constructions. LTE system focus on combining both communication and localization capabilities, as well as location-based services. In LTE Positioning Protocol (LPP) Release 14, three main methods and some auxiliary methods are defined [3], and more attention spent on indoor positioning enhancement for the LTE standard. The large signal bandwidth in LTE enables positioning information real-time transmission for localization, and users can know where they located with not different about indoor and outdoor [7]. Theoretically, LTE coordinated networks can get a positioning accuracy about one meter ideally [8]. But propagation effects always be there, such as shadow and multipath. The deep neural network (DNN) can provide satisfactory results to classification due to its strong robustness and fault tolerance to a wide range of conditions. Positioning systems combined with DNN in various ways have been explored by researchers, especially in fields of time-varying and complex structure. Experimental results show that DNN-based positioning methods can get a state-of-art performance compared with fingerprinting methods [9]. Despite the merit, the mentioned methods are majority developed for 2D scenarios. Due to the serving devices mainly arranged in buildings, such as large shopping malls or school campus, there is a great increasing demand for the indoor location with height information.

One major challenge in LTE 3D indoor location is how to deal with the missing information caused by random fluctuation signals. In [10], a new inference system based on machine learning is proposed to estimate UEs location. The main point is the dealing method to the sparse received information and the median accuracy is 20 m for outdoor. Zhang. We proposed DNN system to generates a coarse positioning estimate and refined by a hidden Markov model [11]. [12] propose a Fingerprint-based Method Based Deep Extreme Learning Machine to extracted features for classification. Xuefeng Yin proposed a novel fingerprint-based localization technique which using physical layer parameters of cellular network to generate feature vector map and a feedforward neural network to estimate the position [13]. In [14], on the other hand, a DNN consisting of a stacked autoencoder (SAE) and a feedforward multi-class classifier is used for building/floor classification. In [15], the author investigates the possibility to use Channel State Information (CSI) extracted from LTE signals for fingerprinting localization both for indoor and outdoor. But it also ignores the difference between floors in the same building.

Considering the challenges, in this paper, we propose a new DNN architecture which combines Autoencoder (AE) to feature extraction from the noisy signal and Recurrent Neural Network (RNN) to deal with the reported data missing for complex floor environments based on LTE physical layer parameters. All parameters we used can be captured by UE's downlink signals of networks. The main contributions of our work are: (1) totally five signal parameters are considered to construct the feature matrix, especially the geo-information of base station is considered. (2) AE is utilized to reduce the feature space dimension and construct the feature matrix. And RNN is used to deal with data missing in complex buildings. (3) the localization framework we proposed considers different types of buildings, such as high-buildings and multi-buildings, mail areas and residences areas, etc.

The rest of the paper is structured as follows. In Sect. 2, we provide an overview of LTE systems and introduces relevant detail of terminologies. Section 3 presents a reliable framework for multi-floor indoor location in different scenarios. In Sect. 4, we show the results of the experiment to confirm the effects of the framework, and finally concludes our work and suggests areas of further research in Sect. 5.

2 Related Technical Background

2.1 Relevant LTE Technical Parameters

The Long Term Evolution (LTE) is an intermediate transitional mobile communication system from 3G to 4G. It inherits most of the standard from the Universal Mobile Telecommunication System (UMTS) to maintain backward compatibility. Moreover, three main methods and some auxiliary methods are defined for positioning. The fundamental cause of rapid promotion of location performance is signal bandwidth spread from 1.4 MHz to 20 MHz. And with that characteristics, we can take out physical layer parameters which cannot use for localization as location features in the 3G system. The parameters relevant for our work are list below.

Reference Signal Received Power (RSRP). It's one of the key parameters in LTE, which represents received signal strength in the wireless network. RSRP is total measured time averaged received signal power at UE from all downlink reference signals carried by a symbol. UE can receive several RSRP values from several transmitters, and it's also the main indicator of choosing the Serving Cell.

Reference Signal Received Quality (RSRQ). RSRQ refers to the quality of received reference signal. Its value ranged from −3 to −19.5, used as a criterion of Cell handover and re-choosing through ranking from largest to smallest.

Signal to Interference Plus Noise Ratio (SINR). In the LTE network, SINR means the ratio of useful received signal power and noise signal power and it also represents communication environment of the channel. Different from RSRQ, SINR puts emphasis on the decision of the size of the transmission data block, the encoding mode, and the modulation mode, etc.

E-UTRAN Cell Identifier (ECI). The ECI is a unique ID of a base station in Public Land Mobile Network (PLMN). Typically, an eNodeB represent by its ECI divided into 3 sectors with 120° to cover the whole area. And it's also the middle node to connect UE and Mobility Management Entity (MME).

Distance from eNodeB to UE (DENU). We choose the distance from UE to its connected eNodeBs as the fifth feature to detect how high the UE locates. Our hypothetical principle is that channels in cities between dense building areas and sparse building areas is two types of channel models, because the channel of high floor is less sheltered by the nearby building than that of low floor. UE in high floor spontaneously can own less shadow environment for its higher than some other architectures, such as buildings, bridges and towers, etc. As shown in Fig. 1, UE in high floor can get an almost direct signal, but UE in low floor get the signal from the same cell is weaker than high ones due to more shadows of buildings obstructing the propagation path.

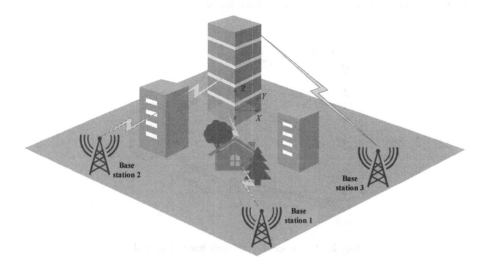

Fig. 1. Signal propagation paths of high floor and low floor.

2.2 The Principle of LTE Cell Selection

In the LTE network, during each call or accessing Internet of UE, there will be measurement data interchanges between terminals and data centers [16]. Measurement data concludes users experiments within the LTE system, and it also reflects the surrounding environments of users, such as natural factors and artificial factors. In our work, we pay more attention to the event that UE hand-off from one base station to another one. As above mentioned, UE locate on different floors have different signal propagation channels, which leads to a connected eNodeB change. Event-based eNodeB switching process is shown in Fig. 2.

The main point of handoff happens or not is when certain standards defined events occur. LTE technical specification defined several events to guide UE report of measurements. Few of our concerned events are as follows:

A1: Event A1 represent the signal quality of Serving Cell is better than the defined threshold (dBm), and it triggered at UE.
A2: Event A2 means signal quality is worse than the threshold.

A3: Event A3 is triggered when a same frequency Neighbor Cell signal quality is better than Serving Cell by certain threshold.

A4: Event A4 is triggered when a different frequency Neighbor Cell signal quality is better than Serving Cell by a certain threshold.

The events triggered mainly by UE measured data, primarily are RSRP, RSRQ and SINR. What information is record depends on UE's surrounding environment that can describe effective features. So, when an event happened in a special scenario, and ECI also can represent the scenario between UE and eNodeB. Geo-information now can get by compared measurement ECI and network parameter list from operators, and we can use the relative distances of them to another feature.

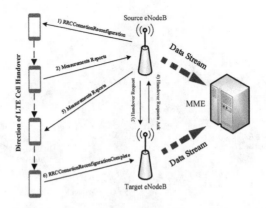

Fig. 2. The process of eNodeB handoff control

3   Proposed Floor Distinction Method

In this section, we mainly concentrate on the detail of designing the reliable neural network framework of floor detection. The framework consists of two parts: features refining and inevitable data missing.

3.1   Feature Parameter Matrix Construction

As mentioned above, we build the feature parameter matrix acquired through UE measurement report and a network parameter list. For measurement report data, we process as (1).

$$MRD_j = \begin{cases} MRD_j, & ECI_j \in \mathbf{ECI} \\ \xi, & ECI_j \notin \mathbf{ECI} \end{cases}, \quad j = 1, 2, \cdots, N \qquad (1)$$

where ξ is a pre-set value vector, and ECI is the data set of all ECIs in the network parameter list. *MRD* is the data vector about received signal quality consist of RSRP, RSRQ and SINR. It constructs it as (2).

$$\mathbf{MRD} = \{RSRP_1,\ RSRQ_1,\ SINR_1,\ \cdots,\ RSRP_n,\ RSRQ_n,\ SINR_n\} \tag{2}$$

where n is the number of being "seen" ECI. So, the ξ is a vector including three factors standing for the default value of RSRP, RSRQ and SINR, which means at the place i UE cannot "see" the eNodeB$_i$. The measurement reports also recorded the phone's longitude and latitude data coordinating along with the timestamp for matching. Under the condition of known Longitude-Latitude information of both UE and eNodeB, the distance of them can be calculated as (3).

$$
\begin{aligned}
d_{1,2}^2 = 2 \cdot [1 &- \cos(lat1 - lat2) \\
&+ \cos(lat1) \cdot \cos(lat2) - \cos(lat1) \cdot \cos(lat2) \cdot \cos(lon1 - lon2)] \\
DENU = 2R &\cdot \arcsin\left(\frac{d_{1,2}}{2}\right)
\end{aligned}
\tag{3}
$$

where the earth is seen as a sphere with radius R. $d_{1,2}$ is the linear distance between UE and base station. Finally, we can get a feature matrix with the floor number as (4).

$$
\begin{aligned}
F &= [MRD,\ ECI,\ DENU] \\
\mathbf{F} &=
\begin{bmatrix}
F_{11} & F_{12} & \cdots & F_{1N} \\
F_{21} & F_{22} & \cdots & F_{2N} \\
\vdots & \vdots & \ddots & \vdots \\
F_{M1} & F_{M2} & \cdots & F_{MN}
\end{bmatrix}
\end{aligned}
\tag{4}
$$

where N is the total number of eNodeB, M is the number of measurement data with timestamp. But it needs to note that some row values of F are null because of internal or external factors, such as different system switching or sudden shade. So, a sparse feature matrix in rows and columns is produced for the next step at last.

3.2 Feature Matrix Refinement

For achieving an accurate positioning result in a 3D indoor environment, we choose 5 parameters as the features to train the network. But some of these parameters are not independent of others, which is harmful to our training network. For one hand, the non-independent parameters input the network for training will make network complexity increase sharply. For the other hand, training the non-independent parameter matrix can reduce the effectiveness of the network. To make better use of the parameters and achieve a satisfactory floor distinction result, we introduce AE to infer the ideal feature matrix from the observation data.

The aim of an autoencoder is to learn a representation (encoding) for a set of data, typically for dimensionality reduction, by training the network to ignore signal "noise." As shown in Fig. 3, x is the input data, and y is the "recovered" data which should be as close to x as possible. $L(x, y)$ is the reconstruction error shown in (5), f_θ is transfer function from the input layer to hidden layer and g_θ is same as f_θ but from hidden layer to output layer.

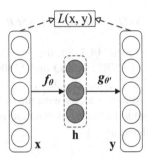

Fig. 3. Autoencoder

$$\arg\min_{\theta,\theta'} L(x,\ y) = \arg\min_{\theta,\theta'} L(x,\ g_{\theta'}(f_\theta(x))) \tag{5}$$

Autoencoder pursues training to replicate its input to its output. The encoding processing can be seen as a feature extraction for the size of the hidden layer is much smaller than the input layer in most cases. This structure forces the autoencoder to engage in dimensionality reduction and learn how to ignore noise to position accuracy.

3.3   Proposed Floor Distinction Method

The proposed localizer is an RNN network which consists of 4 layers. A recurrent neural network (RNN) is a class of artificial neural network where connections between nodes form a directed graph along a sequence. This allows it to exhibit temporal dynamic behavior for a time sequence. RNN can use their internal state (memory) to process sequences of inputs. This makes them applicable to tasks which have high linkages to the backward information and forward information. So, we use RNN to solve the floor distinction problem, as shown in Fig. 4.

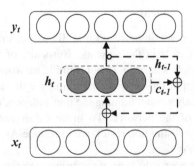

Fig. 4. Recurrent Neural Network

To better illustrate how RNN works, we unfold Figs. 4 to 5. $x^{(t)}$ is the input when the sequence index number is t. $h^{(t)}$ is the hidden state when the sequence index number is t. $o^{(t)}$ is the predicted output when the sequence index number is t. $L^{(t)}$ is the loss function. $y^{(t)}$ is the real output at when trains the sample. U, W and V are the weight matrixes which are to be optimized. We can get $h^{(t)}$ by

$$h^{(t)} = \sigma\left(z^{(t)}\right) = \sigma\left(Ux^{(t)} + Wh^{(t-1)} + b\right) \tag{6}$$

where σ is the *tanh* activation function.

$$o^{(t)} = Vh^{(t)} + c \tag{7}$$

Finally, we can get the estimated output when the sequence index number is t.

$$\hat{y}^{(t)} = \sigma'\left(o^{(t)}\right) \tag{8}$$

where σ' is the *softmax* activation function. And the loss function is defined as:

$$L = \sum_{t=1}^{\tau} L^{(t)} = \sum_{t=1}^{\tau} \left(\hat{y}^{(t)} - y(t)\right)^2 \tag{9}$$

where τ is the residence time in the network. The training phrases use back-propagation algorithm to achieve, which is same as the traditional neural network do.

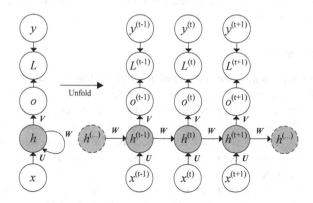

Fig. 5. The RNN unfolded by time

We put the first part of autoencoder which used for feature extraction and the second part of RNN which used for floor distinction together. In particular, the combined model is a network at least 4 layers which can depict the internal relationship between the feature matrix and UE locations. As shown in Fig. 6. Note that we can train the data of different buildings together or separated, but former lead to a rising time complexity to achieve the same accuracy.

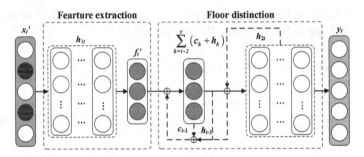

Fig. 6. The architecture of floor distinction based on AE and RNN

4   Experimental Results

In this section, we describe our experimental details and results using AE-RNN framework to confirm its validity in positioning accuracy in a 3D indoor environment. The experiments we chose are 4 different buildings including a teaching building, a shopping mall and two residential buildings. A professional network optimization software equipped with XiaoMi Note3 was recording measurement reports at every floor in all buildings. We extract 80% data randomly as the training and validation dataset, and the others as the testing dataset. We chose at least 4 points at each floor as the testing point and each point collects not less than 1000 piece of data for the consistency and completeness of dataset.

4.1   Data Processing

The original measurement report contained a lot of useless data and some useful but destroyed data should be clean out. Moreover, considering UE's maximum number of neighbor cell is six in TD-LTE network, we just kept the pieces of data containing the largest six RSRP values in the dataset and set other RSRP values ζ_{RSRP}. We set $\zeta = \{\zeta_{RSRP}, \zeta_{RSRQ}, \zeta_{SINR}\}$ is a zero vector because the concrete value of ζ does not affect the final estimation results. After handling the received signal data, we added some geo-information to the dataset. Figure 7 shows the difference of distance from UE to eNodeBs, which measured from same buildings. Although distinguishing higher floors seems harder, there is a rule in distance of UE to eNodeB.

4.2   Model Generation

To verify the performance of the proposed framework, we construct the whole network with 2 hidden layers and the first hidden layer is the feature extraction layer. The output layer of RNN is a multi-label classifier, which the number of nodes equal to one-hot-encoded floor numbers. It makes easy to process for networks to further works. Network parameters in Table 1 summarize according to experimental results or determine a range to optimization.

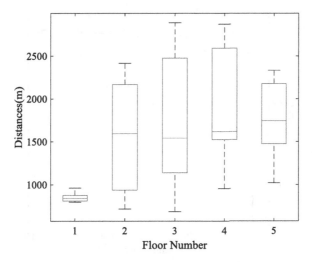

Fig. 7. Distance from UE to base stations

We pay our attention to the floor labels although the positioning accuracy can be further refined because 2D localization methods are sophisticated and perfect enough. In Table 1, the number of neurons C in feature refined layer is the high-light part for its direct influence on positioning accuracy. So, we set different values of C to find its trend for location, as shown in Fig. 8. We can note that when C = 100, the accuracy is tending towards stability, which means we can use 100 dimensions to express data of 784 dimensions in our work.

Table 1. Parameter values of the networks.

Network parameter	Value
Ratio of training data to overall data	80%
AE batch size	50
AE number pochs	784
AE feature layer size	100
RNN batch size	50
RNN number pochs	50
RNN input layer size	100
RNN output layer size	10

4.3   Floor Distinction Performance

In this section, we evaluate the floor distinction performance of our framework compared with fingerprint-based positioning method. In the fingerprint-based method, we choose KNN as the classifier and the K = 3. The training phase used random weight matrixes and bias, and we do not take the training phase in offline into account.

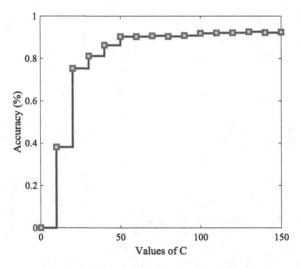

Fig. 8. The influence of value C to floor distinction accuracy

According to the results shown in Table 2, our framework can achieve the best estimation accuracy than others, the hit rate can get 91.28%, nearly 10% higher than traditional fingerprint-based positioning method. But the price is more time needed to position. The reason is RNN network needs to "remember" more information about some periods of time, more time retention in the network, more resources (time and space) consumed on it. In fact, KNN localizer aims to determine the floor position using the least time, but only for single-structured environments. When the environment become complex and unstable, such as human flow or temporary shadow, the method seems to be unreliable. As can be seen, our framework can improve the localization success rate and make the process more reliable. Also, adding extra training data can further affect the reliability of estimation considerably.

Table 2. Floor distinction success rate for different methods.

Method	Success rate (%)	Times (s)
Fingerprint-based	81.12	1.87
AE + RNN	91.28	18.39

5 Conclusions

In this article, we proposed a floor distinction framework consisted of Autoencoders and Recurrent Neural Network in complex environments. We utilize AE to reduce the feature space dimension and RNN, which is a memorable and associative network, to achieve a satisfactory floor distinction result. The proposed framework can not only extract the effective feature matrix from the measurement data which a huge impact on the size of network, but also distinct the number of floors precisely. Experimental results demonstrate that our models provide an efficient generalization performance in complex indoor environments. The framework is also addressed that it can solve the diversity of the positioning problems by modifying the network parameters in more readable manners. The framework can make an approving and reliable floor localization result in complex buildings. Furthermore, how to better use the relevance of the received data and eliminate the noise in the data forms an interesting work in future.

Acknowledgment. This paper is supported by National Natural Science Foundation of China (61571162, 61771186, 61701223); Ministry of Education-China Mobile Research Foundation (MCM20170106); Heilongjiang Province Natural Science Foundation (F2016019); University Nursing Program for Young Scholars with Creative Talents in Heilongjiang Province (UNPYSCT-2017125).

References

1. Filjar, R., Ševrović, M., Dadić, I.: Positioning and localization for Location-based services. In: 21st Telecommunications Forum Telfor (TELFOR), Belgrade, pp. 9–12 (2013)
2. Ma, L., Xu, Y.: Received signal strength recovery in green WLAN indoor positioning system using singular value thresholding. Sensors **15**(1), 1292–1311 (2015)
3. 3GPP Home Page. http://www.3GPP.org
4. del Peral-Rosado, J.A., et al.: Floor detection with indoor vertical positioning in LTE femtocell networks. In: IEEE Globecom Workshop, San Diego, pp. 1–6 (2015)
5. BASRI, C., El Khadimi, A.: Survey on indoor localization system and recent advances of WIFI fingerprinting technique. In: 5th International Conference on Multimedia Computing and Systems (ICMCS), Marrakech, pp. 253–259 (2016)
6. Vo, Q.D., De, P.: A survey of fingerprint-based outdoor localization. IEEE Commun. Surv. Tutor. **18**(1), 491–506 (2016)
7. Zekavat, R., Michael Buehrer, R.: Positioning in LTE. In: Handbook of Position Location: Theory, Practice and Advances, vol. 1, Wiley-IEEE Press (2012). Chapter 32
8. del Peral-Rosado, J.A., López-Salcedo, J.A., Zanier, F., Crisci, M.: Achievable localization accuracy of the positioning reference signal of 3GPP LTE. In: International Conference on Localization and GNSS, Starnberg, pp. 1–6 (2012)
9. Kim, K.S., Lee, S., Huang, K.: A scalable deep neural network architecture for multi-building and multi-floor indoor localization based on Wi-Fi fingerprinting. Big Data Analytics **3**(1), 4 (2018)
10. Ray, A., Deb, S., Monogioudis, P.: Localization of LTE measurement records with missing information. In: The 35th Annual IEEE International Conference on Computer Communications, IEEE INFOCOM 2016, San Francisco, pp. 1–9 (2016)
11. Zhang, W., Liu, K., Zhang, W., Zhang, Y., Gu, J.: Deep neural networks for wireless localization in indoor and outdoor environments. Neurocomputing **194**, 279–287 (2016)
12. Khatab, Z.E., Hajihoseini, A., Ghorashi, S.A.: A fingerprint method for indoor localization using autoencoder based deep extreme learning machine. IEEE Sens. Lett. **2**(1), 1–4 (2018)
13. Ye, X., Yin, X., Cai, X., Pérez Yuste, A., Xu, H.: Neural-network-assisted UE localization using radio-channel fingerprints in LTE networks. IEEE Access **5**, 12071–12087 (2017)
14. Nowicki, M., Wietrzykowski, J.: Low-effort place recognition with WiFi fingerprints using deep learning. In: Szewczyk, R., Zieliński, C., Kaliczyńska, M. (eds.) ICA 2017. AISC, vol. 550, pp. 575–584. Springer, Cham (2017). https://doi.org/10.1007/978-3-319-54042-9_57

15. Pecoraro, G., Di Domenico, S., Cianca, E., De Sanctis, M.: LTE signal fingerprinting localization based on CSI. In: IEEE 13th International Conference on Wireless and Mobile Computing, Networking and Communication, Rome, pp. 1–8 (2017)
16. Sesia, S., Toufik, I., Baker, M.: LTE, The UMTS Long Term Evolution: From Theory to Practice. Wiley (2009)

A Multi-classifier Approach for Fuzzy KNN Based WIFI Indoor Localization

Yuanfeng Du[1,2,3(✉)] and Dongkai Yang[1,2,3]

[1] Beihang University, Beijing, China
yfdu1989@163.com
[2] Shandong Orientation Electronic Technology Co. Ltd., Jinan, China
[3] Postdoctoral Workstation of Jining Hi-Tech Industry Development Zone,
Jining, China

Abstract. WIFI fingerprint positioning technology has been widely studied and developed for a long time and lots of experiment systems have been established. However, the time-varying and nonlinear features of the WIFI signal impede the development in the application level. The performance of existing positioning systems could be very unstable due to the signal varying. Our object is to combine the fuzzy technology and multi-classifier approach to improve the system accuracy and robustness. The proposed method adopts the fuzzy integral to fusion the results obtained from different fuzzy K-nearest neighbor (KNN) classifiers generated by adaBoost. Experiment results demonstrate that our approach improves the average positioning errors and their standard deviations by 21% and 26% separately compared to the traditional KNN algorithm.

Keywords: WIFI fingerprint · Fuzzy · Multi-classifier · AdaBoost

1 Introduction

As the development of information technology, the location based service (LBS) has become more and more important for people's daily lives. The positioning technology based on global navigation satellite system (GNSS) has achieved a great success in outdoor scenarios. However, the complicated environment and the multipath effect cause great difficulties in indoor positioning. Now the research in WIFI fingerprint positioning technology is very popular to promote the development of indoor applications.

Precedent works have considered many algorithms to deal with the WIFI signal fluctuation, such as the widely used KNN, Bayesian [1]. However, how to describe the signal distribution in the area and combat the interference effectively are still big problems. The deep learning algorithm is used in [2] to obtain better accuracy, with higher cost.

Some researchers tried to solve the problem by using the fuzzy technology, which has a strong non-linear characteristic and an anti-interference ability. An effective calculation of Euclidean distance is undertaken by means of fuzzy logic methods. The systems comprising a better understanding of the fuzzy inference technology could provide an improvement of accuracy [3]. Another solution proposed is the use of fuzzy

© ICST Institute for Computer Sciences, Social Informatics and Telecommunications Engineering 2019
Published by Springer Nature Switzerland AG 2019. All Rights Reserved
S. Han et al. (Eds.): AICON 2019, LNICST 287, pp. 393–401, 2019.
https://doi.org/10.1007/978-3-030-22971-9_34

rule-based classification, which divides the RSSI into three linguistic terms, low, medium and high [4–7]. Though the above mentioned fuzzy approaches have made some progresses, they only adopt fuzzy logic without applying detailed fuzzy measurement. On the other hand, some basic multi-classifier technologies, such as bagging [8] and Bayesian fusion [9], are adopted by some studies to improve the positioning system robustness, which provide good research directions.

In this paper, our object is to combine the fuzzy technology and multi-classifier approaches to improve the system accuracy and robustness. We adopt the improved fuzzy KNN algorithm as the basic classifier, which establishes fingerprint database with the average value, the upper quartile, the median and lower quartile of the signal sequence in each grid. Then, the adaBoost algorithm is proposed to obtain sub-classifiers. At last, positioning result is obtained by the fuzzy integral fusion approach. The traditional AP selection and K-means clustering method are also adopted to reduce the computational complexity.

The following parts of this paper are organized as follows: Sect. 2 presents the fuzzy KNN based fingerprint algorithm. Section 3 delineates our proposed system architecture, including the adaBoost algorithm and fuzzy integral fusion approach. Experiment procedures and simulation results in Sect. 4 demonstrates the efficiency of our approach. This is followed by the conclusion in Sect. 5.

2 Fuzzy KNN Based Fingerprinting Algorithm

The widely used KNN algorithm is very practical, and just the average value of the received signal strength (RSS) vector namely S needs to be computed. In the online stage, the real-time RSS vector M is compared with S through Euclidean distance to find the k nearest neighbor nodes. The final positioning result can be obtained as following. l_i is the location of the ith nearest node and l is the positioning result.

$$l = \frac{1}{k} \sum_{i}^{k} l_i \tag{1}$$

Some improved algorithms such as the weighted KNN have been proposed, but there is always only the average feature of each grid for comparison. In this paper, the Fuzzy KNN algorithm is proposed to provide several typical features for comparison. What's more, instead of the absolute weights based on the distances, the relative fuzzy membership degree for each grid is obtained.

During the offline phase, m samples are collected in c grids and the RSS sequence is $R = (R_1, R_2, \ldots, R_c)$, $c = 1, 2, 3 \ldots, L$. L is the number of grids. In grid i, the average value q_{i1}, the upper quartile q_{i2}, the median q_{i3} and lower quartile q_{i4} of the signal sequence $(R_i : R_{i1}, R_{i2}, \ldots, R_{im})$ are calculated and stored as the offline fingerprint database.

Assume the RSS vector R_i expands from small to large, the value of $(q_{i1}, q_{i2}, q_{i3}, q_{i3})$ changes as following.

$$\left(\frac{1}{m} \sum_{j=1}^{m} R_{i,j}, \ R_{i,\left[\frac{(m+1)}{4}\right]}, \ R_{i,\left[\frac{2(m+1)}{4}\right]}, \ R_{i,\left[\frac{3(m+1)}{4}\right]} \right) \tag{2}$$

Where [ ] is the bracket function.

During the online phase, the similarity degree sequence $(t_{i1}, t_{i2}, t_{i3}, \ldots, t_{ic})$ $i = 1, 2, 3, 4$ sorted by average value, upper quartile, the median and the lower quartile are calculated based on Euclidean distance separately. Then, the final membership degree for each grid $D = (\mu_1, \mu_2, \ldots, \mu_c)$ can be obtained as follows. The gird with the largest membership degree will be considered as the positioning results.

$$\mu_j = \sum_{i=1}^{4} \sum_{s=1}^{c} T_{sj}^i \qquad j = 1, 2, 3, \ldots, c$$

$$T_{sj}^i = \begin{cases} \dfrac{1}{K}(K - s + 1) & if \ t_{is} = j \\ \sum_{q=1}^{q} & \\ 0 & else \end{cases} \tag{3}$$

T_{sj}^i is the member of the jth grid of the ith element. K is an adjustable parameter, which means that K grids are chosen in each similarity degree sequence.

3 System Architecture

Based on the basic fuzzy KNN fingerprinting algorithm, the detailed system architecture is shown in Fig. 1. After collecting the fingerprint database, K-means clustering and AP selection are performed, both of which have been proven to be effective in previous papers. As this paper mainly discusses the fingerprint matching approaches, the simple and traditional K-means clustering and maximum selection methods are adopted to make the positioning system executable.

For each cluster, several Fuzzy KNN classifiers are trained based on AdaBoost algorithm. Then, the confusion matrix of each KNN classifier can be obtained by cross validation. After the classifier subset is selected according to our selection criteria, fuzzy measure is trained and stored.

During the online phase, a smoothing filter is adopted to reducing the signal fluctuation. After the cluster ID is decided, the corresponding sub KNN fuzzy classifiers are used to calculate the membership degree of each grid. At last, the positioning result is obtained by fuzzy Integral Fusion.

3.1 AdaBoost Algorithm for Positioning

AdaBoost algorithm trains the same type of basic classifiers based on different training set and combines them together to constitute a stronger classifier, which is the final strong classifier [10]. According to the theoretical proof, as long as each basic classifier's performance is better than random guessing, the error rate of the fusion

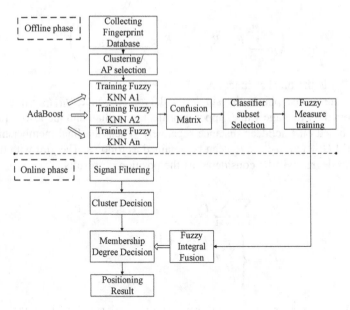

Fig. 1. Detailed system architecture

classifier would tend to zero. And our WIFI positioning classifiers proposed satisfy the assumption. The pseudo code of our method is presented in Fig. 2.

Input: Fingerprint database $R = (R_1, R_2, ..., R_c)\ c = 1, 2, ..., L$

     The expected classifier number t_{max}

     The initial weight of each fingerprint $W_1(i) = 1/(m \times L)$,

     $i = 1, 2, ..., m \times L$

1. $t \leftarrow 0$

2. do $t \leftarrow t + 1$

3. Training the Fuzzy knn C_t based on R and $W_t(i)$

4. Calculate the confusion matrix $M^{(t)}$ of C_t

5. $E_t \leftarrow$ calculate the training error of c_t based on $M^{(t)}$

6. The weight update coefficient $a_t \leftarrow \dfrac{1}{2}\ln[(1-E_t)/E_t]$

7. $W_{t+1}(i) \leftarrow \dfrac{W_t(i)}{Z_t} \times \begin{cases} e^{-a_t}\ \text{if the positioning error} \leq 3m \\ e^{a_t}\ \text{if the positioning error} > 3m \end{cases}$

    Z_t is the normalization coefficient

8. until $t = t_{max}$

Output : C_t and $M^{(t)}$ $k = 1, ..., t_{max}$

Fig. 2. AdaBoost algorithm for positioning

During the loop, the fuzzy KNN should be trained based on R and $W_t(i)$. Firstly, the vector R_i is sorted from small to large according to the RSS value. Then, the average value $q_{i1}^{(t)}$ is calculated.

$$q_{i1}^{(t)} = \sum_{j=1}^{m} R_{i,j} \times W_t(j) \tag{4}$$

Consequently, the offline database of each sub fuzzy KNN is $(q_{i1}^{(t)}, R_{i,r_{0.25}}, R_{i,r_{0.5}}, R_{i,r_{0.75}})$ with r_φ calculated as followed.

$$r_\varphi = P\left(r \mid \sum_{i=1}^{r-1} W_t(i) < \varphi \, \&\&r \mid \sum_{i=1}^{r} W_t(i) > \varphi\right) \tag{5}$$

$$\varphi = 0.25, \, 0.5, \, 0.75$$

The confusion matrix in step 4 is constructed by the cross-validation of the fingerprint database. As there are L grids in the positioning system, the $M^{(t)}$ will be a $L * L$ matrix in which the entry $M_{i,j}^{(t)}$ presents the number of the instances collected in location l_i and assigned to location l_j by the fuzzy KNN classifier.

To meet the target of reducing the positioning error as much as possible, we adjust the fingerprint weight according to whether the error is greater than 3 meters or not.

3.2 Classifier Subset Selection

As proposed in [11], the improvement of multi-classifier approach depends largely on the characteristic that each classifier does not get involved in the same mistake in decision making. Therefore, it is essential to make the correlation of the sub classifiers smaller during the subset selection to provide better improvement of fusion classifier.

In this paper, the generalized diversity (GD) is adopted as the selection criteria [12]. The classifier subset with the largest GD value will be chosen.

$$GD = 1 - \frac{p(2)}{p(1)} \tag{6}$$

$$p(1) = \sum_{t=1}^{T} \frac{t}{T} p_t \quad p(2) = \sum_{t=1}^{T} \frac{t}{T} \frac{t-1}{T-1} p_t \tag{7}$$

$$p_t = \frac{\sum_{i=2}^{L-1} \sum_{j=i-1}^{i+1} M_{i,j}^{(t)}}{\sum_{i=2}^{L-1} \sum_{j=i}^{L} M_{i,j}^{(t)}} \tag{8}$$

p_t is the probability of the tth sub classifier which has the positioning result with error larger than 3 m. T is the number of the selected classifier subsets from t_{max}.

3.3   Fuzzy Measure Training and Integral Fusion

As the decision error distribution of each classifier changes as grids vary, we calculate the fuzzy measure for each grid $g_\lambda^{(i)}$ based on the confusion matrix $M^{(t)}$.

$$g_i^j = \frac{M_{ii}^j}{\sum\limits_{k=1}^{L} M_{ki}^j} \tag{9}$$

$$\lambda_i + 1 = \prod_{j=1}^{L} (1 + \lambda_i g_i^j) \tag{10}$$

Where g_i^j stands for the fuzzy measurement of C_j in grid l_i. Then, λ_i which is the parameter of $g_\lambda^{(i)}$ can be obtained. $Cl^{(j)}$ stands for the jth sub classifier. Consequently, $g_\lambda^{(i)}$ can be obtained and the fuzzy measure training process is completed.

$$g_\lambda^{(i)}(A_j) = g_i^j + g_\lambda^{(i)}(A_{j-1}) + \lambda_i g_i^j g_\lambda^{(j)}(A_{j-1})$$
$$A_j = \{Cl^{(1)}, Cl^{(2)}, \dots, Cl^{(j)}\} \tag{11}$$

For the integral fusion process, the membership degrees $(\mu_i^{(1)}, \mu_i^{(2)}, \dots, \mu_i^{(T)})$ are decided by each fuzzy KNN in the online phase as demonstrated in Sect. 2. And the positioning result can be obtained based on the Choquet fuzzy integral fusion. $(c) \int$ stands for the Choquet integral value of each grid [13]. Therefore, the grid with the largest integral value will be considered as the positioning result.

$$(c) \int f(x)dg = \sum_{i=1}^{n} f(x)[g(A_i) - g(A_{i+1})] \, f(x_1) \leq f(x_2) \leq \dots \leq f(x_n) \tag{12}$$

$$Result = \arg \max_{i=1}^{L}(c) \int (\mu_i^{(1)}, \mu_i^{(2)}, \dots, \mu_i^{(T)})dg_\lambda^{(i)} \tag{13}$$

4   Experiment and Simulation Results

To evaluate the performance of our proposed method, an experiment is carried out on the 5th floor of LaiFuShi piazza in Shanghai with a surface of approximately 80 m by 50 m (see Fig. 3). There are more than 300 IEEE 802.11 WLAN APs in this scenario. During the experiment, we have collected 80 samples of fingerprints from 79 different locations (see dark squares in Fig. 3, respectively), of which 60 samples are used for training and the rest 20 are for testing. Each location is almost 3 m away from each other and MI 2A is used as the mobile terminal, with Android 4.1.1 system.

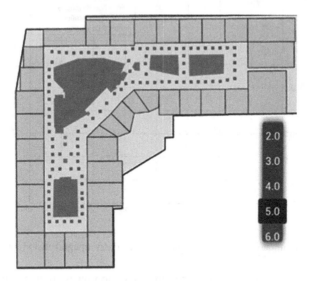

Fig. 3. Experiment scenario

Considering the compromise between system complexity and positioning performance, we adopt the number of selected sub classifier $T = 3$. The results in Table 1 show that only 4.76% of the test points have all the errors of classifiers larger than 3 m. The good diversity of the three classifiers implies high fusion performance.

Table 1. Diversity of the sub fuzzy KNN

Number of sub classifiers with error > 3 m	Zero	One	Two	Three
Number of points	1327	149	104	79
Percentage/%	79.99	8.98	6.27	4.76

The positioning accuracy is compared between the sub fuzzy KNN classifier and the proposed fuzzy integral fusion classifier in the experiment. As shown in Fig. 4, the percentage of test points without error improves from 59.9% to 64.2% and the largest error reduced from 40 m to 32 m, which proves the enhancement of the proposed fusion classifier over all the three sub fuzzy KNN classifiers.

We present some popular positioning matching algorithms for comparison, such as the traditional KNN method, Gauss Bayesian probability algorithm and Kernel-based algorithm. Furthermore, the Voting and Bayesian fusion methods are also evaluated.

As the test and training points are collected in the same locations, many positioning errors are zero and the average error of all the positioning methods are less than 3 m. The evaluation results shown in Table 2 reveal that all the fusion methods, including

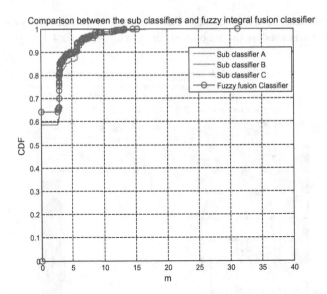

Fig. 4. Comparison of the sub classifier and fuzzy integral fusion classifier

the Voting, Bayesian Fusion and the proposed approach, outperforms the single classifier in terms of the average error distances and their standard deviations. Furthermore, the proposed fuzzy integral fusion approach obtains additional performance improvement.

Table 2. Summary positioning result (meter)

Positioning method	Average error	Standard deviation	90% error
Traditional KNN	1.9725	3.421	6.2
Gauss	2.5083	4.615	6.7
Kernel	1.9222	3.353	5.8
Voting	1.7028	2.81	5.8
Bayesian fusion	1.6809	2.794	5.0
Proposed approach	1.5591	2.598	4.8

5   Conclusion

In this paper, we have proposed a novel multi-classifier approach for fuzzy KNN based WIFI indoor location system. We introduce a new fuzzy KNN classifier based on membership degree. Subsequently, we propose the AdaBoost algorithm together with fuzzy integrate fusion approach in the field of indoor positioning. Practical experiment shows good diversity of selected sub classifiers and the effectiveness of fusion classifier approaches. The proposed approach improves the average positioning errors and their standard deviations by 21% and 26% respectively compared to the traditional KNN algorithm.

References

1. Liu, H., Darabi, H., Banerjee, P., Liu, J.: Survey of wireless indoor positioning techniques and systems. IEEE Trans. Syst. Man Cybern. Part C Appl. Rev. **37**(6), 1067–1080 (2007)
2. Shao, W., Luo, H., Zhao, F., Ma, Y., Zhao, Z., Crivello, A.: Indoor positioning based on fingerprint-image and deep learning. Access IEEE **6**, 74699–74712 (2018)
3. Teuber, A., Eissfeller, B.: WLAN indoor positioning based on Euclidean distances and fuzzy logic. In: Proceedings of the 3rd Workshop on Positioning, Navigation and Communication, Munich, pp. 159–168 (2006)
4. Garcia-Valverde, T., Garcia-Sola, A., Hagras, H.: An adaptive learning fuzzy logic system for indoor localization using Wi-Fi in ambient intelligence environment. In: IEEE World Congress on Computational Intelligence, pp. 25–32 (2012)
5. Li, Y., Liu, X.: Fuzzy logic and neural network based indoor fingerprint positioning algorithms in wifi. Int. J. Comput. Intell. Appl. **13**, 2282–2290 (2014)
6. Alonso, J.M., Ocaña, M., Sotelo, M.A., Bergasa, L.M., Magdalena, L.: WiFi localization system using fuzzy rule-based classification. In: Moreno-Díaz, R., Pichler, F., Quesada-Arencibia, A. (eds.) EUROCAST 2009. LNCS, vol. 5717, pp. 383–390. Springer, Heidelberg (2009). https://doi.org/10.1007/978-3-642-04772-5_50
7. Torteeka, P., Chundi, X.: Indoor positioning based on Wi-Fi fingerprint technique using fuzzy k-nearest neighbor. In: 11th International Bhurban Conference on Applied Sciences & Technology, pp. 461–465 (2014)
8. Trawinski, K., Alonso, J.M., Hernandez, N.: A multiclassifier approach for topology-based WiFi indoor localization. Soft Comput. **17**, 1817–1831 (2013)
9. Shin, J., Jung, S.H., Yoon, G., et al.: Electrical Engineering and Applied Computing, pp. 135–147. Springer, Dordrecht (2011). https://doi.org/10.1007/978-94-007-1192-1
10. Riccardi, A., Fernandez-Navarro, F., Carloni, S.: Cost-sensitive AdaBoost algorithm for ordinal regression based on extreme learning machine. IEEE Trans. Cybern. **44**, 1898–1909 (2014)
11. Kuncheve, L.I.: Combining pattern classifiers: methods and algorithms. Technometrics **47**, 517–518 (2005)
12. Partidge, D.: Network generalization differences quantified. Neural Netw. **9**, 263–271 (1996)
13. Yang, R., Wang, Z.Y., Heng, P.A., et al.: Fuzzy numbers and fuzzification of the Choquet integral. Fuzzy Sets Syst. **153**, 95–113 (2005)

Research on Application and Development of Key Technologies of Dynamic Wireless Charging System in New Intelligent Transportation System

Lina Ma[1]([⊠]), Shi An[1], and Wanlong Zhao[2]

[1] School of Management, Harbin Institute of Technology,
Harbin 150001, Heilongjiang, China
13b910003@hit.edu.cn
[2] College of Underwater Acoustic Engineering, Harbin Engineering University,
Harbin 150001, Heilongjiang, China

Abstract. With the development of electronic science and technology, Intelligent Transportation has entered a new stage. In recent years, IOT (Internet of Things) technology has brought many impacts on people's daily life and social development. IOV (Internet of Vehicle) technology is an important application of IOT technology in Intelligent Transportation System. The rapid development of IOV technology provides a guarantee for Intelligent Transportation. Therefore, accelerating the landing of IOV has a profound impact on the development of new Intelligent Transportation. Dynamic wireless charging technology has become one of the five cutting-edge technologies to accelerate the landing of IOV. Firstly, the article introduces the new Intelligent Transportation System and its key technology. Then the article analyzes the advantages of wireless charging and the composition of wireless energy transmission system. Finally, the article introduces the composition of the dynamic wireless charging system on electric vehicles, the application and development of dynamic wireless charging key technology in new Intelligent Transportation.

Keywords: Intelligent Transportation · Internet of Vehicle ·
Wireless charging · Wireless energy transmission · Electric vehicle

1 Introduction

In recent years, China's economy has risen rapidly, and people's material living standard has improved sharply, automobiles have become the most common vehicles. However, many problems has followed. Such as traffic safety, traffic congestion and transportation efficiency. All of them have tested the ability of city managers. In this context, the role of Intelligent Transportation Systems is particularly important. With the advancement of modern science and technology, new Intelligent Transportation System has seen some initial achievements. The Internet of Things technology has brought many impacts on people's daily life and social development. The Internet of Vehicles technology is an important application of Internet of Things technology in

© ICST Institute for Computer Sciences, Social Informatics and Telecommunications Engineering 2019
Published by Springer Nature Switzerland AG 2019. All Rights Reserved
S. Han et al. (Eds.): AICON 2019, LNICST 287, pp. 402–413, 2019.
https://doi.org/10.1007/978-3-030-22971-9_35

Intelligent Transportation systems. The gradual replacement of traditional energy sources by new energy sources is an important trend in the future. The advantages of electric vehicles are becoming more and more prominent. Therefore, electric vehicles have become an important direction for the development of the automobile industry. However, the inconvenience of charging hinders the development and popularization of electric vehicles seriously. Conventional charging devices have disadvantages, such as poor operability, low safety, and large floor space, which largely limit the large-scale promotion of electric vehicles. In contrast, wireless charging technology can solve the interface limitation problem and security problem faced by traditional conductive charging. Wireless charging technology gradually becomes the main charging way of electric vehicles. However, static wireless charging and wired charging both have the problems of frequent charging and short range. Continuous endurance is very important for public transportation vehicles such as electric buses. In this context, the dynamic wireless charging technology of electric vehicles emerges as the times require, it provides real-time energy supply for the running electric vehicles through non-contact way. Dynamic wireless charging technology has become one of the five cutting-edge technologies to accelerate the landing of IOV. The key technology of dynamic wireless charging has strong research value and broad application prospects in the new Intelligent Transportation.

2 New Generation of Intelligent Transportation and Key Technologies

Intelligent Transportation System, also called Intelligent Transportation System, integrates information technology, data communication technology, electronic control technology and computer technology into the transportation system. It strengthens the relationship among vehicles, roads and person, and it promotes safe and efficient integrated transport system. The Intelligent Transportation system meets the growing demand for public travel and material transportation by creating a transportation system that is fair, efficient, safe, convenient and environmental.

Intelligent Transportation is the hotspot and frontier of the world's transportation development. And Intelligent Transportation is the development direction of the future transportation system. With the continuous innovation of electronic information technology, Intelligent Transportation will enter a new stage. The new Intelligent Transportation effectively integrates IOT, big data, cloud computing, artificial intelligence, sensors, data communication, electronic control, operations research, and automatic control technology into transportation management system. It could strengthen the connection among vehicles, roads and users. Thus it forms an Integrated Transportation System that guarantees safety, upgrades efficiency, improves environment, and saves energy. It establishes all-round function, a real-time, accurate and efficient integrated transportation management system [1].

The new Intelligent Transportation needs to be able to support integrated transportation; it needs the new generation of intelligent infrastructure, including traffic sensor networks, new generation communication systems, new energy distribution systems for extended roads, and many other technical facilities; it needs low-carbon and smart transportation tools; it needs services and management systems that require openness, sharing and coordination; it needs intelligent decision systems based on big data. Therefore, the overall framework of new Intelligent Transportation will take three systems (Intelligent Transportation Service System, Intelligent Transportation Management System and Intelligent Decision Support System), two support technology (Intelligent Transportation Infrastructure, Standards and Technology), and one environment standard (loose and ordered development environment) as the main content of development. Meanwhile new Intelligent Transportation covers the field of urban transportation, roads, railways, aviation, and water transportation. The overall framework of new Intelligent Transportation not only makes arrangements for the development and application of Intelligent Transportation systems, but also promotes the development of Intelligent Transportation advanced technologies and support of emerging strategic industries. Such as new national traffic control networks, cooperative vehicle infrastructure, intelligent vehicle, automatic train operation, integrated hub coordination, high-speed broadband wireless interconnection and high-speed wireless LAN (Local area network). At present, new technologies such as cloud computing, big data, and mobile internet are widely used in the fields of cooperative vehicle infrastructure systems, public travel convenience services, IOT, IOV, driverless, and electric vehicles. The electrification, intelligence and networking of vehicles have become the technological trend of the next Intelligent Transportation System [2, 3].

Besides the Internet and the Internet of Things, Internet of Vehicles becomes another important symbol of the future smart city. Internet of Vehicle is based on the intra-vehicle network, inter-vehicle network and vehicle mobile Internet. According to the agreed communication protocol and data interaction standard, it is a large system network for wireless communication and information exchange between vehicles and X (X: vehicles, roads, pedestrians and the Internet, etc.). It is an integrated network that can achieve intelligent traffic management, intelligent dynamic information service and vehicle intelligent control. It is a typical application of Internet of Things technology in the field of transportation. Internet of Vehicle can realize information sharing and collect information about vehicles, roads and environment through interconnection of vehicle and vehicle, vehicle and people, vehicle and road interconnection. Then it can process, calculate, share and publish collected multi-source data on the information network platform. In addition it can release effective guidance and supervision of vehicles according to different functional requirements, and provide application services of professional multimedia and mobile Internet. Internet of Vehicle technology provides a powerful guarantee for Intelligent Transportation. Accelerating the landing of Internet of Vehicle is significant for accelerating the development of Intelligent Transportation [4]. Five cutting-edge technologies for accelerating Internet of Vehicle include WIFI connection, smart bluetooth, NFC (Near Field Communication), wireless charging, and ethernet security. Driverless technology, wireless charging technology, and intelligent parking technology have been called "Iron riangle" of the future Intelligent Transportation. In a broader perspective, driverless technology is still one of the core components of Intelligent Transportation in the future. The real landing of unmanned driving still requires the support of two other core technologies to jointly construct a complete Intelligent Transportation Ecosystem. One is smart parking technology and the other is wireless charging technology.

3 Electric Car Dynamic Wireless Charging Technology

3.1 Advantages of Wireless Charging Technology

At present, there are two main charging methods for electric vehicles. One is wired charging, which is also called contact charging. Wired charging includes fast charging mode and slow charging mode. The other is wireless charging, which is also called non-contact charging. In the new Intelligent Transportation, wireless charging technology has obvious advantages over wired charging technology.

A comparison of the three charging techniques is shown in Table 1 below. From the Table 1, whether applied to smart devices or other fields, wireless charging technology has obvious advantages over wireless charging technology, which is the main direction of future development (See Table 1).

Table 1. A comparison of the three charging techniques.

Charging mode	Principle	Advantage	Disadvantage
Wired slow charge [5]	The wired slow charging mode generally uses a single-phase 220 V/16 A AC (Alternating Current) power supply. It uses a small AC current to charge a small power for a long time by the charger. Charging time is generally 6 h to 10 h	1. It could reduce cost of charging 2. It could improve charging efficiency 3. It could extend service the life of batteries	1. It is difficult to meet the user's demands of emergency charging and long-distance driving 2. Charging time is long
Wired fast charge [6–8]	The wired fast charging mode generally uses direct current mode with a large current of 150 A to 400 A. Charging time is about 20 min to 2 h	1. It can meet the user's demands of long-time and long-distance driving 2. Charging time is short	1. The high current charging has a negative impact on performance and life of batteries 2. It has a certain impact on the power grid
Wireless charging [9, 10]	The wireless charging is no need the cables to energy transfer. In the wireless charging mode, it need install a vehicle inductive charger on the car	1. It does not need the cables. It uses Conveniently and safely 2. It is conducive to the uniformity of multiple interface standards 3. It could adapt to a variety of harsh environments and weather	1. Equipment charges and maintenance charges are higher 2. Energy loss is relative high. The efficiency of wireless charging needs to be improved

3.2 Dynamic Wireless Charging Technology

Wireless charging technology is derived from radio power transmission technology which is also called wireless energy transmission or radio energy transmission. Wireless energy transfer technology is a new energy transfer technology that can be used to take power from a fixed grid in a non-contact manner with electrical equipment. The wireless energy transfer system is mainly composed of an energy emitting part and an energy receiving part. The transmitting part comprises a grid power supply, a rectifying circuit, a high frequency inverter circuit and a transmitting coil. The receiving part includes a receiving coil, a high frequency rectifying circuit, a load and so on [11]. The Fig. 1 shows a structural topology diagram of wireless energy transfer system (See Fig. 1).

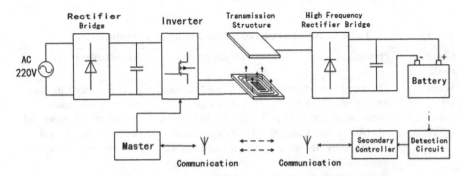

Fig. 1. Structure topology of wireless energy transmission system.

Wireless energy transmission system usually includes inductive energy transmission system and magnetically coupled resonant energy transmission system. The magnetically coupled resonant wireless energy transmission technology uses magnetic near-field coupled resonance mechanism with a wide operating frequency. At the same time, it has a large quality factor Q. Compared with the inductive type, the magnetic coupling type has a longer transmission distance, damage of magnetic coupling type is smaller, so magnetic coupling type is more suitable for dynamic wireless charging of electric vehicles [12]. In the electric vehicle wireless charging system, the most important is the design of the coil coupling structure, which affects the efficiency of the system, anti-offset capability and so on. In the design of the coupling mechanism, high permeability materials are often required to increase the coupling coefficient. Because of the cost, the current scheme mostly uses skeleton-type magnetic cores, including the thin U-shaped, I-type, monorail-type and double-track type of KAIST (Korea Advanced Institute of Science and Technology) of Korea, and the skeleton disc shape of the American Oak Ridge National Laboratory. The structural design of the magnetic core is closely related to the coupling parameter adaptability, magnetic shielding performance, and system cost. In terms of wireless energy transmission system communication problems, Oak Ridge National Laboratory of the United States advocates adopting Internet of vehicle protocol DSRC (Dedicated Short Range Communications) that meets the requirements of US Department of Transportation, and solves the problem of transmitter/receiver offset in wireless charging by communication closed loop.

The important application of wireless charging technology in the field of Intelligent Transportation is mainly to charge electric vehicles. The traditional charging mode limits the development of electric vehicles. Wireless charging technology overcomes the shortcomings of traditional charging technology. The charging device can be installed in a parking space underground or on a wall. No exposed interfaces also prevents the risk of electric shock. Moreover, there is no safety requirement for the plug-in interface, and there are no problems such as mechanical loss or contact loss, which makes the manufacture and maintenance of the charger simpler and cost significantly reduced. But even with wireless charging technology, electric vehicles still have problems such as low battery energy density, short cruising distance, high cost, heavy equipment, and frequent charging. In this context, wireless charging emerges as the times require. The battery is charged in a non-contact way during driving, and the electric energy is supplied in real time. The electric vehicle can be equipped with a fewer batteries, effectively improving the convenience of electric energy supply, and significantly increasing the durability of the electric vehicle [13].

Dynamic charging, that is, charging in the course of driving, can reduce the capacity of on-board batteries and vehicle quality. The dynamic wireless charging technology of electric vehicles mainly includes two types: magnetic coupling type and electromagnetic induction type.

The electric vehicle wireless power supply system consists of two parts: the transmitting part and the receiving part. The transmitting part is composed of a power conversion device, an electromagnetic coupling mechanism, and a power conversion device on the vehicle [14]. The specific system structure is shown in Fig. 2. AC power (AC-DC-AC change) is generated by powering from the grid, rectification, filtering, voltage regulation, and inverter. The energy is transmitted by the magnetic coupling mechanism, and the receiving part supplies the received alternating current (AC-DC) to the electric vehicle.

The wireless power supply system for electric vehicles should ensure that the electric vehicles transmit energy at a certain distance from the ground. The wireless power supply system consists of two subsystems: one system is road system, another system is road surface system. Road system is used for transmitting energy, which includes a rectifier, a high frequency inverter, a primary matching capacitor bank, and a functional rail. Road surface system is used for receiving energy, including receiving coils, secondary matching capacitors and rectifiers. Road system should have strong stability and a low enough price to withstand the harsh road environment. At the same time, the road surface system should have a smaller size and a lighter weight for installation on an electric vehicle.

In summary, the problems that need to be researched in the dynamic wireless charging technology of electric vehicles are as follows:

1. Electromagnetic compatibility: Electromagnetic compatibility problems are closely related to the quality of energy transmission, the electromagnetic interference to the system and the impact on the human body. Only by effectively solving the EMC problems, can the system operate safely, reliably and stably.

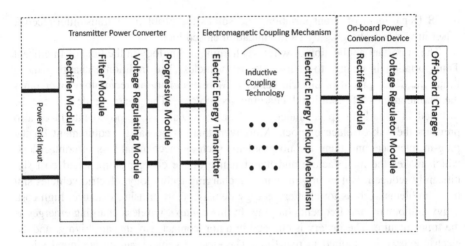

Fig. 2. Structure diagram of electric vehicle wireless power supply system.

2. Robust control of energy transfer: In the dynamic wireless power supply system of bipolar power supply guide rail, energy transfer is in a fast non-linear process, so the stability and response speed of the dynamic wireless power supply system are very important.
3. Coil design: The coil coupling structure is a key issue in the wireless charging system. The excellent coil structure has higher efficiency, lower electromagnetic radiation, and it can also reduce the cost of the power supply track.
4. Power supply efficiency: From the AC power supply to the DC output of the battery, the power supply efficiency determines the competitiveness of electric vehicles and traditional vehicles.
5. Electromagnetic shielding: The dynamic wireless power supply system has a long transmitting terminal and the road must be open, so the magnetic field limitation problem becomes more serious.
6. Power supply track segmentation and road construction: Power supply track segmentation can improve safety and stability, which is easy to maintain. Therefore, it is necessary to consider the track segmentation, control method, and reduce its impact on traffic during road construction.

4 Application and Development of Key Technologies for Dynamic Wireless Charging of Electric Vehicles

From the application and development history of wireless charging technology, the research on wireless charging theory is relatively deep and mature, and there are many practical applications and a few commercial products. At present, the leading countries in the field of dynamic wireless charging on electric vehicles are United States, New Zealand, Germany, Korea, Japan and other countries [15–17].

The University of Auckland in New Zealand worked with the German company Wampfler AG to develop the world's first wireless charging bus in 1997. The underground pavement of bus stop is equipped with 80 A and the radiat with working frequency of 13 kHz. The bus is equipped with ten receiving terminals, which charging power is 30 kW and charging current reaches 250 A. The bus has been operated in the Rotorua Geothermal Park in New Zealand, it effectively overcomes the harsh natural environment of the region. At the same time, Wampfler AG has also developed a 100 kW dynamic wireless power train prototype. The train track is 400 m long. Because of the dynamic power supply, the battery pack is no longer installed on the train. The University of Auckland has also conducted a series of research on the design of coupling mechanisms. In 2010, a double-sided coil consisting of a rectangular core plate and a vertically coiled cable was proposed. Later, a single-sided polarized coil composed of a horizontally wound cable on a magnetic core plate and a double-D-Quadrature (DDQ) pick-up coil structure was proposed [18].

The Oak Ridge National Laboratory of the United States has researched the transmission characteristics and dielectric loss during dynamic wireless charging of electric vehicles. The ground transmitting end is a series connection of two transmitting coils. The research shows that the transmission power and efficiency are greatly affected by the position of electric vehicle. It is necessary to adjust the frequency through the closed loop of 2.4 Ghz communication in order to adapt to the position change [19]. Zeliko Pantic's group of North Carolina State University in the United States has researched the dynamic wireless charging technology of electric vehicles powered by battery and super capacitors, and they discussed the application prospects of this technology in the field of urban transportation. Their research is also based on inductively coupled power transfer technology [20]. In 2013, Professor Chris Mi's team in University of Michigan has achieved radio power transmission at 2 kW to 6 kW with efficiency of over 94%, and the working frequency of the system is less than 200 kHz, which is very suitable for wireless charging of electric vehicles [21]. Stanford University has developed a mobile charging system for electric vehicles, which can charge while driving. The wireless charging efficiency could reach 97% [22].

Germany's VAHLE has developed CPS (Contactless Power Systems) since the end of the 20th century, and then VAHLE has published non-contact power access solutions and related products for ground transportation lines, electric monorail driving systems and transport vehicles. The power capacity of VAHLE's conventional power acquisition device is 500 W to 3 kW, but it is for high-power equipment. Their newly developed special power acquisition device has a single power capacity of 100 kW. It has been successfully operated in Bombardier's train test line.

The KAIST has conducted a lot of research on dynamic wireless charging technology for electric vehicles in recent years, and this kind of electric vehicles based on electric wireless power technology is called OLEV (Online Electric Vehicles). Their research focuses on the design of electromagnetic coupling mechanism and electromagnetic field shielding. Since the first generation was released in February 2009, the generations of OLEV related parameters that Korea has introduced are shown in Fig. 3.

Related parameters of OLEV in Korea					
	1G	2G	3G	3'G	3'G	4G
Vehicle	Car	Bus	SUV	Bus	Train	Bus
Date	Feb.27,2009	July. 14,2009	Aug.14,2009	Jan.31,2010	Mar.9,2010	2010-(under development)
System Spec.	air-gap=1cm efficiency=80%	air-gap=17cm efficiency=72%	air-gap=17cm efficiency=71%	air-gap=20cm efficiency=83%	air-gap=12cm efficiency=74%	air-gap=20cm efficiency=80%
EMF	10mG	51mG	50mG	50mG	50mG	<10mG
Power Rail Width	20cm	140cm	80cm	80cm	80cm	10cm
Pick-up Power	3KW/pick-up	6KW/pick-up	15KW/pick-up	15KW/pick-up	15KW/pick-up	25KW/pick-up
Pick-up Weight	20kg	80 kg	110 kg	110 kg	110 kg	80 kg
Size	55*18*4cm	160*60*11cm	170*80*8cm	170*80*8cm	170*80*8cm	80*100*8cm
All the efficiencies are measured by AC grid voltage to on-board battery terminals.						

Fig. 3. Related parameters of OLEV in Korea.

The first generation of OLEV uses an E-type core with an efficiency of 80% at an air gap of 1 cm. The efficiency decreases with the increase of the air gap, and the efficiency drops sharply with the offset of the receiving terminal. However, it has successfully confirmed the possibility of wireless power supply for electric vehicles. The second generation of OLEV uses a thin U-shaped core that increases the transmission distance from 1 cm to 17 cm and increases the offset tolerance. The third generation of OLEV uses a skeleton core arrangement that enhances compression resistance and reduces cost. The fourth generation of OLEV uses an innovative I-structure power supply track. The receiving coil has a power of 25 kW and a side shifting capability of 24 cm. At the same time, the I-type power supply track is only 10 cm wide, which greatly reduces the cost. In 2012, KAIST has researched two structures of monorail and dual-track. The dual-track divides the magnetic circuit into two parts, making it less susceptible to magnetic saturation. To achieve the same effect, the monorail must have double thickness. But the monorail type can obtain a larger amount of side shift. At present, Korea OLEV mainly adopts dual-track structure. In 2015, the Korean Academy of Higher Science and Technology established a 12 km long dynamic power supply demonstration project for electric buses driving on the road in Yuwei City of South Korea. In the field of wireless power supply technology for railway trains, the KRRI (Korea Railway Research Institute) has researched the whole wireless power supply system for railway trains, and made an experimental device with power of 1 MW and track length of 128M. The coupling mechanism adopts a long straight guide rail at the launching end and enhances the coupling performance by two small U-shaped magnetic cores. Because the track is longer and the inductance is larger, in order to reduce the voltage stress of capacitance, the capacitance is dispersed in the radiation coil [23].

Japan's Toyohashi University of Science and Technology and Ulsan University of Science and Technology in Korea has researched the electric field-coupled electric vehicle dynamic wireless power supply technology, which is coupled to the transmitter end buried in the ground through the receiving end of the wheel. Compared with the magnetic energy coupling of magnetic field coupling, the electric field coupled magnetic field radiation is small, the structure is simpler, the impedance matching is easier, and the dielectric constant of the tire is higher than air, which can improve the transmission efficiency and distance [24]. In 2011, the University of Tokyo in Japan worked with Nagano has developed a contactless power transmission system based on the principle of electromagnetic resonance. Compared with electromagnetic induction transmission system, it has a longer transmission distance and a slightly lower transmission power and efficiency [25].

Research on wireless charging theory in China is relatively late, but universities and institutes in China have researched on technology and application of wireless power transmission.

In October 2011, the "Key Technologies and Application Prospects of Radio Power Transmission" Academic Salon funded by the Chinese Association of Science and Technology was held in Tianjin University of Technology, which was the first academic conference in the field of radio power transmission in China. Subsequently, many academic conferences in the field of radio power transmission were held in China (See Table 2), showing the good development trend and prospects of radio power transmission technology in China [18, 26].

Table 2. A comparison of the three charging techniques.

Conference date	Conference place	Conference topic
In 2011	Tianjin	Key Technologies and Application Prospects of Radio Power Transmission
In 2012	Chongqing	Seminar on Radio Power Transmission Technology
In 2013	Guiyang	Symposium on Key Technologies and Applications of Radio Power Transmission
In 2014	Nanjing	International Symposium on Radio Power Transmission Technology and Applications
In 2015	Wuhan	Academic Conference on Radio Power Transmission Technology and Applications
In 2017	Chongqing	International Symposium on Radio Power Transmission

5 Conclusion

This paper introduces the application and development of dynamic wireless charging technology in the context of a new generation of Intelligent Transportation. With the popularity of electric vehicles, dynamic wireless charging technology has paid more and more attention in the world. The research on dynamic wireless charging technology of electric vehicles is still in the stage of continuous development and improvement, but in the near future, electric vehicles on highways will automatically receive power supply from the road surface below. The new Intelligent Transportation is coming.

Dynamic wireless charging technology can not only provide key supporting technologies for Intelligent Transportation, but also promote the development of Intelligent Transportation.

References

1. Jia, C.: Development and trend of urban Intelligent Transportation system. Sci. Technol. Econ. Guide **26**(07), 42–44 (2018)
2. Lu, X.: Application and research of wireless communication technology in Intelligent Transportation system. Electron. Technol. Softw. Eng. **01**, 31–33 (2017)
3. Zhang, J.: Talking about the application of wireless communication technology in Intelligent Transportation system. Word Technol. Appl. **10**, 18–19 (2015)
4. Cao, J., Zhang, A., Zhang, W.: On the relationship between Internet of Things and Intelligent Transportation. Netw. Technol. **06**, 08–10 (2015)
5. Hu, X.: Smart grid-a development trend of future power grid. Power Syst. Technol. **33**(14), 1–5 (2009)
6. Hu, Z., Song, Y., Xu, Z., et al.: Impacts and utilization of electric vehicles integration into power systems. Proc. CSEE **32**(4), 25–28 (2012)
7. Gao, C., Zhang, L.: A survey of influence of electrics vehicle charging on power grid. Power Syst. Technol. **35**(2), 127–131 (2011)
8. Zhou, L., Huang, Y., Guo, K., et al.: A survey of energy storage technology for micro grid. Power Syst. Prot. Control **39**(7), 147–152 (2011)
9. Huang, X., Tan, L., Chen, Z., et al.: Review and research progress on wireless power transfer technology. Trans. China Electrotech. Soc. **28**(10), 1–11 (2013)
10. Cao, L., Chen, Q., Ren, X., et al.: Review of the efficient wireless power transmission technique for electric vehicles. Trans. China Electrotech. Soc. **27**(08), 1–13 (2012)
11. Wu, X.: Dynamic coupling characteristics of electric vehicles under cooperative work mode. Tianjin University of Technology (2017)
12. Zhang, X., Jin, Y., Yuan, C., et al.: Dynamic wireless charging tight-strong coupling mode analysis of electric vehicles. Power Syst. Autom. **41**(2), 79–83 (2017)
13. Guo, Y., Wang, L., Li, S., Zhang, Y., Liao, C.: Dynamic modeling and characteristic analysis of mobile wireless charging system for electric vehicles. Power Syst. Autom. **41**(2), 73–78 (2017)
14. Guo, C.: Research and design of magnetically coupled resonant wireless charging system. Zhongbei University (2017)
15. Chenglong, X., Bing, S., Ning, Z.: Simulation study on transmission efficiency of wireless charging technology based on electromagnetic induction. Electron. Devices **37**(1), 131–133 (2014)
16. Hu, X.: Design and implementation of wireless charger for lithium ion batteries based on electromagnetic induction. J. Xichang Univ. Nat. Sci. Ed. **28**(1), 61–65 (2014)
17. Zhang, W., White, J.C., Abraham, A.M., et al.: Loosely coupled transformer structure and interoperability study for EV wireless charging systems. IEEE Trans. Power Electron. **30**(11), 6356–6367 (2015)
18. Chen, L., Nagendra, G.R., Boys, J.T., et al.: Double-coupled systems for IPT roadway applications. IEEE J. Emerg. Sel. Top. Power Electron. **3**(1), 37–49 (2015)
19. Miller, J., Onar, C., Chinthavali, M.: Primary-side power flow control of wireless power transfer for electric vehicle charging. IEEE J. Emerg. Sel. Top. Power Electron. **3**(1), 147–162 (2015)

20. Onar, O.C., Miller, J.M., Campbell, S.L., et al.: A novel wireless power transfer for in-motion EV/PHEV charging. In: 28th Annual IEEE Applied Power Electronics Conference and Exposition, 17–21 March 2013, Long Beach, pp. 3073–3080 (2013)

21. Zhang, H., Wang, Z., Li, N., et al.: Analysis of hybrid compensation topology circuit for electric vehicle wireless charging. Power Syst. Autom. **40**(16), 71–75 (2016)

22. Li, B., Liu, C., Chen, Q., et al.: Wireless charging technology for electric vehicles. Jiangsu Electr. Eng. **32**(1), 81–84 (2013)

23. Choi, S.Y., Gu, B.W., Jeong, S.Y., et al.: Advances in wireless power transfer systems for roadway-powered electric vehicles. IEEE J. Emerg. Sel. Top. Power Electron. **3**(1), 18–36 (2015)

24. Kobayashi, D., Imura, T., Hori, Y.: Real-time coupling coefficient estimation and maximum efficiency control on dynamic wireless power transfer for electric vehicles. In: Conference of the IEEE Industrial Electronics Society, 9–12 November 2015, Yokohama, pp. 13–18 (2015)

25. Zhang, J., Liao, G., Wang, F., et al: Research on wireless charging based on electromagnetic induction. Exp. Sci. Technol. 60–62 (2013)

26. Hao, Q., Huang, X., Tan, L., et al.: Maximum power transmission of inductively coupled radio power transmission system based on dynamic tuning. China Sci. **42**(7), 830–837 (2012)

Binocular Vision-Based Human Ranging Algorithm Based on Human Faces Recognition

Xiaolin He, Lin Ma$^{(\boxtimes)}$, and Weixiao Meng

School of Electronics and Information Engineering,
Harbin Institute of Technology, Harbin, China
17s005066@stu.hit.edu.cn, {malin,wxmeng}@hit.edu.cn

Abstract. In the field of security, timely and effective identification is very important for safeguarding public safety, national security and information security. Face recognition is an important technology in these areas. The calculation of range plays an important role in protecting safety and tracking suspects. Binocular stereo vision ranging has wide application in non-contact precise measurement and dangerous scenes. In this paper, a binocular range measurement system based on face recognition is proposed. The system can detect and recognize faces and calculate its real time range. It could realize tracking real time faces and calculate its distance from the cameras and locate them. And it suits the feature of special places of high security and preventing the suspicious people from entering and out.

Keywords: Face recognition · Binocular stereo vision ranging

1 Introduction

With the increasing demand for fast and effective identity recognition in society, the security problem is of great urgency [8]. At the same time, the recognition technology based on biometrics has gradually become a hot spot. Face recognition technology is generally accepted by people because of its non-contact and friendly interface [10]. In many ways of perceiving the world, visual information takes up about 80%. Binocular stereo vision has been widely applied to various aspects of production and life [5], especially in dangerous scenes.

Although the intelligent video surveillance is more and more mature [13], the pressure of people's demand for intellectualization of video analysis is also growing. However, the current monitoring system only support the storage functions. It relies on people to review video data. Then missing detection or erroneous inspection are easy to happen. At the same time, with the increase of the number of monitoring terminals, the resource consumption of human analysis is becoming more and more difficult to accept. So many researches have introduced computer vision technology in video surveillance in order to realize the intelligent video surveillance system [6].

© ICST Institute for Computer Sciences, Social Informatics and Telecommunications Engineering 2019
Published by Springer Nature Switzerland AG 2019. All Rights Reserved
S. Han et al. (Eds.): AICON 2019, LNICST 287, pp. 414–424, 2019.
https://doi.org/10.1007/978-3-030-22971-9_36

Face detection is originally derived from face recognition. Compared with eigenface and fisherface [3], the most obvious feature of the new algorithms for face recognition is the application of automatic recognition technology in the field of face recognition such as Adaboost [4], support vector machine (SVM) [12]. In the early stage of face recognition research, face recognition needs people to face to the camera. So it does not have to take the background information into consideration such as the location of the face. In this system, due to the long distance from people to camera, it's necessary to detect faces first.

Besides, artificial neural network has excellent performance in machine vision, voice recognition, natural language processing. Convolutional Neural Network (CNN) can classify large image data set very well. In the famous Alphago, CNN is applied to analyze the competition and offer decision information [2].

Computer vision technology makes the monitoring system not only see what happens but also understand what happens [9]. Through improving the analysis technology of video data, the system could recognize and identity the unusual things or people and give the alarm in the fastest and best way [7]. In the system we propose, to realize the intelligence of video monitoring system, the monitoring system can not only provide video data passively, but also analyze and process the video contents automatically.

The main contributions of this article are as follows:

(1) We propose a highly robust system to achieve the recognition and positioning of human faces, and it is real-time.
(2) This system can be applied not only in the general environment but also in dangerous scenes. The experimental results show that this system can effectively identify and locate human faces and meet the accuracy requirements.

The remainder of this paper is organized as follows. In Sect. 2, we will introduce the system model. The algorithms will be discussed in Sect. 3, which conclude face detection and recognition and ranging algorithms. Section 4 will provide the implementation and performance analysis. And conclusion will be described finally.

2   Proposed System Model

2.1   Measurement System Overview

The system contains two parts as shown in Fig. 1: one is offline phase to train the face detector and recognizer. Through the training of a large number of offline data and the establishment of a resource bank, a powerful classifier detector can be obtained, which can save a lot of time and improve efficiency when it is used online; the other is online phase to use them and calculate the real time distance. The system has good adaptability and can be applied to various special occasions.

In the offline, face detector and recognizer are built to detect and recognize faces. AdaBoost algorithm is applied to detect faces and its real time performance and accuracy could satisfy our system. At the same time, Convolutional Neural Network trains the faces and gets the face recognizer.

In the online, binocular vision platform works to capture images and the left image is sent to be tested for face detection. If exists, the corresponding right image is also detected. In the online phase, we apply Speeded Up Robust Features Algorithm to match feature points for distance calculation.

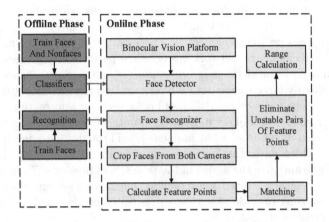

Fig. 1. The flow chart of the system.

2.2   Offline Phase and Online Phase

In the offline phase, the weak face classifier could be obtained by training the faces and non-faces data sets. The results of these weak classifiers can be only slightly better than the results of random guessing. But by cascading these weak classifiers, a strong classifier is obtained.

In the online phase, the binocular vision system will take a series of video streams to the background for processing. After receiving the video stream, the background will firstly detect the face. If there exists human faces, the two faces will be cropped and saved for further process. Then the feature points of the two faces are calculated. The feature points are used to match to calculate the ranging of the faces. The system again removes unstable pairs of feature points before calculating the range of the face. If the person is criminal or someone dangerous, the system will alarm for help to the monitoring platform.

3   Face Recognition and Ranging Algorithm

3.1   Face Detection Algorithm

The first step is to detect faces in pictures. Several methods such as skin color based method are widely used in face detection. AdaBoost algorithm is a main method for face detection and has great advantages over other methods.

It contains thousands of feature matrixes in one picture and the introduction of integral graph can improve the speed and accuracy of detection [11]. Assuming that a picture is $M \times N$ and the gray value of point (x, y) is $P(\alpha, \beta)$, therefore the integral value is:

$$I(x, y) = \sum_{i=0}^{x} \sum_{j=0}^{y} P_{xy}(\alpha, \beta) \tag{1}$$

Adaboost is applied to combine the rectangular feature after calculating the Haar-like feature. As long as its accuracy is better than the random selected feature, it will be chosen as a weak classifier. Every feature can be trained to be a less better weak classifier. Then through training these weak classifiers, strong classifiers could improve the accuracy. The final classifier is to cascade several strong classifiers.

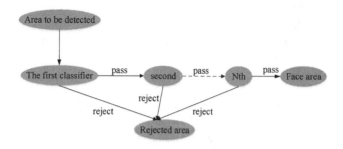

Fig. 2. Cascade classifier.

The cascade algorithm is as shown in Fig. 2. In every classifier, all the regions to be sorting are classified. The one that can reach the threshold will be sent to next classifier. Otherwise, it is considered to be invalid area, and the final face area is obtained after N classifiers. This cascade algorithm can achieve real-time detection effect. Its operation speed is very fast. This is because the face region and the non-face region is extremely asymmetric and the number of areas that can pass the classifier decreases rapidly. So it simplifies the calculation and is very efficient.

3.2 Face Recognition Algorithm

Artificial neural network is designed to imitate the structure of neurons in biological system. It imitates nonlinear processing of information by imitating synaptic connections, structures and functions of brains. The advantage of artificial neural network lies in its high parallel processing, high robustness, high fault tolerance and the correct classification and processing of fuzzy and imprecise information [14]. Convolutional Neural Network develops from multilayer perceptron. It is inspired from the field of biological neuroscience. It simulates the receptive field of the cats' visual cortex. This receptive field is very sensitive to local perception, and the receptive field is tiled to the whole area.

The algorithm flow chart contains 5 main parts:

(1) Input layer. Input layer is the first step of the whole network, and the original image is input directly without so many image preprocessing like other algorithms.
(2) Convolution layer. The convolution layer is the output of the upper layer and the convolution is calculated by a number of convolution cores. Each convolution kernel repeats itself in the entire input region, and the convolution result is a feature graph that forms the input image. The convolution layer is the core of the whole convolution neural network.

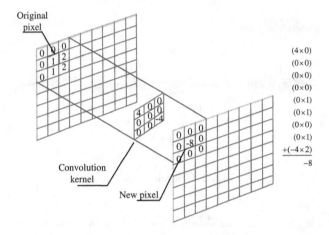

Fig. 3. Convolutional kernel.

Generally a convolution layer contains many convolution kernels (assuming to be n). Every convolution kernel convolutes with all the regions of the picture. Then n corresponding output characteristic maps are obtained. They would be input to the next layer. As shown in Fig. 3, after convoluting the upper image, image data is greatly reduced. However, to keep the size of the same, 0 can be put in the picture.

(3) Pooling. The image scale after convolution layer does not reduce too much. Therefore, pooling is introduced to reduce the dimension of the picture and the computational complexity and enhance the robustness of the network.
(4) Full connection. Many full connection layers are connected to the output layer. And the multiple full connection layers form a shallow layer of multi-layer perceptron.
(5) Output layer of softmax. Softmax is the generalization of the logistic regression model and calculates the maximum likelihood probability. It is a common algorithm used to solve multi-classification problem.

3.3   Ranging Method Based on Feature Extraction

The Speeded Up Robust Features Algorithm is based on iteratively detection and extraction of robust local feature points. Compared with other algorithms, the SURF algorithm has a great improvement in speed and robustness, so it is very suitable for real-time stereo matching [1,7]. The SURF algorithm relies on the Hessian matrix when extracting the feature points. More precisely, it depends on the maximum value of the Hessian matrix in the region. Assuming that somepoint X in the picture, its Hessian matrix is defined as:

$$H(x,\sigma) = \begin{bmatrix} L_{xx}(x,\sigma) \ L_{xy}(x,\sigma) \\ L_{xx}(x,\sigma) \ L_{xy}(x,\sigma) \end{bmatrix} \tag{2}$$

$L_{xx}(x,\sigma)$ indicates the convolution of the second order derivative of Gaussian $\frac{\partial^2 g(\sigma)}{\partial x^2}$ with the image. So do $L_{xy}(x,\sigma)$ and $L_{yy}(x,\sigma)$. The mathematical expression of $g(\sigma)$ is:

$$g(x,y,\sigma) = \frac{1}{2\pi\sigma}e^{-\frac{x^2+y^2}{2\sigma}} \tag{3}$$

The Gauss function needs to be discretized and cut in the actual application. It will be more suitable for the analysis of scale space and reduce the repeat degree of Hessian matrix.

Fig. 4. Match result.

Figure 4 is the result of matching feature points. By using these matched feature points we could calculate its real-time range. The principle of binocular ranging is similar to human eye ranging. So long as the coordinates of the matched feature points are obtained, its range could be calculated. As the Fig. 5 shows, the two cameras are placed in parallel and the horizontal distance is b. One point that should be mentioned is that the two cameras are in the same height. The focal length of the two cameras is f. P is the point in the world coordinate and P_l is the mapped point in the left image and P_r is the mapped point in the right image. (x_l, y_l) is the coordinates of P_l, (x_r, y_r) is the coordinates of P_r. The range could be calculated by the formula:

$$Z = \frac{bf}{x_l - x_r} \tag{4}$$

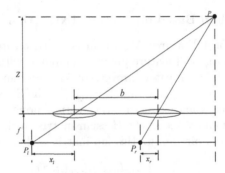

Fig. 5. Binocular ranging principle.

4   Implementation and Performance Analysis

4.1   Offline Training Results

In order to test our proposed method, we make an experiment in our lab, which is located in the Information Building, Science Park of Harbin Institute of Technology, China.

Firstly, offline training is necessary to build face detector and recognizer. To build face detector, 2860 pictures of faces and 4572 pictures of non-faces are used to form the strong classifiers. As shown in Fig. 6, with the increase of the number of weak classifiers, the accuracy rate is increasing. However, with the increase of the weak classifiers, the detection rate will also decrease and the corresponding detection time will increase. So the proper number of classifiers should be selected to balance them.

Secondly, face recognizer is also essential for the system. We use 200 people of their faces pictures and each has 7 pictures of different angles or lights. In the process of training, the number of convolutional kernels in the first layer of CNN is set to be 50, and the second layer to be 70. As shown in Fig. 7 with the increase of learning times, the error rate decreases and finally converges to 3%.

4.2   Online Results

In this experiment, the frequency of the shooting is 5 pairs of pictures per second. Then the pictures of the left and right cameras are sent to detect and recognize. Take the Fig. 8 for example, after human face detection, the position of the face is known. In the left image, (663,417) and (768,536) are the coordinates of the top left corner and lower right corner of the square face area. And in order to ensure real time, only the left image is detected for faces. If there exists, the right image captures the face by default.

Due to the small proportion of the face in the whole image, the size of the face frame is properly enlarged and some part of the body is framed too. It can improve the precision of the feature points matching and avoid the large distance error caused by the lack of matching points.

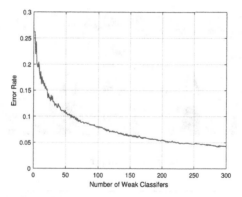

Fig. 6. The error rate of face detector.

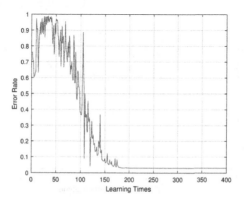

Fig. 7. The error rate of face recognition.

Figure 8 is the final matching result. There are 7 feature points matching pairs.The average distance is 3.64m. While the actual distance is 3.7 m, the absolute error is 0.058 m, and the relative error is 1.6%. The accuracy of the experiment could satisfy the requirement.

Figure 9 is a comparison of the SURF and SIFT algorithms used in the feature point extraction and matching process. From the Fig. 9, the ranging results can be obtained intuitively. Due to the effects of illumination, the SURF algorithm is more suitable for the system than the SIFT algorithm and could match more feature points. And the measurement accuracy is higher. This conclusion can also be drawn from the cumulative distribution function of Fig. 10, and the measurement result of 90% of the measurement results of this system is less than 0.6m, and the relative error of 50% points is less than 10%.

Fig. 8. Matching result.

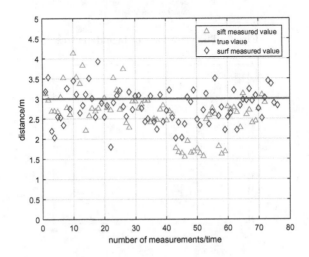

Fig. 9. Measured range.

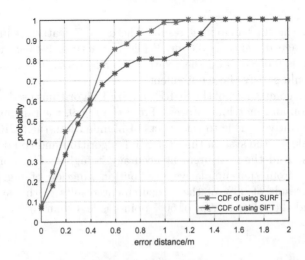

Fig. 10. CDF.

5 Conclusion

In this paper, a binocular distance measurement system based on face recognition is proposed. The AdaBoost algorithm classifies faces and non-faces. CNN is used to recognize different people. SURF algorithm can pick out feature points and match them. Therefore the system could realize tracking real time faces and calculate its distance from the camera and locate them. And it suits the feature of special places of high security and prevents the suspicious people from entering and out to start early-warning.

Acknowledgment. This paper is supported by National Natural Science Foundation of China (61571162, 4181101180), Ministry of Education - China Mobile Research Foundation (MCM20170106) and Heilongjiang Province Natural Science Foundation (F2016019).

References

1. Vinay, A., Hebbar, D., Shekhar, V.S., Murthy, K.N.B., Natarajan, S.: Two novel detector-descriptor based approaches for face recognition using sift and surf. Proc. Comput. Sci. **70**, 185–197 (2015). https://doi.org/10.1016/j.procs.2015.10.070
2. Aloysius, N., Geetha, M.: A review on deep convolutional neural networks. In: 2017 International Conference on Communication and Signal Processing (ICCSP), pp. 0588–0592, April 2017. https://doi.org/10.1109/ICCSP.2017.8286426
3. Belhumeur, P.N., Hespanha, J.P., Kriegman, D.J.: Eigenfaces vs. fisherfaces: recognition using class specific linear projection. IEEE Trans. Pattern Anal. Mach. Intell. **19**(7), 711–720 (1997). https://doi.org/10.1109/34.598228
4. Burduk, R.: The adaboost algorithm with linear modification of the weights. In: Choraś, M., Choraś, R.S. (eds.) Image Processing and Communications Challenges 9, vol. 681, pp. 82–87. Springer, Cham (2018). https://doi.org/10.1007/978-3-319-68720-9_11
5. Chaisorn, L., Wong, Y.: Video analytics for surveillance camera networks. In: 2013 19th IEEE International Conference on Networks (ICON), pp. 1–6, December 2013. https://doi.org/10.1109/ICON.2013.6782002
6. Gao, C., Li, P., Zhang, Y., Liu, J., Wang, L.: People counting based on head detection combining adaboost and CNN in crowded surveillance environment. Neurocomputing **208**, 108–116 (2016). https://doi.org/10.1016/j.neucom.2016.01.097. sI: BridgingSemantic
7. Kokila, R., Sannidhan, M.S., Bhandary, A.: A novel approach for matching composite sketches to mugshot photos using the fusion of SIFT and SURF feature descriptor. In: 2017 International Conference on Advances in Computing, Communications and Informatics (ICACCI), pp. 1458–1464, September 2017. https://doi.org/10.1109/ICACCI.2017.8126046
8. Panagiotou, N., et al.: Intelligent urban data monitoring for smart cities. In: Berendt, B., et al. (eds.) ECML PKDD 2016. LNCS (LNAI), vol. 9853, pp. 177–192. Springer, Cham (2016). https://doi.org/10.1007/978-3-319-46131-1_23
9. Ranganatha, S., Gowramma, Y.P.: An integrated robust approach for fast face tracking in noisy real-world videos with visual constraints. In: 2017 International Conference on Advances in Computing, Communications and Informatics (ICACCI), pp. 772–776, September 2017. https://doi.org/10.1109/ICACCI.2017.8125935

10. Tsai, H.C., Wang, W.C., Wang, J.C., Wang, J.F.: Long distance person identification using height measurement and face recognition. In: TENCON 2009–2009 IEEE Region 10 Conference, pp. 1–4, January 2009. https://doi.org/10.1109/TENCON.2009.5396069
11. Wagh, K.V., Kanade, S.S.: Pedestrian detection using integral channel detection and ADABOOST algorithm, Waknaghat, Shimla, India, pp. 383–387, January 2018
12. Xu, J., Zeng, W., Lan, Y., Guo, J., Cheng, X.: Modeling the parameter interactions in ranking SVM with low-rank approximation. IEEE Trans. Knowl. Data Eng. 1 (2018). https://doi.org/10.1109/TKDE.2018.2851257
13. Yu, X., Ganz, A.: Mass casualty incident surveillance and monitoring using identity aware video analytics. In: 2010 Annual International Conference of the IEEE Engineering in Medicine and Biology, pp. 3755–3758, August 2010. https://doi.org/10.1109/IEMBS.2010.5627536
14. Zarandy, A., Rekeczky, C., Szolgay, P., Chua, L.O.: Overview of CNN research: 25 years history and the current trends, Lisbon, Portugal, pp. 401–404, July 2015

Deep Reinforcement Learning Based Task Offloading in SDN-Enabled Industrial Internet of Things

Jiadai Wang[1], Yurui Cao[1], Jiajia Liu[2(✉)], and Yanning Zhang[2]

[1] School of Cyber Engineering, Xidian University, Xi'an, China
jdwang_xd@163.com
[2] School of Cybersecurity, Northwestern Polytechnical University, Xi'an, China
liujiajia@nwpu.edu.cn

Abstract. Recent advances in communication and sensor network technologies make Industrial Internet of Things (IIoT) a major driving force for future industry. Various devices in wide industry fields generate diverse computation tasks with their distinct service requirements. Note that the distribution of such tasks has essential intrinsic patterns and varies according to factors like region, season and time. Different from previous efforts to develop algorithms in specific scenarios for reducing task execution latency without considering the task generation patterns of IIoT, we propose a DRL-based Task Offloading algorithm (DRLTO) to learn such generation patterns and maximize the task completion rate. A SDN-enabled multi-layer heterogeneous computing framework is also introduced to efficiently assign tasks according to the obtained knowledges towards their features. Extensive experiments validate that our algorithm can not only significantly improve the average task completion rate, but also achieve near-optimal results in lots of IIoT scenarios.

Keywords: IIoT · Task offloading · Deep Reinforcement Learning

1 Introduction

With the development of communication technologies, sensor network technologies, Industrial Wireless Networks (IWNs) and artificial intelligence [1,2], Industrial Internet of Things (IIoT) has been considered as an important driving force of future industry, and can bring great opportunities for high-efficiency production, manpower saving and cost reduction. Various IIoT devices in wide fields such as manufacturing, logistics, retailing and energy sector generate diverse computation tasks with their own service requirements. The distribution of these tasks can vary significantly according to region, season and time. For example, as affected by rainfall, light and weather, monitoring and measuring equipments in agriculture and energy industry can produce seasonal requests. In manufacturing plant, the production process with corresponding task flows may have temporal

S. Han et al. (Eds.): AICON 2019, LNICST 287, pp. 425–437, 2019.
https://doi.org/10.1007/978-3-030-22971-9_37

procedures. The task distribution between residential areas and factories will also change regularly with the crowd mobility. Therefore, IIoT task generation has its own patterns that deserve enough attention.

In IIoT environment, it is difficult to process a large part of computing tasks locally due to their stringent delay requirements or high computation costs. Relying solely on cloud computing or edge computing appeared challenging to meet this situation. Cloud has rich computing resources and storage capacity, however, forwarding huge amounts of data to the remote center for processing may lead to serious network congestion and performance degradation [3]. Edge computing can significantly reduce delay by pushing abundant resources near IIoT devices, nevertheless, its computing power is weaker than cloud computing [4,5]. Therefore, the multi-layer heterogeneous computing framework is much more suitable by combining the advantages of different computing resources to meet IIoT task requirements.

There have been some pioneer research works toward the interplay of edge computing and cloud computing for IIoT. Fu *et al.* [6] designed a flexible and economical scheme to store the data in a secure and searchable manner by integrating the fog computing and cloud computing. Kaur *et al.* [2] proposed a multi-objective evolutionary algorithm using Tchebycheff decomposition for data flow scheduling in edge-cloud IIoT framework. Shi *et al.* [7] presented a real-coded genetic algorithm for task reallocation and retransmission, which aimed to reduce the service latency in cloud-fog integrated IIoT architecture. In addition, a generic architecture is developed in [8] for smart processing and aggregation in large-scale manufacturing control systems. Although these works offer precious insights into resource allocation and task scheduling, it is noticed that they failed to provide a dedicated approach to characterize the essential feature of task generation patterns. In view of this, we propose a Deep Reinforcement Learning (DRL) based algorithm to learn their patterns and perform effective task offloading in IIoT accordingly. The main contributions of this paper are summarized as follows.

- To the best of our knowledge, we are the first to focus on the task generation patterns in IIoT. In particular, we propose a DRL-based Task Offloading algorithm (DRLTO) to learn the task generation pattern, make the appropriate decisions based on the interaction with the environment, then carry on the effective task assignment [9].
- A SDN-enabled multi-layer heterogeneous computing framework is also presented to efficiently allocate tasks according to their characteristics. SDN is adopted to facilitate the logically centralized control of distributed edge network infrastructures and IIoT devices [10].
- Different from the previous works, which considered only on reducing the average execution delay of tasks and neglected the task completion rate, our DRLTO is able to maximize the average task completion rate under the SDN-enabled multi-layer computing framework. As corroborated by extensive experiments, the average task completion rate is distinctly improved by our DRLTO, which is even close to the optimal enumeration algorithm.

The remainder of this paper is organized as follows: Sect. 2 presents the system model of task offloading in SDN-enabled multi-layer heterogeneous computing framework. Then, in Sect. 3, we define the problem of Average Task Completion Rate Maximization (ATCRM) and propose DRLTO as our solution. Following that, Sect. 4 gives extensive performance evaluation. Finally, we conclude this paper in Sect. 5.

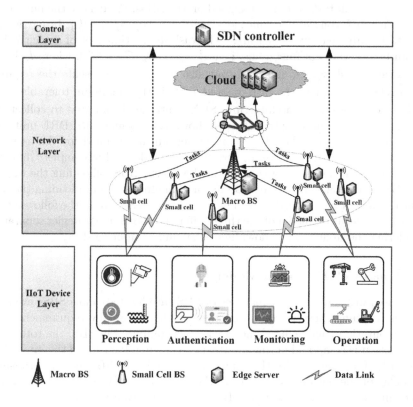

Fig. 1. The SDN-enabled heterogeneous multi-layer computing architecture.

2 System Model

As illustrated in Fig. 1, we consider a SDN-enabled multi-layer heterogeneous computing framework, in which the macro base station with the edge server supports task processing. Small cell base stations with edge servers are also deployed near IIoT devices for achieving high speed network access. We regard base stations with edge servers as edge nodes, and use MBS and SBS to represent the macro base station node and the small cell base station node. For the sake of simplicity, we consider one MBS in our model.

2.1   Task Model

IIoT devices generate various computation tasks for further processing on the edge servers or clouds. We assume that each type of computation task is atomic and cannot be partitioned, and one device only generates one type of tasks. Let $K = \{k_1, k_2, ..., k_{|K|}\}$ denotes the types of IIoT devices and $S = \{s_1, s_2, ..., s_{|S|}\}$ represents the SBSs. IIoT devices communicate with nearby SBSs via wireless data links and all tasks are first assigned on the SBSs. We denote the number of type-k task in L consecutive time slots as $num = \{n_k^1, n_k^2, ..., n_k^L\}$. In particular, these tasks can own diverse features. The task in jth time slot of device k, i.e., a_k^j, can be described in four items, i.e., $a_k^j = (I_k, O_k, C_k, T_k^{\max})$, where I_k is the input size of task a_k^j, O_k is the output size of a_k^j, C_k represents the required CPU cycles to complete the task a_k^j, and $T_k^{\max}$ is the maximum tolerable delay of a_k^j. In our considered architecture, SDN controller is adopted to collect the edge network state and control the task flow. What's more, $|S|$ DRL units are deployed in SDN controller, they can be periodically trained for the assigned tasks on SBSs. Thus the offloading strategy can be decided to complete different types of tasks, i.e., executing the task in the nearby SBS, offloading the task to the MBS which connected to the SBS in wired manner [11], or offloading the task to the cloud. Detailed algorithm will be introduced in Sect. 3. In the following, we present the execution model of the three different offloading strategies separately considering the uplink delay, downlink delay and computing delay.

2.2   Small Cell Execution Model

The processing and storage capacities of SBSs are limited. Thus SBSs are suitable for handling those computation tasks with low latency requirements and less computation complexity. When task a_k^j is computed in SBS, the total time consumption is composed of three parts, i.e., transmission time of the input data I_k from IIoT device to SBS, the computing delay in the SBS and the transmission delay of the output data O_k from the SBS to the device. In particular, the processing delay T_{ks}^j of task a_k^j in SBS s ($s \in S$) is given by

$$T_{ks}^j = \frac{I_k}{r_{ks}^{ul}} + \frac{C_k}{f_{ks}^j} + \frac{O_k}{r_{ks}^{dl}}. \tag{1}$$

Here, r_{ks}^{ul} and r_{ks}^{dl} are the uplink and downlink rate for task a_k^j via wireless transmission, respectively. f_{ks}^j is the processing capacity of SBS s allocated to the a_k^j. The uplink rate r_{ks}^{ul} can be computed by

$$r_{ks}^{ul} = \frac{B^{ul}}{|K|}\log_2\left(1 + \frac{p_k^{ul} g_k}{N_0 B^{ul}/|K|}\right), \tag{2}$$

where B^{ul} is the wireless uplink channel bandwidth which is divided among $|K|$ devices equally, e.g., using OFDMA. p_k^{ul} represents the transmit power of device k, g_k denotes the channel power gains of device k, and N_0 is the noise power spectral density at the receiver. Note that g_k can be calculated by $g_k = (d_k)^{-\alpha}$, where d_k is the distance between IIoT device k and the connected SBS, and α is the path loss factor. After the completion of task a_k^j, the SBS transmits the output data to IIoT device k, and the downlink data rate is given by

$$r_{ks}^{dl} = \frac{B^{dl}}{|K|} \log_2 \left(1 + \frac{p_k^{dl} g_k}{N_0 B^{dl}/|K|} \right), \tag{3}$$

where B^{dl} is the wireless downlink bandwidth and p_k^{dl} is the transmit power of SBS allocated to IIoT device k.

2.3 Macro Cell Execution Model

Since the MBS has stronger computation ability than SBS, computation tasks that have lower delay requirements or need higher computation capacity can be assigned to the MBS from SBS. Let m denotes the MBS. The time consumption of processing task on MBS contains five parts, i.e., the transmission time from IIoT device to SBS via wireless access and SBS to MBS in wired manner, the execution time on MBS, and the transmission time of backhaul from MBS to SBS and SBS to IIoT device. Thus the time consumption T_{km}^j of task a_k^j allocated to MBS m can be calculated as follows

$$T_{km}^j = \frac{I_k}{r_{ks}^{ul}} + \frac{I_k}{B_{sm}^{ul}} + \frac{C_k}{f_{km}^j} + \frac{O_k}{B_{sm}^{dl}} + \frac{O_k}{r_{ks}^{dl}}, \tag{4}$$

where B_{sm}^{ul} and B_{sm}^{dl} are the uplink and downlink data rate between MBS and SBS, and f_{km}^j denotes the processing capacity of MBS m allocated to the task a_k^j.

2.4 Cloud Execution Model

In particular, those tasks that have loose delay requirements and need a large amount of calculation can be assigned to the cloud. Due to the powerful computing capacity of the cloud, the execution time on cloud can be neglected. Thus the processing time of the task a_k^j allocated to the cloud contains the transmission time from IIoT device to SBS, the transmission delay t_c^{ul} from SBS to cloud via core network and t_c^{dl} from cloud to SBS, as well as the time from SBS to IIoT device. The T_{kc}^j is given by

$$T_{kc}^j = \frac{I_k}{r_{ks}^{ul}} + t_c^{ul} + t_c^{dl} + \frac{O_k}{r_{ks}^{dl}}. \tag{5}$$

3 Problem Formulation and DRL-based Solution

3.1 Problem Formulation

As we illustrated above, all tasks are first transmitted to SBS and then they will be assigned corresponding offloading strategies according to their features and the current task generation state. The execution time of task a_k^j is described as follows

$$T_k^j = \delta_k^j T_{ks}^j + \beta_k^j T_{km}^j + \gamma_k^j T_{kc}^j. \tag{6}$$

Here $\delta_k^j, \beta_k^j, \gamma_k^j \in \{0, 1\}$ are the offloading decisions of task a_k^j. $\delta_k^j = 1$ means that task a_k^j will be executed on the SBS, $\beta_k^j = 1$ means that the task a_k^j will be processed on the MBS, and $\gamma_k^j = 1$ means executed on the cloud. Obviously we have that $\delta_k^j + \beta_k^j + \gamma_k^j = 1$.

Average Task Completion Rate Maximization (ATCRM): According to our system model in Sect. 2, IIoT devices generate different types of computation tasks. For each task, it is either computed on the SBS which is close to the IIoT device, or offloaded to the MBS further, or offloaded to the cloud. Since each task has its maximum tolerable delay T_k^{max}, when the execution time T_k^j exceeds T_k^{max}, the task will be dropped. Given the $|K|$ devices and L consecutive time slots, our aim is to maximize the task completion rate within the tasks' tolerable delay. The problem can be formulated as follows

$$\max \sum_{j=1}^{L} \frac{\sum_{k=1}^{|K|} \varphi_k^j}{\sum_{k=1}^{|K|} n_k^j}, \tag{7}$$

where φ_k^j is the successful completion number of a_k^j in time slot j.

3.2 DRL-based Solution

In complex IIoT environment, it is difficult to adapt to the changeable task flow using traditional offloading schemes. Thus, ATCRM problem should be handled more intelligently with learning the task generation pattern. In this section, we propose a DRL based Task Offloading algorithm (DRLTO) to solve the ATCRM problem. As a branch of machine learning, DRL can acquire knowledge in the environment, improve policy to adjust to the changeable IIoT environment and make sequences of decisions to realize the effective task offloading [9]. Its goal is to obtain maximal cumulative rewards. We adopt the effective scheme Deep Q-Network (DQN) to realize our DRLTO, in which the task generation state is adopted as the input of the Deep Neural Network (DNN) and each possible action's Q value as the output. Three key elements of our DRLRO in DQN, i.e., state, action and reward, can be firstly defined as follows.

- **State:** In each time slot, the state vector of our proposed DRLRO can be denoted as $S = \{\{p_k^s\}, \{p_k^m\}, \{p_k^c\}, \forall k \in K\}$. Thereinto, p_k^s, p_k^m, p_k^c represent the number of k-type tasks that are assigned to SBS, MBS and cloud respectively.
- **Action:** The action vector can be given as $A = \{\{\alpha_k^s\}, \{\alpha_k^m\}, \{\alpha_k^c\}, \forall k \in K\}$, while α_k^s, α_k^m, α_k^c denote the action taken by the k-type tasks on SBS, MBS

and cloud, respectively. Reasonable action choices include staying in SBS, offloading q k-type tasks to MBS, and offloading q type-k tasks to cloud. Note that the action is only a part of the assignment process and is not actually performed until final offloading decision has been made.

- **Reward:** In each task assignment step, after taking the reasonable action A, the DRL agent can acquire a certain reward that needs to reflect the objective of our DRLTO, i.e., to maximize the average task completion rate. We define the reward that the DRL agent receives as $R = (\frac{\sum_{k=1}^{|K|} \varphi_k}{\sum_{k=1}^{|K|} n_k})^2$ if the task completion rate increases after doing a reasonable action. Otherwise, the agent will receive reward $R = -1$.

Algorithm 1. DRL based Task Offloading (DRLTO) Algorithm

Require: Discount rate γ, exploration rate ε, replay memory capacity C

1: Initialize replay memory D to capacity C
2: Initialize evaluation DNN with parameters θ
3: Initialize target DNN with parameters $\theta^- = \theta$
4: **for** each episode e **do**
5:     Initialize state S_1
6:     **for** each task assignment step t **do**
7:         Generate random number $\mu \in [0, 1]$
8:         **if** $\mu < \varepsilon$ **then**
9:             Randomly select an action A_t
10:        **else**
11:            Select $A_t = \arg\max_{A_t} Q(S_t, A_t; \theta)$, where Q is estimated by evaluation DNN
12:        **end if**
13:        Execute action A_t in emulator
14:        Observe reward R_t and new state S_{t+1}
15:        Store transition (S_t, A_t, R_t, S_{t+1}) in D
16:        Sample random mini-batch of transitions (S_j, A_j, R_j, S_{j+1}) from D
17:        **if** episode terminates at step$_{j+1}$ **then**
18:            Set $Y_j = R_j$
19:        **else**
20:            Set $Y_j = R_j + \gamma \max_{A_{j+1}} Q'(S_{j+1}, A_{j+1}; \theta^-)$, where Q' is estimated by target DNN
21:        **end if**
22:        Execute gradient descent using MSE function $(Y_j - Q(S_j, A_j; \theta))^2$
23:        Each Z steps reset $\theta^- = \theta$
24:    **end for**
25: **end for**

The training procedure of DRLTO is illustrated in Algorithm 1. In each episode, that is, the task assignment process, according to the task distribution information collected by the SDN controller, DRLTO can make decisions by the evaluation Q-values $Q(S, A; \theta)$ outputted by the evaluation DNN with neural network parameters θ. After choosing action using ε-greedy strategy, the certain reward R can be calculated as we defined above, and the next state S' can also be obtained accordingly. Each transition item (S_j, A_j, R_j, S_{j+1}) is stored in the experience replay memory and will be extracted randomly to execute the training procedure. The parameters θ^- of target DNN are updated on the basis of fixed-Q target strategy [9], namely, θ^- are updated according to θ at regular interval, while θ can be updated by Mean Square Error (MSE) loss function. Through the iteration of the above process, the task offloading decisions can be obtained.

The training process can be periodically executed for the varying task generation pattern. The SDN controller is responsible to send control messages using control plane function, e.g., Open Network Operating System (ONOS) and OpenDayLight (ODL) [12], to each SBS for operating the task flow.

4   Performance Evaluation

4.1   Experimental Settings

We considered a multi-layer heterogeneous computing scenario with the coexistence of centralized cloud, distributed SBS and MBS. A simulator in Python was developed to realize the DRLRO algorithm for smart task offloading in IIoT environment. Based on several in-lab testing applications described in [13], we set the average task input data size between 100 Kb and 500 Kb, and the output size between 5 Kb and 500 Kb. The task requirement of CPU cycles varied from 50 Megacycles to 500 Megacycles. The maximum tolerable delay of task was set between 200 ms and 1000 ms. The DNN structure in DRL was configured as three fully connected layers, and each hidden layer had 50 units. Table 1 presents detailed parameter settings in our experiment.

Three offloading strategies are presented to be our benchmark. (1) Random task offloading: Tasks are randomly offloaded to SBS, MBS or cloud. (2) Classified task offloading: Tasks are classified and offloaded to SBS, MBS and cloud according to their features. Here we use the required CPU cycles and the maximum tolerable delay of the task as classification criteria. Note that this classification is fixed and does not change with the task distribution. (3) Enumeration: Enumerate each possibility and find the optimal solution with high time complexity. All algorithms ran on a workstation with double Intel Xeon E5-2630 V4 2.2 GHz CPUs, 128 GB Random Access Memory (RAM), Nvidia Titan 12G GPU, and Ubuntu 14.04 64-bit operating system.

Table 1. Parameter settings in the simulation

Parameters	Value
Uplink and downlink bandwidth of the SBS	20 MHz
Uplink and downlink bandwidth of the MBS	40 MHz
Transmission rate between SBS and MBS	1 Gbps
Transmit power of IIoT device	100 mW
Distance between IIoT device and SBS	10–50 m
Distance between IIoT device and MBS	80–500 m
Path loss factor	4
Input data size of task	100–500 Kb
Output data size of task	5–100 Kb
Number of the required CPU cycles to complete the task	50–500 Megacycles
Maximum tolerable delay of task	200–1000 ms
Noise power spectral density	-147 dbm/Hz
Number of hidden layers	2
Number of neurons of each hidden layer	50
Replay memory size	2000
Mini-batch size	32
Learning rate	0.001
Target network update rate	500
Reward discount parameter	0.8
ϵ-greedy parameter	0.1

4.2 Numerical Results

From Fig. 2, one can easily observe that with the increase of total processing capacity, the combination of SBS and MBS is much more efficient for ATCRM problem than simple use of the SBS or MBS. This is because the two types of base stations give more options to various tasks. Each type of tasks can select different strategies for processing according to its own characteristics, and thus can also further decentralize the computing load.

For the combination of SBS and MBS, we have done more experiments to compare the proposed DRLTO with three benchmark algorithms, i.e., random task offloading, classified offloading and the enumeration algorithm. In Fig. 3, the experimental results show that with the increasing of total processing capacity, the four algorithms all growing, while our proposed DRLTO algorithm is much better than the random and classified offloading algorithms and is very close to optimal enumeration algorithm that has high complexity. This is because that with the increasing processing capacity, the average task completion rate will also raise as the processing delay of tasks become smaller. Besides, our DRLTO algorithm can adaptively learn the task generation pattern of the IIoT devices,

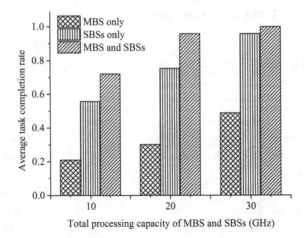

Fig. 2. Performance comparison on the simple use of the SBS or MBS and the combination of SBS and MBS under different total processing capacities.

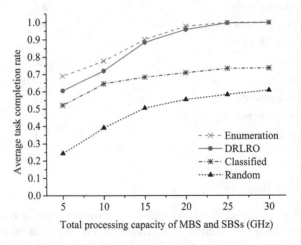

Fig. 3. Performance comparison of the benchmark algorithms and the proposed DRLTO under different total processing capacities.

make the appropriate decision based on the interaction with the environment, thus is more intelligent and better than the random and classified offloading algorithms.

Similar conclusion can also be found in Figs. 4 and 5. In Fig. 4, we set the capacities of MBS and SBS as 10 GHz and 1 GHz respectively. When the processing capacity of MBS is fixed, with the increasing number of SBSs, the DRLTO, random and enumeration algorithms all show growing trends, while the classified task offloading algorithm first tends to invariance, then grows again. This is due to that the classification of tasks is constant in classified algorithm. When the

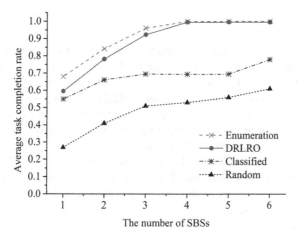

Fig. 4. Comparison of the benchmark algorithms and the proposed DRLTO under different number of SBSs.

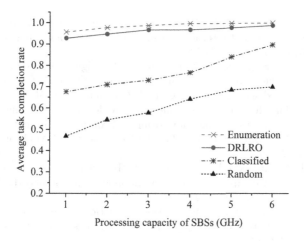

Fig. 5. Performance comparison of the benchmark algorithms and the proposed DRLTO under different processing capacities of SBSs.

number of SBSs is 4 or 5, the increase in processing capacity is not enough to affect the performance of this task offloading algorithm. When the number of deployed SBSs increased to 6, the total processing capacity of the base stations becomes larger, so the result of classified algorithm becomes better. We then set the capacity of MBS as 15 GHz with two SBSs in Fig. 5. The experimental results show that when the number of SBSs is fixed, with the increasing processing capacity of SBS, the four algorithms all growing, while our proposed DRLTO algorithm performs better than the random and classified task offloading algorithms and is close to optimal enumeration algorithm.

5   Conclusion

In this article, we have taken advantage of the IIoT task generation patterns to efficiently enhance the task offloading performance. Under the SDN-enabled multi-layer heterogeneous computing scenario, the aforementioned experimental results have shown that our proposed DRLTO is much more effective than random and classified algorithms, and its performance is very close to the optimal enumeration algorithm in maximizing average task completion rate. This is because our DRLTO can actively learn the task generation patterns through the training process and intelligently choose appropriate action for different types of tasks in complex IIoT environment. Therefore, it is obvious that DRL technology has great potential in smart task offloading and deserves further study. Future work is in progress to supplement more environment details into the state and action vector representation.

References

1. Li, X., Li, D., Wan, J., Liu, C., Imran, M.: Adaptive transmission optimization in SDN-based industrial internet of things with edge computing. IEEE Internet Things J. **5**(3), 1351–1360 (2018)
2. Kaur, K., Garg, S., Aujla, G.S., Kumar, N., Rodrigues, J.J., Guizani, M.: Edge computing in the industrial internet of things environment: software-defined-networks-based edge-cloud interplay. IEEE Commun. Mag. **56**(2), 44–51 (2018)
3. Nuratch, S.: The IIoT devices to cloud gateway design and implementation based on microcontroller for real-time monitoring and control in automation systems. In: 2017 12th IEEE Conference on Industrial Electronics and Applications (ICIEA), pp. 919–923 (2017)
4. Chekired, D.A., Khoukhi, L., Mouftah, H.T.: Industrial IoT data scheduling based on hierarchical fog computing: a key for enabling smart factory. IEEE Trans. Ind. Inform. **14**(10), 4590–4602 (2018)
5. Sun, W., Liu, J., Yue, Y., Zhang, H.: Double auction-based resource allocation for mobile edge computing in industrial internet of things. IEEE Trans. Ind. Inform. **14**(10), 4692–4701 (2018)
6. Fu, J., Liu, Y., Chao, H.-C., Bhargava, B., Zhang, Z.: Secure data storage and searching for industrial IoT by integrating fog computing and cloud computing. IEEE Trans. Ind. Inform. **14**(10), 4519–4528 (2018)
7. Shi, C., et al.: Ultra-low latency cloud-fog computing for industrial internet of things. In: 2018 IEEE Wireless Communications and Networking Conference (WCNC), pp. 1–6 (2018). https://doi.org/10.1109/WCNC.2018.8377192
8. Raileanu, S., Borangiu, T., Morariu, O., Iacob, I.: Edge computing in industrial IoT framework for cloud-based manufacturing control. In: 2018 22nd International Conference on System Theory, Control and Computing (ICSTCC), pp. 261–266. IEEE (2018)
9. Mnih, V., et al.: Human-level control through deep reinforcement learning. Nature **518**(7540), 529 (2015)
10. Qazi, Z.A., Lee, J., Jin, T., Bellala, G., Arndt, M., Noubir, G.: Application-awareness in SDN. In: ACM SIGCOMM Computer Communication Review, vol. 43, pp. 487–488. ACM (2013)

11. Wang, C., Liang, C., Yu, F.R., Chen, Q., Tang, L.: Computation offloading and resource allocation in wireless cellular networks with mobile edge computing. IEEE Trans. Wirel. Commun. **16**(8), 4924–4938 (2017)
12. Bhowmik, S., Tariq, M.A., Koldehofe, B., Durr, F., Kohler, T., Rothermel, K.: High performance publish/subscribe middleware in software-defined networks. IEEE/ACM Trans. Netw. **25**(3), 1501–1516 (2017)
13. Guo, H., Liu, J.: Collaborative computation offloading for multi-access edge computing over fiber-wireless networks. IEEE Trans. Veh. Technol. **67**(5), 4514–4526 (2018)

A Reinforcement Learning Based Task Offloading Scheme for Vehicular Edge Computing Network

Jie Zhang[1], Hongzhi Guo[2], and Jiajia Liu[2(✉)]

[1] School of Cyber Engineering, Xidian University, Xi'an 710071, Shaanxi, China
[2] School of Cybersecurity, Northwestern Polytechnical University,
Xi'an 710072, Shaanxi, China
`liujiajia@nwpu.edu.cn`

Abstract. Recently, the trends of automation and intelligence in vehicular networks have led to the emergence of intelligent connected vehicles (ICVs), and various intelligent applications like autonomous driving have also rapidly developed. Usually, these applications are compute-intensive, and require large amounts of computation resources, which conflicts with resource-limited vehicles. This contradiction becomes a bottleneck in the development of vehicular networks. To address this challenge, the researchers combined mobile edge computing (MEC) with vehicular networks, and proposed vehicular edge computing networks (VECNs). The deploying of MEC servers near the vehicles allows compute-intensive applications to be offloaded to MEC servers for execution, so as to alleviate vehicles' computational pressure. However, the high dynamic feature which makes traditional optimization algorithms like convex/non-convex optimization less suitable for vehicular networks, often lacks adequate consideration in the existing task offloading schemes. Toward this end, we propose a reinforcement learning based task offloading scheme, i.e., a deep Q learning algorithm, to solve the delay minimization problem in VECNs. Extensive numerical results corroborate the superior performance of our proposed scheme on reducing the processing delay of vehicles' computation tasks.

Keywords: Vehicular edge computing networks ·
Mobile edge computing · Reinforcement learning

1 Introduction

In recent years, automation and intelligence have caused extensive discussion in vehicular networks, which has led automakers such as Tesla and Mercedes-Benz

Supported by the National Natural Science Foundation of China (61771374, 61771373, 61801360, and 61601357), in part by China 111 Project (B16037), and in part by the Fundamental Research Fund for the Central Universities (JB171501, JB181506, JB181507, and JB181508).

S. Han et al. (Eds.): AICON 2019, LNICST 287, pp. 438–449, 2019.
https://doi.org/10.1007/978-3-030-22971-9_38

to focus on the research of intelligent connected vehicles (ICVs) [1]. By deploying various sensors (cameras, lidars, millimeter-wave radars, etc.) on the vehicles, an ICV can collect massive data about the information on road traffic and other ICVs. With these information, the ICV can perform a variety of intelligent applications, including autonomous driving, intelligent path planning, in-vehicle remote services, etc. However, the operations of these compute-intensive applications are often accompanied with enormous computation resources consumption, and correspondingly, most of the current vehicles are limited in computation resources, which makes them unable to guarantee the quality of service (QoS) requirements in terms of low latency. This contradiction between resources-limited vehicles and compute-intensive applications becomes a bottleneck in the development of vehicular networks [2].

To meet this challenge, cloud-based vehicular networks which introduce cloud computing into vehicular networks have been seen as an effective solution [3]. In such networks, vehicles' compute-intensive applications can be executed locally on the vehicles' CPUs or offloaded to a remote cloud server, so as to reduce the processing delay. It is undeniable that the introduction of cloud computing has alleviated the computational pressure of vehicles. However, considering that cloud servers are usually located away from vehicles, the data transmission delay over wide area network may result in severely reduced offloading efficiency. In order to address this deficiency, mobile edge computing offloading (MECO) has been considered as a new promising network paradigm [4,5], and has prompted the emergence of vehicular edge computing networks (VECNs). In VECNs, we can provide additional computation resources for vehicles by deploying MEC servers in road side units (RSUs) close to the road. Specifically, a vehicle moving on the road can offload its computation task which is not suitable for local execution to the MEC servers via a road side unit, so as to achieve lower processing delay.

Since its appearance, VECNs have attracted a lot of researchers' attention, and there has been many research works [6–8]. For example, Zhang et al. [6] studied the task offloading problem under delay constraints in cloud-enabled vehicular networks, and adopted contract theory to reduce the energy consumption of computation tasks. Further, in [9], they proposed a cloud-based task offloading framework in order to reduce offloading latency and transmission cost of the computation tasks. In their framework, they considered the effectiveness of vehicle-to-infrastructure (V2I) communications and vehicle-to-vehicle (V2V) communications, and proposed a predictive offloading scheme to solve the problem. Liu et al. [7] proposed a distributed computing offloading algorithm in order to reduce the processing delay of the computation tasks in vehicular networks. The study conducted by Dai et al. [8] investigated the multi-user and multi-server task offloading problem in vehicular networks, and they described it as a mixed integer nonlinear programming problem. To solve this problem, they divided the problem into two sub-problems, and proposed an optimization algorithm to jointly optimize the options of MEC servers and computing offloading.

It is obvious that the existing MECO schemes in VECNs are usually to formalize task offloading problem as an optimization problem and adopt appropriate optimization algorithms, i.e., game-based algorithm and contract-based algorithm, to obtain optimal or near-optimal solution [10]. However, due to fast-moving vehicles and constantly changing communications environment, it is difficult to obtain time-varying optimal solution using traditional optimization algorithms in high dynamic vehicular networks. In such case, machine learning, especially reinforcement learning which can interact with an unknown environment, adapt to environmental changes and take appropriate actions, seems to provide a good solution to this problem.

Recently, a lot of research works have focused on the application of reinforcement learning in vehicular networks [11–13]. For example, Zheng *et al.* [11] proposed a two-stage delay-optimal dynamic virtual radio scheduling scheme, which took channel and queue status information into account. In this paper, the virtual radio resource management was formulated as a partially observed Markov Decision Process (MDP) and then solved by an online distributed learning method. However, for task offloading problem in VECNs, there are currently not much research works using reinforcement learning. In this paper, we propose a reinforcement learning based task offloading scheme to solve the task offloading problem in VECNs, with the goal of minimizing processing delay of vehicles' computation tasks. In particular, the main contributions of this paper are as follows:

- In this paper, we propose a cloud enabled task offloading architecture in VECNs, in which remote cloud server acts as a backup server. In such scenario, we study the task offloading problem with the goal of minimizing processing delay of all the tasks.
- To solve the task offloading problem in our scenario, a reinforcement learning based scheme, i.e., a deep Q learning algorithm, is proposed.
- To verify the performance of our proposed schemes, we conduct a series of simulation experiments, and the numerical results we present demonstrate that our scheme can achieve superior performance on processing delay reduction.

The rest of this paper is organized as follows. In Sect. 2, we describe our proposed cloud enabled task offloading architecture and the system model. Section 3 gives the definition of the task offloading problem in our scenario and our proposed solution. After that, we present our numerical results in Sect. 4. Finally, Sect. 5 concludes the whole paper.

2 System Model

As shown in Fig. 1, there is an unidirectional straight road with N vehicles moving at a constant speed v. Moreover, M road side units (RSUs) are placed next to the road. and each RSU covers a certain range and is connected to a MEC server in order to provide edge computing service to the vehicles. Meanwhile, the remote cloud server thousands of miles away acts as a backup server so as to provide

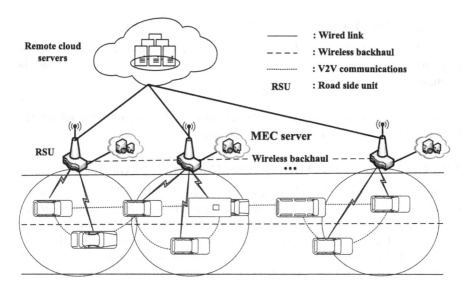

Fig. 1. Cloud enabled task offloading architecture in VECNs.

more computation resources for the vehicles when neither the MEC servers nor the vehicles themselves guarantee the processing delay requirements of the computation tasks. Therefore, for each vehicle, its computation task can be offloaded to the MEC servers or the remote cloud server for lower processing delay. Moreover, there are two modes for the data transmission, i.e., vehicle-to-vehicle (V2V) communications and vehicle-to-infrastructure (V2I) communications.

In order to facilitate the specific description of the problem, we use $\mathcal{N} = \{1, 2, 3, ..., N\}$ and $\mathcal{M} = \{1, 2, 3, ..., M\}$ denote the sets of the vehicles and the MEC servers connected to the RSUs, respectively. At the same time, we assume that only one computation task needs to be accomplished for each vehicle, and its characteristics can be described by four variables: the input data size m_i^{in}, the output data size m_i^{out}, the required CPU cycles to accomplish the task C_i, and the maximum permissible processing delay of the task D_i. So we denote the task of vehicle i as $T_i = \{m_i^{in}, m_i^{out}, C_i, D_i\}$.

According to the foregoing, there are $M + 2$ task offloading decisions for each vehicle, i.e, executing its computation task locally on the vehicle's own CPU, offloading its task to the MEC server connected to RSU j, and offloading its task to the remote cloud server. The task offloading decisions of vehicle i can be denoted as $d_i \in \{0, -1, 1, 2, 3, ..., M\}$, where $d_i = 0$ means that vehicle i decides to execute its computation task locally on its own CPU, $d_i = -1$ is that vehicle i decides to offload its computation task to the remote cloud server, and $d_i = j \, (1 \leq j \leq M)$ means that vehicle i decides to offload its computation task to the MEC server connected to RSU j. After that, for different task offloading decisions, the specific system models are given by the following subsections.

2.1 Executing Locally

While $d_i = 0$, vehicle i decides to accomplish its computation task locally on its own CPU. In such case, the processing time of the computation task can be calculated as

$$t_i^L = C_i/F_L, \tag{1}$$

where F_L is the computation capacity of vehicle i, and we assume that all vehicles have the same computation capacities for simplicity.

2.2 Offloading to the MEC Servers Connected to the RSUs

If vehicle i decides to offload its computation task to the MEC server connected to RSU j, i.e., $d_i = j\,(1 \le j \le M)$, the processing time of the computation task mainly consist of the following parts: the execution time of the task on the MEC server, the transmitting time of the input data from the vehicle to the MEC server, and the transmitting time of the output data from the MEC server to the vehicle. Then the processing time in such case can be given as

$$t_i^{MEC} = C_i/F_M + t_i^{in,trans} + t_i^{out,trans}. \tag{2}$$

Here, the first item is the execution time of the computation task on the MEC server, and F_M is the computation capacity of the MEC server. Also, we assume that all MEC servers have the same computation capacities for simplicity. $t_i^{in,trans}$ and $t_i^{out,trans}$ are the transmitting time of the input data and output data, respectively.

For $t_i^{in,trans}$, since the vehicle chooses the MEC server connected to the RSU within its current communication range, its value can be given by

$$t_i^{in,trans} = m_i^{in}/r_{i,j}^{V2I}, \tag{3}$$

where $r_{i,j}^{V2I}$ is the data transmitting rate between vehicle i and RSU j, and it can be calculated as

$$r_{i,j}^{V2I} = \omega_1 \cdot log_2(1 + \frac{p_{i,j} \cdot g_{i,j}^{V2I}}{\sigma^2 + I_{i,j}}). \tag{4}$$

Here, ω_1 is the channel bandwidth between vehicle i and RSU j, $p_{i,j}$ is the transmit power of vehicle i, $g_{i,j}^{V2I}$ is the channel gain between vehicle i and RSU j, σ^2 is the background noise power, and $I_{i,j}$ denotes the interference at RSU j.

For $t_i^{out,trans}$, due to the different communications modes, it has different expression equations:

$$t_i^{out,trans} = \begin{cases} m_i^{out}/c + m_i^{out}/r_{k,i}^{V2I}, & V2I, \\ m_i^{out}/r_{j,l}^{V2I} + m_i^{out}/r_{l,l+1}^{V2V} + ... + m_i^{out}/r_{l+n,i}^{V2V}, & V2V, \end{cases} \tag{5}$$

where c is the data transmitting rate between the RSUs, and $r_{i,j}^{V2V}$ is the data transmitting rate of V2V communications, which can be calculated as

$$r_{i,j}^{V2V} = \omega_2 \cdot log2(1 + \frac{p_{i,j} \cdot g_{i,j}^{V2V}}{\sigma^2 + A_0 \cdot L^{-2}}). \tag{6}$$

Here, ω_2 and $g_{i,j}^{V2V}$ are the channel bandwidth and channel gain between vehicle i and vehicle j respectively, σ^2 is the background power noise, A_0 is a constant parameter, and L is the distance between vehicle i and vehicle j.

2.3   Offloading to the Remote Cloud Server

If $d_i = -1$, vehicle i decides to offload its computation task to the remote cloud server. In such case, the processing time of the computation task mainly consists the following parts: the transmitting time of the input data from vehicle i to RSU j, the transmitting time of the input data from RSU j to the remote cloud server, and the transmitting time of the output data from RSU k to vehicle i. We ignore the execution time of the computation task because of the powerful computing power of cloud server. Then the processing time of the task can be calculated as

$$t_i^{RCS} = m_i^{in}/r_{i,j}^{V2I} + m_i^{in}/c' + m_i^{out}/r_{k,i}^{V2I}, \tag{7}$$

where c' is the data transmission rate between the RSUs and the remote cloud server.

According to the system model in this section, the processing time of vehicle i's computation task can be given as

$$t_i(d_i) = \begin{cases} t_i^L, & if \ d_i = 0, \\ t_i^{MEC}, & if \ d_i = j, \ 1 \le j \le M, \\ t_i^{RCS} & if \ d_i = -1. \end{cases} \tag{8}$$

3   Problem Formulation and Solution

In this section, we present the definition and formal description of the processing time minimization problem, and propose our solution to this problem.

3.1   Problem Formulation

As discussed in Sect. 2, there are $M+2$ task offloading decisions for each vehicle, i.e., executing its computation task locally on its own CPU, offloading its task to the MEC server connected to RSU j, and offloading its task to the remote cloud server. Due to different computation capacities and transmission efficiency, each type of offloading decisions for the vehicle results in different processing time of its task. Our goal is to minimize the total processing time of all the computation tasks while satisfying their maximum permissible processing time. Specifically, the problem can be given by the following definition.

Definition 1. *Processing Time Minimization under Delay Constraints (PTMDC): In vehicular edge computing networks, given the status of the vehicles (driving speed, information of computation tasks, wireless channel status, etc.), computation capacities of the MEC servers, and maximum permissible processing*

time of the tasks. The PTMDC problem is to find an optimal offloading decisions profile so as to minimize the total processing time of all the computation tasks while satisfying the maximum permissible processing time constraints.

After that, the PTMDC problem can be formulated as

$$\mathbf{P1} : \min_{\{d_i\}} \sum_{i=1}^{N} t_i(d_i)$$

$$s.t. \ C1 : t_i^L \cdot I_{\{d_i=0\}} + t_i^{MEC} \cdot I_{\{d_i=j\}} + t_i^{RCS} \cdot I_{\{d_i=-1\}}$$
$$\leq t_i^{max}, \ \forall \, i \in \mathcal{N}, j \in \mathcal{M},$$

$$C2 : \sum_{i=1}^{N} I_{\{d_i=j\}} \leq K, \forall \, i \in \mathcal{N}, j \in \mathcal{M},$$

$$C3 : d_i \in \{0, -1, 1, 2, ..., M\}, \ \forall \, i \in \mathcal{N},$$

where $I_{\{*\}}$ is an indicator function, and $I_{\{*\}} = 1$ while $*$ is true. K is the number constraint of the wireless channels in RSU j.

3.2   Solution

To solve the problem of PTMDC, we first adopt an enumeration algorithm proposed in [14], in which we enumerate all possible task offloading decisions profiles and choose the profile with minimum processing time. This algorithm can obtain the optimal solution to the PTMDC problem. However, the computational complexity of this algorithm is exponential, so it is not suitable for complex scenes with a large number of vehicles. Therefore, we further propose a reinforcement learning based task offloading scheme, i.e., deep Q learning algorithm, to solve the problem.

Reinforcement learning is a large class in the family of machine learning, and Deepmind's achievements in AlphaGo bring it to the mainstream of artificial intelligence. In the framework of reinforcement learning, agents interact with environment to learn what actions can be taken to maximize long-term rewards in a given environment. This mechanism of reinforcement learning makes its good performance in the dynamic environment of the vehicular networks. In order to solve the PTMDC problem, we propose a deep Q learning algorithm. Next, we will give the details of the algorithm.

Deep Q learning algorithm is an extension of Q learning algorithm. For Q learning algorithm, there are three main elements, i.e., environment state, action, and reward. Specifically, we define these three elements of our algorithm as follows:

– State: we define the system state as the total processing time of the computation tasks $S(t) = \sum_i t_i$, where t_i is the processing time of vehicle i's computation task.

Algorithm 1. Deep Q learning algorithm (DQL).

Input: the initial state information of the environment.
Output: the total processing time and offloading decisions profile.
  Initialize: the replay memory D;
                the main Q network with random weight δ;
                the target Q network with $\delta^- = \delta$;
1: **for** each episode **do**
2:   get the initial state S_1;
3:   **for** $t = 1, 2, 3, ..., T$ **do**
4:     choose a random probability p;
5:     **if** $p \leq \epsilon$ **then**
6:       randomly select an action A_t;
7:     **else**
8:       $A_t = arg \max_a Q(S, A, \delta)$;
9:     **end if**
10:    execute action A_t, obtain the reward R_t, and the next state S_{t+1};
11:    store the experience (S_t, A_t, R_t, S_{t+1}) into the replay memory D;
12:    get a batch of U samples S_i, A_i, R_i, S_{i+1} from the replay memory;
13:    calculate the target Q value Q_i^- from the target deep Q network:
14:      $Q_i^- = R_i + \epsilon Q(S_{i+1}, arg \max_{A'} Q(S_{i+1}, A'; \delta); \delta^-)$;
15:    update the main deep Q network by minimizing the loss:
16:      $L_i(\delta) = \frac{1}{U} \cdot \sum [Q_i^- - Q(S_i, A_i; \delta)]^2$;
17:    perform a gradient descent step on $L(\delta)$;
18:    every G steps, update the target deep Q network weight with rate α:
19:      $\delta^- = \alpha\delta + (1 - \alpha)\delta^-$;
20:   **end for**
21: **end for**

- Action: the set of tasks' offloading decisions $A(t) = \{d_1(t), d_2(t), ..., d_i(t)\}$.
- Reward: the action taken by the agent in each step will receive certain rewards or punishments, we use a reward function to represent it. Specifically, it can be calculated as $(T_L - T)/T_L$, where T_L is the total processing time while all vehicles decide to execute their tasks on their own CPUs, and T is the total processing time by taking selected action in the current state.

The core of Q learning is the matrix Q-table, and the rows and columns of Q-table represent the values of states and actions, respectively. The value of Q-table $Q(S, A)$ measures how well the action taken by the current state is. In the training process of Q learning, we use the Bellman Equation to update the Q-table [15]. However, the states may be infinite in real situations, which causes the Q-table to be very large. To deal with this problem, we implement Q-table via neural networks. Specifically, we use the states and actions as the input of neural networks, and then estimate Q value via neural networks. The combination of neural networks and Q learning is called deep Q learning, and we design our scheme based on this. The neural networks in our scheme contain the main Q network and the target Q network, with weights δ and δ^-, and the main Q network is used to get the current Q value $Q(S, A, \delta)$ while the role of the target Q network is to obtain the target Q value $Q(S, A, \delta\text{-})$. We update the main Q network by minimizing the loss $L_i(\delta)$ and approximate the current Q value. Meanwhile, we calculate the target Q value from the target deep Q network, and update the target deep Q network weight every G steps. Moreover, due to the stability problem of the correlation between states, we store the experience (S_t, A_t, R_t, S_{t+1}) of the current training episode to the replay memory D, and randomly sample the mini-batch from D to update the parameters of the neural networks. The details of the deep Q learning algorithm are shown in Algorithm 1.

4   Performance Evaluation

In this section, we conduct a series of simulation experiments and get some numerical results to evaluate the performance of our proposed algorithm. Without loss of generality, we consider a scenario where there is an unidirectional road, and ten RSUs are equidistantly placed on the road. Moreover, the remote cloud server is assumed to be placed thousands of miles away from the road. For the computation tasks, we assume that the input date sizes are randomly chosen between 500 KB and 1000 KB, and the output data sizes are between 50 KB and 300 KB. The CPU cycles required to accomplish the computation tasks of vehicles are set between 200 Megacycles and 1500 Megacycles, and the maximum permissible processing delays of the computation tasks are in the interval [0.5 s, 2 s]. For communications modes, the wireless bandwidth of the RSUs and the vehicles are set to 40 MHz and 20 MHz, respectively. Meanwhile, the background noise power is −100 dBm. Moreover, the computation capacities of the MEC servers connected to the RSUs are set to 4 GHz, and the computation capacities of the vehicles are 2 GHz.

First, in order to verify that our DQL algorithm can reach a near-optimal solution to the PTMDC problem, we compare the total processing time by adopting two different offloading schemes, i.e., an enumeration algorithm which can achieve an optimal solution to the problem and our DQL algorithm. The experimental results are shown in Fig. 2. We can see that our proposed DQL algorithm can achieve a near-optimal solution.

Figure 3 illustrates the numerical results of the total processing time obtained by three different offloading schemes, i.e., DQL algorithm, DQL algorithm without cloud server and executing all tasks locally, as the number of the computation tasks changes from 20 to 120. From the figure, one can notice that the total processing time obtained by DQL algorithm without cloud server are much less than that while executing all tasks locally. this result shows that MECO has a huge impact on reducing the processing time of vehicles' tasks. In addition, when we take the remote cloud server into account, the total processing time will be twenty to thirty percent less than DQL algorithm without cloud server. Therefore, it is very necessary to introduce the remote cloud server into VECNs.

Meanwhile, we have the experimental results shown in Fig. 4, which illustrate the trends in the number of vehicles choosing different communications modes, i.e., V2I communications and V2V communications, as the number of vehicles

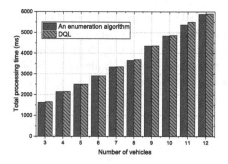

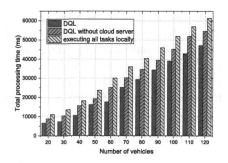

Fig. 2. Comparisons of the total processing time obtained by two algorithms, i.e., an enumeration algorithm and DQL algorithm, as the number of vehicles changes from 3 to 12.

Fig. 3. Comparisons of the total processing time obtained by three schemes, i.e., DQL, DQL without cloud server, and executing all tasks locally, as the number of vehicles changes from 20 to 120.

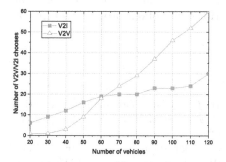

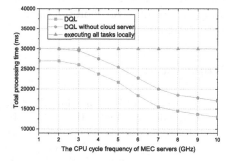

Fig. 4. Trends in the number of vehicles choosing different communications modes, i.e., V2I communications and V2V communications, as the number of vehicles changes from 20 to 120.

Fig. 5. Comparisons of the total processing time obtained by three schemes, i.e., DQL, DQL without cloud server, and executing all tasks locally, as the computation capacities of MEC servers change.

changes from 20 to 120. As can be seen from the figure, both the number of vehicles that choose V2V communications and that of V2I communications increase with the number of vehicles, and the growth rate of the former is larger than that of the latter. In the end, the number of vehicles that choose V2V communications will exceed that of V2I communications. These numerical results show that the number of vehicles has a more significant influence on V2V communications.

Figure 5 shows the changes in the total processing time with the increase in the CPU cycle frequency of the MEC servers connected to the RSUs. Numerical results in Fig. 5 demonstrate that our proposed DQL algorithm can achieve the minimum total processing time of the computation tasks. Specifically, the locally execution time does not change with the CPU cycle frequency of the MEC servers, because local computing does not need the computation capacities of the MEC servers. Also, we can see that the total processing time obtained by

DQL algorithm decrease with the increasing CPU cycle frequency of the MEC servers. However, the rate of decrease in the total processing time increases first and then decreases. This phenomenon indicates that the CPU cycle frequency of the MEC servers has a decisive influence on the result of DQL algorithm when it is not too large. But when it is big enough, the influence of the CPU cycle frequency of the MEC servers becomes small.

5   Conclusions

In this paper, we first presented a cloud enabled task offloading architecture in VECNs, in which the remote cloud server acts as a backup server considering its powerful computation capacities. Then we studied the task offloading problem in such scenario, and we defined the processing time minimization problem under delay constraints. After that, we proposed a reinforcement learning based task offloading scheme, i.e., a deep Q learning algorithm, as our solution. The numerical results corroborated the good performance of our proposed scheme on processing delay reduction.

References

1. Zhu, H., Yuen, K., Mihaylova, L., Leung, H.: Overview of environment perception for intelligent vehicles. IEEE Trans. Intell. Transp. Syst. **18**(10), 2584–2601 (2017). https://doi.org/10.1109/TITS.2017.2658662
2. Vegni, A.M., Loscrí, V.: A survey on vehicular social networks. IEEE Commun. Surv. Tutor. **17**(4), 2397–2419 (2015). https://doi.org/10.1109/COMST.2015.2453481
3. Shojafar, M., Cordeschi, N., Baccarelli, E.: Energy-efficient adaptive resource management for real-time vehicular cloud services. IEEE Trans. Cloud Comput. **7**(1), 196–209 (2019). https://doi.org/10.1109/TCC.2016.2551747
4. Guo, H., Liu, J., Zhang, J., Sun, W., Kato, N.: Mobile-edge computation offloading for ultradense iot networks. IEEE Internet Things J. **5**(6), 4977–4988 (2018). https://doi.org/10.1109/JIOT.2018.2838584
5. Wang, S., Zhang, X., Zhang, Y., Wang, L., Yang, J., Wang, W.: A survey on mobile edge networks: convergence of computing, caching and communications. IEEE Access **5**, 6757–6779 (2017). https://doi.org/10.1109/ACCESS.2017.2685434
6. Zhang, K., Mao, Y., Leng, S., Vinel, A., Zhang, Y.: Delay constrained offloading for mobile edge computing in cloud-enabled vehicular networks. In: 2016 8th International Workshop on Resilient Networks Design and Modeling (RNDM), pp. 288–294, September 2016. https://doi.org/10.1109/RNDM.2016.7608300
7. Liu, Y., Wang, S., Huang, J., Yang, F.: A computation offloading algorithm based on game theory for vehicular edge networks. In: 2018 IEEE International Conference on Communications (ICC), pp. 1–6, May 2018. https://doi.org/10.1109/ICC.2018.8422240
8. Dai, Y., Xu, D., Maharjan, S., Zhang, Y.: Joint load balancing and offloading in vehicular edge computing and networks. IEEE Internet Things J. 1 (2019). https://doi.org/10.1109/JIOT.2018.2876298

9. Zhang, K., Mao, Y., Leng, S., He, Y., Zhang, Y.: Mobile-edge computing for vehicular networks: a promising network paradigm with predictive off-loading. IEEE Veh. Technol. Mag. **12**(2), 36–44 (2017). https://doi.org/10.1109/MVT.2017.2668838

10. Guo, H., Zhang, J., Liu, J.: Fiwi-enhanced vehicular edge computing networks: collaborative task offloading. IEEE Veh. Technol. Mag. **14**(1), 45–53 (2019). https://doi.org/10.1109/MVT.2018.2879537

11. Zheng, Q., Zheng, K., Zhang, H., Leung, V.C.M.: Delay-optimal virtualized radio resource scheduling in software-defined vehicular networks via stochastic learning. IEEE Trans. Veh. Technol. **65**(10), 7857–7867 (2016). https://doi.org/10.1109/TVT.2016.2538461

12. He, Y., Zhao, N., Yin, H.: Integrated networking, caching, and computing for connected vehicles: a deep reinforcement learning approach. IEEE Trans. Veh. Technol. **67**(1), 44–55 (2018). https://doi.org/10.1109/TVT.2017.2760281

13. Ye, H., Li, G.Y.: Deep reinforcement learning for resource allocation in V2V communications. In: 2018 IEEE International Conference on Communications (ICC), pp. 1–6, May 2018. https://doi.org/10.1109/ICC.2018.8422586

14. Guo, H., Liu, J.: Collaborative computation offloading for multiaccess edge computing over fiber-wireless networks. IEEE Trans. Veh. Technol. **67**(5), 4514–4526 (2018). https://doi.org/10.1109/TVT.2018.2790421

15. Li, J., Gao, H., Lv, T., Lu, Y.: Deep reinforcement learning based computation offloading and resource allocation for mec. In: 2018 IEEE Wireless Communications and Networking Conference (WCNC), pp. 1–6, April 2018. https://doi.org/10.1109/WCNC.2018.8377343

Sensor-Based Human Activity Recognition for Smart Healthcare: A Semi-supervised Machine Learning

Abrar Zahin[ID], Le Thanh Tan[ID], and Rose Qingyang Hu$^{(\boxtimes)}$[ID]

Utah State University, Logan, UT 84322-4120, USA
abrarzahin303@gmail.com, {tan.le,rose.hu}@usu.edu

Abstract. Human action recognition is an integral part of smart health monitoring, where intelligence behind the services is obtained and improves through sensor information. It poses tremendous challenges due to huge diversities of human actions and also a large variation in how a particular action can be performed. This problem has been intensified more with the emergence of Internet of Things (IoT), which has resulted in larger datasets acquired by a massive number of sensors. The big data based machine learning is the best candidate to deal with this grand challenge. However, one of the biggest challenges in using large datasets in machine learning is to label sufficient data to train a model accurately. Instead of using expensive supervised learning, we propose a semi-supervised classifier for time-series data. The proposed framework is the joint design of variational auto-encoder (VAE) and convolutional neural network (CNN). In particular, the VAE intends to extract the salient characteristics of human activity data and to provide the useful criteria for the compressed sensing reconstruction, while the CNN aims for extracting the discriminative features and for producing the low-dimension latent codes. Given a combination of labeled and raw time-series data, our architecture utilizes compressed samples from the latent vector in a deconvolutional decoder to reconstruct the input time-series. We intend to train the classifier to detect human actions for smart health systems.

Keywords: Action recognition · Variational auto-encoder · Convolutional neural network · Semi-supervised learning · Internet of Things · Smart health system

1 Introduction

1.1 Motivations

The emerging ubiquitous mobile and sensor-rich devices have led to higher demands for the human action recognition (HAR). Some of the major applications,

This work is supported in part by National Science Foundation under grants NeTS 1423348 and EARS 1547312, in part by Natural Science Foundation of China under grant 61728104, and in part by Intel Corporation.

S. Han et al. (Eds.): AICON 2019, LNICST 287, pp. 450–472, 2019.
https://doi.org/10.1007/978-3-030-22971-9_39

which are benefited from HAR, are daily lifelogging, healthcare, senior care, personal fittings and etc. [1–3]. The efficacy of an HAR system greatly depends on the salient features extracted from the raw signals such as accelerometer readings [4]. There has been extensive research into HAR, but generally, few practical deployed applications have been proposed to address the following arising issues. Firstly, the rapid spread of smart devices have resulted in the scarcity of label data. This has emerged to be a critical issue for developing the learning model, which is capable to learn the salient features and to further recognize the unseen actions. Furthermore, a massive number of sensors will participate in generating big data in an Internet of Thing (IoT) smart health environment. The big data provides more difficulties to the machine learning systems including: *(1) the problem of using compressed sampling to acquire the large datasets, (2) the problem of improving the quality of reconstructed data from large amounts of measurements and (3) the problem of performing data labeling at scale.*

The big data based artificial intelligence (AI) and machine learning are the emerging tools to solve the major problems faced in 5G and beyond networks as well as in industrial IoT systems [6–12]. The innovative These intelligent tools can achieve the goals of acquiring accurate and scalable data in the era of big data. Recent works in compressed sensing (CS) reveal that a signal having a sparse representation in one basis can be recovered from a small number of projections onto a second basis that is incoherent with the first one [5]. Especially, the compressed sampling technology has a capability of receiving the sparse signal at the rates lower than the traditional Nyquist sampling. At receiver side, the signal reconstruction is proposed by solving a convex optimization problem called min-l_l with equality constraints. Some advanced techniques, namely the basic pursuit, the orthogonal matching pursuit, the tree-based orthogonal matching pursuit [5] are also employed to improve the performance of reconstruction.

As a result, many researchers successfully applied the CS technology into various real applications such as cognitive radio networks [6–8] and Smartgrids [9, 10]. In particular, they make efforts to design the CS-based compressive spectrum sensing frameworks [6–8], which operate in distributed manner. Moreover, their proposed models are reliable and appropriate to the practical applications by reducing a hardware complexity. Furthermore, Tan *et al.* [11,12] developed the deep reinforcement learning based framework to solve the joint communication, edge caching and computing design problem in vehicular networks. In particular, they use the classic AI (i.e. the particle swarm optimization scheme) for mobility-aware reward function at the associated large timescale level, while they employ deep reinforcement learning at the small timescale level of their sophisticated twin-timescale solution [11]. These proposed AI schemes are proved to achieve operational excellence and cost efficiency.

1.2   Our Contributions

In this paper, we propose a semi-supervised classifier model, where we employ the deep generative model [16] for recognizing the human activities in the smart healthcare systems. Specifically, the contributions of this paper can be summarized as follows.

1. In particular, the time-series data acquired by sensors can also be represented as an image [13] and the compressed sensing technology developed for image processing would be applied to our data. Then, we use the variational auto-encoder (VAE) [14,15] as the underlying generative model recovery in our proposed compressed sensing algorithm, which provides novel insights into our proposed inexpensive data sampling and acquisition. The core idea of VAE is to learn the true data distribution of a training set in order to generate new data points with some minor variation. It implies that the VAE has the capability of extracting the salient characteristics of human activity data and reliably providing more useful additional criteria for the CS reconstruction objective. According to this idea, our model learns the hidden parameters or the latent codes, which enable it to draw a more precise decision boundaries for the classification than a classifier based on labeled data alone [16].

2. To produce the most defining latent code, we need to capture the discriminative features of the action signal, which are then used for the classification. Therefore, we propose the convolutional neural network (CNN) in the encoder part, which not only extracts the discriminative features but also produces the latent codes in lower dimensions. For the data reconstruction, we employ the deconvolution network in the decoder, where the latent code is the input. The classifier is trained until the reconstruction loss is less than the predetermined threshold. Then the output is the reconstructed signal, which has a higher dimension than the input (i.e. the latent code).

3. To validate our proposed semi-supervised classifier model, we use the data set, namely Actitracker Dataset [17], which contains 2,980,765 samples with six daily attributes. We present experimental results for illustrating the performances of our proposed algorithm such as the VAE loss for training and testing data, the reconstruction loss and the classification accuracy. We also make a fair comparison with the existing works, where our proposed semi-supervised learning method outperforms the supervised learning method in terms of the classification accuracy for the same number of measurements for the Actitracker Dataset.

The outline of this paper is as follows. In Sect. 2, we discuss important related works on machine learning. In Sect. 3, we describe our system model. Section 4 briefly presents the proposed framework of semi-supervised learning for time-series human action. Section 5 presents our performance results followed by our concluding remarks in Sect. 6.

2 The Recent State of Machine Learning Applications: Challenges and Solutions

Deep learning has emerged to be an well-established technique to discover compact and meaningful representations of raw data without relying on domain knowledge [6–12,16,18–20]. In particular, there are four main types of tasks within the field of machine learning, which are referred as the supervised learning, unsupervised learning, semi-supervised learning and reinforcement learning. The main difference between supervised learning and unsupervised learning [16,20] is that supervised learning is done using a ground truth. It implies that we have prior knowledge of what the output values for our samples should be. So given a sample of input data and desired outputs, supervised learning aims for building the best function approximation of the relationship between input and output. In unsupervised learning, we only have input data and do not have corresponding output variables (i.e. the labeled data). Therefore, unsupervised learning aims for inferring the natural structure present within a set of data points. It means that its goal is to model the underlying structure or distribution in the data to learn more about the data. We can readily observe that supervised learning requires a large amount of labeled samples to generalize well but it is an expensive and difficult process. Also in unsupervised learning, there are no correct answers and there is no teacher. To deal with these limitations, semi-supervised learning [16,20] is presented, where it takes a middle ground between supervised learning and unsupervised learning. Here, we have a large amount of input data and only some of the data is labeled. It uses a morsel amount of labeled data bolstering a larger set of unlabeled data. Finally, reinforcement learning [11,12] trains an algorithm with a reward system. Then, it provides feedback, when an artificial intelligence agent performs the best action in a particular situation. In the following, we discuss how these machine learning mechanisms can be applied to the real applications and what are the main constraints of the existing works.

In reinforcement learning, let us focus on the proposed artificial intelligent framework eligible for the real application, which is the example application in edge caching and computing framework in vehicular networks. As we know that the action space and state space are very large. Especially, the scenario of user mobility causes the increase of these spaces. Therefore, we would determine the effective methods to deal with these concerns. [12] is the first step to apply the deep reinforcement learning to edge caching and computing. Here, the deep reinforcement learning is employed for both the large timescale model and the small timescale model. The large timescale model aims for reducing the possible sets of connecting road site units (RSUs) and vehicles for the tagged vehicle, which are then used in the small timescale model. Therefore, the large timescale model roughly estimate the reward and the reserved sets of RSUs and vehicles for the tagged vehicle. However, this initial proposed method cannot work well for the large scale networks, when the number of nodes increase. It means that the proposed method needs to be improved, when we want to deploy it in the practical application. Moreover, the computational complexity of model is still high, and hence it is very hard to apply it to the real application. Motivated from this, Tan et al. [11] develop the particle swarm optimization (PSO) for the large timescale model. In fact, the advanced PSO is used to guarantee the global optimal solutions with the fast convergence and high stability. Because the parameter setting and updating is modified to match well with the dataset in the scenario of edge caching and computing. Moreover, the proposed PSO can avoid the local optimal solutions. Therefore, the solutions in the large timescale model are optimal. Remember that in [12], the large timescale model roughly determine the solutions, i.e. these solutions may not optimal; and the small timescale model needs to correct them. However, in the case that the possible sets of RSUs and vehicles for the tagged vehicle are wrongly chosen, this would cause the wrong decision and/or increase the learning time.

Similarly, many algorithms are proposed to deal with the grand challenges and solutions in supervised learning, unsupervised learning and semi-supervised learning. Let us discuss the action recognition, where one of the most important tasks is the feature extraction. Statistical features such as mean, standard deviation, entropy, correlation coefficients and etc are the most widely used hand-crafted features in the action recognition [21]. Moreover, the advanced eigenvalue models is used for blind feature extraction in [23], where the modern random matrix theory, i.e. the spiked population model, can provide an efficient solution to the problem with unknown information. In [6–8], the spectrum data is transformed into a domain, where it is sparse. For example, a wide-band signal is sampled in the Fourier domain and then is transformed to Wavelet space, where it has a sparse representation. Based on that, salient information is extracted and then is used for data recovery. Similarly, Tamura *et al.* [22] used Fourier transform, Wavelet transform and discrete cosine transform to learn the underlying features. The other application of using CS is data processing in Smartgrids [9,10], where the smart-meter data are projected into Wavelet domain for the further sampling salient extraction. Furthermore, deep neural network [18] and restricted Bozltman machine [19] were proposed as deep learning techniques to extract features. Another deep learning model, namely shift-invariant sparse coding [20] was used to perform unsupervised learning to train an auto-encoder network. In [27], CNN was proposed to recognize human activities using mobile sensors. To exploit the huge unlabeled samples likely to be produced by IoT, semi-supervised learning can be a great alternative. The most recent additions to the conventional semi-supervised algorithms, like transductive support vector machines [20] and semi-supervised support vector machines [16] are belong to the probabilistic model based semi-supervised learning.

In summary, the developed artificial intelligence framework should be eligible for the real application by employing the advanced machine learning mechanism. It can avoid many barriers observed such as the massive devices and big data. It means that the proposed artificial intelligent framework must ensure the optimal solutions with low computational complexity and high stability. Furthermore, there is no machine learning algorithm, which can be efficiently applied to every practical application. Because it totally depends on the characteristics and properties of the observed dataset in every application. To work efficiently with the dataset in the specific application, we must modify the machine learning algorithms and/or combine both the classic and advanced learning methods. The main goal of our paper is to tackle these critical challenges and to develop the algorithms to determine the optimal solutions.

3   System Model

3.1   Applications and Protocol Design

Our proposed semi-supervised classifier can be implemented in a module for various kind of applications in the Smart Healthcare System, i.e. *(1) reporting day to day activities, (2) reporting activities to center for monitoring and (3) life-logging for daily activities.* For simplicity, we consider the six daily activities in our model, namely "Walking", "Jogging", "Upstairs", "Sitting", "Standing" and "Downstairs". Our classifier module can be built with different cascaded classifiers like the action classifiers and the fall-down classifier. The system implementation is presented in Fig. 1, where we consider the classifier models including the wearable sensor devices, the apps (action classifier and other classifier like fall-down detection). Let us consider application 2, i.e. *reporting activities to center for monitoring,* which may be used in the healthcare system at the senior homes. In particular, we consider the reporting activities for fall-down monitoring scenario. For this monitoring, our system model would operate in two modes, i.e. the distributed protocol and the centralized protocol. Let's consider a human activity "Upstairs". Upon receiving the accelerometer data, the sensor will pass it through the action classifier. Then, this app detects the action of "Upstairs", which may cause an accident due to falling down. In the distributed manner, this app sends a command to turn on the camera to monitor the activity of the person going upstairs. It also activates the app of fall-down detection. If the fall classifier detect that a person falls, it then sends a command to the nearest healthcare to take necessary actions. In the centralized mechanism, the cloud is responsible for fall-down detection and there is only app of action classifier at the wearable sensor device. In this centralized manner, the action classifier sends the detected action of "Upstairs" to the cloud. The cloud concurrently send the

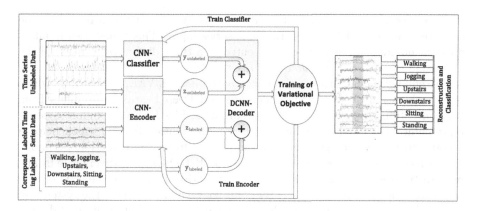

Fig. 1. Semi-supervised classification for time-series human actions in the smart healthcare system

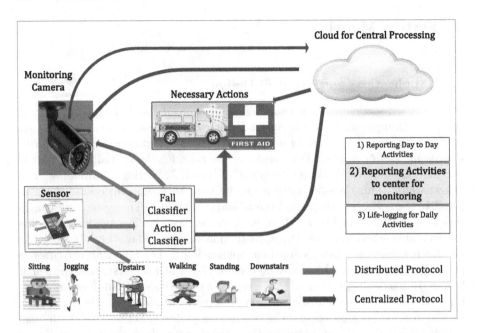

Fig. 2. Real application in the healthcare system using human activity classification

command to activate the camera and start to monitor the person's activity. If the cloud detects the falling, it will call to the healthcare for assistance. Similarly, we have the same procedure with two protocols for the other applications. Detailed operations of the healthcare system using the action classifier is illustrated in Fig. 2.

3.2   Sensor-Based Human Activity Recognition

We consider the recognition of human activities, where the sensor like the accelerometer is used to record the time-series input. This time-series input of different human actions can be represented as a three dimensional image of the dimension $[sample\ size, window\ length, axis]$.

We employ the latent variable generative model, i.e. VAE, for learning, which is a combination of Variational Inference and Deep Learning. It differs from the conventional auto-encoder in two key ways. Firstly, a deterministic latent representation z is replaced by a posterior distribution $q(z|x)$, which helps a decoder to reconstruct an input by sampling z from this posterior. Secondly, the posterior $q(z|x)$ is regularized with Kullback–Leibler (KL) divergence from a prior distribution $p(z)$, where the prior is conventionally chosen to be a Gaussian with zero mean and unit variance. By doing so, we make sure that the system can sample from any point in latent dimensions and still generate valid and diverse outputs.

Let us present the notable contribution of VAE. Firstly, VAE performs a good generalization on reconstructing the approximated input by imposing some restrictions on the latent space. Specifically, by sampling from $q(z|x)$ instead of taking a deterministic z, it forces the model to map an input to a region of space rather than to a single input. It implies that VAE can acquire the salient features of the data, which support for the data reconstruction. Furthermore, the good reconstruction performance depends on estimating a very sharp probability distribution corresponding to a single input in latent space. The KL term in VAE loss function prevents this behavior by training the model to find a solution for low reconstruction error and predicting a posterior distribution close to the prior. In this process, the decoder part of the VAE is capable of reconstructing the sensor data samples from every point in the latent space.

We employ the semi-supervised classification to train the model, where the time-series data are both labeled and unlabeled data. For the unlabeled data, two networks has been trained. The first one is the encoder network $q_\phi(z|X_U)$, where its output is z; while the other is classifier network $q_\phi(y|X_U)$, where its output is y. For our model, both encoder and classifier networks employ the same traditional CNN network. According to the encoder output z and the label y, the decoder would perform the variational inference over them by $p_\theta(\hat{X_U}|z,y)$ and try to approximate the input as likely as possible. For the labeled data, we only train the encoder network $q_\phi(z|X_L)$. Then, we insert its label to the decoder for decoding data. Again, we perform the variational inference over the encoder output and the label by $p_\theta(\hat{X}_L, \hat{Y}_L|z)$ and obtain the reconstructed data. To evaluate the performance, we use the loss function, given as

$$\mathcal{J}_{VAE} = KL(q(z|x)||p(z)) - \mathbb{E}_{q(z|x)}[\log p(x|z)]. \tag{1}$$

Detailed semi-supervised approach for analyzing this loss function would be described in the next section. After a proper training, we store the configured parameters of the classifier $q_\phi(y|x)$ and use them to test the real time-series input. In particular, we implement the classifier module, which takes the raw time-series input from a wearable of an object and classifies a numerous unseen variation of some specific actions.

4   Semi-supervised Learning for Time-Series Human Actions in the Smart Healthcare System

In this section, we provide a comprehensive mathematical formulation for all the core parts of our proposed model, i.e. encoder network, decoder network, classifier network and training model with semi-supervised objective. Before that we present all notations and their descriptions, which are summarized in the Table 1.

Note that we would have the labeled and unlabeled time-series data, which are used to train the model for our proposed semi-supervised classification. For the labeled data, we have the inputs, $\mathbf{X}_L = \{x_1, x_2, \ldots, x_L\}$ and their corresponding labels, $\mathbf{Y}_L = y_1, y_2 \ldots .y_L$, where L is the length of labeled data; while

Table 1. Definition of parameters

Notation	Description
$\circledast$	Convolution operator
$\sum$	Concatenation of feature maps
$(F_E)^i$	Encoder filter for layer i
$(F_D)^i$	Decoder filter for layer i
$M_1 = 1, 2...m_1$	Total filters in layer 1
$M_2 = 1, 2...m_2$	total filters in layer 2
c	Convolved output
c_p	Convolved output after pooling
vec	Vectorize a concatenation
MLP	Multi layer perceptron
FC	Fully connected layer
π	Labels in categorical distribution
$q_\phi(z|x)$	Probability of observing z given x
$q_\phi(y|x)$	Probability of observing y given x
$p_\theta(\hat{x}|z)$	Probability of observing x given z
$q_\phi(y|x)$	Classifier network
ϕ	Weight vector of encoder and classifier
θ	Weight vector of decoder

we only have the inputs, $\mathbf{X}_u = \{x_{l+1}, x_{l+2}, \ldots, x_{l+U}\}$ for the unlabeled data, where U is the length of the unlabeled data. For each data point x_i, there are corresponding latent variables z_i, which are obtained from an encoder structure and are then forwarded to a decoder. At the decoder side, we reconstruct an approximation of the given input of $\hat{\mathbf{X}}_L, \hat{\mathbf{Y}}_L$ and $\hat{\mathbf{X}}_U$ for labeled and unlabeled data, respectively. We train the parameters of ϕ and θ to enhance the overall performance of the model. Recall that ϕ is the weight vector of the encoder and classifier, while θ is the weight vector of the decoder. In the following, we present detailed description of encoder structure, decoder structure, classifier structure and training of the model.

4.1 Encoder Structure

The input data of our proposed encoder model can be recorded from the sensor devices. Usually, human activity data are observed by the tri-axis accelerometer. So the acceleration data are three-dimension (3D) data, which include x, y and z directions. In our encoder convolutional network, there are two kinds of layer, i.e. the convolutional layer and the fully connected layer. To reduce computational complexity, we aim for using the depth-wise separable convolution or 1D convolution [18]. Unlike the traditional CNN, the final layer of encoder in our proposed scheme is replaced by the fully connected layer. In particular, it can output the mean and standard deviation for the distribution of latent code. Furthermore, it can continuously generate the input of the decoder section by sampling the code.

As the observation above, our accelerator input data are the 3D time-series signal, which include x, y and z directions. Therefore, our input data can be categorized as the red-green-blue (RGB) image, which would have been treated successfully by using the conventional CNN. We describe the detailed implementation as follows. WLOG, the dimension of an input time-series signal, D^n is assumed as $(1, T, 3)$, where T is total points of time, the height is 1 and the depth is 3 for x, y and z directions. In the first step, we perform an $1D$ convolution by convolving a single filter m_1 with the input. This operation thus produces a 2D matrix, $\{c^{1,n,m_1}\}$ of $1 \times T$ dimensions, where $m_1 \in [1, 2, \ldots, M_1]$ and M_1 is the number of filters. Then, M_1 filters produce a concatenation of M_1 parameters of c^{1,n,m_1}, which represent all the feature maps of layer 1. We aim for using multiple filters to learn the great variety of patterns. So for a single filter m_1, c^{1,n,m_1} is derived as

$$c^{(1,n,m_1)} = D^{(n)} \circledast F_E^{1,m_1}, \ m_1 \in [1, 2, \ldots, M_1], \tag{2}$$

where F_E^{1,m_1} is the coefficients of the filter m_1. For M_1 filters, the concatenation parameter of $c^{(1,n)}$ is calculated as

$$c^{(1,n)} = \sum_{m_1=1}^{M_1} c^{(1,n,m_1)}. \tag{3}$$

Similarly, we perform another $1D$ convolution in layer 2 and concatenate all the slices. We have

$$c^{(2,n,m_2)} = c^{(1,n)} \circledast F_E^{2,m_2}, \tag{4}$$

$$c^{(2,n)} = \sum_{m_2=1}^{M_2} c^{(2,n,m_2)}, \tag{5}$$

$$C_f = vec c^{(2,n)}, \tag{6}$$

where C_f is the vectorized form of $c^{2,n}$, which has the dimension of $[1 \times dim(c^{2,n})]$. So C_f is gone through the fully-connected layer, which is the design of multi layer perceptron. Its output is given as $FC_1 = MLP(C_f)$, where MLP represents the multi layer perceptron. These fixed latent dimensions of the fully connected layers are then used as the input at the final layer. The outputs are the vector of mean and the vector of standard deviation, $z_n \sim \left(\mu_\phi(FC_1), \sigma_\phi(FC_1)\right)$, which would be used to sample the latent code for the decoder network.

4.2 Decoder Structure

We consider the decoder, which consists of three transposed convolutional layers and three fully connected layers. The implementation of our decoder network is presented as follows. The latent code at a fully connected layer is forwarded to the decoder. The result is the vectorized/flatten form of convolved output at layer 2 in the decoder and is given as

$$vec\ c^{(2,n)} = FC(z_n), \tag{7}$$
$$C_f = vec\ c^{(2,n)}, \tag{8}$$

where FC represents the fully connected layer. This flatten output is gone through the three transposed convolution layers. The outputs at three layers are presented as

$$c^{(2,n)} = C_f \circledast F_D{}^2, \tag{9}$$
$$c^{(3,n)} = c^{(2,n)} \circledast F_D{}^3, \tag{10}$$
$$c^{(4,n)} = c^{(3,n)} \circledast F_D{}^4, \tag{11}$$

where F_D^i represents the coefficient vector of the transposed convolutional filter at layer i, where $i \in \{2, 3, 4\}$. The convolved output are then gone through the other two fully connected layers to reconstruct the approximate version of the input. It implies that the reconstructed data D_{approx} would be given as

$$D_{FC_2} = FC(c^{(4,n)}), \tag{12}$$
$$D_{approx} = FC(D_{FC_2}). \tag{13}$$

4.3 Classifier Structure

We model the classifier structure by using the traditional CNN network, which consists of the convolutional layers, the max-pooling layers, the fully connected layers and the softmax classifier. The last layer, i.e. the softmax classifier, is responsible for providing the probability distribution of the class (or the label). For example, we present our dataset at the numerical results, which has six daily activities, namely "Walking", "Jogging", "Stairs", "Sitting", "Standing" and "Lying Down". We pass the unlabeled time-series data into two 1D convolutional layers (i.e. layers 1 and 2), one 1D max-pooling layer (i.e. layer 3) and three fully connected layers (i.e. layers 4, 5 and 6) and the softmax classifier. In the following, max-pooling operation is down-sampling an input representation to reduce its dimensionality and to allow for assumptions to be made about features contained in the sub-regions. Furthermore, softmax classifier takes a vector of arbitrary real-valued scores form the last layer (c^6 for our case) and squashes it to a vector of values between zero and one, where the summation of all elements equals one. Given unlabeled time-series data x_u, these operations in the classifier network are summarized as

$$C^1 = x_u \circledast F_c{}^1, \tag{14}$$
$$C^2 \sim maxpool(C^1), \tag{15}$$
$$C^3 = C^2 \circledast F_c{}^3, \tag{16}$$
$$C^4 = FC(C^3), \tag{17}$$
$$C^5 = FC(C^4), \tag{18}$$
$$C^6 = FC(C^5), \tag{19}$$
$$f_{c_i} = (C^6)_i, \tag{20}$$
$$q_\phi(y|x_u) = -log \frac{e^{f_{c_i}}}{\sum_{i=1}^{dim(C)} e^{f_{c_i}}}, \tag{21}$$

where f_{c_i} is the ith element of last layer, C^6, $dim(c)$ denotes the total elements of layer C^6, C^i, $i \in \{1, 2, \ldots, 6\}$ are the output of layer i, while $q_\phi(y|x_u)$ is the probability distribution of label y given the unlabeled time-series data x_u.

4.4 Training of Semi-supervised Model for Time-Series Classification

We now present the training steps of the semi-supervised model for both two variational objectives [16], which correspond to the cases of unlabeled data and labeled data.

Variational Objective with Unlabeled Data. In the case of unlabeled data, we treat z and y as latent variables. Therefore, they are considered as the inputs of the decoder by using the operation of concatenation. It means that we train for both the encoder and classifier networks.

$$y = Classifier(x_u), \tag{22}$$
$$z = Encoder(x_u), \tag{23}$$
$$Concatenation(z, y) \rightarrow Decoder. \tag{24}$$

Thus, our variational objective for unlabeled data is

$$\min_{\theta, \phi} \quad KL(q_\phi(y, z|x) \parallel p_\theta(y, z|x)). \tag{25}$$

Here $q_\phi(y, z|x)$ and $p_\theta(y, z|x)$ denotes the approximate posterior distribution of y, z given x and corresponding true distribution respectively.

Proposition 1. *We have the final lower bound for unlabeled data as* $\log p_\theta(x) \geq U(x)$*, where the lower bound,* $U(x)$*, is determined as*

$$U(x) = \mathbb{E}_{q_\phi(y|x)} \left[-\mathcal{M}_{(x,y)} - log \ q_\phi(y|x) \right]. \tag{26}$$

Here, $\mathcal{M}_{(x,y)} = -\mathbb{E}_{q_\phi(z|x)} [\log \ p_\theta(x|y, z)] + K_1 - KL(q_\phi(z|x) \parallel p_\theta(z))$ *and* $K_1 = \mathbb{E}_{q_\phi(z|x)} \log \ p_\theta(y)$.

Proof. The proof is provided in Appendix 7.1.

Variational Objective with Labeled Data. In the case of labeled data, we skip the classifier because we can inject the label from outside. Hence, we use the concatenation of z_L and y_L and then pass the result to the decoder. The procedure is summarized as

$$y_L = \; GivenLabels\;, \tag{27}$$

$$z = Encoder(x_L), \tag{28}$$

$$Concatenation\;(z, y_L) \rightarrow Decoder, \tag{29}$$

where $q_\phi(z, \pi|x, y)$ and $p_\theta(z, \pi|x, y)$ denote by the approximate posterior distribution of (z, π) given (x, y) and its corresponding true distribution, respectively. Thus, the variational objective for labeled data is

$$\min_{\theta, \phi} \quad KL\; q_\phi(z, \pi|x, y)\; \|\; p_\theta(z, \pi|x, y), \tag{30}$$

where $p_\theta(x, y|z, \pi)$ denotes the decoder probability of generating x and y based on the observation z and π, while $q_\phi(z, \pi|x, y)$ represents the probability of correct encoding of z and π given the measurements x and y.

Proposition 2. *We have the final lower bound for labeled data as* $\log p_\theta(x, y) \geq L(x, y)$, *where the lower bound,* $L(x, y)$, *is determined as*

$$L(x, y) = -\mathcal{M}_{(x,y)} - KL\,[\; q_\phi(\pi|x)\|p_\theta(\pi|y)]\,. \tag{31}$$

Here, $\mathcal{M}_{(x,y)} = -\mathbb{E}_{q_\phi(z|x)}\,[\log\; p_\theta(x|y, z)] + K_1 - KL(q_\phi(z|x)\; \|\; p_\theta(z))$ *and* $K_1 = \mathbb{E}_{q_\phi(z|x)}\log\; p_\theta(y)$, *while the Kullback-Leibler divergence function is* $KL\,[\; q_\phi(\pi|x)\|p_\theta(\pi|y)] = \mathbb{E}_{q_\phi(\pi|x)}\,[-\log\; p_\theta(\pi, |y) + \log q_\phi(\pi|x)]$.

Proof. The proof is provided in Appendix 7.2.

The total VAE loss is computed by adding both the labeled loss and the unlabeled loss as

$$\mathcal{J} = \sum_{(x,y)\sim \hat{p_l}} L(x, y) + \sum_{(x)\sim \hat{p_u}} U(x). \tag{32}$$

As stated before, the whole point of semi-supervised learning is train encoder and classifier network at the same time. Hence, in spite of having labels (for labeled case), we need to train the classifier with labeled data too, if we want to use this distribution as a classifier. Thus, according to [16], a classification loss has been added with (32).

$$\mathcal{J}^\alpha = \mathcal{J} + \alpha * E_{(x,y)}[-\log q_\phi(y|x)]. \tag{33}$$

In the above function α is an hyperparameter which adjusts the contributions of the classifier in the learning process. During the training process, the stochastic gradient descent of $\mathcal{J}$ is computed at each training step to update the parameters θ and ϕ. We summarize the training procedure in Algorithm 1.

Algorithm 1. Semi-supervised Learning for Time-series Classification in the Smart Healthcare System

---

1: **Input:** Labeled Data: X_L, Y_L, Unlabeled Data: X_U, Test Data: X_T
2: **Output:** Labels for Test Data
3: Get samples from Labeled & Unlabeled Data and initialize parameters ϕ and θ
4: **while** *Training* **do**
5:     **for** *Labeled Data:* X_L, Y_L **do**
6:         $X_L \rightarrow Encoder$
7:         *Compute* z_n
8:         *Concatenate* z_n & Y_L
9:         $z_n, Y_L \rightarrow Decoder$
10:        *Calculate* $L(x, y)$
11:    **end for**
12:    **for** *Unlabeled Data:* X_U **do**
13:        $X_U \rightarrow Encoder$
14:        *Compute* z_n
15:        $X_U \rightarrow Classifier$
16:        *Compute* Y_U
17:        *Concatenate* z_n & Y_U
18:        $z_n, Y_U \rightarrow Decoder$
19:        *Calculate* $U(x)$
20:    **end for**
21:    Compute $\mathcal{J} = \sum_{(x,y) \sim \hat{p_l}} L(x, y) + \sum_{(x) \sim \hat{p_u}} U(x)$
22:    Update $\mathcal{J}$ with Adam Optimizer
23: **end while**
24: **while** *Testing* **do**
25:    Evaluate Model on Test data to calculate VAE loss
26:    Evaluate Classifier on Test data
27:    Evaluate Reconstruction loss by *L2norm*
28: **end while**

---

5   Experimental Analysis

For the experiment of our semi-supervised algorithm we selected publicly available Actitracker dataset [2], which contains six daily activities, i.e. walking, jogging, upstairs, downstairs, sitting, standing. This dataset is collected in an controlled laboratory environment, where it is recorded from 36 users. The dataset from these users is collected from their cellphone operating at 20 Hz sampling rate, which results in 29,000 frames. In this analysis, we present our experimental results of training and testing data, where the evaluated performances are the VAE loss, the reconstruction loss and the classification loss. Our simulation model is based on 6-dimensional hidden variable z. We assume that an amount of labeled data equals that of unlabeled data. The representation of our model is summarized in Table 2.

5.1   VAE Loss for Training and Test Data

In Fig. 3, we present the VAE loss of training data for three different learning rates of 0.001, 0.0001 and 0.00001. Recall that loss function of VAE is composed of two terms, i.e. the reconstruction loss and the regularization term. Here, the reconstruction loss is the expected value of negative likelihood of all data points. This term encourages the decoder reconstruct our input data, whereas the regularization term is the measurement of information lost while approximating p with q. The VAE loss for training data is the addition from both the labeled loss and the unlabeled loss, whereas for test case, the input data is passed through the unlabeled structure to measure the loss. It is easily observed that as a hyper parameter, learning rate plays a crucial role in calculating the loss. Similarly, we test our model with the learning rates of 0.001, 0.0001 and 0.00001. In particular, the VAE loss of testing data is illustrated in Fig. 4.

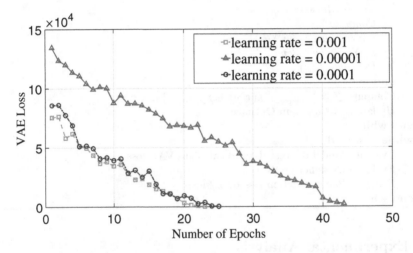

Fig. 3. VAE loss of training data for three different learning rates 0.001, 0.00001 and 0.0001

We have the following observations from these experimental results. Firstly, we train our model for both labeled and unlabeled data as well as experiment the efficacy of our model in terms of VAE loss on test data. It is readily seen that the VAE loss reaches the minimum value, when the number of epochs is nearly 50. During training, we test our model on testing data with the trained model parameters of ϕ and θ after every 5 epochs. The VAE losses from both training and testing data for learning rate of 0.00001 shows a gradual and slow decay. However, they ultimately reaches the considerably low losses, i.e. 215.314 and 121.457, respectively. For other two learning rates of 0.001 and 0.0001, the VAE losses start with the comparatively low loss. Then, they quickly reach the negative values before even reaching considerably low values. This is because

Table 2. Representation of our model

Encoder structure	
Layer 1	*60 conv 1D filters*
Layer 2	*180 conv 1D filters*
Layer 3	*FC with 120 units*
Layer 4	*FC with 90 units*
Classifier structure	
Layer 5	*FC with 6 units*
Layer 6	*60 conv 1D filters*
Layer 6	*max pool size 20*
Layer 7	*180 conv 1D filters*
Layer 8	*FC with 100 units*
Layer 9	*FC with 100 units*
Decoder structure	
Layer 10	*FC with 90 units*
Layer 11	*FC with 90 units*
Layer 12	*FC with 90 units*
Layer 13	*60 conv 2D Transpose filters*
Layer 14	*120 conv 2D Transpose filters*
Layer 15	*60 conv 2D Transpose filters*
Layer 16	*FC with 9 units*

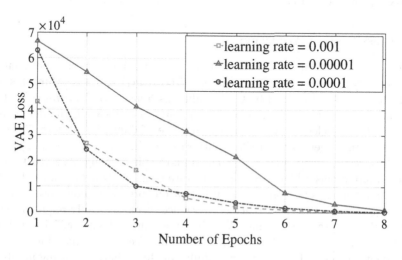

Fig. 4. VAE loss of testing data for three different learning rates 0.001, 0.00001 and 0.0001

(1) *the VAE excellently extract the most salient characteristics of human activity data, which generate the useful criteria for the compressed sensing recovery*; (2) *furthermore, our proposed CNN successfully extracts the most discriminative features, which provide the essential low-dimension latent codes.* So our joint design significantly improves training stability and efficiency, because it has capability of tuning the loss multipliers automatically. Additionally, our proposed mechanism makes better use of the training data and achieves a high accuracy even with a limited amount of labeled data available for training. Thank to the discriminative performances and the regularization effects, which enhance our proposed method on real dataset in the semi-supervised setting.

5.2   Reconstruction Loss

One of the major objectives in our proposed model is to reconstruct the input time-series by performing semi-supervised learning. We evaluate the reconstruction loss based on $L2$ *norm*. If our true input and approximated input are defined as x_i and x_r respectively, then $L2$ *norm* for computing reconstruction loss can be defined as follows. For N samples, this quantity is calculated as

$$\mathcal{R}_{Loss} = \sum_{n=1}^{N}(x_i - x_r)^2. \tag{34}$$

We experiment the reconstruction loss on our train data. For test case, we consider data points x of both labeled and unlabeled data. Then, we compute the reconstruction loss of the final output by using $L2$ *norm*. Our analysis of reconstruction loss with two different learning rates 0.001 and 0.0001 for 500 epochs is provided in Fig. 5.

5.3   Classification Accuracy:

Finally, we present our comparison of the classification accuracy between our proposed model (termed as *Semi-supervised Learning*) and a benchmark supervised learning model trained by CNN (called as *Supervised Learning*). We train both the supervised learning model and semi-supervised learning model by using 20% and 25% labeled data. For a learning rate of 0.00001 and with 500 iterations our semi-supervised classifier outperforms the supervised one by 5.28% and 5.15% respectively (Figs. 6 and 7). Moreover, it is easily observed that our proposed model has a higher convergence rate than the benchmark model. This observation confirms theoretical analysis that our proposed model does not typically require more epochs to reach convergence, because it only requires a small amount of data used for training. We also experimented with 30% labeled data but in that case we found no significant difference in classification accuracy after 500 iterations. Thus, we can rightfully conclude that, increasing number of labeled data will not make our semi-supervised model more constructive than the supervised one. It implies that our model can work efficiently with any scenario

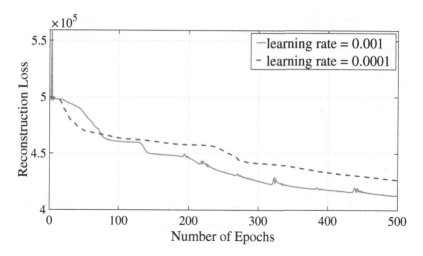

Fig. 5. Reconstruction loss of training data for two different learning rates 0.001 and 0.0001

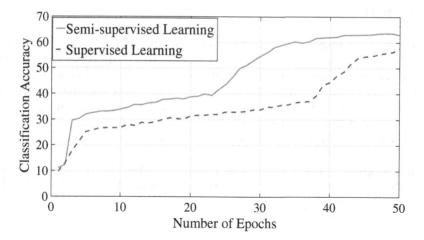

Fig. 6. Classification comparison for 20% labeled data

of big data applications, while the benchmark supervised learning model only achieves a good performance on small data. The desired experimental results demonstrate that our proposed model is benefited by the joint design of variational auto-encoder and convolutional neural network.

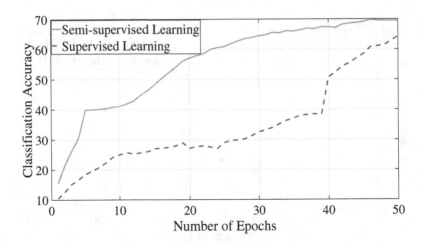

Fig. 7. Classification comparison for 25% labeled data

6 Conclusion

In this paper, we proposed a semi-supervised classifier which extracts salient and discriminative features to train a classifier in order to recognize numerous human actions. The experimental result has shown that with a small amount of labeled data our model outperforms the conventional supervised learning. For further study, experiments with larger datasets are needed to study the efficacy of the proposed model. We also aim to use fall action datasets in order to develop a fall classifier for a comprehensive smart home monitoring solution.

Acknowledgment. The research of A. Zahin, L. T. Tan and R. Q. Hu was supported in part by National Science Foundation under grants NeTS 1423348 and EARS 1547312, in part by Natural Science Foundation of China under grant 61728104, and in part by Intel Corporation.

7 APPENDIX

7.1 Variational Objective with Unlabeled Data

Recall that in the case of unlabeled data, we treat z and y as latent variables and we train a encoder and classifier network. Thus, our variational objective for unlabeled data is

$$\min_{\theta,\phi} \quad KL(q_\phi(y, z|x) \parallel p_\theta(y, z|x)),$$

where KL is the Kullback-Leibler divergence function between the two distributions, which can be obtained as $KL(q\|p) = \int_{-\infty}^{+\infty} q_i log(q_i/p_i)$. So we have

$$KL(q_\phi(y,z|x) \parallel p_\theta(y,z|x)) = \int_{-\infty}^{+\infty} q_\phi(y,z|x)) \log \frac{q_\phi(y,z|x)}{p_\theta(y,z|x)} \, dy \, dz$$

$$= \mathbb{E}_{q_\phi(y,z|x)} \left[\log \frac{q_\phi(y,z|x)}{p_\theta(y,z|x)} \right].$$

From Baye's Rule, we know that $p(y,z|x) = \left[\dfrac{p(x|y,z)p(y)p(z)}{p(x)} \right]$. Thus, we can write

$$KL(q_\phi(y,z|x) \parallel p_\theta(y,z|x)) = \mathbb{E}_{q_\phi(y,z|x)} [\log q_\phi(y,z|x) - \log p_\theta(x|y,z) \\ - \log p_\theta(y) - \log p_\theta(z) + \log p_\theta(x)].$$

So we obtain

$$\log p_\theta(x) = KL(q_\phi(y,z|x) \parallel p_\theta(y,z|x)) \\ + \mathbb{E}_{q_\phi(y,z|x)} [\log p_\theta(y) + \log p_\theta(x|y,z) - \log q_\phi(y,z|x) + \log p_\theta(z)] \quad (35)$$

As KL-divergence describes the similarity between two distributions, it is always a non-negative term. So, we characterize $\log p_\theta(x)$ in (35) as follows:

$$log\ p_\theta(x) \geq \mathbb{E}_{q_\phi(y,z|x)} \left[\log \frac{p_\theta(x|y,z)p_\theta(y)p_\theta(z)}{q_\phi(y,z|x)} \right],$$

$$\geq \mathbb{E}_{q_\phi(y,z|x)} [\log\ p_\theta(x|y,z) + \log\ p_\theta(y) + \log\ p_\theta(z) \\ - log\ q_\phi(y,z|x)],$$

$$\geq \mathbb{E}_{q_\phi(y|x)} \left[\mathbb{E}_{q_\phi(z|x)} [\log\ p_\theta(x|y,z) + \log\ p_\theta(y) \\ + log\ p_\theta(z) - log\ q_\phi(y|x) - log\ q_\phi(z|x)] \right].$$

Finally, we obtain

$$\log p_\theta(x) \geq \mathbb{E}_{q_\phi(y|x)} \left[\mathbb{E}_{q_\phi(z|x)} [\log\ p_\theta(x|y,z)] + K_1 \\ - KL(q_\phi(z|x) \parallel p_\theta(z)) - \log\ q_\phi(y|x) \right]. \quad (36)$$

where $K_1 = \mathbb{E}_{q_\phi(z|x)} \log p_\theta(y) = \log p_\theta(y)$. Here, $p_\theta(y)$ is considered as a constant. Because $p(y) = p(y|\pi)p(\pi)$ is a Dirichlet- multinomial distribution and for unlabeled case, we assume that each label y is equally likely.

We further define $\mathcal{M}_{(x,y)}$ as

$$-\mathcal{M}_{(x,y)} = \mathbb{E}_{q_\phi(z|x)} [\log\ p_\theta(x|y,z)] + K_1 - KL(q_\phi(z|x) \parallel p_\theta(z)).$$

Then, we get

$$log\ p_\theta(x) \geq \mathbb{E}_{q_\phi(y|x)} \left[-\mathcal{M}_{(x,y)} - log\ q_\phi(y|x) \right]. \quad (37)$$

So we explicitly write the expectation with respect to y. Hence, we get

$$log\ p_\theta(x) \geq \sum_y q_\phi(y|x) \left[-\mathcal{M}_{(x,y)} - log\ q_\phi(y|x) \right]. \quad (38)$$

Therefore, we have completed the proof of Proposition 1.

7.2   Variational Objective with Labeled Data

For the labeled case, both (x, y) and (z, π) are treated as unknown latent variables. The variational inferences for both z and π use a fully posterior dependent on only x. It means that we can derive $q(z, \pi)$ and $p(y)$ as follows:

$$q(z, \pi) = q(z, \pi|x) = q(z|X) * q(\pi|X),$$
$$p(y) = Cat(y|\pi).$$

Here, "Cat" represents a categorical distribution, which is a discrete probability distribution. It describes the possible results of a random variable that can take one of π possible categories, with the probability of each category separately specified. For our case, $\pi = 6$ as we have six daily activities. Furthermore, α represents a hyperparameter, which controls the weight of how strongly we want to train our classifier. Note that in order to train a classifier for the labeled case, we also aim for choosing π such that it only depends on x. By doing so, this enforces the classifier to work as the conventional classifier. It means that the classifier network $q_\phi(y|x)$ will also classify the x_L and compare its performance with the true labels. So we have

$$\min KL \ q_\phi(z, \pi|x, y) \ || \ p_\theta(z, \pi|x, y).$$

By exploiting Kullback-Leibler divergence function, we obtain

$$KL \ q_\phi(z, \pi|x, y) \ || \ p_\theta(z, \pi|x, y) = \mathbb{E}_{q_\phi(z, \pi|x, y)} \left[log \ q_\phi(z, \pi|x, y) - log \ p_\theta(z, \pi|x, y) \right].$$

According to Baye's Rule, we have $p(z, \pi|x, y) = \left[\dfrac{p(x, y|z, \pi)p(z, \pi)}{p(x, y)} \right]$. Thus, we can write $KL \ q_\phi(z, \pi|x, y) \ || \ p_\theta(z, \pi|x, y)$ as

$$KL \ q_\phi(z, \pi|x, y) \ || \ p_\theta(z, \pi|x, y) = \mathbb{E}_{q_\phi(z, \pi|x, y)} \left[log \ q_\phi(z, \pi|x, y) - log \ p_\theta(x, y|z, \pi) \right.$$
$$\left. - log \ p_\theta(z, \pi) + log \ p_\theta(x, y) \right].$$

Using the simple manipulations, $log \ p_\theta(x, y)$ can be calculated as

$$log \ p_\theta(x, y) = KL(\ q_\phi(z, \pi|x, y) || p_\theta(z, \pi|x, y))$$
$$+ \mathbb{E}_{q_\phi(z, \pi|x, y)} \left[log \ p_\theta(x, y|z, \pi) + log \ p_\theta(z, \pi) - log \ q_\phi(z, \pi|x, y) \right].$$

Recall that KL-divergence describes the similarity between two distributions. Hence, it is always a positive term. So we characterize $log \ p_\theta(x, y)$ in (39) as follows:

$$log \ p_\theta(x, y) \geq \mathbb{E}_{q_\phi(z, \pi|x, y)} \left[log \ p_\theta(x, y|z, \pi) + log \ p_\theta(z, \pi) - log \ q_\phi(z, \pi|x, y) \right].$$

According to the probability chain rule, we have $P(A, B|C, D) = P(A|B, C, D) * P(B|C, D)$. By employing the simple manipulations, we obtain

$$\log p_\theta(x, y) \geq \mathbb{E}_{q_\phi(z,\pi|x,y)} \left[\log\ p_\theta(x, |y, z, \pi) + \log\ p_\theta(y|z, \pi) \right.$$
$$\left. + \log\ p_\theta(z, \pi) - \log\ q_\phi(z, \pi|x, y) \right],$$
$$\geq \mathbb{E}_{q_\phi(z,\pi|x,y)} \left[\log\ p_\theta(x, |y, z, \pi) + \log\ p_\theta(y, z, \pi) \right.$$
$$\left. - \log\ q_\phi(z, \pi|x, y) \right],$$
$$\geq \mathbb{E}_{q_\phi(z,\pi|x,y)} \left[\log\ p_\theta(x, |y, z, \pi) + \log\ p_\theta(y, \pi) \right.$$
$$\left. + \log\ p_\theta(z) - \log\ q_\phi(z, \pi|x, y) \right],$$
$$\geq \mathbb{E}_{q_\phi(z,\pi|x,y)} \left[\log\ p_\theta(x, |y, z, \pi) + \log\ p_\theta(\pi|y) \right.$$
$$\left. + \log\ p_\theta(y) + \log\ p_\theta(z) - \log\ q_\phi(z, \pi|x, y) \right].$$

We now separate $\mathbb{E}_{q_\phi(z|x)}$ and $\mathbb{E}_{q_\phi(\pi|x)}$. This is because for labeled case, $z|x$ and $\pi|x$ are two different networks and thus they are independent. We then obtain

$$\log p_\theta(x, y) \geq \mathbb{E}_{q_\phi(z|x)} \left[\log\ p_\theta(x|y, z) + \log\ p_\theta(y) + \log\ p_\theta(z) \right.$$
$$\left. - \log q_\phi(z|x) \right] + \mathbb{E}_{q_\phi(\pi|x)} \left[\log p_\theta(\pi|y) - \log q_\phi(\pi|x) \right].$$

From (37), the first expectation at the RHS is exactly equal to $\mathcal{M}_{(x,y)}$. So we can write

$$\log p_\theta(x, y) \geq -\mathcal{M}_{(x,y)} - \mathbb{E}_{q_\phi(\pi|x)} \left[-\log\ p_\theta(\pi, |y) + \log q_\phi(\pi|x) \right].$$

Note that the remaining expectation is the KL divergence form. Finally, the labeled loss $\log p_\theta(x, y)$ has the lower bound as

$$\log p_\theta(x, y) \geq -\mathcal{M}_{(x,y)} - KL(\ q_\phi(\pi|x)\ ||\ p_\theta(\pi|y)). \tag{39}$$

Hence, we have completed the proof of Proposition 2.

References

1. Chennuru, S., Chen, P.-W., Zhu, J., Zhang, J.Y.: Mobile lifelogger – recording, indexing, and understanding a mobile user's life. In: Gris, M., Yang, G. (eds.) Mobi-CASE 2010. LNICST, vol. 76, pp. 263–281. Springer, Heidelberg (2012). https://doi.org/10.1007/978-3-642-29336-8_15
2. Forster, K., Roggen, D., Troster, G.: Unsupervised classifier self-calibration through repeated context occurrences: is there robustness against sensor displacement to gain? In: Proceedings of ISWC (2009)
3. Wu, P., Zhu, J., Zhang, J.Y.: Mobisens: a versatile mobile sensing platform for real-world applications. Mobile Netw. Appl. **18**(1), 60–80 (2013)
4. Zhang, M., Sawchuk, A.A.: A feature selection-based framework for human activity recognition using wearable multimodal sensors. In: Proceedings of ICST (2011)
5. Candes, E.J., Tao, T.: Near-optimal signal recovery from random projections: universal encoding strategies? IEEE Trans. Inf. Theory **52**(12), 5406–5425 (2006)
6. Thanh, T.L., Yun, K.H., Quoc, B.V.N.: Projected Barzilai-Borwein methods applied to distributed compressive spectrum sensing. In: Proceedings of IEEE DyS-PAN (2010)

7. Tan, L.T., Kong, H.Y.: A novel and efficient mixed-signal compressed sensing for wide-band cognitive radio. In: Proceedings of IFOST (2010)
8. Le, T.T., Kong, H.Y.: Using subspace pursuit algorithm to improve performance of the distributed compressive wide-band spectrum sensing. J. Electromagn. Eng. Sci. 11(4), 250–256 (2011)
9. Tan, L.T., Le, L.B.: Compressed sensing based data processing and MAC protocol design for smartgrids. In: Proceedings of IEEE WCNC (2015)
10. Tan, L.T., Le, L.B.: Joint data compression and MAC protocol design for smartgrids with renewable energy. Wirel. Commun. Mob. Com. 16(16), 2590–2604 (2016)
11. Tan, L.T., Hu, R.Q., Hanzo, L.: Twin-timescale artificial intelligence aided mobility-aware edge caching and computing in vehicular networks. IEEE Trans. Veh. Technol. 68, 3086–3099 (2019)
12. Tan, L.T., Hu, R.Q.: Mobility-aware edge caching and computing framework in vehicle networks: a deep reinforcement learning. IEEE Trans. Veh. Technol. 67(11), 10190–10203 (2018)
13. Wang, Z., Oates, T.: Encoding time-series as images for visual inspection and classification using tiled convolutional neural networks. In: Proceedings of AAAI (2011)
14. Dhar, M., Grover, A., Ermon, S.: Modeling sparse deviations for compressed sensing using generative models. In: Proceedings of ICML (2018)
15. Mardani, M., et al.: Deep generative adversarial neural networks for compressive sensing MRI. IEEE Trans. Med. Imaging 38(1), 167–179 (2019)
16. Kingma, D.P., Mohamed, S., Rezende, D.J., Welling, M.: Semi-supervised learning with deep generative models. In: Proceedings of Advances in Neural Information Processing Systems (2014)
17. Lockhart, J.W., Weiss, G.M., Xue, J.C., Gallagher, S.T., Grosner, A.B., Pulickal, T.T.: Design considerations for the WISDM smart phone-based sensor mining architecture. In: Proceedings of Fifth IWK DSD ACM (2011)
18. Plotz, T., Hammerla, N.Y., Olivier, P.: Feature learning for activity recognition in ubiquitous computing. In: Proceedings of Twenty-Second IJCAI (2011)
19. Hinton, G., Osindero, S., Teh, Y.-W.: A fast learning algorithm for deep belief nets. Neural Comput. 18(7), 1527–1554 (2006)
20. Joachims, T.: Transductive inference for text classification using support vector machines. In: Proceedings of ICML (1999)
21. Figo, D., Diniz, P.C., Ferreira, D.R., Cardoso, J.M.: Preprocessing techniques for context recognition from accelerometer data. Pers. Ubiquit. Comput. 4(7), 645–662 (2010)
22. Tamura, T., Sekine, M., Ogawa, M., Togawa, T., Fukui, Y.: Classification of acceleration waveforms during walking by wavelet transform. Methods Inf. Med. 36(4–5), 356–359 (1997)
23. Le, T.T., Kong, H.Y.: Performance of spiked population models for spectrum sensing. J. Electromagn. Eng. Sci. 12(3), 203–209 (2012)
24. Vollmer, C., Gross, H.-M., Eggert, J.P.: Learning features for activity recognition with shift-invariant sparse coding. In: Proceedings of ICANN (2013)
25. Blum, A., Chawla, S.: Learning from labeled and unlabeled data using graph mincuts. In: Proceedings of ICML, pp. 19–26 (2001)
26. Cote, M., Larochelle, H.: An infinite restricted Boltzmann machine. Neural Comput. 28(7), 1265–1288 (2016)
27. Zeng, M., et al.: Convolutional neural networks for human activity recognition using mobile sensors. In: Proceedings of MobiCASE (2014)

CoLoRSim: A Highly Scalable ICN Simulation Platform

Hongyi Li[1(✉)] and Hongbin Luo[2]

[1] Beijing Jiaotong University, Beijing, China
16120084@bjtu.edu.cn
[2] Beihang University, Beijing, China
luohb@buaa.edu.cn

Abstract. In the past few years, Internet usage is shifting from host-to-host communication to content distribution. As a result, information-centric networking (ICN) is emerging as a promising candidate paradigm for the future Internet. Meanwhile, many researchers have developed specified simulation platforms for the ICN architecture they proposed, to evaluate the performances in the research stage. In this paper, we present a simulation platform for a recent proposed ICN architecture named CoLoR. With the help of this simulation platform, performance for CoLoR can be evaluated through large-scale simulations. New protocols designed for CoLoR can also be studied.

Keywords: CoLoRSim · CoLoR architecture ·
Information–centric networking · INET

1 Introduction

As a promising candidate paradigm of the future Internet, information-centric networking (ICN) is envisioned to advocate the efficient usage of the network resource. Over the past few years, many researchers put lots of efforts on ICN and a lot of different ICN architectures [1] have been proposed in order to fit the requirements of different networking environments and address a series of limitations of the current Internet, including the efficient delivery of information to the users, mobility management and security enforcement.

Instead of assigning IP addresses to hosts, ICN assigns a globally unique name to a piece of content. To obtain content, a consumer sends out a request carrying the name of the desired content to the network. The network will forward the request to the closest caching node. The caching node returns the content by using data packets carrying the same content name. The intermediate nodes along the forwarding path can cache the content for serving subsequent requests for the same content.

In our previous work, we have proposed a new ICN architecture called CoLoR [2], whose intrinsic idea is to couple service location with inter-domain routing, but to decouple them from forwarding. Taking the advantages of CoLoR, many issues can be addressed. For example, the in-network caching of CoLoR can help Internet Service Providers (ISPs) reduce content retrieval latency and improves users' Quality-of-Experience (QoE), since the desired content may be retrieved from a nearby caching

S. Han et al. (Eds.): AICON 2019, LNICST 287, pp. 473–485, 2019.
https://doi.org/10.1007/978-3-030-22971-9_40

node instead of a remote server [3]. CoLoR can also help address the mobility issues [4] and improve network security [5].

In our previous research work, we put lots of efforts into developing a real-world prototype to evaluate the feasibility and performance of CoLoR. However, due to the limitations of machines and the complexity of implementations, the prototype size is restricted in 40-60 nodes, which has not reached the realistic Internet scale. As such, there is a need to develop a simulation platform for CoLoR in large-scale network topologies.

To address the above issues, in this paper, we present CoLoRSim, a highly scalable simulation platform for CoLoR based on the well-known simulator of OMNeT++ and INET framework [6, 7]. Especially, we make the following main contributions.

First, we designed and realized the main components of CoLoRSim, which includes a topology generator, a platform configuration module, the resource manager, the border routers and other components.

Second, we evaluate the relationship between the time consumption and topology scale. We draw the conclusion that when the topology contains 10000 autonomous systems (Ases, or domains) simulation will consume about four hours and 16.5G memory.

The rest of this paper is organized as follows. In Sect. 2, we summarize several ICN simulators. In Sect. 3, we briefly introduce CoLoR architecture. In Sect. 4, we introduce the system-level architecture of the developed simulation platform and the node structure of resource manager and border router. We also present how to extend this simulator. Finally, we conclude the paper in Sect. 6.

2 Related Work

For researchers, building a prototype system for a new ICN architecture is hard and expensive, especially when a large-scale network is needed. In such a situation, simulation is a better choice. Various simulation platforms have been developed for different ICN architectures. ndnSIM [8], which implements Named Data Network (NDN)/ Content-Centric Network (CCN) [9] communication model, has been built based on ns-3. ccnSIM [10] for NDN/CCN has been developed based on OMNeT++. In Table 1, we list several ICN open source simulators.

Table 1. Summary of several simulators

Simulator	Architecture	Language	Operation system
ICNsim	Others	OMNeT++, C/C++	Linux, FreeBSD
Icarus	Caching	Python	Linux, Mac
CCN-Lite	CCN/NDN	OMNeT++, C	Linux, Mac, Win
CCNPL-sim	CCN/NDN	C++	Linux
NDNsim	CCN/NDN	NS-3, C++, Python	Linux, Mac
ccnSim	CCN/NDN	OMNet++, C++	Linux

3 A Brief Introduction to CoLoR

CoLoR architecture assumes that the future Internet is still comprised of ASes. CoLoR architecture separates inter-domain routing from intra-domain routing explicitly. Every domain in CoLoR architecture can choose its network architectures according to its demand, such as IPv4, IPv6, and others. Meanwhile, inter-domain routing is based on path identifier (PID). Every inter-domain path connecting two domains will be assigned a unique PID negotiated by the two domains. Border routers located in the border of domains need to store the intra-domain and inter-domain routing tables. For example, R2 in Fig. 1 has an inter-domain routing table like the one shown in the down left corner of Fig. 1. Each inter-domain routing entry contains the destination domain of the PID, the value of the PID, the prefix length of the PID, and preference value if multiple inter-domain paths exist.

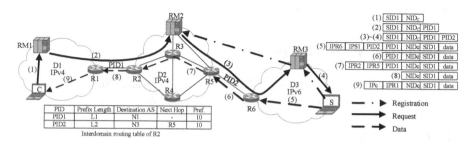

Fig. 1. Illustration of basic mechanisms of CoLoR architecture.

In particular, the PID of a path is not advertised through the Internet. It will only be kept secret by the two connected domains. By default, a user needs to send a request message which is routed to the receiver through the network, and then the receiver sends the desired content back to the user. Such a default-off communication model is more secure than the default-on communication model employed by the current Internet.

A globally unique node identifier (NID) is assigned to every component, and a globally unique service identifier (SID) is assigned to every piece of content in CoLoR. A logic centralized resource manager (RM) is deployed in every domain to manage node information, service information and inter-domain path information.

Figure 1 illustrates how a request message is routed from a user to the content provider. We assume that service provider S1 has registered service whose SID is SID1 in the network. The procedure is illustrated by dash lines in Fig. 1. When a user C wants to obtain content, whose SID is SID1, it sends a request message to its local resource manager (RM1) by using local routing mechanism, such as IPv4 in Fig. 1. Request message carries SID1 and NIDc of C. When RM1 receives the request message, it looks up the service information table and finds out that this request message should be forwarded to RM2 in D2. According to Fig. 1, RM1 appends PID1 at the end of the request message and sends the request message to RM2. When RM2 receives the request message, it looks up the service information table and finds out that this message should be forwarded to RM3 in D3. RM2 appends PID2 at the end of the request message and sends the request message to RM3, as illustrated by (3) in Fig. 1. While RM3 receives the request message, it looks up in its service information table and finds out that the desired service is hosted by service provider S1. It sends the request message to S1, as illustrated by (4) in Fig. 1.

When S1 receives the request message, it sends the requested content back by using several data packets. Each of these data packets contains the information of SID1, NIDc, PID2, PID1. RM3 encapsulates an IPv6 header to the data packets and sends them to the border router R6, as illustrated by (5) in Fig. 1. When R6 receives the data packet, it strips the IPv6 header and PID2. Then R6 sends the data packet to R5, as illustrated by (6) in Fig. 1. While R5 receives a data packet, it forwards the data packet to R2 after encapsulating an IPv4 header to the data packet, as illustrated by (7) in Fig. 1. R2 strips the IPv6 header and PID1 and then sends the data packet to R1 as illustrated by (8) in Fig. 1. Finally, R1 sends the data packet to user S1 by using local routing mechanism, as illustrated by (9) in Fig. 1.

4 Simulation Model Design

A new simulation platform is developed based on OMNeT++ and INET framework in order to evaluate the performance of the CoLoR architecture.

4.1 Design Goals

The development of CoLoRSim takes following goals into consideration.

- Full support for CoLoR architecture
- Compatibility with original INET modules
- Auto-configuration for parameters
- Extensible architecture
- Applicable to large-scale network simulations

4.2 Simulator Architecture

As introduced in previous sections, the main system elements of CoLoR architecture include resource manager, border router, client/server. In this section, we describe the system-level architecture and node structure of CoLoRSim.

Figure 2 shows the architecture of CoLoRSim. There are eight blocks in it: topology generator, platform configuration, communication protocol, user-defined modules, mapping information tables, OMNeT++ platform interface, and internal/external analysis tools. The advantage of this architecture is that resource manager and border router can share the same communication protocol block and carry out different operations by replacing different user-defined modules.

Three different types of flows are defined, including internal input/output flow, external input/output flow, and control flow. Internal input/output flow represents communications via message or inter-module communication mechanism provided by

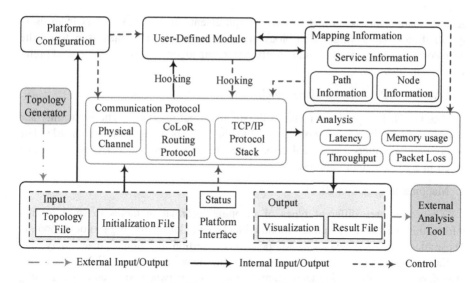

Fig. 2. The architecture of CoLoRSim

OMNeT++. External input/output flow represents communications via regular text files, JSON files, XML files, and even network connections. The control flow represents communications via signals.

Three different types of flows are defined, including internal input/output flow, external input/output flow, and control flow. Internal input/output flow represents communications via message or inter-module communication mechanism provided by OMNeT++. External input/output flow represents communications via regular text files, JSON files, XML files, and even network connections. The control flow represents communications via signals.

1. Topology Generator Block

New protocols should be tested under different topologies. To this end, a topology generator is developed, to avoid the errors in manual topology generation. The topology generator accepts flexible network parameter settings, including the number of ASes and the degree distribution of the network. The output files of the topology generator include an AS-level network description file and corresponding initialization file. Each node in the network description file represents an autonomous system consisting of a resource manager, border routers, clients, servers and other IPv4 or IPv6 routers.

2. Platform Configuration Block

A large number of parameters need to be set before starting a simulation. If all parameters are placed in the initialization file, the size of the initialization file will explode with the number of nodes, increasing the time of initialization. In addition, multiple initialization files need to be generated if the protocols are tested under different situations. Therefore, in CoLoRSim, the platform configuration block can generate parameters according to users' requirements or read parameters from users specified files. The configuration block of the current version enables users to set the inter-domain path prefixes through prefix generating algorithms or pre-generated prefix assignment files.

3. OMNeT++ Platform Interface Block

The OMNeT++ platform includes input and output interfaces. The input interface enables users to import a topology file and the corresponding initialization file. The output interface offers a graphical display, performance chart and statistics that can be saved in a file for future analysis.

4. Mapping Information Block

There are three different types of mapping information tables to store routing information used by user-defined-module blocks and CoLoR routing protocol module. These blocks provide several basic operations: insertion, deletion, update, query, and verification. Service information table stores the mapping between SIDs and service providers. Node information table stores the mapping between NIDs and local routing identifiers, such as mapping between NIDs and IPv4 addresses. The path information table stores the mapping between PIDs and destination autonomous systems. The key shared between two adjacent ASes will also be stored in path information module.

5. Analysis Block

Two different types of analysis blocks are provided in CoLoRSim: internal analysis block (Analysis block) and external analysis tools block. Internal analysis block collects critical statistics from user-defined-module blocks and communication protocol block, such as latency, throughput, and packet loss. These statistics can be stored by the output interfaces provided by OMNeT++ platform interface block. An in-depth understanding of all collected data is gotten by using external analysis tools.

6. Communication Protocols Block

Communication protocols block provides protocols from physical layer to network layer. The basic structure of this block is shown as Fig. 3. Communication protocol block includes physical layer protocols, link layer protocols, and network protocols. We use physical layer modules, link layer modules, and some existing network layer modules. Only wired network is taken into consideration, where Point-to-Point (PPP) and Ethernet protocols are supported.

The network layer supports different protocols. First, we implement a CoLoR routing protocol module which supports an inter-domain routing protocol based on PIDs and an intra-domain routing protocol based on NIDs. CoLoR routing protocol block also translate NIDs and PIDs into local routing identifiers. Second, routing protocols used in the current Internet is also supported. Because local routing protocols are selected by network administrators, different autonomous systems may choose different protocols. Thus, we simplify the change of local routing protocol module, without modifying other modules. The CoLoR routing protocol module detects the type of local routing protocol and encapsulates correct information into packets sent to the down layers.

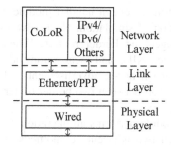

Fig. 3. The structure of communication protocols block

7. User Defined Modules Block

Communication protocols block only focuses on routing and transmitting messages. As a message is detected by communication protocol block, the message will be forwarded to a user-defined module according to the type of the message and the destination port number. User-defined module will call its own handleMessage() function when receiving the message. A user-defined module is usually designed for one type of message. Several related functions have been implemented:

Client module is used to generate request flow subject to a probability distribution, such as Poisson distribution. This module is also used to handle received data packets.

Server module is used to handle received request packets and generate data flow corresponding to the requested service. The characteristics of data flows are subject to probability distributions or characteristics inferred from real Internet flow data.

Request packet handler module of border routers and resource managers performs request packet processing, request packet verification, and any other operations on request packets. This module may modify requests based on its local policy or drop illegal packets if the packet verification fails. For example, when a request packet should be forwarded to another autonomous system, a PID should be encapsulated into it. When a border router receives a request, the router calculates a message authentication code and drop the packet if the calculated code is not the same as the code carried in the request packet.

Data packet handler module behaves similarly to request handler module. This module is equipped with border routers and resource managers. This module performs data packet processing, data packet verification, and any other operations on data packets. This module needs to modify packet and drop illegal packets. For example, when a data packet is forwarded to another border router located in another domain, a PID is popped. This module will also use message authentication code to detect if a packet is modified by attackers.

Service registration packet handler module is equipped with servers, border routers, and resource managers. Servers use this module to generate service information and announce it to its local resource manager. When receiving the service advertisement messages, resource manager adds new entries into service information table and make announcements to the parent autonomous systems and peer autonomous systems, according to the local policy defined by users.

Node registration packet/management handler module performs automatic configuration during the early period of simulation. Node advertisements will be generated and send to resource manager and border routers. When node advertisements are received, the mapping between NIDs and local routing identifiers can be established based on the information carried in the advertisements. This module can also interchange inter-domain information between two border routers and send the information to the resource manager.

PID updating handler module performs all operations about path prefixes, such as periodic negotiation between two adjacent autonomous systems, advertisements for newly negotiated path prefixes.

Those modules can be equipped according to the types of nodes. For example, a resource manager is equipped with all these modules except client module and server module. For different types of nodes, the same type of user-defined modules has some differences. For example, request packet handler module of resource manager needs to query its database to decide how and where to forward this request, while requests packet handler module of border routers do packet verification instead.

8. Extensibility

Extensibility provides the ability to add new functions without modifying existing modules. In our simulation platform, we provide hooking interfaces between communication protocols block and user-defined module block.

The first step to use hooking module is to specify the hooking function. When the hooking module receives a message from other modules, the hooking module will call the function we specify previously. By specifying different functions, we can change one node's behavior. For example, to record the PID sequences carried by a request, the client module can be modified to extract PID sequence and save it to a file. But such a method requires recompiling simulation platform, which may take long time and cause new issues. A hooking module can address this issue. We can develop new functions separately without modifying existing modules. Then, by modifying the parameters of hooking module and the hooking module will load the functions automatically and perform the corresponding functions.

4.3 Node Structure

In the previous sections, we describe the system-level design of CoLoRSim. This section further shows the node structure design based on the CoLoRSim. Each node contains the communication protocol block, the user-defined module block, and information table block. However, different user-defined module blocks are defined for different types of nodes.

1. Resource manager

The structure of resource manager is shown as Fig. 4. Resource manager is equipped with five types of user-defined modules, i.e., request packet handler, service registration handler, PID updating handler and node management handler.

When a message arrives at a resource manager, the physic layer and linker layer module process this message firstly. Then the message will be sent to the IPv4 or IPv6

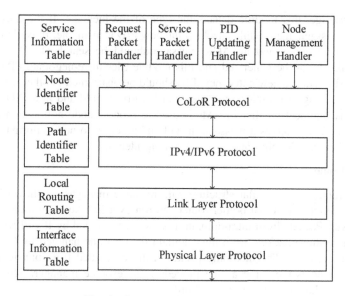

Fig. 4. Structure of resource manager

protocol module. The message will be sent to the CoLoR protocol module if the destination IP address belongs to this resource manager. Message received by CoLoR protocol module will be sent to a user-defined module according to the type of message. For example, if a request packet is received, this message is sent to request packet handler. As the message arrives at a user-defined module, these modules will take actions.

When user-defined modules send out messages, the CoLoR protocol module will receive those messages and get the destination of those messages. CoLoR protocol module will encapsulate corresponding control information into packets according to its local routing protocols. For example, if the local routing protocol is IPv4, then the IPv4 address of the destination will be encapsulated into control information. IPv4 or IPv6 protocol modules can process received messages from CoLoR protocol module according to the control information. After processed by link layer and physical layer module, the message will finally be sent to other nodes.

Request packet handlers in RMs get requested SID and query it in the service information table. In addition, this module decides which node or which domain this message should be forwarded to.

Service registration packet handlers in RMs will get the SID, NID of provider, the autonomous system the provider is located in and other information about this service. A new service entry will be added into service information table. Service registration handler will also send an acknowledgment (ACK) message to the source of the received registration message and register this service to its parent autonomous systems if possible.

PID updating handlers in RMs are used to negotiate new PIDs with the adjacent ASes and distribute new PIDs to nodes in the same domain. When receiving a PID updating message, this module detects the type of the message. If the message is a negotiation message, the module checks if the new PID is available. If available, a new entry should be added and an ACK message should be sent back. Otherwise, an available PID should be generated and this module tries to re-negotiate PID with the other one. After adding new entry, new PID should be distributed to other nodes in this domain by sending distribution messages which carry the old and new PIDs.

Node management handler in RMs is used to process node notification message. When this module receives a message, it will add an entry to node information table. This entry contains the NID and its local routing identifier.

2. Border Router

Border router has a similar structure with resource manager, as shown in Fig. 5. The biggest difference is that border router can run over link layer protocol instead of network layer. Packets from intra-domain links will be handled by IPv4/IPv6 protocol module, while those packets from inter-domain links can be handled by CoLoR protocol module directly. The incoming packets will be handled from physical layer to application layer as the same as the procedure in resource manager. The outgoing packets will be handled in the reversed order.

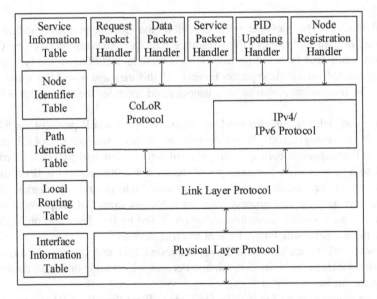

Fig. 5. Structure of border router

Request packet handlers in BRs forwards request packets according to the result querying from path information table. Data packet handler in BRs checks if data packets are legal and forward legal packets according to the routing entry queried from path information table. Service packet handlers in BRs only forwards registration message. PID updating handlers in BRs receives PID distribution message and update corresponding entries in its path information table. Node management handlers in BRs announce its information including its own NID, its local routing identifier to the RM and other border routers. Node management handlers also update the node information table as receiving advertisements.

3. Client/Server

Structure of client module, as shown in Fig. 6, is similar with border router. The request packet handler is replaced by a client module or server module. A service registration packet handler is replaced with service generating handler. In client/server, all received requests should be forwarded to server module and all data packets should be forwarded to client module. Service registration handler module generates service registration messages and sends them to its local resource manager.

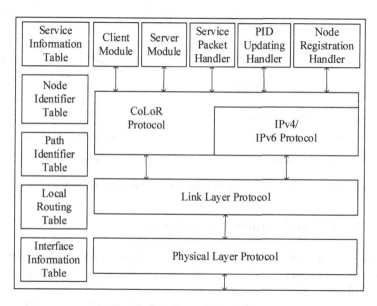

Fig. 6. Structure of client/server

5 Evaluation

In this section, we evaluate the performance of the CoLoRSim. The CPU of the server is Intel Xeon E7-4820 @ 2.0 GHz. The total memory size is 128G and the capacity of hard drives is 900 GB.

We define two different phases of simulation, initialization phase, and simulation phase. The initialization phase begins with reading topology from files and ends with the first event occurring. The simulation phase begins with the first event and end with the last event.

Different topologies are adopted, containing different numbers of autonomous systems. Each node in our topology will generate 500 requests and corresponding 500 data packets whose length is 1000 bytes.

We measure the time usage and peak memory usage of the initialization process and simulation process. The simulation time is set to 8000 s.

Figure 7(a) and (b) show that both time usage and memory usage are almost proportional to the size of the simulation networks in both initialization and simulation phase. When we simulate a network that contains 8,000 autonomous systems, about 56,000 nodes, CoLoRSim consumes about 12G memory and 200 min. As the number of autonomous systems reaches 10000, we need 16.5 G memory and 4 h.

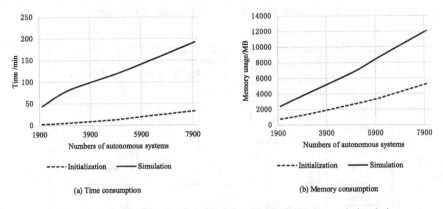

(a) Time consumption   (b) Memory consumption

Fig. 7. Time and memory consumption during initialization and simulation

6   Conclusions and Future Perspectives

In this paper, we present the design of a simulation platform for the CoLoR architecture based on OMNeT++ and INET framework. The system-level architecture of the whole simulation platform and the node structures of resource manager, border router, client and server are introduced in detail. The performance of CoLoRSim is evaluated, and the relationship between resource consumption and topology scale is also demonstrated.

In the future, we will enhance the compatibility of wireless link in CoLoRSim, such as IEEE 802.11. The parallel simulation will also be introduced to speed up the simulation, and the memory usage will be optimized.

References

1. Xylomenos, G., et al.: A survey of information-centric networking research. IEEE Commun. Surv. Tutor. **16**(2), 1024–1049 (2014)
2. Luo, H., Chen, Z., Cui, J., Zhang, H., Zukerman, M., Qiao, C.: CoLoR: an information-centric internet architecture for innovations. IEEE Netw. **28**(3), 4–10 (2014)
3. Zhang, M., Tang, J., Rao, Y., Luo, H., Zhang, H.: Degree-based probabilistic caching in content-centric networking. China Commun. **14**(3), 158–168 (2017)

4. Ying, R., Hongbin, L., Deyun, G., Huachun, Z., Hongke, Z.: LBMA: a novel locator based mobility support approach in named data networking. China Commun. **11**(4), 111–120 (2014)
5. Luo, H., Chen, Z., Li, J., Vasilakos, A.V.: Preventing distributed denial-of-service flooding attacks with dynamic path identifiers. IEEE Trans. Inf. Forensics Secur. **12**(8), 1801–1815 (2017)
6. OMNeT++. https://omnetpp.org/. Accessed 20 Dec 2018
7. INET Framework. https://inet.omnetpp.org/. Accessed 20 Dec 2018
8. Mastorakis, S., Afanasyev, A., Zhang, L.: On the evolution of ndnSIM. ACM SIGCOMM Comput. Commun. Rev. **47**(3), 19–33 (2017)
9. Jacobson, V., Smetters, D.K., Thornton, J.D., Plass, M.F., Briggs, N.H., Braynard, R.L.: Networking named content. In: Proceedings of the 5th International Conference on Emerging Networking Experiments and Technologies - CoNEXT 2009, Rome, Italy, pp. 1–12. ACM Press (2009)
10. Chiocchetti, R., Rossi, D., Rossini, G.: ccnSIM: an highly scalable CCN simulator. In: 2013 IEEE International Conference on Communications (ICC), pp. 2309–2314. IEEE, Budapest, Hungary (2013)

Manifold Learning Based Super Resolution for Mixed-Resolution Multi-view Video in Visual Internet of Things

Yuan Zhou[1,3(✉)], Ying Wang[2], Yeda Zhang[3], Xiaoting Du[3], Hui Liu[1], and Chuo Li[3]

[1] The National Ocean Technology Center, Tianjin 300111, China
zhouyuan@tju.edu.cn
[2] Unit 61660 of PLA, Beijing 100089, China
[3] Tianjin University, Tianjin 300072, China

Abstract. In a Visual Internet of Things (VIoT), the video sequences of different viewpoints are captured by different visual sensors and transmitted simultaneously, which puts a huge burden on storage and bandwidth resources. Mixed-resolution multi-view video format can alleviate the burden on the limited storage and bandwidth resources. However, the low resolution view need to be up-sampled to provide high quality visual experiences to the users. Therefore, a super resolution (SR) algorithm to reconstruct the low resolution view is highly desirable. In this paper, we propose a new two-stage super resolution method. In the first depth-assisted high frequency synthesis stage, depth image based rendering (DIBR) is used to project a high resolution view to a low resolution view to estimate the super resolution result. Then in the second high frequency compensation stage, the local block matching model based on manifold learning is used to enhance the super resolution result. The experimental results demonstrate that our method is capable to achieving a PSNR gain up to 4.76 dB over bicubic baseline and recover details in edge regions, without sacrificing the quality of smooth areas.

Keywords: Visual Internet of Things · Super resolution · Manifold learning

1 Introduction

In recent years, the field of Visual Internet of Things (VIoT) has attracted a lot of research attention and provided a broad variety of application, such as security surveillance, smart homes, health-care [5,14]. VIoT is comprised of a large number of visual sensors, each of which captures massive video information

Supported by organization NSFC61571326.

about target events, and transmits them to a central base station or a data sink. However, the video sequences of different viewpoints are captured by different visual sensors and transmitted simultaneously in a common VIoT, which puts a huge burden on storage and bandwidth resources. In order to reduce the amount of data to be compressed, the mixed-resolution (MR) multi-view video format is introduced [13]. In the MR video format, some visual sensors acquire viewpoints at high resolution (HR), while others are captured at low resolution (LR). This significantly reduces the amount of data for storage and transmission for multi-view video applications.

Recently, Brust et al. propose mixed resolution multi-view coding framework for mobile devices, where one of the views is coded entirely at a lower spatial resolution than the others [3]. The multi-view video plus depth (MVD) representation and coding scheme are proposed in [1,11], which provide a multi-view texture scene and the corresponding depth map. These methods can provide fairly good results in bitrate reduction. However, the decoded low-resolution view in these aforementioned work is of poor visual quality compared with the high resolution view, since these methods do not compensate for the quality differences between the views.

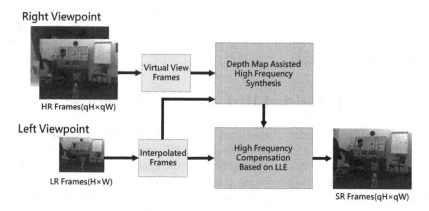

Fig. 1. The framework of our proposed method. The high resolution right view assists the SR of low resolution left view. The SR method contains two stages: (1) the depth map assisted high frequency component synthesis (DHFS) stage; and (2) the high frequency compensation (HFCOM) stage.

We consider situations where two views are of different spatial resolutions. According to binocular suppression theory [2], the human visual system (HVS) perceives high frequency information from the high resolution view, such that one can approximately perceive a visual feeling of the high resolution view. However, such approximate feeling will cause visual uncomfortableness. In order to tackle this deficiency, a super resolution (SR) algorithm to reconstruct the low resolution view is highly desirable. In general, super resolution algorithms can be categorized into three classes, namely the interpolation-based [18], reconstruction-based [16] and example-based approaches [4,15]. In recent years, these SR resolution methods have been applied to multi-view video applications gradually. Besides, for multi-view video SR, high frequency information from neighboring high-resolution views can be used to increase the visual quality of the low-resolution camera video sequence [9,10,17].

In this paper, we propose a novel multi-view video SR method assisted by virtual views. Unlike the aforementioned papers intending to obtain more accurate high frequency information from adjacent high resolution views, we present an example learning based method to compensate the synthesized high resolution information. Figure 1 depicts the framework of our proposed method, which consists of two stages: (1) the depth map assisted high frequency component synthesis (DHFS) stage; and (2) the high frequency compensation (HFCOM) stage. To better recover high frequency information, we mainly contribute to the multi-view video SR in the following two aspects:

(1) In the first stage, we measure the similarity of the virtual and interpolated views using both the spatial and depth information to locate mismatched regions, and reduce erroneous high frequency added to the interpolated view; and

(2) In the second stage, a block matching method based on locally linear embedding (LLE), a representative algorithm in manifold learning, is used to compensate the synthesized high frequency component and reconstruct the missing high frequency component in the mismatched regions, which is able to remarkably improve the quality of reconstruction, especially for the non-parallel multi-view video sequences.

2   The Depth Assisted High Frequency Synthesis

In the original high frequency synthesis method [8], the high frequency component is directly extracted from the virtual view V_L^v and added to the interpolated view V_L^i. However, this virtual view generated using the depth-image-based rendering (DIBR) [6] method contains correspondence errors such as cracks and occlusions attributable to the inherent defects of DIBR. As a result, the high frequency component extracted from the correspondence errors will cause obvious mismatching in the SR result. Therefore, a similarity check between the virtual view V_L^v and the interpolated view V_L^i is employed to identify mismatched regions, and the high frequency part of the projection points in V_L^v that fail in the similarity check would not be added to the corresponding position of V_L^i.

Similarity is measured by calculating the sum of the absolute differences (SAD) of corresponding image blocks centered around (u', v') between the virtual view V_L^v and the interpolated view V_L^i. To further utilize the depth information, we also calculate SAD of the corresponding depth map blocks centered around (u', v') between the virtual depth map D_L^v and the original depth map D_L. The total SAD of the corresponding blocks in the color images and depth maps is shown as follows

$$SAD = \sum_{(u',\,v')\in S} \left| V_L^v\left(u',\,v'\right) - V_L^i\left(u',\,v'\right) \right| +$$

$$\sum_{(u',\,v')\in S} \left| D_L\left(u',\,v'\right) - D_L^v\left(u',\,v'\right) \right| \tag{1}$$

where S is the block range, and $D_L^v\left(u',\,v'\right)$ is the projected virtual depth map, which is mentioned in the last section.

The occlusion and crack areas in virtual view will have obvious difference with the interpolated view, and the depth value of these areas in the virtual depth map would also have difference with the original depth map, these would lead to a large SAD value. If the SAD value of block S is larger than a threshold T_s, all the pixels in block S of V_L^v are refilled by the interpolated pixels from V_L^i, and we mark $M\left(u',\,v'\right) = 0$, or all the pixels in block S remain to be virtual view pixels and $M\left(u',\,v'\right) = 1$. Here, M is a mask matrix that indicates whether or not a pixel is from the virtual view.

After the similarity check, the virtual view result can be refined. One can extract the low frequency component of V_L^v using a Gaussian filter F and add the high frequency component, which is the difference of the original virtual view frame and its low frequency component, to the interpolated view to obtain the (DHFS) result V_L^{SYN} as follows

$$V_L^{SYN} = V_L^i + (V_L^v - F(V_L^v)) \times M. \tag{2}$$

3 High Frequency Compensation Based on Manifold Learning

In our high frequency compensation model, we use the local linear embedding (LLE) [12] algorithm, which is a representative algorithm in manifold learning, to enhance the high frequency synthesized in the first stage. The DHFS super resolution result V_L^{SYN} is assumed as the HR space, while its down sample denoted by $V_{L_d}^{SYN}$ is assumed as the LR space. Unlike using the whole training set as the searching range, we determine a much smaller searching range centering around the LR image patch. Thus, block matching is processed between the low-resolution frame V_L and $V_{L_d}^{SYN}$ in a small searching range, and then a fusion of the high frequency information extracted from the matched blocks is added to the interpolated image to enhance the SR result.

Figure 2 illustrates the manifold learning based high frequency compensation model, where x_n indicates the image patches in the low-resolution frame V_L, while y_n refers to the SR result corresponding to x_n. Here, $y_n = y_n^I + y_n^H$, where y_n^I denotes the interpolation result of y_n and y_n^H is the high frequency part reconstructed by the LLE algorithm. The high frequency compensation (HFCOM) algorithm follows three steps:

(1) Determine the local searching range. To enhance the current patch x_n in V_L, a corresponding local neighbor area R_n in $V_{L_d}^{SYN}$ is determined as

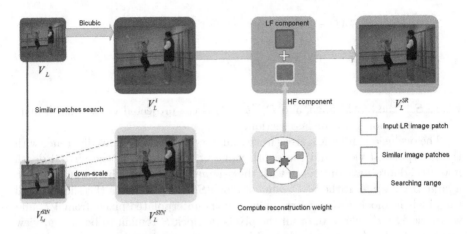

Fig. 2. Manifold learning based high frequency compensation model.

the searching area. The size of the searching area is determined by whether or not x_n is a high-frequency missing patch. A high-frequency missing patch is determined to the ratio of the number of interpolated pixels to the whole patch. For each patch x_n, we calculate

$$\lambda_{x_n} = 1 - \frac{\sum\limits_{(i,j) \in R_n} M(i,j)}{S' \times S'} \tag{3}$$

where, S' is the size of block x_n. M is the mask map calculated in last section. If λ_{x_n} is larger than threshold λ_0, x_n is determined as a high-frequency missing patch, and the search range of x_n will be the whole image space of $V_{L_d}^{SYN}$. Otherwise, the search range will be a small square area that centers around x_n.

(2) Search similar image patches and obtain reconstruction weights. Then several similar patches of x_n are searched in R_n and indicated as x_n^k. The reconstruction weights W_n are computed by minimizing the local reconstruction error.

The Euclidean distance is used to define neighbors and reconstruct weights of x_n. Several similar patches, which have the smallest Euclidean distance with x_n, are found and marked as $x_n, k = 1, \ldots, K$. By minimizing the local reconstruction error for x_n, the optimality is achieved:

$$\varepsilon_n = \left\| x_n - \sum_{k=1}^{K} w_k x_n^k \right\| \quad s.t. \sum_{k=1}^{K} w_k = 1. \tag{4}$$

Apparently, minimizing ε_n subject to the constraints is a constrained least square problem. Define a local Gram matrix

$$G_n \triangleq (x_n I^T - X_n)^T (x_n I^T - X_n) \tag{5}$$

where I is a column vector of ones and X_n is a matrix with its columns being the neighbors of x_n. An efficient way to solving (10) is to solve $G_n W_n = I$, and then normalize the weights. Then, the reconstruction weights W_n of patch x_n is attainted.

(3) **Reconstruct the high frequency component.** These similar patches have corresponding image patches in V_L^{SYN}, which are indicated as y_n^k. Finally, by fusing the high frequency part of y_n^k under the same reconstruction weights W_n, the high frequency part y_n^H is reconstructed.

The high-frequency part of x_n is reconstructed based on the corresponding HR patches with the aid of weigh matrix W_n and the high-frequency parts of y_n^k as shown

$$y_n^H = \sum_{k=1}^{K} w_k \left(y_n^k - F\left(y_n^k \right) \right) \tag{6}$$

where F is the Gaussian used to obtain the low frequency component. And the reconstructed patch is

$$y_n = y_n^I + y_n^H \tag{7}$$

After repeating the above steps for all the patches in V_L, all the reconstructed patches are obtained. In order to enforce the inter-patch relationships and to weaken the block effects, the pixels in overlapping region of the reconstructed image are averaged.

4   Experimental Results

4.1   Parameters Setting

We test our SR method on typical multi-view video sequences, including both parallel and non-parallel camera video sequences, such as *Ballet* and *Breakdancer*. The low resolution video sequence is generated by downsampling one of the HR view sequences. A 5×5 Gaussian kernel is been used to blur the original high-resolution view prior to down-sampling. The down-sampling factor is two for both the horizontal and vertical directions.

4.2   Experiment Result on Multi-view Video

Table 1 shows the PSNR and SSIM values of the final super-resolution results obtained by the proposed method, bicubic interpolation, the original HFSYN [7], and VVA [10]. The PSNR and SSIM values were calculated over several the frames of each test video and then averaged. It can be seen that the proposed method is able to significantly boost the PSNR performance. For instance, the proposed method achieves average gains of 4.76 dB over the bicubic interpolation method, 4.10dB over [7] and 2.84 dB over [10]. As for SSIM, it achieves average gains of 0.0304 over the bicubic interpolation method, 0.0309 and 0.0203 over [7] and [10], respectively.

Table 1. PSNR (dB) and SSIM comparative results of different methods.

Dataset	Bicubic	HFSYN [7]	VVA [10]	Proposed
BookArrial	32.44/0.9101	33.92/0.9256	35.11/0.9451	**37.16/0.9580**
DoorFlowers	32.81/0.9262	34.05/0.9375	35.68/0.9459	**37.72/0.9615**
LeavingLaptop	32.77/0.9094	34.04/0.9253	35.15/0.9273	**37.63/0.9578**
Champtower	33.06/0.9656	33.80/0.9614	35.50/0.9688	**39.39/0.9854**
Pantomime	32.54/0.9598	34.17/0.9634	34.85/0.9721	**39.46/0.9869**
Ballet	33.79/0.9231	33.61/0.8962	33.95/0.9205	**37.36/0.9433**
Breakdancer	36.95/0.9064	35.38/0.8876	36.30/0.8909	**38.96/0.9206**
Average	33.48/0.9286	34.14/0.9281	35.40/0.9387	**38.24/0.9590**

(a) Bicubic (33.87 / 0.9231)   (b) HFSYN (33.66 / 0.8960)

(c) VVA (34.04 / 0.9207)   (d) Proposed (**37.37 / 0.9431**)

Fig. 3. *Ballet* SR result. The visual results and PSNR(dB)/SSIM values of different methods. Our method recover the finest strip pattern.

Figures 3 and 4 show sample frames from the video sequences *Ballet* and *Doorflowers* with a up-scaling factor of two. The Bicubic method is used as the baseline. Figures 3(b) and 4(b) are the original high frequency synthesis (HFSYN) result. The HFSYN method [7] is capable of restoring image details,

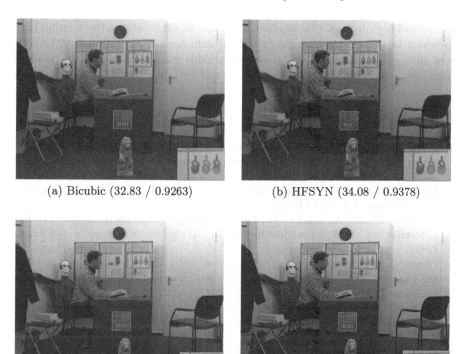

<table>
<tr><td>(a) Bicubic (32.83 / 0.9263)</td><td>(b) HFSYN (34.08 / 0.9378)</td></tr>
<tr><td>(c) VVA (35.67 / 0.9460)</td><td>(d) Proposed (37.63 / 0.9615)</td></tr>
</table>

(a) Bicubic (32.83 / 0.9263)   (b) HFSYN (34.08 / 0.9378)

(c) VVA (35.67 / 0.9460)   (d) Proposed (**37.63** / **0.9615**)

Fig. 4. *Doorflowers* SR result. The visual results and PSNR(dB)/SSIM values of different methods. Our method reconstructs the clearest boundary.

albeit with evident artifacts along the boundary between the object and the background. These artifacts are caused by mismatched high frequency components. Figures 3(c) and 4(c) are virtual view assisted SR (VVA) result. The VVA method [10] can process a much better visual quality than HFSYN result, but still suffers from some undesirable stair-like artifacts and distortion. The results produced by our proposed method as presented in Figs. 3(d) and 4(d) can reconstruct sharper edges and yield better structure details. Our method can effectively tackle the mismatch problem. Neither stair-like nor substantial blurring artifacts occur in our recovering method, showing much better visual results than other comparative methods.

5 Conclusion

In this paper, we propose a novel two-stage method for efficient mixed-resolution multiview super resolution based on refined virtual view synthesis and manifold learning. The first depth map assisted high frequency component synthesis stage can effectively reduce mismatching regions in the synthesis virtual view.

The second high frequency compensation stage can reconstruct the missing high frequency in the mismatching regions and enhance the visual quality. Experiment shows that our method can get remarkable gain in both quantitative and qualitative result.

References

1. Aflaki, P., et al.: Coding of mixed-resolution multiview video in 3D video application. In: 2013 20th IEEE International Conference on Image Processing (ICIP), pp. 1704–1708. IEEE (2013)
2. Blake, R.: Threshold conditions for binocular rivalry. J. Exp. Psychol. Hum. Percept. Perform. **3**(2), 251 (1977)
3. Brust, H., Smolic, A., Mueller, K., Tech, G., Wiegand, T.: Mixed resolution coding of stereoscopic video for mobile devices. In: 3DTV Conference, pp. 1–4. Citeseer (2009)
4. Chang, H., Yeung, D.Y., Xiong, Y.: Super-resolution through neighbor embedding. In: Proceedings of the 2004 IEEE Computer Society Conference on Computer Vision and Pattern Recognition CVPR 2004, p. I (2004)
5. Cruz, M.A.A.D., Rodrigues, J.J.P.C., Al-Muhtadi, J., Korotaev, V., Albuquerque, V.H.C.: A reference model for internet of things middleware. IEEE Internet Things J. **99**, 1 (2018)
6. Fehn, C.: Depth-image-based rendering (DIBR), compression, and transmission for a new approach on 3D-TV. In: Stereoscopic Displays and Virtual Reality Systems XI, vol. 5291, pp. 93–105. International Society for Optics and Photonics (2004)
7. Garcia, D.C., Dorea, C., de Queiroz, R.L.: Super resolution for multiview images using depth information. IEEE Trans. Circuits Syst. Video Technol. **22**(9), 1249–1256 (2012)
8. Garcia, D.C., Drea, C., Queiroz, R.L.D.: Super-resolution for multiview images using depth information. In: IEEE International Conference on Image Processing, pp. 1793–1796 (2010)
9. Jain, A.K., Nguyen, T.Q.: Video super-resolution for mixed resolution stereo. In: 2013 20th IEEE International Conference on Image Processing (ICIP), pp. 962–966. IEEE (2013)
10. Jin, Z., Tillo, T., Yao, C., Xiao, J., Zhao, Y.: Virtual-view-assisted video super-resolution and enhancement. IEEE Trans. Circuits Syst. Video Technol. **26**(3), 467–478 (2016)
11. Merkle, P., Smolic, A., Muller, K., Wiegand, T.: Multi-view video plus depth representation and coding. In: IEEE International Conference on Image Processing. ICIP 2007, vol. 1, pp. 1–201. IEEE (2007)
12. Roweis, S.T., Saul, L.K.: Nonlinear dimensionality reduction by locally linear embedding. Science **290**(5500), 2323 (2000)
13. Sawhney, H.S., Guo, Y., Hanna, K., Kumar, R., Adkins, S., Zhou, S.: Hybrid stereo camera: an IBR approach for synthesis of very high resolution stereoscopic image sequences. In: Proceedings of the 28th Annual Conference on Computer Graphics and Interactive Techniques. pp. 451–460. ACM (2001)
14. Sezer, O.B., Dogdu, E., Ozbayoglu, A.M.: Context aware computing, learning and big data in internet of things: a survey. IEEE Internet Things J. **5**(1), 1–27 (2017)
15. Yang, C.Y., Huang, J.B., Yang, M.H.: Exploiting self-similarities for single frame super-resolution. In: Asian Conference on Computer Vision, pp. 497–510 (2010)

16. Zhang, J., Cao, Y., Wang, Z.: A simultaneous method for 3D video super-resolution and high-quality depth estimation. In: ICIP, pp. 1346–1350 (2013)
17. Zhang, J., Cao, Y., Zha, Z.J., Zheng, Z., Chen, C.W., Wang, Z.: A unified scheme for super-resolution and depth estimation from asymmetric stereoscopic video. IEEE Trans. Circuits Syst. Video Technol. **26**(3), 479–493 (2016)
18. Zhang, X., Wu, X.: Image interpolation by adaptive 2-D autoregressive modeling and soft-decision estimation. IEEE Trans. Image Process. **17**(6), 887–896 (2008)

Posture Recognition and Heading Estimation Based on Machine Learning Using MEMS Sensors

Boyuan Wang[1]($\boxtimes$) iD, Xuelin Liu[1], Baoguo Yu[2,3], Ruicai Jia[2,3], and Lu Huang[2,3]

[1] College of Information and Communication Engineering,
Harbin Engineering University, Harbin 150001, China
boyuan@hrbeu.edu.cn
[2] The 54th Research Institute of China Electronics Technology Group
Corporation, Shijiazhuang 050081, China
[3] State Key Laboratory of Satellite Navigation System and Equipment
Technology, Shijiazhuang 050081, China

Abstract. With the popularity of smartphones and the performance improvement of embedded sensor, the smartphone has become the most important terminal device in motion recognition and indoor positioning. In this paper, the methods of the smartphone posture recognition and the pedestrian heading estimation are proposed. We analyze the signal characteristic of the accelerometer and the gyroscope, the representative feature information is extracted and a classifier based on DT model is proposed. Besides, considering the different postures of the smartphone, we propose an improved heading estimation method, which utilizes a weighted-average operation and combines the principal component analysis-based (PCA-based) method and the angle deviation method innovatively. The results of the experiments show that the average accuracy of posture recognition is nearly 97.1%, which can satisfy the pattern recognition in the process of pedestrian navigation. The average error of the proposed heading estimation is 6.2° and the performance is improved than the single PCA-based and angle deviation method.

Keywords: Posture recognition · Machine learning · Heading estimation · MEMS sensors

1 Introduction

Location-based Service (LBS) has become an indispensable service in people's social life, and its key is the acquisition of location information [1]. Traditional LBS relies mainly on global navigation satellite systems (GNSS), such as GPS, Beidou, Glonass and Galileo systems [2]. GNSS can achieve a global wide coverage and the positioning accuracy with civil signals can be better than 10 m. However, due to the influence of signal occlusion, reflection and multipath effect in indoor environment, the effectiveness of satellite navigation signals in indoor environment is difficult to be guaranteed, which greatly restricts the development of LBS in indoor environment [3]. In recent

© ICST Institute for Computer Sciences, Social Informatics and Telecommunications Engineering 2019
Published by Springer Nature Switzerland AG 2019. All Rights Reserved
S. Han et al. (Eds.): AICON 2019, LNICST 287, pp. 496–508, 2019.
https://doi.org/10.1007/978-3-030-22971-9_42

years, more and more attentions have been paid to the indoor positioning, the indoor positioning systems based on different technical systems have also been widely established. Current indoor positioning technologies mainly include WIFI fingerprint [4], Bluetooth [5], pedestrian dead reckoning (PDR) [6], RFID [7], Ultra-wide Bandwidth (UWB) [8], ultrasound [9] and visible light positioning [10].

PDR positioning technology uses the built-in MEMS inertial sensors of the smartphone to calculate the relative position of pedestrian movement, the MEMS inertial sensors include accelerometer, gyroscope and magnetometer. However, in the process of pedestrians using smartphones, the posture of device will constantly change. The traditional PDR method requires pedestrians to keep their device in front of their bodies stably. However, this requirement is unrealistic in the actual navigation process. Therefore, this paper analyses the habits of pedestrians using mobile phones and uses machine learning algorithm to design classifiers for the recognition of different smartphone postures.

Current pattern recognition methods can be divided into two categories [11]: the method based on the environmental sensors and the recognition based on the mobile sensors. The method based on the environmental sensors uses the infrastructure (such as camera networks or wireless access points) to perceive human activities. Mobile sensor-based method usually uses the built-in MEMS inertial sensors in smartphones, such as accelerometers, gyroscopes, magnetometers, etc. to identify pedestrian behavior patterns. At present, mobile sensor-based methods have become very popular. Because they have no coverage restrictions and can work anywhere. At the same time, the smartphone is the devices which is more closely related to people, thus no additional deployment cost is needed [12]. For using the smartphone in indoor positioning, the motions can also be divided into two categories: one is to describe the overall movement of pedestrians, including walking, running, standing, upstairs, downstairs, elevator and so on. The other is different postures that represent people holding the smartphone, such as reading information, watching navigation interface, making calls, swinging with arms, putting it in pockets and so on. This paper mainly aims at the second type of pattern recognition, which can further assist indoor pedestrian navigation by recognizing different phone postures. Some recognition methods of motion mode recognition are also proposed, including artificial neural network (ANN) [13], support vector machine (SVM) [14], decision tree (DT) [15] and other classifiers, they are used to recognize the motion modes, capture the transition between different modes and assist the PDR.

In general, PDR includes three modules: step detection, step length estimation and heading estimation, in which the heading estimation is the most difficult and greatly influenced by the smartphone posture. The heading offset between different phone postures is estimated, and the actual heading is obtained by adding the offset to the orientation, but the offset is not constant in actual environment. In [16], the principal component analysis (PCA) of horizontal acceleration is applied to estimate the heading, but because of the poor precision of gyroscope embedded smartphone, the attitude matrix is not always accurate.

In this paper, a classifier with DT model which can recognize the current posture of the smartphone is designed. A pre-processing for the raw data from the MEMS sensors is carried out to eliminate the influence of noises and 4 phone postures are defined. Simultaneously, the feature data in time and frequency domain are extracted from the filtered signals. Furthermore, a novel heading determination method is proposed. By combining the PCA-based method and the angle deviation method, the estimated heading has higher accuracy.

2 Approach

2.1 MEMS Data Pre-processing

The errors of MEMS IMU can be divided into static error, dynamic error and random error. Static and dynamic errors are generally considered to be deterministic errors related to the velocity and acceleration of the carrier motion, which can be compensated by experimental calibration. Random drift is an important characteristic of the gyroscope, a lot of works have been done in the measurement and modeling of the gyroscope drift. However, due to the low measuring accuracy of the MEMS sensor, the performance of the calibrated IMU cannot satisfy the requirements of the indoor pedestrian positioning system. Therefore, to improve the performance of smartphone posture recognition and pedestrian heading estimation, it is necessary to pre-process the raw data output from the MEMS sensors embedded in the smartphone. This paper uses a 10th order Butterworth filter with a 12 Hz cut-off frequency to effectively eliminate the high-frequency noise interference of the MEMS signal.

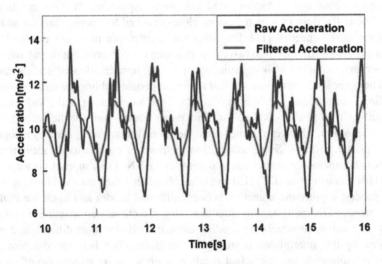

Fig. 1. Raw acceleration signal and filtered acceleration signal.

As shown in Fig. 1, we can see that the raw signals from MEMS sensors contain many clutters and noises, the low-pass filtering removes the high-frequency components of the noise, the filtered signals are smoother and the waveforms can be seen more clearly. This pre-processing operation is necessary for extracting feature information from the MEMS sensor and enables the process of smartphone posture recognition and pedestrian heading estimation.

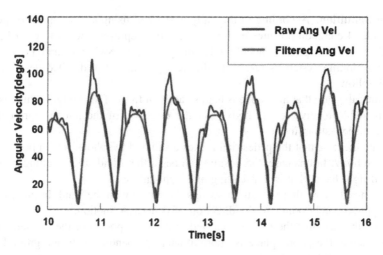

Fig. 2. Raw angel velocity signal and filtered angel velocity signal.

In general, all the coordinate systems of the accelerometer, gyroscope and magnetometer embedded in the smartphone are consistent, which are also the same as the coordinate system of the smartphone. Thus, we introduce the coordinate system of the smartphone, as shown in Fig. 2. We place the smartphone on the horizontal plane, the screen center is the origin of the coordinate system; the X axis is parallel to the short side of smartphone and the direction is horizontal to the right; the Y axis is parallel to the long side of smartphone and the direction is horizontal to the forward; the Z axis is upward and perpendicular to the screen (Fig. 3).

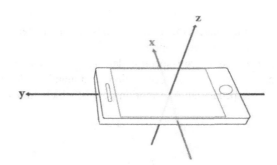

Fig. 3. The coordinate system of the embedded sensors.

2.2   Posture Recognition

The posture recognition is that we collect the current sensor signal, based on our predefined pattern categories and the data characteristics of the sensors, we can determine the current smartphone postures. The posture recognition in this paper includes three modules: postures definition, feature information extraction and class determination.

Posture Definition. According to the daily custom of using smartphones for people, we consider 4 common postures in this paper, which represent the posture for holding or placing the smartphone, including Holding, Calling, Swinging and Pocket. The indoor positioning system is related to different postures. The detailed description is listed as follow:

Holding: the case that the phone is held steadily in front of the body. In this case, the phone is stable relative to the body, and the direction of the phone represents the direction of pedestrian motion.

Calling: the case that the pedestrian makes a call and the phone screen points to the side of the body. In this case, the posture can be further divided into calling with left-hand and right-hand, that is, left-calling and right-calling.

Swinging: the case that pedestrian swings the phone with the hand. In this case, the phone approximately points to the direction of pedestrian motion.

Pocket: the case that the phone is carried in the front pocket of the trousers. In this case, we define the phone plane is approximately perpendicular to the ground when pedestrian is in static state.

Feature Information Extraction. The filtered IMU signal cannot completely satisfy the requirement of the posture recognition. We still need to extract feature information from the filtered accelerometer and gyroscope signals in a sliding window. The size of the sliding window is set to 256 samples with 50% overlap.

The module values of acceleration and angular velocity are denoted by

$$a_{mv} = \sqrt{(a_x^2 + a_y^2 + a_z^2)} \tag{1}$$

$$\omega_{mv} = \sqrt{(\omega_x^2 + \omega_y^2 + \omega_z^2)} \tag{2}$$

where a_x, a_y and a_z are the measurements from 3-axis accelerometer, ω_x, ω_y and ω_z are the measurements from 3-axis gyroscope.

We choose variance and energy spectral density as the feature information for posture recognition. The variances of accelerations and angular velocities describe the amplitude change of the pedestrian in a motion period, which are calculated by

$$\sigma_a^2 = \frac{\sum(a - \bar{a})}{N} \tag{3}$$

$$\sigma_\omega^2 = \frac{\sum(\omega - \bar{\omega})}{N} \tag{4}$$

In this paper, for the accelerometer and gyroscope signals, the variances of the module value and each axis value are extracted, which are denoted by

$$\sigma_a^2 = [\sigma_{ax}^2, \sigma_{ay}^2, \sigma_{az}^2, \sigma_{amv}^2] \tag{5}$$

$$\sigma_\omega^2 = [\sigma_{\omega x}^2, \sigma_{\omega y}^2, \sigma_{\omega z}^2, \sigma_{\omega mv}^2] \tag{6}$$

where σ_a^2 and σ_ω^2 are the acceleration variance vector and the angular velocity variance vector, respectively. They form the time-domain feature. The characteristics of acceleration variances with four postures during walking are shown in Fig. 4.

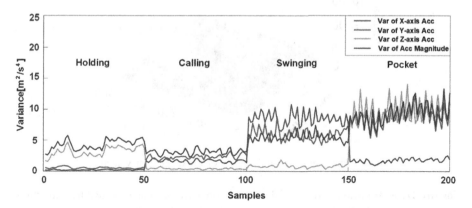

Fig. 4. The variances of accelerations with four phone poses while pedestrian is walking.

The time-frequency analysis of accelerations and angular velocities is performed by the Short Time Fourier Transform (STFT). As shown in Figs. 5 and 6, the subject walks with four phone postures, in the order of Holding, Calling, Swinging and Pocket. The period of each posture is 100 s. As shown in Fig. 6, it can be found that the energy spectral density of Z-axis angular velocities $e_{\omega z}$ shows significant peaks from 200 s to 300 s, this is due to the phone swings around Z-axis during the swinging of the hand. When the phone is carried in pocket, the phone is fixed relative to the thigh and rotates with the thigh. The energy spectral density of X-axis angular velocities $e_{\omega x}$ shows significant peaks from 300 s to 400 s in Fig. 5. The frequency-domain feature vector is expressed as $e = [e_a, e_{\omega x}, e_{\omega z}]$.

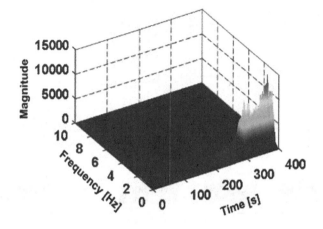

Fig. 5. The energy spectral density of X-axis angular velocities.

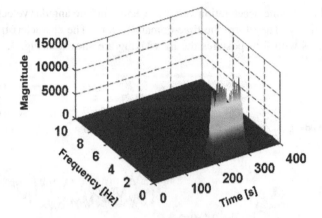

Fig. 6. The energy spectral density of Z-axis angular velocities.

Posture Determination. After the device posture definition and the feature extraction, we begin to identify the postures according to the defined categories. DT is a nonparametric classifier that has tree structure, each node represents a classification, the advantage of DT is it can directly reflect the classification process and the characteristics of the data, is easy to understand and implement. In this paper, the DT model is utilized as the classifier to classify four device postures.

The feature vector $f = [\sigma_a^2, \sigma_\omega^2, e]$ consists of the variances and the energy spectral density of accelerometer and gyroscope signals, which is chosen as the input vector of classifier and the output is the current posture. All feature data are divided into two groups, one group is training dataset for training the classifier parameters and the other group is testing dataset for verifying the recognition accuracy of the trained classifier. ε_a, $\varepsilon_{\omega z}$, λ_a, λ_ω, η_a and η_ω are the parameters of classifier. The flowchart of the classifier based on DT model is shown in Fig. 7.

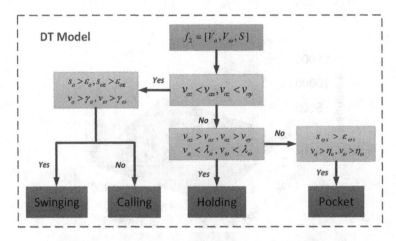

Fig. 7. The DT classifier for smartphone posture classification.

2.3 Heading Estimation Based on Smartphone Posture

To simplify the computational complexity and avoid the cumulative error caused by the integral operation of gyroscope data. The pedestrian's heading is estimated only by the accelerometer and magnetometer in this paper. Due to the magnetometer is easily disturbed by the environment, thus, our positioning work is carried out in an approximate laboratory environment to guarantee the availability of magnetometer.

We propose a novel method for estimating the heading, which combines the heading deviation determination and the PCA-based heading estimation. The Degrees of Freedom (DOF) of the smartphone is very high during the navigation process, there is a deviation between the direction of smartphone and the direction of pedestrian motion. The orientation readings from the smartphone cannot always represent the actual headings.

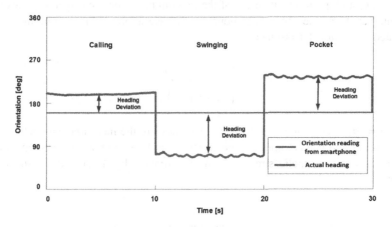

Fig. 8. The heading deviations for Holding and Calling with left-hand and right-hand.

As shown in Fig. 8, the actual heading of pedestrian can be obtained by the orientation readings from smartphone and the heading deviations. It is needed to be highlighted that the deviations are different for making a call with different hands, it is known by the directions of each accelerometer axis and described as Table 1.

Table 1. The directions of accelerometer axes for calling.

Posture	Hand	Directions of accelerometer axes		
		X-axis	Y-axis	Z-axis
Calling	Left-hand	Above and front	Above and back	Right
	Right-hand	Under and back	Above and back	Left

The directions of X-axis in vertical plane are opposite for making a call with left-hand and right-hand. Therefore, it can be determined based on the readings of accelerometer X-axis. The heading estimated by angle deviations are denoted by

$$\theta_1 = \theta_o - \theta_d \tag{7}$$

where θ_o is the orientation information from the smartphone and θ_d is the heading deviation. However, the deviations are varying in the navigation, especially for Calling and Pocket modes. Relative to the initial direction of the phone, once the phone direction has changed a lot, the obtained deviations cannot be adaptive to estimate the actual heading. Therefore, PCA method is utilized to estimate the actual heading. The PCA-based method is based on a fact that the largest variations of horizontal accelerations represent the direction of pedestrian motion, thus horizontal accelerations are needed to calculate. We obtain the horizontal accelerations using the estimated gravity vector.

$$g = -(g_x, g_y, g_z) \tag{8}$$

where g_x, g_y and g_z are the averages of the measurements on the respective axes in the time interval. Then, the vertical components of accelerations and magnetic strengths are estimated by vector dot product.

$$\begin{cases} a_v = \left(\frac{a \cdot g}{g \cdot g}\right)g \\ m_v = \left(\frac{m \cdot g}{g \cdot g}\right)g \end{cases} \tag{9}$$

where $a = (a_x, a_y, a_z)$ and $m = (m_x, m_y, m_z)$, they are the measurement vectors of the accelerometer and magnetometer respectively. Therefore, the horizontal components of accelerations and magnetic strength scan be estimated by moving the vertical components out.

$$\begin{cases} a_h = a - a_v \\ m_h = m - m_v \end{cases} \tag{10}$$

The obtained horizontal acceleration components are used as the input of PCA and the first eigenvector is regarded as the motion vector, which represents the pedestrian's direction and is denoted by

$$v = (v_x, v_y, v_z) \tag{11}$$

Then, the eigen vector v is utilized to calculate the heading θ_2 with the horizontal magnetic vector.

$$\theta_2 = \arccos(\frac{v \cdot m_h}{|v||m_h|}) \tag{12}$$

By analyzing the experimental data, we find that the headings estimated by the angle deviations are availability when the motion vector v is perpendicular to the abscissa-axis of phone. However, the abscissa-axis is approximate to Z-axis of acceleration for Calling and Swinging. Therefore, a weighted estimation algorithm is presented.

$$\begin{cases} \theta = \theta_1, & \varepsilon - 90° < \delta_1 \\ \theta = (1-\kappa) \cdot \theta_1 + \kappa \cdot \theta_2, & \delta_1 < \varepsilon - 90° < \delta_2 \\ \theta = \theta_2, & \varepsilon - 90° > \delta_2 \end{cases} \tag{13}$$

where θ is the estimated heading by the angel deviations and motion vector obtained by PCA, ε is the angle between the motion vector v and the Z-axis of acceleration, δ_1 and δ_2 are the thresholds for judging the attitude of the smartphone.

In the case that $\varepsilon - 90° < \delta_1$, that is, the v is nearly perpendicular to the Z-axis of phone and the angle deviations can be credible, so the θ_1 obtained by angle deviations is taken as the final estimated heading. In the case that $\varepsilon - 90° > \delta_2$, the angle deviations cannot be used and the estimated heading is equal to θ_2 obtained by the motion vector. For $\delta_1 < \varepsilon - 90° < \delta_2$, the heading θ is estimated by the weighted average operation of θ_1 and θ_2, the weighted coefficient are calculated by

$$\kappa = \frac{(\varepsilon - 90 - \delta_1)}{\delta_2 - \delta_1} \tag{14}$$

3   Experiments and Results

3.1   Experiment Field and Setup

In this section, the posture recognition and heading estimation experiments are introduced to verify the performance of the proposed methods. The experimental site is in an office building. The handheld terminal is Xiaomi MIX2 smartphone and the sampling frequency is set to 100 Hz.

3.2   Posture Recognition Experiment

We selected 10 testers to verify the posture recognition performance and the subjects move with different postures. The total data collection duration of each participant is about 10 min. The size of the sliding window for feature extraction is set to 256 samples with 50% overlap. In this experiment, 60% of the feature data are chosen for training dataset and 40% are chosen for testing dataset. The instances for testing are listed in Table 2.

Table 2. The instances of postures for testing.

	Holding	Calling	Swinging	Pocket
Walking	500	500	500	500

As shown in Table 3, the lowest accuracy of the posture recognition is 96.4% and 2.7% instances are mistaken as Swinging, this is because the phone rotates in both postures and the periodicities of the motion are similar. The highest accuracy is

Table 3. Confusion matrix for phone poses recognition.

	Holding	Calling	Swinging	Pocket
Holding	**97.3%**	1.1%	0.2%	1.4%
Calling	1.7%	**96.6%**	0.5%	1.2%
Swinging	0.2%	0.5%	**98.2%**	1.1%
Pocket	0.6%	0.3%	2.7%	**96.4%**

Swinging and can be to 98.2%, and only 0.2% instances are misclassified as Holding, this is because the postures of Holding and Calling are more stable, Swinging is significantly different from the two postures. The average accuracy is 97.1%, which can satisfy the pattern recognition in the process of pedestrian navigation.

To prove that the proposed algorithm can effectively improve the recognition accuracy, we introduce the SVM algorithm and carry out the comparative experiments. As shown in Fig. 9, the recognition accuracy of our proposed method is 8.4% higher than that of SVM method on average.

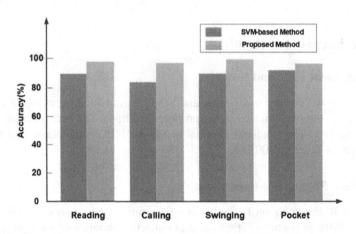

Fig. 9. The compare for the recognition accuracies of SVM and proposed method.

3.3   Heading Estimation Experiment

To verify the performance of the proposed heading estimation method, the PCA-based method and the angle deviation method are also introduced. For the comparison experiment, the smartphone is in Swinging posture. The results of the experiments are illustrated in Fig. 8. The 50% heading estimation errors for the proposed method, PCA-based and angle deviation method are 6.7°, 7.8° and 11.8°, respectively. The 75% absolute estimation errors of heading are 11.4°, 13.6° and 22.1°, respectively, The average error is 6.2°. The proposed method combines the motion axis estimated by PCA and the angle deviation, the final pedestrian's heading are obtained by the weighted average operation. Therefore, we can obviously see that the performance of the proposed method is much better (Fig. 10).

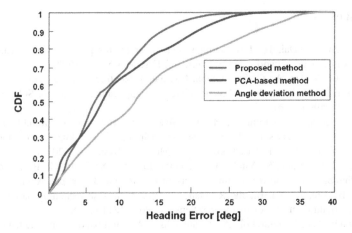

Fig. 10. The cumulative error distribution of heading estimation with the proposed method, PCA-based method and the angle deviation method.

4   Conclusions and Future Works

In this paper, the posture recognition and heading estimation method based on machine learning is proposed. The data are all from the MEMS sensors embedded in a smartphone. According to the analysis of accelerometer and gyroscope signals, the representative feature information is extracted, including the statistic feature and the frequency-domain feature. By comparing the characteristics of various features in different postures, a DT model for recognizing postures is designed. Besides, considering the attitude of the smartphone in different postures, we present an improved heading estimation method, which combines the PCA-based method and the angle deviation method innovatively. The results of the experiments show that the average accuracy of posture recognition is nearly 97.1%, which can satisfy the pattern recognition in the process of pedestrian navigation. The average error of heading estimation is 6.2°. The result of the comparison experiment shows that the performance of the proposed heading estimation method is better than the single PCA-based and angle deviation method. With the methods of this paper, the performance of the indoor pedestrian positioning will also be improved.

For the future works, we plan to research more advanced machine learning algorithms for the mode recognition of the pedestrian and smartphone. We also hope to apply the motion mode recognition to more fields of LBS.

Acknowledgments. This work was supported in part by the Fundamental Research Funds for the Central Universities under Grant HEUCF180801, and in part by the National Key Research and Development Plan of China under Grant 2016YFB0502100 and Grant 2016YFB0502103.

References

1. He, X., Jin, R., Dai, H.: Leveraging spatial diversity for privacy-aware location based services in mobile networks. IEEE Trans. Inf. Forensics Secur. **70**(99), 1 (2018)
2. Perrone, G., Vallan, A.: GNSS - Global Navigation Satellite Systems (2008)
3. Kaplan, E.D.: Understanding GPS: principles and application. J. Atmos. Solar Terr. Phys. **59**(5), 598–599 (1996)
4. Torressospedra, J., Montoliu, R., Mendozasilva, G. M., Belmonte, O., Rambla, D., Huerta, J.: Providing databases for different indoor positioning technologies: pros and cons of magnetic field and Wi-Fi based positioning. Mob. Inf. Syst. 1–22 (2016)
5. Mingchi, L.U., Wang, S., Yunke, L.I., Yuanfa, J.I., Sun, X., Deng, G.: Bluetooth location algorithm based on feature matching and distance weighting. J. Comput. Appl. 45–54 (2018)
6. Wang, B., Liu, X., Yu, B., Jia, R., Gan, X.: Pedestrian dead reckoning based on motion mode recognition using a smartphone. Sensors **18**(6), 1811 (2018)
7. Forouzannezhad, P., Jafargholi, A., Jahanbakhshi, A.: Multiband compact antenna for near-field and far-field RFID and wireless portable applications. IET Microw. Antenna. Propag. **11**(4), 535–541 (2017)
8. Zhang, C., Kuhn, M.J., Merkl, B.C., Fathy, A.E., Mahfouz, M.R.: Real-time noncoherent UWB positioning radar with millimeter range accuracy: theory and experiment. IEEE Trans. Microw. Theory Tech. **58**(1), 9–20 (2010)
9. Qi, J., Liu, G.P.: A robust high-accuracy ultrasound indoor positioning system based on a wireless sensor network. Sensors **17**(11), 2554 (2017)
10. Kuo, Y.S., Pannuto, P., Dutta, P.: Demo: Luxapose: indoor positioning with mobile phones and visible light. In: International Conference on Mobile Computing & Networking, pp. 5–11 (2014)
11. Gu, F., Khoshelham, K., Valaee, S., Shang, J., Zhang, R.: Locomotion activity recognition using stacked denoising autoencoders. IEEE Internet Things J. **5**(3), 2085–2093 (2018)
12. Jian, K.W., Liang, D., Xiao, W.: Real-time physical activity classification and tracking using wearble sensors. In: International Conference on Information, pp. 1–6 (2008)
13. Shin, B., Kim, C., Kim, J., Lee, S., Kee, C., Lee, T.: Motion recognition-based 3D pedestrian navigation system using smartphone. IEEE Sens. J. **16**(18), 6977–6989 (2016)
14. Ling, P., Jingbin, L., Robert, G., Yuwei, C., Heidi, K., Ruizhi, C.: Using LS-SVM based motion recognition for smartphone indoor wireless positioning. Sensors **12**(5), 6155–6175 (2012)
15. Rautaray, S.S., Agrawal, A.: Vision based hand gesture recognition for human computer interaction: a survey. Artif. Intell. Rev. **43**(1), 1–54 (2015)
16. Deng, Z., Si, W., Qu, Z., Xin, L., Na, Z.: Heading estimation fusing inertial sensors and landmarks for indoor navigation using a smartphone in the pocket. Eurasip J. Wirel. Comm. Netw. **2017**(1), 160 (2017)

Author Index

Printed in the United States
By Bookmasters